Housebuilder's
Bible 10

ovolo

Housebuilder's Bible™ 10

Ovolo Books
www.ovolobooks.co.uk

Tenth edition published April 2013

ISBN 978-1-9059-5946-4

For more information on Ovolo Books please visit
www.ovolobooks.co.uk
or email: info@ovolobooks.co.uk

Picture Acknowledgments
Firminger & Firminger Ltd, www.londonloftconversions.co.uk.
Robert Cooper, www.rclandforce.co.uk.
Trevor Bounford, www.bounford.com.
T.J.Crump Oakwrights Ltd, www.oakwrights.co.uk

CONTENTS

CHAPTER 8
HEATING & PLUMBING 160

CHAPTER 9
WIRING 192

CHAPTER 10
FINISHES 204

CHAPTER 11
ROOM BY ROOM 228

CHAPTER 12
ADDING EXTRA SPACE 252

CONTENTS

FOREWORD

I FIRST DISCOVERED THE Housebuilder's Bible when editing a feature on Mark Brinkley's own self-build home – the Bible's original 'benchmark house', back in 1994. Mark was a classic self-publicist author, posing for the shots of the house with his book unashamedly clutched to his chest for a bit of free promotion. Fourteen years and eight editions later, the improbably named 'Housebuilder's Bible' has gone on to sell over 140,000 copies and is consistently in the Amazon best sellers charts: an astonishing feat for a book about building houses.

Intrigued by the bold – and I have to say I thought foolishly brave – title, I decided to read the Bible and appropriately enough, it proved revelatory. Mark has managed to dissect and analyse the housebuilding process in a way quite unlike anything I had ever read, or have read since, examining each key decision and the factors that influence cost, quality and build speed.

What made the book so riveting was its refreshingly honest approach, and its wry, knowing, cynical humour. Not surprisingly for a subject that has received very little academic analysis that is in any way decipherable, the Bible has proved a hit with professional builders and self-builders alike.

Now in its Tenth Edition, Mark no longer typesets the book, stuffs the mail order envelopes himself or gets his offspring to design the cover. This latest edition has a more ergonomic new look and a new size. The Bible may look different, but it has not lost any of its charm or humour, and remains an incredibly interesting and useful read.

MICHAEL HOLMES
Editor-in-Chief of *Homebuilding & Renovating* magazine and presenter of TV's *Build, Buy, or Restore*

1
BEFORE YOU START

THE BUILDERS' DILEMMA

THE TRIANGLE ON the right represents the age-old conundrum for all builders and would-be builders. It is said that you can have any two of these points in a building job but only at the expense of the third. Thus you can have a good, cheap job but it won't be quick, or a cheap, quick job that won't be any good.

So when you hear claims – as you may – of people having built (or more likely 'put up') a house in just eight weeks you can reply, confidently, "Ah, but how much did it cost you?" And, similarly, if you meet someone who claims to have built a house for £35 per sq ft, you can look them in the eye and

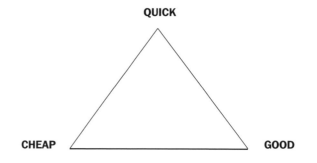

exclaim "I bet it took you years" – and you'll be right. So before you set out to build a new house, first examine your motives and see where you fit into the triangle.

THE CHEAP HOUSE

The average new house is

You can have any two of the three options in the triangle (above) but you will sacrifice the third! Make sure you know which one you are prepared to sacrifice.

constructed entirely by builders, takes about 6-8 months to complete and costs around £90 per sq ft (that's £800ish per sq m). It is built to standards that meet – and do not exceed – the current building regulations.

If you want to maximise the

House Prices v Brickie Rates in Cambridge

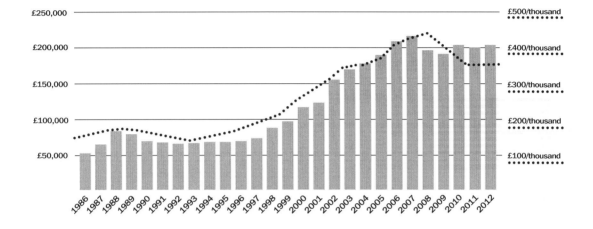

financial return on your new house – in all but the most up-market areas – it pays to keep it dead simple. Whether you plan to actually be a hands-on builder or not, for the cost-effective house the following advice should be carried out to the letter.

Dispense with any notions of individual design. Aim for a four-square box drawn up by a technician or a surveyor or better still from some already existing book of house plans – in fact anyone except an architect.

Avoid all of the following:

▓ layouts with more than four external corners

▓ anything round or curved

▓ anything poking out through the roof (dormers, chimneys)

▓ anything other than large format concrete tiles on the roof

▓ anything other than face brickwork on external walls

▓ anything other than straight stairs

▓ complicated sites (unless at a bargain price)

▓ fancy Continental plumbing systems

▓ trying to build an 'Eco' house

▓ big glazed features

▓ underfloor heating

▓ central vacuum cleaning systems

▓ kitchens that don't come from Ikea or B&Q

▓ bathrooms that don't come from B&Q or Bathstore

▓ anything but boring plastic windows

▓ home cinema rooms

▓ handmade anything at all (bricks, tiles, etc)

▓ Agas

There is a remarkable correlation between house prices and building trade rates, as illustrated by this graph. The gray bars show average house prices in my local town, Cambridge. The dotted line indicates the brickies' rate per thousand bricks laid, something of a benchmark for all the building trades and currently around £360/ thousand. Whereas the prices of building materials seems to be rather less than general inflation, the cost of labour seems to follow house price rises.

▓ garages – especially with remote-controlled doors

▓ porches and entrance canopies

▓ conservatories

▓ built-in cupboards

▓ hardwood floors

▓ data cabling

▓ any lighting that doesn't hang from a pendant in the middle of each room

▓ almost everything second-hand – it's only been salvaged because it's worth more than new.

What you will end up with will have all the charm of a Fifties council house. But if space for bucks is your main motive in taking on a construction project, then you'll be very happy. Much of the book that follows is concerned with the options that might turn a cheap house into a good house and

Chapter 1

therefore much of the book will be of little relevance to you. I have, however, always tried to indicate what the cheapest option is in each element of the house.

THE QUICK HOUSE

The quick house will almost certainly be a kit house, which is largely prefabricated in a workshop or factory. It will also, very likely, be a timber-framed house, or maybe a SIPs house, which is a variation on timber frame that is gaining in popularity. Don't worry if you have no idea what SIPs stands for.

But are they really quicker? What really takes up a builder's time is the finishing tasks and these are pretty much the same whatever your chosen building methods.

THE GOOD HOUSE

Most would-be individual housebuilders are not hard up nor in a hurry – at least they're not when they're just planning it all; they might beg to differ when they're halfway through building. They can afford to browse and contemplate and research. They will look at many different options before embarking and will probably be keen that the finished product should somehow be an expression of their personality as well as a way of meeting their individual needs in a way that an off-the-peg house couldn't hope to.

Even if you are building for resale rather than personal occupation, you are more than likely to want to build an attractive house that passers-by will come to admire and occupants will love to call their home.

After all, the house is likely to be standing long after any transient profit is banked and spent, and may well still be there when they are burying your grandchildren. To build well, you have to know what's going on and not just rely on experts: the more you are involved in the

design, the more you will appreciate the outcome, and the more you are involved in the building, the better that outcome will be.

IS THIS BOOK FOR YOU?

What follows is housebuilding's original bodice ripper, a warts-n-all rough guide. It is not a DIY manual (there are enough of those) and it is not a disguised advertisement (I'm not selling anything apart from this book). Although primarily concerned with new housebuilding, there is also much information specifically tailored for people converting or restoring existing properties.

Many of the tricks and tips described I have learnt the hard way since I started building in 1980. As the old saw goes: experience is the best education, but it is also the most expensive. My hope is that some of my 'experience' and research will help you avoid expensive pitfalls, many of which I've had the doubtful pleasure of falling victim to myself.

In short, the aim of this book is to enable you to build a good house cheaply and quickly. Now hang on a minute, I thought that wasn't possible.

HOUSEBUILDING IN THE UK

Housebuilding in Britain has always been a boom or bust activity, and this has never been more clearly illustrated than in recent times.

My experience of the property business began in the Eighties (in my late twenties) and it is worth recalling what went on then, for the benefit of younger readers. That period saw a surge in private housebuilding, caused partly by post-war baby-boomers (like me) entering the housing market and

partly by people choosing to live in smaller groups. This increased demand also led to a huge increase in house prices which, in turn, encouraged more people to jump onto the home ownership bandwagon, encouraged by the Thatcher government which made property-owning a key plank of its programme.

THE 1988 SLUMP

This particular bandwagon came juddering to a halt on August 1, 1988 when Nigel Lawson, then Chancellor of the Exchequer (but now better known for being Nigella's dad) stopped a tax perk known as double mortgage tax relief.

I remember the day well. I was property developing at the time, owed the bank about a quarter of a million and had just learned that I was to become a father for the first time. It was also the day my business partner and I completed on the purchase of a rather large barn for conversion in Comberton, a village near Cambridge. The timing was about as bad as it could be.

Double mortgage tax relief sounds like rather an obscure tax perk, as indeed it was; these days we have no tax relief of any description on mortgages but, back in 1988, both halves of an unmarried couple could claim tax relief on a mortgage, which was worth a few bob. It was an anomaly and Chancellor Lawson strove to eliminate anomalies.

The problem was that he announced his intention to do so in his budget speech in March, telling us all that the elimination of this particular anomaly would take place at midnight on the 31st of July. People who, in more normal times, would never have considered house purchase together were suddenly bounced into it by a fear that it was now or never for the housing ladder. The housing market, already toppy, duly went ballistic for four months in the rush to get sales completed before the Chancellor's cut off point.

In Cambridge, average house prices jumped by 25 per cent overnight. Many of the 'Lawson couples' lived to regret the unwarranted emotional entanglement caused by this feverish speculation. All of them lived to regret the financial chaos brought on by the price bubble bursting on August 1st that year. For almost all of them, it would be ten years before the houses they bought at ridiculous prices in 1988 would be worth as much again.

For us property developers, it was more painful still. But then, as a group, we have never elicited much sympathy. What happened on August 1st was distinctly eerie. The housing market just came to a standstill. Viewing stopped. Offers to buy were withdrawn. People just lost interest in buying homes altogether. The events of 2008, when the property market also stopped dead in its tracks, were eerily reminiscent, although there was no pivotal moment as happened in 1988.

Back then, prices didn't fall immediately. But, with hardly any house sales happening, it was hard to know what house prices were really doing. However, over the next year or two it became apparent that all the estate agents' talk of the market "just taking a breather'"was bull and, as the number of sales continued to decline, the rout set in. Things weren't helped at all by another of Nigel Lawson's foibles, the decision to peg the pound to the Deutschmark (remember that currency?) which led to interest rates going up and up – the base rate was 15 per cent from October 1989 to October 1990. As you can imagine, housebuilders took a bath.

It wasn't until 1993 that house prices stopped falling. Even then, the recovery was painfully slow. Rather than being a return

to the good old days before Lawson's bubble when house prices gently rose year-on-year (or so it seemed), everything remained resolutely frozen. Newspapers were full of stories of families stuck in 'negative equity' and of unhappy young homeowners just handing their keys back to the mortgage lenders and going back to live with Mum and Dad.

The climate all changed once again with the election of New Labour in 1997. Strange to think of a supposedly left-wing government riding to the rescue of the property-owning classes but then life was ever full of such ironies.

The fact is that average house prices were back to roughly the same level in May 1997 as they had been on that fateful day nine years earlier when Nigel Lawson delivered his now infamous budget speech.

From 1997, house prices started rising once again, just as they did from the Fifties through till 1988. This situation continued for another ten years until it finally started unravelling in late 2007, brought on by the global credit crunch that made it much harder to borrow money. I wrote in the 8th edition that "if the past tells us anything, it's that the longer the good times roll in property, the bigger the hangover.'" Well we had a ten-year boom: I think it would be prudent to look forward to a few years' bust. If the 1988 experience is to be repeated, then the good times might be not return before 2018. In my gloomier moments, I think maybe that's it forever, and that stagnant or depressed house prices are here to stay.

What's changed this time around is that mortgage lending seems to have dried up. It's not altogether clear (from an early 2013 viewpoint) whether this is because the banks won't lend or people don't want to borrow, but what's amazing is that house prices have held up so well because

turnover is right down.

HOW WE BUILD HOUSES

There are many unusual aspects to the British housebuilding scene besides the topsy-turvy nature of the housing market. Particularly pertinent to this book is the way we go about building homes – more particularly who builds them.

If you were to imagine a pie chart representing the total number of houses built each year in the UK there would be three slices in it marked:

■ speculative housebuilders (the vast proportion);

■ social housing (a small but reasonable slice); and

■ others (another still reasonable slice – maybe 15 per cent)

This type of arrangement has existed for decades. The big housebuilders got hold of giant estates of land to develop (or re-develop in the case of city centre regeneration), and they sold the lion's share off privately. In exchange for getting the planning permission, the councils would insist that they also built some social housing. This was a fine arrangement as long as the big builders continued to make money, but since 2007 this relationship has all begun to look a little strained. In fact, the credit crunch has blown it apart.

Let's look with the middle slice, social housing. This is mostly homes built by housing associations for rent or shared ownership. Social housing has more or less taken over from the council housing schemes, which were such a feature of the middle years of the 20th century. It's an area alive with innovation and some fascinating schemes have been built in the past few years. Indeed standards for social housing have been consistently higher than those used in the private sector, because the government and councils have insisted on it.

Now let's move on to the first category, speculative housebuilders. In Britain not only is speculative housebuilding by far the most common method of delivering new home, but this huge market is dominated by comparatively few names.

In fact, the top twenty speculative housebuilders knock out around 75 per cent of new homes. And they do rather "knock them out'." There are a similar number of regional housebuilders and then there are the small housebuilders, doing anything from one site of maybe twenty at any one time, right down to the general builders who occasionally do a spec build.

And then there are the others. Sorry if I make it appear as though we are constantly sliding down the pyramid towards the bottom of the heap. Because this book is primarily intended for the builders down here at the bottom of the housebuilding heap. The small builders and the others. Particularly the others.

In many ways, this 'others' grouping is by far the most interesting. Although it may account for less than 15 per cent or so of new homes, that still amounts to between 12,000 and 20,000 each year. And the great bulk of these are built by individuals for their own occupation – what the media and everyone else has learned to call 'selfbuild'.

The crucial, defining distinction between selfbuild and 'spec' building is that selfbuilding is done for your own occupation and is, consequently, out of the tax net. It's not being carried out as a trade and therefore there is no profit being made and no income tax to pay. And additionally there is no capital gains tax to pay because principal residences are tax-exempt and always have been in this country.

In the next section (and indeed throughout the book) I will be looking in greater detail at some of the pros and cons of selfbuild, but before getting stuck into that I think it's important to point out that there is a huge grey blanket of an area spread out between the sort of selfbuild featured in Channel 4's 'Grand Designs' and the output of a small spec builder who builds a house or two for sale every year and every so often builds a new one for himself – that way netting a nice little tax free earner. I have often heard builders referring to odd plots of land they own as 'their pension' and all good pensions should be tax free, shouldn't they?

Many good people, academics amongst them, have tried to assess the size of the UK selfbuild market and they get into all sorts of difficulties because selfbuild is not a clearly defined entity. The first 10,000 selfbuilds are easy to spot – they show up on the VAT returns – but the next 10,000 get murkier and murkier the higher the total gets. Hence I quite like the term 'others'. It covers a lot of nefarious undertakings.

SELFBUILD

Not that long ago, back in the Seventies and Eighties, selfbuild had a decidedly alternative flavour to it. Selfbuild was usually group selfbuild. This typically involved a number of individuals or families pooling their labour to build homes for themselves in a little estate.

Group selfbuild enjoyed a boom in the Eighties but came horribly unstuck when the Lawson bubble burst in 1988. Groups were left with homes worth less than they had paid for them and some of these schemes were abandoned half-built. Private group selfbuild all but disappeared off the radar screens after this.

But group selfbuild also existed in another guise where the schemes were done for rent rather than ownership – it's now known as Community Selfbuild – and this small sector continues to flourish although it rarely accounts for more than a dozen schemes each year.

In order to form a Community Selfbuild group, you need to have identified a number of people living in the same area who are in genuine housing need. Whereas the country is stuffed full of people in genuine housing need, not many of them have the time or inclination to go about meeting it by building a house which they then have to rent. So it remains a bit of a niche. The emphasis is often on building cheaply, simply and in an environmentally sound way.

Interestingly, the Coalition's first housing minister, Grant Shapps, was very keen to revitalise community selfbuild and has put in place plans to make it far easier for such groups to form and build. A the time of writing, this all remains largely speculative, but we are beginning to see schemes coming forward such as co-housing and Community Land Trusts (lots in Devon).

Whilst this specialised niche is alive and thriving, it is dwarfed by the mainstream selfbuild market, which consists of people acting as what the Americans sometimes call *paper contractors* – do-it-yourself property developers.

This group tend to be fairly well-off and tend to build relatively high spec houses; some estimates reckon that over a third of all detached housing in the UK is now selfbuilt. For many of this new breed of selfbuilder there will be little or no physical involvement in the construction of their homes; they are instead providing the nous (and money) to get a plot of land purchased and to build a new home on it.

Throughout the postwar years, this

activity for your spare time that should gain you more in a year than your regular salary? With the benefits completely tax-free? If so, you are looking at self build. It is all based on the fact that the cost of a serviced building plot added to the cost of building a house on it using subcontractors is significantly less than the finished value of the property. Typically the savings will be around 25 per cent and on a £160,000 home this can be £40,000.'

Sounds too good to be true? You guessed it. Whilst many people do end up with pleasing results like this, it's not easy and many people don't make any money at all. With the more recent housing boom now well and truly over, it will be interesting to see just how resilient self build remains this time. The good news is that property slumps turn up loads of buying opportunities, as developers offload plots they can't afford to finance on debt.

LAND COSTS ARE THE KEY

The way in which prices for building plots are set is based on subtracting the building costs from the estimated value of the completed house. For example, if the estate agent or surveyor marketing a plot reckons that a nicely finished house might fetch £300,000 and that it might cost around £120,000 to build, then they will probably recommend that the plot be sold for around £130,000, maybe more, leaving a small element of profit for the

group was typically buying and doing up old wrecks of houses, but as the wrecks with the most potential have mostly been snapped up now, their attention has moved on to building from scratch. Now it is recognised that there is such a thing as a self build industry that supports many specialist businesses, three national magazines – 'Build It', 'Selfbuild & Design' and 'Homebuilding & Renovating' – and various exhibitions up and down the land. Not to mention, of course, its very own TV programme, Grand Designs, which more than anything has promoted the idea that self build is a noble activity, or at least an aspirational one.

And whilst the credit crunch has affected all areas of homebuilding, self build is one niche which the storm clouds seem mostly to have

Despite, or maybe because of, their simplicity, Walter Segal houses are instantly recognisable, even though the designs have undergone a few modifications over the years

passed by. The number of self builds is down about 15 per cent from their peak in 2007, but the average spend has increased by a similar amount. Self build has gone up-market.

So why do people self build? There are two distinct camps here. One is to work your way up the property ladder (aka making a bit of money): the other is to individuate – to get exactly what you want (aka spending a bit of money). Much of the sales literature used to attract individuals to build their own homes is based on the former premise – that there is a large, tax-free profit to be had. Whilst the responsible end of the market likes to rein in such claims, you still come across examples of this hype. Here's one I dredged from my archives:

'Interested in a management

builder. There is obviously a return here but the problem is that there are many more costs involved than just the plot price and the building costs.

If house prices increase by 15 per cent during the time it takes you to build, all appears well and good and you do appear to get a fantastic return on your efforts; but if house prices don't go up you'll have to throw an almighty number of hours at your building project if you are to keep costs down to a level at which you appear to make a profit of more than a few per cent.

The bulk of the profit in a greenfield housing site tends to go to the landowner who succeeded in gaining planning permission to turn whatever was there into building land.

In most parts of the UK, agricultural land is worth around £3,000 per acre, although after many years in the doldrums, this now appears to be rapidly rising. In contrast, in SE England at least, half-acre building plots are still fetching over a hundred times as much.

One effect of this relationship between land costs and finished housing costs is that building plots tend to go up in value faster than house prices when house prices are rising; conversely, plot prices fall further than house prices when house prices slump.

As the money men would put it, land prices are geared to house prices so they experience faster rates of growth and decline.

UNDERSTANDING THE COSTS

If you just add plot costs and building costs together you'd see a 20-30 per cent profit (this is the margin that the press get so excited about), but a more thorough analysis reveals that the figure is nowhere near this amount. In particular, finance

costs eat into the gross profit at an alarming rate and the effect of a) interest rates going up and b) failure to obtain a quick sale are disastrous.

Anyone who borrows to finance a project as large as a new house is extremely vulnerable to changes in interest rates.

When interest rates start to rise, professional developers get squeezed not just by the extra cost of this finance but also by the fact that the level of sales tend to decline, sometimes accompanied by the dreaded fall in house prices. Housebuilders are very vulnerable in these circumstances and what looks like a healthy profit on a house can evaporate within a matter of weeks.

A selfbuilder is in a subtly different situation to a speculative developer and this may mean that they are able to hang on to more of this gross profit margin. The selfbuilder doesn't need to find a buyer and therefore has no selling costs; also the selfbuilder can keep construction costs down by carrying out supervision and some construction work. Against this, however, it is unlikely that they can build as cheaply as a professional developer, whatever construction methods they use.

WHERE ARE THE SAVINGS?

The costs of the average residential building job are made up of around 50 per cent on-site labour and 50 per cent materials. In theory, you could therefore achieve savings of around 50 per cent on construction costs if you carried out all the labour yourself – but here we have to look at some rather complex actuarial calculations about the value of your time and the cost of borrowed money. Only if you are both rich and unemployed can you afford to ignore these calculations.

Most DIY projects are of low value (say,

less than £1,000) and have little effect on house values. They are carried out because the occupants appreciate their amenity value. However, larger building projects – extensions, conversions, rehabilitations and especially new housebuilding – call for much closer assessment of your labour input.

By taking on even part of the work yourself, you are in effect becoming a speculative builder whose work will be rewarded by an increase in the value of your property. The more work you carry out yourself, the less you pay to others and the greater your eventual profit (in theory).

The problem with this sort of work is that your labours are far more likely to be rewarded in line with property price movements rather than with how hard or well you yourself work. In boom times your rate per hour may appear to be enormous (and you'd probably think yourself very clever for embarking on this nice little tax-free earner); however, building through a slump puts all that into a new perspective, and many DIY builders will have found that they have actually lost money – and the more masochistic will have converted that into a loss per hour which begins to make slavery look like an attractive alternative.

Most people would not consider carrying out all the work themselves. In fact, the vast majority of people would have no more wish to take on such a task than they would choose to educate their children at home; life simply isn't that long.

There are, however, many people who find their work is seasonal, intermittent or out of normal working hours, to whom a high level of involvement in a building project makes good sense. They will tend to be practical and experienced in problem solving and those that are already running their own business will have much of the

Where the Money Goes

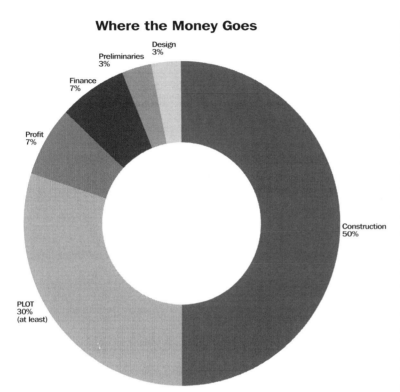

Design 3%

Preliminaries 3%

Finance 7%

Profit 7%

PLOT 30% (at least)

Construction 50%

follow the economic cycle, so that in boom times the rates can go sky high, whereas in busts they fall back pretty quickly.

MANAGEMENT WITH A BROOM

For every seven or eight hours spent on construction, one hour has to be put into servicing the site. This can involve any and everything from sweeping up and unloading lorries to meeting building inspectors and buying materials. Many selfbuilders take on this 'management with a broom' role thinking that they may not be able to plaster a wall or fit a staircase, but they had no trouble organising the school run, therefore...

Be warned. You'd be right to think that the organisational skills are not in themselves exceptional, but their efficient execution is very dependent on a reasonable working knowledge of the building trades' and the local building practices and prices.

After three or four projects, you'll start to get halfway good; if it's your first time, most people find it an almighty struggle and you'll be unlikely to do it well. Your subcontractors will very quickly realise they are working for a novice and the less scrupulous ones may be tempted to take advantage of this and to cut corners or to bodge, particularly if you've negotiated 'keen' labour prices.

Whilst your building inspector should ensure that the structure is adequate, very little professional checking takes place above foundation level and, in any event,

organisational backup in place already. The extra costs involved will not be enormous and even if their work only nets them £2.50 per hour, that's still more than they'd get doing nothing.

However, for many people selfbuilding may just prove to be a lousy option. They will be committing themselves to 2,000-3,000 hours work – often very hard and dirty work – putting up an overpriced structure to a design that isn't very good in the vague hope of making a 'dream home' and a 'fantastic windfall profit' to boot. Ask yourself two questions:

1. If it is that easy to make money, why don't more selfbuilders turn into professional property developers?

2. If builders' profits are so exorbitantly high, how come so many of them keep going bust?

I started as a selfbuilder (albeit with a renovation not a new build) and went on to become a 'professional' (in that other people paid me for my labours), often working alongside selfbuilders. It'll come as no surprise when I report that the hours are long, the work is backbreaking and the pay is often crap. The pay rates usually

This doughnut chart shows the breakdown of costs on a typical small developer model. The 30 per cent plot cost is variable in the extreme: it can be as much as 50 per cent in the more expensive areas – but the final profit figure is still fairly realistic. Even in the good times, the big plc housebuilders rarely made profits of more than 10 per cent per unit sold

Chapter 1

Comparison of Costs: Developer v Kit Home Selfbuilder

	DEVELOPER	SELFBUILDER	
Plot	£140,000	£140,000	
Stamp Duty	£1,500	£1,500	No stamp duty on purchases under £125,000. Above this, it's 1% of transaction costs
Community Infrastructure Levy	£20,000	£20,000	
Purchasing Legals	£500	£500	
Survey Fees	£600	£600	
Design Work	£3,000	£0	Design fees included in kit house purchase
Planning Fee	£800	£800	
Building Control	£900	£900	
Structural Warranties	£800	£1,000	
Insurance	£600	£600	
Infrastructure Charge	£650	£650	
Water Connection	£600	£600	
Electricity Connection	£750	£750	
Build Costs	£150,000	£160,000	This covers a kit house plus follow-on trades. Savings could be enhanced with DIY work
Selling Costs	£7,000	£0	
Finance @6% for Plot (18months)	£16,400	£16,400	
Finance @ 6% for Build Costs	£6,000	£6,400	
Total Development Costs	£350,100	£350,700	
Projected Sale Price	£400,000	£400,000	
Profit Before Tax	£49,900	£49,300	
Profit after Tax at 40%	£29,940	no tax	

building regulations do not cover most of the finishing trades.

Furthermore, don't kid yourself that you're doing away with the overheads of employing a main contractor by managing the project yourself. Your phone bill will be up by £100-£200 a quarter; your mileage will increase two or three fold, even if you are living on site; you will need site insurance; you will suffer damage to materials which will have to be replaced at your own expense; you will end up with leftovers that you cannot easily get rid of; and at the end of the job, you'll have to chase yourself to get all those little snags finished.

More than half of a main contractor's mark-up goes on paying overheads that would be common to professionals and amateurs alike. And there is still the tricky little matter of finance. There are many other costs besides plot and building costs, and they all conspire to eat away your paper profit.

STILL WANT TO SELFBUILD?

Having got all that off my chest, I will also readily point out that I have met many selfbuilders who have made a tidy packet out of their dealings. Nevertheless, I would argue that the rewards of selfbuilding are not chiefly financial. What it really allows is the freedom to design and build a new house to your specifications, something that you will not be able to do by any other route.

For many people selfbuilding represents one of the great challenges in life. The more they are involved in the project, the more they get out of it and the whole attraction of selfbuild is the pure adventure of it all. If this is your motivation then more power to your elbow.

You may well end up just a little disappointed by the outcome and will perhaps be haunted by a whole host of 'what ifs' and 'if onlys.' Fear not, this is an experience common to all designers and builders. You'll just have to do it all again.

However, if your motivation is mainly financial then I warn you to look very carefully at the sums involved.

Yes, you can save money selfbuilding but it may not be as much as you might first expect.

Don't ignore the well-trodden route of hiring a designer (who in turn manages the job for you) just because you think it will be expensive.

Don't forget that property developing

(for that's what you're doing) is a risky business.

Unlike many financial products that are now sold with warnings attached, building plots and the houses that go on them are sold on the understanding that the buyer knows the risks involved. You are assumed to be a sophisticated investor; make sure that you actually are.

EMOTIONAL INVESTMENT

The selfbuilder has an emotional investment in their project and really wants to believe that all their work actually makes sense financially; on the other side, the professional builder has good financial reasons for not wanting to exaggerate the profitability of any scheme they undertake. To do so would be to hand money over to the taxman. Thus the professional builder will account for every cost they possibly can whereas the selfbuilder will be inclined to overlook many of the legitimate overheads in order to make the final sum look more pleasing.

Nowhere is this discrepancy greater

How Big Is That House

	M²	FT²	RANGE OF BUILDING COSTS
One-bedroom flat	40	430	£30,000-£45,000
Terraced two-bedroom house	60	650	£50,000-£70,000
Semi-detached, 3 bedrooms	90	970	£80,000-£120,000
Detached 3/4 bedrooms	130	1,400	£120,000-£180,000
Large detached 4/5 bedrooms	200	2,150	£180,000-£300,000

than in the area of finance. To a developer, finance is just another job cost, essentially no different than the cost of the land or the building costs. When the house is sold on, they will total up all the loan interest they have paid and add it in as a legitimate business cost.

The selfbuilder is in a rather different position. They may – probably will – already have a mortgage before they even think of taking on a major project like a new house or a major renovation. By transferring this mortgage from an existing house to a building plot they are not necessarily altering their cashflow at all and do not have to add this cost into their calculations.

What they are doing is exchanging a year or two's hardship (such as living with the in-laws or in a caravan on site) for the opportunity to live in a bigger or better house than they could otherwise afford. Whilst a cost accountant would probably say that the selfbuilders are deceiving themselves, it seems to me to be a perfectly legitimate approach to things.

If there is a danger for the selfbuilder in all this, it is that they will tend to get greedy and to overreach themselves. It is notoriously difficult to accurately predict building costs and the world is full of people with a vested interest in making building costs look cheaper than they actually are. Getting prices out of builders and subcontractors is often much easier said than done and the chances are that most selfbuilders will have to commit themselves to a building project before they have a clear idea of the actual costs. Often people realise at a comparatively late stage that they can't afford the scheme they have embarked on and desperately look for ways of reducing the costs.

Many will complain bitterly just how expensive builders are when the root of the problem is that they always had inflated expectations of what they could achieve with the money at their disposal.

Many people are bounced into becoming project managers because they think it is bound to be cheaper to build

Selfbuild allows you to choose the type of house you want (planners permitting)! Selfbuild covers virtually anything that isn't developed by a builder for sale. You can lay every brick – or none. The choices are yours

directly with subcontractors. This is not the way to become a selfbuilder; it's the way to become a headless chicken. Even hard-bitten professionals have problems reconciling their dreams with their budgets and it is essentially in response to this problem that I wrote this book – to help put you, the person paying all the bills, back in control of the situation.

THE MODEL HOUSE

EVERY EDITION OF the Housebuilder's Bible – until this one – has had a benchmark house. It's almost invariably been a four bedroom detached house, built in the year before publication, usually built by selfbuilders or sometimes a small developer. The idea has been to extract the information from the project and to feed it into the new edition.

But this approach comes with a problem attached. The houses are never the same and so comparing them with one another is impossible. For instance, I can't tell you how much cheaper it was to build in 1994 than it was in 2010, the last time I did this exercise, because the houses were quite different.

So for this, the 10th edition, I am doing it differently. I've created a model house which will run through future editions. It's not a house that's ever been built: it's a virtual house consisting of nothing more than a series of numbers, areas and volumes which reflect what goes on in a typical house. For it turns out that the homes I have analysed, though individual, are not so very different from one another and that many of the key measurements are remarkably similar. It's all very well having a unique benchmark house in each edition, but as no one is setting out to build the self same house, it's only of

academic interest to the reader.

The New Model House

The house has an internal floor area of 160 m², divided between two floors. That's pretty much average for a UK selfbuild, and average for all the benchmark houses I have used over the years which run from 110 sq m up to 220 sq m.

The house itself is rectangular measuring 13 m x 7.3 m externally. As the walls are 375 mm wide, the internal dimensions are 12.25 m x 6.55 m, or 80 sq m per floor. Double this and you get your 160 sq m (note that I don't discount the area taken up by the stairwell). There is a pitched roof with gable end walls at either end of the house.

A chimney? A good question. Every benchmark house I have used, until the 9th edition, had a fire or at least a wood stove and therefore a chimney. The 9th edition broke with this because it featured two homes which were specifically low energy – one being a Passivhaus – and neither of them had a conventional central heating system, nor a fire. So my model house, in the spirit of a brave new future, has no fire and no chimney either, but you can look elsewhere to find the cost of adding these.

In fact there are a lot of things like stoves that selfbuilders aspire to which can be taken out of a model house and it begins to look suspiciously cheap to build. But therein lies an important lesson. Much of the rising cost of building a house – and it has risen a lot in the 20 years I have been writing about it – is down to consumer preferences. Not just wood stoves, but fancy kitchens with granite worktops, hardwood flooring, wet rooms, LED lighting schemes, glass balustrades, not to mention various forms of renewable heating.

The model house can take them all, but it doesn't have to either. At it's most basic, it's a very simple build. There is no garage either. That's probably a bit unlikely for a detached house these days but once again it's fairly easy to cost as an extra.

What's interesting is that the cost of building this model house is less than £150,000, a lot less than £1,000 per sq m. 'Homebuilding & Renovating' magazine publishes a build cost calculator which you can find on their website (look under the Advice Section) and it shows that building at around this cost is quite common in many parts of the country, whichever build route you choose.

An awful lot of this has to do with the standard you choose to build and how many expensive fittings you chose to put in place. For instance, whether you are happy with radiators (cheap) or you want to splash out on underfloor heating. Or whether you go for concrete roof tiles or something like natural slate or handmade clay tiles.

It's also interesting to reflect that actual building costs haven't changed a huge amount over the years. Builders certainly aren't taking home more money and many materials haven't altered much in price for years, though some have been affected by commodity prices increases. The big increase in housebuilding costs since I started this project twenty years ago has mostly been down to consumer preferences for more stuff and more expensive stuff.

The Model House cost table is on the opposite page. Each individual row is discussed in detail in the relevant chapter and there is a more detailed cost table to be found there. The following page shows the assumptions that went into creating the model house..

Model Housebuilding Cost Summary

	MATERIALS	LABOUR	PLANT	FEES	SUBTOTAL	TOTAL
CH 6 GROUNDWORKS						£ 22,000
Groundworks	£ 6,200	£2,800	£2,300		£11,300	
Drains & Services	£3,200	£2,200		£5,300	£10,700	
CH 7 SUPERSTRUCTURE						£42,700
Inner Skin	£ 1,500	£ 2,500			£4,000	
Steels & Lintels	£900	£200			£1,100	
External Brickwork	£ 3,800	£ 4,600			£ 8,400	
Insulation	£3,300	£ 1,400			£ 4,700	
Joinery	£ 7,200	£1,100			£ 8,300	
Internal Floors	£ 1,300	£ 1,300			£ 2,600	
Internal Walls	£ 1,000	£ 1,300			£ 2,300	
Roof Carpentry	£ 2,000	£ 1,200			£ 3,200	
Roof Cover (slates)	£ 4,100	£ 2,600			£ 6,700	
Rainwater/Fascia	£ 600	£ 800			£ 1,400	
CH 8 HEATING	£ 3,000	£ 2,300				£5,300
CH 9 ELECTRICS	£ 2,700	£ 3,700				£ 6,400
CH 10 FINISHES						£33,100
Plastering & Screeding	£ 3,500	£ 6,100			£ 9,600	
Wall & Floor Finishes	£ 5,500	£ 3,000			£ 8,500	
Second Fix Carpentry	£ 2,700	£ 2,400			£ 5,100	
Painting	£ 500	£ 2,700			£ 3,200	
Externals & Paving	£ 3,200	£ 3,500			£ 6,700	
CH 11 ROOM BY ROOM						£13,900
Kitchen	£ 9,800	£ 1,500			£ 11,300	
Bathroom	£ 1,300	£ 1,300			£ 2,600	
CH 13 PRELIMS			£6,000			£ 6,000
PROFESSIONALS (CHS 4 & 5)				£8,000		£8,000
Rounded Totals	£ 67,000	£ 49,000	£ 8,000	£ 13,000		£ 137,000
Int FloorArea in m^2			160			
	Cost/m^2		£ 856			
	Cost/ft^2		£ 80			

Chapter 1

The Model House Assumptions

BASICS Two storey, rectangular house. No garage

External Dimensions	m	13.0 x 7.3
Internal Dimensions	m	12.25 x 6.55

ITEM	UNIT	VALUE	RANGE	COMMENTS
GENERAL				
Internal floor area (two floors)	m²	160	110-200	Twice internal dimensions
House perimeter	m	40	33-60	
House Footprint	m²	95	60-110	Area of external dimensions
Oversite area	m²	140	120-240	50% larger than footprint
Oversite excavation volume	m³	35	21-42	Depth dependent but usually around 0.25m
Heated volume	m3	430	244-536	Int gr floor area x 5.4
Upstairs Floor Area	m²	80		
SUPERSTRUCTURE				
Setting Out Foundations	m²	120	95-200	Footprint plus 25%
Foundation length	lin m	70	45-100	
Excavating Foundations	m³	40	22-55	Assume Length x 0.6 width x 1.0 deep
Readymix (600mm deep)	m³	25	10-50	Dependent on depth
Footings (550 deep)	m²	40	18-30	Dependent on depth of readymix
House Floor Slab Area	m²	95	60-110	Same as Footprint
Screed	m²	80	55-100	Int floor area, one floor
Foul Drains	m	40	15-50	Site specific
Rainwater Drains	m	60	25-75	Site specific
Service Trenching	m	15	15-25	Site specific
External Wall Area inc Openings (Gross)	m²	235	150-250	House perimeter x 5.4, plus 2 gables
Combined Gable Area (35° pitch)	m²	19		Worked with roof calcs, but used as part of ext wall calcs
Joinery Area	m²	35	18-40	Often surprisingly close to 35m²
Ext Wall Area minus Openings (Net)	m²	200	115-215	
Inner Skin (gross)	m²	220	125-220	Note it's around 7% less than external measurements
Inner skin area (net)	m²	185	110-200	
Ext Lintels	No	16		Typical for 35m² of Joinery
Possible Lintel Length	m	25		Typical for 35m² of Joinery
Windowboards	m	20		Typical for 35m² of Joinery
Chimney	m²			The model house has no chimney!
First Floor Area	m²	80		The stairwell will, in practice, reduce it by a little
INSULATION				
Insulation GF	m²	80		Derived from Screed measuerments
Insulation Ext Walls	m²	200		Derived from Ext Walls (Net) measurements
Insulation Ceiling	m²	80		Derived from First Floor Area
Insulation Sound Floor	m²	75		Derived from First Floor Area
Insulation Sound Walls	m²	60		Derived from Int Walls (Studwork)

BEFORE YOU START

ITEMS	UNIT	VALUE	RANGE	COMMENTS
INTERNALS				
Internal room-dividing wall area (net)	m²	130	86-185	Net means door openings have been deducted. Ext walls not included here
Internal Walls masonry	m²	70		Helpful to split internal walls by type
Internal walls studwork	m²	60		Helpful to split internal walls by type
Steel Beams	No	2	0-5	Most houses of this size have a beam or two, but its not a prerequisite
Plastered area	m²	490	380-650	Sum of plastered walls and ceilings: if alternative mats used, then further breakdown required
Plastered walls net of openings	m²	350	280-420	Worked out on a room-by-room basis
Plastered Ceilings	m²	140	110-240	Worked out on room-by-room basis; calcs are complex with sloping ceilings, none on model house
Coving	m	150	115-175	Ceiling-wall junction measurement, worked out on a room-by-room basis
Architraves	m	130	110-200	Door openings have (conventionally) 5.1m of architrave each side
Skirtings	m	120	100-160	Wall -floor junction measurement, worked out on a room-by-room basis
Internal Doors	No	13	12-14	Remarkable how small the range is. Maybe not.
Door Lining Lengths	m	65	60-75	Conventionally 5.1m per opening
ROOF				
Roof Cover (in plan)	m²	100	70-150	Generally 10% more than footprint due to overhangs.
Roof Cover (actual 35° pitch, dual pitch)	m2	122	120-213	35° roof usually 20% larger: 45° roof usually 40% larger
Chimney	No	0	0-2	There is no chimney on the model house
Rainwater (Gutters and Downpipes)	m	45	36-95	
Eaves	m	26	20-35	Varies depending on roof shape: here it's combined front and back elevations
Ridge	m	13.2	4-15	Varies depending on roof shape: here it's half the eaves length
Hips	m	0	0-10	Model house does not have a hipped roof
Verges (Bargeboards)	m	18	0-20	The verge is the gable-roof junction. Model house has gables at both ends of roof.
Scaffold Run	m	40	33-60	Taken from house perimeter
FINISHES				
Rigid kitchen units	m³	10	4-13	Unusual way to estimate kitchen costs but can be quite helpful
Worktops	lin m	10	8-12	Even small houses seem to have long worktops these days
Kitchen sinks	No	2		
Bathrooms	No	2.5		2.5 means there are two bathrooms upstairs and a small WC downstairs: bog standard
Hardwood Flooring	m²	60	0-115	Flooring costs equate to internal floor area but the split is elective
Floor Tiling	m²	30	0-65	
Carpet	m²	70	0-95	
Wall Tiling	m²	40	10-60	10 is a minimum: above this it's elective
EXTERNALS				
Base Preparation	m²	160	120-160	Surprisingly similar results from all manner of houses
Driveway	m²	140	100-160	
Block Paving	m²	20	0-160	
Paving slabs	m²	15	0-60	
Fencing	m	30	0-50	
Close boarded Fencing	m	15	0-25	
Turfing	m²	140	0-140	
GARAGE	No	0	0-1	Garage is excluded from model house. Cost £8k for single; £12k for double.

CASE STUDY

I MAY HAVE abandoned the idea of a benchmark house in this edition but a case study is still a useful guide to what's happening in the real world. I've included a very interesting house built by an old schoolfriend of mine, Michael Goodhart. I hadn't clapped eyes on Michael since about 1965 and I'd completely lost touch with him, but whilst I'd been wheeling away in the nether regions of property development and writing, he'd been carving out a career as a conservation architect in Leicester. But us baby boomers are getting older and Michael and his wife, children's author Pippa Goodhart, had long had their eyes on a family-owned piece of land in the village outside Cambridge where Pippa had grown up and where some other members of Michael's family lived.

Now stop right here. Those of you without access to land and who could only dream of getting a plot in a nice

village outside Cambridge will be turning green with envy at this point.

You are probably thinking this all reeks of privilege and silver spoons. But not so fast. This was no hand-me-down building plot. It was very difficult to achieve planning permission and it wasn't at all straightforward to negotiate terms with the Council and the rest of the family. It's quite a complex story, not atypical of the hurdles faced by today's self builders.

Micheal's first proposal did actually get planning permission, but it had a very tight access down the side of his sister's house. It would have turned a valued strip of his sister's garden into his driveway. So he put in for an alternative planning permission which accessed the house via a cul-de-sac of 1980s sheltered bungalows. The council didn't like this and turned it down, possibly reasoning that you shouldn't mix private and social housing, or more likely that a single house wasn't a good use of this plot.

Michael and Pippa went to appeal and during this time government planning policy changed: the old reqirement for high density was ditched in favour of a more laissez-faire approach. The net result is that they got permission for the house with the alternative access and, in the process, gained a lovely, private, south-facing garden on the other side of the house. The council still managed to charge them £5,785 for easements and access across what effectively was a ransome strip but this would have cost considerably more, had the site not already had planning permission. The council also got their hands on another £5,000 for a Section 106 agreement, but in light of what seems to be coming our way (or many areas is now upon us)with the Community Infrastructure Levy, it seems the Goodharts got away relatively lightly.

The family decided that they wanted to keep the design fairly simple in

SOUTH / GARDEN ELEVATION   EXTERNAL FINISHES

ROOF : GREY AND PHITOVOLTAIC INTERLOCKING TILES

WALLS : WANEY EDGED ELM BOARDING BUFF COLOURED FACING BRICKS

WINDOWS : PAINTED TIMBER/OAK SILLS

DOORS & BALLUSTRADE - SEASONED OAK

GUTTERS, RWPS & BUTTS - UPVC/CC ALUM,

PORCH : GREEN OAK

NORTH / FRONT ELEVATION

WEST ELEVATION   EAST ELEVATION

REVISION A : 30/8/2010

1
With a large collection of books to display, together with somewhere inviting to sit and read them, Michael and Pippa built a landing library, lined with shelves. The shelves are backed in bright lime green and back lit. The library landing leads onto a generous balcony that overlooks the garden

2
The balcony is shaded from the glare of its southern aspect by a deep roof overhang. The waney edge oak weatherboarding helps link the building to the well-landscaped garden

both concept and execution, and chose to build using a largely conventional masonry superstructure. Having said that, this being 2012, the house bristles with new technologies such as air source heat pumps, underfloor heating and computer-controlled lighting. But it's the personal touches which mark this house out.Michael and Pippa were living in Leicestershire during the build and at first he was only able to manage a weekly visit, so much of the responsibility for the construction fell on the shoulders of one or two trusted individuals, notably Norman Wells who acted as foreman whilst undertaking a lot of the carpentry and joinery work. Michael's role was therefore somewhere between client, architect and co-ordinator. He spent a great deal of time assembling a crew to get the project through to completion and, by and large, his thorough preparation paid dividends. Towards the end of the build Michael spent more time on site, so was able to react speedily, for example, commissioning hand-made tiles at very short notice. Being hands on allowed him to create special finishing touches.

Michael said: "Both of us wanted a good workspace; something we didn't have in our previous home. Hence the large through-room studio upstairs with 'his and hers' ends for desks, and built-in shelving and cupboards.

We also had a large collection of books which we wanted to house and display, together with somewhere inviting to sit and read them. So we've built a landing library (top of page opposite) lined with shelves that are backed in bright lime green, and lit to stunning effect. You can step from that library-landing, through an arch of books around French windows, onto a generous balcony that overlooks the garden. Cedar-lined, and with lighting for evenings, the balcony is shaded from the glare of its southern aspect by a deep roof over-hang."

The slate kitchen work-tops, window sills, and a panel within the mantelpiece all come from the Burlington quarry in the Lake District which Michael had used on a previous job. Pippa and Michael toured the quarry and chose the slate workshops before the

build, so the choices of stone are individual to them. Some of that slate has been carved beautifully by Eric Marland to create number and name plates for the house. They also commissioned the artist Susan Moxley to create two stained glass windows placed at the front of the house. And Pippa's sister, Jo Eddleston, made some beautiful glass tiles featuring butterflies and dragon flies in shiny metallic insets which adorn the bathroom and wet room.

Points of Interest

The house is an interesting mix of the economic and the exotic. The basic shell couldn't be simpler – a rectangular shape built in brick and block under a trussed roof which

First floor joists are I-beams – an engineered solution, combining lightness with strength. They are sitting on high insulation thin blocks

is covered with simple Stonewold tiles. Much of the distinctive feel of Silver Grove derives from the use of waney-edged elm planks and oak framing around the upper storey which reflects some of the neighbouring houses and references the Arts & Crafts style. This is further emphasized by the beautiful oak-framed porch with a cedar shingle roof which reaches forward in a welcoming manner.

The house is heated via an air-source heat pump which supplies both hot water and an underfloor heating system. The only supplementary heating is a wood-burning stove, seated in the kitchen area, and whose wood supply is neatly housed outside the potting shed, a keenly

1
First floor studwork walls before insulation and plasterboarding. The flooring is Caberdek board, which provides high levels of acoustic performance

2
Loft space is built up from a hybrid roof design which doesn't use conventional attic trusses. The space is unheated but is used as a games room and for storage. It's not included in the floor area measurements for the house

3
Gangnail trusses on the south side where the roof pitch changes from 35 deg to 25 deg, to get a big overhang on the south roof to create summer shading

4
As part off the house's low energy concept Redland's photovoltaic tiles are integrated into the Stonewold roof tiles

5
Plasterer Mick Firek working in the garage. The walls are insulated because the garage is outside the heated envelope

6
The balcony area under construction showing the structural first floor walls in contrast to the studwork walls in picture 1

Right
3D drawing showing the house in its location – including the relocated parking spaces

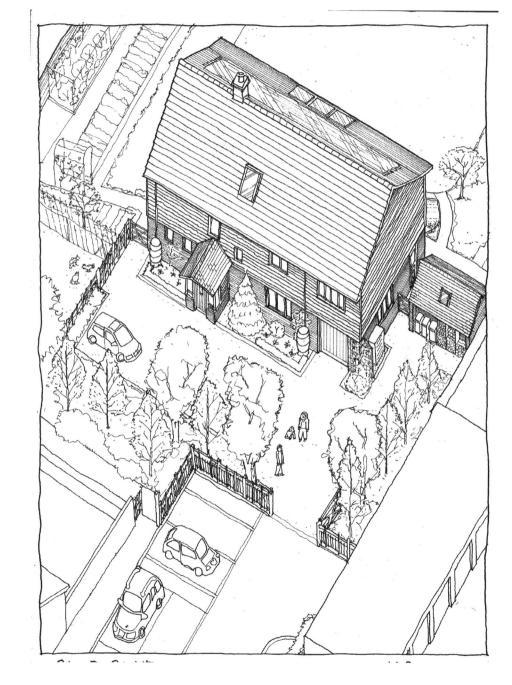

anticipated annexe, constructed simultaneously with the house. Whilst many self builds take years to establish a garden, Michael and Pippa had undertaken the landscaping, built a pond and were growing their own vegetables before they had even moved in.

One of the more unusual features in the house is the computer controlled system by Lighting Sensations. It enables banks of lights to be switched in harmony to create lighting scenes, rather than adjusting each light individually. The system cost just over £5,000, and involved a lot of extra wiring as well, but the main benefit is the convenience of being easily-able to change the light settings in the main rooms to accommodate what is going on.

What We Learned

Michael commented: "We learned the importance of providing unimpeded access to enable tradesmen to get on with their work. If you are paying by the day, you want to make that day as productive as possible. On

Around £38,000 of the budget was spent on external fencing, hard landscaping and planting – most of which was already in place (with plants established) before Michael and Pippa moved in

the other hand, if paying for the job, you don't want to make the job difficult. Frustrations with the client are likely to reflect in the tradesman's motivation and commitment to the job.

"We were surprised to find that bespoke pieces from crafts people cost so little, as a proportion of the overall build cost. Those things made for a personal and particular build, and yet weren't extravagant.

"I under-estimated the skill required for much of the work. I was especially impressed by

1

Cylinder cupboard with split unit above. Also visible are the manifolds for the first floor underfloor heating and the controls for the roof mounted solar panels

2

The external unit of the Air Source Heat Pump – which provides heat for the underfloor heating

3

Rear elevation clearly showing the two different solar roof panels. The larger display is solar pv – generating electricity, whist the smaller ones over the balcony are solar thermal – helping heat the hot water

the ground-workers, masons, woodworkers, electrician, plumbers, tiler and decorator. They worked with energy and commitment, often using exceptional intuitive ability enhanced by years of experience. It was wonderful to watch, and heartening to have that work being done on our home."

On Costs

It's a very interesting case study as regards costs. On the face of it there are several items that seem very expensive, certainly as

SILVER GROVE COSTS

Groundworks	£18,000
Drains + Services	£4,000
Service Connections	£3,000
Inner Skin	£11,500
Ext Cladding/Porch/Balcony	£20,000
Chimney	£2,000
Joinery	£34,000
Int Floor	£3,500
Int walls	£2,000
Roof Carpentry	£6,500
Roof Cover	£32,500
Rainwater/Fascia	£2,500
Insulation	£3,500
Plumbing & Heating	£20,500
Electrics and Lighting	£37,000
Plastering/Screeding	£13,500
2nd Fix Carpentry	£18,000
Wall/Floor Finishes	£19,000
Painting & Decorating	£7,000
Kitchen	£32,000
Bathrooms	£6,500
Externals	£38,000
Prelims/Scaffolding	£8,500
TOTAL	**£343,000**
INTERNAL FLOOR AREA	**213m²**
COST/m²	**£1,610/m²**

compared with my model house.
■ There is a huge amount spent
on garden and externals works
(£38,000 or 12 per cent of the
total). But much of this was
down to having a very large
driveway connecting to the
re-negotaited entrance, and
having to supply public parking
spaces because the new entrance
had ploughed through the ones
that were there.. The planners
also insisted that the 250 sq m
of paving was permeable which
added considerably to costs, both

the 300 mm permeable driveway
foundations (£8,000) and the
specialised paving (£15,000). The
foundations and the drainage,
the conventional bits of the
substructure, were relatively
modest at around £18,000.
■ The roof is covered in run-of-
the-mill Stonewold roof tiles,
cost just £4,250. But the roof
also features solar PV (£21,850)
and solar thermal (£3,500) which
bump up the roofing costs nearly
six-fold. The solar PV qualified for
the first tranche of the Feed-in-

1
*The woodburning stove
provides additional
heating for the kitchen/
living area at the heart of
the house*

2
*Wood flooring used
through the main
downstairs living areas
is ideal for use with
underfloor heating*

Tariff which paid 41p/kWh over a
25 year period and was, therefore,
an attractive investment in its
own right. You could say that
this was as much about pension
planning as it was construction
costs. The feed-in-tariff still
exists but the amounts paid out
are much lower today, and set
to go lower still. Note, however,
that the cost of installing solar PV
has just about halved since early
2012, so it doesn't necessarily
make it a bad deal.
■ The heating system is

3
The staircase and book landing add to the Arts and Crafts feel of the house

3
The staircase and book landing add to the Arts and Crafts feel of the house

4
Family/kitchen area is a welcoming space that includes slate kitchen worktops from the Burlington Quarry in the Lake District

5
The front-to-back office includes refitted shelving and workspace at opposite ends for Michael and Pippa

6
The potting shed is an unusually sophisticated structure

7
The north-facing side of the potting shed has a deep roof overhang protecting the log and bin store from the elements

expensive, at £22,000: the model house notches up just £5,000-odd, but that's a gas boiler and radiator jobbie. The Goodhart's have gone for a top of the range heating system with underfloor heating on both floors (£8,400) and a Daikin Altherm air source heat pump and a Grant Duowave 250lt hot water cylinder, supplied and fitted for £11,000.

■ The electrics. Again, they have splashed out on electrics, going for a computer-controlled lighting system and numerous fancy bits. In total, they spent £37,000 on electrics and their new home: in comparison, the model house spends just £6,400.

■ Much of the other spending on this house isn't out of line with the model house, given that the Goodhart's house is much bigger and also includes an integral garage (17 sq m) and a large potting shed (9 sq m), neither of which is separated out from the other costs. Considering there is much fine finishing work here and numerous arts and crafts features like carved Burlington slate and fitted bookshelves, it makes a very interesting case study and an overall spend of £343,000 (or £1,600 per sq m) begins to look like very good value.

■ On the other hand, Michael's considerable skills and time are not costed. As he was both designer and project manager, you might anticipate that were he to charge for such services, it might add between 10 per cent and 15 per cent to the overall costs. You can find out for yourself as he's now available for hire to other self builders and renovators. The sort of level of detail you get in an Arts & Crafts inspired new home is never cheap compared to the more industrial output of the mass housebuilders (something akin to my model house), but it more usually costs over £2,000 per sq m. Bringing a project of this standard in under £2,000 per sq m in SE England is some feat

Fact File

NAMES: Michael and Pippa Goodhart (Tel 01223 841420 or michael.goodhart@hotmail.co.uk)

PROFESSIONS: Conservation/Selfbuild Architect and Children's Author

LOCATION: Cambridgeshire

HOUSE: 4 bedroom, 213m² plus integral double garage and large potting shed

CONSTRUCTION: Traditional masonry build, mostly timber clad

PLOT COST: £350,000

BUILD COST: £340,000, £1,420/m²

ADDITIONAL COSTS: £17,300 (access and easements: £5,785, Section 106 £5,047, plus fees and insurances)

WARRANTY: Not taken

FINANCE: NatWest offset flexible mortgage

VALUE TODAY: c £850,000

PITFALLS

FINDING LAND

Every year in Britain between 10,000 and 15,000 selfbuilds, and probably as many major renovations and conversions, are completed. This number has held rather steady for many years, despite some people predicting that we would run out of plots and that every tumbledown old wreck had already been tarted up. The ravages of the credit crunch have only managed to dent the total a little – the overall number is down about 15 per cent over the past five years even though the total spend seems to be much the same. It seems there are fewer houses being built, but they each cost more than they used to. In fact, selfbuild is one of the few bright spots in the construction industry. The opportunities are out there - the business is being done. So, the question is, why do people find it so hard to get started?

I fear that the answer can be summarised in one uncompromising phrase – unrealistic expectations. Or, to put it another way, the opportunities are rather more expensive than people can afford.

The property market is pretty ruthless in valuing opportunity and the idea that you can pick up a really nice building plot for next to nothing is fallacious. The selfbuild exhibitions are full of people who are 'seriously looking at building a house' who basically can't afford to, or at least can't afford it in the expensive areas they already live in. They will make enquiries, log onto websites and register interest, and even buy books, without ever really realising that they haven't got the wherewithal to make it happen. It doesn't help matters that TV still has lots of programmes about doing up property and 'making it all happen': this just pulls even more people into the whirlpool. Without some serious financial

assets and/or income, it's not really going to happen. After two or three frustrating years, would-be builders withdraw, saying they wanted to do it but they couldn't find a plot. But there are plots, and some people do make it happen.

So what are the essential ingredients for people who do manage get on and make it happen? I think they tend to fall into three camps. Either they are rich and can afford to pay the prices needed to secure prime building plots. Or they are lucky and happen to already own a piece of land which is developable. Or they are not too fussy about where they live and will buy anything that comes up - within reason. This last group are the really keen selfbuilders who tend to do it over and over again because they love the whole process of building houses.

There are always dozens of opportunities on offer in every county during the course of a year: if people are deadly serious, they will find something. If they are just sticking a toe in the water, they will always find a reason to not go for a property or they will never bid enough to get it. Or they will complain that they can't afford the prices being asked.

PROFESSIONAL PLOT FINDING

Plot finding is actually becoming more organised and more professional. There are plot finding websites out there that will allow you to zoom-in in aerial photograph mode and get a pretty good idea of what the place is like before you visit.

You can subscribe to plot databases for individual counties and you can also check details of recent planning permissions granted in your district so you get advance warning of plots before they even come to market. Even so, tracking down opportunities is a time consuming process and it pays to be professional about it: always think like a developer, because that is what you are.

According to Buildstore, which runs the Plotsearch database, the average cost of a plot in Surrey is £350,000 whereas in Aberdeenshire it is just £40,000. Those are the two extremes. It follows directly from this that selfbuild in Surrey is somewhat different to selfbuild as practiced in Aberdeenshire. In Surrey, selfbuilders tend to either be replacing their own dilapidated houses or building in their back garden whilst selling off their original house; in Scotland, there is a more conventional selfbuild market with plots being bought by 'ordinary people'. It also means that selfbuild is far more common in the cheaper areas.

Of the 15,000 selfbuilds taking place each year in the UK, over half the total

are in Wales, Scotland or Northern Ireland whose combined population is just 10 million, compared to 50 million people living in England.

Single plots in SE England are so expensive that they attract professional developers whereas in the rest of the country they tend to be sold to amateurs wishing to build for themselves.

So it pays to be realistic. If you live somewhere expensive, you need a plot or a lot of money to make it happen; alternatively, you can move somewhere cheaper and upset the locals with all your flash big-city money. The opportunities are out there.

UNCONSENTED LAND

There are several companies selling 'land' for knock down prices, usually just a few thousand pounds. The adverts seem very enticing but, if you keep your wits about you, you will realise that this land has no planning permission and has very little chance of ever getting planning permission. It's on the wrong side of the planning boundaries and planning boundaries very rarely move, despite what the sales literature would have you believe. Usually the giveaway is that they advise you not to bother with a solicitor. Here's what Gladwish Land Sales suggests: 'No Solicitors necessary! Unlike buying a house, when buying land you do not need to ensure vacant possession (unless you want to scare birds away) nor do you have to ensure all the fixtures stay. Most land that we sell is cheaper than buying a car. Do you use a solicitor to buy a car? The car could be stolen and the log book a forgery! With land, nobody can steal the land you buy and the transfer document you get, once signed, is irrevocable.'

All true. All true. But a solicitor might also advise you not to bother. It gets worse.

I have to hand a glossy brochure from an outfit calling itself UK Land Investments Group, head office in Berkeley Square in London, no less. They offer an 'unparalleled level of expertise' and a 'rare blend of knowledge and practical know-how which sets us apart' (who writes this guff?) and suggest that this is an opportunity for serious investors or, as they get called in Berkeley Square, private clients. Plots in East Sussex are being offered for £7,500. Better still, you can pay your 10 per cent deposit with a credit card. No need to bother with expensive solicitors. And you will become the proud owner of a slice of a field in Sussex with no realistic hope of becoming a building plot this side of the 22nd century.

There is nothing illegal about all this. They don't make any false claims. They make it clear the plots don't have planning permission. They do, sort of, insinuate that they will get planning permission but are very careful with their choice of words here. 'We negotiate with local councils on your behalf so that you don't have to worry about getting planning permission.' That's good wording, isn't it? You 'don't have to worry about it' because nothing is ever going to happen on that front.

The moral? Don't buy land without planning permission from anybody unless you are certain what you are letting yourself in for. If you are tempted by any plot always talk to local planners who will be able to tell you about the history of any applications and the likelihood of getting planning consent

MECHANICS OF PROPERTY PURCHASE

There are basically five methods by which property (including building plots) can change hands in these islands.

■ Public auction: The best thing about

Settlement Boundaries

this is that it's open. It gives the seller (or vendor in these circles) a legally binding agreement. On the other hand the expensive pre-sale work has to be undertaken with no guarantee of success. Sometimes, in the excitement of an auction, it doesn't get done at all. A 10 per cent deposit is usually taken at the auction so the buyer has to have funds to hand.

■ Formal tender: as practiced in Scotland. Once a bid is accepted, the deal becomes legally binding.

Otherwise similar to the auction in terms of pros and cons.

■ Informal tender: buyers are asked to send in sealed bids for the property by a fixed date, together with details of their own financial position. All the bids are opened at the same time and the sale is agreed, usually with the party considered to be in the best position to buy. Buyers are wary and object to the decision being made in private and with no opportunity to increase their bid. However it's probably less

Development is controlled around every settlement in the country. The usual way of doing this is to draw dotted lines on a map, known as framework boundaries. Outside the land is deemed to be agricultural and changes hands at £5,000 an acre. Inside land costs over £1m an acre in southern England

stressful than an auction and gives more flexibility to the vendor.

■ Informal telephone auction: the common method of property sales everywhere outside Scotland. It gives much more flexibility to both sides. This is both its strength and its weakness – you get flaky offers from purchasers and you get gazumping and other evils because the contracts are not binding until physically exchanged. Furthermore, when there are more than three buyers competing for one property, it can get very difficult to organise proceedings because someone is often away or can't make up their mind. In these situations agents often decide to switch to informal tender (see previous point), to close the deal.

■ Private sales: often referred to as 'Sale by Private Treaty'. If a buyer and a seller can agree on a price, then there is no obligation for them to go through the more public channels indicated above. A lot of land changes hands this way. You'd be surprised. Or may be you wouldn't.

The actual process of buying land (or derelict buildings) is similar to that involved in buying houses. You usually employ solicitors and surveyors to ensure that you are not buying a pig in a poke. Likewise with plots, you want to ensure that you can build what you want on it at a price you can afford. But, the whole process of buying plots (and, especially, renovation opportunities) is more complex because there are more things that can go wrong. When buying an existing property at least you know that it is there, even if it might just fall down next week! With a building plot you are buying nothing more than a field that comes with a promise, a hope for the future. And unlike the conventional house market, the chances are that you will have to purchase your plot without knowing exactly what you can build.

THE LIMITS OF PROFESSIONAL HELP

You don't have to hire any help but it's usual to do so because the stakes are high and you don't want to make a silly mistake. If you hire the services of a solicitor or a licensed conveyancer, look for a property specialist. If you are buying in an area new to you, you'd be well advised to look for a local rather than sticking with someone you've used before who might be 200

miles away. Now is the time you need as much information, official and unofficial, as you can get. A good solicitor will uncover more than just that which is revealed by undertaking searches and checking for legal complications and boundaries.

One common pitfall occurs when the planning permission only allows you to build on one part of the site – a frequent occurrence when close to village framework boundaries and the like. Some solicitors spot this, others don't. You should be able to check this yourself on the web: I was able to download my own parish development plan within three minutes of typing the name of my district council into Google (clue – look for the Local Plan maps). But even the best solicitor is not going to be able to advise you as to whether the plot is an A1 purchase because there are a number of other areas that are outside the remit of even the most scrupulous legal beaver.

PURCHASE TAXES

You pay exactly the same taxes on land purchase as you do on house purchase. It's called stamp duty. The government likes stamp duty and they like increasing it: it's a stealth tax because, although people don't like it, it's not going to lose them the next election, and it's relatively easy to police. Only the buyer pays the stamp duty, which gives self builders a small advantage because they are usually buying cheap (plots) and building expensive (houses).

Note that stamp duty is payable on the total value so if you move up a stamp duty tax band then you will pay the higher rate on the total amount. So a house or a plot bought for £249,000 would be charged stamp duty of £2,490 (one per cent of the total), whereas a house or plot bought for £250,000 would be charged £7,500 (three per cent of the total).

Stamp duty rates in the UK are still relatively low compared to other countries, so expect to see these rates continue to rise.

Any other charges? There are fees payable to bodies like the Land Registry (around £200) and for council searches, maybe another £200, but they are not significant in the scheme of things. And of course your legal fees.

RENOVATE OR REBUILD?

As virgin, greenfield building sites become more and more difficult to obtain, increasing numbers of people are looking to purchase dilapidated dwellings that they then seek to demolish and to build afresh. These are basically recycled building sites, sometimes referred to as brownfield sites.

Planning permission is usually much easier to obtain on a site with established residential usage and there are also usually considerable savings to be made because the service connections are already in place. A few sites will have problems with contaminated ground, but mostly the requirements of today's foundations to go much deeper than was previously thought necessary mean that any existing foundations will be excavated and disposed of. In addition to buying a serviced plot, you have an existing structure from which you may well be able to salvage some useful materials.

So far so good. The decision to demolish, however, is often not as clear-cut as this. For a start, few people care to sell their existing properties at building plot prices. To do so is to admit that your home is worthless which can be a bitter pill to swallow, even if it's true. In any event it's usually the case that the house is not worthless, it's just old and dilapidated and with a little bit of tender loving care and a whole lot of money it could continue to make a very serviceable home. So problem number one is the extra expense of buying such a site. Then you are faced with a decision whether to knock down and start again or whether to work with what is already there. Now here things start to get complicated because the chances are that it is not a clear-cut issue, most renovation opportunities fall somewhere between the two extremes. Added to which it is a fiendishly difficult exercise to compare costs between the two approaches because this major decision has to be made at a pre-plan stage and you will have to work with ballpark figures. Whether the building is worth saving at all is an issue that only you (and the planners) can decide – each case has to be argued on its merits and there is little point making any broad generalisations here..

COMPARISON COSTS

Rebuilding from scratch is almost always cheaper than major renovations. It's hard to be too precise as to why this should be but that's the way it goes. For instance, the typical price for building a new home is currently around £900-£1,200/sq m of internal floor area. For barn conversions, the ballpark costs tend to start at £1,200/sq m. At first this appears to be counter-intuitive: after all, with a major renovation or conversion, you already have much of the superstructure in place and

so, logically, you might think that the job would be that much less in scale. But logic and conversions don't sit that well together and experience tends to suggest that major conversions soak up money like a sponge.

Of course, it depends how major your major works are. But restoring a near-derelict superstructure is never quick and even minor repairs seem to cost.

IS IT A PLOT AT ALL?

Don't assume that any building that has once been occupied by humans will automatically qualify for residential planning permission. Councils take widely differing attitudes to what constitutes abandonment and the

If you can find a bungalow on a big plot and buy it at the right price it may be possible to get permission for a larger replacement home. It is a well-trodden route that can be cost-effective, but it is not a certainty, and there will be costs involved

most telling factor in whether or not an old building can be converted into a new home is usually the quality of the building, not its previous usage. Always check on the status of a derelict property in the local plan to see whether redevelopment is likely to be controversial. Often the planners will allow the conversion of a particularly fine old barn just to stop it from disintegrating and sometimes this permission is dependent on the structure being maintained, even when this is a costly and relatively dangerous course to take. There have been cases of planning permission being withdrawn from barn conversions after the builder has undertaken demolition of a few select walls.

LEGAL PITFALLS

The prospect of buying a duff plot is a nightmare that haunts professional builders as much as amateurs, and the consequences of doing so are likely to be with you for many a year to come. There is no absolutely foolproof way of avoiding the lemons but a little diligence (and a good lawyer) employed at the pre-contract stages of negotiations should uncover most of the problems.

LEGAL COVENANTS

Building plots are often sold with legal constraints over what may and what may not be done to them. The most common form of constraint is the covenant whereby the vendor (i.e. the person selling the plot) requires that the purchaser should fulfill a number of conditions. Many of these might not cost a euro – i.e. no caravans to be stored in the back garden or no trees to be planted where they might block someone else's view – but others can involve substantial costs.

The commonest type of covenant deals with boundary fencing and would read something like this: 'The purchaser covenants to erect six foot high fencing to the southern and eastern boundaries of the plot before any building work takes place.'

Sometimes the covenant will be very much more specific and ask for a brick wall nine inches thick or something like that. A condition such as this is expensive to meet and should really be reflected in a lower plot price.

It is also common now to find covenants preventing any further development. The point behind such conditions is not to preserve the unique beauty of your setting but to hold on to any uplift in value you may be clever enough to negotiate with the planners. Covenants have beneficiaries

Stamp Duty

PLOT OR PROPERTY PRICE	DUTY
Up to £125,000	0%
£125,001-£250,000	1%
£250,001-£500,000	3%
£500,001-£1million	4%
£1 million - £2 million	5%
over £2 million	7%

Rates as of 2013

and you can usually remove covenants if you are prepared to throw money at the beneficiaries. The going-rate for buying off a no-development covenant is around 50 per cent of the value created – an arm and a leg, in other words.

Sometimes there are some very old covenants lurking on the deeds and it's long since ceased to be clear who exactly the beneficiary is. Maybe they have died and their heirs are not very apparent: unfortunately, covenants don't disappear with the death of the beneficiary. In such cases, you can insure against anyone coming forward and laying claim to the uplift.

BOUNDARY DISPUTES

It is unfortunately very common to encounter problems with fuzzy boundaries. Just because someone offers a piece of land for sale, it doesn't follow that they own all of it – or even any of it sometimes. Plot boundaries are usually drawn in title deeds as relatively thick lines on OS maps and there is frequently lots of room for disagreement about where exactly these lines are on the ground.

Matters have been improving over the years as owners start to register their plots with the Land Registry but there are still over four million properties in the UK not registered and many of the large estates that

routinely off-load land haven't bothered to register.

In 2003 an amended Land Registration Act was passed, which establishes a framework for registering boundaries using satellite positioning technology. This should mean that having established site boundaries with sellers and neighbours on paper there should be no room for dispute when translating these to the site..

RANSOM STRIPS

Another potential problem occurs when someone else owns part of the land needed to successfully develop a plot. Typically, this is land needed to access the plot. This is sometimes referred to as a ransom strip. Ransom strips can usually be bought off although you may be staggered to find out that you will be required to pay over as much as half of the plot value – they are not called ransom strips for nothing.

RIGHTS OF WAY AND WAYLEAVES

There are any number of complications that should, repeat should, be uncovered by your solicitor's search: rights of way crossing the plot, existing wayleaves for services and cables to cross the plot, complex shared ownership of access roads, to name but three. Even if you can live with these arrangements, they may well affect resale values and make finance much harder to get and insurance more expensive. Many of these problems can be sorted out by throwing money at them – but the canny buyer should ensure it's the vendor's money not theirs.

USING OPTIONS

If there are major problems to sort out (as discussed above) in order to turn the bit of land you want to build on into a legitimate building plot, you might consider taking

Chapter 3

out an option, rather than pressing ahead with a more straightforward purchase.

What is an option to buy? The bare bones of a contract might look like this: you agree a price on a plot of land (though even this doesn't have to be fixed in stone). This remains in place for, say, two or three years; the length of the option is entirely up to you. During that time the vendor is prohibited from selling to anyone else. Some contracts involve interest payments to the vendor: this acts as a spur to the purchaser to get on with it and protects the vendor from time-wasters. The big plus from the purchaser's point of view is that an option protects you from gazumping and other forms of treachery.

How much would you be expected to pay for an option? Well, that depends. If the planning angle is difficult and you are taking on the costs of obtaining planning permission (which could be several thousand), then there may well be no payment made to the vendor at all. They would be very happy for someone else to do all this work for them. However if market conditions are buoyant, then you may have to part with up to five per cent of the plot price just to tempt the vendor into an option. Also the buyer may want to make the plot price conditional on what you manage to squeeze out of planning so that the price is £120,000 if you get permission for one house but £200,000 if you get permission for two.

If there is a pitfall in all this, it is that you can spend a lot of money and get nowhere. But that's a pitfall that all property developers have to face.

PLANNING TRAPS

Ever since they introduced the concept of planning permission in 1947, it's got progressively harder to obtain. Every government makes noises about reforming the planning system but that has invariably been code for introducing yet more controls. The current government, the Coalition, have made a great song and dance about reforming planning and have trumpeted their reduction of 1,000 plus pages of guidance into one simple 52-page document, the National Planning Policy Framework, or NPPF. But it doesn't seem to have made much difference on the ground. The planners, albeit accountable to elected local councillors, now have considerable and arbitrary powers over what you can and cannot do on a piece of land that you nominally own; in effect there is a level of 'state ownership' over each and every building plot and you must fulfill the conditions placed on you before you can begin to put your own ideas in place.

TIME LAPSES

One potential problem for the unwary is the fact that planning permission has a time limit on it. This time limit was reduced from five years to just three in 2004. The key thing is to check when the permission will expire because, currently, there is no guarantee that it will be easy to renew.

Once the work has begun, you no longer have to apply for planning permission. Exactly what the definition is of 'work having been started' is a grey area, but it is usually accepted that if you have laid the footings then you have started. So if time is running short and you don't have the wherewithal to complete the building work, you can ensure your planning permission is permanent by undertaking just the foundations and footings.

PLANNING CONCERNS

The planners are concerned with far more than whether a particular plot can be zoned for building. Some of the major areas they are likely to look at will be:

■ size of the house: is it 'too big for the plot?'
■ site of the house: don't assume you can build anywhere on the plot
■ neighbours' privacy and right to light
■ style of the house: design and materials 'must be in keeping'
■ vehicular access and turning heads: a particular problem on narrow fronted plots, less than 12m wide. The highways department insists that not only will adequate visibility splays be provided, but that there must be adequate room on site for cars to turn around or, as they say in planning speak, 'enter and leave in a forward gear.'
■ trees and hedges: often have to be retained or replanted.

VISIBILITY SPLAYS

Plots need access and this can of itself prove to be quite a planning nightmare. The Highways Department has a little routine known as the visibility splay – which prevents some plots ever being developed. The idea is that each new entrance onto the public highway should be safe and that to be safe it should have clear vision in both directions. In addition to this, the visibility splays have depth as well. At slow speed limits, you need clearance up to 2.4m back from

Visibility Splays

SPEED LIMIT OBSTRUCTIONS FOR:	CLEAR OF
20mph	45m each side
30mph	90m each side
40mph	120m each side
50mph	160m each side
60mph	215m each side
70mph	295m each side

Frustrated selfbuilder Tim Cox proudly displays one of his tiny preserved trees. Huntingdonshire DC thoughtfully slapped TPOs across most of his road frontage, which had the effect of disrupting his development plans

the carriageway: this increases to 4.2m at the higher speed limits. In effect, you have to imagine two triangles of visibility on each side of your site access. These are guidelines. You may well be able to develop a site where the visibility is marginal – i.e. it nearly meets the guidelines. But if you have, for instance, a large wall in your way then you have big problems.

It may be that you can negotiate with (bribe) a neighbour to reduce the height of a hedge or move a fence in order to meet the criteria. You may even have a ransom hedge on your hands.

ACCESS FOR FIRE ENGINES

In the Building Regulations, there is a requirement for a fire appliance to be able to get within a minimum distance of the house along a route of minimum width and to be able to turn around, yet this is not considered at the planning stage.

It would be quite possible for a purchaser of a plot/barn with planning consent to find they could not legally live in it. My good contact, Charlie Duke in Devon, has come across this tricky little scenario three times – it's a particular pitfall for barn conversions where access can be unconventional with narrow access or tight turnarounds.

TREE PRESERVATION ORDERS

Tree Preservation Orders (casually referred to in these circles as TPOs) can be slapped on inconvenient trees just to make life difficult for you. It doesn't have to be a big oak tree either: they can place TPOs on a tree with a girth of just 75mm or, failing that, little clusters of trees as well. Many people have been caught out over the years by inquiring if there were any TPOs in force at such and such a site, only to be told: 'There didn't use to be, but there will be within half an hour!' Well, it's never quite that brazen but it does happen – it's not an urban myth.

However, you can avoid this particular nightmare by asking to inspect the TPO register for your area; TPOs are a matter of public record and you aren't obliged to reveal your hand in order to take a look at it. If your site is TPO-free, you can then cut down anything

that might cause problems in future. In fact, if gaining planning permission could be at all contentious, I would recommend you do just that.

CONSERVATION AREAS

These are areas defined by the planners as being especially sensitive and on which they maintain a whole raft of extra controls over what you can and can't do – for instance you need to fill out a three-page application in order to fell a tree.

Conservation areas are typically the older parts of a town or the core area of a village, perhaps surrounding the village green, and the fact that you are buying in such an area should be apparent when you purchase – after all it is usually used as an additional sales bullet in the blurb and passes as an excuse to hoick the price. It affects new builders less than renovators because new build is already subject to stringent planning controls. But be aware that you will be unlikely to get permission for anything unusual in a conservation area.

Logically the issue of conservation areas ought to be dealt with by regular planning controls but logic and local government make uneasy bedfellows and regular planners do not deal with conservation area issues. There is of course a trap in here waiting to catch the unwary: if, for instance, you apply to build an extension to an existing house in a conservation area, which involves the removal of some existing structure, you

Chapter 3

could find that your permission to build the extension gets approved by planning but your permission to demolish what already exists is turned down by the conservation department. This is known, technically, as being kiboshed.

LISTING

The other great wedge of planning control concerns the listing of buildings thought to be of merit and which, therefore, need extra protection from unscrupulous owners and developers. The Department of Culture, Media and Sport (DCMS), taking advice from English Heritage, Historic Scotland and Cadw in Wales, compile the lists of protected buildings. The following tend to be listed:
- pre-1700 in anything like original condition
- most from 1700 to 1840
- those of quality and character from 1840-1914
- post-1914, only the very highest quality.

England & Wales have 500,000 listed buildings. Grade 1 accounts for just two per cent (i.e. 10,000), Grade II* is four per cent (20,000) and Grade II, the rest. Listing protects the interior and the exterior, as well as objects or structures fixed to the building, and objects and structures within the curtilage of the building, present before 1948. The curtilage is

I am not alone in thinking that the listing of our nation's housing stock has gone too far. Here's a prime example from Cambridgeshire. Fake leaded lights? I don't mind. Aluminium patio doors? No problem, if you like them. But this house is listed. Who are we kidding?

a fancy word for the outbuildings and garden walls: very often barn conversions are covered by listing arrangements because they are within the curtilage of a listed farmhouse.

If you want to undertake any building work on a listed building you are required to apply for listed building consent, whether or not you need planning permission. There is dispute over just what constitutes 'building work.' Repainting the windows usually doesn't, but something like re-pointing usually does. Obtaining listed building consent is often a slow business – anticipate at least a three month delay.

Listed building officers are attached to each planning department and these are the people to head for in order to glean more information.

EXPENSIVE REQUIREMENTS

When considering the problem from a perspective of hidden costs, it is the planners' interest in the design and materials of the house that is of most concern. Sometimes these concerns are easily predictable: if, for instance, you are building in one of the stone belts where there is a uniform vernacular style (as in the Cotswolds or the Yorkshire Dales), you will not be surprised to learn that you must build with similar materials. Expensive but not unexpected. However, most of Britain does not have a uniform building style and lowland England in particular is characterised by its great variety of building styles and materials. Despite this diversity, the planners can insist on any number of design details, examples of which now follow.

SLATE ROOFS

Even in East Anglia, home of the (cheap) pantile, planners are frequently known to insist on slate roofs despite the fact that most roofing slate came from North Wales and wouldn't have been known in England before the railway age.

DISLIKE OF ROOFLIGHTS

They sometimes insist on dormer roof windows. A small dormer will add at least £400-£500 to construction costs; in comparison, a flat opening roof light (eg a Velux) would cost no more than £250. Paradoxically, on barn conversions the reverse is true: planners hate dormers on barns.

ALTERING ROOF PITCHES

A common planners' ruse. A steeper roof pitch is more expensive because it increases the roof area. A 45° pitched roof covers an area 16 per cent larger than one at 35° and will add around this much to roofing costs. On the other hand, a 45° pitch on a roof makes any future loft conversion far easier.

CHANGING EXTERNAL MATERIALS

Unless they insist on an expensive stone facing, the materials cost of differing wall constructions is not that large. And the brick market is such that insistence on a different kind of brick is unlikely to have a huge effect on price. For more detail on the mechanics of planning permission, see Chapter 4.

Only when a house has detailed planning consent without any reserve matters is it possible to accurately budget the above-ground costs of construction. However, below ground, we come up against another set of unpredictable variable costs, determined to make a mockery of your budget.

The development costs of any new home can expand considerably because of problems encountered on site. These potential pitfalls fall into two main areas: problems encountered with the site itself, and difficulties encountered in getting access and supplying services to the site.

ARCHAEOLOGICAL REMAINS

You may be a fan of Tony Robinson and 'Time Team' but having a site with archaeology on it is a mixed blessing for housebuilders. Curse might be a better word for it. When you put in a planning application your site is routinely assessed by archaeologists with reference to your county historic environment records. If they think you will be digging into archaeology, then you will be required to undertake – and pay for – an evaluation that has to be carried out by an approved archaeological contractor.

Archaeology is not cheap. An evaluation will cost you £1,000 to £2,000 if your development is in a rural location. In an ancient town or city you might look at £3,000 to £10,000. An excavation, which may follow if anything of interest is found, will easily double these figures. Having an archeologist on site will add £120 - £200 per day, and if the site produces interesting archeology these will need to be doubled to take into account report writing. If you're really unlucky and they find something good you'll need an evaluation, and excavation and then a watching brief of service runs etc.

The best solution to avoiding heavy archaeological costs is to do your homework before you buy the land. Every city and council has a Historic Environment Record, and these are available to the public. Check what has been found on your site, or within a 100m radius. Take advice from the development control archaeologist, and any other archaeologist you can find.

TOO MUCH NATURE

If the Roman coins don't get you, then great crested newts might. There are three groups of animals whose presence on your site you may have cause to regret; slow worms, bats and newts. All are protected and all can present major headaches for developers, even on single-unit sites.

If there are known issues with your site – such as it lying within an SSSI (Site of Special Scientific Interest) – then the consequences should be made clear with the granting of planning permission. However, if there is the mere suspicion that sensitive flora or fauna is present on your site, you could be in for some expensive delays.

Chapter 3

I know of a selfbuilder in Essex who spent over £5,000 on measures to allay concern that he was damaging a Great Crested Newt breeding site. After two years of owning the site, Great Crested Newts had yet to be encountered at all but this didn't prove anything so he had no choice but to become a registered newt handler and to establish newt protection fences around his building plot.

And at the 2008 Homebuilding & Renovating show at the NEC, I met with a barn converter in Cheshire who was having to provide a 2m high bat-box stretching from one end of her barn to the other, completely spoiling the desired for open ceiling look she was hoping to achieve.

COUNCIL PAYMENTS (CILS)

The fact that there is lots of money in land deals hasn't escaped the notice of cash-starved governments and councils. For years, they have been clawing back some of these paper profits, insisting that developers build affordable housing and contributing to community thingies like playgrounds and schools.

In the past, selfbuilders haven't been greatly affected by all this, but in recent times these community fees have begun to trickle down to single sites and planning permissions have come attached with demands for many thousands of pounds.

Now there is a new charge, the Community Infrastructure Levy, or CIL, which seeks to bring some clarity to the situation. Instead of negotiating each site individually, as used to happen under the old Section 106 agreements, CIL will set a tariff for each area, based on the size of the house you plan to build, and you'll just have to cough up. It will affect everyone building a new house, unless it's deemed to be an affordable house. The levy varies

enormously depending on where you live, but nowhere is it going to be less than tens of thousands.

At time of writing (January 2013), there may be some dispensations in the pipeline, in order to encourage selfbuild. But it's just not clear what lies in store. Suffice to say, you won't get very far with a selfbuild project and not come across the Community Infrastructure Levy. And curse. For the latest information, you might do worse than check the Selfbuild Portal which will keep you up to date on what lies in store.

PROBLEM PLOTS

Next on the list of potential booby traps is the problem of difficult ground. There are three basic causes of alarming cost expansion:

- slopes
- bad ground
- trees.

Straightforward excavation and foundation work can be relatively cheap. Typically, the groundworks make up 10 per cent or less of the overall build cost on a new house. On a straightforward site, this is usually around £100 per square metre of footprint (i.e. the area you are enclosing). However any of the above problems encountered on site could conspire to make things a lot more expensive and, if you have more than one of these problems, expect your foundation costs to treble.

For more detail on these problems and how they are overcome, read Chapter 6: Groundworks. Here I simply want to give a few pointers about what to look for in assessing plots.

VISUAL INSPECTION

The first step in assessing any building

plot is to take a walk over the site and the surrounding area. Be on the look out for clues as to what may have gone on in the past. Some points to watch out for are:

- foundations of former buildings on site
- evidence of drains, old watercourses or wells
- subsidence cracks in neighbouring buildings
- overhead cables
- springy ground – suggests high water table
- slopes greater than 1:25
- trees within 30m of your proposed foundations – species, size and girth should be noted
- any evidence of ground having been disturbed or used as a dump.

BACKGROUND DETECTION

Investigations with local council, service companies, etc, should reveal more historical and geographical data on which to assess likely problems. Talk to neighbours, local builders or building inspectors who may well know the lie of the land.

TRIAL PITS AND BORINGS

To dig or not to dig, that is the question. Whether it is better to leave everything to chance and let the building inspector decide how deep your foundations must go when the time comes, or investigate in detail beforehand and risk having to do more than you really need. Many cautious builders now tend to dig trial holes as a matter of course, whatever the history or geology of the ground. The normal practice is for the pits to be dug to a depth of 3m (close to, but not under, the foundations) in the presence of a structural engineer who takes a long gander at the ground conditions before the digger fills the holes back in. The engineer then decides whether the house

foundations can proceed as normal or whether a more complicated foundation solution is needed.

Expect to pay an engineer between £150 and £300 for this service, though their fees will be much higher if special foundation designs are needed; a JCB for an hour should cost an additional £50-£100 (depending on travel time). Augered boreholes are another alternative – likely to cost around £300 each (and you'll need two) but a good option when access to JCBs is not possible or you have other problems like high water tables.

But there is also a natural tendency for the experts, having been called in, to suggest very expensive, fee-swelling, solutions when they may not be necessary. Jeremy Bulbrook built three houses in the Cambridgeshire Fenland town of March during 2001 and he

When digging a trial hole, the convention is to go down somewhat deeper than the proposed (or existing) foundations. Normally, you dig two or three trial holes just outside the proposed footprint – not under it

ended up feeling badly let down by his professional advice: 'I had a couple of boreholes drilled on my architect's suggestion. The soil report that came back from these recommended a piled foundation, on the basis that the first two metres or so could possibly be made-up ground, even though it was gravel/sand.

'My building inspector asked why I hadn't spoken to them first. He said that they would have been happy with strip footings, but as a recommendation for piles had been made, they had no choice but to force me down the piled route.

'Now whilst I don't want the houses to fall down,' he adds, 'I do wonder if some of the engineers that produce these reports are too scared to say that strip footings would be OK, because if it goes wrong in the future, then they have

to bear some responsibility. After all, it doesn't cost an engineer a penny more to say he would recommend piled foundations. In fact he may earn more, if he gets to design the footings as well.

'If I was starting again, I would definitely talk to the building inspectors first. There's always the risk that when you dig you find something unexpected, but that could still happen even if you have boreholes drilled,' he said.

In some extreme situations the professional fees can end up costing more than the foundations. I have reports of people having spent around £5,000 on site investigations in areas where mining activity may or may not have occurred; boreholes down to 30 metres are very expensive. Self builder Archie Hunter's case is a classic: he undertook a full geological survey which established that he didn't need a specialist raft foundation which he reckoned would have cost him an extra £2,000. 'Look we've saved over £2,000 on the cost of the foundations. OK, it cost over £4,500 to save this money but what the hell!'

CONTAMINATED LAND

Where the problems with the site are caused by the natural characteristics of the land, the solutions are usually fairly straightforward, if expensive. However, there is now a trend towards recycling building land and an increasing number of new homes are being built on sites that have had buildings on them before – these sites are sometimes known as brownfield sites. If the previous building was a house or a

Chapter 3

Pitfalls Checklist

Before buying a plot of land, you should check the following points. None of them is a reason for not buying, but all of them present potential extra costs, which you need to be aware of and, perhaps, this knowledge may even enable you to negotiate a lower price:
- are the described boundaries accurate?
- are there any restrictive covenants on the plot?
- are there rights of way crossing the plot?
- would you own all the land necessary for access and services? If not, are wayleaves readily obtainable?
- are there any tree preservation orders?
- are there any other 'legal encumbrances' which might hinder you in any way?
- is access adequate for cars?
- What are the requirements for visibilty splays?
- is the plot wide enough? Plots narrower than 12m can present problems for turning vehicles.
- are there any planning conditions in effect?
- does planning permission apply to the whole of the plot?
- when does planning permission run out?
- Is there a slope steeper than 1:25?
- what are ground conditions like?
- is there evidence of existing drains on site?
- are there any large trees within 30m?
- are there any overhead cables to be moved?
- are there likely problems with services?

Many of these potential administrative snags should be unearthed by your solicitor. The more technical ones are normally dealt with by building professionals – i.e. architects and structural engineers. If the plot looks dodgy in any way, don't hesitate to get help. Consider commissioning a feasibility study from your designer before contracts are exchanged – because this should unearth most of the bugs.

At the end of the day though, it's caveat emptor – buyer beware – because you are where the buck stops and it'll be down to you to sort out any do-dos.

---

barn, then a pollution problem is unlikely but if the site has been used as a tip or as an industrial plant then it is quite likely that the ground may contain a whole cocktail of nasties such as heavy metals, toxic chemicals or methane gas. Now local authorities up and down the land are currently preparing registers of contaminated land and they will be empowered to issue Remediation Notices, which will require the landowner to make the site safe, which usually means either excavating and burying the pollutants elsewhere (the Foot and Mouth option) or encasing them in concrete or clay (the Chernobyl option). Sometimes the solution may be relatively cheap – for instance specifying sulphur-resistant cement – but it will be some time before housebuilders are able to accurately budget for contamination problems.

ACCESS & SERVICES
When assessing a plot or a barn, you should take note of the distance you think you will have to take the services and the access you will have to build. Many backland developments come onto the market these days – typically the rear of someone's garden – and the prices asked for these sites are often little different to the prices asked for somewhere with a road frontage. Yet the budget cost of laying private driveways, drains, water and electricity combined with providing fencing is upwards of £100 per metre; that means that a plot set 50m back from a road is going to cost at least £5,000 more to develop than one with a road frontage. Whereas the layout of vehicle access arrangements are usually easy to work out, finding out about the services requires detective work.

DRIVEWAYS
The basic cost of laying a drive can be budgeted at around £80-£100 per linear metre, rather more if it is required to be fenced off as well. Often there is extra work involved in connecting to the public highway: typically you may have to construct a dropped kerb if you are crossing a raised pavement, at the very least you will have to provide a small apron of asphalt or tarmac so that there is no unsightly gap between your drive and the public highway. In some situations you may be required to create a visibility splay, which may involve removing existing obstructions and rebuilding them further back from the road.

On the other hand, you may have to construct a bridge over a ditch or even make an opening through an existing building. There are, in fact, so many potential access problems that it is almost pointless trying to summarise them – you will, in all probability, discover them when you first visit the site. Just be aware that whilst a straightforward highway junction will cost a couple of hundred quid, complicated access arrangements may well set you back several thousand pounds.

SERVICE CONNECTIONS
Gas, electricity, water, sewage, phones. Together, these constitute the services and you need to have them (or as many as you

can get) to turn a building plot into a home. Just how much this will cost you will vary enormously, depending largely on your site layout. Generally speaking, the further the services have to run, the more expensive it will get.

You'd think that the utility businesses would be delighted to have new customers and would bend over backwards to help accommodate them and get them connected for next to nothing. The reality is usually very different: selfbuilders struggle with service connections. They are costly, lead times are unpredictable and there are often strange administrative hoops to be jumped through.

Utilities have been largely privatised for twenty or thirty years now, yet the new connection work tends to be carried out by the same old institutions that ran the publicly-owned boards, and there is very little evidence of competition having come into play. BT run the copper phone cables, water and sewage are the domain of your local water company and electricity rests with the same electricity outfit that's been in place since the year dot. Gas infrastructure is now run, confusingly, by National Grid, but that's simply down to clever financial engineering.

A selfbuilder's first port of call is to get in touch with the local service providers and to ask for a quotation for a new supply. It's one area where Google is still pretty useless – search terms like selfbuild new supply turn up all manner of strange things, but not the New Homes Department of your local utilities. You have to persist! Eventually you will find the people you need.

Bear in mind that you don't have to own a plot of land to generate a quotation. Thus, getting new connection prices is often one of the first tasks to undertake when assessing the viability of a plot purchase. Sometimes, the resulting high connection fees can be enough to render a project unviable.

OVERHEAD CABLES

Power cables running across your plot are bad news. They may intersect with your proposed building, in which case they will have to be moved; even if they don't they will detract from the resale value of the property. Burying them is the obvious solution but it can be horribly expensive; even a low voltage cable can cost over £40 per m to bury, which can easily make a short diversion cost £5,000 or more. Again, the trick is to get quotations for this before entering into any contract to buy.

EXISTING DRAINS AND WATER MAINS

This is one real nightmare for rookies and professionals alike: existing drains and water mains running across your proposed building. Do whatever you can to find out if they are present, but sometimes there are no records and no surface evidence. Drains vary in their importance; small runs connecting one or two households to a sewer may very easily be diverted – depending on the lie of the land – but sewers and pumped drains cannot readily be moved and discovering one of these in your footings is a Grade A disaster, though thankfully this doesn't happen too often. The situation with mains is very similar; you probably will not be able to build within 2 or 3m. Again the key is to find out as much as possible about the plot before you exchange contracts to purchase. If there is any doubt in your mind, then try and place a retention in the sale contract which is only payable should nothing untoward be found under the ground.

BAD DESIGN

There is a dangerous tendency for selfbuilders to cut right back on the design costs in order to cram more features into the house. I've been into new homes, which are about as attractive as a cardboard box but are stuffed to the gunnels with home theatres, central vacuum systems, sprinklers, heat recovery systems, Agas, closed-circuit TV, saunas, gyms, you name it. It turns out the plans for the house were knocked out by some bloke in his spare time for about £300 because they thought that six grand for a proper architect was a rip-off. Well, maybe it is, maybe it isn't but, in terms of payback, good design really does seem to pay for itself and good design rarely (never) comes cheap. Skimping on design comes about from concentrating on the cost of everything rather than the value.

BORROWING MONEY

I have already touched on the perils of property developing on borrowed money but it would be amiss not to touch on them once more because borrowing money, large dollops of the stuff, is perhaps the most dangerous peril of all.

If you already have a large mortgage and feel comfortable that you can meet the repayments, then the fact that you transfer this mortgage to an unbuilt or partially built property should not make very much difference to you. But never forget that there are many things that can come between you and the large paper profit that you start out with. Don't assume that this profit will flow effortlessly to you as you complete your building programme. Always be prepared for a situation where you cannot sell the finished house at the price you hoped for, or indeed at any price at all.

OVER-SPECIFYING

It is said that the three most important factors in property development are location, location and location. Like many other sayings, there is a pearl of wisdom

Chapter 3

How To Treble Your Build Costs

Based on Model House size, 160m²	Cheap, no probs Cost/m²		Mid Range Cost/m²		Expensive Cost/m²		Elective element
Foundations/Ground Floor	£75	£12,000	£100	£16,000	£150	£24,000	
Drains & services In	£35	£5,600	£50	£8,000	£100	£16,000	
Service Connection charges	£30	£4,800	£30	£4,800	£50	£8,000	
Inner Skin	£30	£4,800	£35	£5,600	£35	£5,600	£800
Internal walls	£10	£1,600	£15	£2,400	£20	£3,200	£1,600
First Floor	£15	£2,400	£24	£3,840	£40	£6,400	£4,000
Cladding	£50	£8,000	£100	£16,000	£200	£32,000	£24,000
Chimney	£0	£0	£20	£3,200	£100	£16,000	£16,000
Joinery	£45	£7,200	£90	£14,400	£150	£24,000	£16,800
Roof Carp	£20	£3,200	£40	£6,400	£80	£12,800	£9,600
Roof Cover	£30	£4,800	£60	£9,600	£125	£20,000	£15,200
Insulation	£25	£4,000	£35	£5,600	£60	£9,600	£5,600
Rainwater/Fascia	£10	£1,600	£20	£3,200	£40	£6,400	£4,800
Plastering/Screeding	£60	£9,600	£75	£12,000	£100	£16,000	£6,400
Painting	£20	£3,200	£40	£6,400	£80	£12,800	£9,600
Wall Tiling/Floor Finishes	£30	£4,800	£60	£9,600	£120	£19,200	£14,400
2nd Fix joinery	£35	£5,600	£50	£8,000	£150	£24,000	£18,400
Electrics & Home Cabling	£35	£5,600	£50	£8,000	£150	£24,000	£18,400
Heating	£30	£4,800	£50	£8,000	£150	£24,000	£19,200
Sanitaryware & Plumbing	£25	£4,000	£40	£6,400	£100	£16,000	£12,000
Kitchen	£40	£6,400	£80	£12,800	£150	£24,000	£17,600
Externals	£50	£8,000	£80	£12,800	£150	£24,000	£16,000
Prelims	£30	£4,800	£50	£8,000	£100	£16,000	£11,200
Professionals	£50	£8,000	£80	£12,800	£150	£24,000	£16,000
ROUNDED TOTALS	£800	£125,000	£1,300	£204,000	£2,600	£408,000	£257,600

DIFFERENCE BETWEEN CHEAPEST AND MOST EXPENSIVE	£283,000
ELECTIVE	£257,600
% ELECTIVE	91%

Cost variations

The purpose of this table is to draw your attention to the huge cost variations between cheap and expensive, and the reasons for those variations. The left hand columns are loosely based on this editions's all-so-cheap-and-cheerful model house. The middle columns show just how much more it can be if the site is difficult to build on and the specification is upped. The right hand columns the bankers' bonus costs, with no expense spared. Finally, there is a column marked elective extras, those additional costs, which result directly from you choosing something more expensive than the basic.

here and one that rookie housebuilders would do well to heed. Building plots, just like existing houses, have to be assessed in relation to the neighbourhood they are located in and what goes on around them. If you are interested in maximising the return on your investment, then don't fall into the trap of specifying a luxury house on a plot that is surrounded by houses of a much lower quality. Rich people like to live in quiet secluded neighbourhoods, well away from the noise and grime of traffic and industry, and close to other rich people; poor people don't get the choice and have to make do.

If you have no intention of moving for many years to come and really don't give a hoot that your house is next to a council estate or a rubbish tip or a chicken farm, then go ahead and build your mansion on that nice cheap plot you found. However, if you are hoping to maximise your profit, it pays to take careful heed of the location you are building in and to specify a house in keeping with the neighbourhood. This is not hard to do, just look around and see who your would-be neighbours are and, more importantly, how much their houses are worth.

A well-built new house will tend to attract a premium price, perhaps as much as 15-20 per cent more than second-hand stock nearby but it is vital that you realise that however much money you pour into your house, you will not improve much on this premium.

This is a particular problem for selfbuilders in SE England who have to compete with each other and end up chasing up prices paid for quite humble plots of land. Naturally enough, they want to build the best house they can afford because they want to live in it but this often means ignoring the time honoured rules about the importance of location.

The general inexperience of selfbuild purchasers also means that the lessons contained in this chapter are frequently ignored or, more likely, just not known about so that there is often precious little difference in price between an A plus plot and a C minus.

Most estate agents have only the dimmest ideas about building costs and tend to value properties and plots far more by amenity and location than by assessing what the development costs might be. It is up to the buyers to assess these costs and the likely resale value. This is particularly so with barn conversions: these are usually considerably more expensive to build than equivalent new houses but the prices paid for derelict barns with planning permission don't reflect this at all.

GET THE RIGHT DESIGN

DESIGN

HOUSE DESIGN is undoubtedly the trickiest issue faced by every potential builder. The central point that shouldn't be forgotten is that you want to build the best possible house for a price you can afford. Easily written, but how the hell do you do it? What is the 'best possible' house? And how do you go about designing it?

Questions abound. Is an architect necessarily an expensive option? What about using a designer who is not a qualified architect? Isn't it cheaper to use a package build design? Won't the planners force me to redesign the whole thing in any event?

Well steady on, I'll cover these issues in due course. But first let's take a look at the design process because...well, it's a good place to start. The design process can be subdivided into number of parts, some fixed points with known costs and others elastic in the extreme. Below is a list of the stages that you need to go through. You don't have to do it in this order (you could for instance apply for building regulations approval before you have planning permission) but it would be frankly very strange not to do it this way.

- site survey and feasibility study
- design process, leading to sketches of options
- commission drawings for planning permission
- submit plans for planning permission (fee)
- try and negotiate positive planning outcome
- do this over and over again till outcome is positive
- detailed designs and specifications
- submit detailed designs for building regulations approval (fee)

SITE SURVEY

Unless you are very confident of your surveying and drafting abilities, you should have a professional carry out an accurate site survey to measure and plot all the existing buildings, boundaries, levels, access arrangements, trees, drains, neighbouring buildings and any other information thought to be relevant. On simple sites this might cost £200, but expect to pay over £500 on large or complex sites. If by chance you've read the previous chapter then you'll realise that a smart plot buyer will have carried out much of this work before signing any contracts. Don't rely on professionals to sort these problems out for you after the event.

FEASIBILITY STUDY/ SKETCHES

Assuming you have a plot and a budget,

DESIGN

the most important questions are: what can you build on it and how much will it cost? It may seem very early in the whole mysterious design process but you have already reached crunch point: this is the key moment when you start to commission the whole building process and at this point your decisions will have costly implications down the line. I have distinguished between a stage called feasibility study and another called sketches of options; this is helpful in understanding how one grows out of the other but in reality there is no hard and fast dividing line between them and how you and your designer get from an empty page to a full planning application is a very individual thing.

Nevertheless, there tends to be a clear path, which leads from the site survey stage into a feasibility stage (which, if you like, is about eliminating impractical options) into outlining practical solutions and, from there, plumping for your best choice, at which point the designer changes gear and looks at the nitty-gritty decisions, which spring from the choices you have made.

A professional at £30-£50 per hour may seem a luxury, but they will (or at least should) understand the issues and concentrate your thinking on the relevant areas. There may or may not be any consultation with local planners at this stage, depending on how confident you or your agent feels. If doing it yourself, then a visit to the planners

would be advisable. Note this once used to be a free service, but wily planning officers now often charge for 'pre-application advice'. My local council now charges just over £100 for such a meeting.

Use books of house plans for inspiration (despite the fact that they're mostly anything but), but

It is important to have an accurate site survey, especially in situations like this, where there are substanstantial differences in level

do not expect to fit an existing plan on to your plot; the chances of it working without amendment are small and amending existing plans can be almost as expensive as starting from scratch.

The cost of this stage is naturally very open-ended: some short-of-work designers will undertake the early parts

Chapter 6

permission drawings to present to the local planning department. Budget anything from £200 for pre-drawn plans through to £6,000 for architect one-offs.

For a detailed look at the mechanics of applying for planning permission, and the likely fees, see the following section. There are a number of plans and drawings that the planners require and your chosen designer/agent should know this rigmarole backwards – indeed if they don't I would tend to be rather suspicious.

WORKING DETAILS

If designing from scratch, it is conventional not to decide on all the construction details until planning constraints are established. This is simply to avoid having to do things twice. However, construction details on conventional houses are remarkably similar and often the details can be lifted from previous jobs. On simple projects, the plans, construction details and specification (known as the spec with a hard or soft 'c' – the choice is yours) can all be contained on two sheets of A1 (840 x 592 mm) plans which would detail:

- floor plans
- foundation plan
- drainage plan
- first floor joist layout
- roof truss/rafter layout
- N,E,S and W elevations (or views)
- section or sections through the middle of the house,

of this process for free on the understanding that more work will follow. For many independent designers and architects, the early part of the process is the most challenging and the most interesting and they would anticipate spending around a third of their time on this stage. The biggest variable is you, the client. The more sussed out you are, the better your brief, and the shorter and cheaper this process will be.

Even if you are planning to build a kit house or use an off-the-shelf design, it is still worthwhile getting a professional designer to undertake some sort of study if only to sort out practicalities like drain runs (though note that many kit suppliers have their own designers

A model of the PassivHaus in Denby Dale which was featured in the Ninth edition of 'The Housebuilder's Bible'. The owners used this model to help gain planning permission

who will undertake this work).

PLANNING DRAWINGS

A good designer with a thorough working knowledge of local practices and trends will be able to help you marry your ideas with the views of the planners, hopefully pre-empting any potential areas of conflict. Planning departments are surprisingly diverse in their ideas, often reflecting the individual tastes of the chief planning officer, and knowing the whys and wherefores of local planning decisions is one way in which local knowledge scores heavily over nationwide services.

Whoever you choose, they will have to produce a set (in fact several sets) of planning showing room heights, floor levels, wall constructions, joist depths, staircase dimensions

▓ window and door schedule (list of joinery manufacturers' codes)

▓ text explaining construction standards (lots of B.S. numbers here).

On more complicated jobs, there may be extra plans perhaps running to many pages, showing various complicated details like eaves or dormer windows. Up-market jobs tend to have the specification written separately from the drawings and a serious architectural practice may write a specification running to fifty pages or more. How much of this is necessary depends on a) the complexity of the work and b) the attitude of the client. Rookie builders would be well advised not to attempt anything too unusual first time around, in which case the standard two-sheet plans are probably adequate. Many experienced subcontractors never look at plans in any event – quite a few can't read – and complex plans could be wasted on many.

I know of a number of small builders who basically dispense with the working drawings stage. They work from little more than the planning drawings which can be littered with notes like 'To be confirmed on site' or 'To Building Inspector's Satisfaction'; they are on site every day and they prefer to work out these details as they go along. Once you've done it a few times, it works fine provided you stick to fairly standard solutions (they do). But if you are new to this game and/or you can't be there on site a good deal, then you would do well not to skimp on working drawings as these form, in effect, your detailed instructions to your builder.

Much of this detailed work and,

in particular, the writing of the specification, forms the very heart of any forthcoming building contract. If you want an element of protection from the perils of badly executed building work, then a professionally written specification is worth far more than any off-the-peg contract you might be tempted to sign.

In budget terms, these design details are the area with the most variance. If purchasing a set of predetermined house plans (typically for £300-£500), then all this detailed work will be included with the plans so the effective cost is zero. If using a package build, then again these details will come integrated with the package. But be wary of assuming that pre-drawn plans are necessarily the cheapest option because 90 per cent of the time they require significant amendments and sometimes it proves to be just as expensive as starting with a blank sheet of paper. However, even a one-off design may cost no more than a few hundred pounds if it sticks to tried and tested solutions; on the other hand, this part of the design work can also very easily cost £2,000-£4,000 for unusual houses, as unusual features take time to design, not to mention build. Here you would expect workshop joinery, arched openings, fancy staircases, patterned brickwork – generally expensive features, which are also expensive to design.

If you are building to a tight budget and are happy with conventional solutions, then make it clear that you do not want unusual detailing and, as a result, a) your working details should not cost too much, b) your house isn't likely to be expensive to build and c) it is much less likely to run over budget.

The danger in trying to put a price to

all this is that you may lose sight of the fact that, as with so many things in life, you get what you pay for; if someone knocks up a set of plans for you over a couple of weekends for a few hundred quid, the chances are that your finished house will reflect the fact. On the other hand, if you are interested in creating a wonderful one-off home, you'd be daft to skimp on the design stages.

If you want to save money, you'd probably do better to build a smaller house. There is a real conundrum in here. People don't want to be ripped off by some fancy-dan architect charging the earth. Yet a good architect can often justify the fees because they actually add value to the finished product. If an architect or designer can do the business, then the thousands of pounds they charge is money well spent.

STRUCTURAL ENGINEER

Having been called in during the digging of the trial hole, if the designs take on any non-standard features, the structural engineer may have to make another appearance. All beams, lintels, roofs and foundations (the so-called structural elements) of a building require proof that they are sufficient to do the job asked of them. Standard solutions to standard problems are regarded as tried and tested, but anything out of the ordinary will require 'proving' to the satisfaction of the building inspector. A structural engineer will calculate the forces applied to beams or foundations and come up with adequate solutions. If the ground you plan to build on is at all dodgy, then an engineer will be required to prove your foundation design; also many very ordinary situations like using steel beams or opening up a loft space require structural proving. If you want to build in timber frame without going via a specialist supplier, you need to get the design proved by a specialist timber engineer.

Detailed drawings and structural calculations (if needed) are presented to the local council's building control department for examination.

SUB-DESIGNS

Design and specification of finishes is often left to the client or builder to sort out and this is more often than not passed down the line to the tradesmen involved on the job. Therefore, the plumber designs the central heating system, the electrician designs the lighting, a kitchen specialist will take over design of the kitchen. This sort of arrangement obviously works, as it is what happens in 90 per cent of homes built, but arguably it could be much better co-ordinated by a single designer.

On large commercial contracts specialist professionals who draw up a specification and then arrange quotes from it deal with all these areas separately. One-off housing is really too small to justify the expense of all these extra professionals and much of the work, designed and installed by the various tradesmen, is consequently very unimaginative. The degree of competence varies enormously: many act as much as salesmen as designers and most make no charge provided you buy their product, which is all very well but it makes you very vulnerable to uncompetitive practices.

It's really a very difficult area to negotiate, even for hard-bitten professionals. Many architects are not qualified to give advice on, say, lighting design or interior decorating. If you are happy with tried and tested solutions to

problems then you will be well advised to keep it simple and deal directly with your chosen contractor; if, however, you want to explore the many and varied options open to you, then you could do worse than read the rest of this book...

IN CONCLUSION

Design and professional expenses are the hardest areas to budget for because they are so variable. To a large extent they are dependent on the brief that you, as a client, present to the designers. An off-the-peg house plan can be purchased for a few hundred pounds but will very probably require a great deal of alteration to fit both the site and your ideas. In contrast, an architect might charge over £5,000 for designing a detached four bedroomed house; however, it does not follow that the off-the-peg plans are necessarily better value. The resulting house might be £5,000 less expensive to build and might also be worth £10,000 more when finished! Here you must use your own judgement and intuition.

PLANNING PERMISSION

Planning permission and building regulations are two big hurdles that every would-be housebuilder will have to jump. They are complex and not easily mastered, and many building professionals have bald patches on their heads where they have torn their hair out from negotiating paths through or around the maze of regulations and precedents that govern our construction activities. For a rookie builder this can all seem rather daunting, especially when you're not even clear what the difference is between planning permission and

building regulations – or regs as they are known in the trade, as in 'God, there's been another bloody change in the regs.' The regs are dealt with later in this chapter – first planning permission.

WHAT EXACTLY IS IT?

Various Acts of Parliament (notably the Town and Country Planning Acts) require that local authorities should control what can be built where, and how buildings (and land) should or should not be used. Planning permission is not concerned with how you build – that's the building regs – nor with who owns the land on which you wish to build. There are many small construction projects that do not require planning permission but something of the size of a new house invariably does.

The power-that-bees in this respect is your local council. Not your County or Metropolitan Council, but your District or City council. In Scotland and N Ireland the system works slightly differently, as it does in National Parks, but then they wouldn't want to make it too straightforward, would they? It gets worse. Officially, the licence to build is granted by the elected councillors, but every council has a full-time planning department staffed by planning officers, and these are the people who actually deal with planning applications. Indeed, the chief planning officer has powers to make certain decisions off his or her own bat. Even when they choose not to exercise these powers they make 'recommendations' to the committee of councillors as to whether an application should be accepted or refused. The planning committee rarely goes against the recommendations of its planning officers.

Planning Terms Explained

1 OUTLINE

Often used by landowners who are trying to find out whether development would be acceptable in principle without going through the hassle of having detailed plans drawn up. Outline permission to build is what turns a garden or a field into a building plot; getting it makes you seriously rich but it doesn't, on its own, allow you to build. Outline permission lasts for five years, but a detailed application must be agreed within three years or else the permission lapses.

2 FULL APPLICATION

As its name suggests, a full planning application seeks to approve both the principle and the details of development. It lasts for three years.

3 APPROVAL OR RESERVED MATTERS

This is used to convert outline permission to detailed.

4 RENEWAL

Planning permission can be renewed, but only if consent has not expired so this route is used to get an extension to an existing permission. If the permission has lapsed, then a new application has to be made.

5 RELAXATION

Sometimes planning permission comes with a load of irksome conditions. You can apply to have these lifted at a later date but don't hold out too much hope.

6 AMENDMENTS

If you purchase a plot with detailed permission for a house that you don't actually want to build, you may be able to amend the plans without submitting a whole new application. There is no charge for amendment but if your changes are substantial the planners may not accept them as amendments and you'll be back to square one

7 EXTENSIONS / CONVERSIONS

If your building project involves work to an existing structure, you may not need planning permission. Phone your local council's planning department and ask their advice. Or check the government website www.planningportal.gov.uk for planning in England & Wales. Scotland and N. Ireland have their own sites.

FOREPLAY

You don't have to have any contact at all with the planners before submitting your application, but it is commonplace to do so. Tactics are involved here and there is no such thing as a correct way of going about it – every case stands on its own. On the one hand, you don't want to be faced with the expense of drawing up plans only for the planners to fall about laughing at the very thought that anyone could build on that piece of land; on the other hand, if you wander into the planning department with questions like 'What sort of house could I build on this spot?' then you are inviting the planners to design the house for you. This they won't do, but what will happen

is that they will get in their minds all kinds of constraints that will severely limit your options: 'You must do...' and 'You can't have...' Like our legal system and our parliament, our planning system is adversarial; you may not get exactly what you want out of it – most planning decisions are the result of compromise – but you stand a far better chance of getting more of what you want if you choose the battleground on which to fight; i.e. submit plans with minimal reference to the planners. Getting the planners too closely involved before submitting your application can be seen as ceding this battleground.

In the past few years, planning departments have been under cost

constraints and are under pressure to maximise income. One clever ruse they have come up with is charging for pre-application advice, a service they were once happy to dispense for free. Now it may be that your planning application is not terribly controversial and that the planners will be delighted with your ideas. In which case you may think I am a paranoid old nutter. But don't forget that it's your money and that they have the right to make you shell out for things that you think are completely unnecessary. Adopting a 'lie down and think of England' pose may earn you brownie points at City Hall but may also fire off alarm bells around the corner at the bank or building society.

SUBMITTING AN APPLICATION

The mechanics of submitting an application are straightforward but time and tree-consuming. There are, however, several different types of planning permission that can be granted and these are summarised in the box on the previous page.

APPLICATION FORMS

The actual application consists of a number of forms that you have to fill out, together with your plans and your cheque. Exact requirements vary a little from council to council but are not likely to be less than six copies of each of the following, though to be fair most councils now encourage online applications:
▓ location plan (taken off OS map at a scale of 1:1250)
▓ existing site plan (boundaries outlined in red) at 1:500
▓ proposed site plan – showing position of house, garage, driveway, access
▓ layout plans and elevations of any existing structures on site
▓ layout plans and elevations of proposed dwelling at 1:100 or 1:50
▓ details of materials to be used
▓ details of trees to be felled.
▓ Design & Access statement

In addition to these, it often helps to have three-dimensional bird's-eye view drawings (isometric projections), which show how the house fits with its neighbours. Planning officers and committee members like a nice drawing, just like the rest of us, and apocryphal evidence suggests that they are likely to be better disposed towards a well presented application. Some people even go to the trouble of building scale models. This is probably over the top for routine applications but if there are close neighbours who will be affected by the new buildings, it does help to have a contextual drawing or two so they can see just how the development sits in relation to what is already there.

You can of course now do all this online. Again, the Planning Portal website is the place to go for the low down (www.plannningportal.gov.uk). When I last checked, there was a series of short You Tube videos explaining how to do an application online, featuring a young man called Toby with a distinctive Bristolian accent. All very charming. A bit like Ricky Gervais explaining how to do your tax returns. I don't know what happens in Scotland and N Ireland, but planning applications are seemingly headed into the online world.

OWNERSHIP CERTIFICATE

You also have to fill out a form stating ownership of the land in question. You don't actually have to own land in order to apply for planning permission over it but you are required to notify the owner of your intentions.

FEES

Outline fees in England are £385 for each 0.1 hectare (or 1,000 sq m which is a small plot) of site area applied for. Detailed permission for one dwelling is also £385 and if you apply for outline and then move on to a detailed application it will cost you twice £385; interestingly, when I first published this book in 1995, the fee was £160, so it has more than doubled in 18 years. The only way to avoid this double fee is to go straight for detailed permission, which involves more costly drawings: in some situations this is a risk worth taking but if the application is likely to be controversial, just go for the outline. There are no fees for consultation with planners or for making amendments to plans to satisfy planners' concerns.

CHANCES OF SUCCESS

After submitting your application, the planners then go to work on assessing it. These days they all seem to work in teams, and this makes it even harder to get any sense out of them as to how they think the application is progressing. They are meant to take eight weeks to reach a determination, but in practice it depends on how busy they are – it can all take much longer. This in turn has led to pressure from central government and targets have been set to turn round planning applications more quickly; all that has happened is that applications are more likely to be rejected. As recently as 2002, only one in five applications were rejected; today it appears to be around one in three. Which only makes your task ever more daunting. Don't despair.

Keep ringing them to find out what's happening to your application; sooner or later they will reach some sort of provisional verdict and this is the point at which negotiations start. If they are completely hostile, then you may do better to withdraw the application and start anew; if they express some reservations (they usually do), then you must be prepared to compromise hard. Eventually, the planning officials will either grant planning permission (unlikely on a new house) or refer it to the planning committee of the local council who, typically, meet once a month. This referral will come with a recommendation either way, which the committee habitually accepts. Planning permission is often granted with conditions attached; if you are Sainsburys wanting to build a supermarket, these conditions may be something big, but for a one-off housebuilder they are not likely to be terribly onerous though in some parts of England additional money is being asked for 'planning gain' – this can run to several thousand pounds.

This routine is currently being replaced by the Community Infrastructure Levy (CIL) which will require the payment of a large sum of money to the council, for the granting of planning permission for creating a new home. This has nothing to do with planning fees.

REASONS FOR REFUSAL

There can be any number of reasons why planners take a negative view of your proposals. In rural districts the land is zoned (via the 'local plans', which you can inspect at your library or online), and if you are applying to build in a non-building zone then you've got your work cut out trying to get anywhere. Assuming they accept that the site is suitable for development, here are several reasons why they may still not play ball:

▨ lack of adequate parking
▨ can't turn a car around on the hard standing
▨ overlooking neighbours
▨ roof too high
▨ house too big for plot
▨ not enough garden
▨ development out of keeping with neighbourhood
▨ wrong position on the plot
▨ don't like your choice of materials or overall design.

I could go on. Suffice it to say that many of these reasons are perfectly justifiable and if you weren't so greedy and pig-headed you would be able to see the sense in them. But applicants are apt to feel aggrieved whenever the outcome goes against them.

LOBBYING

You don't have to take the views of the planning officials lying down. Many people have taken to lobbying their councillors to overrule the recommendation for refusal. This is real grass roots politics and in many parts of the world sums of money would change hands in order to get planning permissions through on the nod, but in Britain, of course, we don't do that. I don't wish to sound too sarcastic because, by and large, this is true – people tend not to go into local politics for money, but they do have a tendency towards self-importance and many are not averse to a little bit of flattery. This is the network at work: it all depends on personalities and who you do or do not know.

Even if you don't get very far with councillors, you should at least consider lobbying your neighbours. A couple of letters from neighbours saying positive things about your plans is worth a lot at a planning committee meeting. However, there is every chance that your neighbours may not feel as enthusiastic about your plans as you do and this tactic can backfire.

APPEALS v NEW APPLICATIONS

If you shoot your bolt and, despite all your lobbying, your application is refused you are faced with three choices:
▨ give up
▨ submit a new application
▨ appeal.

The first is the cheapest but it doesn't get you very far. If you want to persist, then there is no reason why you can't go to appeal on your first application whilst simultaneously submitting a new one. Surprisingly, there is no charge for making an appeal but it does take time, around six months, and many people can't wait that long, especially if there's borrowed money riding on it. Appeals are presided over by an independent inspector, often a QC, sometimes an architect, and on small projects like individual housebuilding the usual way of going about it is to produce written evidence. Basically, you must write your side of the story and explain to the inspector why you think you should have been granted planning permission in the first place. On the due date the inspector will visit the site and shortly afterwards they will make their ruling known. That's it. There are alternative methods of appeal, notably using the informal hearing method, which gathers all the interested parties together to discuss the issue at hand, but the written representation is the simplest and least time-consuming (as well as cheapest, if you are paying a professional to act for you).

Only one in three appeals succeed and from my limited experience it is difficult to predict the outcome in advance, so you are taking a big gamble in going to appeal. You can hire a professional to make the appeal for you, but this will be expensive and may not add to your chances. As there is no further drawing work to be undertaken – you can't amend your plans between first refusal and appeal – the appeal process can easily be undertaken by any lay person capable of using pen and paper, although a thorough understanding of planning issues will

Chapter 4

obviously stand you in good stead.

For many people, it will be cheaper and much quicker to submit a new planning application. When an application is refused, the planners have to state grounds for refusal. In an ideal world these issues could have been sorted out before the application ever came before the committee, but sometimes it takes a refusal to actually bring the problems out into the open. Armed with refusal reasons, you can make suitable amendments in your next application and, provided you can genuinely sort out the issues, you should have a much better chance of gaining planning permission, although the outcome is likely to be some way from your original ideas.

Changes to the planning system are always being mooted but all that ever seems to happen on the ground is that the whole process becomes ever more troublesome and time consuming. And I haven't even discussed Listed Building Consents – these can take over a year to obtain! Good luck.

BUILDING REGULATIONS

As mentioned at the beginning of the previous section, the building regs are a different matter altogether from planning permission. As with planning permission, there are a number of small works that are exempted from having building regulations applied to them, but again a project as large as a house will invariably fall inside building control.

Each local council has a building control department that employs building inspectors, who both assess plans submitted to them and visit sites to ensure that the plans are actually put into practice. The plans submitted to building control are more detailed than those used for gaining planning permission and so this work is usually commissioned as an additional service after a successful planning application.

It is worth noting, however, that much of the detail needed to satisfy building regulations is to do with written specifications rather than drawings and that much of this is standard to all housing. Phrases peppered with BS numbers and sentences finishing with 'to the satisfaction of the building inspector' are commonly placed in specifications precisely to meet the regs. Furthermore, what is often the most important part of an inspector's job, checking that the foundations are adequate, can really only be done on site.

Getting approval for building regulations is not a political matter and there are no committees to go before or councillors to lobby. You just have to reach agreement with your appointed building inspector – which, by and large, means doing as he (occasionally she) says. If you stick to conventional methods of construction this is generally not too difficult. However, expect problems if you are inclined to unusual techniques.

WHAT ARE THEY?

The building regulations actually consist of a number of separate booklets known as Approved Documents, generally referred to as Parts. Each part is given a letter and currently the English & Welsh versions of these run from Part A (which deals with Structure) to Part P (Electrics). You can buy the complete pack of 14 parts for £60.00. You can also download all the parts for free from the Planning Portal website (www.planningportal.gov. uk). Scotland and Northern Ireland have their own building regulations, which are very similar but employ different labelling systems. Wales has always had its lot thrown in with England, but this is currently changing and Wales is soon to have devolved regs, though whether this is really helpful to anyone is open to doubt.

The building regs are technical publications and most builders have never clapped eyes on them; instead they rely on their designer to have satisfied the regs in the drawings and their building inspector to put them straight if the situation on site requires it.

The building regs are always getting tightened and their scope is forever being increased. What started life as a motley collection of bye-laws, which attempted to eliminate jerrybuilding practices in Victorian times has grown into a sophisticated instrument of social engineering, most obviously in the introduction of disabled access regulations in 1999.

Currently we are in the middle of a period of rapid review – for which read expansion – of all the building regulations and many of the professionals from whom we seek guidance on these matters are themselves quite at sea. Building inspectors are consequently prone to making inconsistent decisions and not applying the letter of the law because they frequently either don't know it or don't much like it.

BUILDING CONTROL FEES

Local authority fees are no longer set nationally. However the fees for new houses tend to cluster around the £700 mark. My local authority charges £195 for plan approval and an additional £490

Building Regulations Guide

Building Regulations by Name

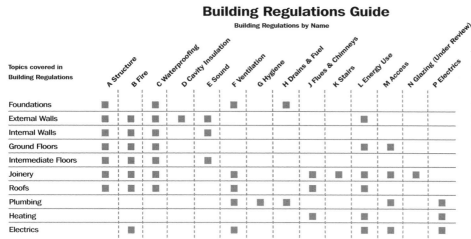

Topics covered in Building Regulations	A Structure	B Fire	C Waterproofing	D Cavity Insulation	E Sound	F Ventilation	G Hygiene	H Drains & Fuel	J Flues & Chimneys	K Stairs	L Energy Use	M Access	N Glazing (Under Review)	P Electrics
Foundations	■		■			■	■							
External Walls	■	■	■	■	■						■			
Internal Walls	■	■	■		■									
Ground Floors	■	■	■								■	■		
Intermediate Floors	■	■	■		■									
Joinery	■	■	■			■		■	■		■	■	■	
Roofs	■	■	■			■			■					
Plumbing						■	■	■				■		■
Heating								■			■		■	
Electrics		■				■					■	■		■

This chart is designed to give you some inkling of the areas the building regs are involved in. The lettering across the top refers to the Approved Documents that go to make up the English & Welsh regulations and the rows refer to the main areas of concern. Thus Part F, the Ventilation regs, has bearing on foundations (suspended ground floors), joinery (trickle vents), roofs (roof ventilation), plumbing (bathrooms need extract fans) and electrics (fans again).

for site inspections on new houses up to 300 sq m internal floor area (both these figures include VAT). With smaller works like extensions, the fees are correspondingly less. VAT is charged on building control fees for new dwellings (unlike planning application fees) and is generally not reclaimable.

WARRANTIES

Whilst planning is exclusively the domain of the local councils, building control has been 'privatised.' For many years there was only one other option to local authority inspections and that was the National House Builders Council (the NHBC), who run a building control scheme for their members side-by-side with their 10-year warranty. The NHBC is a force to be reckoned with in new housebuilding and it publishes its own standards that are far more wide-ranging than the government's building regulations. Professional housebuilders are mostly members because the 10-year warranty scheme is seen as essential to

secure sales; besides this fact, the NHBC's fees for administering building control are a little lower than those charged by local councils.

The NHBC is aimed at professional builders and charges a one-off joining fee of over £500 plus an annual membership of at least £250 dependent on how many houses you build.

Since 1997, others have been allowed to undertake the building control function and gradually over the years a number have risen to prominence. The whole issue gets confused here because we are really getting into the world of insurance and this, arguably, doesn't have much to do with design, which is the subject of this chapter. But the point is that these private building control inspectors all offer a structural warranty, dependent on them having undertaken inspections of the house under construction.

Many self builders require a warranty because the mortgage provider insists. Even when mortgage finance is not

being sought, a warranty is reckoned to be a good idea because a re-sale within the first ten years will almost always require a warranty to be in place, and they are much more expensive to issue retrospectively.

Some good providers of private building inspections and warranties, apart from the NHBC, are Premier Guarantee, LABC (which is a private arm of the council building inspectors, who don't on their own provide warranties, and SelfbuildZone, which is a one stop shop aimed at all the insuarnce needs of self builders. If you want to explore still further, Google "Approved Inspectors" and look through the Construction Industry Council's website where they keep a log of both individual and corporate building inspectors.

CERTIFICATION

There is an alternative to buying structural warranties. If you employ a professional – usually an architect, but it can be a surveyor – you can have them certify that the work has been carried out correctly. It's not quite the same as a warranty, as any later claim you might have would be against your professional – i.e. you have to sue them – rather than an insurance company, but most mortgage lenders are happy to accept an architect's certification. Your fee for this would be negotiated independently with your architect, but bear in mind that many architects don't like certifying work (understandably – it's quite a risk and it has to be backed by expensive professional indemnity insurance) and will try and steer you towards using the NHBC. It is also worth bearing in mind that if you are financing your housebuilding by means other than a regular mortgage, then a warranty is not needed at all, although absence of one could make resale within ten years more difficult.

Finally, a note for barn converters. You can get warranty scheme for conversions, though these are both costlier and of shorter duration than their newbuild equivalents. Also note that there is more on the ins and outs of warranties in the Insurance section of Chapter 5.

THE PARTY WALL ACT

There is more to the red tape than just planning permission and building regulations. If you are lucky these two will be the only bits you encounter but there are other things to consider as well. Close to a neighbour? Within six metres? You may have to treat with The Party Wall Act, which has been in effect in 1996 throughout England and Wales – prior to that it was restricted to London. The idea behind this piece of legislation is to protect the neighbouring properties from damage when your construction work is carried out. The Act is very specific about

just where and when it comes into effect.

If your foundations are to be deeper than your neighbour's buildings, you must observe the Party Wall Act provisions if you are within three metres of those buildings – note not boundary, but buildings. In addition to this, there is a provision which states that if you are building much deeper than the neighbouring house's foundations, then you may still be affected by the provisions of the Act at a distance of six metres. You draw a line at 45 deg down from the bottom of your neighbour's foundations and if it strikes your projected foundation works within six metres, then Ka Boom – you are in the net. It's likely to be pointed out to you when you put a full planning application in.

If the Party Wall Act does come into effect – and in many urban areas it is likely to if you want to build a basement or if you have to pile – you are obliged to notify your neighbour and to assuage their concerns that your building work may damage their property. Often this can be done with an informal exchange of letters but, if the neighbour is worried about what you are up to, then he or she is entitled to hire, at your expense, a qualified structural engineer or surveyor to verify your plans.

You must state whether you propose to strengthen or safeguard the foundations of the building or structure belonging to the adjoining owner. Such aspects need to be considered at the design stage of the project to avoid unexpected costs arising. This can, naturally, become a long and involved process, as the two surveyors have to reach agreement about just how the work should be undertaken. Your neighbour cannot prevent you

undertaking this work but they can delay you. If the next door building is split into flats, then you have to entreat with each occupier individually. Doesn't that prospect fill you with joy? You can obtain a Party Wall Act Explanatory Booklet for free off the web at www.communities. gov.uk – type 'party wall' in the search field.

CHOOSING A DESIGNER

There are two distinct approaches to house design. One is to hire a designer (be they architect or not) and to let them get on with the task of melding your ideas with their expertise; the other is to approach a package build company who specialise in selling standard houses, which can be adapted to particular needs. In some ways the differences are not that great – after all both involve building houses – but conceptually it's the difference between painting from scratch and painting by numbers.

PACKAGE BUILD

Whilst the creative types would probably be appalled at the idea that you could buy an off-the-peg kit house, package-build does have one big advantage going for it and that is WYSIWYG. For those not up in computing circles, WYSIWYG (pronounced Whizz-Ee-Wig) stands for What You See Is What You Get, and it describes perfectly the attraction of the package-build philosophy in that you know in advance what your home will look like. Furthermore, you know you'll have a conventional, re-saleable property because it wouldn't be on offer if it wasn't. This is a very comforting and reassuring selling factor for self builders, who are terrified of losing their construction virginity to some way-out weirdo architect with ideas.

Package builds will almost certainly not be the cheapest route to a finished house: in fact, as reference to the next section of this chapter will show, they are often considerably more expensive than the route taken by volume developers. However, they do offer the novice housebuilder something that few architects ever do and that is a price in advance – though I should add that in reality they only offer a price for the parts of the house they actually supply and erect, which is often no more than a quarter or a third of the total building costs.

Take a hill-trekking holiday in the Himalayas as a comparison. Many people would want to go on such a holiday first time with a package deal, but having done it once, would realise that it was not so difficult to organise and that, if they ever went again, they would go on their own, have more independence and save money. Housebuilding is not so dissimilar; the comfort of having a professional organisation behind you in your first venture and a feeling that you know what the final bill will be is worth a lot more than the vague hope that you just might be saving money.

What buyers of package building services should realise is that they are not getting free design. Rather, the design work is being paid for within the package price. The package build companies all employ architects or designers and these people get paid just like their freelance cousins, and who do you think pays their salaries? Now the logic of using pre-drawn house plans is that the whole design process is reduced to a matter of a bit of photocopying

which should be much cheaper for all concerned. However, British planning restrictions being what they are today, there are virtually no uncomplicated building plots on which you can plonk an off-the-peg house: the houses all require 'adaptation', which is tantamount to admitting that the brochure designs are just sales hooks to entice you, and that the actual house you have built will have had a fair amount of additional design work done to it in order to get it to fit both your ideas and the limitations of the plot. This extra work is invariably charged and you may well end up having a package build company designing your home from scratch.

Which begs the question 'Why start with an off-the-peg design at all?' In theory, a freelance architect or architectural designer should be able to provide a similar service to a package build designer and really shouldn't cost any more. But, for many people, the prospect of hiring a freelance is off-putting and not just because they think it will be expensive.

If you happen to know somebody in the trade, then there is every chance that you'll appoint them (however inappropriate) just because it takes away the difficult task of finding a compatible stranger. Many people without any contacts will, however, be lured into the package build option just because it's there. Eyeing up package build companies is like visiting Amsterdam's red light district: you can trawl up and down all night looking at the wares on offer but you don't have to consummate any deals if you don't like what's on offer. However, involving freelance architects and designers is much more personal: if you don't know them then it is akin to going on a blind date. You may or

may not end up in bed together but you have to go through a courting stage just to find out where you want it to end up. It's a time-consuming and involved process and the outcome is just as likely to hinge on personal – not to say sexual – chemistry as it is on the designer's suitability and competence to carry out your brief.

Of course it doesn't have to be thus. If you're the professional, organised type, there is absolutely nothing to prevent you having a sort of beauty contest between three or four designers, in which you interview them and ask to see photographs of their previous work, ask for references and even ask them to prepare a quotation for design work, and possibly building work as well. The fact that architects hate this sort of thing is by-the-by: you'll be paying their bills and there is no reason at all why you shouldn't organise a parade of talents so that you can make an informed judgement.

Red light districts, blind dates, and beauty contests – it's all getting a bit far away from building houses. So who are all these people?

WHAT'S IN A NAME?
ARCHITECT

Use of the very word architect is a touchy subject. The general public thinks an architect is someone who designs houses but the title architect is, in Britain at least, protected in law, just like the titles doctor and lawyer. To be qualified to call yourself an architect you must have completed seven years' training and passed all the relevant exams; an architect will regard him or herself as the natural choice for a commission such as designing an individual house and most architects love to take on such projects; trouble is, they may be rather high falutin' for your simple project and – worse fears – expensive. Just how expensive an architect is depends on how desperate they are for work but what can't be denied is that architects design only a small fraction of new homes in this country.

Traditionally, architects worked on a percentage fee basis; three per cent of the contract value to prepare plans for planning permission, another three per cent for working details and doing the tendering work and yet another three per cent for administering the contract and (if you are lucky) certifying that the work has been done correctly – that's nine per cent in total for the full works. However this particular tradition is dying out and now architects work for what they can get.

Designers and architects have even been known to give quotations in advance for their work so they are showing every sign of rushing headlong into the 2lst century.

A newly qualified rookie might cost less than a technician – say £200 per day – whereas a top-notch, in-demand architect could go out at that much per hour. One of our internationally renowned architects quotes £70,000 for designing and administering a one-off house – more than most more humble abodes cost to build. That's exceptional – although the house probably would be as well. But fees of £15,000 - £25,000 for up-market projects costing a quarter of a million to build are now commonplace. But there are still loads of small architectural practices that work for much less.

Qualified architects are required to register with the Architects Registration Board. There is a body called the Architects Registration Council, who you can call to check whether someone who is calling themselves an architect is fully qualified.

If they then choose to join the Royal Institute of British Architecture (RIBA) or its Celtic equivalents, they are able to call themselves Chartered Architects. The RIBA runs a nationwide Client's Advisory Service, which will supply a list of suitable local practices who are actively looking for your sort of business.

There is a collection of architects (known as the Association of SelfBuild Architects or ASBA) who got together to cater specifically for selfbuilders and although as a collection of individuals it can't guarantee excellence, it has done some innovative marketing – including quoting for architectural services on a unit area cost basis. Incidentally, this rate was, until recently, around £30 per sq m, about the same as the cost of wall-to-wall carpeting.

Another useful lead is Design for Homes, a body set up to promote the use of architects in housing. The Design for Homes website has a searchable catalogue of architects where you can view their work.

ARCHITECTURAL TECHNOLOGISTS

There is a second body, the Chartered Institute of Architectural Technologists, which issues a quite separate qualification (architects would say it is a lesser one), which is relevant in the field of house design. Traditionally this group was thought of as mere draughtsmen, beavering away in offices, turning architect's sketches into working drawings, but many of them work in practice independently. And some of them are very good. CIAT oversees and publishes a Directory of Practices and a regional list of self-employed members interested in taking on new work.

BUILDING SURVEYORS

Chartered building surveyors carry out lots of good design work. The problem is finding them. As a professional body, they are administered by the Royal Institute of Chartered Surveyors (known as the RICS) but this amorphous group includes every flavour of surveyor including estate agents and building inspectors. The key is to find the right grouping – the Chartered Building Surveyors. If you ask for a list by post, you'll wait a long time but again you can search by region on the web at www.rics.org/resources.

MANY OTHERS

There is in fact no requirement for anyone to have any qualifications to design houses. The country is stuffed full of unqualified but nevertheless competent designers. Some may have undertaken some architectural studies but never qualified, some may have qualifications in other related fields, notably structural engineers, quantity surveyors and building inspectors. And there are whole rafts of individuals who are 'qualified by experience' – often designer builders – who do perfectly good work, some of it every bit as good as professional architects turn out. Obviously these designers are not regulated in the way that architects and surveyors are and you should be aware that if you hire an unqualified designer they are unlikely to carry professional indemnity insurance; on the other hand, unqualified designers are likely to steer you down a route where insurance is handled by third parties, such as the NHBC, so this is not actually as big a risk as you might imagine. You pays your money, you takes your choice.

DESIGN AND BUILD

This is a method of building that straddles the traditional distinction between designers and builders. In some ways it is similar to package build in that you are faced with an all-in-one solution but, unlike package build, there are usually no pre-drawn plans on the table, so in other respects, design and build is more akin to hiring a freelance designer.

In fact many design and build businesses are based around the skills of a designer who also happens to run a construction business. It is hard to generalise because individual businesses will go about things in markedly different ways.

I worked in a design and build business for ten years from 1986 to 1996 and if anything characterised this particular business it was the wide variety of projects taken on; some clients used us just as designers, some just as builders, most as both. Some clients subjected us to beauty contests, some to competitive tendering, some to both of these and some to neither, preferring to work in an atmosphere of trust all the way from initial contact to completion of building work.

Unqualified designers will tend to be a little cheaper and will also tend to be a little less imaginative, which can be a good thing if you want to build cheaply. Engineers and surveyors in particular have a reputation for designing to a cost, something which has been known to elude more up-market architects.

CAD PACKAGES

Computer-aided design (CAD) has been around for decades but architects tend to look down their noses at it all: they continue to sketch stuff on paper in the time honoured fashion and then hire a 'CAD operator' to turn their works of art into engineered drawings.

Operating a full blown CAD package (the market leader is AutoCAD) is no mean feat but what has changed recently is that there are a number of really very cheap 3D software products around, which anyone can pick up and play around with on their home PC. And some of it is very powerful indeed – a good example is ArCon's 3D Architect that costs around £255. If you like working with computers and you have plans for a home, you will probably love building virtual homes on screen and it may well help you work out some of your ideas.

DIY DESIGN

You can, of course, go the whole hog and design your own home. It's not as unusual as all that and it's not desperately difficult to undertake planning drawings – I once wrote an article for 'Homebuilding & Renovating' magazine about a 77-year old grandmother who did just that, having sacked her architect because he kept trying to 'improve' her plans. She knew what she wanted and successfully undertook all the negotiations with the planners.

However, there is a large chasm of knowledge between doing outline sketches and filling in all the construction details, a chasm which can only realistically be filled by training and/or experience (preferably both). Most DIY designers get an experienced professional on board at some stage if only to satisfy all the building regulations – as indeed did my intrepid lady client.

The problem with DIY design is that it's difficult to get pleasing results if it's your first time. Design sense and spatial awareness are not skills that can be quickly or easily mastered and you have to be supremely confident in your own abilities to be entirely happy with your own work. Fine if what you were producing was just a set of drawings but, of course, it's not, it's a recipe for a real, live house.

People are naturally afraid that they will be building an ugly or impractical structure and so the vast majorities are keen to get some professional opinion on board. Most architects expect to feed in ideas and improvements to your initial ideas and most people reckon that they are very good at this and welcome the added input. But not everyone.

There is in fact a groundswell of opinion that rates building professionals in general and architects in particular as nothing less than a cancer working to destroy an otherwise simple and healthy process called building. Here's building pundit Colin Harding quoted in 'Building Magazine' in 1999:

'Very few architects have the construction management skills to justify their claims to be team leaders. Most of the contracts we work on suffer to a varying degree as a direct result of the designer's failure to do their job properly and professionally. Typical lapses are:

▇ specifying inappropriate materials and systems, then being incapable of devising professional solutions to overcome the technical problems created

▇ lack of knowledge of basic construction techniques

▇ no understanding of buildability

▇ unwillingness to accept budget constraints

■ inability to manage the design process so that information is often late or inaccurate.

'What is so disappointing is that, in my opinion, the standard of professionalism among architects is still falling,' he wrote.

Harding's is not a lone voice. Here's selfbuilder Rick Hughes's assessment of the service he received on his project in Swansea: 'I would never use an architect again, this practice has proved difficult, frustrating, incredibly slow, and, although very good on conceptual items, struggle greatly once things leave the drawing board and enter the real world.'

Hmm. Doesn't look good, does it? But in defence of architects I hear of rather more successful relationships than failures. Indeed I have heard many selfbuilders go as far as to say that their project would have been hell without an architect on board and that using one had got them a far nicer house for much less money.

Try this one for a counter blast from home extender Marc Arnall: 'I decided to build an extension and, in order to save money, I wanted to use a person to draw the plans as opposed to using an architect. Meanwhile I talked to an architect that I knew, after explaining to him that, unfortunately, I couldn't afford to make use of his services. He was most understanding and offered to check over my ideas and costings, with no charge to me.

'The end result? Richard (the architect) has designed a far better extension, organised and put in my planning application, organised a good discount with suppliers and has reduced my costings by some £8,000. He is going to supervise the work, thereby ensuring

that I comply with all regulations and that any labour I hire fulfills his/her part of the deal. Thank goodness for architects!'

Well this game of architectural ping-pong could go on all night. It seems you either love 'em or hate 'em. What would be fair to say though is that there is a significant minority of architect/client relationships that are bedeviled with problems and that if you choose to work with an architect, choose very carefully. By and large, the design professionals who are not qualified architects don't arouse nearly so many hackles. It must be something they do to them in architecture school during those long seven years.

THE SELECTION PROCEDURE

Building is one of the ultimate network businesses, there being very little formal long-term work around so it is not surprising that your designer should arrive on your (yet to be) doorstep by word of mouth. But bear in mind that all designers have tastes and quirks that are individual to them and even the simplest house commission is likely to receive radically different treatments. Make sure that you can at least live with your chosen designer's ideas by taking a look at their previous stuff. And you really should, if possible, talk to their previous clients. If you have very particular ideas yourself, then you would be well advised to seek out a like-minded soul.

One of the keys to hiring an architect or designer and not paying through the nose is to be very upfront about money from the first meeting. Conventionally, architects like to work on a percentage fee basis but there is no reason why you should: some argue it encourages

architects to make you spend more than you want. You could, for instance, ask for an estimate to undertake the design of your house and specify that your project should cost no more than £XX,000 and that it has to be designed to a budget. Some designers will flee a mile when faced by such demands but a surprising number will actually appreciate such specific requests from their clients – they get very tired of the polite to-ing and fro-ing that goes on around issues like this. The more specific your brief is, the better pleased you will be with the results.

If it's a safe, packaged product that you are looking for then the package build route may well be your best choice. Package build also wins out if speed of construction is paramount. There is much going for the package build route but it won't get you a unique nor a cheap home. Whilst you would expect to turn to a freelance designer for a one-off house, surprising as it may seem, I think they are also the route to use if you want to build very cheaply, though I doubt very much if it would be the same designer for both options.

TIMBER FRAME PACKAGE BUILD

When arranging the running order for the 'Housebuilder's Bible', I initially thought that I should put this section into the superstructure chapter, up there with walls and roofs. Because, if you buy a timber frame kit, then it's basically the superstructure you are buying. Logic would seem to dictate that that's where it should go, and indeed there is a piece on timber frame as an inner skin up there in Chapter 7. If you want to know what a timber frame wall is, or what a Structural Insulated Panel is, look in that Chapter. And there's a brief discussion of the merits of lightweight versus heavyweight building in the Green Chapter, as well (Ch 14). But the main piece is here in the chapter on Design. In truth, it was a close call. But I believe that the main reason for choosing a timber frame package build (and the same goes for its close cousin, Structural Insulated Panels or SIPS) is not to do with the merits or otherwise of selecting timber or SIPS as your walling material, but rather to do with selecting a specialist custom home builder as your supplier; the fact that they choose to build with timber is secondary. And, as if to prove my point, there are one or two package home suppliers who don't build in timber frame. So it's the fact that it's package build, which makes it end up here in the Design chapter.

In England, Wales and Ireland (though not Scotland), the building trade traditionally builds houses using masonry blockwork for the structural walls. In Scotland, they love timber frame and it accounts for the majority of new houses there. In the rest of Britain, builders are of course happy to use timber in the roof and usually for the floors above ground level so, in a sense, even these houses have some timber framing in them but masonry walls have been the preferred way of building homes since we ran out of forests around three hundred years ago.

Timber frame houses in Europe have developed down a very different path to North America. North Americans build their timber homes on site: we tend to make them in factories, far away from the building site, and consequently timber frame housebuilding is a very different process to 'normal' housebuilding.

It's harder for builders to 'add value' by using timber frame or SIPS. By taking much of the labour input off-site and putting it into a factory, builders are in effect doing themselves out of a job and there is little incentive for them to change their ways. Architects are similarly disadvantaged in that timber frame construction

Although they produce many styles people often associate timber frame maker Potton with their Heritage range

requires an extra stage of panel drawing and extra structural calculation, both of which are technical in nature and best dealt with by specialists. There is thus an unwritten understanding between design professionals and builders to leave things as they are.

ADVANTAGES

Selfbuilders, of course, don't have to run along with the crowd and selfbuilders throughout the UK have taken to timber frame in a big way for much the same reasons as Scotland as a whole has. Not only is a timber frame house potentially much quicker to build than a masonry one, but − because the frame itself is largely hollow − it is easy to insulate

Chapter 4

to a high standard and yet still maintain a clear cavity between the frame and the outside walling material. Timber frame houses are therefore inherently energy efficient and they are warm and comfortable to live in, even in the depths of the coldest winters.

At least as important as any technical differences between the building systems is the question of procurement. I've touched on the fact that most architects and most builders like to use traditional masonry construction because it suits their own purposes. Because of this, there has grown up a quite distinct timber frame industry in the UK which has had to specialise in meeting all or most of the would-be housebuilder's needs. A timber frame company can't just build a factory, set up its jigs and wait for the orders to come rolling in – they won't. Instead they have to go out and grow the business by attracting the end users. As there are few independent architects prompting clients down the timber frame route, the companies themselves need to attract selfbuilders at the initial design stage and, by and large, they do this with attractive brochures of houses they have already built or a set of off-the-peg house types, which you can choose or adapt to your own requirements. In effect, most timber frame companies design your house as well as provide and erect the superstructure.

It follows therefore that the frame is only one part of the service provided by these

SIP panels: an alternative to timber framed walls

businesses. What they are really about is what is known as design and build or what the Americans call custom home building where you can pitch up with a few ideas, maybe a few sketches, and they will transform these into a workable home, delivered and erected on your site.

The fact that your superstructure is made of timber is almost incidental to the procurement process – in order to sell you a frame kit, it is first necessary for them to capture your imagination and your confidence. Often they have a range of standard house types from which you can choose or adapt but most of them admit to rarely, if ever, building these standard houses.

These days, selfbuild clients are choosing to have a much greater say in how their houses should look and function and

consequently most timber frame houses start life as a sketch done by the selfbuilder or a more detailed drawing carried out by their architect.

Even companies with an established reputation for standard house ranges such as Potton find they are doing more and more 'one-offs'.

THE BUSINESSES

There are a surprising number of frame businesses throughout the country catering for the selfbuilder. By and large, they tend to offer a similar range of services. Almost all the businesses offer a design service to turn your preliminary drawings into a fully engineered structure. In this respect a timber frame house is quite different to a masonry brick and block house: the design for a timber frame structure needs to be proved so that the building inspector is satisfied that it won't collapse in a heap or that it won't take off in the wind. This work is normally carried out in-house, though you can commission a structural engineer to undertake it for you if you want. To do it on a one-off basis is a complex and time-consuming process and you also need to draw up technical drawings for the timber frame wall panels which, by hand, can take almost as long as it does to actually assemble them. This is all work that can be carried out easily on a computer and this is another contributory factor helping to develop the timber frame industry into a unique

Timber frame comes in many different guises. Above: A green oak house from TJ Crump Oakwrights mixing traditional idioms with masses of glass and open plan living

Right: German factory housebuilder Baufritz have been supplying the UK for a number of years – they specialise in biologically healthy buildings

entity, quite distinct from the mainstream building industry.

Beyond the design and assembly of the timber frame, the businesses offer various levels of service from frame erection right through to a complete build, often known as a turnkey service.

Chapter 4

Many of the businesses tend to offer different levels of service depending on distance – for instance, they will be happy to quote for an entire build or a waterproof shell within, say, a forty mile radius but beyond that feel that they are bound to be uncompetitive. Others have developed contacts all over the country and feel comfortable taking on entire builds far away from home – indeed some of the timber frame builders think nothing of going overseas. If anything characterises the industry it is the word flexibility. Having said that, it often pays dividends to work with a local business – the level of service is usually better.

Some of the businesses are known for specific styles or designs. Market leader Potton are best known for their Heritage range, half-timbered Tudor cottages. They have spawned several imitators. There are a clutch of Scandinavian or Scandinavian-inspired companies, a couple of American ones and an increasing number from Germany and places further east like Poland and Lithuania. There are also a small number specialising in SIPS, as opposed to timber frame. The selfbuild magazines are the best place to get information and contact details and the selfbuild exhibitions, particularly the annual jamboree at Birmingham's NEC in March or April, are where you can most easily make face-to-face contact.

The majority of frame companies offer to work with any and every style. In all there are around sixty businesses active in the field, although around half are based in Scotland, reflecting the popularity of timber frame there. Many of the larger firms have joined together to form an umbrella group known as the UK Timber Frame Association. SIPS have their own trade association – uksips. org. Oak framers are something of a race apart – they don't do trade associations! There are one or two offering to do very similar things with steel frames and Design & Materials is unique in working in a similar method to timber frame companies but actually supplying masonry materials to build houses in the traditional way.

Generally, the concept homes are expensive; for instance, a Potton Heritage home of equivalent size to a developer's house is going to cost about 15-20 per cent more to build. However, if you strip out the vernacular elements of the Potton Heritage style – notably the posts and beams – the cost differential all but vanishes. Typically the price of the kit is between a third and a quarter of the overall build costs though the amount of goods supplied with the kit varies quite considerably.

When making comparisons you have to become adept at looking at the small print to see what's provided and what isn't. The Scandinavian kit home suppliers tend to provide the bulk of what you need but at a considerable price; they also have a nasty habit of listing their floor areas gross – that is including the external walls – which makes the homes appear to be 15 per cent larger than the competition, which works with net floor areas. Watch out for this. In Scotland, the timber frame market is more mature than elsewhere and there tends to be a standard Scottish package (which includes the plasterboard), which makes cost comparisons more straightforward.

PREPAYMENT ISSUES

Because a large amount of work is being carried out off-site, most timber frame companies want some form of prepayment. The timing and amounts of deposit required vary enormously from some businesses that want 100 per cent of the frame costs before delivery to others who expect payment after work has been carried out.

From a client's point of view, the nightmare lurking over the horizon is that the company they are dealing with may be about to go bust and that their cheque will be cashed before anything has arrived on site. Timber frame companies are no more secure than any other type of business and one piece of advice frequently given to selfbuilders is 'never pay for anything upfront'. On the other hand, the suppliers have legitimate fears that the customer can't or won't pay and many have learned the hard way that a contract as large as a timber frame house, usually measured in tens of thousands of pounds, should not be undertaken without some form of deposit and some form of guarantee that the client is able to pay. Unlike other expensive items such as cars, timber frame kits are bespoke and can't just be sold on to another customer.

One way around this problem is to use a solicitor's stakeholder account where the majority of your payment is lodged, usually about a week before delivery of the main frame. This way the supplier can see that you have cleared funds in place, but they are not drawn down until the frame is on site. Another often acceptable solution, used widely for car purchases, is to get a bankers' draft or a building society cheque – i.e. the sort of cheque that won't bounce – made out to the supplier a week or so before delivery. This is then shown but not handed over until goods are on site.

However, this raises another problem for selfbuilders borrowing to fund their build. Many lenders will not release funds against goods still being fabricated in a factory and consequently many selfbuilders get caught in a Catch 22 situation where they are unable to proceed.

However, there are now mortgage products on the market, like Buildstore's Accelerator Mortgage, which are designed to unlock funds before a critical stage is reached. Alternatively, many timber frame suppliers will accept undertakings from lenders to pay them directly on delivery.

The important thing to bear in mind is that you must plan ahead and discuss the matter with your chosen supplier and your lender.

SHAPE AND SIZE

Before you even approach a designer or a package company, you would do well to take on board a few home truths about the cost implications of your design decisions. If you are after cheap space, then you need to build your house in a simple shape, preferably a simple box with a simple roof. This doesn't have to look cheap – indeed it doesn't have to be cheap – but the point is that it is almost always going to be the simplest (and therefore cheapest) form of construction available to you. Many traditional houses take this form and they are not all peasants' cottages.

So why should a rectangular box shape be cheaper than say two rectangular box shapes stuck together? In a word: junctions. You are introducing junctions at every stage of the building process and junctions always involve head scratching and usually expensive detailing. Your brickwork will take just that little bit longer to build, your carpentry will become just that little bit more

complicated, your roofing will become much more complicated.

However, it is important not to exaggerate the cost implications of building complex shapes: I estimate that the cost effect of these junctions is probably of the order of between 0.5 and one per cent on your total building budget per junction. Therefore if you were to build in an L shape, for instance, you would scarcely notice the extra cost.

But wherever you interrupt the basic shell shape of a house you are adding junction costs and if you choose a complex form with extensions, dormers, porches and the like then you can take it that the overall cost will increase by much more than the unit cost per square metre at which you build the main shell.

CIRCULATION SPACE

There is another hidden cost brought about by using non-standard shapes in house design and this is to do with having adequate circulation space – i.e. hallways, stairwells and landings. This is virtually impossible to quantify because no two situations are the same, but the basic tenet holds that the more complex your form, the more difficult it becomes to provide adequate circulation space or, put another way, the more space you end up using just to get around from A to B. For instance, in our lean, box-design developer house, circulation space occupies just over 18 sq m, which is 16 per cent of the internal floor area. That's a pretty tight ratio.

Reconfigure the house in a 'T' shape and you'll probably be looking at circulation space taking up 25 per cent or more of your internal floor area. Now you may not mind that, you might even want a minstrel's gallery set under a glass atrium in your entrance hallway, but do

be aware of the constraints you put on your space by choosing more complex designs.

Bear in mind also that the current trend for heavily insulated walls comes at a cost of reducing internal floor area. A Passivhaus wall, with its 300 mm wide cavities, may eat up as much as five per cent of the internal floor area.

PROJECT MANAGEMENT

WHAT EXACTLY is project management? It's become a buzzword among builders who assume that it's the be-all and end-all of running a building site. There are now professional project managers who apparently keep building sites going armed only with a mobile phone and a fast car, the yuppies of the building trade. It's all about networking and contacts, being at the very centre of a huge web of information.

Well, yes, there is this aspect, but don't get carried away. Really, project management is nothing new; it's what contractors have always done, which is to organise building work. There is power here and if you've never employed anyone other than a baby-sitter that is an undoubted attraction to many of us frustrated prefects. But, as the old saw goes, with that power comes a responsibility and, in the case

of the contractor, that responsibility is considerable, because whilst you are hopefully making a bit on everybody's labour you also have to pick up the tabs for everybody's cock-ups. You are where the buck stops.

So, project management goes on at every building site, even out-of-the-way ones where they've never even heard of it. It's really rather a holdall term that covers just about every non-manual aspect of running a building site. And there are no rules as to who can and who can't be a project manager; it could be the selfbuilding client, or their architect or quantity surveyor, or it could be the main contractor or their foreman. And of course it doesn't all have to be carried out by one individual – the various functions may be split between people, though when this happens you can expect even more cock-ups than usual.

RAISING FINANCE

The first step in the management of a project such as building a house is to have the finance organised to pay for it. For the majority of selfbuilders and small developers that translates as how much you are able to borrow. Well, how do you go about borrowing on a property that doesn't even exist? You will find it a lot easier to borrow money if you have a) substantial assets and b) substantial income, preferably both. If you don't fall into either of these categories then you are by no means ruled out of the game; you'll just have to work harder at impressing the mortgage lender.

There are currently around 10 institutions actively seeking selfbuild borrowers; some of these are prepared to lend up to 75 per cent of the finished value of the property and several will potentially lend rather more than this – though most will expect you to come up with a hefty deposit for land purchase. Credit has undoubtedly got tighter since 2007 but the market is still active and is likely to remain so because, by and large, the lenders have had good experiences lending to selfbuilders.

Norwich & Peterborough is a building society with a long-term track record in selfbuild: they will lend 75 per cent of the plot value and 75 per cent of the cost of building. Loan to value percentages have been higher in the past but, hell, this is 2013 and we've had a credit crunch. What did you expect? Buildstore has also made a speciality out of selfbuild finance, introducing the Accelerator Mortgage, which enables you to borrow ahead of the pre-arranged stage payments.

As with conventional mortgages, the amount you can borrow is dependent on your income. The conservative approach is to restrict the borrowing levels to three times the main income or two and a half times the combined incomes. But the actual limits depend a lot on market conditions and when banks are keen to lend then the multiplier tends to stretch upwards. If you are self-employed or you actively want to sell on the finished property for a profit, then the regular avenues may well be closed to you but there are still a number of specialist brokers who it is worth approaching, many of whom advertise in the selfbuild magazines. Another very useful contact is the Ecology Building Society who are particularly helpful in lending to those undertaking unusual constructions and renovations which mainstream lenders shy away from. Professional developers have traditionally borrowed from the major clearing banks but there are a number of finance boutiques catering for them

as well. A good place to check who is currently active in this field is the small ads in Housebuilder magazine, which can be accessed online.

YOUR PRESENTATION

Many lenders recommend that you contact them early, when you are still at the dreaming stage. If you have an existing mortgage, start by talking to this source and trying to gauge their attitude to your ideas. Talk in broad sweeps about what you are trying to achieve and try and winkle out of them how far they will be prepared to come along with you. Together you may be able to shape up a budget to work to.

If you feel they are being unduly negative, then start looking at other lenders. The lenders themselves are tending towards centralised decision making, which can make things more transparent but also rather less flexible.

When the time comes to act, you will in all probability have to act quickly and you will need whatever ammunition you can get hold of – agent's details of the proposed purchase, copy of planning permission, your salary details, a building budget. If you've no plans, then show them a copy of this book and say you've read it from cover to cover – that'll impress them. You shouldn't have to show any plans at this stage because it is ludicrous to expect there to be any yet but this is one area where the timber frame package companies tend to win out because you can actually present a budget AND a plan, even if the house you end up building is nothing like this.

SCHEDULING

Unlike conventional mortgage lending, development loans and selfbuild mortgages are released in stages as the work progresses. For someone new to this,

it can be a daunting process, especially if they have to borrow to complete the plot purchase for a house that's not even designed, let alone built.

The key to doing this is to prepare a schedule of works, the sort of thing that is outlined in the diagram overleaf. This shows how a typical British house is built, taking around eight months to complete. The costings are for a total build of just under £180,000, enough to construct a four-bedroomed house. It's interesting to note that the rate of spending is surprisingly constant throughout the job.

Eight months is generally a good time to set to build a simple house, unless you plan to take on a lot of the work yourself, in which case it is likely to take a whole lot longer. As you can see from the timeline, there are nearly twenty major tasks to accomplish, all needing co-ordinating and timetabling so that they occur in the right order at the right time. At this speed, you are actually paying the wages of three men to be on site continually and if that were how houses got built there really wouldn't be any problems trying to schedule a workforce. But in reality each house is built by upwards of 30 people, each with different skills and each with their own schedules to work to; you can't expect everyone to turn up at the drop of a hat so you have to programme some slack into the schedule to allow for this.

SPEEDY BUILDS

Some houses do get built in much less time than eight months. If you want to build quickly, then either be prepared to spend good money on professional supervision of the whole construction process or to have a half-finished house with lots of snags, which will probably never get sorted out.

It's quite feasible to build a house from

Chapter 5

Eight-Month Time Schedule

Time line	January	February	March	April	May	June	July	August	September
Groundworks	▨								
Groud Floor Walls		▨ £25,000							
First Floor		▨							
Upper Floor Walls			▨ £50,000						
Roof Carpentry				▨					
Roof Cover				▨					
Scaffolding			▨▨▨▨▨▨						
Rainwater/Fascias					▨				
Internal Studwork					▨ £75,000				
Wiring (1st fix)					▨				
Plumbing (1st fix)					▨ £100,000				
Plastering/Screeding						▨			
Carpentry (2nd fix)						▨▨▨▨ £125,000			
Kitchen								▨	
Wiring (2nd fix)								▨	
Plumbing (2nd fix)							▨▨▨▨		
Decorating							▨▨▨▨▨▨▨▨		
Externals	▨						▨▨▨▨ £160,000		
Snagging									▨

An idealised timeline for a project such as a large detached four-bedroomed house. Eight months is a typical time for a professional housebuilder to take, without exactly busting a gut. It's comfortable. It represents around 3,500 hours work, or three guys for 30 weeks. The rate of spending is pretty constant at around £4,250 a week.

scratch in just three months but in order to do so you have to concertina all the events and, realistically, this means planning the whole process months in advance so that everybody involved in the construction knows exactly what they are required to do and when they are required to do it, just the sort of intricate project planning for which British builders are famous! It also requires that the correct materials be delivered to site on the appropriate day (ditto British builder's merchants). Speedy builds? It can be done, but...be prepared to spend the time you saved in the building process planning the whole thing instead.

STAGE PAYMENTS

What are the key stages or landmarks which trigger release of development funds? Each lender seems to use slightly different criteria to define when each

stage is completed but a typical regime would involve four or five stage payments coinciding with:
■ groundworks complete (say 15 per cent)
■ first floor joists (say 30 per cent)
■ structure roofed in and watertight (say 50 per cent)
■ plastered out (say 75 per cent)
■ finished.

Normally the lender will insist on a surveyor making a site visit to check that the work has progressed as far as you claim, although some of the more intrepid bank managers will do this checking themselves.

MANAGING CASHFLOW

One critical point to take note of is that the lenders only ever release payments after a stage is completed, so that you have

to be able to float the works between the payments. This fact has undone many a small builder in the past and will doubtless continue to do so in future; typically, the builder runs out of cash towards the end of the job and gets stuck in a Catch-22 where they can't get the final (largest) instalment of the loan because they haven't finished building and they can't finish building because they haven't got the final stage of the loan. A tricky little pitfall made all the worse because builders (and surveyors) habitually underestimate the cost of finishing building works off and the time that the finishing soaks up.

One of the major advantages of building reasonably quickly is that the strain on cashflow is minimised because the subcontractors may well be happy for you to withhold payment for a couple of weeks until the next stage payment is authorised; if that couple of weeks becomes a few months, then this option is effectively removed. However, there are now mortgage products on the market, like Buildstore's Accelerator Mortgage, designed to unlock funds before a critical stage is reached.

There is another little pitfall here awaiting the slower-than-average selfbuilder: the VAT reclaim procedure. The what? Check out the VAT section of this chapter.

WHERE DO WE LIVE?

Selfbuilders are faced with the problem of finding somewhere to live during the construction of their new home. The lucky ones can stay on in their existing homes and, if the market is rising, enjoy a two for one tax-free punt on the property market whilst their build takes place. However, the majority are faced with having to sell up their existing home in order to raise enough money to buy the plot. In this situation you have to find somewhere short-term.

The two main options are a short-term rental or a caravan on site. The first is expensive, often costing rather more than servicing a mortgage, and you can use this fact to try and persuade your mortgage lender not to have to make you sell up in the first place. The caravan is seen as the cheap and cheerful option but it's not without its hidden costs as well.

Usually people buy static caravans. Purchase costs vary from around £2,000 to £6,000 depending on size and quality. Add to this the costs of getting it to site and installing it once there, usually between £500-£1,000. Many firms supplying static caravans will buy them back from you although only expect to get between a half and two thirds what you paid.

You need to have drainage, water

and electricity supplies sorted before the installation which can make it hard to move into directly from selling an existing house. Also consider the cost of storing your possessions. Quotes to do this professionally usually come in at around £50 per month plus the added cost (say £500) of moving everything twice. Amateur storage is feasible but often results in damaged furniture – fabrics, bedding, books, pictures should not be stored in unheated sheds through a winter if you value them at all.

WORKING WITH BUILDERS

The question everybody wants answered is: 'How do I find a good builder?' I suspect that people have been asking the same question all over the world for several thousand years now and I've yet to come across a convincing answer. I'm not going to even try. Instead I think it's a good idea to look at the question from a number of different angles, to try and grasp just what it is that goes wrong with construction work that causes people to tear their hair out with exasperation. In an effort to close in on the main question, I'll take a look at several supplementary questions

DO I NEED A BUILDER AT ALL?

The building trade is a free market but, all in all, it's not a very good advert for the free market. It is widely perceived as being expensive, inadequate and inefficient, certainly when it comes to domestic work. Indeed one of the main drivers behind selfbuilders' willingness to take on the project management role themselves is a widespread lack of trust with general builders.

When times are tough in the building trade, builders are falling over themselves

to try and get work but an alarming number are simultaneously going bust. On the other hand, when times are good it can be extremely hard to even get builders to quote for work – some of the more reliable builders I know get booked up with work for over a year. The problem becomes one of finding a builder at any price rather than one at the right price. There is an added danger that less scrupulous builders will take your job on knowing full well they are inadequately resourced, hoping their contact book will see them through. Mistakes multiply when main contractors get stretched beyond their capabilities.

WHAT'S A GENERAL BUILDER'S MARGIN?

I frequently get asked this question at selfbuild shows and seminars. Behind the question is the widely held belief that general builders are an expensive waste of space and that by dispensing with a general builder you will immediately be doubling your potential profit.

I have always been uneasy with this proposition: having worked as a general builder for many years I know just how hard it is to turn a good profit on domestic building work, even when the initial margins look quite inviting.

The builder's profit margin can be looked at in a number of ways. Part of it is made up of business overheads that can't be ascribed to any particular job: phone bills, office rents and rates, vehicle costs, insurances. Another slice goes towards the time of a general builder – you might call this project management. This would include some admin work on your particular job and some general work, like estimating, that has to be spread across all jobs. Combine these two slices together and they probably add between 15 per cent and 20 per cent to your raw job costs – that is time-on-the-tools,

Chapter 5

plant hire and materials.

Then there is a third slice, which is in some ways the interesting one. You can look at it as speculative profit or you can look at it from the builder's point of view as risk money. This third slice may lift the margin from around 20 per cent (break-even, if you like) right up to 40 per cent or 60 per cent or more. If the builder is very busy, he is likely to up his price because he doesn't really need the work. But if he doesn't like the look of the job (or of you), then he may adjust the price upwards as an insurance against things going wrong.

Many builders would be happy to take work on at a margin of 15 per cent or maybe a little bit more if they could be guaranteed they would actually make that much – ie on a cost plus basis - but if asked to supply a fixed-price quotation, they will hide behind a much higher figure, having learned from bitter experience how easy it is to lose money on tightly quoted fixed price contracts.

Each builder will assess the risk involved in signing a fixed-price contract differently and it's this, more than anything, which explains the enormous variations you see in quotations. So in answer to the original question, how much is a builder's margin, I think the answer is anywhere between 15 per cent over raw costs up to… 50 per cent, 80 per cent, frankly there is no upper limit.

SO, IS A BUILDER, A GENERAL BUILDER, NECESSARY?

The main ingredient that a general builder brings to the party is this magic phrase 'project management'. Co-ordination of material deliveries, subcontractors, building inspectors, plant hire, office administration, you name it. Anyone who has ever managed a business of whatever size will know that it's time consuming and anyone who has ever managed a building business

will know that it's almost impossible to get it just right. Rookie builders with experience in management can and frequently do take on the role (and risk) of a general builder and do the hiring and firing of tradesmen together with all the other activities. However what should not be underestimated is the amount of time and energy this all takes up. Realistically, you need some sort of professional management help if you can't be on site every day (although not necessarily all day). For many people, hiring a general builder makes a lot of sense.

WHY AREN'T BUILDERS ANY GOOD?

However much sense it makes in theory, in practice many people end up feeling let down by their main contractor. More often than not, this is because contractors tend to be incredibly busy people and they are forever juggling timetables and deadlines. Whilst the typical general contractor would make a good project manager on one particular job, the wheels start to fall off when the number of sites being supervised gets above three. Yet in order to make a decent living and to keep a run of work going for various tradesmen, most general contractors simply have to keep going at several jobs simultaneously. I know from experience that it's incredibly demanding and stressful trying to co-ordinate building work going on across a wide area. As a builder you may start out with the best intentions in the world but you rapidly end up employing the same knee-jerk excuses used by everyone else in the trade (and despised by its clientele). Appointments start to get missed, calls start to go unanswered, promises start getting broken.

WHY CAN'T BUILDERS DELIVER?

I'm not sure there is an easy answer to

this. The glib answer is 'You try doing it and see if you are any better'. But that's not terribly helpful. In truth, most general contractors do deliver eventually but often at a standard well below their customers' expectations. So perhaps the advice should be by all means use a main contractor but don't set your standards too high. Or perhaps we are not prepared to pay enough for the level of service we want.

WHAT SCARES THE BUILDERS?

Money for a start. It is an axiom often repeated that you should avoid paying a builder upfront for anything, wherever possible. However, there is another side of this coin – it is the builder who is consequently extending you credit, which immediately puts him at a disadvantage. And despite the so-called power of the consumer these days, the levels of unsecured credit you are likely to get from a builder are way beyond anything else you are going to be offered on the high street.

Try buying a new car by offering to pay in 30 days only if you are completely satisfied and then withholding five per cent of the price for six months. Little wonder that so many builders experience cashflow problems. Sure, they are buying their materials on credit but this only lasts 30 to 60 days and the subcontract labour they employ will down tools if not paid much more quickly than that.

So one way you can smooth your relationship with your builder is to agree how payments will be met before the contract starts and then stick rigidly to those terms. If you are having to borrow large dollops of money to finance your building work and this money is only released in stages, then be open with your builder about this and make it clear just what he has to do to trigger the stage payments – at least he'll know that you are being realistic about money.

One of the bugbears of today's builder is to be told at the end of the job that although the client is perfectly happy with the finished result, the final £20,000 is going to have to wait a bit because they've overspent and run out of money: yet it happens all the time, builders getting used as sources of interest-free finance.

Another frequent scam foisted on builders is the excuse that the money is locked into a 30 or 60 day savings account and that payment is being withheld until the full withdrawal period is up. The builder is quite likely to be struggling with an overdraft as big as a mortgage. Yet such behaviour by clients is all too common and is verging on being really abusive but when the builder is the creditor he can basically do very little about it.

As you can see, the builder is actually in a very vulnerable position. But clients play still worse tricks; some will withhold payment of many thousands of pounds on the flimsiest of excuses, such as resolving a few snags that might be worth just a few hundred pounds at most. Sometimes these machinations are born of frustration with the performance of the builder but sometimes the client uses these excuses to cover up for the fact that they never had enough money in the first place. Yes, these are the real cowboy clients.

My business was 'locked out' on a couple of occasions on the excuse that the standard of workmanship was not good enough when subsequently it emerged the real reason was that the client was in financial difficulties and simply had no way to settle the bill. Rather than admit to the humiliation of being unable to settle a debt, it is altogether easier and more convenient to tell everyone that the builder is an incompetent rogue

Selfbuilder Stuart Meier's Guide to Project Management

Add up the appropriate factor from each box to give an overall multiplier for your eight months....

Experience

I've done numerous previous projects successfully:	factor 0
I've done quite a bit before, I'm tediously well organised:	factor +50%
I've never tried and my wife thinks I'll lose control:	factor +300%

Complexity

Everyone says it's a very boring design:	factor 0
It has a few unusual features:	factor +50%
Architect is really chuffed with it:	factor +200%

Site

Flat open site with loads of room:	factor 0
It's a bit tight around the edges, and slopes too:	factor +50%
On a clifftop with 4wd access only:	factor +200%

Publicity

"Good lord, no":	factor 0
Grand Designs want to film it:	factor +50%
Grand Designs are GOING to film it:	factor +200%

from whom you have had to withhold money or, even more likely, submitted an extortionate bill for the extras.

Whilst the client is telling everyone who will listen just how awful the builders are and receiving a sympathetic ear, able to point to work which is half finished in evidence, the builder is often forced to bear such indignities in silence. Often the amounts at dispute are too large for the small claims court but not large enough to warrant risking a full-blown legal challenge and many thousands of pounds get written off this way. Clients withholding money for whatever reason is easily the commonest reason for builders going bust and it can happen to even the best builders.

DOES THE BUILDER CHOOSE THE CLIENT?

Small wonder then that builders are just

as wary of potential customers as the customers are of them. The vetting process that goes on between contractors and clients is very much a two-way thing and part of the skill of being a good builder is one who knows which clients to work with and which to avoid. Your builder chooses you as much as you choose your builder. It's back to that marriage thing again. More often than not, a builder who suspects that a job is a potential lemon will not even bother to quote for it or, if they do, they will add a very high percentage to the overall profit figure to cover their back should they win the contract.

WHAT'S WRONG WITH COMPETITIVE TENDERING?

One practice that is prevalent is for busy builders to get together and divide up the work in a way (and for a price) that suits them – it's called covering. It works like this. A job is put out to tender – typically by an architect – to four or five local builders. Some of them are so busy that they simply don't want to take on any more work. Architects tend to regard refusals to quote rather badly and the builders feel that, rather than risking losing the possibility of quoting for future work, they would like to put in some price, any price. So the next step is to chat with the competition – it's not hard, it happens naturally anyway – and soon an informal cartel is in place.

Reg: 'Have you been asked to quote for the Old Rectory job at Chipping Butty?'

Charlie: 'Yes. I like the look of it.'

Reg: 'I really can't see any way we could do that one – could you do us a favour and cover us.'

Charlie: 'Sure – I've no doubt you'll be able to return the favour soon.'

So Charlie puts in his price and tells Reg to put in a price maybe £20,000 higher. Reg knows he won't get the job but he hasn't spent any time or money quoting for it and he hasn't upset the architect so he'll stand a chance next time around when he does want the work.

Occasionally the builders know all the other tenderers on any given job – in matters like this the grapevine works extremely efficiently – so that there are cases where every builder on the tendering list has been in on the scam. They all know who is providing the lowest quote and, consequently, the lowest quote is in reality quite a high one. Such a complete stitch-up is perhaps rare but frequently two or three of the quotes will be for show purposes only.

Partly this problem stems from the way building work is procured in the first place. And in particular the practice of builders quoting for free causes a lot of problems. It

sounds too good to be true and of course it is. It takes a good deal of time to generate an accurate quotation and most builders simply send tender documents off to a quantity surveyor who carries out the work for them (for a scaled fee, depending on the size of the job). Now builders often end up quoting for five or six jobs in order to win one, so the overheads of quoting for jobs they don't get becomes a significant business expense in itself. Anything that helps to ease the load of having to quote for jobs is manna from heaven for builders so you can see the attraction of any informal price fixing arrangements they might concoct.

ARE THERE ANY OTHER OPTIONS?

What's advantageous to the builder is obviously less welcome news for the consumer. What ways are there for clients to avoid being on the wrong end of one of these cartels? The obvious one is to avoid using general contractors at all, as previously discussed.

You can elect to be your own main contractor and hire all the labour yourself but for many busy people this is an unrealistic option and in many parts of the country it is becoming harder and harder to track down good labour. Alternatively, you can hire a project manager who will do all this work for you for a fee. However, such people are thin on the ground and there are potential contractual problems when the job overruns or goes wrong in some way. There is also little guarantee that the project manager will succeed in hiring the best labour at the best price unless you hold him to a fixed price for the whole job – in which case – hey presto! – he's just become a general builder.

A third approach is to select a builder first, preferably even before the design stage, and to work in a sort of loose

partnership with them throughout the project. Design and build – it's a buzzword in big commercial construction at the moment (where, incidentally, the problems are remarkably similar if only on a different scale).

Rather than trying to tie builders down to the lowest possible price for a set of plans they have had no part in formulating, start by asking them what they think are the most cost effective ways of getting what you want and who is the best person to design such a house. This way you can work to the strengths of your builder and hopefully use these to drive down costs.

Some builders will respond very positively to such an approach – others will run a mile, much preferring to work in the traditional ways. And whilst a more open, trusting approach to building can reap dividends, it's also not without its share of problems.

Just because you start out talking partnering and understanding doesn't mean that you'll end up there – and untangling a messy design and build contract can be more work than sorting out the more traditional adversarial way of working. However, I do feel there is a lot to be said for it, particularly if you don't want to get keel-hauled by builders putting huge risk margins on your job. If the builder is prepared to open his books for you to see his costs, then maybe a cost plus arrangement has a chance of working. You need to keep on top of the costs as they arise and monitor, monitor, monitor. But if the job runs to an agreed programme, then the cost overruns should be minimal. Tip here: a job that finishes on time never goes over budget (well hardly ever).

WHAT MAKES A GOOD BUILDER?

Hugely successful contractors (or project managers if you prefer) are a rare breed.

Though they almost invariably have their roots in one of the building trades, the skills that are required for managing building work are quite different. Good, clear communication is perhaps the most important and, if you are weighing up potential contractors, it is probably the aspect to which you should give the most careful consideration. After all if you can understand what they are on about then chances are that they will understand what you are on about and anyone working for them will understand their instructions. Of the things that go wrong on building sites 90 per cent go wrong because of misunderstandings or plain bad instructions.

In some ways this is good news, because if you meet someone face to face then you do at least get an immediate impression. If you can understand them it doesn't mean they will do a good job but there is a much higher chance that they'll do the job you want them to do rather than one they want to do. This calls into question your judgement of character: can you tell the difference between the hard-working, trustworthy, reliable characters and the shifty, slapdash and chaotic ones? It's terribly difficult, particularly as long exposure to the building game has a habit of turning the most upright people ever so slightly cynical and bitter. I suspect that the truth is it's always a bit of a gamble; there is no cast-iron way of making sure you are entering into a marriage made in heaven. This doesn't mean that it's not worth taking some elementary precautions.

HOW TO SELECT A GOOD BUILDER

1 Try and start with a sensible shortlist. Get one or two of the bigger local builders on board whom you suspect will do a good job even though you expect they might be expensive. Try and choose the smaller ones from recommendations rather than pins in the 'Yellow Pages'.

2 Don't waste everybody's time by selecting fifteen or twenty contractors. It's much better to have three of four who you contact (even visit) personally beforehand to see if they have the time or the inclination to do your job. If the response is lukewarm, don't bother to send documents for quotation, look elsewhere.

3 If you want to check on financial standing and/or membership of trade organisations now is the time to do it. Don't get someone to quote for your work if you are going to reject them later because they don't meet your standards.

4 The more detailed your plans, the more meaningful will be the quotations. Ideally, you should send drawings already approved by the building inspector. If you have a separate written specification, the process of quotation becomes much more straightforward (and therefore tends to increase accuracy).

5 Ask what the day-work rates are and what mark-ups will be applied to materials supplied, which were specifically excluded from the quotation – usually done to allow you to make up your mind nearer the time.

6 Be suspicious of very low quotations. Often you may find that most of the replies cluster around a figure (say £70,000) but one comes in way below (say £45,000). Without revealing your hand, try and elicit how this quotation was arrived at: what does this guy do that the others don't know about? Why is he so desperate for the work? It may just be the cheap one is the only one not in on the price fixing scam but, even so, be wary.

7 If there is no clear winner on price, then have a second informal round of interviews (probably by phone) to elicit more information. Are they busy? Are they *very* busy? If you haven't got a contract specifying a completion date, find out when could they start and how long would they take? Who would actually be running the job? Could you meet this person on their current site (good chance for a snoop)? Do they have a mobile number? Are they contactable out of hours?

8 If all still equal, then go for the best communicator. The one who you understand best, or just get on with best, will also be the one who will understand you best. It's that old chemistry at work again. If you've got to this stage and still haven't made up your mind, then trust your instinct.

Some of the very best of our small builders are extremely unambitious and don't go out chasing work. They keep a gang of three, four or five guys going and will turn work away rather than take on twice their normal workload. They don't advertise and you won't find them in the 'Yellow Pages'. Often they don't even do quotations. Clients willingly wait months, even years, to get hold of these builders and work is almost always carried out in a spirit of trust and co-operation, usually with very few subcontractors involved at all. If you value quality above price and informality above deadlines then this may be the route for you. If there are any of these mediaeval craft gangs in your neck of the woods, chances are your architect or building inspector will know of them.

WHAT MAKES A GOOD CLIENT?

Be straight about money. If money is tight then sit down at the beginning of the job and discuss how and when payments will be made. Don't leave it until the end.

Communicate well. Choose a builder you can talk to easily and one who you in turn understand. If you choose to use a main contractor, then work with him all the time.

Don't issue instructions to the subcontractors over the head of the main contractor. There is a chain of command and you should stick to it. It's sometimes very tempting to short-circuit it but it very quickly gets messy. This dictum gets terribly hard to stick to when the main contractor has gone AWOL.

If you enter into a written contract, then understand what the basic terms are. This applies even if the arrangement is less formal.

Don't be afraid to ask questions. If the job starts taking off on a course you hadn't envisaged, then find out why at once.

Realise that part of the key to getting good building work done is to be a good client, which translates as being a good manager. Don't be a passive consumer. And avoid letting things decline into a 'them and us' situation.

Don't keep changing your mind. And don't abuse the 'free quotation' ethos that general contractors operate on. It's one thing to get a free quotation at the outset of the job, it's quite another to demand costed alternative quotes for every finish item in your house. Main contractors spend an inordinate amount of time generating quotations and the more they are asked to provide them, the less time they have to spend on managing their business.

If you want to withhold money because you feel something has not been done satisfactorily then be specific about exactly how much you are withholding and why. Explain what you want the builder to do in order for you to release the payment.

This still doesn't guarantee success. But if you as a client play your part to the full and don't mess your builder around, then you won't be doing your chances of success

any harm. In my experience, a good client is the single most important element of a successful building project – indeed, good clients tend to get good building work done for them. And if there is a key to being a good client, it is to understand just what your role is and playing it to the full.

HIRING SUBBIES

If you've chosen to dispense with the main contractor then you'll almost certainly be in the business of hiring subcontractors. Project management – piece of piss, mate. Subcontractors – no problem – there are simple ground rules, aren't there! Well there are. They go something like this. What should happen is:

▨ never hire anybody who hasn't been personally recommended to you
▨ always check on their previous work
▨ always get three quotations in writing
▨ never hire anybody on an hourly rate; get all work priced beforehand
▨ check to see if they are members of a reputable trade organisation
▨ check to see what guarantee they offer
▨ never pay up front
▨ always get 'extras' priced and put in writing before they are carried out
▨ impose a time schedule with penalties for late completion.
All sounds good, sensible stuff.

WHAT ACTUALLY HAPPENS:

▨ *never hire anyone who hasn't been personally recommended to you:* You might have to wait a long time.
▨ *always check on their previous work:* Has anyone seriously got time to do this? Chasing up old working contacts for subcontractors who may only be on site for a day or two doesn't feature highly on most 'To Do' lists.
▨ *always get three quotations in writing:*

You must be joking. You may have to approach about ten to get three to respond in writing and even then you may have to wait (and chase) for two months.
▨ *never hire anybody on an hourly rate; get all work priced before hand:* Fine for most trades, but sometimes this is totally impractical. You have to have a detailed specification ready and chances are, if you are trying to save money, you won't have.
▨ *check to see if they are members of a reputable trade organisation:* They'll probably be more expensive if they are.
▨ *check to see what guarantee they offer:* Worth checking on for kitchens and plumbing but a bit meaningless for most subbies. They've either done it right or they haven't and you'll have to check.
▨ *never pay up front:* Good advice for anybody anytime. Sometimes it's very hard to keep.
▨ *always get 'extras' put in writing before they are carried out:* Alright in principle but, again, sometimes totally impractical if you are in a hurry (you will be). Get a site diary instead. If you want it to go down in writing be prepared to do the writing yourself.
▨ *impose a time schedule with penalties for late completion:* Risk losing your subbies.

WHAT IS A SUBCONTRACTOR?

Legally a subcontractor (or subbie) is a worker who gets hired and paid by a main contractor. If a subcontractor works directly for you then they are, strictly speaking, not subcontractors at all but ordinary (or main) contractors.

The difference is crucial because if you become a main contractor you also become responsible for policing your subcontractors' tax affairs – lots of unpaid admin! However, if you are the client, this all flows over your head – i.e. you don't have to know anything about it. Even though your subbies won't be subbies at all when they are working for you, everybody still refers to them as subbies.

Generally speaking, when we say 'subbies' we are referring to tradesmen providing a specific skill, like a plumber or a brickie. Sometimes subbies will be one-man bands. Sometimes they will be small firms employing several people. The one-man bands will tend to work for a cheaper hourly rate but may well be just as expensive when it comes to quoted works.

ESSENTIAL SUBBIES
Generally, you will be able to build a house by hiring the following characters:
▓ groundworkers. Someone with a JCB and access to a lorry
▓ brickwork (brickies). Often overlaps with groundworkers – one of the two (or you) will have to lay the drains. Often work in gangs of three (two brickies/one labourer). Don't usually supply materials
▓ carpenters (chippies, or joiners up north and in Scotland). Often work in twos (no labourer). Don't usually supply materials
▓ roofers. Most often hired in small gangs who supply and fix, sometimes doing the scaffolding as well
▓ plasterers/dry liners. Mixture of one-man bands and small firms
▓ plumbers. Same mixture of one-man bands and small firms
▓ electricians. Same mixture
▓ decorators. Most self builders do this themselves but there are plenty of 'professionals' around.

There are a number of other specialist subbies who you may want to use: glaziers, garage door fitters, kitchen specialists, pavers and drive layers, landscapers, scaffolders. Refer to Chapter 12 on 'Shopping' for more details.

CHOOSING A GOOD SUBBIE
I'd like to come up with an easy rule for picking good subbies but I don't know what it is. If you've found one perhaps you would let me know. Obviously, you can go to great lengths to see that you appoint a master, but this can be very time-consuming and if the guy is only going to be on site for a few days it seems like a big case of overkill. Generally, contractors and subbies know the going rates for various trades and they can usually work out an amicable agreement over a cup of tea and a ten minute chat and this is how 99 per cent of subbies get hired. It's easy come, easy go and if someone is useless they usually get asked to move on. However, if you want to ensure high standards from the start then you have to do a great deal more work, taking up references and talking to other contacts.

NB Don't forget the builders' dilemma. High standards don't tend to go with cheap prices. You gets one or you gets the other.

LABOUR-ONLY v SUPPLY & FIX
Subbies tend to come in two distinct flavours. The labour-only subbies are usually hired singly or in small informal gangs. They tend to be concentrated in the heavy building side (brickworkers, carpenters, plasterers). Many of the later trades – i.e. those concerned with finishes – are more often organised by small businesses, which prefer to sell a package whereby they supply the materials and the labour to fix the materials: typically, roofers, plumbers, electricians, glaziers and kitchen fitters. These supply and fix subbies will tend to be more organised – you'll be able to get quotes out of them – and possibly a little more expensive, particularly as they are in the business of marking-up materials they buy on your behalf. In effect, you are introducing an extra layer of management, which has to be paid for.

From a small builder's point of view, the big advantage of hiring small firms, rather than singletons, is that cost control becomes much clearer. If someone is quoting to supply and fit a kitchen into your new house for £15,000 then you know in advance what the damage is. However, if you rely on your own buying power plus Jim's joinery skills (paid for on an hourly rate) then you will just have to hope that it'll be less than £15,000; logic says it should be, but such finishing jobs have a habit of running over budget. You could ask Jim to quote to install your kitchen but Jim might well be reluctant to do so, especially if you are supplying the kitchen fittings. And what about co-ordinating with the plumber, the electrician and the tiler? Who will do this? If it's to be you and they end up keeping Jim waiting (they will) then it's you who is taking advantage of Jim's fixed price and he'd have every right to cry foul. This sort of finishing work involves so much intricate planning that it is unrealistic to expect every part of it to be quoted for separately, so it tends to be either subbed out in its entirety or done on a time and materials basis.

DAYWORK v PRICED WORK
Daywork is the term commonly used to describe payments by the hour (or day) and it contrasts with priced work, where payments are related to specific works having been completed. For example, a brickie on daywork might hope to get paid, say, £150 per day: if he was on a price, he would hope to get paid something like £300 for every 1000 bricks laid. All

things being equal, you would hope that he would lay about 500 bricks per day whichever system was being used to pay him, but human nature being what it is, it is widely assumed that the person paying the brickie will get better value from priced work. Many advisors say you should only ever hire builders on a price work basis but there are many situations where a daywork arrangement is both easier and more flexible.

If you are building to a tight budget, price work is almost certainly the route to take. For a rookie builder this is perhaps doubly important because you don't know what's in a day's work. Ask yourself how many doors a chippie should be able to hang in a day; if you haven't got a clue then you qualify as a rookie builder.

The main problem with always insisting on price work stems from the fact that it is, contractually, a much tighter type of agreement and that, for it to work, you need to be able to describe the work accurately before you can readily ask for it to be quoted. So really you need to have a professionally written specification for it all to make sense to subcontractors. It's not enough to say, 'Here is a set of plans. How much will you charge to put the brickwork and blockwork up?' because there are any number of little incidentals that increase the size of this work and make a mockery of your attempts to limit the damage.

MEASURED RATES

Another problem is that many subbies find plans about as easy to read as you do. This is less of a problem with the finishing trades where they can come and give the house a once over and don't have to resort to plans, but often the hardest parts of a job to quote are the first parts when no house shell yet exists. Here a common ruse is to agree a rate for each section of work

(say £400 per 1000 bricks laid) and then to total up when the work is completed. This is a perfectly sensible way of going about it and protects the subbie from any dispute about differences between what's on the plan and what actually got built: however, there is a great scope here for disagreements over the quantities actually built. Even qualified quantity surveyors will disagree by two or three per cent and they work to an agreed set of measuring rules: a contractor and a subcontractor may end up 10 per cent apart.

Note also that brickies like to 'measure through openings' for both brickwork and blockwork. Thus they don't deduct anything from the overall surface areas to account for windows and doors, which can account for as much as 25 per cent of the area being built up. In return, they normally fit the joinery in as they go without any extra charge.

CASH PAYMENTS

One of the big advantages of organising your own building work is the ability to negotiate discounts with tradesmen in return for paying them in cash. This is, of course, illegal and any serious publication such as this cannot, naturally, condone such behaviour. But cash payments for casual work are not going to stop because I start being self-righteous.

The normal builder's scam is to take off VAT in exchange for payments in cash, but this does not make much sense in new housebuilding because almost all the work is zero-rated so you are not paying it in the first place. Unlike the professional contractor, a selfbuilder is not required to police subcontractors' tax arrangements and if you choose to pay them in cash then that is a matter between you and them – it is not illegal simply to pay cash. Should the subcontractor then fail to declare this

income it is they who are committing an offence, though subsequent inquiries might get back to you to uncover these payments.

Cash payments actually do very little to benefit the new housebuilder unless they are used to negotiate lower prices from subcontractors, something most subbies are reluctant to do.

CONTRACTS
'DO I NEED ONE?'

You've already got one. It's a principle of contract law that every time you buy something or hire someone (or something) you enter into a contract. Any item you purchase should perform adequately, any person you hire should carry out the work described competently and you, in turn, should pay them the agreed amount. In essence, it's that simple and this basic principle holds whether you are hiring a baby-sitter or constructing the Channel Tunnel.

All building work is covered by these principles – after all it's why builders are referred to as contractors – and don't think that just because you haven't got a written contract then you have no redress should things go wrong. However, it is also true to say that if things do go wrong, the more written evidence you can produce to show how and why, the stronger your case will be.

If you can produce a written contract, signed by the builder, to say that he should have been finished by the end of August, and it's now November and you still haven't got any glazing in, then you've got a pretty good case for withholding payment. Without something written down, it's your word against his and – well there might just be two sides to the story: you're not in a completely hopeless position, but your case is much weaker.

'SO A WRITTEN CONTRACT IS ESSENTIAL?'

Not at all. It's actually one of the most overrated of safety features devised by professionals largely to justify their fat fees. Take the aforementioned Channel Tunnel, the largest construction project undertaken in these parts in recent times. Teams of lawyers were drafted in by both sides to negotiate contracts designed to be as watertight as they hope the tunnel will be. Did it get the tunnel built on time and to budget? Of course not. Re-enter those same teams of lawyers to argue about compensation, etc. Who benefits out of all this? The contractors, Eurotunnel and its shareholders – or the lawyers?

'IT'S ALL DOWN TO A HANDSHAKE?'

Not at all. That's throwing the baby out with the bath water. The basis of a building contract is that the client contracts to pay a specified sum in return for completion of a list of specified tasks. The more detailed this list, the stronger the contract becomes. If you have a professionally drawn up specification of works, then you already have about as good a contract as you can get. Signing a formal written contract for work that is only specified in the loosest terms is, in comparison, a complete waste of time and money.

'YOU THINK ACCEPTANCE OF A QUOTE IS ENOUGH?'

Yes. If a builder has seen whatever plans and specifications you have, by quoting for them he is committing himself to carry out the work competently. If there are further conditions you wish to set (such as time limits), then you should add these to your specifications. Should it later prove that your specifications are inadequate then so be it; the situation would be no better had you signed a written contract.

'IS THE SPEC WITH MY OFF-THE-PEG PLANS?'

You've missed the point. No contract is ever completely watertight. The more detail you put into a contract, the tighter it gets. There isn't a point at which it suddenly becomes OK; rather you get what you pay for. It's like asking how much life insurance is enough when you know that there's a 99 per cent chance that you won't need any and a one per cent chance that twenty million would be very useful. Very detailed specifications are time-consuming to produce and are, therefore, expensive; only you can decide whether you need one.

'BUT I'M PLANNING TO ORGANISE THE WORK MYSELF?'

It's unusual to sign contracts with labour-only subcontractors or indeed to put anything down in writing. Normally, the work is described verbally or with reference to any plans and specifications to hand. However, the contractual principles involved in hiring subcontractors are no different and neither are your chances of redress, should things go wrong.

One of the penalties of building on the cheap is that you are more exposed to bad practice, but hopefully you can compensate to some extent by your frequent site presence. In the absence of any written undertakings, keep a site diary to record the comings and goings and at least you'll have some written evidence in case of trouble. Even to be able to say, 'Gary and Pete were there just two days in that week and no-one else turned up till the 27th,' puts you in a much stronger position than saying 'they were hardly ever there'.

'I SAY. I SAY, I SAY'

The above section appeared verbatim in the original edition of the 'Housebuilder's Bible' and its assertion that you don't need a contract has caused one or two people to hop up and down with indignation. Perhaps they have a point. The fact that I've never built with contracts doesn't necessarily prove that they are a waste of time.

Julian Owen, a well known self build architect, pointed out that he was required professionally to work with a contract and that they didn't have to be expensive or difficult to understand. He particularly favours the simple 16-page JCT Minor Works Contract that is written in clear English and helps all sides to understand their responsibilities. I won't argue against this proposal but I stand by my original line that a contract is no substitute for a detailed written specification of work.

There's also the little point that a builder faced with a formal looking contract to sign will react by upping his quote. And if he sees penalty clauses, he will up his quote even more.

'ANYTHING ELSE TO SORT OUT?

There are some things that you need to be clear about that are not to do with the technical specifics of building. The formal way of dealing with them would be to enclose the terms along with the plans and specs you send for quotation; by putting in a quotation, the contractor implicitly accepts your terms. However, you could choose to sort these terms out more informally after acceptance of quotation; if you are confident that the terms are not too onerous on the builder, he should be happy to accept and, if he isn't, then you've just been given the clearest indication you'll ever get that this marriage was not made in heaven. Reconsider. Sorting out these matters is in the interest of both parties and very often the first move will come from the builder.

Chapter 5

INSURANCE

For terms and rates, see 'Insurance' section later in this chapter. Whoever is organising the building work should have cover. Make sure it's in place.

PAYMENTS

Agree payment terms. If a lender is advancing your money in stages, be open with the builder about when and what these stages are. Generally it's the builder who is advancing you credit and this makes him even more vulnerable than you are.

RETENTION

It is quite common to withhold a little money (between two and five per cent) until snags are adequately sorted out. However, don't try and spring this on a builder halfway through a job as if it was a matter of course. It's not. Furthermore, it's always a delicate issue – it reeks of a lack of trust – and some perfectly good builders find it all rather insulting and choose to steer clear of such contracts. After all, how would you feel if five per cent of your pay was withheld until such time as your employers saw fit. An awful lot of builders, when faced with a retention clause, just add the sum onto their initial quotation.

There is an additional problem with retentions. How do you define the end of the job? What is *practical completion*? People often take possession of their new home or extension long before the builder is really ready to hand over and what tends to happen is that a rolling snags list develops. Some items are clearly down to the builder to complete satisfactorily, some are extras, and many snags are rather indeterminate contractually. You could argue that the job is not completed until the snags list is finalled off, but if so, what is the retention money being held back for? Snagging the

snags? If that's what you want, then really you are looking for a guarantee, which is a slightly different matter.

TIME PENALTIES

Usually, these take the form of damages, which are to be deducted from the overall contract value if the work is not completed to an agreed schedule. For some reason I've not been able to fathom, these are conventionally referred to as liquidated damages. Again, it's one to sort out right at the outset and it's a very adversarial condition to place on a builder.

Time penalties make sense when you will suffer financial hardship (such as paying extra rent). However, when a job overruns it is more often than not very hard to decide who is to blame. You have to be prepared to keep your side of the bargain, which means no delays in agreed payments along the route and no changes to the specification of works. This still leaves the messy grey area of unavoidable delays (weather, strikes, illness, disputes with architects) which could keep an impartial referee busy for weeks. You need a very tight specification to be able to argue your side effectively.

These added conditions are really nothing more than specialised forms of insurance and if you load a contract with retention clauses and time penalties you can expect to pay more overall for the works described.

EXTRAS

The biggest single contractual nightmare any builder faces is how to adequately negotiate what the trade calls variations but what everyone else refers to as extras. People call them extras because, like Topsy, they seem to grow and grow. Some do shrink (hence variations being a more accurate term) but for every one that

shrinks or even disappears there must be a dozen that expand. It's a particularly critical problem with renovations and smaller works (where often 40 per cent of the final bill is made up of items not originally quoted for) but the new housebuilder is not immune from catching these particular bugs. If you've got plenty of time and money and like a nice loose specification where you can make up your mind as you go along then you'll be wondering what all the fuss is about, but if you belong to the 95 per cent of builders who break out into a sweat every time a bank statement arrives you will want to know how to avoid these nightmares.

The good news is that you can inoculate yourself against most of them. The bad news is that immunisation is itself expensive and time-consuming. Many extras can be avoided by having a professionally written specification, but people wanting to save money will probably have avoided paying for one in the first place and are usually the same people who can least afford extras.

As if the fact that extras occur at all isn't bad enough, when they do occur, you, the client, are negotiating with a gun to your head; you can hardly hire another builder just to do the extras. If you've gone in a bit hard at the beginning, including onerous time penalties and retentions, you can be sure that the builders will have their revenge here. Not only can they potentially stitch you up pricewise, but also they have a cast-iron excuse for blowing your time penalty clauses out of the water. Even if things haven't descended to this sabre rattling, adversarial level there is still ample scope to misunderstand and to misconstrue – 'Oh I didn't realise that meant the glass had to be toughened as well.' 'Well that's an extra £200.' If you are the kind of client who expects your builder to give you fully costed options for free throughout the job, as in 'How much extra would it be if we had a bidet in the kitchen?' you probably deserve to pay over the odds in any event.

Each little decision forms a mini-contract in itself and accounting for them can take up over half the total admin time spent on a job. The golden rules are:
- make it clear that extras need to be authorised by you before work starts on them
- always negotiate extras direct with the main contractor – that is the person with whom you placed the initial contract, not with anyone working for them
- write down what you've agreed – even if it's just in a site diary.

The reasons for extras are many and various. Sometimes it is down to unquantifiable works discovered after the building work has begun – in new building this type of problem usually occurs underground. Most often it is down to the client adding to the original specification of works as the job progresses or, as it's known in the trade, 'changing their bloody minds again'. There are two specialised forms of extras, or variables, which deserve closer attention.

PRIME COST SUMS
PC sums are not a new form of anti-sexist arithmetic but a good old builder's routine for dealing with loose specifications. PC sums are put into contracts to allow you, the client, the freedom to select a particular product at a later date. For instance, you might put a PC sum of £500 for a bathroom suite into a specification. The contractor will have included this amount in the quotation but the actual figure you pay will be down to which bathroom suite you choose.

There is a nasty little problem here because things like bathroom suites have list prices and they have trade prices – indeed the trade price is a matter for negotiation. Don't bulldoze in and buy the kit yourself, because the builder (or perhaps plumber in this case) is expecting to make a profit on this deal and they would have every right to expect you to reimburse them for their lost profit.

The normal arrangement is that the builder buys what you specify and that you get to pay list price and the builder pockets the difference between list price and his trade price, but this can work out very expensive, particularly if you up the spec. There is no reason why you shouldn't negotiate a radically different deal whereby you pay trade prices, but make damn sure that you negotiate it beforehand – preferably right at the beginning. Again, the sure way to avoid these sorts of problems is to have a tight specification and that means one without PC sums. This requires decisions on things like kitchen and bathroom finishes before the job starts.

PROVISIONAL SUMS
Like their cousins, the PC sums, the provisional sums are placed in contracts where there is an element of doubt about the amount of work to be carried out. They are much more common in renovations than in new building but there are nevertheless areas – notably underground works – which most builders will only estimate rather than enter into a fixed price quotation. Understandably so. It's a buck-passing device, a way of saying that if there's more work to do than can reasonably be anticipated, then you, dear client, will be the one who has to pay. Well, you knew it was a risky game. Provisional sums are just one of the things that makes building work such a gamble. You can try to force contractors to take on the risk themselves but their

understandable response is to hoick prices through the roof; more realistically you can establish guidelines for how provisional works will be charged: a labour rate, a mark-up applied to materials, that sort of thing.

RUNNING A SITE
Plan your site as if you were Wellington planning the downfall of Napoleon, or Montgomery about to attack Rommel. Think of it as a military campaign. Montgomery defeated Rommel because he realised that a battlefield was like a building site and that the best building sites were well organised with things happening when and where you wanted them to happen.

Don't just order 14,000 bricks and think how clever you are to have got them so cheaply. Think about how much space 14,000 bricks will take up, where that space is to be found, who or what will put them there, whether they will stay there when you dig a trench in front of them and whether your hod carriers will be able to get to them if there are 200 sq m of concrete blocks stacked in front. Build the house in your head before you pick up a shovel in anger and you will be some way towards having a strategy for negotiating the obstacles that you will encounter along the way.

Always assume the worst. Plan for rain, lots of it; plan for sub-zero temperatures in which your tap freezes and your bricklaying sand sets hard like rock; plan for delays as your subbies slip off to finish another job. Don't be gobsmacked if materials turn up damaged or if the wrong materials get delivered or if nothing gets delivered at all. Keep calm when your mortgage advance fails to come through on time and four large roofers move threateningly towards

Chapter 5

you demanding payment.

It'll be alright. It won't be that bad.

WHO? WHEN? WITH WHAT?

I cannot stress how much it is worth sitting down with a blank sheet of paper before you start building. In my experience, builders actually find this incredibly hard; they are, by nature it would seem, always wanting to 'push on' or 'get ahead' and they think admin is for accountants and blank sheets of paper are for poets.

It's almost as if the child in us can't resist the lure of the sandcastle whereby you start digging and piling and gradually the structure appears as if by magic, because everyone is digging and piling. Perhaps it is the natural way to build – after all how many children do you see designing sandcastles before going onto the beach. Natural or not, building this way is a luxury, which only the rich and frivolous can afford.

Your preparation doesn't have to look incredibly professional – it may indeed look like nothing so much as a glorified shopping list – but it does need to identify who is going to do what, when and with what. As a rule of thumb, every hour spent planning the job beforehand saves between three and four hours tying up the loose ends at the end of the job.

Some of these whos? and with whats? will be blank at the beginning of the job – for instance, you may not know your plumber or your plasterers at that stage – but the key point to take on here is that you need to identify a time by which you should make a decision, otherwise you will lose the so-called critical path and the whole building programme will slide gently off the rails.

HOW TO FINISH

Following on from this thread, there is another identifiable problem which you need to address from the word go and that is to do with the finishing details, the key ones listed below:

- kitchen
- bathroom furniture
- light fittings
- socket placement
- decorating schemes
- wall tiles
- floor finishes
- shelving, cupboards
- pavings, driveway finishes.

Very often, and quite understandably, people don't want to make decisions about these features until the structure is finished and they can walk around it and visualise everything. Architects' drawings (and 3D computer walk-throughs) are no substitute for being there any more than watching 'The Travel Show' is a substitute for going on holiday. The ability to successfully visualise completed building projects when they are still on plan is something that is generally only picked up after years of experience. If you feel unhappy about making these crucial buying decisions before you have a building you can walk around, then be realistic about the scheduling of these delayed purchases.

Refer back to the eight-month building schedule that appears at the beginning of this chapter. Notice that your first fix wiring and plumbing are taking place whilst the roofing is being completed, in Month 4. Well first fix wiring and plumbing can't actually take place until there has been some decision making about what is being wired and plumbed in and this effectively means that you will have had to plan both the kitchen and the bathroom layouts, even if you have yet to decide on what the fittings are to be. Usually these layout options will have been drawn in on the initial plans but note also that the

socket outlet and lighting positions will also have to be linked in at this stage and this will affect your positioning of beds and desks and TVs, which is normally left off the plans.

PLAN FOR A PAUSE

If you refer back to the timeline diagram at the beginning of this chapter, you will note that the finishes are booked in to Month 6. Note also that the plastering stage isn't booked to be completed before the middle of Month 5 and realistically this is the point at which the visually challenged can at last see what their schemings have produced.

Most people are surprised to find that some rooms seem larger than they had imagined, some seem smaller, some lighter, some darker. If you are of the sandcastle persuasion of builder, you've reached the natural point at which decision making about finishes should take place. Well you know, a dark oak kitchen would look just so, or perhaps you feel like stretching to those sensational Provençal tiles you saw in the Fired Earth catalogue, which would look a wow behind the bath. Now phone up your chosen supplier, be they B&Q or Smallbone kitchens.

'Yes, madam, we'd be pleased to supply you with these items. They will be shipped to you in six weeks time.'

'Six weeks! But I've only got ten days!'

'Well perhaps madam would like to choose from our Salmon Slash range, which can be delivered to you in three working days.'

'But I don't like any of those.'

I could go on but my point is made. If you want the time to step back and think and then seek out obscure items, and you don't want to do it before your house is plastered out, then plan a quiet period in the building programme so that you can engage on a second stage of the planning. If you are working to stage payments, then try and arrange for a stage payment to coincide with the completion of the plastering stage so that the financial pressure is taken off.

SITE TIDY

A clean site is a happy site. It is also a more productive site and a safer site. However, keeping a site tidy takes time and some people regard this as wasted time. It's not. Take time out each day to clear away the crap and to return tools to the spot where they should be kept and it will repay dividends in time saved later on.

Subcontractors tend to be very messy; if someone is working for you on a price then they will tend to think that clearing up after them is your business. Typically, the issue doesn't even get discussed when the subbies are being hired but as a general rule if the subbies are supplying materials then they should be responsible for seeing that they clear their waste away after they've finished – after all, in this instance they own the waste materials.

On the other hand if you are supplying materials then they are yours and it's down to you to decide what to do with them. If you demand that your subbies spend half an hour at the end of each day clearing up their own mess they may well turn around and demand extra money for work which would normally be done by an apprentice (whatever happened to them?). Clean subbies are a blessing, but if yours aren't don't just stand there and moan, get on with it yourself.

RUBBISH DISPOSAL

Often the reason a site degenerates into something resembling the aftermath of a small bomb is that there is no coherent way of disposing of all the rubbish. Indeed, many

builders are a) loath to spend money on keeping a site clean and b) loath to throw anything away because it might come in handy later on the job, or on another job. There is a balance to be struck here between a sensible amount of recycling of waste materials and a stubborn refusal to admit that 98 per cent of what is not used the first time will never get used anywhere else. What this invariably hides is the refusal to admit to an earlier buying mistake.

The easiest option for most small sites is to have a skip on site all the time. It costs around £10 per week to keep a skip in an off-the-road location, which I reckon is very good value. The expense comes when skips are exchanged – expect an exchange to cost £150 or more, depending on your location, but don't forget that you can have sand and aggregates delivered economically in the new skip, which can make a considerable saving. Many builders are tempted to economise on the rubbish and let the pile grow bigger and bigger, thinking that they'll sort it out later on.

Just piling rubbish up in one corner can cause more problems than it solves – a windy day may send it all out over the site again, and into your neighbours' gardens as well. Another solution is to dig a pit on site, which you will cover on completion – this sounds attractive but it is usually rather a dodgy way of going about things because you'll find that covering it over is easier said than done and you'll be unlikely to use the resulting land for anything useful because it will keep subsiding. Bonfires are OK for disposing of timber offcuts but most building waste is either inert (which won't burn) or is plastic (which shouldn't be burnt).

Whatever you do, do plan to do something. Building work produces copious quantities of all kinds of waste and it won't just go away.

SITE SECURITY

Theft is a problem on building sites the world over. It's usually on a small scale and it's typically tools that get nicked, often by casual ne'er-do-wells rather than organised gangs. Fortunately, the way most sites work, the early stages of the work involve a large amount of largely low value commodities like concrete and blocks, which are not easily stolen. Only after the shell is watertight (and hopefully lockable) do the expensive fittings arrive on site. If you want to beat the threat of any potential theft, then don't provide any tempting morsels for light fingers:

▦ Have valuable materials (joinery, sanitaryware, kitchen goods) on site for as short a time as possible before fixing.

▦ If you have nowhere to lock up kit like cement mixers, barrows and handtools then at least hide them so that the casual visitor does not see them from the road.

▦ Take small tools (especially power tools) home with you.

▦ Get the windows glazed and the external doors hung as soon as is practicably possible.

▦ If your site is particularly vulnerable, consider building the detached garage first (if you have one) to use as a strong room. Alternatively, do what many of the professionals do and hire a container for the duration.

▦ Temporary fencing-off is expensive and usually unjustified on small sites. However, it may be worth considering if you are in a particularly high crime area or if your site is particularly hazardous and it is likely that people may be wandering around after hours. You can hire 2m high steel fencing such as SGB's Heras Readifence for around 50p per metre per week – less for longer periods. If you need security fencing for more than five months it will probably repay you to buy it and re-sell when you have finished.

Chapter 5

SITE SAFETY

Building sites are by their very nature dangerous places. We demand finished buildings that are themselves structurally sound, weatherproof and safe to live-in but in order to create them we have to go through a series of steps, which are inherently unsafe. Anyone managing small building sites is legally required to be aware of these risks and to take measures to minimise their impact. New housebuilding is actually one of the safer sectors of the construction industry – a fact borne out by lower insurance premiums – but there are still a large number of potential hazards to be negotiated.

EXCAVATIONS

Trench work is usually fairly safe at levels down to about 1m (waist height), but thereafter the dangers of trench collapse become very much greater. There are well proven techniques for shoring up trenches and if you are not sure what you are doing then for God's sake get hold of someone who is.

Deep foundations are potentially very dangerous and you need to guard against not just trench collapse but also materials and people falling down into them. If you are working close to or underpinning an existing structure there is the additional problem that you could undermine it and cause a potentially catastrophic collapse.

Another problem to always be aware of is encountering buried cables and pipes, something that is common when you are opening roads to make service connections.

You can reduce this risk by doing your homework and trying to establish just where cables are likely to be buried.

PLANT

Control machinery. Heavy plant can kill or maim if not properly controlled. If you get behind the wheel of a dumper truck don't play silly buggers, be very wary. They are not difficult to drive but they can be difficult to control, particularly if it's wet and muddy. They can easily end up crushing someone. Dumpers are often used to pour concrete into foundations and this frequently leads to accidents. Also, ensure cement mixers are properly seated before you start loading.

Temporary fencing may be relatively expensive, but it can be a good investment as building materials are a surprisingly flexible currency

LADDERS

Don't be tempted to be macho – anchor the top end on to something secure. Don't make do with funky old ladders with broken rungs. And wonky step ladders are a nightmare you can live without.

SCAFFOLDING

Don't be afraid to spend money on extra scaffolding. If you are uneasy about doing some task off a ladder (or a scaffold tower) then get proper scaffolding erected. It's surprisingly cheap and you'll get the job done in half the time. Also be very wary about 'rearranging' scaffolding. Usually, this means nicking boards off the scaffolding to use elsewhere. Think who might be going to use the scaffolding in the near future and make sure they know what's been going on.

POWER TOOLS

If you don't already have a kit of power tools but are planning to buy some, then buy 110v ones rather than 240v. You'll need a transformer to get them to work but they are far safer. When you hire power tools you should be offered a choice of 110 or 240v. If you are committed to using 240v power tools then ensure that your temporary electricity supply is protected with RCDs (Residual Current Devices)

ELECTRIC CABLES

Long extension leads are a menace (though sometimes unavoidable). Try and avoid trailing them across site where vehicles may drive over them. Get a cordless screwdriver – they are brilliant and you won't need all those extension leads. Cables on building sites tend to get gashed and generally bashed about and it's not unusual for bare wires to get exposed. Keep your eyes open for this sort of thing and if you come across badly frayed cable then replace it, don't bodge it with insulating tape.

STEEL TOE-CAPS

Bruised and broken toes are still one of the commonest of accidents. Yet you still see subbies wearing trainers on site. If you are buying purpose made shoes, get some with steel toe caps (from most builder's merchants from around £30). If you manage to acquire a pair with Doctor Martens written on them you'll have a valuable fashion accessory to boot. Most builder's merchants also do a line of steel toe-capped wellies.

HEAD INJURIES

Most 'serious' sites insist on hard hats

being worn at all times, yet you won't even find a hard hat on most small sites – which is a shame because small sites are no less dangerous and, when people are working above you, a hard hat makes good sense. Yet, because they have an image of being 'for the big boys only,' the small builders and their subbies tend to shun them at all times. At least make an effort. Have a couple of hard hats on site and wear them when people are working on scaffolding above you.

SHARPS

Remove nails from loose timber lying around site. Common sense really but it usually gets overlooked. If you keep a clean and tidy site, this will be no extra work. If you don't then chances are the only way you'll even know that nails are lying in wait is when you tread on them. Ouch.

LIFTING

Back injuries are by far the commonest cause of lost time for builders. They can usually be easily avoided by asking for some help when lifting heavy objects like bags of cement. Again, don't feel you have to be macho just because you're on a building site. Ask for help.

MINOR ACCIDENTS

Have a small first aid kit on site. Most injuries are minor and can readily be treated with TCP and a bandage.

CDM REGS

In 1995, there was a significant upgrade to the health and safety regulations in respect to building sites when the Construction (Design and Management) Regulations came into effect. They were amended in 2007 although the difference this made to small sites was marginal. The key point

in these regulations is that building work should be organised in accordance with a Health and Safety Plan, which should be written by the designer and administered by the main contractor.

If you are deemed to be a domestic client – definition: someone who is having work carried out on their own home, or that of a family member, whether for profit or not – your job does not come under the CDM umbrella. Or, at least you do not have to notify the HSE that your job is taking place, which is critical in all this. However, professional developers have to go through a number of hoops in order to comply with CDM and if you don't know the score, you probably ought to start by looking for someone who does – an agent. And if you are a professional builder working for a domestic client you will still have some CDM responsibilities

It's a technical subject and there's not room to cover it all here; the Health & Safety Executive (HSE) publish several booklets and I recommend one called Health and Safety in Construction, available from HSE Books, and also available for free download. It's currently 141 pages and it's not terribly relevant to small selfbuild sites, but it's about the most pertinent guidance there is. Some local authority building regs departments and the NHBC now offer a CDM co-ordination service for professional developers: the going rate appears to be around £750.

INSURANCE & WARRANTIES

There is a great deal of risk involved in building. One of the keys to successful building is to be able to manage this risk so that it doesn't overwhelm you, and one of the most useful tools, in this respect,

Chapter 5

is insurance. Risk comes in two flavours, physical and financial. The physical risk on building sites is largely a health and safety matter and managing that risk is looked at in the previous section 'Running a site'. But there is an overlap between the two types of risk because an injured subbie or passer-by may well choose to sue you for negligence and so the first (and arguably most important) layer of insurance rears up at you. In fact, you need two separate policies in place to cover this risk because the risk to the general public is dealt with quite differently to the risk to people working for you.

EMPLOYER'S LIABILITY

If you employ any subcontractors – and if you undertake your own project management you are deemed to be an employer, at least from an insurance angle – and any one of these subcontractors then has an accident, which might be construed to be your fault, then they can sue you. If this is a serious accident the sums of money at stake will be large. Most policies now cover you for £10 million. A general builder is required by law to have an Employer's Liability policy in place and if you, as a client, are using a general contractor then you don't need your own policy in place as well. But you should check to see if your chosen contractor's policy is in place.

PUBLIC LIABILITY

This covers people (or objects) who you are not employing but might, nevertheless, still have cause to regret your building site ever existed. Maybe the mud from your site led to an accident, maybe your scaffolding fell down on someone's car, or maybe some kids were playing in your foundation trenches when... This is 'what if' insurance with a vengeance, but although the chances of a claim are small, any such claim could be extraordinarily large. Most standard policies cover you for £2 million worth of damage.

CONTRACT WORKS INSURANCE

Financial risk can never be entirely covered – for instance no one is going to insure you against your finished house being worth less than it cost to build. But there are various catastrophes that you can, to a certain extent, guard yourself from. The basic level of insurance here is covered by the Contract Works or All Risks policy, used to cover theft of plant and materials from site (usually with a hefty excess) together with fire or structural damage to any structures that you may be working on. Your lender will probably insist that you have all risks cover just as a conventional mortgage lender will insist that buildings insurance is in place on any property they mortgage.

If you are employing a builder to erect your house, again you shouldn't need to take out your own policy as well but again you must check to see that they have current all risks insurance in place and that it's large enough to cover the value of your completed house – very often the policies stipulate a maximum contract value above which they won't pay out.

One important point to note is that contract works insurance does not cover any existing structure you may be altering, converting or extending. You would be expected to have this covered by a regular buildings insurance policy.

There is another particular problem, which occurs with unconverted barns with valuable planning permission riding on the back of them. The nominal value of the structure may be very low indeed – in fact it may well be a liability rather than an asset – but the planning permission depends on the building continuing to exist. Were it to burn down before conversion work is started, you could theoretically have the planning permission revoked, which would be far more expensive than replacing the original fabric. So the risk you are insuring in these cases is not the value of the building but the value of the planning permission. Make sure that your insurance company understands the difference.

Contracts Works or All Risks policies are not mandatory and they usually come with dozens of options for you to pick and choose just which risks you want to cover. These go from the catastrophic (such as the building being destroyed) down to the inconvenient (such as some kid nicking your power tools). Just where you draw the line and just what excess you choose to bear yourself has an enormous impact on the cost of the policy.

There are only a handful of insurance companies active in the construction market and most of them are open to the needs of self builders as well as the professionals. The names with the track records currently are DMS Insurance, Selfbuildzone, Self-builder.com and Buildstore via their Buildcare package.

Expect to pay around 0.5 per cent of the total project value to get most of the cover you really need to build with a safety net. That translates at around £800 for a typical, four-bedroom detached house. Small builders pay much the same rate on their overall turnover. This would cover you for all the main areas that professional builders are supposed to cover, being employer's liability, public liability and all risks insurance, all summarised above.

If you are self building, then these policies cease to have any validity once you have completed and so then you need to transfer to regular building and contents policies.

WARRANTIES

Most people have heard of the NHBC (the National Housebuilding Council) – usually because it's being attacked in yet another TV programme about bad housebuilding practices. But most people are only dimly aware that the NHBC is actually an insurance company and that the so-called NHBC guarantee is really nothing more than a latent defects policy. A what?

If you buy a car or a computer, it is usual for it to come with a one-year or two-year guarantee, provided free of charge by the manufacturer. The new homes market once operated in exactly the same way – i.e. the builder supplied their own guarantee – but back in the Thirties depression, there was such a huge number of housebuilders going bust that the house-buying public lost all confidence in the guarantees being offered by individual builders. Those housebuilders who remained in business decided to pool together the risk and that's how the NHBC was born. It's really rather a peculiar organisation because it's part policeman, part arbitrator, part insurer and partly a club for housebuilders. The builders themselves pay the premiums (based on their turnover and their claims record) and sell it to the purchasers as a ten-year guarantee. But it's not the same thing as buildings or contents insurance and many house buyers have had cause to feel very poorly done by the NHBC policies when they finally get around to reading the small print and find out just how little is covered.

Over the past fifteen years, however, there have been a lot of changes in this area. For a start there is some competition, principally from Premier Guarantee, Local Authority Building Control (LABC) and Selfbuildzone. Partly driven by this competition, and partly by wave after wave of bad publicity, the NHBC has substantially improved its terms of cover

to include things like roof tiles and double glazing. In 1998, the NHBC introduced a policy called Solo aimed specifically at selfbuilders. Zurich CustomBuild had been around for a lot longer and was market leader but on recent form Zurich quotes have been coming out considerably more expensive and in 2009 they dropped out of the selfbuild market altogether. Premier Guarantee is relatively new; they only do warranties and they work with a team of independent inspectors across the UK and Ireland. Many of the selfbuild insurance brokers have links with them. The LABC, the organisation representing the good old council building inspectors, has joined the fray with a warranty, which operates completely separately from the normal building inspections. Selfbuildzone started life as a provider of conventional site insurance but has expanded its offering to include warranties: it tends to be the most competitive. Others can also come into the market now; Google 'Approved Inspectors' and you'll find rafts of them.

How do warranties work? Initially, you submit your plans, which are scrutinized and sometimes returned for one or two amendments. The warranty providers then carry out onsite inspections to see if you are building what your plans suggest you should be building. Unlike traditional building inspections, which take place at pre-arranged landmarks, the warranty inspectors habitually turn up randomly, although you usually get warned of their visit beforehand. Having satisfied themselves that you have carried out the building work correctly, you then get a completion certificate. If you are just building an extension, that is basically the end of the story.

The crucial difference between ordinary building control and a warranty scheme is that the latter is turned into an insurance

policy, which allows you to make a claim against the builder (or its insurance company) in the event of defects arising in the future. But, of course, you have to pay for this policy and, for selfbuilders, it's an expensive exercise – invariably costing over £1,000 per dwelling and up to £3,000 for larger ones. You don't have to have it in place but you may well find your mortgage lenders insist on some form of warranty.

Local authority building control doesn't come with any guarantee. The local authority building inspectors have the power to act as construction policemen, making you redo bits of your work so as to satisfy the building regs. And they are able to issue (or withhold) a completion certificate for your works, which is a mighty handy thing to have when you come to sell your house. But you have no redress against them if their inspections should prove to be negligent.

ARCHITECT'S CERTIFICATES

There is an alternative to buying warranties. If an architect is supervising your job (or in some cases a surveyor or a chartered builder), you can elect to have them issue progress (and completion) certificates throughout the job which say, in effect, that the work has been done to their satisfaction.

Most lenders are more than happy to take the word of a suitably qualified (and insured) professional instead of a latent defects warranty such as NHBC Solo. However, your professional is unlikely to provide such a service for free and the overall cost may well end up being very similar to third party insurance.

There is a pitfall here too for the unwary. Your architect is not an insurance company and making a claim against an architect is no easy matter. If your double glazing (say) was to fail after five years you would have difficulty establishing whether this failure was down to poor design or to manufacturing defect. If you think the blame lies with your architect's design or supervision, you would then have to pursue the architect for compensation.

Now it is part of a properly qualified architect's job to have Professional Indemnity (PI) insurance in place for just such eventualities so they can't just roll over and play dead the moment you get heavy, but what isn't often understood is that their insurance policy will cover their costs but not yours. And unless you have all costs awarded to you (which is extremely rare) then you are likely to end up with huge legal bills.

So, another financial risk looms and, lo and behold, there is yet another policy available to cover this particular risk, although I only know of one such policy, the Selfbuild Legal Protection scheme. It will pay reasonable legal expenses for actions you might wish to take against a whole raft of characters over and beyond your architect: your main contractor, your subbies, your materials suppliers, even your solicitor. It costs about £125 and is valid for up to two years after you move in.

What if you are using a designer who doesn't carry PI insurance? Many very good house designers are not formally qualified and would find it very difficult to get PI cover. In these instances, your protection would lie in using one of the third party warranty providers instead. Once your plans are accepted by the likes of the NHBC, then they are taking on responsibility for their outcome.

BOOK-KEEPING

SITE DIARY
Even if you loathe the thought of record keeping, do try and keep a site diary and write down a summary of every day's action:

- weather
- what work was done
- who was on site and how many hours they worked
- quotations, orders, deliveries, shopping trips
- payments made
- contacts made, phone numbers
- site visits by building inspectors, architects, surveyors, etc
- comments, feedback from casual visitors, neighbours
- accidents (however small), breakages, theft.

This not only provides a fascinating historical record, but a site diary has a more immediate benefit if a dispute arises; you have a written record of transactions as they occur. Whether you choose to work with or without a formal contract, a site diary will provide you with loads of unexpected ammunition should things ever turn nasty.

BASIC ACCOUNTS
What level of accounts you keep on a project like a selfbuilt house is very much up to you. Because you are able to reclaim VAT on most purchases going into a newly built house, it is a must to keep every VAT receipt that comes your way (I recommend a lever-arch file and a hole puncher for filing). When the time comes to make your claim, you will have to total all the figures, but whether it's worth keeping a running total of costs going whilst the job is in progress is doubtful.

Running trading accounts with builder's merchants and plant hire shops can be a big help; not only is buying more convenient (and often cheaper) but just the fact that tax invoices get sent by post to your home address makes it much easier to keep tabs on paperwork. Trading accounts is a subject dealt with in greater length in Chapter 13 'Shopping'.

MANAGEMENT ACCOUNTS
If money is tight then you should consider putting a lot more effort into job accounting. You need an early warning system in place to warn you when costs start to overshoot. The key to doing this is to split your whole project down into a number of little joblets such as groundworks, external masonry, roofing, etc. Prepare a detailed budget for your house showing how much you expect to spend on each joblet and prepare a job schedule sheet showing how long each stage of the job should take. Analyse costs as they occur and use your site diary to estimate how much of each stage is completed each week.

You don't go into a project like building a new home without some sort of a budget. Sticking to the budget is obviously crucial to the success of the project, but in my experience you are more likely to come adrift through making an unrealistic budget in the first place rather than overspending on budgeted items. The other great budget breaker is the unavoidable extras (often to do with extra foundations or drains). There is only one safe way around this and that is to make a largish – say five per cent – contingency sum available for such eventualities. If your budget doesn't stretch to this, then how about building a smaller house? The more loosely organised your management of the job is, the higher the chance there is of encountering unavoidable extras. No amount of clever management accounting will make up for an incomplete specification.

CORRESPONDENCE
Keep handy copies of all correspondence

to do with your house from plot purchase to suppliers' terms. Some of this now happens using email, but an awful lot still gets done on paper. Even if it's email, it's still not a bad idea to print it out and keep a hard copy. A lever-arch file with about ten sub-dividers should be sufficient. Don't forget that correspondence means keeping copies of your letters as well as ones received, so work out some system of making and keeping copies of your side.

When you express any kind of an interest in building, you soon find yourself getting snowed under with mailshots for this, that or the other. Some of this is junk, some of it is incredibly useful, but you will need to be on the ball about organising it or you'll never be able to retrieve the useful bits when you need them. Again, a subdivided lever-arch file is a real winner here, though you may need to invest in a heavy-duty hole puncher (c. £25) to pierce the thicker tomes. In addition, get a pack of cardboard magazine files,

Concessions for VAT on listed buildings have now been removed

which you can use to hold really thick literature like you get from kit home suppliers and certain kitchen manufacturers.

VAT

VAT rates can change. Indeed they may well do during the lifespan of this edition. It only takes a single announcement in the House of Commons. This edition is based on the situation that applied in early 2013. All prices mentioned in this book are VAT-free (unless

Chapter 5

otherwise stated). If there are major changes, they are likely to receive wide publicity but if you are not sure what has happened, you are advised to contact the VAT query line – 0845 0109000. The peculiar situation that self build finds itself in is about to be described in some detail but it's worth noting here that you can download the self build VAT reclaim form from the Revenue & Customs website on www.hmrc.gov.uk (hint: look for Notice 431NB (for newbuild) or 431C (for conversions) in the VAT section.

New housebuilding (and conversions of non-domestic property into homes) enjoy a privileged position in the UK VAT world. They are mostly zero-rated. This means, in layman's terms, that you can reclaim almost all the VAT charged to you in the course of creating your new house. This is something of an anomaly. Since the introduction of VAT in 1983, almost all other building work has been standard-rated, which means that you cannot reclaim the VAT.

The reason new housebuilding survives VAT-free is that VAT cannot be levied on second-hand house sales since such sales are private, and so it would be regarded as inequitable for new housebuilders to have to charge VAT on their product when 90 per cent of all house sales escape it. Nevertheless, the imposition of VAT on new housebuilding is a possibility that all new housebuilders must face and it's recently come to the fore in the political debate about the future of housing.

Change may well be on the way during the lifetime of this edition so that VAT reclaims may become a thing of the past. Having warned you of that, the changes in VAT rules for homebuilders recently have actually been pretty helpful. The definition of a non-domestic property was widened in 2001 to include anything that hadn't been lived in for ten years so conversions of all

kinds of buildings into homes was brought into the zero-VAT net – prior to that they had to have been unoccupied since 1973.

Gordon Brown, as Chancellor, also introduced a new 5 per cent VAT band, which applies to work on properties empty for more than two years and also to changing the number of living units in a building. This latter was presumably brought in to encourage builders to convert large houses into flats but it seems to equally well apply to people who want to turn a block of flats into a large house.

Thus far, the Coalition government hasn't sort to undo any of these tax advantages, but it could of course all change. Fingers crossed.

RECLAIMING VAT

So much for politics. Here follows an explanation of the VAT position in Great Britain as of 2013. The position varies depending on how you organise your construction. If you are a professional builder undertaking a spec build for the first time, it could hardly be simpler; you just reclaim the VAT inputs each quarter when you do your VAT returns. The only complexities come with certain costs where VAT is not reclaimable. More on these in a minute. For self builders, HMRC runs a special scheme called VAT refunds for DIY builders and converters. Really, this claim pack is a must-have item unless, of course, you think the government deserves the money more than you do. You can use the DIY reclaim scheme even if you have very little input into a new house: if a builder undertakes a turnkey project for you, you can still reclaim VAT on items like fencing and paint that you might put in yourself.

How you run a job has a bearing on the VAT situation. Design fees and professional services are not normally eligible for VAT

refunds but if you start by appointing a builder who provides design as part of the overall package (as you might with many timber frame companies), then it's all considered one design and build contract and you can reclaim all fees (provided the invoicing doesn't separate out the fees from the construction). It's called creative invoicing.

If you are taking on the project management yourself, there are quite a few ground rules you need to be aware of.

You can't reclaim VAT from subcontractors for their labour, or on supply and fix contracts. If it's a regular new build, then make sure they don't charge VAT in the first place. Just to make things complicated, if the project you are undertaking is classed as a conversion, not a new build, then you are able to reclaim VAT on labour, even though VAT on the labour should be being charged at the reduced rate of five per cent – you have to ensure that it is.

You can only make one claim and this must be within three months of completion. Completion is not the same thing as occupation: they expect you may well occupy before technical completion but if the delay between the two is longer than six months then they become suspicious and will demand explanation. Tread cautiously here.

Valid VAT receipts, made out to you, must support all purchases you wish to reclaim the VAT on. A VAT receipt is one that includes the supplier's VAT No (but doesn't necessarily separate out the VAT). Credit card slips, cheque stubs, delivery notes are not VAT receipts. Also Customs & Excise want to see the originals; they don't accept photocopies. Note also that if some of your material supplies are purchased through a subcontractor who is not VAT registered, you will not be able to reclaim

VAT – the original invoice must be made out to you.

WHAT IS ZERO-RATED?

As discussed already, recent changes in VAT rules have somewhat simplified the rules and made definitions of what can and cannot be zero-rated much easier to grasp. There are two areas to consider. Firstly, how does the job as a whole stack up in the VAT reclaim stakes? And secondly, which costs incurred can you reclaim?

The first area has always been looked on as a minefield. If you are in doubt, you can get hold of the rules on the web at www. hmrc.gov.uk where you want to get hold of two documents, VAT notice 708 (Buildings and Construction) and VAT information sheet 0501 (which explains the 2001 changes in a mere 11 pages). There are of course still grey areas – for instance what happens when you convert a pub that has a self-contained flat – but it's still simpler than it was. A bit. And no, building new holiday lets doesn't qualify for zero-rating. What's in and what isn't is all determined with reference to these lengthy documents.

Provided you can establish that your project is a new build, almost all the construction costs are eligible for zero-rating of VAT. That is to say, those suppliers who are knowingly supplying a zero-rated project should not add VAT to their invoices and if VAT is applied (currently at 20 per cent) you should be able to reclaim it. The situation with conversions is subtly different. Here you are expected to pay VAT on all supplies, including labour albeit at the reduced rate of five per cent. You can still reclaim using the DIY builders VAT refund system.

As your house nears completion, you will find a number of items that HMRC, in their wisdom, regard as fittings that lie outside the zero-rating net. If there is any

ground rule at all it is that if the items are fixed into the building then they are zero-rated but if they are removable then you must pay the VAT.

However, there are many exceptions to this rule and the rules are often subject to review. I present the following list for general guidance only; the VAT office may view things differently and please don't jump down my throat if you find you are unable to reclaim VAT on something I've said you can. It's the VAT office you should be arguing with and, if you're canny, you will do this before you start construction. VAT Notice 431 includes a similar list, which you should refer to for the latest views from the VAT office.

Having tried to get myself off this particular hook, let's look at the current state of play. Personally, I find this catalogue of what's in and what's out ridiculous, and I'd be tempted to laugh at it if there wasn't so much damn money riding on it. Don't keep telling your VAT official that 'This is crazy!'; they know it and they've heard it a thousand times before.

■ Kitchens: Fitted kitchens are zero-rated but white goods (cookers, washing machines, dishwashers, etc.) are not. There is no distinction made between integrated and freestanding equipment – you must pay VAT on them – so things like waste disposal units and water softeners are standard-rated. However there are some zero-rated appliances, most notably cooker hoods and built-in vacuum cleaners.

■ Agas: standard-rated except when they have an integral boiler; then they are regarded as part of the heating system and VAT can be reclaimed.

■ Fitted cupboards: At present the ruling seems to be this – if you build the cupboards (ie fitting doors across alcoves formed in the walls) then it seems that you

can reclaim the VAT on all the materials, but if you buy in fitted cupboards then you can't. If that's not clear then ask your VAT office.

■ Flooring: All forms of carpeting are standard-rated. Everything else is zero-rated.

■ Heating/plumbing/sanitaryware: All zero-rated except water treatment units. Fireplaces are also zero-rated. Solar panels, heat recovery systems and air conditioning also qualify for zero-rating.

■ Electrics: All zero-rated. Light fittings should be OK provided they are fitted, but a zealous inspector may disagree.

■ Alarms: Both smoke alarms and burglar alarms are zero-rated. Also fire safety equipment is now zero-rated.

■ Furnishings: Movable furniture is invariably standard-rated. The status of fitted shelves is unclear. Curtains and blinds are standard-rated but you can reclaim VAT on curtain rails.

■ Decorating: Paint is zero-rated and you shouldn't have any problem with wallpaper. Also, if you want to have decorative finishes (like pine matchboarding) you should be able to reclaim the VAT.

■ Garages and driveways: Zero-rated, but note that other outbuildings are standard rated.

■ Landscaping: They will generally accept a limited amount of turfing and paving as zero-rated. The rule seems to be that if the landscaping is included as part of the planning permission, then it's zero-rated. Otherwise it's standard rated.

■ Swimming pools: Standard-rated unless it's inside a building, which is at least attached to the main house.

■ Outbuildings/conservatories: Detached outbuildings (except garages) are standard-rated. However, attached extensions like conservatories are zero-rated. The rule seems to be if it's attached, it's zero-rated: if it's detached, you have to pay the VAT. The only exception is the detached garage (see above).

■ Plant hire, scaffolding: These are standard-rated items, which you cannot reclaim, although note that scaffolding erection and dismantling is technically zero-rated whilst the hire is not. Therefore, you can save money by getting your scaffolder to invoice separately for the two services.

■ Professional fees: standard-rated.

END OF THE PARTY

A selfbuilder can only make one reclaim from the VAT office and so when it's done, it's done. This presents a major cashflow problem to many as there is usually several thousand pounds waiting to be reclaimed, several thousand pounds which most selfbuilders could well use to finish off their project; many end up forgoing further VAT reclaims in order to get their hands on this money before the house is complete. If you employ a VAT registered builder to construct your house this reclaim problem does not occur as the builder's invoices are zero-rated for all but the exempt items though note that you can still use the DIY reclaim scheme if you buy just the odd can of paint and a few curtain rails on your own account.

LISTED BUILDINGS

Listed buildings used to enjoy a semi-privileged VAT position in that whilst repairs were standard rated, improvements were zero-rated. Lots of fun was had by designers and builders, trying to show that a repair was actually an improvement, but this game was stopped in its tracks by Chancellor George Osborne who made all listed building work standard rated (i.e. 20 per cent VAT) in 2012.

VAT IN THE EU

The VAT regimes for new housebuilding vary substantially around the EU. There is no such thing as zero-rating anywhere else (as far as I can establish). In the Republic of Ireland, VAT is collected at over 20 per cent on all building materials though there is a tax break if you employ a registered builder on a new house – you pay VAT at 12.5 per cent instead.

But one piece of good news is that if you are undertaking zero-rated building in the UK you can reclaim VAT on materials purchased anywhere in the EC. Also note that there is an increasing cross-Channel trade in light goods, which currently seem to be significantly cheaper in France and Belgium than in the UK.

OTHER TAXES

Whereas professionals and selfbuilders are on a level playing field when it comes to VAT, selfbuild really comes into its own when you start to look at other taxes. If you are building your one and only house, then you really don't have to pay any taxes at all on the profits you make. The two taxes that you might expect to get clobbered by are income tax and capital gains tax (CGT). If you are a professional, you will get caught by one of these two. Typically, income tax is levied on you if your livelihood involves building homes for sale, and CGT cuts in if you buy and sell second homes or houses to let out. Here you would be expected to pay income tax on any rental income, and CGT on any gains you make when you come to sell the house. However, neither income tax nor CGT have ever been levied on 'your principal private residence' so any profits you make on your private homebuilding are consequently tax-free. Even if you sell off part of your garden for someone else

to build a house, you don't pay any tax on the proceeds, although you can trip into the tax net if the garden area exceeds 0.5 hectares.

Now the selfbuilders' tax exempt status raises a few interesting possibilities. What if you move into a house you have built, make it your 'principal private residence', and then sell it shortly afterwards? What if you step from one selfbuild house to another to another? Welcome to the world of the serial selfbuilder. It's actually a long established practice in the UK. I remember a builder doing exactly this in the Cambridgeshire village I grew up in. My parents bought a house from him in 1950. By the time we left the village when I was 13, he'd moved house about five times and was at work on another, all in the same village.

Many small builders live a semi-nomadic, selfbuild lifestyle like this, interspersing regular work with the odd homebuilding or renovating project. As long as you establish each house as your 'principal private residence' you should be in the clear tax-wise, although there are signs that the Revenue is beginning to take an interest in this area. There is no published guidance on how long you have to stay in a house before it is accepted as your 'principal private residence' that would distinguish you from a commercial developer but 12 months is often quoted as a broadly acceptable period. The key point to establish isn't how long you live in a house but that the project wasn't undertaken with profit in mind. 'Private residence relief is not intended to relieve speculative gains,' reads the Inland Revenue Help Sheet 283. 'Relief is not therefore available where you acquire or spend money on your dwelling-house wholly or partly to realise a gain on its disposal.' Ominous wording, especially as it could be applied to just about anyone who ever bought a house in Britain. It's worth bearing in mind. Although the number of people pursued for tax on their 'speculative' profits on selfbuild is tiny, it would be as well not to make too much of a song and dance about how much money you may have made.

In reality, not that many people will keep on moving house and building and moving and building indefinitely. Whilst it's a great way to build up equity and reduce mortgages, it doesn't actually bring in any extra cash (unless you start trading down) and it's also pretty exhausting and doesn't fit easily into the requirements of family life. But it probably beats babysitting as a way of eking out a little bit extra. Until such time as the property market decides to take another tumble…

6
GROUNDWORKS

GROUNDWORKS IS THE term used to describe all the things that builders do beneath ground level. It's actually a hotch potch of different activities – excavation, drainage, service connections, concreting, some brickwork.

The advent of JCBs, readymix concrete and plastic drainware has taken a lot of the graft out of this part of building, but it still remains an exacting and potentially hazardous task. It is also incredibly messy, especially when there's rain about. Whilst neighbours will look on in horror as you recreate the battlefield of the Somme, you must shrug your shoulders and utter asinine comments like 'You can't make an omelette without breaking eggs'.

Groundworks is really a question of getting from A to B as cheaply and easily as possible. There are many reasons for using something other than the standard solutions for your underground work, but all of them involve sorting out or avoiding problems, not increasing amenity value. This is not to say that the housebuilder does not face choices of how best to get the groundworks completed, but these choices are for the most part to do with ease, speed and cost of installation. This chapter concentrates on these issues as well as taking a closer look at how some of the problems, outlined in Chapter 3 'Pitfalls', are solved.

Given a straightforward site and a straightforward house design, the groundworks can progress with remarkable speed at a comparatively low cost. However, a problem site can easily double the base costs, so I cannot emphasise enough how important it is to thoroughly analyse the costs involved in just getting your house out of the ground.

Groundworks is also one of the areas of housebuilding most prone to mistakes being made. The setting out of foundations and levels and the correct siting of drain terminals is not a job to be undertaken lightly; add a slope into the equation and you have a job to tax the most skilled surveyor. Yet the supervision of groundworking is often left to harassed digger drivers who 'want to get on with it' and often barely refer to any plans that may have been drawn up. The horror stories that you occasionally hear of completed houses having to be taken down because they were put up in the wrong place are a testament to the consequences of rushed excavations.

Groundworks Costs Summary for Model House

	Quantity	Rate	Materials	Labour	Plant	Rounded Total
EXCAVATION						
Clearing Oversite/Site Strip	35 m³	£ 17 per m³	£ 600			
Setting Out	120 m²	£ 3 per m²	£ 360			
Excavating and Muck Away	40 m³	£ 17 per m³	£ 680			
Dumper Hire	5 days	£ 80 per day	£ 400			
Total excavation						**£ 2,000**
FOUNDATIONS						
Foundation labour	40 m³	£10 per m³	£ 400			
Readymix in Trenches	25 m³	£75 per m³	£ 1,880	£ 300		
Footings	40 m²	£46 per m²	£ 1,290	£ 560		
Total foundations						**£ 4,400**
GROUND FLOOR						
Beam and Block floor	80 m²	£ 31 per m²	£ 1,600	£ 840	£ 300	
150mm Celotex Insulation	80 m²	£ 17 per m²	£ 1,120	£ 240		
DPM	80 m²	£ 2 per m²	£ 30	£ 120		
50mm Leanmix concrete	80m²	£ 7 per m²	£ 320	£ 240		
TOTAL GROUND FLOOR						**£ 4,800**
TOTALS			£ 6,200	£ 2,800	£ 2,300	£ 11,300
Overall Footprint	95 m²					
Internal Floor Area	160m²					
Cost per m² Footprint	£ 119 m²					
Cost per m² Floor Area	£71 m²					

£2,000 is at the low end of excavation costs. If there is any slope on the site that needs excavating, or if deeper trenches are required, the costs will multiply. See section on Slopes, Bad Ground and Trees. Similarly, foundation costs can also escalate. On many sites now, engineered foundations are required, so that overall costs can stretch to as much as £30,000 in some situations.

NB Insulation Costs are combined into one category in the Model House Table so figures reflect this

THE NEED FOR ACCURACY

If you've never been involved in setting out foundations, you can sit back and laugh at the incompetence; not until it's just you and a stroppy JCB driver do you begin to realise just how difficult it iw easy it is to go badly wrong. Of all the areas of housebuilding, grouvndworks is the one that needs the most management and the best management. If you are a DIY project manager, this is the big one. Crack this and you will have no problems on down the line.

Most builders choose to subcontract all the groundworks but, whilst this makes it very much easier to navigate this stage, it is still vital to check that you are getting exactly what you asked for. You must check that the foundations are in the right place, are square, and are at the right height (this last can be difficult to measure). You must check that the access arrangements have been properly constructed, with falls going the right way and that the drains and the services have been installed correctly. Your building inspector will provide some guidance and should be able to pinpoint errors and bad practice but is not paid to be a surveyor and will have no idea if your trenches are off-square or in the wrong position. It is much harder to ferret out mistakes on groundworking than on later parts of the build and usually much more expensive to rectify at a later date.

On traditional masonry work, accuracy is not so important because the bricklayers can correct errors in setting out and levels − to a certain extent − as they go about their work. But most of the so-called modern methods of construction − timber or steel frame, SIPs, ICFs or thin-joint masonry − have little room for error and the tolerance

Excavation and Foundations Prices

KEY ELEMENT PRICES	
Groundworker	£ 18 per hr
JCB Hire with driver	£ 30 per hr
JCB digs in easy ground	5m³ per hr
JCB Digs in hard ground	2m³ per hr
20 tonne lorry	£ 80 per load
20 tonne lorry holds	12m³ spoil
Landfill tax (inert)	£ 2.50 tonne
Spoil bulk up rate	1.3m³ per m³ in the ground
Readymix Concrete	£ 75 per m³
Concrete Pump Hire	£ 300 per day
Dumper Hire	£ 80 day
Setting Out Foundations	5 min per m²
Foundation Preparation	5 min per m²
Foundation Pouring	30 min per m²

COMPOSITE RATES FOR EXCAVATION	
Easy Dig Excavation rates	
Excavation with JCB	£ 6m³
Muck away in lorry rate	£ 7m³
Plus Landfill tax	£ 4m³
Total	£ 17m³

HARD GROUND EXCAVATION RATES	
Excavation with JCB	£ 15m³
Muck away in lorry rate	£ 7m³
Plus Landfill tax	£ 4m³
Total	£ 26m³

Variations

I have made a distinction between easy and difficult excavation to reflect the fact that it's a job that can vary enormously in time and cost. This sort of thing can make it difficult to estimate groundworks – especially if you are digging out a basement, which may be as much as 200m³ for a detached house.

standards are much more exacting. TRADA, the timber people, suggest the following standards for foundations under a timber frame house:

■ Wall lengths should be within 10mm of plans
■ Diagonals: 5mm up to 10m, or 10mm over 10m
■ Floor slabs level to 5mm
Sounds easy. Good luck.

EXCAVATIONS

A flat site is a cheap site; clearing debris off the oversite will not take long and digging normal depth foundations for a four-bedroom house will take a JCB no more than a day. Note, however, that the crucial task of setting out the foundations on the ground has to be carried out after the undergrowth is stripped away. It's not a job to rush, especially if you are new to the game, and so you ideally want to leave a couple of days between site clearance and the start of excavation.

Unless you are working in a confined area where mechanical plant cannot reach, then you will want to get hold of a JCB or some similar digger. Some builders have diggers and digger drivers in their armoury, but most just have contacts with guys who are self-employed and own their own machine. They tend to charge for travelling time so it's worth getting someone local and – depending on how busy they are – they often charge for a minimum of half a day even when they're only around for a couple of hours. But at around £150-£200 per day for driver plus JCB, they can do the work of around ten to twenty men and therefore represent a bargain not to be sniffed at. They can also do a lot of damage. The one-man-band digger drivers tend to be the most helpful, but they do like to get on with it. If you're not 100 per cent on top of what's to be done then chances are that you'll get rushed into mistakes. Trench excavations happen remarkably quickly: expect around 50m per day, enough for a small house.

DEMOLITION MAN?

If you've an existing structure to demolish, then you'll have a choice of taking it down slowly and salvaging materials, or getting a machine to demolish it which is not very green but it's far more exciting. I'd suggest that it is almost entirely dependent on the value of the salvaged materials. There are also health considerations, whichever method you employ: watch out for asbestos, which was very common in much of the 20th century housing now being demolished.

MUCK AWAY

Charming expression for getting rid of the spoil. The topsoil is stripped off and stored on site for later use, but the subsoil is usually dumped somewhere else. Many digger drivers operate in tandem with a 15 or 20 tonne lorry and will have local dumping contacts. Alternatively, it is worth chasing up local landowners to see if they have any holes to fill. Subsoil taken out of

the ground 'bulks-up' at least 30 per cent when piled in a heap (or on a lorry). This means that just under 12 m³ dug out of the ground will fill the 15 m³ space on a 20-tonne lorry: those sorts of calculations are typical when doing muck away sums – a cubic metre in the ground tends to weigh between 1.5 and two tonnes. Some ground conditions, notably clay, bulk-up at much more than 30 per cent: a 50 per cent or even 60 per cent bulk-up rate can be expected. Make sure if you get a quote per cubic metre whether you are dealing with muck in the ground or bulked-up on the lorry.

The reality of foundations for many people. You dig 'em – they fill up with water before you can order the readymix

LANDFILL TAX

Landfill tax was introduced in 1996 and it's one of those taxes that gets subjected to an escalator. This means it keeps going up, rather like the taxes on petrol, cigarettes and alcohol. Unlike these, you don't really notice landfill tax, until you come to start to clear building sites.

There is an important distinction between inert waste and man-made stuff. Inert is a term used to cover ground you might dig out in the course of excavations. It still gets taxed but at a much lower rate, currently £2.50 per tonne. In contrast, the man-made waste gets really clobbered, and the current rate is £64 per tonne.. That makes it diabolically expensive and if you have man-made waste you would probably do rather better to find someplace else to put it, rather than a muck away lorry.

The tax is paid when spoil is tipped at a licensed pit and even the inert rate (i.e. £2.50 per tonne) has had the effect of increasing the cost of a 20-tonne muck-away lorry by £50, something like 40 per cent of the overall cost.

All the more reason to find a friendly farmer with a hole to fill. Many builders are choosing to put all excavated spoil in the back garden, then compacting it with heavy machinery and placing topsoil back on top. It's an option to consider but it's just not possible on all sites.

On many sites you will be unable to get heavy plant like JCBs to the back of the house once you have completed the trench excavations. If you have plans for landscaping or drainage or even plan to build a swimming pool or a summer house at a later date, this may be your only opportunity to get the groundwork done quickly and cheaply and a change of plan or an oversight can have costly ramifications later. Another area to sort out on day one is the site access; it pays to get your drive leveled and hardcored as early as possible.

SUMMARY

To work out your likely excavation and muck away costs,

Traditional Strip Footings

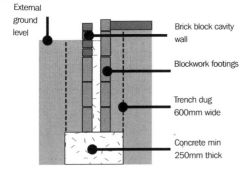

External ground level

Brick block cavity wall

Blockwork footings

Trench dug 600mm wide

Concrete min 250mm thick

Trenchfill

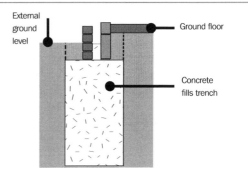

External ground level

Ground floor

Concrete fills trench

Footings Key Rates

7N Concrete Blocks	£ 6.25 / m²
Trenchblock 300 mm	£ 30 / m²
Celcon Blocks	£ 7 / m²
Regrade Bricks	£ 10 / m²
Common bricks	£ 16 / m²
Blockwork mortar	£ 0.90 / m²
Brickwork mortar	£ 2.40 / m²
DPC	£ 1.00 / m
Readymix Concrete	£ 75 / m³

Meter rates for Footings	Labour	Materials	Combined
Lay Footings (100mm blocks, vertical)	£ 11	£ 8	£ 19
Lay face bricks	£ 23	£ 18	£ 41
Lay 300 mm Trenchblocks	£ 14	£ 30	£ 44
Alternative to footings			
Readymix Trenchfill 600 mm wide	£ 5	£ 45	£ 50
Readymix Trenchfill 450mm wide	£ 6	£ 34	£40

first work out the volume you need to remove. If it's fairly easy digging, it's likely to cost around £6 per m³ to dig out of the ground and an additional £10 to £12 per m3 to remove it to a licensed tip (of which £3-£4 will be tax). If the digging is hard (rock, for instance) the excavations costs can double or even treble but the muck away costs should be unaffected.

FOUNDATIONS

If you ever get involved in working around the foundations of some pre-20th century buildings, as you might if you were building an extension on to a Victorian house, you will be amazed at how shallow and how basic the existing foundations appear to be compared with what we have to build off now.

'How come this house is still standing?' will be your first thought. Followed by 'If these foundations have supported this house for so long, what am I doing messing around a metre further down below ground?' Both good questions. Neither has a simple answer.

The history of foundations is vaguely interesting and a little instructive. The current idea of building up off slabs of concrete at depths of a metre or more below ground level is relatively new, very much a 20th century innovation. The Victorians used to step the walls out at the base, pyramid style, over a depth of just three or four brick courses, that way spreading the load of the house across a wider area. These below-ground courses were known as footings and the footings were effectively the foundations. Today we still refer to footings but we put concrete foundations under them. 21st century footings are simply the brick or blockwork sandwiched between the concrete foundations and the damp proof course that is usually installed at 150mm above ground level.

When concrete foundations were first adopted widely, in the Twenties, they were sold to builders as being a cheaper and quicker method of building-in adequate load bearing. In fact, the load imposed by a typical house (which maybe weighs around 100 tonnes in total) really isn't that great – it's similar (on a weight per area basis) to that imposed on the ground by your feet when you stand up. The problems arise from the fact that the ground has a nasty habit of shifting about which itself has a nasty habit of causing all manner of disruption on the very rigid structures placed on it. Building foundations out of concrete may sound very hard and solid but when the ground starts moving then they look as feeble and spindly as you could want. Consequently, foundations have been getting deeper and deeper over the years in an attempt to get down below the trouble zone.

The Building Research Establishment investigated the phenomenon of ground movement in the early Nineties and found a site that regularly heaved up and down by 50mm over the course of a year, not to mention a 60mm sideways movement as well. Mostly it's sites with large trees and clay soils but it's also rather unpredictable so consequently the momentum is towards deeper and deeper foundations, which means more and more concrete. This usually works but we still have a large number of new houses (approx 1,000 a year) that subsequently suffer from foundation failure.

The best advice is to follow the advice you are given as closely as you can – don't cut corners. Readymix concrete and excavations are moderately expensive but nothing like as expensive as having to fix later failures.

As foundation requirements have grown deeper over the years, two options have evolved about how to construct them – at least on largely problem-free sites. One is to pour the minimum amount of concrete possible into the foundation trenches and then build upwards in brick or blockwork – this is known as strip foundations. The other system reverses this logic altogether and pours as much concrete as possible into the trench before starting on the bricklaying – this is usually called trenchfill. Both methods have pros and cons.

The traditional method, laying footings below ground level, is cheap on materials but heavy on labour; it is also slower. In contrast, trenchfill is much quicker but, of course, uses more concrete. When pouring concrete into clay soils, you will probably have to use the trenchfill method.

An important consideration when designing foundations is to set the level of the concrete so that it 'works blocks'. Blocks are laid either flat in courses of 110mm or in the vertical in courses of 225mm (ish). If you have surveyed the site accurately, you will know exactly where the damp proof course will be so you can ensure that you stop the concrete at 225, 450 or 675mm below that point. That ensures that you keep the fiddling about and cutting to a minimum – provided, of course, that you pour your foundations level!

The depth and length of the trenches are not in your control, but the trench width is largely down to which bucket the JCB uses to dig with (the general choices being 450 and 600mm wide). Using a 450mm wide bucket is going to reduce the amount of readymix used by a quarter (as well as reducing

excavation costs) but it is not to be recommended to rookie builders. Cavity walls – generally now 350mm wide and set to get wider still as cavity widths get increased to cope with ever more insulation – sit uncomfortably on such a narrow trench; internal load bearing wall foundations are obviously less of a problem, but the key factor in all this is accurate setting out of trenches.

Unless you are an experienced surveyor, you really want to play safe and set trenches at 600mm wide.

GROUND FLOORS

The 'industry standard' is to build a concrete or masonry ground floor and a timber first floor. This is how 90 per cent of single homes are built in the UK. Only in Scotland does the practice change – there they still love timber ground floors. First floors, known as intermediate floors, are in a section all of their own in the next chapter. Here, I just look at ground floors.

Comparing floor costs is a bit of a nightmare. The problem is to know where to begin and end. I was struck by this looking around Buildstore's permanent exhibition space at their National Selfbuild and Renovation Centre in Swindon. There they have a small display showing the main floor types, being timber, solid slab and pre-cast concrete suspended floors.

On the solid slab exhibit I counted seven different layers in the sandwich: from the bottom, hardcore, sand, damp proof membrane (DPM), concrete, insulation, screed, floor cover. In total, nearly 500mm in depth. That's just phenomenal. If it were all, miraculously, to turn to jelly, you would be wading about up to your knees in floor.

Chapter 6

Groundfloor Key Rates

	MATERIALS UNIT COST	LABOUR M2 RATES	COMBINED M2 RATES	M2 RATES
Beam and Block Floor (inc blocks)		£ 20	£ 11	£ 31
Hanson Jet Floor (insulation but no concrete)		£ 19	£ 11	£ 30
Hollow core floor		£ 30	£ 11	£ 41
Crane Hire	£300 / day			
Telescopic Vents	£ 2.50 each	£ 0.60	£ 1.50	£ 2
Airbricks	£ 3.50 each	£ 1	na	£ 1
100 m² DPM	£ 30 roll	£ 0.40	£ 1.60	£ 2
125 mm Celotex Insulation		£ 11	£ 3	£ 14
150 mm Celotex Insulation		£ 14	£ 3	£ 17
175 mm Expanded Polystyrene		£ 8	£ 3	£11
65mm Readymixed Screed		£ 8	£ 7	£ 15
50mm Gypsum Screed		£ 20	S & F only	£ 20
100mm Concrete	£ 75 m³	£ 8	£ 8	£ 15
Reinforcing Mesh		£ 4	£ 3	£ 7
150mm Hardcore	£ 32 m³	£ 5	£ 7	£ 12
Sand Blinding over hardcore	£ 32 m³	£ 2	£ 2	£ 4
50 x 200mm Joists	£ 3 m	£ 10	£ 14	£ 24
50 x 200mm I beams	£ 7 m	£ 18	£ 9	£ 27
22mm Chipboard		£ 5	£ 5	£ 10

Ground Floor: All-in Rates per Square Metre		
Concrete Slab (Un-reinforced)	£ 62	inc 125mm Celotex and 65mm screed finish
Concrete Slab (Reinforced)	£ 68	inc 125mm Celotex and 65mm screed finish
Beam and block floor	£ 61	inc 125mm Celotex and 65mm screed finish
Hollow core floor	£ 70	inc 125mm Celotex and 65mm screed finish
Hanson Jet Floor	£ 50	inc 65mm Screed Finish (insulation built-in)
Insulated Timber joist ground floor	£ 65	inc base concrete and chipboard floor cover
Insulated I-beam ground floor	£ 68	inc base concrete and chipboard floor cover

AN IMPORTANT DISTINCTION

Groundworks are conventionally costed 'up to DPC level' which means that floor finishes are ignored. But because underfloor insulation is now mandatory, there are solutions around that provide insulation and consequently the All-in Rates per Square Metre include costs for a semi-finished floor — i.e. a screed or at least some chipboard on top of the structure. Underfloor heating is ignored but it tends to add about another £20/m² to the costs.

Add in a little re-inforcement in the concrete (not uncommon), maybe some underfloor heating pipes laid on some sort of backing board in the screed, and another plastic DPM layer above the concrete (sometimes specified) and you have a very complex as well as a very thick construction.

The problem from a costing point of view is that the floor finishes are usually considered separately. On top of that, it's also common practice to consider the intermediate layers such as the underfloor heating and the screed in yet another compartment. Yet they are also all related. Ideally, you need to start with your floor finish and work downwards to get your most cost effective floor.

SOLID SLABS

A solid concrete slab is usually laid 100mm thick over a layer of compacted hardcore. This is the most labour intensive system and, conversely, the cheapest on materials, which makes it suitable for DIY builders with access to cheap or free labour.

You have a choice of placing the insulation layer – you have to have an insulation layer – either above or below the concrete.

It's sort of conventional to finish a

concrete slab floor off with a cement screed on top, laid at a later stage of the build. But there is no requirement to do so and some builders dispense with the screed layer, choosing to get a smooth finish on the concrete using a power floater. There is no reason why you couldn't place your insulation beneath your slab, and sink your underfloor heating pipes (if you want them) into the concrete: it's just that not many people think this far ahead.

PRE-CAST FLOORING

Pre-cast concrete floors are a factory-produced alternative to ground-bearing slabs. Because of the added transport costs, they are rarely economic over small areas, say below 50 sq m, so you don't see them used for house extensions but they become an increasingly cost-effective solution as the floor area increases. The increasing popularity of pre-cast floors has been driven by a number of factors:

- floors can be laid in a day and worked on the next day
- no wet trades involved - no readymix lorries required
- have to be used on sites where there would otherwise be excessive backfill under the ground-bearing slab
- they can be used on intermediate floors as well as ground floors

Perhaps the main downside to using pre-cast floors is that each one needs to be manufactured

to order and you may well find that you have to wait six to eight weeks for them to be delivered. If you plan on using a pre-cast floor, then you must plan well ahead. The other issue that needs attention is the requirement for ventilation in the void under the floor: this is achieved with airbricks built into the external wall, usually with offset ducts placed within the cavity.

BEAM AND BLOCK

Beam and block is the cheapest and commonest form of precast floor: it consists of number of evenly spaced concrete beams, similar to timber joists, infilled with normal building blocks. It has been gaining in popularity with developers since it first appeared in the Seventies, largely

The concept behind the beam and block floor is dead simple. The concrete beams form an upturned 'T' section, enabling the blocks to sit loosely between the beams. This technique was introduced in the 1970s and has been widely taken up across the country. Builders like them because they are quick, dry and relatively easy to use, but they are expensive on smaller footprints, below 100m²

because it's fast and largely dry.

As with all pre-cast options, beam and block floors are provided by specialists who work from drawings supplied. A number of businesses cater for this market and many have links with builders merchants who act as middlemen. The floors are designed to work with standard concrete blocks (ie 100 x 225 x 440mm) as used in wall construction.

There is often more than one way to run the beams and you may be able to take advantage of a system like Rackham's 225 beams that can span up to 8m and can sometimes enable you to do away with sleeper walls within the main floor area.

Another thing to watch out for is the 1:300 camber on these

pre-stressed beams. It's surprisingly large: as much as 13mm on a 4m long beam. If you lay a screed over the floor you can of course get a level finish but if you want a dry finish or a floating floor, consider the fact that the floor won't be level.

INSULATED BEAM FLOORS

A variation on the standard beam and block floor uses polystyrene infill blocks to fill the voids between the beams. They have become increasingly popular as a ground floor option since changes to the building regs in 2002 brought in a requirement for floor insulation, previously a green option only. It's a little more expensive than a block infill floor but it does away with an added layer – you can, and indeed must, just place a structural screed on top of it before you have a working platform. This can make it difficult to work with underfloor heating unless you add another screed layer above. The best-known insulated floor beam system is

Hanson's Jet Floor.

Whilst these flooring systems undoubtedly work well and have been tried and tested over many years, they do suffer from cold bridging at the edges where the heat is able to divert away from the beams into the walls. If you want a cold-bridge free foundations, you need to look at using an insulated polystyrene raft, where the walls themselves are built up off the insulated base. Two systems which achieve this are Isoquick and Insulslab SFRC.

HOLLOW CORE

Hollow core planks are another form of craned-in precast floor though this time more commonly used as an intermediate floor. Instead of concrete beams being laid and infilled with blocks, the whole floor is laid in a series of wide concrete planks - hollowed out to reduce the weight, hence the name. Hollowcore is the most expensive of the pre-cast options but leaves you maximum flexibility: you don't have to align your internal walls above load-bearing walls or supporting beams – you can build anything anywhere. However, the internal walls where the planks meet end-to-end have to be double thickness in order to have adequate bearing. Hollowcore floors are prized for their soundproofing qualities and are thus commonly used in apartments.

HYBRIDS

Most pre-cast floors are topped off with a cement screed, if only to get a smooth surface on which to lay a floor cover. But there are a number of options that require a structural screed or concrete slab in order to gain sufficient strength. The insulated beam floor is one example but there are others, used widely in Continental Europe, sometimes known as lattice girder plate floors. The best-known example in the UK is Hanson's Omnia.

The advantage of using such a system is that you can get greater spans per floor depth. Indeed, you can get a span of over 9m on just a 250mm depth floor.

TIMBER

Suspended timber ground floors could potentially be very cheap and simple to build. They were commonly installed by the Victorians but have gone out of fashion for two reasons. Firstly, a requirement, which has come into the building regs, to cover the ground beneath a timber ground floor with a concrete capping capable of withstanding the passage of moisture, which adds at least £5 per sq m to costs; secondly by the added complexity of fixing underfloor insulation from above. Upstairs, of course, no such extra work applies and here timber joisting is easily the cheapest option.

On the ground floor, timber still makes a lot of sense if you want a timber floor cover because you can have an entirely dry construction. Around half the cost of a timber ground floor goes into the sheeting (usually chipboard or plywood) that is laid over the joists and where a plank floor finish is desired this sheeting can be dispensed with. The problem with doing this is that either the planking will be exposed for the duration of construction, which will almost certainly lead to damage, or some form of temporary sheeting will have to be installed which will cancel out most of the perceived cost advantages. However, the technique works well with reclaimed boards that need to be sanded and sealed and can serve as both temporary and finished floor covering.

INSULATION

Underfloor insulation on the ground floor is not quite mandatory but recent changes to the building regs make it expensive to avoid. There are several methods of insulation available. The cheapest and most readily understood is to lay flooring grade expanded polystyrene at 200mm thickness over the sub-floor and under the screed or chipboard. Or you can use a thinner layer (around 125mm) of one of the more efficient insulation boards such as Knauf's Polyfoam, Kingspan or Celotex.

These techniques of underfloor insulation are relatively new and there are possibly problems building up in the future should the insulation not prove to be as rigid as expected: ensure that the insulation you specify is flooring-grade. More cautious builders will continue to use some form of reinforcement in their screeds to counteract any such failures.

Aficionados of underfloor heating will wonder what all the fuss is about. Such systems only work well with very high levels of underfloor insulation – otherwise much of the heat would be lost – and, whatever problems there may have been with underfloor heating systems, laying insulation under heavy cement screeds does not appear to be one of them.

SLOPES, BAD GROUND & TREES

If you have worked through the book to this point from 'Pitfalls' you will have twigged that, although groundworks can work out to be relatively cheap, they can also turn into a budget-crippling nightmare. Whether you have or haven't, the crucial groundworky bits went as follows:

There are three basic causes of alarming cost expansion:
- slopes
- bad ground
- trees.

SLOPES

Obviously, it all depends on how much it slopes, but even quite gentle slopes can create havoc with a tight budget. Brinkley's Slope Law states that, no matter how you deal with it, each one degree of slope will add £1,500 to your development costs. Obviously this represents an enormous over-simplification of different situations but you will be disappointed to discover that it rarely works out less than this and sometimes it can be a whole lot more, especially if you are constructing a mansion larger than 200 sq m. The fact is, you just can't get away with building a sloping house and so adjustments have to be made between the lie of the land and the lie of your house and these adjustments are expensive. It's not just excavating out the ground so you can build on the level; if the slope is greater than five degrees, there are complications with access roads and pavings, drains, and landscaping. Steeper still and you are likely to require retaining walls and possibly even safety railing. Aficionados of Grand Designs may remember a couple in Bath, filmed in 2007, who managed to spend £300,000 taking out a slope before they even got to dig their foundations. According to my law, they must have had a 200 deg slope, which is going it some, so be warned it's not really a law at all. I expect you already realised that.

Brinkley's Slope Law

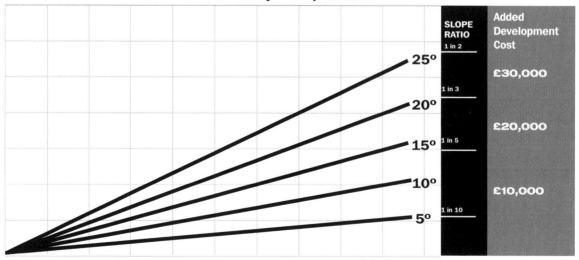

Chapter 6

Faced with a sloping site, there are basically three options for the new housebuilder.

Building on a slope is expensive however you approach it

EXCAVATE AND CART AWAY
Here you dig a large, house-sized hole out of your slope, dispose of all the excavations and fit the house into the hole. This is perhaps the simplest and the one that the planners are likely to prefer, as it will keep your roofline low. There will be the cost of excavation and carting away which, depending on the lie of the ground, could easily cost £2,000-£10,000. Add to this the cost of any retaining walls that might have to be built: budget £100 per lin m for a one metre high retaining wall, and bear in mind that retaining walls get wider as they get higher, so tall ones are exponentially more expensive

BUILD OUT FROM HIGH POINT
Here you substitute the cost

of excavating with the cost of building supporting walls. There may not be much to choose between the two in cost terms, but this method is likely to leave you with expensive steps to build up to the back/front of the house. The overall structure is also likely to be far more imposing and, consequently, much less likely to pass muster with the planners.

FIT HOUSE TO SLOPE
Arrange the house as a series of steps, running up the slope. Building basements and/or mezzanine split-levels may well be architecturally the most pleasing but it is also the most expensive. Split-levels have cost implications at almost every stage of the building works: stepped foundations, shuttering for floor slabs, special stair joinery, complex service routes, and complex roof details. Split-level building adds between 10

and 20 per cent to your overall building costs.

Whichever method you choose to overcome the problems set by a sloping site, you will be faced with extra landscaping expenses – steps, turfed banks, rockeries. Although these costs can generally be deferred over a number of years, they will add significantly to the overall development. The extra thousands might be better spent on building a semi-submerged basement.

BAD GROUND
A variety of problems are dealt with under the category of bad ground. The commonest are clay soils and the presence of tree roots, but also you must be prepared for bog conditions, mining subsidence, wells, water courses, old factory workings, disued refuse tips, even problems when ancient remains are discovered. It's worth carrying out any amount of detective work to ascertain exactly what has happened on your site because the ramifications can be expensive.

A site appraisal is likely (but not definitely) going to uncover the problems you will meet below ground and your foundation design is almost definitely going to be in the hands of an engineer.

The key to understanding the cost implications of these alternative foundation solutions is to hang on to the ballpark figure that applies to normal

Raft and Piles

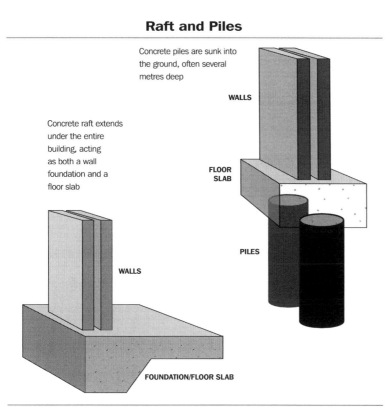

Concrete piles are sunk into the ground, often several metres deep

WALLS

Concrete raft extends under the entire building, acting as both a wall foundation and a floor slab

FLOOR SLAB

PILES

WALLS

FOUNDATION/FLOOR SLAB

groundworks. This is currently around £100 per sq m of footprint covered. This includes the cost of providing foundations, below ground walling and a ground floor to the externally measured areas of house and any outbuildings such as garages.

There are three likely solutions to bad ground:
- deeper foundations (sometimes reinforced with steel)
- raft foundations
- piling.

DEEPER FOUNDATIONS

You will have to excavate to good bearing ground (if it's there). If it's just a question of going down to 2.5m, you may get away with the regular trenchfill foundation. But this will be expensive; it will add around £3 to the ballpark footprint figure (remember base equals £100 per sq m) for every 100mm deeper you have to dig.

So if, for instance, you were asked to dig foundations 2m deep all round instead of the standard 1m depth, it would ratchet your overall footprint costs up from around £100 per sq m footprint to £130 per sq m footprint. Deeper than 2m, it starts to look like other, engineered systems will save

you money – see next items. Trouble is, if you are discovering how bad it all is as you dig, then it's realistically too late to switch to one of the alternative foundations systems.

CLAYBOARDS

One technique commonly used in clay areas is to fit a collapsible board against the side of the trench, rather like lining paper on the side of a cake tin. The idea is that clayboard is flexible enough to allow the clay to heave without moving the enclosed concrete foundations. There are a number of dedicated products available for this application; the two best known are Claymaster which is made of polystyrene and Clayboard which uses a honeycomb filler very similar to that used in moulded doors.

RAFTS

On a problem-free site, the floor slab is laid a couple of stages further on than the foundations. However, with rafts, you pour the foundation concrete together with the floor slab concrete in one operation. With various cambered design profiles and a whole mass of steel reinforcement, you create a concrete raft, which will move as one. If subsidence occurs, the raft will absorb the changes without imposing extra strains on the superstructure above.

A raft foundation uses vast amounts of concrete and steel and is unlikely to cost less than £135 per sq m footprint. There have also been a few high profile problems with raft foundations where the raft as a whole starts shifting; leaving the house above perched at a precarious angle. They are not a solution for every site.

Chapter 6

PILING

Increasingly specified as the engineering solution of choice for difficult sites, piling is also reckoned to be cost effective in situations where foundations would otherwise have to be deeper than 2m. The number of piles and the depth of each pile can only be determined by a test pile being dug (budget £300), but a typical installation would place piles 2.5m apart under every load-bearing wall (including detached garages) and each pile would go down till solid ground was reached. All the piles are then filled with concrete (either poured wet or precast) and tied together with a concrete ground beam, which would be all that you would eventually see of the operation, and would look much like a regular trenchfill concrete foundation. Budget prices are £30 per m depth for individual piles (depth anywhere from 3-10m) and £60 per lin m for ground beams. There are various other techniques that can be used as an alternative to concrete piling or reinforced rafts but these are really the province of the specialist engineer. One interesting option is Abbey Pynford's Housedeck, which is designed to be cost effective for single house developments; it's actually a floating or suspended raft, which gives you a well-insulated slab. Housedeck will typically cost between £15,000 and £25,000 for a 150 sq m footprint. Abbey Pynford's Phil Jones commented to me: 'Our unit area rate gets lower as the footprint increases, up to about 250 sq m. We are never going to be competitive with simple strip foundations but we find that Housedeck starts to make sense if you have to dig down more than 1.5 metres'.

Tree Table

Common species of tree VERY THIRSTY	MATURE HEIGHT	Distance at which tree roots cease to have any effect on foundations SAFE DISTANCE	Distance within which specialist foundations will be required DIG DOWN 2.5M
Elm	24m	30m	within 12m
Oak	20m	25m	within 10m
Poplar	25m	30m	within 12m
Willow	16-24m	20-25m	within 2m
Hawthorn	10m	12m	within 4m
Cypress	20m	15m	within 5m
MODERATELY THIRSTY			
Chestnut	20m	15m	not required
Lime	22m	16m	not required
Beech	20m	15m	not required
Ash	23m	18m	not required
Plane	26m	20m	not required
Sycamore	22m	16m	not required
Apple	10m	8m	not required
Most conifers	20m	8m	not required
NOT VERY THIRSTY			
Birch	14m	7m	not required
Elder	10m	5m	not required
Hornbeam	17m	8m	not required
Hazel	8m	4m	not required

TREES

There are two different ways in which trees may affect your development costs. One is visual; planners and neighbours may view the importance of your trees quite differently from you. The other is to do with the effect of tree roots on your foundations. A site with mature trees will tend to look immediately attractive but you should pay close attention to just where these trees are located in relation to your proposed foundations.

TREE ROOTS

Tree root systems can spread a very long way from the trunks and they can suck water from even greater distances causing movement and shrinkage in soils, which is bad news for house foundations. The solution to this problem is not to cut down the offending trees – this can actually make the situation worse for up to ten years afterwards – but to have deeper foundations, or specialist ones. The NHBC publishes tables showing the foundation depth needed for different tree species at varying distances but this is too technical in scope for this humble work: the summary table is designed to let you roughly gauge the effect on construction costs. There are four variables that determine the foundation depth when tree roots are present; these are:

■ shrinkability of the soil – clay soils are bad news

■ water demand from tree species: some species such as poplar, willow and elm, are very thirsty whereas others, such as beech and birch, have much less impact on your foundations

■ mature height of tree species

■ distance of tree from foundations

The worst-case scenario would be to have a tall and thirsty tree, located 7m (or less) from your foundations, which are in clay. God help you! The NHBC would want you to dig foundations over 3m deep or use piles or rafts. And, of course, it would cost.

ACTION

If your plot has any of these problems it will pay dividends to seek advice at survey stage. The person who would normally deal with such matters is a structural engineer, but if you are employing a designer to solve your problems, it would be as well not to engage another professional off your own bat; let the designer choose how (and who) best to overcome the difficulties. A possible source of free and impartial advice is your local building inspector.

If there is good news in here it is that there is now effectively some sort of cap on the amount your foundation costs may grow. The new techniques coming

on stream – especially piling and ground beams – are slowly but surely getting cheaper. If you have bad ground, your total groundworks costs (including laying of the ground floor) may well double from a base of around £100 per sq m footprint, but they are unlikely to treble. If you are excavating blind – ie without a clue what lies beneath – then a contingency fund of around £80 per sq m of footprint would be a good idea.

SERVICES

The service connections are an administrative heavyweight. The actual amount of work is often relatively small but it will usually take many hours sorting out just what goes where. Most of the utility companies have something like a New Homes Division, which is what you need to get hold of. This will arrange site surveys and quotations for installation and also offer advice about the do's and don'ts. It is quite possible to lay drains and services in the same trench and this is usually the cheapest option – providing of course that your connections are all in the same direction.

WATER

New homes (and conversions of existing buildings) in England and Wales are almost always fitted with water meters, which are themselves almost always fitted as near to the highway as possible – though there is a move afoot to start fitting internal water meters. The water company will usually put a temporary standpipe next to the meter, which will enable you to have a water supply on site immediately, and it is worth considering just where the meter is best located so as to avoid traffic.

You need to lay your water pipe at least 750mm below ground so as to avoid frost – and your water company will want to inspect this before you close the trench. If your main drain run goes more or less in the direction you want to go, you can often lay it in the same trench. You don't have to duct it except where it comes through the foundations of the house; if you bring it up into the house against an outside wall or through a suspended floor, you need to lag the pipe with insulation as it comes up out of the ground (again to avoid frost damage). These days people tend to use alkathene (aka MDPE) for water mains and it will pay you to use a wide bore 25mm pipe (which costs around £20 per 25m roll) if you are considering a mains pressure hot water system. Avoid underground joints at all cost – you are responsible for leaks on your side of the meter.

ELECTRICITY

Included in your quotation for electricity supply will be (hopefully) enough plastic ducting for you to get from the local supply to your meter. The route you take between these two points is up to you but the ducting should be buried 450mm below ground level. These days the local electricity companies prefer you to locate your meter in a white plastic box, recessed into your wall; whilst convenient (allowing for meter reading when you are not at home), they are pretty ugly and if you haven't got anywhere you can hide them you can insist on an indoor meter.

It is very useful to have a temporary supply to site whilst construction is underway but you have to do a bit of construction work first to create a

Chapter 6

Ballpark Costs For Drains

	PIPE	EXCAVATION	ACCESSORIES	MATERIALS	TIME IN MINS	LAB @ £18/HR	COMBINED
Foul Drain Runs	£ 24	£ 4	£ 4	£ 32	80	£ 25	£ 55
Rainwater Drain Runs	£ 24	£ 4	£ 4	£ 32	60	£ 18	£ 50
Service Trenching		£ 4		£ 4	40	£ 12	£ 16

suitable housing for it.

GAS

If you have a mains gas supply to lay, then you are usually best advised to install ducting, available free from Transco (now part of National Grid) at the groundworks stage. You are conventionally aiming to get from the gas main to an external meter box, which you can place pretty much where you please. Transco should supply a semi-concealed meter box that is mostly buried in the ground and is much less obtrusive than the wall boxes. The incoming gas service pipe which connects the gas main with your meter should be buried at least 375mm below ground level.

TELECOMS, CABLE

Both BT and the cable companies will supply plastic ducting for free. The BT supply may be overhead, in which case, you needn't trouble yourself with underground routes. If you have to go underground, the routes and the depths of these runs are up to you, although note that the preference is for the line to come out of the ground on the outside wall of the house, rather than inside.

Mains water, electricity, gas and telecoms are often laid in ducting, which is laid across the site during the drain-laying excavations. The water company will want to inspect the ducting but the other services will let you fend for yourself, so you need to

know exactly where you want them to run. Industry standards are to set electricity and gas mains at least 450mm below ground level.

INFRASTRUCTURE CHARGE

First introduced in England and Wales in 1990 to help pay for environmental improvements, these charges are raised by the local water companies and are additional to their already high connection fees. The infrastructure charge is nothing more or less than a tax on new building. It's applied to every new dwelling created – including flats converted from existing houses – and it is applied at exactly the same level regardless of the size of the dwelling.

Until 1994, water companies were free to set their own charges and – surprise, surprise – they tended to charge the earth (often over £1,500) but then OFWAT, the water regulator, stepped in and set a ceiling for the infrastructure charges which was much lower but has recently begun to creep relentlessly upwards again (£328 for water and an additional £328 for mains drainage connections in 2012). In Scotland and N Ireland the situation is very different; there the water industry is still publicly owned and infrastructure charges are unheard of.

DRAINAGE

First things first: it is important to understand the difference between foulwater and rainwater.

Key Costs

KEY ELEMENT COSTS DRAINAGE	
Road Openings	£400-£8,000
Septic Tanks and drainage	£ 4000 plus
Mini Treatment Works	£ 7,000 plus
Cesspool	£ 5,000
Soakaway	£ 80-£200
Storm Drain Connection	£ 500
Main Drain Interceptor	£ 250

■ Foulwater is the waste generated by normal household usage - flushing loos, emptying baths and sinks, washing machines, dishwashers etc. Foulwater is sometimes subdivided as black water (toilets) and grey water (most other outlets).

■ Rainwater, as its name suggests, is what falls out of the sky and flows down the gutters and downpipes from off the roof.

Generally our sewage systems are working at near capacity levels and therefore it is a standard requirement that rainwater is not added to the load. Hence it is normal to lay two separate drain systems to dispose of their respective wastes in different ways. In certain locations it may be possible to run rainwater into the main sewerage system (refer to your water company) but it would be unwise to assume that this is the case. You will need to prove that there is no alternative.

Rainwater drains typically cost more to install than foulwater drains. Bear in mind that there are often downpipes at every corner of the house and this contributes to some very long drain runs.

When planning rainwater drains it is sometimes possible to replace a relatively expensive underground drain run with a relatively cheap gutter run overhead. Alternatively, you can sometimes use a larger size of guttering, which will enable you to cut down on the number of downpipes and therefore the length of rainwater drains. But I digress; this stuff really belongs in the section on rainwater – see Chapter 7 'Superstructure.'

WHERE TO?

In assessing the likely costs of any individual scheme there is one overriding question that must be answered at the outset. That is, 'Where the hell am I going to dump all this crap?' There are other questions as well, notably: 'How do I get it there?' but 'Where to?' is the 'big one'. So, although it may seem illogical to start at the end, we'll look at the drainage options this way around.

RUNNING INTO THE MAIN DRAINS

Even a relatively simple mains drainage connection can be an expensive business. In England and Wales, you'll have to pay a sewage infrastructure charge from which off-mains disposal is exempt. Locating main drains can be a problem; the water companies hold what records exist and, whilst access is open to all, accuracy is not guaranteed.

The amount of work in excavating and connecting to the main drain (usually referred to as 'doing a road opening') can vary enormously depending on the depth of the drain, whether there are vacant junctions (known as laterals) already present to connect on to, the presence/absence of other utilities and the attitudes and charges of local authorities and water companies.

To open a public highway you must contact the council highways department in order to purchase a road-opening permit, now generally known as a Street Works Licence (prices very variable but probably going to set you back as much as £300 in total). Inspections of the opening and connection need to be carried out by a) your water company, b) your own building inspector and c) the council highways department who inspect no less than five times to ensure the surface reinstatement is in order. A busy road may require traffic lights and if your main drain runs under the other side of the road, the whole process becomes very much more complicated.

The water company is going to insist that you employ a competent groundworker to make the connection and therefore it is a sensible idea to get some quotes for this work before proceeding.

BACKDROP MANHOLES

It is much cheaper, easier and safer to lay house drains at depths of between 600 and 1200mm below ground level. Normally, drains are best laid at gentle falls (around 1:80) and sharp inclines are discouraged. If your main drain level is way beneath your optimum house drain level, you will probably find it easiest to construct a backdrop manhole near your boundary line. A backdrop manhole works a bit like a waterfall: it's a sudden drop from one level to another and it requires special construction methods and access arrangements.

PUMPS

If your main road drain is higher than your house drains you have the option of pumping the waste up hill. This is often done by building in a tank of some description, similar to a small septic tank (say, 2m deep and 1m in diameter) into which the house drains run, and fitting either a solid handling pump or a macerator or grinder pump. The macerator pump is the more expensive but allows the waste to be expelled in a 32 or 50mm pipe, which makes it a better bet for long distances. A control panel is placed somewhere indoors or in a weatherproof casing.

Expensive though a pump is, it can be cost effective to install one when the main drain connection is further than 300m away, even if it is downhill. This is because it can pump out into a small bore pipe that can be laid in a flat trench, much reducing excavation costs. On the other hand, any system that works by gravity alone is ultimately preferable because it isn't going to break down.

Budget between £2,000 and £4,000 for making a road opening and maybe a further £3,000 if you need a pumping station. Occasionally road openings can be done for less but don't count on it. Recently the tendency is upwards, not down, and some self builders are being quoted ridiculous amounts, like £8,000, for a simple T-off a main drain just 3m away. And another instance of £10,000 for a double sewer and storm drain connection across a very quiet road. When cost start getting silly like this, it might be time to look at the alternative, an off-mains solution.

Chapter 6

OFF-MAINS DRAINAGE

The simplest and the cheapest off-mains solution is usually to install a septic tank. It's a tried and tested method and there are millions of them in operation, dotted around the countryside – it's a very rural thing. A septic tank is one of the simpler concepts to understand in the field of sewage treatment: it is an underground chamber (traditionally constructed of brick, more recently from concrete or GRP), into which your foul waste system empties. There is no power needed, there are no moving parts and, as long as the solids at the bottom of the tank are regularly pumped out (or desludged), then the septic tank should give decades of trouble-free service.

The cost of the tanks varies depending on the volumes they are designed to deal with but single household units are often priced between £400 and £600. Added to this is the cost of the groundworkers installing the tanks (often around £1,500) and the cost of excavating and installing a herringbone soakaway system - again depending on the volumes to be dealt with and also ground porosity. It would be wise to budget £4,000 to £5,000 for a new septic tank system.

Hoowever, simple septic tanks won't work in every location. The Environment Agency will be taking a look at your site and may well come to the conclusion that your ground

conditions require something else, typically a sewage treatment plant, which is like a septic tank on steroids. Well, it has a power source to speed up the digestion process.

The simpler plants use a little power to drive an air pump whilst the unique Klargester Biodisc is designed around a series of rotating metal discs. And there is one, the Bio Bubble, which acts like a super-super-charged septic tank and eats the solids as well

The advent of plastic pipes has made laying drains easier. Pre-formed inspection pits have a number of outlets. Laying in pea gravel helps protect the pipes. Building inspectors will usually want to have sight at this stage

as the liquor and therefore doesn't need any desludging.

CONSENT TO DISCHARGE

In England and Wales, sewage disposal comes under the aegis of the Environment Agency and they have a say in what you can and can't do. They used to operate a permit system called A Consent to Discharge but this has been replaced (in 2010) by a Water Discharge Consent, known as EPP2, which makes the process much easier if you are using conventional solutions, but much more expensive if you plan anything unusual. If you use a EPP2 registered supplier, such as Klargester, then provided you follow the instructions and take out a service contract, your site is deemed to qualify. If you choose something or someone who hasn't registered, then you have to convince the Agency that what you are doing is adequate and you also have to buy a permit (no less than £885 in 2012).

The situtaion in Scotland and N.Ireland is different but they too seem to be in the business of inroducing something like EPP2 in the near future.

ALTERNATIVE OPTIONS

There is a growing interest in alternative forms of sewage disposal. Some of these are seen as being greener than the conventional methods but it's a tag that many of the alternative practitioners themselves are

Model House Drainage and Services

	LENGTH OF RUN	RATE PER m RUN	MATERIALS	LABOUR	COST
Foul Drains	40m	£ 55	£ 1,240	£ 960	£ 2,200
Rainwater Drains	60m	£ 50	£ 1,250	£ 1080	£ 2,940
Service Trenching	15m	£ 16	£ 60	£ 180	£ 240
TOTAL			£ 3,200	£ 2,220	£ 5,400

Model House - Service Connection Costs

Electrics	£ 2,500
Mains Gas	£ 250
Water (inc infrastructure charge of £450)	£ 1,800
Road Connection for Drains	£ 750
TOTAL	£ 5,300

reluctant to emphasise: most readily admit that there is a time and place for almost all the sewage systems on the market and it is often stretching things a bit far to make out a case that any one system is greener than another.

The best known of the alternative disposal systems is the use of reed beds (aka Constructed Wetland Sewage Systems). A reed bed system can be used to upgrade the effluent coming out of a tank so that it meets the same discharge standards as a package treatment plant and can, therefore, be discharged into a watercourse. Although it sounds very organic and natural, successful reed bed drainage involves a surprising amount of construction and no way is this a cheap option – installation costs are similar to a package treatment plant and you require an area the size of half a tennis court. And like a septic tank or package treatment plant, you still have to pump out the solids, which are collected in a primary settlement tank. Reed beds also require some weekly maintenance so they tend to attract enthusiasts

rather than the fit-and-forget brigade.

Reed bed treatment is well accepted as a sewage treatment method and is now being specified on a large scale by some of our water companies. There are however other options, including the use of dry composting toilets. Increasingly, self builders are turning their attention to the whole picture of water and waste management and seeking to combine aspects such as rainwater harvesting and grey water recycling with efficient treatment of sewage waste.

Normally it is a principle of all foulwater drainage systems that rainwater should be disposed of separately: the problem being that whereas most sewage digestion systems need a steady supply of blackwater to keep working smoothly, rainfall has a habit of arriving in large quantities which can disrupt the workings of the sewage systems. However, if rainwater is being collected separately, it is usually used to flush toilets and this way the two systems can be effectively combined at one stage removed.

SITING OF TANKS

Any off-mains drainage system that uses a tank which needs desludging (and that includes most of the options) has to consider tanker access – 30m is reckoned to be the limit that a tanker's hose can extend to. In Scotland, tanks must be a minimum of 15m from the house. No minimum exists in England and Wales but if you have a sensitive nose you would do well to stick to the Scottish standards.

RAINWATER DISPOSAL
SOAKAWAYS

The normal destination of rainwater is a simple soakaway that is nothing more than a 1m deep hole in the ground, usually filled with free draining hardcore or brick rubble. Soakaways are conventionally sited 5m away from buildings, but the building inspector must be convinced that the water will percolate away. In heavy clay soils, for instance, a soakaway may not be appropriate and you may have to look at other ways of disposing of rainwater.

STORM DRAINS

Common in urban areas, rare in the country, they are actually designed to stop the roads flooding, but can sometimes be used for house rainwater. Budget £500 to make a connection to a storm drain. Storm drains are often over 100 years old and in a poor state of repair, and locating them can be a hit and miss affair. Typically, these are managed by the highways department of the local council (rather than the local water company) and they often flatly refuse to accept any additional rainwater discharge, even when it is obviously the best option. If you have well-honed negotiating skills, here's a

Chapter 6

Eight Drain Tips

1 THE PLANS NEED...

Drawings and specifications should include drain layout, invert levels (depths), junctions, inspection chambers and access (rodding) points.

2 PLASTIC OR CLAY?

Although the trade is still split between using clay and plastic (uPVC) drainage, someone new to the game would do well to use plastic. There is little to choose between the systems on price but the plastic systems are more user-friendly. There are six major players in this field and, underground at least, there is little to choose between them on quality or price. Osma are the market leaders and their installation guide tells you much of what you need to know about laying drains. They do a free (but slow) design service but you must know your main drain invert (drain depth) levels for it to be worthwhile.

3 BUYING PLASTIC PIPE

Plastic pipe is sold with heavy discounts off list price. A new house project should be able to get discounts of 30-40 per cent. All the manufacturers produce guttering and internal waste fittings as well and, if you combine your order, you will have more muscle to negotiate better discounts.

4 EXCAVATION OF TRENCHES

Drain trenches are normally 450mm wide (the width of a digger's narrow bucket). If drains are to run parallel and close to wall foundation trenches, then you will be doing yourself a favour if you can set the drains higher than the concrete in the adjacent trench – NB this won't work with trenchfilled foundations. Where this is not possible, drains will have to be concreted-in, whereas they are normally just bedded in pea shingle.

---

good place to use them.

RAINWATER INTO MAIN DRAINS

Attitudes to this vary from area to area, but nowhere is it encouraged. But when soakaways and storm drains are impracticable, this course will often be accepted as a last resort. There must be an interceptor between the two drain systems to prevent unpleasant pongs coming back up the rainwater gullies.

SUDS

SUDS stands for Sustainable Urban Drainage Schemes and they have been quite the buzziest thing in rainwater management for several years now. The idea of SUDS is that they will stop flash flooding caused by rainwater cascading off hard surfaces like roofs and roadways, and that instead rainwater will collect in oversized soakaways or sometimes above ground

in ponds, known as swales (not to be confused with S Wales which is a place where it rains an awful lot). Now really SUDS are applicable to housing estates and businesses like Tesco which are about to cover a square mile of open countryside in metal, concrete and tarmac, but the system being what it is, we now find selfbuilders on single plots asking to have a SUDS plan in place in order to win planning permission. To my way of thinking, there isn't really much difference between SUDS and a good old-fashioned soakaway, but there are dozens of companies out there that will sell you dedicated SUDS kit which you may have to specify to meet the regs.

One interesting SUDS development I have seen is to use the water stored in a SUDS system as a heat source for ground-source heat pumps or, to be more accurate in this instance, water-

source heat pumps. Whether this would work better than burying the pipes underground is something that is open to debate, but it's always nice to see people trying something new and here you get two sustainable developments (ie SUDS and heat pumps) rolled into one!

RAINWATER HARVESTING

There are now a handful of businesses in the UK selling (mostly German) gear with which you can filter, collect and pump rainwater around the house for flushing loos. More information can be found on this in Chapter 10 'Green issues'.

ROUTES

This is the other major decision to be made when looking at drain runs. The idea is to get from the house to the final dumping point with as few bends as possible. Drains have a tendency to get blocked so access is important at

5 DRAIN SIZES AND DEPTHS

100mm drain (the standard) is going to be adequate for all situations where there are less than five loos. There is no set depth, but less than 600mm and you may have to cover the pipe with paving slabs, deeper than 1200mm and you will have problems working. The optimum fall is 1:80 which is equivalent to 250mm on a 20m run. If you have to cope with gradients much steeper than this then take specialist advice - don't assume that drains will work just because they are going downhill.

6 PEA SHINGLE

Plastic pipe should be bedded on pea shingle, which is a particularly fine grade of gravel. Allow one ton of pea shingle for every 8 lin m of drain. When calculating excavation quantities, allow for 80 per cent of excavated material to go back into the trenches once the pipes are laid.

7 RODDING ACCESS

It is good practice not to have to rod from inside the house, so try to give every waste point a direct run to a manhole rather than joining drain runs together under the house in the assumption that they can be rodded from above.

8 DRAINS UNDER DRIVEWAYS

Plastic drains are prone to deformation if loads are placed upon them. They therefore require more protection than clay drains. This becomes an issue if you are laying drains under roads or drives: anything less than 900 mm deep will require some form of concrete capping over the drain.

all but the gentlest bends, and access is expensive.

BALLPARK DRAIN RUN COSTS

Straight 110mm plastic drain runs can be machine excavated (to average depths), laid and buried for around £30 per lin m. The building inspector may allow you to have a few gentle radius bends on your drain runs, provided they don't prevent rodding – that is clearing future blockages with drain rods – but generally the accepted practice is to have access to the drains every time there is a bend. The addition of inspection chambers, gullies, rodding access, etc ('fittings') more or less doubles the basic metre rate for drain laying to between £50 and £60 per lin m – the cost of one manhole is equivalent to 10 lin m of straight drains. So the general idea is to plan your drain runs with as few bends as possible.

7
SUPERSTRUCTURE

INTRODUCTION

SUPERSTRUCTURE IS A long and pretentious word and I would like to use some funky Anglo-Saxon alternative, altogether more down-to-earth. Trouble is, I don't know one. Some use the term shell – as in 'Putting up the Shell' – and perhaps this isn't bad, especially if you think of it in terms of sea shells, not egg shells. But, to confuse matters, the outer walls that make up the shell get referred to as skins or, sometimes, leaves; one suggests bodies, the other trees, neither eggs nor sea creatures. It all seems a bit of a mess; hence I'll stick with the term Superstructure.

Definition? Well you have hopefully figured it out by now – it's all the above ground bits of a house up to but excluding the finishes and the wiring and piping. Literally, the super (i.e. above) structure as opposed to the sub (i.e. below or under)

structure. So in Superstructure we'll look at walls (as in inner and outer skins), external doors and windows, roofs and all the fiddly bits that hold them together. Floors? The ground floor details are in the previous chapter, the first floor and above – known as intermediate floors – are buried in this chapter. If you buy a factory-built house, it's the superstructure that you are getting. Or at least part of the superstructure. The roof covers and the external wall finishes are conventionally left to you to sort out, along with the substructural works and the finishes.

INNER SKIN

The load bearing walls are sometimes referred to as the inner skin: they almost always are if the house is being built in blockwork, but many aren't these days so it's hard sometimes to tell just where

the skin is inner, outer or something in between. Anyway, how you build these ranks as one of the most crucial decisions you have to make when commissioning a new home. In fact, it rather defines the build method. Will it be done on-site with brick and blocklayers or built off-site in a factory? Or by some other method entirely?

I'll start with a look at how blockwork homes work. This remains the No 1 housebuilding method in the UK as a whole. Its only serious rival, at least in terms of numbers built, is timber frame, and I'll therefore make this section a bit of a compare and contrast between the two methods. The other build systems are looked at in the next section, Alternative Skins.

CAVITIES

You can't really get a handle on blockwork houses without looking at the whole issue of wall cavities because without cavities

Inner Skin Key Cost per Meter

	BASIC MATERIALS	ACCESSORIES (INCLUDING MORTAR)	TIME TAKEN IN MINUTES	LABOUR AT AT £18/HR	COMBINED
MASONRY MATERIALS					
Celcon 100mm blocks	£ 7	£ 1	35	£ 11	£ 19
Hemelite blocks	£ 7	£ 1	35	£ 11	£ 19
Thin Joint Blocks	£ 7	£ 2	25	£ 8	£ 17
TIMBER FRAME					
47x90mm Frame	£ 3	£ 6	50	£ 15	£ 24
47x140mm Frame	£ 5	£ 6	50	£ 15	£ 26

Timber frame is costed as if it was being built on site, which it rarely is in the UK. Normally it's created in a factory and erected on site, a much quicker process. Also note that though timber frame external walls are more expensive than masonry ones, the reverse is true on internal walls. Overall, there is very little difference in cost between the two main walling systems.

Model House Inner Skin Costs

Inner Skin Area - minus joinery openings	185m²	
Celcon-type blocks laid in mortar	£ 8m²	£ 1,500
Inner Skin Area - measured straight through openings	220m²	
Blocklaying price based on above	£ 11.00m²	£ 2,500
Total Inner Skin Blocklaying cost (exc lintels, see next section)		**£ 4,000**
Switch to 140mm Timber Frame		£ 5,000
Switch to 185mm Timber Frame		£ 6,500

The brickies have a cute habit of measuring their work straight through joinery openings. Hence, the different areas for the Inner Skin. The logic is that they spend time fixing joinery, not charged elsewhere. But the overall effect is to make blockwork more expensive than its headline rate suggests.

there could be no blockwork. Cavities enabled builders to incorporate large format concrete blocks – which became widely available in the 1930s – into house walls whilst retaining a brick skin on the outside. Prior to this, brick walls had been built nine inches thick (i.e. a double skin of bricks), which was both slower and more expensive.

The cavity was advertised as being an 'improvement' in house construction because it introduced a barrier across which rain supposedly couldn't jump. But rain often does find a route across cavities: they are very difficult to build well, easy to get wrong. For along with cavity walls came brick ties (to knit the inner and outer walls together), returns (for joinery to sit in) and cavity trays (to divert water trickling down the inner skin across to the outer skin). Cavities had a nasty habit of filling up with bits of crud, or snots as they are lovingly

referred to, which would cling to the ties and form tracks for the water to cross the cavity. As regards protecting the house from water damage, cavity walls are only marginally better than solid walls.

In the Eighties, we started to become concerned about heat loss through walls and builders began to put insulation into the cavities. Now you might think that these two alternative uses for a cavity – i.e. to stop water going one way and heat the other – are completely at odds with one another and, essentially, you'd be dead right. Yet, bit by bit, builders are learning that insulation and cavities are not an impossible marriage and many builders are now enthusiastically stuffing their cavities with all manner of insulants without suffering horrendous damp penetration problems. But an even greater number of housebuilders continued to build homes with empty cavities; up till 2002, over half

of all new homes in Britain were built this way – i.e. with no insulation in the cavity.

LINTELS AND WALL TIES
Cavity walls need to be knitted together. And the openings in them need to be bridged. And the bases of them need protection against rising damp. All told there are a number of things you have to think about when you build a cavity wall. The knitting together is done with wall ties, once galvanised steel, now stainless steel, placed in regular patterns, dictated by the building regs. Lintels are needed over window and door openings. These are now usually steel and they need to bear at least 150 mm at either end of the openings they bridge.

You also have to consider how water will behave inside a cavity: it has a tendency to funnel across to the inner skin so you have to take great care to ensure that any

Steel Lintel Key Rates

Convention is that steel lintels need 150mm bearing at each end

Thus a 1200 mm wide window requires 1500 mm lintel, or 1.5 m

These costs are averages per metre run:

Regular Type	£ 28
Heavy Duty	£ 50
Box Type (internal)	£ 17
Timber Frame Type	£ 13
Single Skin for Garage	£ 80
Masonry Cast Cills	£30

Steel Beams and Lintel Costs

Heavy duty RSJ (ie UB 203x133x30kg)	£ 35 per metre run
Lighter RSJ for short spans <4m	£ 25 per metre run
Labour to set	£ 75 each

Model House Steel Beam and Lintel Costs

	Materials	Labour	Total
2 Universal Beams (RSJs)	£200	£200	£400
15 No Steel Lintels (Windows, Door Openings)	£700	inc blockwork	£700
Total	£900	£200	£1,100

water trickling down the inner face of the cavity has to be directed outwards above openings. There are a number of companies producing cavity tray products designed to keep cavities dry, a very specialised niche within the building trade.

BLOCKS

Typically, building blocks are made of cement and various aggregates like sand and stone. In many countries blocks are manufactured with feature finishes and are used extensively, instead of bricks or stone, as external wall finishes in their own right. But in Britain this hasn't proved to be a popular technique, except where cheaper substitutes for stone are sought. So when we look at building blocks we are analysing how well they perform structurally, not how good they look.

BLOCK STRENGTH

Block strength is calculated in Newton / sq mm, known in the trade as 'Newtons' or just plain 'N'. Roughly speaking the more cement in the block, the higher the strength (or the more Newtons it is said to have). Most blocks qualify for the basic 3.5N strength, though some applications require 7N blocks (i.e. below ground and,

some say, floor blocks). You will find a number of 'utility blocks' on the market but their strength is not guaranteed. Having said that, there aren't many applications in housebuilding that call for extra-strength blocks.

BLOCK TYPES

There is an industry standard size of block, which is 440 mm by 215mm. This is the equivalent of six standard bricks and you need 10 of these blocks to build a square metre of wall: they are conventionally bought by the square metre – a ten-pack. They are usually 100 mm thick, though some of the super-lightweight varieties are thicker in order to get their insulation values up to par.

THE DENSE BLOCK

Uncomfortably heavy to lift, they are usually used below ground, often at 7N strength. Cheap – full loads cost just around £6.00 /sq m.

LIGHTWEIGHT CLINKER BLOCKS

Almost half the weight of a dense block, these are often used on the inner leaf of insulated cavities and in partition walls. They provide an excellent keying surface

for plasters. They are also widely used in beam-and-block flooring; they are very similarly priced to dense blocks.

AERATED BLOCKS

Introduced from Scandinavia in the Sixties, these blocks have become a huge hit in the UK market and more than 70 per cent of new homes use them somewhere. There are three manufacturers, Celcon, Thermalite and Tarmac, who bought the fourth, Durox, which is still obtainable as a separate brand. Their big plus is (or was) that they packed enough insulating properties into them to allow builders to carry on with empty cavities. Current U values are now too demanding for this solution to be acceptable.

Brickies love aircrete blocks because they are light and easy to cut. Plasterers are not quite so fond of them: they have a reputation for movement which causes plaster to crack. This is one of the reasons for the rapid uptake of plasterboard stuck onto walls (dot and dab), taking over from the old wet plastering routines.

TRADE RATES

An all-in rate of between £10 and £12 /sq m for laying blocks is OK, depending on area.

All-in rate means that your brickies would fix wall ties, cavity wall insulation, joinery, lintels, airbricks, DPCs, etc. as they go, but excludes the cost of laying an outer skin, which likely as not will be in a different material.

Using an all-in rate saves the hassle of measuring non-standard runs like chimneys. A two-and-one gang should be able to lay between 30 and 40 sq m of blocks in a day. Combined with the cost of blocks and mortar, it creates an inner skin walling cost of around £20 /sq m, against which all other options have to be compared. Note that when working on measured rates, brickies conventionally treat joinery openings as if they were part of their work (which arguably they are, as they fit the joinery as they go). This makes a considerable difference to overall costs, as highlighted in the Inner Skin table.

INSULATION

The preferred way for the majority of English builders to knock-out the inner skin/cavity detail up till 2002 was to use an aircrete block and an empty cavity. That all changed with the introduction of the new thermal standards in 2002. Builders are faced with four basic options: fill the cavity with insulation, put insulation in the cavity but leave a gap (known as partial fill), insulate on the inside of the wall or on the outside of the outer wall.

CAVITY FILL INSULATION

This is both cheap and easy to do – but you do lose your empty cavity. Cavity batts designed to completely fill the void between the walls – known as Full Fill – are usually made out of one of the woolly insulators such as glass fibre or mineral wool; these are 'wicked' (rhymes with licked) to stay rigid and are cut to fit in around cavity ties. An alternative would be

to blow the insulation (either polystyrene beads or glass fibre) into the cavity after construction. Cavity fill is only acceptable in the more sheltered parts of the country: in the rainswept west, you have to maintain a 50 mm air gap in the cavity. In other words, you look for a partially filled cavity solution.

The Cavity Wall

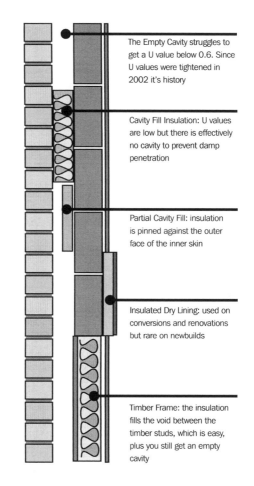

The Empty Cavity struggles to get a U value below 0.6. Since U values were tightened in 2002 it's history

Cavity Fill Insulation: U values are low but there is effectively no cavity to prevent damp penetration

Partial Cavity Fill: insulation is pinned against the outer face of the inner skin

Insulated Dry Lining: used on conversions and renovations but rare on newbuilds

Timber Frame: the insulation fills the void between the timber studs, which is easy, plus you still get an empty cavity

PARTIAL FILL

Most of the regular insulation materials are available in formats designed to partially fill the cavity. Despite making special 'retaining' wall ties available (which, at 25p each, actually cost more than the insulation), the wet Tuesday in February syndrome means that it is often extremely difficult for brickies to maintain a partially clear cavity. If you want a decent amount of insulation plus a 50 mm cavity, your overall wall thickness is starting to blow up to 300 mm plus, and this starts to eat a significant chunk out of your internal floor area.

INSULATED DRY LINING

This method involves using either plasterboard laminated to insulation and sticking the whole thing on the room side (i.e. inside) of the inner skin wall. Or, more frequently, insulation fixed to the wall with battens onto which the plasterboard is fixed. The insulation value depends on the choice and depth of insulation. Although it gets around the problem of having to partially fill the cavity wall, it leaves a number of cold bridges between floors and where internal walls meet external walls and this makes it hard to meet the U-value ratings now required for walls. It's often used in renovations where you don't want to disturb the outer wall but it's not common in newbuild.

EXTERNAL INSULATION

Also rarely used in new build, but there is nothing to stop you placing insulation on the outside of your walls and finishing off with a waterproof render. It's really only a common practice when renovating or upgrading existing structures, which either don't have a cavity or have reason not to insulate the inside. It actually works pretty well in that you make the whole structure inherently warm.

THIN-JOINT BLOCKWORK

Thin-joint or glue mortars are widely used in Germany and were introduced into Britain by Durox in 1991 but their uptake hasn't been as fast as the manufacturers would like and their use has been limited in the housebuilding arena.

There are two key elements that make it different to conventional blockwork. Firstly, it uses a very sticky mortar, more akin to tile adhesive than a traditional sand and cement mix. This thin-layer mortar starts to set within ten minutes and this makes it possible to work with much bigger block sizes - this is the second key element and the one from which the speed advantages derive. The limit on block size is set by what a man can easily handle: in fact, in response to feedback from site, Celcon's currently preferred size – 610 x 270 mm – is slightly smaller than the format they launched with. Blocklayers who have moved over to thin-layer reckon that it's around 30 per cent quicker. Any increase in material costs is more than offset by a decrease in labour rates.

The techniques used are quite different to mortared blockwork. In many ways, it's closer to carpentry than masonry: tooling up for thin-joint blockwork also requires a bandsaw, a mortar spreader, a block rasp, a mortar whisk and a wall tie puncher – you can't use traditional wall ties. Thin-layer work also requires a very level base to work off; with just a 2 mm bed between the blocks you can't make good any initial errors as you go. As with many of these new techniques, the problem for would-be adopters is that there simply aren't any (or at least many) blocklayers around who know anything about thin-joint. When faced with the thin-joint option, the knee-jerk reaction is to hoick the labour rates up through the roof when, going on the evidence, they ought to be actually lowering them.

TIMBER FRAME

Tinkering around with where you put the insulation in relation to the blockwork is all very well but there is a mainstream alternative that enables you to place the insulation inside the wall, which is, in many ways, the most elegant solution. We are, of course, talking timber frame here. The past few years have not been easy for timber frame. In the years leading up to the banking crisis, there had been a boom, as new markets opened up for timber frame in social and mainstream housing, but since 2007 volume housebuilding has tailed off and there simply hasn't been enough business to sustain everyone. Furthermore, changes to the building regulations have forced the industry to re-assess the way it builds, demanding further investment. Many have chosen, or have been forced, to pack up shop and look for gainful employ elsewhere, but this means that the businesses which carry on are leaner and fitter and better prepared for the future.

What is interesting is that, despite the economic downturn, innovation continues to flourish and there now appears to be more choice available for customers than there was back in the boom times. What we once routinely referred to as timber frame is now a collection of varied offsite construction systems, and it can be difficult for selfbuilders to navigate through the options. The strand that unites them all is that they offer factory-built superstructures and this, in turn, offers rapid and precise build times.

BACKGROUND

In North America, timber framed housing is almost always constructed on site by teams of carpenters armed with chainsaws in a process known as stickbuild. But the Europeans — starting with the Swedes in the 1920s — have always preferred the idea of pre-fabricating their timber homes and shipping them to site on the backs of lorries. Timber frame in the UK could have gone down either route but, with little native timber suitable for housebuilding

Timber Frame Walls

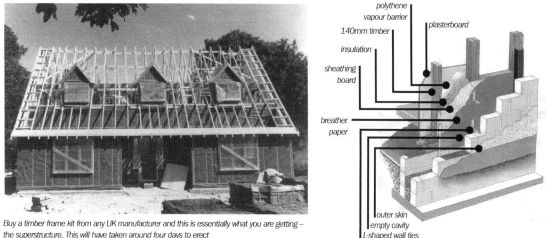

Buy a timber frame kit from any UK manufacturer and this is essentially what you are getting – the superstructure. This will have taken around four days to erect

Labels on diagram: polythene vapour barrier; 140mm timber; insulation; sheathing board; breather paper; plasterboard; outer skin; empty cavity; L-shaped wall ties

and without a pool of stickbuilding carpenters, factory pre-fabrication was always favorite to win out, despite the fact that the initial boom in timber frame was largely financed by American oil money looking to house workers in the Aberdeen area in the 1960s.

But whereas the Continentals veered towards building pre-finished, or closed-panel, homes, the Brits stuck with a more rustic, open-panel approach which simply concerned itself with getting the basic timber structure up and then fitting out all the insulation, services and plasterboard on site. The structure itself was usually built from studwork covered with OSB (Oriented Strand Board) for bracing, and one of the main advantages it held over masonry construction was that it allowed ample space for mineral wool insulation and yet still retained an empty cavity.

An alternative version of timber frame used a mixture of solid timber posts and beams and infilled with studwork, apeing the methods used by the Tudors. This style continues to thrive, having morphed into green oak building, a style almost unique to Britain – elsewhere they use softwoods to achieve the same effect. It's never going to compete with the standard form of timber building on cost grounds – green oak superstructures are usually around 30 per cent more than conventional framing – but it comes with an inbuilt sense of style and substance which people seem more than happy to pay a premium for.

The original open-panel style of timber frame is now under threat as tighter building regulations have forced a re-think. Open-panel timber frame was based on using the 38x89 CLS stud which, once braced with OSB, forms a strong box-like structure. However, an 89 mm depth is no longer an adequate width for the insulation required to meet building regulations and in the past five years alternative approaches

have come to the fore. Some stuck with the narrow studs and started adding extra layers of insulation, others began using 140 mm wide studwork which allowed ample space for insulation, but added significantly to costs. But Part L, the energy efficiency section of the regs, continues to tighten, and combined with many planners now insisting on compliance with the Code for Sustainable Homes, it looks like the days of using open-panel building systems are numbered.

SIPS

Structural Insulated Panels (or SIPS) have been a beneficiary of these changes. SIPS have been used for decades in North America (though never more than a niche product) and first appeared in the UK around the turn of the millennium. They offer better insulation levels for a given wall thickness because they use far less timber, their strength coming instead from bonding the insulation with the wall panels. SIPS were, however, rather more expensive than conventional timber frame; but with each change to Part L, the price gap decreases and coupled with the convenience of having the insulation already in place, SIPS have been taking market share from timber frame.

HYBRIDS

For many years, framed construction seemed to be turning into a battle between SIPS and conventional timber frame, but what now seems to be happening is that new hybrid forms are appearing that seem to have a foot in both camps. The hybrids seem to have bought into the idea that frames should be pre-injected with insulation, but have stuck with a framework of timber, or sometimes steel.

There are several businesses working this furrough. Some are still in the development process such as Eco Mech, based on Merseyside, who are developing a steel framed made to measure system. Others, such as Mantle Building Systems, have a hybrid solution, somewhere between Stressed Skin Panels and regular SIPS systems. They use very little timber in the frames and the casing is a cementatious board, rather than a timber-based OSB.

Val-U-Therm is another interesting development which has already has considerable success, having been used to build over 500 houses. It's a system developed by Bryan Woodley and it is currently licenced to two UK manufacturers who target the self build market, Scotframe and Flight Timber. It's a timber frame building system which used a largely plant-based insulation foam which is factory-injected into the panels. The technology behind the injection is German, but the plant matter used in the insulation is locally sourced.

CLOSE PANEL TIMBER FRAME

A sort of halfway house between regular timber frame, as practised in the UK, and prefabs is the closed panel systems, as used by the Germans and the Swedes. Here the wall, floor and roof sections are finished in the factory, right down to the services and decorations, and then craned into place on site. It's quicker than regular or open panel methods, which require internal finishing on site, but it only suits builders who are very organised and know exactly what they want. It has been tried once or twice in the UK but has never really caught on because the average British client wants the flexibility to change their mind every two days or so. However, whenever a German factory house builder appears on Grand Designs, the world and their aunt goes weak at the knees about how amazing it all is and just why can't we in Britain build that way as well. So much so that there are now about a dozen of these companies setting up in the UK. Amazing the methods maybe, but they are not cheap. Even when sourced from Poland, the resulting houses are costing over £1,500 /sq m and thus they are aiming mostly at the top end of the market.

GREEN OAK/POST AND BEAM

The traditional way, that is to say Tudor way, of building large timber houses was to erect a large post and beam skeleton (usually using oak) and then to hang the house off it. Whereas modern, industrial timber frame is a fast, lightweight, cheap way of erecting walls, here we are working in an altogether different idiom. Post and beam housing has undergone a revival in recent years and it's used for both retro designs (Border Oak, Potton Heritage) and modern (Carpenter Oak). It's also essentially the form you get when you take on a timber barn conversion. It's very good

for creating large open-plan spaces as you don't require structural walls. However, you do require an external weatherproof cladding. Here you have basically two options, infill between the posts or build an external cladding around the structure. The infill technique used to be carried out with wattle and daub but today's insulation requirements rely on rather more hi-tech solutions. Attention has to be paid to the fact that the oak posts shrink so that what starts out as a nice tightly fitting infill panel can work itself loose by Year Three. This is addressed by using flexible foam gaskets, which expand to take up the slack.

Post and beam frames are of course load-bearing but often houses can be designed around them so that the loads bear on external walls instead. Consequently, the cost of the posts and beams is almost always an extra, from the pure construction cost point of view, to the cost of building the house in a simplified, modern format.

A typical large detached house (they are rarely small) will use between 20 and 30 cu m of green oak to make up the frame. The cost of the oak alone will be at least £15,000 (it's around £700 per cu m for French oak, even more for English) and the cost of making up and erecting the frame will be around three times as much as this on top – it's a slow, painstaking business.

The point I am labouring to get to is that green oak frames are expensive and completely unnecessary – a complete luxury, in other words. You won't build a green oak home for under £1,300 /sq m and a more realistic budget is up near the £1,800 /sq m. You may save a bit by switching to a softwood – Douglas Fir gets used on occasion – but saving money isn't what this is all about, is it? But what's just as interesting, to my mind, is that there are a number of small developers out there who willingly pay all that extra money to get an oak framed house because they can make it back and more on the asking price. It's the added wow factor.

PODS AND PREFABS

The past few years have seen renewed interest in prefabrication as a solution to our housing needs. Bathroom pods in particular are migrating from commercial office space into housing. They are assembled and finished in a factory and then craned into place on site, bolted into place and the plumbing is connected from the outside. Completely prefabricated dwellings are also back – steel-framed containers have been used to build hotels and MacDonalds for years and now innovative housing groups such as the Peabody Trust have started using them as well. However, neither pods nor prefabs are likely to be of the remotest interest to self builders or small developers because, to make economic sense, you have to replicate the work many times – opinions vary as to how much many consists of but it's not less than 30 and it may be as much as 100.

Timber and steel frame homes are normally supplied in what kitchen suppliers would call a flat pack state, wall and floor units ready to be assembled on site. In contrast, pods and prefab units are supplied as ready assembled units – indeed they tend to have as much work done in the factory as possible. Transportation thus becomes the limiting factor – you can't realistically transport

anything that won't fit onto the back of a lorry.

ICFS

Another technique. Another three letter acronym. Just to prove not all innovation is happening in the lightweight framing, this one uses polystyrene moulds and lots of concrete. ICF stands for Insulated Concrete Forms.

There is an umbrella group, known as the ICFA (Insulating Concrete Formwork Association), which acts as a point of reference. In 2012, it had eight members active in the UK market.

The idea behind ICFs is that you start with a delivery of hollow polystyrene blocks (or sometimes panels) which you then stack up into a house shape. You stop at each floor and get lorry loads of

Closed-panel construction sees al floor and roof sections finished in the factory, right down to the services and decorations. This Baufritz home was built entirely in Germany for final assembly in the UK

readymix, which you pour into the hollows in the polystyrene walls. It's a clever variation on how concrete building work is usually carried out, where you take down the formwork after the concrete has set. With ICFs, the polystyrene acts initially as formwork (or mould) for the concrete and stays in place to become the insulation for the finished house.

The polystyrene can be covered on the outside with polymer (flexible) renders; inside, however, there are many unusual techniques for fixing internal walls, frames and floor joists, which would probably completely flummox the average British builder. And whilst the idea is engagingly simple, it's not without its problems as I've seen on site when the wet concrete sometimes bursts through the side of the polystyrene blocks.

ICFs have an undoubted appeal to people wanting to take a hands-on approach to building their own walls. They don't require bricklayers and blocklayers, anybody can do it. However, there are some cost implications that have to be addressed. Even using your own sweat labour, ICFs are more expensive than blockwork or timber frame.

In their defence, the ICF suppliers point out that overall wall costs are often pretty much the same as blockwork or timber frame, at around £80 /sq m, but that's really only true where you want to use a rendered exterior finish which can sit directly on the polystyrene wall formers.

A Beco Wallform pour taking place on a selfbuild in Banbury, Oxfordshire. For a long time, Beco were the only ICF show in town, but several alternative suppliers have appeared. Together they have formed an ICF Association to help raise the profile

STEEL

In some parts of the world – notably Australia – steel-framed housing is big bananas. In Britain, its heyday came and went in the Forties in the post-war prefab boomlet. Since then, it's remained something of a curio. There are two approaches, mirroring timber frame. You can have a post and beam structure (which is what most office buildings are) or you can build lightweight wall panels (which is where most of the housebuilders' interest is). Advocates reckon it's superior to timber frame in many ways – it's lightweight, it's fast, it's accurate – but it's mostly been aimed at the mass-housing end of the spectrum.

For several years, British Steel's Surebuild was the only game in town and they regularly produced about 1,000 homes a year from an antiquated plant in South Wales. Now if you Google Surebuild, you'll only find historical references to it. British Steel got taken over by Corus, who in turn got taken over by India's Tata Steel and the housebuilding bit got put out to grass. There are often new businesses which start out to "introduce" steel frame to the UK market, but they never seem to get any traction and so this sector really remain a housing by-water, though of course it is very much No 1 in the commercial world.

OTHERS

Having been very traditional in our approach to homebuilding for decades, suddenly there has been an explosion of interest in how differently we might do it in future. All I've tried to do here is summarise some of the methods which are putting themselves across as mainstream alternatives. There are several more ethnic methods about which I know very little and can't really do much more than point you in the right direction.

Here are some useful contacts:
■ Earth-sheltered or underground homes: these take the concept of a basement to its logical conclusion and build the entire house underground. Actually, more typically, earth is banked up on three sides so that you still end up with one wall of

glass. However don't assume this is a natty way of avoiding the planners. Current contact via website www.besa-uk.org

■ Centre for Earthen Architecture, University of Plymouth, Nottle Street, Plymouth (01752 233630). All things to do with building in cob and earth, increasingly of interest in restorations. Linda Watson runs courses and acts as an informal contact for other regional groups.

■ Straw bale homes: a small phenomenon in North America, they have started to sprout in Britain and Ireland as well. Our best known straw bale builder is Barbara Jones who runs Straw Bales Futures (aka Amazon Nails).

■ Hemp: architect Ralph Carpenter of Modece Architects is

The advantages of thin-bed masonry are many. But, as with all new techniques, there are disadvantages as well. Here builder Steve Hicks returns to a thin-joint site after a 200 mile round trip to collect the steel bed reinforcement mesh. If you want to try something different, don't expect the local building suppliers to have everything you need on tap

the man - 01284 761141.

■ Centre for Alternative Technology, Machynlleth, Powys (01654 702400). Mine of information, especially on timber and also straw bales. Wide number of residential courses on offer and good bookshop with details of all these and more.

PERFORMANCE STANDARDS

Actually, it gets even more complex still. The past few years have witnessed an explosion of interest in novel forms of construction using unusual materials. In truth, I've only really scratched the surface here and there is lots of things happening here which are difficult to write about in a compendium such as this partly because I don't know much about them but also because they have a habit of not hanging around too long so that any lengthy investigation in one edition would be redundant in the next. Every other episode of 'Grand Designs' seems to feature a new take on building homes which promises to turn the construction world upside down: only I've been around long enough to know that, by and large, they don't.

But there is one aspect which is worth mentioning and that's Performance Standards. What? Well, in particular I want to draw your attention to the Passivhaus Standard because it is making waves and because it's the gold standard of low-energy homebuilding. There are other standards you might aspire to,

notably the higher levels of the Code for Sustainable Homes, but I reckon the Passivhaus standard is the best. There is much more on this elsewhere in the book. But the point I am labouring to make here is that you can use any kind of construction type to make a high performance home — the standards are rarely prescriptive. Leading on from this, what really matters more than the materials or system you choose is the quality of the building work. All these construction systems are capable of delivering fine homes, in the right hands: equally, they can all turn out to be nightmares. It's not a question of deciding which is best: just seek out people who know what they are doing and you'll probably be fine.

OUTER SKINS

If you're reading the book conventionally (i.e. from front to back), you will have noticed that a previous section, 'Inner skins', started with a short (very short) history lesson about the introduction of cavity walls into British housebuilding in about 1930. If you weren't paying attention, the cavity splits the external walls into an inner and outer skin. Whilst there have been numerous developments and changes in the techniques used to build the structural inner skin, the outer skin has remained largely unchanged over the years. Other than some very modern houses, which tend to swap glass or terracotta rainscreens for cavity walls, most of the materials used to clad homes

External Claddings

	Basic materials	Accessories	Materials	Tme in mins	Labour at £18/hr	materials + labour
Heavy Claddings						
Brickwork @ £265/k	£ 16	£ 2	£ 18	75	£ 23	£ 41
Brickwork @ £700/k	£ 42	£ 2	£ 44	75	£ 23	£ 67
Natural Stone	£ 50	£ 2	£ 52	180	£ 54	£ 106
Artificial Stone	£ 20	£ 2	£ 22	120	£ 36	£ 58
Stone Cladding	£ 40	£ 2	£ 42	120	£ 36	£ 78
Painted Render on Blockwork	£ 15	£ 1	£ 16	110	£ 33	£ 49
Lightweight Claddings						
Painted Render on Mesh	£ 16	£ 2	£ 18	90	£ 27	£ 45
Monocouche Render on board	£ 24	£ 3	£ 27	70	£ 21	£ 48
Tile Hanging	£ 27	£ 7	£ 34	70	£ 21	£ 55
Sawn & Stained Weatherboard	£ 13	£ 5	£ 18	60	£ 18	£ 36
Unpainted Cedar	£ 28	£ 5	£ 33	50	£ 15	£ 48

Model House Brickwork

	Area in m²	Rate	Materials	Labour	Total
Brickwork @ £265/k	200	£41	£3,600	£4.600	£8,200

haven't changed that much.

The basic choices are fairly limited. Brick – still easily No 1 in England; stone – expensive, tending to be used where local styles dictate; renders – top choice in the wetter parts; or lightweight claddings such as timber boarding or tiles – commonly used for odd decorative panels but rarely for whole houses.

There is surprisingly little difference between the prices you pay for external claddings. It's hard to build an outer skin for less than £40 /sq m and it's not difficult to vastly increase this figure if you specify expensive materials and finishes. Before embarking on a look at what the regular options are, a word about mixing up walling materials, something that's become very popular with developers. Mixing materials invariably creates an extra layer of complexity and therefore adds to costs. Not only are different materials and

trades being brought in for relatively small amounts of work, but junction details need to be built in as well. It's difficult to be too precise about this because every situation is different but bear in mind that simplicity helps if your primary aim is to hold down costs.

BRICK

Bricks remain the preferred material for external walls throughout England and Wales. They are reasonably cheap, they are well understood by the building trade, they can look attractive and, above all, they are durable. Not only should a brick wall not need any further care after construction, it should actually improve with age.

There are dozens of brick manufacturers and thousands of bricks to choose from. There is also a substantial business in reclaiming bricks from old buildings – though it only amounts to one per cent of

total brick sales, that's still 40 million bricks reclaimed each year. If you are limited by budget you will probably find your choice is rather narrow, but if you are prepared to pay more than £300 per 1,000 (that's 30p per brick) then a whole world of choice opens up.

Choosing a brick is quite an involved process and it is notoriously difficult to visualise what a brick wall will look like from a manufacturer's display board. Most British bricks are baked clay and these are the ones to go for if you are seeking out a character brick. There are other materials, notably concrete and sandlime, that get used to make bricks but the overall effect tends to be industrial looking and, crucially, there are no great price savings to be had – unlike in the world of roof tiles and block paving where concrete is invariably cheaper than clay.

There are two technical ratings for clay

Five Vernacular Claddings

Brick Noggins

Flint Panels

Pargetting

Half Timbering

Painted Shiplap

bricks that you should know about, to do with frost resistance and salt content. The frost rating is broken down into three categories being F (high), M (medium) and O (appalling), and the salt rating is split into just two categories, L (low) and N (normal). What does it matter? With frost, the problem is spalling, where the face of the brick starts crumbling away. Very soft bricks, rated O, would not be acceptable in any situation in the UK where they would be exposed to the elements – i.e. outside – but only severe frost areas (Scotland, the Welsh mountains and the English Lakes and Pennines) would require an F-rated brick. M-rated bricks are fine for almost all applications outside these areas, but note that in certain exposed spots (notably chimneys) you will be asked to add copings and overhanging courses if not using an F-rated brick.

The matter of low or normal salt content is not as important to housebuilders. In very wet areas (usually within sight of the Irish Sea) it is advisable to avoid bricks with an N rating as you may be asked to use sulphate-resisting cement. A merchant will be able to advise as to a brick's rating – but what if you're using second-hand bricks? You'll have to check your source and convince the building inspector that they are suitable for outdoor use. The building inspector will very probably have seen the brick before and will be able to assess its suitability. But do check before forking out. Take samples into the building control office if necessary.

ENGINEERING BRICKS

These are particularly hard-wearing and strong. Not only do they offer much greater structural support (and so they are a natural choice for supporting steel beams) but they are also extremely moisture-resistant. This second quality, combined with some very low prices, has seen engineering bricks being widely used as a damp-proof course (DPC). The semi-gloss finish on the bricks (which are either blood red or slate blue) can be used to good effect in creating two-tone effect brickwork both at DPC level and elsewhere on brick elevations.

SPECIALS

This is the term given to bricks that aren't a standard rectangular box shape. These get used, typically, on details like cills and brick wall cappings where you want to stop rainwater pooling. Some of the more common specials are readily available but many have to be made to order, which is a) expensive and b) time-consuming. If your chosen design incorporates specials then don't assume that they will just turn up with the rest of the bricks; you may have to wait another two months.

In response to these problems with procuring specials, there are now brick-bonding services which will cut and glue ordinary bricks into out-of-the-ordinary shapes. At between £3 and £4 per brick they are a little cheaper than unusual specials and with a turnaround of one week, rather than six, they are a whole lot quicker. It's a particularly useful service if you are using a second-hand brick from which you could never otherwise hope to obtain specials. Try Brickability.

BRICKIES' RATES

As of 2013, our local rate is sticking around £360 per 1,000 face bricks laid, over double what it was in 1995 and surprisingly little changed on what it was back in the pre-credit crunch days. In some cheaper areas it's still down around the £300 per 1,000 mark whilst in London it's above £500 per 1,000. On typical British residential sites, a two-and-one gang (that's two brickies serviced by one labourer) will lay 1,000 bricks a day – though normally they alternate between brick and blockwork. There are 60 bricks per square metre on single skin work. A rate such as this would normally include extra work like corners and reveals and fixing joinery and insulation, but not overly-fiddly details like dogs-toothing gables, which would be negotiated separately. If paying brickies by the square metre, be clear whether or not your square metres are 'solid' (i.e. include openings). The conventional arrangement is to measure straight through openings: there is however no additional charge for building frames into the openings.

BRICK FACTORS

Suppliers have developed specialised antennae for detecting new housebuilding activity: note that if you phone up a merchant inquiring after bricks, the first thing you get asked is: 'Where is the site?' Why do they all want to know? Well, brick merchants get money for simply identifying (or 'covering') a new site, even if they don't get the subsequent order. So the moment they inform the manufacturer that there is a new house going to be built in Pig Lane, they clock a commission, rising to near 20 per cent if it turns into a sale. They also shut out competitors from this particular deal – only the initial contact gets offered the commission.

It would probably be better if you didn't know that. It's a cosy little relationship between manufacturers and merchants that reeks of rip-off Britain. But would you get your bricks cheaper if it didn't happen? Maybe. The businesses which survive in this niche are called brick factors and the good factors have ever such long antennae.

A brick factor will wave brick panels in front of you with gusto and the bricks will not be identifiable as Ibstocks or Hansons but have names like Mellow Red or Autumn Gold – renaming the bricks makes it harder for you to get alternative quotes. Don't get me wrong: dealing with brick factors can be fun and some of them do terrific deals, but there is more than a hint of the Middle Eastern souk about the whole process. As far as I can ascertain, this rigmarole is more or less restricted to bricks, although it is rumoured to occur with up-market roof tiles and pavings.

MORTAR

You can't lay bricks without mortar and mortar actually makes up around 20 per cent of the area of a brick wall. So what the mortar looks like is arguably as important as what the bricks look like. The current fashion is for very pale mortars, aping the lime mortars that the Victorians used. One way to get this is to use pure lime mortars instead of cement, but lime mortars are expensive and not as easy to use as cement. If you want the look but not the hassle, you can use white cement (Snowcrete) and sand mixed with plasticiser. There is a much longer section on mortars in Chapter 12.

RENDER

Rendering is the term most commonly used for an external plastered finish. It's widely used in Scotland, where it's known as harling, and in Ireland. There is a reason for this: it's better at keeping rain out than brick, and therefore the wetter the region, the more you see render being used.

Two alternative techniques are used to get a rendered finish – rendering directly on to blockwork or rendering on to metal-lathing like Riblath or Renderlath, nailed on to battens. The first would normally be used on masonry-built houses, the second on timber frame, though note that the Scottish preference is to build a masonry block wall around a timber frame superstructure and then to render (or harl) the surface of the blockwork.

Render is also widely used against insulation backgrounds, as you would expect to find with Insulated Concrete Formwork walls, or external insulation systems.

DECORATIVE RENDER

A nearly lost art, which is undergoing a revival. The finish is rather like an upmarket artex applied to the face to enliven the appearance. In East Anglia, it is known as pargetting.

SINGLE COAT OR MONOCOUCHE RENDERS

Monocouche is French for single layer or bed. Conventionally, both lime and cement renders have been mixed on site with sand and applied in a series of layers or coats, never less than two and sometimes three or more. In contrast, a monocouche render is supplied in bag form ready for mixing with water: it can be applied by hand trowel or sprayed on. It's a practice which has spread here from the Continent and many of the big names in this field — Sto, Knauf Marmorit, Weber — are German in origin. These renders are use white cement and are pre-coloured so that what you are applying is as much a decorative finish as it is a weatherproofing layer. As they can be applied in one coat — typically around 15 mm thick — they are much less labour intensive process than traditional renders. The downside is of course the material cost — a 25 kg bags cost anywhere between £8-£10 each and only covers a square metre of wall area. This compares with a materials cost on a traditional cement render of around £1/sq m. But of course, the monocouche render systems claw much of this added cost back through reduced labour costs, not to mention eliminating the need for subsequent painting. Another advantage of monocouche renders is that they have additives placed in them which make them more flexible and help to eliminate cracking. The additives vary, depending on the make-up, but they typically include acrylics, polymers and silicates, sometimes giving rise to alternative names, such as "acrylic renders." Not all plasterers are entirely happy to apply monocouche renders in just one coat, and a site I visited recently in London has had two coats applied by hand for an overall cost of around £35/sq m. This compares with around £20/sq m for a traditional two-coat cement render, or £30/sq m for a three-coat finish.

LIME

Green builders love lime and happily apply it to all manner of unlikely surfaces such as straw bale and cob. But lime works just as well on more standard materials like blockwork, and it too has some advantages over cement renders, in that lime is inherently more flexible than cement and you are less likely to have problems with moisture getting trapped within the wall – a noted problem when cement renders are applied to old walls. Lime also tends to look very appealing, though to keep it looking good it does require frequent coats of limewash. Building limes are available in a variety of formats from the very traditional lime putties (which are bought wet, by the tub) through a number of distinct bagged products — hydraulic limes — which behave rather like a weak cement. They need to be mixed on site with sand, and are hand trowelled in the traditional way. Limes are a little more expensive than standard cement renders, but shouldn't really take any longer to apply. For lovers of tradition and modern methods of construction, there are one or two lime-based monocouche renders. Look out for K-Rend (K-Lime) and Baumit.

TIMBER AND BOARDS

Plain timber boarding (sometimes known as clapboarding) is coming back into fashion with the increasing popularity of barn conversions. There are several different style. Roughsawn timber (featheredge) looks more rustic; planed timber (shiplap) can look a shade more sophisticated. In their raw states, they make remarkably cheap claddings, costing between £10 and £12/sq m (materials only). But they drink wood stains by the gallon and, of course, they require extensive maintenance to keep looking the business. If you pay for the labour, then weatherboard is actually one of the most expensive of claddings after thirty years has elapsed.

Step forward a number of timber or near-timber solutions that don't require staining in the first place, let alone frequent re-applications. Cedar – usually Western Red Cedar – is the best-known timber promising to be fit and forget. It's five times the price of basic sawn featheredge but it lasts for 60 years. Roughly, anyway. It's being sold on the proposition that it lasts 60 years and there are many acres of cedar claddings going up all over the place in locations that are often hard to reach so it had better last 60 years! It goes a mellow silvery-grey after a couple of years.

There are a number of mid-priced alternatives between cedar and the basic whitewood boards. Native larch is sometimes specified – it's a little cheaper than cedar. There are some interesting heat-treated timbers coming onto the market: one is Thermowood, from Finland, which is a treated redwood with a 30 year lifespan. Another is Accoya, a pine which has been treated with vinegar and heat, and boasts a 50 year lifespan. And both Eternit (Weatherboard) and James Hardie (Hardiplank) produce convincing pre-painted fibre-cement boards for slightly less than genuine timber boards. Right at the bottom end of the spectrum is uPVC: sure, it doesn't rot but it doesn't really have much going for it as a cladding.

There are also a number of semi-industrial boards which can be used to clad buildings. These live really in the commercial sectors of the building trade but one or two adventurous architects sometimes specify them on housing.

Incidentally, with all external timber that requires painting or staining, it is good practice to put at least one coat of paint or stain on the boards on the ground before fixing. Timber shrinks, and if the whole board is not covered with a uniform colour you will end up with 1-2 mm flesh-coloured strips wherever boards overlap.

VERTICAL TILING

Using vertical tiling is another Victorian building feature that is coming back into fashion, particularly in SE England. Costs are very similar to plain tiles laid on roofs, although vertical hanging tends to be a little more expensive because there is more work involved in cutting corners, angles and around openings. Generally it looks best with small format plain tiles or slate and it is more important to select a good looking (i.e. expensive) tile for a wall than it is for a roof. Cedar, in the form of small tiles called shingles, also features as wall cladding.

RAINSCREENS

There is a modern variation on vertical tiling, which is the terracotta rainscreen. This is commonly used in commercial developments and city centre blocks of flats and is beginning to transfer across to housing. Rainscreens are normally fixed to some steel or aluminium support rails, which replace the more traditional timber battens. Look for products such as Hanson's LockClad or Wienerberberger's ArGeTon.

There is another variation on the rainscreen idea, and that is to fit a brick slip cladding which is commonly used to update older homes. It's primarily a way of adding external insulation to an existing wall, and the brick slips are glued into the insulation channels formed in the insulation.

Rainscreens and brick slip claddings tend to be done on a supply and fit basis and they also tend to be expensive, but they come into their own when renovating existing walls where extra insulation is required but space is limited. They typically add only 50 mm or 60 mm to the wall width.

STONE

If you live in one of the so-called stone belts you may well have to build in stone to satisfy the local planners. You may actually want to build in stone – it's usually very attractive – but it's likely to be very much more expensive than the developer's standbys: brick and render.

There are basically three approaches: you can use real stone quarried out of some hillside, you can use reconstituted stone, which is stone dust glued together with cement, or you can use stone cladding which usually gets stuck on the outside of cheaply erected blockwork.

NATURAL STONE

Building stone tends to be a very local affair. It was, after all, hewn from quarries and, in the days before cheap transportation, could only be carried the shortest of distances. Many of these old stone quarries survive and supply the demands of the local construction trade. In some areas there are thriving second-hand markets in stone walling materials, yet nowhere is natural stone a cheap material. You may be given brownie points for using natural stone in your house – more likely the local planners will insist on it – but you'll probably be adding £10,000 to the overall cost.

The cost of laying stone varies a little depending on its characteristics and whether it's coursed or not, but a good stone mason would hope to lay around 3 sq m a day. He would also be hoping to earn around £200 a day so you can tell what sort of price per square metre you should be looking at here.

RECONSTITUTED STONE

A cheaper alternative is to use a reconstituted stone. Bradstone is the best known and the largest producer. Although, to the practised eye, reconstituted stone will never look as good as the real thing, it will cost about half as much and, if done well, looks as good as many of the cheaper bricks.

STONE CLADDING

Stone cladding has got a reputation for being naff as hell, but this is because it's often associated with people who fix it to their brick terrace houses to 'make a statement' (such as 'I'm naff as hell'). Out of context like that it does look more than a touch ridiculous, but on a new house in a stone village chances are most casual passers-by would not even know it was stone cladding. However, artificial stone claddings are now virtually unobtainable and natural stone cladding is very expensive – it is unlikely to cost less than £50/sq m – so if you are starting from scratch you might just as well use real stone.

One interesting option is to use reconstituted stone cladding. It sounds awful but Fernhill produce a very convincing product which is set in moulds and is so realistic that it's virtually impossible to tell from the real thing. But realism comes at a price: it costs around £35-£45 /sq m to buy the tiles and laying is as expensive as brickwork. It can be placed on a polystyrene backing (useful for people building with ICFs) but it's usually stuck onto an outer blockwork wall.

RUBBLE WALLS

If you know the right quarries this kind of walling material can be extremely cheap to buy, but it tends to be very time-consuming to lay. Traditionally, rubble walling was independent of any backing materials, but now it is much cheaper to lay if it is set against a background of blockwork – which makes it a bit like very rough pebble dash. Each area of the country has its own local 'rubble' stones and seaside locations often tend to find theirs on the nearby beaches.

In East Anglia, flint is the usual material and prices vary enormously depending on how it is finished. Flint can be laid as wholestones – which gives a rough 'agricultural' look – or it can be knapped, which involves breaking the stones open to reveal a shiny black inside which is then set as the facework. Wholestone is available for under £20 per tonne, but knapped flint is up to ten times this amount. Expect to pay around £6-10/sq m for rough walling materials (inc sand and cement) and around £80 /sq m for laying. As you can see from these prices, laying is slow. It is, however, not particularly difficult and it could well suit a DIY builder who has more time than money. You can now buy pre-finished flint blocks, which take all the hard work out of it – you just lay them like a conventional block.

PORCHES AND BAYS

Thus far I've been looking at exterior finishes but there is, of course, much more to the external design of a house than just the materials used. Features like bay windows and porches have been coming right back into fashion despite the fact that they are expensive to build. It's quite hard to separate out how much extra these features cost because they tend to get lost in the whole job costings.

A bay window, for instance, involves minor additions to almost

Traditional house design demands that the front door should wear a hat, but just how ornate the porch should be is strictly a matter of taste

every aspect of the construction – excavations, foundations, flooring, brickwork, joinery, roofing, guttering, carpentry and decorating (to name just nine). Individually these changes are not great but added together I estimate that a two-storey bay may add as much three per cent to the costs of erecting the house superstructure. For an area less than 3 sq m that's expensive – getting on for double the amount spent on ordinary living space.

Porches are easier to quantify, although bear in mind that the standard of construction varies enormously from something little

more than a rain shelter to what amounts to a mini-extension. Being (usually) rectangular in shape, porches are not appreciably more expensive to construct than the main structure, but bear in mind that any complications that might ensue will end up taking a disproportionate amount of supervision time. One recent development is companies producing GRP bolt-on porches and bay window canopies; it's proved to be a big hit with developers. One company, Stormking, produces a whole range of architectural conceits such as pseudo-lead infill panels and clock towers. Their bolt-on porches start at just over £100.

CILLS AND ARCHES

One of the classiest effects you can get on external facades is to use feature lintels above and cills below your openings. There are a number of options for doing this. The cills and lintels can be formed from special bricks or made on site with a granite and cement mixture, which is fine if they get painted afterwards. Another variation is to have reconstituted stone ones made up in a workshop: this is the most expensive option but also probably the most attractive.

Insetting joinery into the facade is not merely a decorative process. By its very nature it helps to protect windows and doors from the worst of the weather, and the building regulations acknowledge this by making recessed joinery compulsory in Scotland and in many exposed parts of the rest of the country.

Chapter 7

DON'T RUIN IT

Having gone to all that trouble to get good-looking materials correctly proportioned, it is worth taking on board a cautionary word about the effect of those little elements, which can ruin the overall effect - like a wart on the face of a much loved friend (shouldn't that have been a carbuncle? Ed). Whether you go for period charm or ultra-modernism really makes no difference, just think about the details - remember the devil is in the details. Here are a few style tips:

■ rainwater downpipes – the fewer the better
■ plastic meter boxes – hide them round the side
■ security floodlighting – don't point it straight at people walking towards it
■ alarm bells – potential burglars will still see them on a side wall
■ satellite dishes – they can sometimes go out in the garden.

INSULATION

All materials insulate to a greater or lesser extent – see section on U-values in Chapter 13 – but only since the Seventies have we seen the widespread adoption of materials that do very little else except insulate. By and large, these materials are not prohibitively expensive and most will pay for themselves within a few years. So whilst you could design your home to avoid using insulation wherever possible, there would be very little point in doing so.

There are several materials available to insulate housing. All have pros and cons and not all are suitable in every application; mostly they are available in a number of different formats – often in combination with other materials like chipboard and plasterboard – which

makes describing them all extremely complicated. The basics are as follows. First the woolly ones.

GLASS FIBRE

Cheap, reasonably good insulator. Excellent when laid flat in lofts but when placed in walls it will sag. But help is at hand: it can be 'wicked', which stiffens it up and allows it to be placed into wall cavities without risk of sagging or, as they say in insulation speak, to 'perform well in the vertical'. Here they tend to get referred to as batts as in cavity batts or timber frame batts. Although nearly double the price of unwicked quilts, they are still good value compared to other materials.

MINERAL WOOL

In most ways it performs very similarly to glass fibre and can also be wicked to perform well in the vertical. However, mineral wool is noticeably superior to glass (and almost all other insulation materials) in terms of fire resistance. It is usually priced to compete with glass though sometimes it is five to ten per cent more. The Danish company, Rockwool, dominates production and it's often referred to by this trade name.

SHEEPS WOOL

The natural product on which both glass wool and mineral wool are based. In many ways it performs very similarly to its synthetic cousins but it's obviously much nicer to work with – the synthetic ones are notoriously itchy and unpleasant, especially glass wool. It's only really appeared as an option in the past few years and it appeals mostly to people wanting to build using natural products wherever possible. They also need deep wallets because it's around five times the price of the synthetic wools.

EXPANDED POLYSTYRENE

Now it's on to plastics. The most familiar plastic insulation is expanded polystyrene. It gets used in buildings in two formats. The first is as a vast amorphous mass of little white beads that get blown into cavity walls from lorries. The second is in rigid boards; here two brands dominate, Jablite and Kaycell – builders often refer it to as Jablite. It performs very similarly to glass and mineral wool in terms of insulation capabilities (but not fire protection) and is similarly cheaply priced. Used widely in cavity wall construction (in both formats) and underfloor insulation (where the regs now require at least 100 mm of EPS). It is much the cheapest material when you are having to build with a partial cavity fill.

EXTRUDED POLYSTYRENE

This is a different version of polystyrene that is much denser and much stronger - expanded polystyrene sheets are notoriously brittle. In terms of insulation capabilities it lies midway between expanded polystyrene and the polyurethane family of insulants, but its big selling point is that it is resistant to water penetration. It's great under floors and below ground but it's a bit pricey to use elsewhere. Businesses to check out are Dow Chemicals, who make Styrofoam, and Knauf Insulation, makers of Polyfoam.

POLYURETHANE FAMILY

The most efficient of the mass market insulators, it is usually sold in rigid sheet format, usually foil backed. However, it is pricey even if you buy second hand, where a company called Seconds & Co is busy. The domestic market is dominated by two manufacturers, Celotex and Kingspan, though others are beginning to appear.

A big problem with polyurethane

Insulation options

	Underfloor	External wall	Flat ceiling	Sloping roof
Approx U value requirement	0.16	0.20	0.10	0.16
Glass/rock wool	INADVISABLE	150mm	300mm	200mm + Foam
Cost/m^2		£6	£5	£12
Expanded Polystyrene	175 mm	150mm	INADVISABLE	300mm
Cost/m^2	£8	£7		£20
Extruded Polystyrene	140 mm	100mm	INADVISABLE	INADVISABLE
Cost/m^2	£17	£12		
Polyiso foam boards	125 mm	80mm	200mm	180mm
Cost/m^2	£11	£7	£23	£18
Blown fibre	INADVISABLE	180mm	300mm	200mm + Foam
Cost/m^2		£10	£20	£20
Sheeps Wool Batts	INADVISABLE	140mm	300mm	DIFFICULT
Cost/m^2		£12	£26	

The insulation levels shown in the table above should meet the requirements of the 2010 Part L regulations in England & Wales, though explicit U values are no longer published. 2013 Building Regs may get a little more exacting

Model House Insulation

Time taken to fix normal depth	10 Min/m^2	Cost to fix normal depth	£3/m^2
Time taken to fix superinsulation depth	15 Min/m^2	Cost to fix superinsulation	£5/m^2

	Area	Used	Materials	Labour	Combined	costs/m^2
Under Ground Floor	80m^2	175mm	EPS	£ 700	£ 200	£ 900
Extrenal Walls	200m^2	150mm	Rockwool	£ 1,800	£ 600	£ 2,400
Ceiling above First Floor	80m^2	300mm	Rockwool	£ 400	£ 200	£ 600
Soundproofing Int Walls	60m^2	100mm	Rockwool	£ 200	£ 200	£ 400
Soundproofing Int Floor	80m^2	100mm	Rockwool	£ 200	£ 200	£ 400
Total				£ 3,300	£ 1,400	£ 4,700

has been that its production involved the use of CFCs, now implicated in the demise of the ozone layer. This has led the manufacturers on a frantic search to find ways of making their boards with a different blowing agent, and this has produced a range of similar insulation boards made with either polyisocyanurate foam or phenolic foam. In terms of performance they are both very similar to the older polyurethanes.

Despite their cost, polyurethane (and substitutes) are being increasingly specified because their superior performance as insulators means that they are space efficient – in that you can get the desired insulation levels from a thinner sheet – and that means there are sometimes reductions in other construction costs. Basically these boards are twice as good but three times the cost of the basic insulators, expanded polystyrene and the wools.

Another application for the polyurethanes is to get blown into cavities and increasingly under old roofs to keep them going a bit longer. It's expensive and traditionalists howl with indignation when they see it done but it works.

CELLULOSE FIBRE

This is sometimes promoted as a green alternative to the other materials. For a start, it's made from recycled newspapers (so that's where they go) and it can also be used in timber frame walls without a vapour barrier, which is reckoned, by some, to be an advantage. It has one major disadvantage in that it is not available in a sheet form so it has to be blown in by specialists. There is one main manufacturer in the UK, Excel Industries, who market their product as Warmcel.

UNUSUAL INSULATIONS

There are numerous other materials being used as insulants, and new ones coming onto the market all the time. At the hi-tec end of things, there are vacuum-insulated panels (VIPs) which are horribly expensive, terribly thin and only last for 30 years (Nanopore is the best known name). Then there are the aerogels, of which Spacetherm is the best known example. It's rather brittle and dusty to use, but it has its place where you want good insulation and don't have very much space. Foamglas is another hi-tec insulant: it is made of crushed glass and carbon and is totally impervious to water, rot, vermin or any sort of damage.

Then there are various natural insulation materials. Apart from Warmcel and Sheep's Wool(already covered), look out for Hemp Insulation (Isonat), Hemcrete (a lime-hemp mixture), and Pavatex (wood fibre board). These materials are usually used with timber framed houses where the emphasis is on breathing walls - i.e. ones built without a conventional vapour barrier. There are usually bought via specialist supplier's: Mike Wye Associates is a useful contact as they maintain an online price list.

MULITIFOILS

A controversial group of insulation materials, which work on the Bacofoil-behind-the-radiator principle. That is to say they have shiny reflective barriers which bounce the heat back into the room. There are three, Actis (from France), Alreflex 2L2 (from Holland) and Airtec (British), which have some body

to them and therefore tend to act like conventional insulation, though none is thicker than 25 mm. The use of multifoils is based on their manufacturers' claims that they are equivalent in insulation value to around 250 mm of mineral wool, which makes them suitable for use in sloping roof spaces. This claim is, to put it mildly, controversial and when placed into a guarded hot box, the traditional method of measuring U values, multifoils only perform to the equivalent of 80 mm of mineral wool. Nevertheless, multifoils have established a foothold in the insulation market, thanks to their endorsement by BM Trada, a prominent third party certifier, and whether you choose to believe the claims of their manufacturers, or not, it would be churlish of me not to mention their existence.

Multifoils are getting used in conjunction with other materials, such as plastic insulation boards, and the authorities are far happier to accept these combination applications.

BUYING TIPS

Generally the best place to buy insulation materials is from the insulation specialists. Sheffield Insulation (SIG) and Encon are the best-known national distributors but there are numerous local ones listed in 'Yellow Pages' under Insulation Materials. Some of the insulation installers are worth checking out for supply only. The supply and fix services offered are often a good deal; it is hard to beat them on price (or speed) except where you are not paying for site labour.

A great online resource if you want to know more is Greenspec.co.uk. It has bags of information on the different types of insulation available.

COLD BRIDGING

Cold bridging is what happens when parts of your insulated shell are interrupted by things that don't insulate very well. What on earth am I talking about? The returns where cavity walls join around window and door openings are the best-known example, but there are many others. The timber studs in a timber frame wall or the rafters in a roof, the edge of a floor where it meets the foundation walls. All effectively leak heat rather faster than their better insulated surroundings. Even things like steel wall ties, used to tie cavities together, act as heat sinks. Now the more insulation you stuff into your fabric, the greater the relative importance of cold bridging becomes. As insulation levels rise, there are more and more products appearing that address cold bridging effects, most notably the group of products known as cavity closers, which you use in the gap around window and door openings.

In super-efficient low-energy designs, such as Passivhaus, the cold bridging issue becomes critical and designers go to great lengths to avoid any route by which heat can be transferred.

JOINERY

We've reached the external joinery section. It's a complicated part of the book with a lot of information to absorb. In previous editions, I subdivided this section into three parts; windows, doors and glazing. This sort of reflected the traditional way of building houses where the window frames and door frames were built into the walls by the bricklayers as a first fix process and then the windows were glazed and the doors hung and both were painted as part of the second fix.

Some sites still operate like this but the trend now is to get the windows and

doors glazed and decorated in a distant factory, to be fitted much later in the build process and now the bricklayers have to fit just sub-frames or cavity closers around the openings. This means that the glazing is increasingly carried out off-site and so ceases to be a separate consideration to buying windows and doors.

Building regulations are also driving change here. The principle driver is the requirement for greater energy efficiency, which has brought in increasingly sophisticated levels of double glazing and draught proofing; but in addition to this, many windows have to act as controlled ventilation channels and as fire escape routes, and some have to be assessed for security, sound proofing and safety as well. External doors are required

1

Vertical brick joints should be aligned. Here the red line shows how the brick edges should fall. You can see how the brick edges are thrown out of alignment by the placing of a 1200mm wide window

2

Obviously a house built with traditional timber windows. Wrong. These are uPVC. The house is built by Bellway Homes. Actually, these windows were so realistically woody-looking that I had to sneak up and touch them to be sure they were in fact plastic

to fulfil a number of additional functions; besides being energy efficient to a degree unthought of a few years ago, they must meet the demands of the disabled access regulations.

So this section is designed to deal with the technicalities of windows, doors and glazing. The choices and the costings are looked at in the follow-on sections.

ENERGY EFFICIENCY

There have been huge changes here over the years I have been producing this book (i.e. since 1995), principally to do with the adoption of double glazing. Unless you are concerned with repairing a listed building, your new windows will have to be double glazed and not just run-of-the-mill double glazed but double glazed to a standard

unheard of even a few years ago.

DOUBLE GLAZING

The idea of double glazing is to reduce heat loss and, to a lesser extent, increase sound insulation. The work is done not so much by the extra pane of glass but by the air between the two panes, known as the air gap. The early forms of double glazing were a significant improvement on single glazing. U-values, the common measurement of heat loss, for single glazing tends to be up around 5.0; in contrast, a basic double glazed sealed unit scores around 3.0. But the technology of double glazing has kept on developing and the most advanced glazing systems available today have U values under 1.0. That means the heat lost through the glazing would be just a fifth of what single glazing, with its score of 5.0, would suffer.

The most recent changes in our thermal building regs reflect this changing state of affairs and now suggest that windows have a U-value of no more than 1.6, that glazed doors are no worse than 2.0 and that largely solid doors should 3.0 or better. What was a state-of-the-art window ten years ago now won't even pass muster. It's not exactly Pentium processor type change but it's still a lot for the dear old building industry to cope with.

And if anything, the future looks like it will be triple glazing, where U values fall still further and costs continue to rise. Triple glazing is still aspirational in the UK, but it's now a recognised option from local suppliers, not just something that has to be imported from somewhere cold.

ADDRESSING FAILURE IN SEALED UNITS

In fact the building trade took a long while to come to grips with basic double glazing. There was a horribly high failure rate, usually manifesting itself in the form of misting between the panes. The air in the air gap was sealed, and was meant to stay sealed, but when the edge seals broke down, the air would mix with moist external air and condensation would take place.

Hundreds of thousands of double glazed units have failed this way over the years and only recently has the industry worked out how to combat the problem. Builders were using the wrong kind of sealants and squeezing glazing units into

The trend towards factory-glazing of windows has been accompanied by the uptake of cavity closers, pictured here, which you build into the wall as it goes up. The windows and doors are clipped in later when the damage can be minimised

rebates that weren't designed to take them. The results were that the units got wet around the edges and the seals disintegrated.

Double glazing failure was one of the 'bete noirs' of the warranty providers because they didn't include them in their ten-year guarantees – something which the new housebuyers never seemed to twig until they came to make a claim. But such is the confidence in the new installation techniques that the NHBC have, since 2000, added sealed unit failure to the list of items covered by their latent defects policies, provided that installation follows some key guidelines.

The key change has been the uptake of drained and vented bottom rails that allow any accumulated moisture to either drain away or evaporate before it starts doing damage to the seals. Deeper glazing rebates in the joinery help matters as well and these are becoming mandatory thanks to changes in the thermal regs. Misting in units was a problem for both timber and PVC windows but the problems were worse with timber because these were often site glazed, rather badly.

In fact, the adoption of factory glazing has almost eliminated the old problems we once had with sealed unit failure. Keith Topliss of Howarth Windows told me in 2008 that "90 per cent of our glazing problems now come from the 10 per cent of site glazed installations that we still supply."

IMPROVING SEALED UNITS

Various measures improve the efficiency of double glazing. The simplest is to increase the distance between the panes. A 6 mm gap was the old standard. By upping this to 16 mm or 20 mm you reduce heat loss by nearly 25 per cent. It's easy for the glazing manufactures to alter the gap and there is no cost penalty here. The difficulty comes in building joinery that will take deep units like this. The uPVC manufacturers didn't have any problems but the timber window makers proved very reluctant to switch to wider glazing rebates though the new legislation effectively insists on it – the old high performance windows are now the standard.

The next trick is to fill the air gap between panes with something other than air. The inert gas argon is the common choice (though some use krypton). Argon filling tends to add about £5 /sq m to the costs of the units and it results in only a marginal improvement in efficiency, typically between five per cent and ten per cent.

Then switch to coated, low emissivity (or Low-e) glass. Low-e glass works by absorbing short wave solar heat, just like other glass, but then acting as a reflective shield to the long wave heat emanating from inside the house. In effect it introduces a layer of one-way insulation into the sealed unit.

Low-e is applied as a micron-thin coating to the inside of the inner pane and, although some people claim to be able to tell the difference between low-e coated and uncoated glass – apparently it has a blue tint – I can't. Low-e coating is a developing technology and there are now hard coatings and soft coatings with varying emissivity levels. Soft coatings are better and, needless to say, more expensive. A hard coat will reduce the overall U-value by 25 per cent; a soft coat by as much as 35 per cent.

Another emerging technique is to use warm edge spacers around the sealed units. Traditionally, the spacers have been made of aluminium which is, of course, a very good heat conductor. A classic case of cold bridging. By replacing the aluminium with something less conductive (typically plastic) you get a much more even U-value across the entire sealed unit. The smaller the units, the bigger difference warm edgings make.

Beyond this, there are adjustments you can make to the frames, which can have a major impact on heat loss. And ultimately, you can add an extra sheet of glass and move to triple glazing, which also improves efficiency by around 25 per cent. Triple glazing is also much better for sound proofing. Add all these 25 per cents here and 35 per cents there plus the odd ten per cent and you can see how a state of the art double or triple glazed unit can get a very low U-value, far in excess of what is required by the new UK regs. Triple glazing with insulated frames is how you get the very low U values, down at 0.8 or so.

REPLACING OLD WINDOWS

The 2002 building reg changes brought about another significant change in that, for the first time, replacement windows were required to meet the new standards as well. This has become a largely self-policing process whereby glazing firms have to be accredited by a body known as FENSA (England & Wales only). If they are, they can issue a certificate to say that the job they have carried out met the relevant standards, without you having to trouble the local building inspector. This information may later be required as part of your seller's pack so there is a semblance of a stick here to get you to comply. Expect the glazing firms to stop selling units that don't have a U-value figure of 1.6 or less. And expect the joinery firms to stop making windows that can't take at least 24 mm wide double glazed units.

One area that will remain exempt from the new requirements is listed buildings. English Heritage doesn't buy the new regs – they see it as a uPVC window salesmen's licence to rip out all that is wooden and lovely with our national treasures. The exemption may also apply to properties situated in Conservation Areas though this isn't abundantly clear. The conservators' point is that thick windows (whether uPVC or timber) don't look as good as thin ones.

ENERGY RATINGS

I have been idly talking about U values and windows and doors as though they behaved just like walls or roofs, which is where you more commonly come across U value figures. Of course, joinery really isn't directly comparable with walls and roofs because the primary function is to let the light in or to gain access.

Windows in particular are quite capable of gaining heat when the sun shines and some of the more energy efficient windows, facing south, are thought to be net heat contributors throughout the course of a year. So the simple concept of U values tends to break down when looking at glazed elements.

Step forward the idea of having energy ratings for joinery, just like fridges, washing machines and, more recently, boilers. The advantage of the system is that it looks at the whole assembly, not just the glazing and it also takes into account other factors such as solar overheating in summer and air leakage. The downside of energy rating is that it tends to favour big plain windows and marks down some of the more traditional window styles, such as the sliding sash, which may do little for the look of our homes in years to come.

AIR TIGHTNESS AND COLD BRIDGING

Almost as critical to the energy performance of windows and doors as their overall energy ratings, is the methods used to fit them into the external walls and the draught-proofing of the opening parts when in contact with the fixed parts. Draught-proofing is now pretty well built into doors and windows but gaps around the frames, where they are built into walls, are still left very much up to the guys on site. It's not unusual to see large gaps under lintels, for instance, which would later be covered over with plasterboard: this makes a mockery of fitting high cost double glazed units.

Many suppliers are developing subframe assembly systems, which address some of these issues. The subframes, or cavity closers, fit into the cavity and are built-in as the wall goes up. They address the old problem of cold bridging where the internal skin was taken around a corner (known as a return) to form an opening for a window or a door, but they also act as a clip-in frame for the window to later be placed directly into, without having to mess around with any screws.

EGRESS WINDOWS

In 2002, the fire regs (Part B in England & Wales) were amended to make it a requirement that every habitable room above ground floor had to have access to an easy means of escape via what has come to be known as an egress window. This is defined as follows:

- must have an openable area not less than 0.33 sq m
- the opening dimensions must be at least 450 mm wide and 450 mm high
- the opening must be within 1100 mm of the floor
- if it's a sloping roof, then the distance between the cill and the eaves shouldn't be more than 1700 mm.

For many windows, this doesn't present a problem but a few designs have had to be re-engineered to make them pass muster. The simulated-sash windows, which open outwards aren't acceptable in their original format and neither are narrow windows with fixed vertical bars. However, with a bit of imagination, they can be reconfigured - there is in fact a detail now known as a flying mullion, which sounds like a fish but is actually a bar built into the opening casement.

So building in egress windows into your

house shouldn't present a problem but it may call for one or two adaptations.

SAFETY GLAZING

Another important factor to consider is the regs requirement (Part N in England & Wales) for safety glazing on:

- any window less than 800 mm off floor level
- any window less than 300 mm from a door
- all doors and sidelights where pane width is greater than 250 mm
- internal glazed doors with pane sizes more than 250 mm x 250 mm.

What do they mean by 'safety glazing?' There are two common forms of clear, strengthened glass:

- toughened: baked hard to about five times the strength of float glass and, when broken, shatters into (hopefully) harmless lumps. Toughened glass costs about 50 per cent more than the standard float glass.
- laminated: consists of two sheets of ordinary glass sandwiched around a plastic film: when hit it breaks but doesn't collapse. This is now how most car windscreens are made.

Laminated glass is conventionally 6.4 mm thick and it costs around double standard float glass, considerably more than toughened glass. Consequently for these applications, toughened glass is now almost universally specified, but laminated glass is preferable if you are worried about security; it's harder to break through. Laminated glass is normally preferred for applications like conservatory roofs.

CLEANING WINDOWS

It's not a requirement stemming from the regs, but arguably its something of a safety-led innovation. Self-cleaning glass. All the big producers seem to have something

on the market now. St. Gobain's is called Bioclean, Pilkington's version is Activ (why do they all sound like yoghurt?) Like Low-e glass, it uses a transparent coating but this one is hydrophilic (literally 'water-loving') mineral material, so that water spreads out over the surface of the coating and causes a washing effect when it comes into contact with the window. The water then quickly evaporates, leaving no marks from dried drops of water. They don't actually claim that you'll never need to clean windows again, rather that you won't need to clean them so often.

VENTILATION

One of the less popular demands of the regulations (Part F in England & Wales) is that the frames should be capable of supplying background ventilation around the house. This is usually achieved by adding trickle vents to the head of the frame, though some versions slip the vents into the subframe where it is much less visible.

Most people don't even notice the presence of trickle vents in their window frames but a surprising number develop a deep aversion to them. The good news is that you can avoid using trickle vents if you build an alternative ventilation system into your house. The obvious choice is to switch to a whole house ventilation system (see the section on Ventilation) but this is an expensive option for most homes. Those of you aiming for a low-energy home will probably be fitting a whole house ventilation system in any event but note that if you are building on a noisy site (i.e. near a main road or under a flight path) you may be required to use an alternative to trickle venting because they are just as good at letting sound pass through as air.

Many windows are supplied with trickle vents as standard. If you wish to avoid them, for whatever reason, make sure that your joinery supplier knows about this well in advance otherwise you may well end up getting them anyway.

SCOTLAND, WALES AND IRELAND

If that lot is not complicated enough, bear in mind that I have been writing about England where one set of building regulations apply. Scotland has its own set, Northern Ireland another and the Irish Republic yet another. And Wales has recently decided to branch out on its own and leave the English regs behind. Whilst the basic regulations covering all these territories are very similar, there are lots of little differences and the changes that do come into effect all happen on different timescales. Scotland in particular has a very annoying stipulation that the energy efficiency standard of new windows is dependent on the efficiency of the heating system. Whilst I am sure it gives a warm glow to those in the Scottish parliament to know that devolution is working, it's hard to see who really benefits from such a regulation.

This is a nightmare scenario for the manufacturers. What they of course seek is one range of windows and doors that will be admissible in all territories, which tends to mean that the territory with the toughest regs sets the standard for all the others. Incidentally, none of these specifications apply to conservatories, as long as they are physically separated from the main house, or heated envelope as they tend to say in these circles.

CHOOSING WINDOWS

Timber or plastic? Or something else entirely? Pre-glazed or finished on site? Modern or traditional? Made-to-measure or off-the-peg? What sort of opening

mechanism? There are, in truth, a lot of questions facing you when it comes to window selection. You have, in fact, a microcosm of the UK housebuilding scene right here in one product group.

There is quite a good chance that you won't have to go through all these decision processes, at least in any great detail, if you work with a designer or a package company who steer towards a window that just happens to work with their chosen design. For instance, if you are building in the Georgian rectory style, you will almost certainly be wanting to use a Georgian sash-style window.

Windows and, to a lesser extent, doors, are absolutely critical to your overall house design and generally there is a window that works for every house design so you would be most unlikely – indeed extremely badly advised – to fit the wrong style of window into the wrong façade. Not that the typical homeowner on the typical suburban street would know this: bear witness to the dreadful mish-mash of styles and materials used in the great replacement window craze of the Eighties and Nineties. But an awful lot of contemporary housing isn't tied to any style in particular and this leaves a wide range of choices available.

WINDOW OPENINGS

With new housing, it's a bit different, because you are not replacing anything. Yet new housebuilding window styles tend to be pretty conservative. There is a reason for this. The openings are almost always worked out from a limited range of options. All the main manufacturers selling into this market are geared up to thousands of windows (and doors) to fit these openings. There are cost and time penalties for varying away from these openings, so everyone sticks to these openings. What exactly are they?

The window opening heights are easy to fathom: they are in 150 mm steps, which represents two bricks courses – the height options are 450, 600, 750, 900, 1050, 1200, 1350, 1500 mm. The width options – 488, 630, 915, 1200, 1770 mm – would at first glance seem to be selected by a random number machine. It appears that the widths were changed in the early Eighties after a directive from Brussels indicated that the 300 mm brick was about to take over Europe and that they'd better have joinery to suit. The joinery manufacturers all obliged but bricks remain 215 mm long! This is most noticeable on the 1200 wide windows, which disrupt the vertical joints on face brickwork.

The big joinery companies made their mark by turning out these modular sized windows by the tens of thousands. But the product they produced was a very basic unglazed, unpainted timber frame. You can still buy your joinery like this and indeed, in terms of headline prices, off-the-peg timber joinery still looks much cheaper than any of the pre-finished alternatives.

The old British joinery businesses have all been taken over now but the same factories still churn out these windows by the truckload. Names to look out for are Jeld Wen, who took over two of the big names in this business, Boulton & Paul and John Carr, Premdor and Magnet. Of these manufacturers, Magnet are alone in maintaining a substantial branch network of depots through which they sell exclusively. All the others sell through the established builder's merchants. There are numerous others in this business like Howarth Timber who sell directly to housebuilders and the trade.

When plastic windows appeared on the scene, back in the Seventies, they were being sold almost exclusively into the replacement market and the businesses were all geared up to make one-offs. It took a long time for the uPVC manufacturers to realise that the new housebuilders only really wanted about five different window sizes and that there were economies of scale to be had here by aping the likes of Boulton & Paul. The plastic window merchants started making basic windows in the same old modular sizes and then improved on the process by introducing clip-in cavity closers which let you push a finished window into place, long after the brickies had left site. This fitting system is now available on most types of window.

TIMBER v PVC

Thus far I have simplified it into timber v plastic but the reality is more complex. There are different timber species, available at a huge range of costs and different performance characteristics. uPVC is uPVC but the windows made out of it vary considerably in quality. And there are other options, notably the composite windows, which are usually made largely of timber but come with a more durable external covering.

SOFTWOODS

If you choose to have your windows supplied cheaply from a volume manufacturer then they will almost certainly be made from European Redwood, probably from Scandinavia. Although it is not particularly durable, it can be readily treated with wood preservatives; more importantly it is the cheapest type of suitable timber. It machines well and generally looks good, which makes it suitable for translucent finishes like wood staining.

Many so-called quality window producers complain of the low standards of the volume producers. They may have a

point, but it is worth bearing in mind that these standards have improved substantially in recent years. All timber is now vacuum treated with preservatives, opening casements are draught stripped and window locks and ventilation are now fitted as standard. Much of what people used to demand from a so-called high performance window is now available right throughout the ranges.

There really isn't a lot to choose between the quality of the joinery turned out by the volume timber manufacturers, though the finer detailing does vary a little. Occasionally, you will find that one is offering much better terms than the others and you may have cause to switch horses. This is usually possible because, despite the different naming systems they use, the sizes are standard and therefore interchangeable.

BESPOKE TIMBER

There are better woods to use for external joinery but they are all very much more expensive and won't necessarily result in better (or longer-lasting) windows. Most hardwoods are inherently more durable than softwoods – oak, teak and Brazilian mahogany are particularly suitable – and there are some North American softwoods, such as Douglas Fir, which are nearly as durable as the better hardwoods – certainly durable enough not to require treatment with wood preservative.

The big joinery manufacturers offer 'hardwood' alternatives in most of their ranges, at around double the cost of the softwood windows, but you don't get any choice as to which hardwood. If you particularly wanted something like Douglas Fir for your windows then you would have to search out a small joinery shop to make them for you; this route would probably treble the cost of using a bog standard casement from a volume producer.

A new arrival on the scene is improved timber, the best known example being Accoya. It's expensive, but it promised a timber finish that can be guaranteed for 50 years, although it will still require occasional re-staining.

UPVC

Generally speaking, uPVC is now cheaper than softwood on a like for like basis. What I mean by this is that uPVC is almost invariably supplied ready-glazed whereas timber windows are still sometimes bought without glazing, so comparison isn't as straightforward as it might be.

Timber can only be the cheaper option if you want to put a lot of your own unpaid labour into glazing and decorating. Note, however, that the wood-grain effect uPVC windows are at least 50 per cent more than the plain white ones.

The question is, is uPVC any good? Well, uPVC windows have a stranglehold on the replacement market. What sells them is the fact that they are usually replacing clapped-out timber or steel windows, which may have been in place for fifty years or more, and they are offering comfort and warmth together with the promise of being maintenance free.

It's actually too early to say if uPVC windows will be trouble-free (uPVC guttering certainly isn't), but the indications are that they are performing well. uPVC as a material may last for 30 or 40 years but it's hard to repair: in contrast, timber windows can last much longer - if they are regularly painted or stained.

Note also that Greenpeace have been leading a vociferous campaign against the use of uPVC in buildings. They argue that both the production and the eventual disposal of uPVC is a toxic process involving the release of a number of unpleasant chemicals, dioxins being the

Joinery Rules Of Thumb Costings

■ The Model House has 35m² of external joinery: that is windows, doors and patio doors

■ As a rough guide, you can assume that your joinery area is likely to be 20% of your internal floor area

FACTORS WHICH INCREASE THE BASIC RATE

Windows and doors are not sold by the square metre. However you can calculate a square metre rate (by dividing the total spend by the opening area) and this gives a helpful rule of thumb on how much the joinery costs. Note

■ Doors - more expensive than windows. Patio doors, French doors will add extra

■ Small windows - the unit cost increases dramatically

■ Unusual styles - sash windows, curved work, leaded lights - all extra

■ Non standard sizes - usually add between 25% and 40%

Typical Square Metre Window and External Door Costs

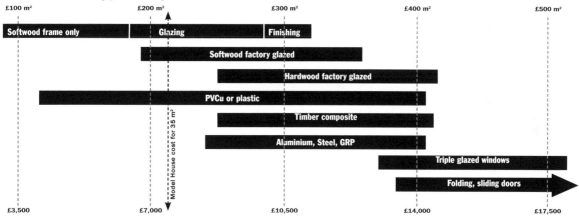

most prominent. Their claims are naturally denied by the British Plastics Federation. What Greenpeace have succeeded in doing is making uPVC rather unfashionable: it gets blacklisted from projects with green sensibilities, along with cement.

There are alternative materials. Glass is used a lot for doors and is starting to be used for windows as well. Pultec (now trading as Yprado)has an interesting range of pultruded glass fibre joinery. If you don't want the hassle of timber and just don't like uPVC, check them out. Not only do

they promise no maintenance, but they are available in a wide range of colours.

COMPOSITES

There are a number of suppliers who offer timber on the inside and uPVC or aluminium on the outside, thus combining the good looks of timber with a more durable exterior. They are usually imported, mostly from North American and Scandinavia. Best known of these is Andersen Windows, an American joinery giant, who produce a huge range of timber

doors and windows with an external uPVC coating An awful lot of good European windows are owned by the same company, VKR Holdings, (Velux, SP Fonster, Rationel, Velfac, Loewen) but there are others such as Nor-Dan, and Pro Tec, Composite windows are approximately double the price of basic timber or uPVC, but note that if you want sliding sash style windows, the US designs are good value. Also check window dimensions: most of these importers will make to order but if they are working off modular sizes, then they may not be readily

Chapter 7

substitutable for UK drawings.

COMPARING COSTS

The formal way of getting joinery priced is to first design the elevations with the windows and doors drawn, then to turn this into a joinery schedule (a shopping list), which you can use to garnish quotations from. The problem with doing things this way is that there are some styles of windows, notably the imported ones, which don't work to standard UK sizes and if you want to take advantage of their best prices you have to redraw your elevations to accommodate them. Which may bring knock-on costs elsewhere, as other aspects of the design have to be reconfigured. There is thus a huge inbuilt advantage to manufacturers and designers working with a limited number of door and window openings and this is how houses tend to be designed in the UK.

If you have set your heart on using North Americans windows, let your designer know about this right away so that the openings can be incorporated into your design from the off.

Joinery is an expensive feature in the overall budget. It frequently makes up between five per cent and 10 per cent of the final figure, and there is a large price gap between the basic stuff and the top of the range, whatever material you choose to use. If you want a shortcut price guide, look out for the cost of a unit like a 1200x1200 mm window and use this to extrapolate upwards.

A basic unit in a simple configuration, say a double casement window with one opening panel, will cost around £200 fully glazed and finished. You can easily spend double or triple this amount by changing styles or materials. If you are using a joinery catalogue for pricing purposes, bear in mind that most items are normally sold at big discounts to the published prices. 30 per cent or 35 per cent off are often taken as read and big volumes or good haggling skills can easily increase this discount.

One of the things that throws people out is that the headline rates for timber windows from the large joinery manufacturers appears to be low, much lower than any of the finished windows. A raw timber window needs glazing, needs detailing around the openings and needs decorating as well: the combined costs of these items is more than double the cost of the raw timber window.

If you account for these extra items as the window table does, then you find that uPVC is now the cheapest way to build a window, by some margin.

SECURITY

Factory-glazed windows are available in some styles (not sashes), which meet a British security standard known as BS 7950. Rather than just testing the individual locks or the glass, BS 7950 tests the whole window assembly in situ. Typically such a window will have laminated glass on the external face and shootbolt espagnolette locking mechanisms. To get windows to this standard, they really need to have been factory glazed but this doesn't mean they have to be plastic – most of the big timber joinery manufactures now produce BS 5750 windows.

THE STYLES

The British window is an unusual beast, not found outside these islands. Although made by industrial methods, the styles are mostly very traditional. Work your way through a joinery catalogue and you will see Cottage Style (with cute glazing bars), Narrow Module (just so on barn conversions), All Bar (Georgian-style), Swept Head (now mercifully going out of fashion), not to mention bay

windows and a whole range of sliding sash windows, which are made to an entirely different set of sizes. It's really a question of matching the style of window to your overall house style. If you are working in a vernacular idiom (i.e. something olde worlde) then you'll find something out there to suit. If you want something modern, you may have to look elsewhere, probably towards the continental tilt-and-turn style windows, though increasingly UK manufacturers have ranges which will suit.

SLIDING SASH

The vertical sliding sash was the mainstay of Georgian and Victorian housebuilders but was mostly overlooked in the 20th century in favour of hinged windows, although its popularity never died out in North America where it remains the most popular window design. It's now mainly used by designers wanting to replicate an olde-worlde look or in the window replacement market. Although sliding sash is thought of as very traditional, there are a lot of modern refinements brought into the design and manufacture of them and they are available in a range of materials. For instance, many of the modern ones have a tilt facility that allows you to clean the windows from the inside.

At the top end of the range, there are restoration specialists like Mumford & Wood who are producing a product very similar to what the Georgians built. And the sash window is not restricted to timber: there are a number of uPVC fabricators; Masterframe is a particularly notable example as they have a plastic product that is almost indistinguishable from timber.

OPENING SYSTEMS

There are some surprising differences in the ways we operate windows throughout

Joinery Schedule

SOFTWOOD DOUBLE GLAZED	Areas WIDTH IN M	HEIGHT IN M	AREA IN M²	ITEM COST	Fitting costs FITTING COST	COMBINED COST
Kitchen French Doors	1.8	2.1	3.8	£ 800	£ 160	£ 960
Kitchen Window	2.1	1.2	2.5	£ 500	£ 40	£ 540
Utility Door	0.9	2.1	1.9	£ 400	£ 130	£ 530
Utility Window	1.2	1.2	1.4	£300	£20	£320
Dining Room Window	2.1	1.2	2.5	£ 500	£ 40	£ 540
Front Door	2.0	2.1	4.2	£800	£220	£1,020
WC Window	0.5	0.7	0.3	£ 100	£ 20	£ 120
Lounge Patio Door	3.2	2.1	6.7	£ 1,300	£ 300	£ 1,600
Bedroom 1 Window	1.8	2.1	3.7	£ 700	£ 60	£ 760
En-suite Window	1.2	1.2	1.4	£ 300	£ 20	£ 320
Bathroom Window	1.2	1.2	1.4	£ 300	£ 20	£ 320
Bedroom 2 Window	1.5	1.2	1.8	£ 400	£ 30	£ 430
Bedroom 3 Window	1.5	1.2	1.8	£ 400	£ 30	£ 430
Bedroom 4 Window	1.5	1.2	1.8	£ 400	£ 30	£ 430
House Total			35	£ 7,200	£ 1,100	£ 8,300
Costs/m²				£206		

the world. British windows tend to be side hung and open outwards using a simple stay to hold the window open: perhaps, unsurprisingly, this is at the cheap and cheerful end of the spectrum.

The French make windows in a similar fashion but they tend to open inwards (because of all those external shutters). Almost all German windows use the much more sophisticated tilt-and-turn mechanism, which enables them to pivot open inwards along the bottom edge (tilting) for ventilation purposes or, alternatively, inwards along one side (turning).

North America uses both sliding sashes and outwards opening windows but their windows tend to operate on a screw thread mechanism. If you import windows, you will find these options tend to come as standard (depending on where you are importing from) but you can specify them

as extras on some British designs, if you know what to ask for. However, if you want to stick to traditional British looks, then you will probably want to stick with British furniture though you might want easy clean or projecting hinges, which enable you to reach the outside of the glass from the inside or maybe coloured fittings tickle your fancy.

Most timber windows are available in either a stain basecoat or a white primed finish. The default is the stain basecoat because you can paint or stain on top of that but you will be saving yourself time and money by getting the primed finish if you are going to paint over the top. Just remember that all these options will delay your delivery schedules by weeks so they are only an option if you are planning well ahead. Increasingly, we are being offered pre-finished timber windows, which makes

sense, especially if you are using one of the clip-in cavity lock systems.

ROOFLIGHTS

A word about rooflights and, in particular, Velux windows. They are another form of composite window, being basically timber windows encased in an aluminium cladding, but they have revolutionised loft living by being simple to install, and near-problem-free in operation. Supply-only they cost around £200/sq m including the essential roof flashings, very little more than the standard price for good quality timber or uPVC windows. Velux is not the only company making rooflights but they are the trailblazers and still enjoy by far the largest market share in this specialist market: but watch out for Fakro, a Polish company also reckoned to be very good.

Chapter 7

BARN CONVERSIONS

Conversions usually pose problems quite different from new builds. There may be existing windows to match but more often than not you will be punching new holes in an existing wall and hoping to fit something that looks in keeping with the period of the original building. Incidentally, the expression 'punching holes' is very hip in barn converting circles at the moment, used widely by both planners and architects, so much so that you might be forgiven for thinking that the decision on where exactly to punch those holes is the be-all and end-all of barn design.

As you may have noted, made-to-order joinery tends to cost an arm and a leg and specifying it is one of the factors which makes converting barns more expensive than building new. However, if you want to keep costs down there are a number of options that may be of interest to you (or your planners) that can be bought off the shelf. First, the oh-so-modern looking 'top hung' window can actually look just-so in a barn elevation; certainly less obtrusive than the cottage or swept head styles. Also note that the narrow module casement windows tend to look better than standard-width windows in barn-type buildings.

DETAILING

The Victorians set their windows and doors back into the brickwork. Not only does this decrease the effects of weathering on joinery but it tends to look better as well. However, it is an expensive way of going about things, primarily because it requires a masonry projecting cill underneath and some form of arched lintel overhead, adding perhaps £100 per opening.

Today's volume joinery is made with integral cill sections and is designed to fit just 25 mm back from the outside face of the brickwork. This is easy and cheap – but it also looks cheap, especially in brick facades. Rendered and timbered exteriors normally feature cottagey windows perched on the external face, but traditionally brickwork was associated with recessed joinery. Consider recessing your joinery if you are building in brick or stone:

- it will be cheaper than specifying hardwood in windows
- it will almost certainly look better
- a softwood window, set back, will probably perform better than an exposed hardwood one.

Look at the relative performance of Victorian sash windows and timber or steel casements on 20th century housing. By and large the old sash windows last about 100 years, or three-times as long as exposed casements.

If you live in an area rated severe weather exposure (and this includes all Scotland and Northern Ireland), you will have no choice but to recess your windows into the walls. Note also, however, that if you plan to sit your window deeper than normal, you may not be able to use some of the new cavity closers on offer and you may also have problems with exposed lintels above the window.

If you are engaged on a Passivhaus build, then the placing of the windows in the wall is a critical matter. Get it wrong and you can create horrible thermal bridges which will render your triple glazing and insulated cills next to useless.

EXTERNAL DOORS

Many of the things that I've written about windows apply equally to external doors. Furthermore, there is a polite convention that your choice of door should not clash with your choice of window – a convention that's well worth following whatever your chosen style. As with windows, the door manufacturers tend to stick to pretty conventional ideas and all produce variations on some remarkably similar themes. One of the more daring ideas is to put a little bit of stained glass in the pocket window on some of the designs. By and large, the best that can be said about the design of these doors is that 'it blends in quite well' or 'isn't that unobtrusive?' If you want a door that makes a statement about you – and, after all, the front door is the first thing visitors come into contact with – then you'll have to look to a bespoke joiner's shop or a salvage yard. Either way expect to pay.

MATERIALS

Timber is still the most widely used material for external doors (just) but whereas it once enjoyed a near monopoly it now has to share the field with other materials. As with windows, timber doors are the cheapest to buy off the shelf but they are not universally loved by developers because they are prone to twisting and warping, entailing unwelcome call backs. Switching to hardwood doors is one option but, by all accounts, hardwood doors are almost as likely to move as softwood ones. A reasonable compromise for those who want something better than a softwood door but are not keen on specifying tropical hardwood is to go for hemlock, a durable North American softwood particularly well suited to doors.

What are the other options? All are more expensive than softwood and all share the plus point that they are dimensionally stable – which no timber door will ever be. Steel is the cheapest alternative; widely used in North America, it has an aura of security about it that is perhaps unjustified, since a door is no stronger than its frame (which is usually softwood) or its locks (which are no different whatever the door). Steel takes paint well but is susceptible to bodywork damage just like a car. The most interesting of the alternative materials is GRP – that's glass reinforced fibre or good ol' Glass . It's well established in the garage door market but is now beginning to make inroads into house doors. The wood-grained effect is far more realistic than anything uPVC can achieve and the material can be stained to match other joinery.

GLAZED DOORS

The idea of opening up a largish hole in the house facing the garden is attractive to most of us; it's a sort of poor man's conservatory. You have a basic choice here between sliding doors and hinged ones, which we conventionally refer to as French doors (though the French, more accurately, call them porte fenêtre or window doors). There is not an awful lot to choose between them pricewise, but the overall visual effect can be very different. You see, the patio door is that rarity in new housebuilding, an essentially modern design feature, a sort of junior relative of the glass walled office block.

If you are spending money (lots of it) on creating an olde worlde look, then a set of patio doors – even with leaded lights – is going to look out of place. In contrast, a pair of French terrace doors tends to add a little bit of Brideshead to the elevation; they're nothing if not old-fashioned. French doors may look the part, but the timber ones are notoriously fickle in their behaviour and are a bugger to hang well. Too tight and you'll forever be planing bits off every time it rains: too loose and the wind will whistle through them as if they were wide open.

Patio doors, whether sliding or hung, present security problems. French doors

are also relatively easy to force open; this can be countered to some extent by fitting sliding and locking bolts to both doors, not just the first leaf to open. They are also unusual for external doors in that they open outwards, which leaves their hinge knuckles exposed and vulnerable to being cut off, though there is a little gizmo called a hinge bolt that can counteract this. Patio doors present a different problem in that they have frequently been prised, frame and all, from their moorings; very often they are secured only by three screws at either end.

FOLDING SLIDING DOORS

A more recent trend is the development of folding sliding doors, which combine features of the patio and French door but are used to create much wider openings. Folding sliding doors were first introduced into the UK in the late 1980s and hey mark a logical progression for large glazed openings

The doors run in trackways located both above and below the opening, just like a sliding patio door. However, the individual doors are hinged together so that they concertina into a very small space. This means that virtually the entire door frame can be opened up, unlike patio doors where one section must remain fixed in place. This open aspect appeals to anyone who likes the idea of the house and the garden merging into one on a bright summer's day.

One thing to consider is how the doors sit when fully open, as they must extend either inwards or outwards by the width of a door leaf. The neatest arrangement is usually to have them opening inwards but to do this you ideally want to create a large return space for them to sit against, but this isn't always practicable or feasible. You also have to decide whether to split the arrangement in two so that you have doors closing each side. For easy access, many people chose

to have a solitary 'traffic door' on one side, which acts like one side of a pair of French doors, allowing all the other door leaves to stack up on the other side only when the weather is suitable.

Folding sliding doors are almost invariably made to measure, so there can never be such a thing as a price list. However, generally costs start at around £800 per leaf (door) and rise to around £1400, depending on the materials used, so a seven-leaf door would cost between £6,000 and £10,000. Generally, the more leaves used, the more expensive, so sometimes you can save a little money by specifying a smaller number of wider doors (hint: aluminium door leaves can be as wide as 1200 mm).

HANDLES

Whilst in theory there are innumerable materials that you could use to make door handles from, in practice the range is surprisingly limited: aluminium, wrought iron or brass (or rather brass effect). Aluminium has the reputation for being cheap (though there are some very expensive aluminium fittings available) and brass is the preferred material for most developers, both inside and out. Its styling is usually either Victorian (plain) or Georgian (fancy scrolled edges). Black wrought iron is favoured for the country cottage look, but is out of place on anything else. If you want something a bit different, look out for modern stainless steel designs (check out Allgoods) or even plastic.

HEAT LOSS

With regards to overall heating costs, the role of doors is pretty negligible, largely because their overall area is small compared to other elements in the house. However you have to consider the U-value of your external doors as well as your

Chapter 7

windows. Generally, the double glazed sealed units score rather better than the solid bits of the door so glazed doors – defined as being 50 per cent glazed or more - have lower values imposed on them than solid ones. Anticipate that door suppliers will tweak their product to meet these figures but it may be a problem if you are using a small joinery manufacturer or are importing doors.

INTERMEDIATE FLOORS

The ground floor has been looked at in the previous chapter, Groundworks. Any floors above ground level (inc floors over basements) are referred to as intermediate floors; they act as both floors for the rooms above and ceilings for the rooms below. This makes the issues we need to look at rather different. Intermediate floors only have to be thermally insulated if they are above features like garages; on the other hand, you have to consider sound insulation, which you don't on ground floors.

The structural elements of intermediate floors are pretty similar to ground floors. Obviously, the ground-bearing slab is not an option but otherwise you have the same choice to make between timber or concrete suspended floors. Timber floors are traditional and remain the cheapest option. The main reason for switching to something else is to get better soundproofing. Paradoxically, timber floors don't have to be poor in this department but it's a widely held perception that they will be.

TRADITIONAL JOISTS

The standard way to build intermediate floors in both masonry homes and timber framed ones has been to lay sawn timber joists across the floor. Span tables exist to show you just how deep your joists need to be to avoid flexing unacceptably. Once you get to a span of around five metres, you struggle to find a joist deep enough to cope, so most conventional house designs stick to spans under five metres and place load-bearing walls in the appropriate places to pick up the joists.

There are routines for dealing with openings around staircases – lots of doubling up of joists - and supporting partition walls above – more doubling up. And nowadays chippies join joists using steel hangers. There are also some elaborate rules about just where you should and shouldn't notch and drill holes through joists, rules which are routinely ignored by plumbers and electricians.

To provide stability, the joists need to be braced together: this is achieved with either diagonal struts or solid bridgings. As you can see, whilst the basic idea of laying floor joists is simplicity itself, there are a number of additional factors to consider that make it a whole lot more complex and a whole lot slower than it might be. So much so that the traditional sawn joist floor is rapidly being replaced by….

I-BEAM FLOORS

This is an American innovation, which uses thin, lightweight timber RSJs. Like many building innovations, the I-beam has actually been around for decades. I am reliably informed that there is an estate of houses in Redditch built out of nothing but I-beams in the Seventies. Having never been to Redditch, I'll have to take it on trust. But it wasn't until the mid-Nineties that anyone really started to push I-beams in a big way. That's when Trus Joist MacMillan started advertising them as SilentFloor.

What's the proposition? Well you pay more for an I-beam than you do for a sawn timber joist. Almost twice as much in fact on a linear metre basis. But in return you get a product that takes half the time to install, and is far easier to install services through. Instead of having to drill holes or make notches, you just tap on a preformed knock-out and you are through. And the squeaks? Well, one of the main problems with timber when used in floors is that it shrinks as it dries out. A 200 mm deep timber joist may well measure just 195 mm after a warm, centrally heated winter and this causes not only squeaking floors but can also lead to problems with showers and baths where the mastic seals fail. An engineered I-beam cannot shrink because the web (the upright bit) is made of OSB, or some similar plywood-like board.

I-beams are also capable of spanning up to six metres, which gives them an additional edge. If you are interested in I-beams (and there are now several manufacturers), you have to order in advance, just as you would with roof trusses. They are invariably sold as an engineered solution, made up specifically for your site.

As an alternative to the solid I-beam floor joists, look out for the hollow Posi-Joist, which is gaining popularity and is somewhat easier for stringing services through, especially ventilation ducting.

JOIST HANGERS

How do you sit a timber joist on a wall? You build in on top of your blockwork and then fill in the gaps between the joist ends with odd bits of block: what could be simpler? Well that's how it was done for years on building sites up and down the land. But the energy wonks have cause to believe that this is very sloppy and contributes hugely to unwarranted air leaks. Not only do the brickies take very little care in filling in this void, but then the joists shrink by five per cent or more, as discussed, making air leakage paths almost inevitable.

The building regs require you to pay a little more attention to this detail. They would really like joists (and I-beams) to be hung off external walls using joist hangers, but this is a fiddly detail and builders have been allowed to lay joists onto the walls, provided close attention is paid to mastic-ing around the joist ends to ensure there will be no air leakage. It's a detail that will become far more critical in the future when air tightness testing will be taken seriously. Incidentally, this is unlikely to be a problem in timber frame designs.

SOUND INSULATION

In 2003, I spent the night in a very beautiful detached new house which had cost well over £300,000 to build. Whilst the thermal U-values had been engineered down to amazingly low levels by the use of SIPS panel construction, as far as I could see – and hear – no attention at all had been paid to internal sound-proofing and I could hear all too clearly what was going on in the rest of the house during the night. God knows what they thought of my snoring! The floors were the simplest construction imaginable: hardwood planks over timber joists above a single skin of plasterboard. The walls were just as basic.

Such construction details have caused a lot of problems for a lot of people over the years. It's the simplest and the cheapest floor detail you can build and, over the past fifty years or so, it's got both simpler and cheaper to build. Manufactured boards have taken the place of denser materials and they have tended to grow less dense over time as suppliers strove to drive down costs. It all contributed to a sustained decline in soundproofing standards which many new homeowners have had cause to complain about.

The building regs didn't have anything to say about this trend. They concerned themselves solely with stopping noise passing through party walls and floors between flats and terraced housing. That state of affairs changed in 2004 when Part E, the bit of the regs that deals with soundproofing, was re-worked. But it's a very basic improvement that is called for. You may want to do better. Here follows some costed suggestions; if you want to know more about what a decibel is, have a look at the section in the last chapter entitled Sound Advice.

▓ the naked floor option. Construction - timber joists or I beams, chipboard cover, single sheet of plasterboard underneath. Cost: effectively minus zero as you aren't allowed to build like this anymore. Likely decibel reduction? Around 35 dB on the lab test scale.

▓ the English building reg requirement within the home (E2): adds insulation in joist space and a ceiling board that is slightly heavier than what we have been getting used to. British Gypsum has a product called Wallboard Ten because it weighs 10 kg/sq m, which is the building reg requirement. Cost: zero. Hoped for decibel reduction: 40dB. You can improve this rating a little by putting in more insulation into the joist space. Don't pack it tight – 80 per cent depth is reckoned to be ideal for sound absorption.

▓ add a carpet and underlay above. Dramatic improvement in impact sound going down. Slight improvement in airborne sound coming up! If you really don't want carpet upstairs, add a resilient layer (an acoustic underlay) between the chipboard and the floor cover. Acoustilay and Ecoustic are two brand names costing between £10 and £20/sq m, depending on

your spec. Reduces sound transmission by around 5dB.

▓ use two layers of plasterboard or a heavier building board such as Fermacell on the ceiling. Added cost, maybe £5/sq m. Sound transmission reduction: 3dB.

▓ improve this by a further 2dB by introducing resilient bars, fixed to the underside of the joists. You fix the plasterboard to the resilient bars. These metal strips, costing just 65p per linear metre, act to separate the ceiling boards from the floor joists. Isolation is one of the keys to improving sound insulation. The very best way of building isolation into a floor is to separate the ceiling joists from the floor joists, but this makes for a lot of extra work and a very deep floor void.

▓ add a floating floor above. There are numerous proprietary acoustic floor systems on the market: the insulation manufacturers all seem to make them, as do the plasterboard makers. They are rated either lightweight - aimed at impact noise mainly – or heavyweight. The heavyweight ones are usually made up of layers of heavy board products with names like SoundPlank. Overall, with attention to flanking sounds as well, heavy floating floors will add about 5dB to decibel reduction, cost maybe £5/sq m and add 50 mm to your floor depth.

PRECAST CONCRETE FLOORS

As a complete alternative, you can switch to a masonry floor system. You see an immediate substantial jump in airborne sound reduction between floors, of the order of 15dB, though impact sound reduction requires a bit more thought. However, there is also a substantial cost penalty for switching away from timber or I-beam joists.

As with ground floors, the choice is either a beam and block floor or a hollow core plank floor. The planks are better acoustically but are more expensive and are more taxing to install; they require double thickness supporting walls unless the planks span between external walls. Both masonry systems can perform well but beam and block in particular is prone to catastrophic acoustic failures. Why? Because the blocks get left out. Or taken out to make a path for plumbing or soil stacks. Whatever you make a floor out of, if you start punching holes in it, it won't work.

You also have to pay attention to how best to finish a masonry floor. Underneath, you have a problem in that you need a service void in which to run lighting cables. You can either fix battens into the floor or hang the plasterboard off special clips. Above, you have a problem with the camber on the floor beams and the manufacturers want you to lay a screed. Fine, if you want underfloor heating, but expensive if you don't.

Interestingly, the cost of installing a precast intermediate floor is not dissimilar to improving a timber floor to the standard of a precast one.

SCREEDFLO ACOUSTIC FLOORING

An innovation I first came across in 2008 is a flooring system that combines the simplicity if timber I-beams with an anhydrite screed covering, making it ideal for sound reduction and also underfloor heating. A floor which behaves like a solid concrete floor, designed to be built into a lightweight timber frame construction. I don't know what the price is like yet, but it does represent a bit of a breakthrough in the UK intermediate floor market.

PARTY FLOORS

Having gone into some detail on how to improve sound insulation levels on intermediate floors, it's worth adding that if you are involved in constructing party floors

– that is floors between flats - you have to meet some very tight sound reduction standards. And you will very possibly be asked to have your floor (and party walls) tested to see if they work as designed. See the section called 'All about Noise' in the last chapter to find out more.

Also note a couple of little points. First, carpet still works pretty well as a sound-proofer. I know it's out of fashion but a good carpet laid over a thick underlay does wonders for keeping the noise down, at least as good as many of the other more expensive solutions I have been writing about. And downlighters. Very fashionable, I know. But making holes in the ceiling is bad news noise-wise.

FLOOR FINISHES

The lowest grade of timber floor covering in widespread use, chipboard, is made out of tiny wood particles suspended in a sea of glue. It's around half the price of the much stronger plywood but is not nearly as durable. The NHBC requires that all chipboard used in new housing should be moisture resistant, but this is far from being weatherproof and it is not recommended that chipboard be built into a house before the structure is watertight – but nevertheless it regularly is.

Chipboard is now frequently laid as part of a floating floor: that is to say that it is laid – or rather wedged-in without any fixings at all – on top of polystyrene floor insulation sheets on the ground floor, or acoustic insulation sheets on intermediate floors.

Problems have been encountered with chipboard sheeting curling at the edges and with sheets getting wet and consequently expanding and cracking walls above. In theory, there is much to recommend floating chipboard floors, especially where a carpeted finish is required, and costs are no higher than the traditional cement screed

topping given to ground floors. In practice it pays to use the technique with caution; lay timber battens underneath where extra support is needed such as underneath stud walls, at external doorways and at the foot of staircases.

INTERNAL WALLS & BEAMS

The traditional routine for internal partition walls is to build blockwork walls downstairs and timber studwork upstairs. Internal studwork is a little cheaper and quicker to build than blockwork. By the way, don't assume from this that timber frame houses are cheaper to build than block built ones: the external walls are slightly more expensive to build than their blockwork equivalents.

If you opt for studwork, then you have another choice to make; timber or steel? The use of lightweight steel channel is rapidly gaining momentum with the major housebuilders. When you have people who know what they are doing and a decent sized run of a few houses, then steel framed walling systems are cheaper than timber or block. GypWall is the best known system. Increasingly, we are seeing dry lining gangs offering a steel stud wall installations service as well as plasterboarding.

Which to choose? Well the main issues to consider here are load-bearing and sound. Do you need internal load-bearing walls? Most two storey houses with spans of more than 5 m (which is most of them) will require some way of taking the load of the first floor joists: if the span is more than 5 or 6 m, then you can't run joists (or concrete floors) across the gap without a break, and that break has to be either a load-bearing wall or a structural beam. Now you can have internal load-bearing walls built in

First Floor Square Metre Rates

	Materials	Time in mins	Labour @ £18/hr	M² rates
Joists	£ 7	45	£ 13.50	£ 21
I beams	£ 14	30	£ 9.00	£ 23
T&G Chipboard	£ 5	15	£ 4.50	£ 10
Weatherdeck 22mm	£ 7	15	£ 4.50	£ 12
Acoustic Quilt	£ 3	10	£ 3.00	£ 6
Acosustic Upgrades for Party Floors	£ 18	40	£ 12.00	£ 30
Beam and block (above ground floor)	£ 20	35	£ 10.50	£ 31
Hollow core	£ 30	30	£ 9.00	£ 39
Readymixed cement screed 65mm	£ 8	20	£ 7.00	£ 15
Gypsum screeds 50mm	£ 20	supply and fix only		£ 20
FIRST FLOOR OPTIONS - PER SQUARE METRE				
Timber or I beam floors to 40dB (Part E2)		£ 40		
Timber or I beam floors to Party Floor standard		£ 70		
Beam and Block floor with screed to 40db (Part E2)		£ 50		
Beam and Block floor with screed to Party Floor Standard		£ 55		
Hollow core floor with screed		£ 55		

It's not easy making floor cost comparisons! I have ignored floor finishes altogether, although they are themselves affected by how the sub-floor has been built. I have also ignored the cost of laying services within the floor void - a task much simpler on timber floors than masonry ones, which require some sort of false ceiling below to be added on.

Model House Internal Floor

	MATERIALS	LABOUR	TOTAL
Timber Joists with Acoustic Insulation u 22mm Weatherdeck			
Area 80m²	£1,300	£1,300	£2,600

timber - most timber frame houses do just that - but conventionally you need to add extra support down at foundation level, usually in the form of a trench foundation. So you can see that load-bearing walls are quite a bit more expensive to build than simple partition walls. At roof level, the issue is rarely critical because most roofs are designed to spread the load from side to side, across the wallplates, so no load gets transferred down to internal walls. This is why traditionally internal partition walls are blockwork downstairs and timber stud upstairs. We are beginning to go around in circles!

SOUND ISSUES

Builders instinctively go for blockwork if load-bearing capacity is important. The other reason why they like blockwork is of course soundproofing. Generally a block wall is pretty good at soundproofing between rooms. Until 2004, the building regs didn't address the issue of soundproofing within homes but now they call for a minimum of 40dB sound resistance which, in truth, isn't very difficult or exacting. If you are building in timber or steel channel, you will have to add a little insulation into the void and use a slightly heavier than normal plasterboard (such as British Gypsum's Ten). A greatly improved method is to fix double thickness boards to each face of the wall. Or switch to a much heavier building board such as Fermacell, popular in any event with selfbuilders because it's much easier to finish than plasterboard.

You can go to great lengths to soundproof your bedroom walls but bear in mind that a bedroom is only as soundproof as its weakest link and that's usually the door. Unless you go to the considerable expense of fitting an acoustic doorset, then you'd probably do well not to get too fussed about the whole process. Other design tips are to place built-in cupboards between rooms you want to isolate, and to avoid placing electrical switches and socket plates in noise-sensitive walls.

STEEL BEAMS

Every designer will tell you that you can build rooms to any size that you want – 'your imagination is the limit' or some such nonsense. But they may not explain that once a room gets wider than the normal span for a floor joist you will run into extra costs because you have to fit a beam across the middle to split the loading. This width

varies with the size and frequency of the floor joists, but once you get over 4 m, your costs start to rise substantially. Well, they do if you are working with timber joists: some of the alternative materials mentioned in the flooring section (i.e. concrete precast floors and timber I beams) are capable of much longer spans.

Steel beams themselves are not wildly expensive but fixing them is a lot of work, no matter which method you use. If they are set inside the floor void, the floor joists will all have to be hung off the steel; if the steel is put below the ceiling then it will have to be boxed in with plasterboard.

Steel also needs looking after; it needs a coat of paint and it needs protecting from the threat of fire – usually this is achieved by fixing two thicknesses of plasterboard around it, although there are fire-proofing paints that can be applied as an alternative. Despite its inherent strength, steel is actually one of the

first things to give in a serious fire, so steel beams normally get extra fire protection.

Inserting a steel beam of around 5 m length is likely to add around £300 to construction costs. You will also be required to supply calculations to prove that the beam is adequate for the span: a structural engineer will need to be hired and this may well cost more than the beam itself.

OTHER BEAMS

Timber framers tend to use specialised beams when they want to create wider than average rooms. If you are using a post and beam system of construction such as employed by some timber frame companies like Potton Timber or Border Oak, the solution comes complete with the house as they use the massive post and beam timbers to hang the rest of the house off.

A more usual situation is to use a flitch beam, which is a piece of

1
Engineered joists like these PosiJoists don't twist or squeak like traditional joists and they are very easy to run services through

2
In order to stop unwanted air leakage, the building regs now call for floor joists to be hung off steel joist hangers rather than the more traditional method of building the joists into the wall

steel sandwiched between timbers. Flitch beams can be made up on site and are subject to the same sort of cost provisos as regular steel beams. There are various other types and styles of timber beam available; one worthy of mention is the glulam (pronounced glue-lam) beam that is made up of hundreds of small timber sections glued and laminated together. Glulam beams are rather more expensive than steel on a strength for price basis but they have the big advantage that they look good, good enough to leave exposed even though they look a little too modern for some traditional tastes. Most specialist timber merchants will stock several sizes from around £20-£50 per lin. m depending on girth.

ROOF CARCASSING

There are two major competing

Internal Wall Square Metre Rates

	Basic Materials	Acoustic Insulation	COMBINED Materials	Time in mins	Labour @ £18/hr	Combined
100mm Blockwork	£ 8		£ 8	35	£ 11	£ 19
90mm Timber Studwork	£ 4	£ 3	£ 7	25	£ 8	£ 15
Steel Channel	£ 3	£ 3	£ 6	20	£ 6	£ 12
Acoustic Upgrades for Timber Party Walls	£ 6			30	£ 9	£ 15

Model House Internal Walls

	Area in m²	Rate	Materials	Labour	Cost
Blockwork Walls (downstairs)	70	£19	£600	£800	£1,400
Studwork Walls (upstairs)	60	£15	£400	£500	£900
Rounded Totals			**£1,000**	**£1,300**	**£2,300**

techniques for building roofs. Traditionally, roof timbers were measured, cut and assembled on site – a skilled job involving complex setting-out procedures and cutting lots of obscure angles and notches. Traditional roof carpentry is an art form in itself and it has its own rich jargon involving the likes of rafters, purlins, collars and birdsmouths. However, the rise of the prefabricated roof truss is slowly but surely putting an end to all this. With trussed roofs, the brainwork is done by computer, the cutting by machine and the jargon is reduced to fink and fan, the two commonest truss designs. Erecting a series of roof trusses is generally a straightforward matter – hoist them into place, straighten them up, nail them on and add diagonal bracing.

On a simple rectangular box-shaped structure, roof trusses are about three times quicker to erect than traditional roofs and, because of the inherent strength of each individual truss, they use considerably less timber – usually about 30 per cent less by volume.

Whereas traditional cut roofs are built from sawn carcassing, readily purchased from any builder's merchant, trussed roofing tends to get fabricated by specialists. Not that this should present a problem to builders: provided you can present a set of dimensioned plans, you will get a quote back usually within a few days. You can contact specialists or you can take your plans to any builder's merchant who will do the donkey work for you.

If you choose to build using trusses, bear in mind that prefabricated roof trusses are sensitive things and they perform well only if they are treated well:
▓ care should be taken not to put any twist or undue load on to them, both whilst being handled and when being stored before erection
▓ they should be stored upright on bearers (not n standing on their feet)
▓ they should never be altered on site. They can't be cut around chimneys and openings, so you must get the plan accurately built

Another tip is to set the truss spacings as accurately as possible using a 600 mm spacing. This will pay dividends when

it comes to tacking the metric length plasterboard sheets to the ceilings formed by the trusses.

So why doesn't everybody use roof trusses? Well, mostly they do but there are some situations where the traditional cut roof holds sway:
▓ roof truss manufacturers sometimes get very busy and cannot deliver for several weeks
▓ complicated roof shapes take longer to build whichever system you use and the difference in erection speeds – which is the trusses' big selling point – is much less marked.

Consequently, many builders specify trusses for their main roofs, but prefer to stick with the traditional methods when it comes to odd jobs like building dormer windows, porches or garages.

ATTIC TRUSSES
There is another reason why many builders dislike the trussed roof; it effectively eliminates use of the loft space for anything other than storage. The cross-members, which make up each truss cannot easily

Chapter 7

Jargon Buster

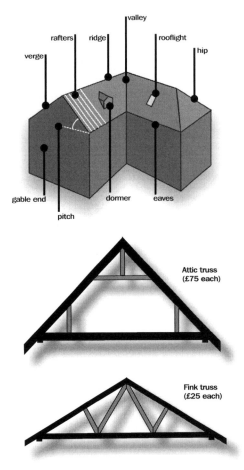

Attic truss
(£75 each)

Fink truss
(£25 each)

be removed or altered and this makes it much harder and more expensive to open up the roof space at a later date. There is, however, the possibility of using specialised attic trusses, which are designed to leave the main loft space open so that any future loft conversion can be arranged with a minimum of fuss and expense. However, whilst the speed of installation is maintained, attic trusses are between two and three times the price of regular ones and this means that they effectively lose their cost advantage over traditionally cut roofs.

ROOM IN THE ROOF DESIGNS

Where overall roof heights are restricted, it is common to build the upper storey of a house projecting partly into the roofspace. When added to an existing dwelling this is usually referred to as a loft conversion but in a new build the convention is to give the upper floor at least a metre of vertical wall before the sloping (or raked) ceiling cuts in. This type of design is sometimes known as a one-and-a-half storey house.

If you are going for a room in the roof design – and many timber frame companies specialise in this style of home – there are a number of knock-on effects which you should be aware of. The internal sloping ceilings on these houses greatly limit what goes on underneath them; beds are usually OK, cupboards are difficult and planning a bathroom in such a space is something you should consider very carefully. You can end up with a lot of expensive dead space; you may like the idea of under-eaves cupboards or a basin in a sloping alcove, but you'll probably live to regret it and end up wishing for convenience rather than character.

When comparing floor space costs, consider space under raked ceilings to be worth just that little bit less than space with full-height ceilings.

The prefabricated roof truss works most effectively when you are designing roofs that sit entirely above the upstairs room space. Then the horizontal section of the trusses can sit directly onto the wallplates at the top of the surrounding walls and form the ceiling joists for the upstairs rooms. When you introduce a raked ceiling you change the truss loadings and start having to use much wider rafter sections, and if you have long sloping ceilings you will have to introduce a midway support beam known as a purlin. In effect you are back to constructing a traditional roof, so again the supposed economies of prefabricated trusses largely disappear.

However, there are roofing systems

Roof Carpentry Costs

Roof areas measured 'in plan': that is to say, the roof pitch is ignored

	Materials	Time in minutes	Labour	Combined
Traditional or cut roof	£ 25	110	£ 33	£ 58
Fink Truss Roof	£ 20	40	£ 12	£ 32
Attic Truss Roof	£ 35	40	£ 12	£ 47
Panelised roof (simple design)	£ 45	12	£ 4	£ 49

Model House Roof Carpentry Costs

Note these are 'in plan' measurements

Plan Area In m²		Materials	Labour	Total
House Roof Area (Trusses)	100m²	£2,000	£ 1,200	£ 3,200

I have simplified the roof carpentry tables right down to four options, and glossed over complexity such as valleys and dormers. Obviously, simple roofs are much easier to build, whichever system you use, but the trusses and panels work best with glorified sheds. This edition's model house used ordinary fink trusses on the roof, where the roof space is not utilised. There is no garage, no chimney, not even a hip or a dormer. It's oh-so-simple.

appearing now which address these problems, replacing rafters altogether with a series of insulated panels stretching from the ridge down to the eaves. It's a variation on the theme of using attic trusses to create an open space in the roof but its selling point is that it is lightweight and quick to install. We are essentially talking about SIPS construction here (see section under Inner Skins, where it's used as load-bearing walling). There used to be specialist SIPS roofing businesses about but these days you would do best to locate a more generalist SIPS supplier/installer.

VAULTED CEILINGS

Some designs call for the room in the roof idea to be extended all the way up to the ridge beam at the apex of the roof. Here you have no flat ceiling area at all. This is a visually dramatic effect, often employed in barn conversions and new oak buildings where you have attractive timber rafters which are worth displaying in their own right. This is a world away from prefabricated roofing trusses, employing techniques of roof design similar to those used in mediaeval times.

ROOF WINDOWS

Once you have opted for a room in the roof design, you have to sort out how you will treat the windows for these rooms. When your natural window height coincides with a sloping ceiling you have two choices. You can 'go with the roofline' and fit a sloping rooflight window or you can 'break through the roofline' and build a dormer.

A dormer window is a fiddly construction. However it is formed, it involves building a sort of miniature house with walls, roof and a window and then joining it seamlessly on to the main roof structure. Whilst this may appeal to the model makers amongst you, harassed builders in a hurry will not appreciate all this intricate detailing.

People buying kit homes with dormers placed on the roof might think that they are avoiding all this hassle, but they will find that finishing dormer details is still a time-consuming business. The roofers have to form valleys and often stepped lead flashings, plasterers or bricklayers have to come back to fill in tiny wall spaces on the outside, and even tacking plasterboard on the inside calls for an ability to think three dimensionally. Another pitfall associated with some dormer designs occurs when they break the eaves gutter line of the main house, which results in extra rainwater downpipes; I have seen various ways

people have tried to disguise this detail but none of them look particularly convincing.

Planners permitting, you can of course forget about dormers and fit opening roof lights. Velux is the big name in this field (though there are several others) and Velux rooflights are very quick and easy to install; on a new building an opening rooflight will cost between £150 and £300 depending on size and will add virtually nothing to labour cost – it taking no longer to install than it does to fit the roof covering over the same space. In comparison, a simple dormer is likely to cost over £1,000. It may well be that your overall desired effect demands dormer windows in your roof and, if so, so be it. Just be aware that these types of windows (like bay windows) are not only expensive in themselves but are also heavy on management time. Unless very well planned out, they are more than likely to cause snags further on down the line.

If you are converting a barn you are likely to find that the planners will not allow dormer windows and will force you to use a rooflight. In response to this, Velux have produced a range of conservation rooflights that are designed to blend in with centuries-old buildings whilst still providing ease of opening and double-glazing expected of modern roof windows.

Chapter 7

These conservation rooflights are however priced at a 30 per cent premium to standard rooflights.

SUNPIPES

For those of you still in the dark, a sunpipe or light pipe is a highly reflective tube that allows you to pipe daylight from a roof down into the house. What you actually see is a transparent dome sitting on your roof and a translucent light diffuser – looking for all the world like an electric lampshade – fitted onto the ceiling of the room below. What you get is a credible amount of natural daylight into the darkest recesses of your home. A medium sized 350 mm light pipe will produce much more light than a 100W bulb even on a dull winter's day and will be adequate to light a room up to 15 sq m. At around £300, they are similar in cost to rooflights but they can have advantages in certain situations - you can bend the pipes round corners if necessary.

EDGE DETAILS

One important detail to consider when thinking about roof designs is how to treat the roof edges. The ridges, hips and valleys will be sorted out by the roofing contractors, but the eaves and verge details are largely a matter of roof carpentry. Here, it makes no difference whether you've built a traditional cut roof or a trussed rafter one; you still have to sort out some sort of effective junction between the roof cover and the underlying structure.

EAVES

There are numerous variations on this theme, none of which is likely to cost less than about £20 per lin m to fix (excluding decorating costs). If there is an industry standard detail it is the closed or boxed eaves. The vertical section is the fascia board: the horizontal bit under it, returning to the wall, is the soffit. One of the emerging trends here is for builders to use uPVC sections. uPVC has all but taken over the guttering and downpipe market and it's a small step to switch from timber to uPVC for the supporting fascia boards as well. Check out Omnico's Cellular Systems. This work is often carried out on a supply and fix basis by specialists.

An alternative is to have open eaves. These are reckoned to look less modern and often more attractive. Some designs dispense with fascia boards altogether and allow guttering to be strapped on to the rafter feet - this is a particularly useful technique to employ with timber barn conversions where a fascia would look out of place - but the more usual method dispenses with just the soffit boards and leaves the rafter feet exposed. An open eaves detail is a little more expensive than boxed or soffitted eaves as you still have to provide a plywood plate (albeit above the rafter feet to catch the felt) and you are left with fiddly finishing details on the exposed underside.

More expensive still is to use the Georgian-style parapet. Here you build your external walls up above the eaves line and collect the rainwater draining off the roof in a hidden lead gutter behind the parapet. This technique was once common in inner-city housing terraces and large country houses, but nowadays tends to look a little bit pretentious – unless you happen to be building a large Georgian-style house.

VERGES

Verges are only found over gable ends, so many houses without gables will have only eaves details. There are, again, two classic treatments of verge junction details. One is to lay the tiles or slates straight on to a bead of cement at the top of the supporting gable wall, the other is to oversail the wall and to finish the roof cover over a (usually timber) bargeboard. Each technique has its merits. The direct method can look horribly cheap but, equally well, is capable of being enhanced by using some fancy dog's-tooth brickwork: the bargeboard method is rather easier to install (it too can be enlivened by adding decorative effects).

VENTILATION

It is surprising to many people that roof timbers do not need to be treated with preservatives (unless you live in a long-horn beetle area, mostly south of London) but you do need to consider moisture penetration very carefully.

For a conventional trussed roof, where the upstairs living space does not project into the roofspace, the ventilation requirements are satisfied by the provision of a 10 mm continuous air gap all the way around the eaves. You might think that this is a very straightforward matter, but there is also concern that a ventilation gap shouldn't become an open doorway to birds and insects, and therefore there has grown up a whole industry making plastic roof vents that let air in and keep bugs out. There are several different types; some are cut into the soffit boards, some are nailed on top of the fascia and some get fixed between the rafters.

RIDGE VENTILATION

When you have a room in the roof design, roof ventilation becomes a more complex problem and care has to be taken to leave an airflow gap between the roofing felt and the insulation surrounding the living space. There is also a requirement for ventilation at the top of the roof, the ridge, and this can be expensive to achieve.

One way of achieving this is to fit a

ventilated ridge, a plastic extrusion which fits under the ridge tiles: this has the advantage of being visually unobtrusive but it comes at a cost of around £20 per lin m, much more than the cost of the ridge tiles themselves. Alternatively there are several formats of ridge ventilation tiles now available: they are invariably expensive – expect to pay between £30 and £50 each – and unlike the dry ridge systems they are all too obvious from the ground.

Roof or ridge vented tiles are also useful with an internal soil pipe or an extract fan that are most conveniently ducted up through the roof space. Glidevale produce the most complete catalogue of roof ventilation and also some of the best solutions for these types of problems.

If you are working with a handmade tile, Tudor Roof Tiles produces an Invisible Venting System that uses the natural camber present on most handmade tiles to provide adequate ventilation space to take the foul air away from extractor fans and soil pipes.

UNVENTED ROOFS

If all this ventilation seems to be more trouble than it's worth, then you'll want to know about other options. In fact, if you were building a room-in-the-roof design then you would also be well advised to use an alternative because they are likely to be cheaper and easier.

If you are building a new house with a pitched roof, you will find that there simply isn't the depth of rafter to stuff insulation in and still have room for a 50 mm vent gap under the roof. But just when all seems lost, Tyvek and the breathable membranes ride in to the rescue. These materials are at once waterproof and vapour permeable and their manufacturers have convinced the authorities that if you specify one of these so-called breathable membranes instead of traditional roofing felt, then you don't need to have the 50 mm vent gap within the rafter space and you don't need to worry about eaves

Contrast these two roofs. Both are 'room in the roof' designs but the one on the right uses attic trusses, while the one above is built on site. They both might have used attic trusses but on the site above the builder was told there would be a delay of several weeks to get trusses on site – so he handbuilt it instead

and ridge ventilation. Although they are expensive compared to roofing felt, you claw this money back by saving on other materials.

It's not quite true to say you don't need a vent gap at all because most designs call for counter battening under the tiles or slates – this effectively gives you a vent gap on the outside of the roof, above the rafter line.

There are many variations on the unvented roof design, sometimes known as a warm roof design. It's complicated in Scotland by the requirement for roof sarking, which is a layer of solid timber boarding traditionally nailed over the rafters, but the insulation manufacturers and the breathable membrane suppliers all have details showing ways of satisfying both the U-value requirements and moisture management – every roof design has to pass what is called a Condensation Risk Analysis.

CONDENSATION PROBLEMS

A little discussed but widespread

Roof Ventilation Detail

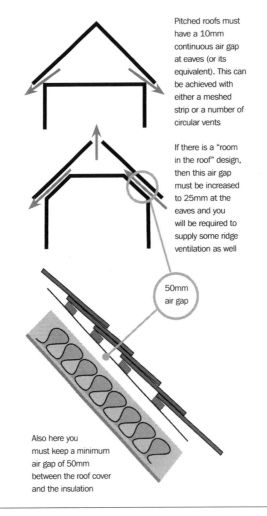

Pitched roofs must have a 10mm continuous air gap at eaves (or its equivalent). This can be achieved with either a meshed strip or a number of circular vents

If there is a "room in the roof" design, then this air gap must be increased to 25mm at the eaves and you will be required to supply some ridge ventilation as well

50mm air gap

Also here you must keep a minimum air gap of 50mm between the roof cover and the insulation

point under the felt where it proceeds to drip down onto the ceiling. It seems to make no difference whether you fit felt or a breathable membrane.

The most effective solution is to build in some form of ridge venting. Combined with the eaves venting, this creates a stack effect that keeps the air flowing through the loft. Without ridge vents, the air inside the loft frequently hangs around for a long time.

Guidance on condensation in new roofs has recently (2011) changed so that it's no longer adequate just to fit a breathable membrane under the roof with eaves vents. High-level or ridge venting is required as well.

ROOF COVERS

There are many different materials you can use to cover your roof but before we go on to examine them, consider first that virtually every housing estate in the country has a concrete tiled roof. Why? Simply a question of cost – concrete tiles are an amazingly cheap way to provide a roof cover and, designed well, they can look very effective. Sometimes but not, unfortunately, always.

Another plus point for concrete interlocking tiles is that they can be laid at very shallow pitches, some at as little as 14°, whereas the more traditional tiles often demand roof pitches of 35°. Low-pitched roofs have two advantages over steep-pitched roofs: their surface area is less – this makes for savings on roofing materials – and they are less visible, therefore the visual impact of any roof covering is diminished. Note, however, that if you are trying to recreate an older style of building, a low-pitched roof will probably look out of place.

CONCRETE v CLAY

In contrast to concrete, a clay tile is seen

problem concerns condensation in lofts. It's a feature of cold roofs where there is unused loftspace. The insulation gets placed at ceiling level, leaving a large mass of air inside the roof but outside the heated envelope of the building. Roofs

such as these require venting at eaves level – already covered – but this isn't always enough to stop condensation. The roof cover itself can get very, very cold, especially on clear cold nights, and the moisture in the air in the loft finds a dew as an upmarket product and people often enthuse about how much better they look but, as ever, it's a question of personal taste. Concrete and clay can look virtually identical when laid – the difference becomes apparent as they weather. After ten years a concrete tile looks washed out, the colour flat, the roof lifeless. In contrast, the look of clay actually improves with age as it develops an interesting patina. Clay tiles hold their value too - see if you can find a concrete tile in a salvage yard.

The price differential between concrete and clay used to be wide but it has been steadily falling in recent years - currently there is a 20 per cent premium for clay.

At the really cheap end, concrete has the market more or less to itself with what are known as large format or interlocking tiles – often measuring 330 x 270 mm, the size of six plain tiles; you don't need very many and this fact alone makes them much quicker to lay. Large format tiles start losing their cost advantage on complex roof shapes with lots of cuts, so you tend to see them on very simple roof designs.

Small format tiles, known as plain tiles, are available from a wide range of suppliers in both concrete and clay. At the top end of the plain tile market come the handmade clay tiles: these are something else and, like handmade bricks, they tend to lend a strong vernacular flavour to any building they are put on. However, handmade clay tiles are also amazingly expensive, costing around five times as much to supply and fix as the basic concrete interlocking tile.

The roof tile market in the UK is dominated by two giants, Redland (now part of Monier) and Marley Eternit. Redland sets the standards to which others aspire and if you want to get a better understanding of the possibilities with tile coverings, you should get hold of their Guide to Roofing; it's free and

it's an incredibly useful booklet which will tell you more than you will ever want to know about roof tiling. It's also available for download from their website. Redland tends to be more expensive than the competition (at least on single site developments) and you may find better prices if you chase Marley roofing or one of the smaller manufacturers such as Sandtoft, Russell or Redbank.

Most roofing contractors have cosy relationships with one particular manufacturer and you may well find that it pays you not to be too picky as to whose tile goes on your roof. Handmade tiles tend to be the province of smaller producers: if you have a deep wallet, look at Keymer and Tudor, who produce visually stunning roof tiles that are brand new yet manage to look at least 200 years old.

If you crave the look of a traditionally tiled roof but your budget doesn't stretch that far, Forticrete produce a large format concrete tile called the Gemini, which simulates the plain tile look by planting a groove down the middle of a large format tile. Slightly more expensive but arguably better looking comes Sandtoft's 20/20 and HF's Beauvoise, imported from France: both are middle format clay tiles.

SLATE

Slate became the preferred roofing choice of the Victorians when the railways provided access to the cheap Welsh slate quarries. The Welsh slate is still there in Snowdonia but it is no longer cheap; indeed it is up there with handmade tiles and thatch as one of the most expensive options for the pitched roof. In rural areas, slate is unlikely to be most people's first choice. However, planners often insist on slate roofs for the flimsiest of reasons and it is as well to be aware of that possibility.

If you want slate but are reluctant to pay the going rate for new Welsh slate there are

a number of other options. You can look to source your slate from Spain or even further afield: prices are much cheaper than Welsh slate but quality has been patchy and it's worth looking out for slate carrying a 30-year guarantee. Alternatively you can track down a supplier of second hand slate. Prices are similar to imported slate and quality is similarly variable but, if you know what to look for, it's relatively easy to assess the quality of a recycled slate and it can make a very good buy. There are also a number of slate substitutes on the market. The cheapest are the fibre cement slates but these are liable to warp and discolour over time.

There are also a number of interesting slate products, usually made out of reconstituted slate dust. Redland produce the best-known reconstituted slate called the Cambrian and Marley Eternit have one called the Melbourn: they are, in fact, not traditional slates at all but interlocking tiles. It is a mid-priced alternative to the natural slates and unimpressive artificials. However, many planning officers will insist on you using natural slates, even though they couldn't tell the difference when laid on a roof.

Then again, you could stop messing around and just fit Welsh slate. The reason it's more expensive is that it's simply better than the alternatives and that's entirely down to geology. If you are looking for a reasonably local, thoroughly natural and incredibly durable roof covering, Welsh slate is the one.

STONE BELT ROOFING

Don't think that you can get away with just a stone facade if you live in an area where stone is the predominant building material. For sure, you will be required to lay a stone tile roof to match your neighbours. Local material prices vary

Roof Cover Costs (supply and fix)m²

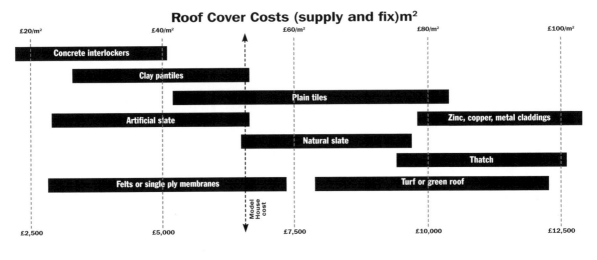

Model House Roof Cover Costs

	Amount	Rate	Materials	Labour	Cost
Spanish Slates	122m²	£ 55	£ 4,100	£ 2,600	£ 6,700

from quarry to quarry but are invariably high. I was quoted 'a penny a square inch' (£16/per sq m) by one salvage yard for Westmoreland slate, which puts it on a par with the other very expensive roof covers you could possibly choose. There are numerous cheaper, artificial alternatives around that will not look in the least bit convincing but using them may save you several thousand pounds. Again you face a tricky task reconciling your budget with the demands of your local planners.

SHINGLES

Another old vernacular stand-by is the cedar shingle. A shingle is a tile fashioned out of cedar wood and is usually supplied in random widths to give a broken up effect. It is a reasonably hard wearing material – though not as good as clay, slate or concrete – and it is used just as often

to do vertical wall panels as it is pitched roofing. Cedar is a naturally durable timber that doesn't require any treatment or staining, and if you covet a genuine timber house then shingles will be your chosen roofing material.

THATCH

This is really one for enthusiasts but new thatched homes are getting built in small but increasing numbers. Not only is it very expensive, but there are numerous regulations about where thatch can go on new buildings. The one that used to trip people up was a requirement for thatched roofs to be at least 12 metres from another house but if you pay close attention to the internal fire proofing arrangements, using a set of guidelines known as the Dorset model, you should find that this requirement can be relaxed. Thatch is

not something that can be added as an afterthought; if you are really serious about it you must design the roof around the thatch. You are more likely to come across thatch if you are involved in renovating or converting.

TURF OR GREEN ROOFS

Turf roofing is vernacular in places like Iceland but in the UK it's distinctly organic. There have been a number of new turf roof houses in the last few years and they always make for very interesting features. No, you don't have to mow them, not if you get your planting right. Their success depends to a large extent on having a top notch underlay and here Erisco Bauder seems to be the company of choice.

I'm afraid I am rather critical of the whole green roof thing. Whilst it may all look rather cool, it's an expensive pain to have to build one, using lots of very non-organic plastic underlays and often having to strengthen the rafters in order to take the extra weight.

SHEET ROOFING

Sheet roofing is often associated with flat roofing and there isn't a great deal of flat roofing being installed today, certainly not in the domestic market. There is nothing intrinsically wrong with flat roofing, but too much cheap felt got stuck on too many cheap extensions in the Sixties and Seventies and the bitter taste of continual roof repairs has yet to fade away.

You might, however, be considering flat roofing for, say, a roof garden or a balcony. Be aware that the durability of a flat roof is almost entirely dependent on how much you spend on it. Mastic asphalt was the first of the manufactured flat roofing materials. A two-layer system, which is hot poured over the roof area, it has many advantages over other systems because it can easily form complex shapes.

Asphalt is also easily repaired and refurbished but its big disadvantage is that it requires hot working with consequent fire risk. It is now often used in conjunction with paving slabs on areas where there will be foot traffic. Because it was relatively pricey, it came to be replaced in the domestic market by felt, or built-up multilayer bitumen impregnated felt to give it its correct title. It was introduced in the 1940s and has been used extensively on flat-roofed extensions during the past 60 years.

Over the years, the product has

been improved: the cheaper systems have a design life of no more than ten years but you can specify better options, which will last three times as long.

In the Sixties, another flat roofing cover was developed, originally made from uPVC but now usually made using a plastic known as TPO. The single-ply systems produced by the likes of Sarnafil have become a major force in flat roofing because they are low maintenance and long lasting.

The other option is to opt for sheet metal coverings such as lead, zinc or copper. Lead is rarely used these days apart from providing waterproofing details or flashings for pitched roof junctions, but the other metals are increasingly being used

Coursed stone tiling: the courses get narrower as you move up the roof. An attractive vernacular feature but time consuming and therefore expensive to achieve

on upmarket projects, usually driven by architects. Zinc is currently in vogue as it's the most neutral colour of the metal roofs, but stainless steel and copper are arguably more durable. None of them will cost any less than £100/sq m, invariably supplied and fixed by specialist contractors.

TILE WEIGHT

Roofing materials vary enormously in weight. For example:

Lightweight slate   20 kg/sq m
Concrete interlocking tile 45 kg/sq m
Plain tile   90 kg/sq m

Does this matter? Well, it matters to the roof designer that the timbers holding up the roof should be strong enough to bear the imposed load but the effect on cost is surprisingly

Chapter 7

Roof Edge and Rainwater Gear Costs – per Linear Metre

	Materials	Time in Mins	Labour @ £18/hr	Combined Rates
Timber Fascias & Soffits	£ 5	45	£ 14	£ 19
Timber Bargeboards	£5	30	£9	£14
uPVC Fascias & Soffits	£ 8	45	£ 14	£ 22
uPVC Rainwater Gear	£ 8	15	£ 5	£ 13
Metal Rainwater Gear	£20	15	£5	£25
Stainless Steel Cappings	£8	15	£5	£13

Model House Costs

	m	Rate	Materials	Labour	Combined
Timber Fascias + Soffits	26	£ 19	£ 130	£ 360	£ 490
Timber Bargeboards	18	£14	£ 100	£ 250	£350
uPVC Rainwater Gear	45	£ 13	£ 350	£ 230	£ 580
ROUNDED TOTAL			£ 600	£ 800	£ 1,400

small, particularly if roof trusses are being used. The cost of using a roof truss system for a heavy roof covering will add about ten per cent to the truss cost – probably less than £200 for a detached house.

FELT AND BATTENS

Building regulations require that whatever (pitched) roof covering you decide on there should be a layer of roofing felt underneath. At a cost of less than 50p/sq m this is no great cost and it has the added advantage for quick builders of providing a temporary waterproof cover for work going on below. Felting takes place simultaneously with battening, which is necessary to provide fixings for the tiles or slates. On all but the largest houses, the whole process of felting and battening usually takes roofers no more than a day and costs around £2/sq m.

Don't make the mistake of felting and battening before choosing a roof covering: the spacing of the battens is set by the gauge of slate or tile and the gauges are very variable. Note that the Scottish practice is to build a solid timber sarking layer on top of the rafters before laying felts: this adds

significantly to the roofing costs but makes a much stronger structure.

Felts are now tending to get replaced by breathable membranes – Tyvek remains the best known but there are many others such as Klober, Monarperm 450 and Daltex Roofshield. Although expensive, two to three times the price of ordinary roofing felt, these membranes enable water vapour inside the roof space to permeate through them thus eliminating the need for other expensive ventilation gear.

ADDITIONAL FITTINGS

As most roofing is carried out by specialist contractors, usually on a supply and fix basis, there is perhaps not the need to know so much about the intricacies of roofing. However, there is a lot more to a roof than slates or tiles and on a typical detached house the actual roof tiles may make up no more than 50 per cent of the overall roofing material costs. The most visible additional element is the ridge and/ or hip tiles (usually around 20 per cent of cost); the underfelt and battens (15 per cent) are the other significant costs.

Ventilation gear, which is often fitted by roofers, is another expensive item.

EDGE DETAILS
HIP TREATMENTS

The hip is the name given to an external angle in a roof – an internal angle is called a valley – and the standard way of finishing a hip is to use something very similar to a conventional ridge tile, although the hipped version is sometimes slightly differently shaped. This is a cheap and quick specification and it is really the only practical way of finishing a concrete interlocking tiled roof. However, if you are planning on a plain tiled roof there is an alternative, which is to fix bonnets, which look very rural and vernacular. However, bonneted hips are way more expensive both in labour and materials (you'll need something like ten bonnets per linear metre as opposed to two hip tiles) and the rate per linear meter works out at over £40. An even more expensive option, which is most often seen on slate roofs, is to cut the tiles or slates to meet exactly over the hip. This is known as a close-mitred hip and it tends to be preferred by those going for neat, unfussy solutions. It is heavy on the old labour and it relies on underlying lead soakers to be effective, which makes it cost in excess of £50 per lin m.

Bonnets and close-mitred hips may sound like unnecessary extravagances, but although they are way more expensive than hip tiles, the total length of hips to cover is often not that much and specifying something different here has a marked effect on kerb appeal.

VALLEYS

Another cost-sensitive area of roofing is the valley, which is formed when two rooflines meet on an internal corner. The valley is not as visually prominent as the hip and this makes it a candidate for treating as cheaply as possible. The commonest way of doing this is by fitting a purpose-made valley gutter and cutting the tiles or slates around it. Here, glass is tending to replace lead; it's quite a bit cheaper and much quicker to lay but labour costs are still significant. Valley gutters cost around £20 per lin m when done in glass, rising to £30 per lin m when finished in lead.

On plain tile roofs there is the alternative of using purpose-made valley tiles. These are very similar to inverted bonnet hip tiles. Again, this is an expensive option − £45 per lin m − but it is worth considering around features like dormer windows where the valleys are visible from the ground.

VERGES

If you are roofing up to a gable wall, you will need to form some effective junction at the verge. The simplest method is to lay a mini-soffit board (known as an undercloak) on top of the brickwork (or timber bargeboard if one is specified), run the roof cover up to the edge of the undercloak and then fill the void between with cement. Such an arrangement costs no more than £3 per lin m to execute and is no different whether the roof cover is slate, tile or stone. There are alternatives − Redland make a concrete wrap-over tile that can be used with certain tile covers and there is even a plastic verge system. However, these other methods all cost around double the cement undercloak technique and they add nothing to the look of your roof edge.

An interesting innovation in this field is a product called Roofblock. This is a masonry alternative to fixing fascias, soffits and bargeboards − i.e. all the roof edge details that drive builders mad. With Roofblock you simply lay a special shaped block on top of the wall and the detail is sorted. It does equally well for eaves and verges.

Three Hip Treatments

Hip tiles, £12/m run

Bonnets, £50/m run

Close mitred hips, £60/m run

DECORATIVE ACCESSORIES

Whilst most fittings are purely functional, occasionally a decorative touch can make a very plain roof exciting. Caught by the general trend for all things vernacular, roofing manufacturers have been busy reproducing Victorian embellishments like cockscomb ridge tiles and fleur-de-lys finials. Handle with care; in the right place these can look fantastic but on most roofs they look plain silly. Similarly, two-tone effect roofing (either with contrasting tile colours or accentuated ridge tiles) is invariably very striking – but that doesn't always mean it works. If you see a roof you like, photograph it and show it to your roofer for quotation. Chances are it will be out of your price bracket!

DRY TECH SYSTEMS

The parts of the roof most vulnerable to weather damage are the perimeter areas like ridges, hips and verges. The traditional way of fixing ridge, hip and verge tiles is to bed them in cement. For some time now the tile manufacturers have been trying to persuade us to use dry systems, which clip together with a series of mechanical fixings, but there is a general reluctance to take up their offers partly because of the higher prices charged for these fittings and partly because the look is even more modern and nondescript than the conventional roof. In Scotland, dry verges are the norm and housebuilders seeking a low maintenance finish are also specifying them – cement fillets on roof edges are notoriously brittle.

RAINWATER

Getting rainwater off roofs and down into the drainage systems is one of the small but very important details that can make or break the appearance of a house. Done well, with appropriate materials, it can add a little to the overall visual appeal of a house. However, done badly, it can ruin a fancy facade. The key to getting the look right is the placing of the downpipes and, as a general rule, the fewer the better.

PLASTIC

The low maintenance, low budget option is plastic (uPVC). There are around half a dozen manufacturers in the UK and they all sell through the builder's merchants. Note that there is a compatibility problem here: even though the designs are very similar, the rival manufacturers' products rarely fit each other, so don't mix and match your guttering. Generally uPVC guttering is available in four colours: black, brown, grey and white. There are also a range of sizes and styles: both half-round and square-box are common plus there are a few more ornate sections such as ogee.

When designing rainwater systems, you have to bear in mind the likely flow rates that naturally tend to vary with the area of roof being drained: if your roof areas are large you may find yourself having to fit more downpipes than you wish and one way around this is to use a larger guttering and downpipe. The manufacturers all hold data to help you specify appropriate sizes. For instance, Osma produce a StormLine gutter section, which will drain over 100 sq m of roof area, as opposed to the 57 sq m maximum specified for their standard RoundLine section. Now, this guttering is over twice the price of the RoundLine, but specifying it can sometimes actually save money by cutting down on both the number of downpipes and the length of underground drainage work.

Fixing uPVC guttering off scaffolding is at best a semi-skilled job easily mastered by a competent DIYer – the manufacturers all have concise installation guides. But note that whilst it is a relatively easy task to do from scaffolding, it can be a very dangerous and difficult thing to undertake using just a ladder. Also you need to pay attention to the brackets used to hold the gutters and downpipes in place.

There is quite a choice available, designed to cope with the whole range of materials that you may have to fix into or around. Note that there are adjustable brackets available, which can accommodate situations where you are unable to fix into your preferred location - very useful when working with uneven surfaces that you might expect to find on barn conversions or stone buildings.

There is a current trend to install guttering and downpipes together with plastic fascias and soffits: it makes sense, as the work takes place in the same locations. There are businesses such as Omnico which produce all the necessary fittings – i.e. rainwater gear and fascias.

There are two perceived drawbacks to using plastic guttering. One is that, as discussed, it all looks a little naff; the other is that it isn't actually any good. uPVC guttering generally, and the rubber jointing gaskets in particular, seem to break down under the effects of bright sunlight and the effective lifespan of a uPVC rainwater system is probably only about 15-20 years. Expect to start replacing bits after this time.

OTHER OPTIONS

All the other options are more expensive but all promise greater durability. The traditional British material used for guttering before the advent of plastic was cast-iron and this is still widely available in a range of period details. It is now mostly used on conservation work and listed buildings. With proper maintenance (which means repainting every five years or so), cast-iron guttering does last a long time – there are many examples of Victorian rainwater systems still in good working order.

Copper is another material, widely used on the Continent. It's very resistant to the elements and doesn't need any painting. Copper of course changes colour over time to eventually achieve a lime-green patina, which will suit some properties better than others. Copper is also used with chain pipes, an interesting technique that does away with the conventional enclosed downpipe and allows the rainwater to run down a chain to the ground - only to be recommended when you

have a good overhang on your eaves.

Aluminium and plastic-coated steel are also used. Aluminium now tends to be the province of specialist suppliers who provide seamless welding. Both these systems are available in a wide range of colours and promise many years' maintenance free

Roofblock is an innovative way of connecting the walls with the roof, a detail which normally takes time and is known to cause problems. Here it's achieved with these pre-formed concrete blocks which are designed to make the tasks of both the brickie and the roofer a little simpler

service.

RAINWATER HARVESTING

There is no reason to stop you putting some of this mildly acidic rainwater to good use before pouring it all away. Many people will be interested in building-in rainwater butts and these can be made much more useful and more productive if they are designed in from the beginning. For around £10, you can add a rain diverter to your downpipes, which will not only redirect your rain into a tank but is also intelligent enough to know when the tank is full and then redirect the rain back down the downpipe. If you want to use the rainwater for domestic purposes – and there's good money to be saved here - you are talking more serious underground storage tanks and pumps. May I refer you to the section called 'Saving Water' in Chapter 14.

HEATING & PLUMBING

ON HEAT

DECIDING ON A heating system is one of the biggest bugbears facing a would-be housebuilder. And it's getting ever more complex, as the better insulated new homes we are building require less and less in the way of conventional heating. It's such a complex field and there are so many options available that it is terribly easy to get swamped by the sheer volume of information. It's all very well saying something smarmy like 'You should choose the system that suits you best' but that doesn't actually make it any easier to know what that system might be. There's nothing for it but to start at the beginning. A little background on the physics of heat will improve your understanding of all the areas discussed. Here answered for you are five questions that you'd never even think to ask.

WHAT IS HEAT?

Heat is a by-product of 'work' going on or, if you like, energy being spent. Heat is most commonly found where one substance is in the process of breaking down into its constituent parts. Our bodies (like our houses) leak heat and this leaked heat must be replaced, which we do by eating (calories are a measurement of energy, there are 13 calories in a kilowatt hour). The colder it is outside our bodies and our houses, the more heat we leak and the more energy we have to take on board to stay warm.

WHAT IS 'FEELING WARM?'

The rate at which we lose heat determines how hot or cold we feel. 'Feeling cold' is a signal that we are losing high and potentially dangerous amounts of heat; 'feeling warm' signals that all is OK.

WHAT DETERMINES HOW WARM WE FEEL?

■ The insulating effect (U value) of our clothes (or duvets, or houses)
■ The temperature of the surrounding air
■ Wind speed (wind chill factor)
■ Level of water vapour around
■ Whether our skin is wet or dry
■ How much heat is being 'given off' (radiated) by surrounding objects (including the sun).

When assessing heating systems, we use air temperature as a shorthand indicator of background comfort but it is important to be aware that air temperature is just one of several factors at play. Anyone who has ever had a thermostatic control dial in their home will be well aware that what's warm on a dry day can be 2 deg or 3 deg C too cold on a wet or a windy day.

Heat transfers via three different methods: conduction, convection and radiation. Conduction is the passage of heat through a solid – the classic example is the poker placed in the open fire that soon gets too hot to hold. Convection is what happens to heat when it transfers into a gas (typically air) – it rises. Radiant heat is the glow you feel on your face when you are standing near a bonfire; the air temperature may be minus 10 deg C but you feel as warm as toast. We don't often feel conducted heat but most heating systems deliver a mixture of the other two, convection and radiation.

Convected heat (or warm air) is characterised by being very responsive – i.e. you feel warm very quickly – but it can also be rather unpleasant, drying the throat and watering the eyes – think of the fan heaters in cars. In contrast, radiant heat you hardly notice. We experience it from things like underfloor heating systems, night storage radiators and Agas. Despite their name, radiators deliver a mix of all three forms of heat. The air convects through them, they are hot to touch (conduction) and you are aware of their warmth if you sit nearby (radiation). All heating systems deliver heat by all three methods but the mix varies according to the delivery system.

SO WHAT'S THE PERFECT HEATING SYSTEM?

I haven't really been much help here, have I? You just need to understand that you must make a series of compromises and your aim is to make the least bad compromise.

WATTS IT ALL ABOUT?

Finally a word about how we measure power output, because I know everyone finds it confusing, not least because there are different systems of measurement in operation. Here I try to plump for one, the watt (W), and its big brother the kilowatt

(kW) which is, as you might hope, 1,000 watts. British Thermal Units (BTU) are an imperial alternative that sometimes still get used in the world of boilers (not to mention America) :

$$1W = 3.41 \text{ BTU}$$
$$1kW = 3,410 \text{ BTU}.$$

These are all measurements of the rate of heat output. However, you will also be frequently coming across the kilowatt-hour (kWh), which is a measurement of heat actually consumed.

The simplest way to understand the difference is to think of an old-fashioned two-bar electric fire: each bar puts out 1kW of heat. If you leave one bar on for one hour, it will have used 1kWh of energy: if you put both bars on, its output will obviously double and that kWh will have been burned in half the time. So its output is measured in kilowatts but the power actually used is measured in kilowatt-hours – output through time.

STANDARD HEATING

All this theory is fine but how well does a standard central heating system stack up? The 'wet' central heating system described below has been pretty much standard in British housing since 1970, both for newbuilds and refurbishments. It may now be under threat from several new fangled systems, but most people would still think of it as the norm. It's still a good place to start.

HEAT LOSS CALCULATION

The plumber usually carries this out on a room-by-room basis, and the results are used to assess the size of the radiators needed in each room. The boiler is sized

up by adding all the outputs of the radiators and adding 'a bit.' As insulation levels have risen and space heating demand has fallen, the critical factor in deciding boiler size is now delivery of adequate quantities of hot water to the taps.

BOILER

The boiler is fitted against an outside wall and the exhaust gases are ducted horizontally outside, by way of a balanced flue. The boiler heats water passing through it and this water is then pumped through the primaries (large copper pipes) and thence to the cylinder and radiators. Or, if it's a combi boiler, directly around the pipes without going through a cylinder of any sort.

CYLINDER

Placed in the airing cupboard, this acts like a giant (bath-sized) kettle for heating domestic hot water (DHW). It starts to empty every time a hot tap is turned on; it is simultaneously filled from a tank of cold water in the loft space which, in turn, is filled from the water main. The cylinder is indirect which means that the water inside it never passes directly through the boiler but rather gets heated at one stage removed by the boiler water passing through copper loops inside the cylinder.

RADIATORS

These are fitted and connected by two copper pipe circuits: one – the flow – takes the hot water from the boiler around the circuit, the other – the return – takes the cooler water coming out of the radiators back to the boiler. A small plastic tank (feed and expansion tank) is placed in the loft which gives the hot water in the circuit space to expand – which it does as it gets hotter. Mains pressure systems are rapidly replacing gravity for delivering hot water around the house, but let's not get ahead of ourselves. More on these later.

CONTROLS

The system is electrically pumped to supply even heat around the house. There is a programmer and a couple of thermostats which turn the system on/off and also switch motorised valves so that the hot water pumped from the boiler can be switched between heating the water in the cylinder or circulating around the radiators. The radiators may also have their own thermostatic valves, or TRVs.

LABOUR CONTENT

In a new four-bedroom house, the pipework and control cabling will be 'first fixed' in three to four days; first fixing needs to take place after the structure is up but before the plastering starts. The 'second fix' (including hanging radiators) will take five to six days. Conventionally, the heating engineer also fits the sanitaryware, does the kitchen plumbing and the above ground waste runs, and all this work tends to get lumped into one quotation and carried out together.

OPEN FIRES

Many large family homes are still built with an open fire in the living room, or a wood burning stove. Despite modern central heating being quite adequate to provide warmth in the most extreme winter conditions, housebuyers are still apparently happy to pay thousands for a real fire. Whereas central heating is regarded in entirely functional terms (fuel efficiency, programmed control, water pressures, etc), the open fire or stove is altogether much more of a romantic dream – and a very potent one. So what if 70 per cent of the heat goes up the chimney and it needs daily cleaning? To the average British household,

a fire in the living room is as fundamental as sex in the bedroom.

Because fires are both expensive to install and largely unnecessary, the current trend is to only see them specified on up-market homes.

THE FABRIC EFFECT

One of the most important things determining your choice of heating system is the energy efficiency of the structure you are trying to heat. The more clothes you wrap around the building, the less heat is required, so the smaller and cheaper your heating system needs to be.

At the extreme end of things – and here we are talking about the most exacting energy efficiency standards around (such as PassivHaus) – you don't really need a conventional heating system at all because 90 per cent of what you require comes from incidental sources; that is people, pets, appliances and lights. And lots of self builders now build relatively low energy homes (some way short of PassivHaus standard) without recourse to traditional central heating.

But don't be sucked into thinking you can build a house without any heating at all. There are times, when it's just so damn cold and nobody is around to provide incidental heat, when you really do have to have some strategy in place to deliver heat around the house.

What you should be aware of is what the heat demand will actually be. This makes it much easier to comprehend how effective the various solutions you chose to look at will be.

RENEWABLE HEAT INCENTIVE

This is a subsidy scheme designed to encourage low carbon heating systems, in particular heat pumps, biomass and solar thermal water heating. It was first suggested

early in 2010 and at time of writing (Dec 2012) only indicative amounts have been published for consultation, but the idea is to pay money on an annual basis to people who install these green-tinged heating systems. .

At the terms indicated, the Renewable Heat Incentive will make it very advantageous to install heat pumps and/or biomass boilers, and conversely the economics of installing conventional gas or oil-fired boilers will take a knock. The problem is that as the scheme is a subsidy, it may a) never see the light of day b) get cut back or c) get turned off at a moment's notice.

I am hesitant, therefore, to recommend that you plan your entire heating system around the subsidy harvest that is the Renewable Heat Incentive. But you should at least be aware of its existence: the scheme is administered by the Energy savings Trust.

WHICH FUEL?

When considering which fuel to use to provide space heating and domestic hot water (DHW) there are a number of considerations:

Availability
- Installation and storage costs
- Capabilities of each fuel
- Fuel costs
- Environmental impact
- Subsidies

AVAILABILITY

Piped gas is currently available to over 70 per cent of UK households, which includes almost all urban areas. However, large tracts of rural Britain and Ireland are deemed too remote to justify laying gas mains and most of these areas will never have the option of a piped gas supply. If in doubt, a phone call to the local office of National Grid

Fuel: Effective Costs Compared

	FUEL COST/KWH	EFFECTIVE COST	APPLIANCE OR BOILER EFFICIENCY
ELECTRICITY			
Daytime Peak Rate	14.5p	100%	14.5p
Off Peak Rate	6.0p	100%	6.0p
Heat Pump (CoP of 4)vvv	14.5p	400%	3.6p
Heat Pump (CoP of 3)	14.5p	300%	4.8p
Heat Pump (CoP of 2)	14.5p	200%	7.3p
MAINS GAS			
Elderly Cast Iron Boiler	4.5p	60%	7.5p
Condensing Boiler	4.5p	90%	5.0p
LPG			
Elderly Cast Iron Boiler	6.6p	60%	11.0p
Condensing Boiler	6.6p	90%	7.3p
OIL			
Elderly Cast Iron Boiler	6.2p	70%	8.9p
Condensing Boiler	5.2p	95%	6.9p
SOLID FUEL			
Wood Pellet	5.7p	85%	6.7p
Coal Fired Boiler	6.6p	75%	8.8p

All figures include VAT at 5%

Fuel costs from Notingham Energy Partnership Jan 2013

will illuminate the situation in your area. Sometimes an initial enquiry will trigger the offer to extend a gas main along a side road.

The other fuels touched on here are available everywhere except the remotest corners.

INSTALLATION
ELECTRICITY

Installation to a new site is charged on a time and materials basis. Even when it's straightforward it is unlikely to be less than £300. However, as its use in modern housing is universal, when considering electricity as a heat source it is effectively there for nothing. An Economy 10 (two-rate) meter can be installed at no extra cost and is generally worth doing even if you don't plan to use electric heating. Three phase supply may be useful if you are considering a heat pump bigger than 12kW.

GAS

British Gas (now National Grid) subsidises the installation costs because they want new customers. If gas supply is adjacent then connection is usually free. Longer distances are possible, subject to negotiation with National Grid new supplies. Beyond a distance of a couple of hundred metres or so, it becomes prohibitively expensive unless the cost of connection can be borne with neighbours.

OIL

The costs are solely to do with onsite storage. Storage tanks are now all plastic and you have a choice of double or single skin. Go for double – they are much simpler, although more expensive. You can make a single skin tank into a double one if you build a masonry bund around it, but it's best avoided. At the moment you may be required to have a double skin or bunded tank if there is a danger that your heating oil would spill out into a watercourse. Single skin tanks start at around £300, double skinned ones are roughly twice the price so that a 2500lt bunded tank costs around £900. If you are building for a largish detached house you would do well to get the large tank size that should be enough to last a year at a time. Other costs you may have to take into consideration are supporting piers, initial placement, measuring gauge, filter, fire check valve and microbore connection to boiler, in all maybe an additional £300.

Recent upgrading of the regulations means that ideally an oil tank should be placed 1.8m from the house and 760mm from a boundary, although if you build a reasonably fireproof structure these distances can be relaxed. Oil tanks are also ugly and their careless siting can spoil an otherwise attractive elevation. They can be buried underground (like a petrol station) but the cost here soars to more than £3,000. Camouflaging with trellis and climbers is a cheaper option but allows access for tank replacement.

LIQUID PETROLEUM GAS (LPG)

Storage tank needs to be 3m from any buildings or boundaries so there are comparatively few sites that it is suited to. Calor Gas is the biggest supplier and they take on full responsibility for installation and maintenance of tanks. They usually charge around £300 to install a tank: this includes pipe laying to the boiler. Note that alternative suppliers such as Shell supply tanks for free - but you are then bound to use them as suppliers. Bulk gas tanks are even more of an eyesore than oil tanks and their placing is a matter that the planners will want to consider − don't plump for an LPG supply as an afterthought, you may be letting yourself in for big problems. Note that, like oil tanks, LPG tanks can be buried

underground but this is likely to cost much more.

SOLID FUEL

This all-embracing term includes just about everything you can burn which isn't a liquid (oil) or a gas. In the 20th century, this list would have included a range of coals and coal derivatives like anthracite but hardly anyone is burning such polluting fuels anymore, at least certainly no one is installing new coal burning stoves. Today we are looking at biofuels, which refers to fuels that are derived from wood or fast growing plants. In particular, there is a growing interest in pellet fuels, which are made of wood compressed to have similar calorific value to heating oil. If you plan to use wood or one of the biofuels, then it is important to build somewhere dry to store it; this takes space but can be an attractive feature in its own right. Balcas, the Irish pellet fuel supplier, likes to "blow in" pellets in 3 tonne loads: you need a pellet bunker to be able to take this much.

CAPABILITIES
GAS

Gas is the preferred fuel for most people and gas is at the leading edge of heating technology. Around 85 per cent of central heating systems run on mains gas and, where it is available, it is the overwhelming choice in new developments (although subsidies are set to change this situation). The market responds to this by making far more gas-burning products available - and at keener prices. Another plus for gas is that it is, arguably, the best fuel for cooking.

LPG

Despite having a tiny fraction of the market (around 2 per cent), LPG versions of many gas boilers are available, though usually around 10 - 15 per cent more expensive −

LPG boilers can be converted to mains gas. Note that LPG can also be used for cooking

OIL

Oil-fired systems account for around 10 per cent of the market overall, and have been much the most popular choice in rural areas where mains gas is not an option. In the past ten years, the dominance of oil in rural areas has begun to wane, challenged by biomass and heat pumps, not to mention cripplingly high oil prices. Oil boiler prices are 20-50 per cent more than gas equivalents, though this is partly because they use the more efficient pressure jet burner which reduces running costs. Oil cannot be used to cook with (unless using an oil-fired range).

SOLID FUEL

Solid fuel heating systems are available as kitchen ranges, living room stoves or utility room boilers. Anything that the other fuels can do, solid fuel can do; compared to the other fuels, though, solid fuel heating is unresponsive, inefficient and plain hard work. Wood-burning stoves struggle to generate enough heat for DHW and wet heating systems combined, but appliances like pellet boilers are quite capable of keeping a large house heated throughout the winter.

ELECTRICITY

This was always looked on as the poor relation in the space heating field. Installation costs were low but running costs were invariably high so it really wasn't widely used, except in flats where flue and chimney options were limited. However, the development of the heat pump market has begun to change the perception of electric heating and as long as oil prices remain high relative to electricity prices, this is a trend that will be likely to continue.

Although heat pump installation is expensive, the running costs are (or should be!) as low as gas.

SOLAR POWER SOURCES

The problem with most of the genuinely renewable alternatives is that they don't provide an all round energy solution: they'll give you some of your hot water, some of your electricity but you will still need some form of fossil fuel backup. For instance, warm water solar panels are, at best, a top-up source that can provide most of the hot water for a UK house in summer and less than 15 per cent in winter. Using solar power is unlikely to save more than 10 per cent of overall fuel bills, whichever system you use for your main heat source.

ELECTRICITY

Electricity is charged by the kWh and so price comparisons are straightforward. Electricity suppliers (RECs) are free to set their own tariffs and there is some variation between them. And since 1999, domestic customers in England, Wales and Scotland have been free to buy their electricity from a range of suppliers - currently over 30 and rising. Check out one of the comparison websites such as UK Power. Not only are there more suppliers but also each has its own tariffs and its own payment options. Your electricity bills can be reduced by careful shopping about, by using as much cheap-rate night-time electricity as possible (look to use Economy 7 tariffs or similar) and by paying your bills by direct debit – usually worth a 5 per cent reduction on its own. You can increase your bills by between 5 and 10 per cent by opting for a green tariff, which promises to match your demand with a similar amount of electricity generated by renewable sources such as solar panels and wind power.

Note that one of the alternative suppliers

Fuel Fudge

This table shows the carbon dioxide emissions of all the main home heating fuels and how they are treated by Part L, the energy efficiency regs.

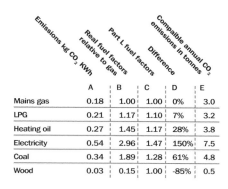

	A	B	C	D	E
Mains gas	0.18	1.00	1.00	0%	3.0
LPG	0.21	1.17	1.10	7%	3.2
Heating oil	0.27	1.45	1.17	28%	3.8
Electricity	0.54	2.96	1.47	150%	7.5
Coal	0.34	1.89	1.28	61%	4.8
Wood	0.03	0.15	1.00	-85%	0.5

A CO_2 emissions in kg per kWh burned.

B how these compare with mains gas, which is the base reference fuel with a score of 1.0.

C how the fuels are scored in Part L. Thus an oil-fired house has to be 17% more energy efficient than a gas-fired one, even though oil emits 45% more CO_2.

D the difference between the real fuel factors and Part L's fuel factors, expressed as a percentage. Note how leniently electric heating is treated.

E the same fudge, expressed in tonnes of CO_2 released per annum, by a new house for its space heating and hot water requirements. Thus even after an electrically heated house has been designed to be 47% more energy efficient than a mains gas heated house, it can still release over 4 tonnes more CO_2 and still beat the regs.

One of the effects of this fuel factor fudge is to make it extremely favourbale for installers electric ground source heat pumps. Heat your home with one of these and passing Part L becomes pretty easy.

Chapter 8

Heating: Key Materials Prices

Gas Condensing Boiler and Flue	£750
Gas Condensing Combi Boiler and Flue	£850
Oil Condensing Boiler and Flue	£1,400
Mains Pressure Cylinder	£600
Primaries/Valves/Pumps	£300
Radiator and Pipework	£70
Heating Controls and Wiring	£200
TRV	£10
Room Thermostats	£60
Elctric Heat Mats	£12 /m²
Underfloor Heating pipework	£15 /m²
Oil Tank	£1,200

Plumber's Key Rates £30/hr

Fit Boiler & Flue	12 hr	£360
Fit Cylinder	8 hr	£240
Fit tanks in Loft	8 hr	£240
Connect Primary Pipework	8 hr	£240
Fix one radiator and pipe	2 hr	£60
Fit Heating Control	6 hr	£180
Fit Individual Room Stats	2 hr	£60
Commission System	8 hr	£240
Place and Plumb-in Oil Tank	6 hr	£180
Lay underfloor heating	20 mins/m²	£10

Model House Heating Costs

	MATERIALS	HOURS	LABOUR	TOTAL
Gas Condensing Boiler and Flue	£750	12	£380	£1,100
14 Radiators	£1,120	28	£840	£1,960
Mains Pressure Cylinder	£600	8	£240	£840
Primaries	£300	16	£480	£780
Commission System		8	£240	£240
ROUNDED TOTALS	£3,000	78	£2,300	£5,300

is British Gas who promise great savings simply by combining the two utility bills. It seems almost fatuous, but apparently something like one hour in four spent working for a utility company is spent collecting the monies it is owed, so there is certainly logic in offering to combine the billing.

GAS

Gas is also billed in kWhs which makes comparison with electricity easy – again, refer to websites such as UK Power. How much of the gas you consume actually ends up heating your house depends on the efficiency of your boiler, hence the variable efficiency ratios suggested in the accompanying table. The comments about combining utility bills apply just as much to the gas industry as the electricity industry and you can now purchase your gas from a number of suppliers, including electricity companies.

LPG

Although there is no tariff as such, Calor Gas – the main supplier – make a charge of around £60 per annum for tank rental. One of the issues with using LPG as a main fuel is that you get tied into an exclusive contract with one supplier, who owns the tank. It's the one fuel where you can't readily switch suppliers. For local prices, check Yellow Pages under Gas Suppliers or Bottled Gas.

OIL

The most common fuel of this type is known as 28-second burning oil, or kerosene. Every rural district has a choice of several suppliers and there are frequently buying co-operatives in place, which can slightly soften the impact of the bills. Note that there is usually a significant seasonal price fluctuation, and having a tank large enough to allow buying once a year - in summer - will lower your fuel bills.

SOLID FUEL

These days solid fuel means biofuels. Transport costs are a big issue here because it doesn't make sense to ship wood long distances just for burning. So either buy

Comparative Heating Costs

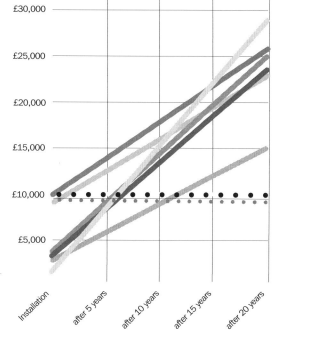

Legend:
- ALL ELECTRIC HEATING
- LPG CONDENSING BOILER
- OIL FIRED CONDENSING BOILER
- GROUND SOURCE HEAT PUMP
- GAS CONDENSING BOILER
- PELLET BOILER

Y-axis: £30,000 / £25,000 / £20,000 / £15,000 / £10,000 / £5,000

X-axis: Installation / after 5 years / after 10 years / after 15 years / after 20 years

This graph attempts to show how the various heating options work out financially by comparing capital costs with running costs. The Renewable Heat Incentive skews the calculations: the capital costs are the same but the running costs are paid back to you by the government.

wood locally or look at pellets, which are compressed wood. If you can track a pellet fuel supplier down and get a price of under £300 a tonne, you have an economic proposition in front of you. Divide the tonne price by 4,800 and you get the cost per kWh. £300 a tonne converts to around 6.25p per kWh, similar price to heating oil. Note, there are worries about wood and pellet prices: if biomass burning at power stations takes off, then prices may just sky rocket, quite unrelated to oil prices.

ENVIRONMENTAL IMPACT
Gas is the cleanest of the fossil fuels in that it produces very little sulphur dioxide or nitrous oxide (the acid rain gases).

It's also efficient in that little is lost in transmission from source to end-user and so its combustion produces comparatively little Carbon dioxide. Liquid Petroleum Gas is a more processed form and results in carbon emissions 20 per cent greater than mains gas.

Oil is a slightly dirtier fuel than gas (acid rain wise) and produces around 35 per cent more Carbon dioxide than gas. Transporting oil around the world is cheap but occasionally hazardous when tankers run aground.

Electricity is a form of converted energy so it is much processed before it enters the home. It is generated in a number of ways – by burning coal, oil, gas and other

fossil fuels, by hydroelectricity, by wind and solar power and, most controversially, by nuclear fission. Some of these are clean, some are not, whilst nuclear power is, paradoxically, both the cleanest major energy source available and potentially the most dangerous. Whatever the merits or demerits of electricity generation, much of its energy is lost in transmission along the national grid, which adds to its expense and reinforces its poor environmental rating. Despite the existence of so-called green tariffs, electricity in all forms is reckoned to produce nearly three times as much Carbon dioxide per kilowatt-hour as mains gas.

Coal, and British Coal in particular, is a dirty fuel, which contributes loads

Plumbing Systems Compared

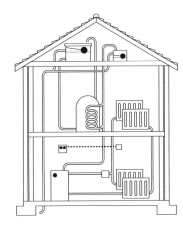

TRADITIONAL BRITISH METHOD
Tanks in the loft and a hot water cylinder

COMBIS
No water storage involved at all. The cold feeds all come off the mains. The hot water is heated instantly as it passes through the combi boiler

of sulphur to the atmosphere. Despite cutbacks in coal mining, it remains the one British fossil fuel with long-term reserves. There may well be a renaissance in coal burning over the next few years: technology moves on and there are ways of consuming coal which don't pollute like the bad old days, but at the moment it's a case of watch this space.

Biofuels also release Carbon dioxide but because the Carbon dioxide has never been fossilized it doesn't add to the Carbon dioxide already in the atmosphere. Therefore they are regarded as a green fuel source. Actually, this view is very contentious. The powers that be regard wood burning as green, but many commentators (myself included) think it would be better if we used wood in buildings rather than gave out subsidies to burn it. Strange world.

BOILERS

Boilers are rated according to the power they can produce. Manufacturers used to work in BTU (British Thermal Units) but now everyone seems to have adopted kilowatts (kW) which are, in truth, much simpler. Just remember:

1kW = 3410 BTU.

A small application - like a one-bedroom flat – might use a 6kW boiler; a large Victorian vicarage would require something in excess of 30kW. A new four-bedroom house built to the latest thermal regulations will need – well read on, it's a bit controversial.

Conventionally, boilers are sized by totalling the radiator output (worked out from the heat calculation) and adding a bit for heating domestic hot water (DHW), and then going to the nearest size above.

This is a bit hit-and-miss, to say the least. For a more detailed explanation of heat calculations, see Chapter 14.

The industry standard is to design heating systems capable of keeping the house around 21 deg C warmer than the temperature outside. Now in a new house built to current regulations, the amount of heat needed to keep the structure 21 deg C warmer than outside is surprisingly small. As a rule of thumb, you need no more than 15 watts per cubic metre of living space. Take a largish 200 sq m five-bedroomed house as an example. It will have around 450 cu m of heated living space and this means that the heating requirement is 6,750 Watts (15 x 450) or 6.75kW. However, any gas or oil-fired boiler fitted into this house is going to be much bigger than this because it has to heat the domestic hot water in a reasonable timespan. A bath or a power shower will drain heat away at a rate of 1kWh every 90 seconds or so, so you would actually require a 40kW boiler to replace hot water as fast as you consume it. Now arguably the best way of counteracting this problem is to store hot water in a cylinder so that you effectively buffer the demand. This means you can afford to reduce the boiler size. Smaller boilers are not only cheaper but run more efficiently. Some newer boiler models are capable of modulating the burner so that they can burn lean and green at around 6kW when they are just being called on to do the space heating, but can also ramp up the power output to 24kW or even 30kW when the hot water tank needs filling. If you fit a decent sized cylinder (say 140 litres), you should be able to use a 12kW boiler and still enjoy hot baths — see later section on Recovery Rates.

BOILER HEAT EXCHANGERS

The old style gas and oil-fired boilers used cast iron heat exchangers and worked by heating this cast-iron, which holds heat well and, in turn, transfers the heat through to the hot water. They were characterised by being easy to install, reliable but inefficient. The cast-iron takes a comparatively long time to heat up and a correspondingly long time to cool down - hence the inefficiency of heat transfer.

Twenty-first century boilers – which include the combi and condensing boilers – are made with copper or other lightweight metal heat exchangers and operate with a much lower water content. Some of them have two heat exchangers, made of different materials. They are more efficient but have to be much more carefully commissioned, and it is vital that the correct corrosion inhibitors are present. They also need more servicing.

COMBINATION BOILERS

A combi has a second heat exchanger in the boiler, which works as an instantaneous water heater, in the manner of the once popular Ascot water heaters, used to heat water bound directly for the hot tap. This second heat exchanger adds 50-80 per cent to the price of the boiler but this cost penalty is clawed back by the elimination of hot water storage (in cylinders), and tanks and associated pipework in the loft. All in all, it is cheaper to install than a conventional system. Combi boilers are now well established in the UK - they account for well over 50 per cent of all new boiler sales - and continental manufacturers like Vaillant and Vokera dominate the market. Low flow rates mean they are not that wonderful for applications such as showers but they are good choices for households with erratic lifestyles, coming and going at all hours. The relatively low water content heat exchangers also mean they need rather more careful commissioning by the plumber and, even so, the heat exchangers scale up in hard water areas. Hard water scaling isn't a terminal problem – you can get the boilers de-scaled – but it won't do any harm to fit some sort of scale-inhibiting device as well.

CONDENSING BOILERS

Condensing boilers, also known as energy efficient boilers, work by having extra large heat exchangers (or, in some designs, a second one) that extract a much greater proportion of the usable energy from the fuel. The exhaust gas comes out at a surprisingly low temperature, usually around 50 deg C to 60 deg C as opposed to 250 deg C on a conventional boiler and as a result the flue pipe from a condenser can be plastic. They also give off a mildly acid condensate which should be piped into the soil stack or to an outside gully. To cope

with the condensation, the heat exchangers are made of aluminium or stainless steel - one of the main reasons for their extra expense. Condensing technology isn't specific to one class of boiler: they can be stand-alones, combis or all-in-one system boilers, wall mounted or floor mounted, gas or oil-fired.

Condensing boilers have been around since the Eighties but it took changes to the building regulations to make us use them. Their market share has jumped from something like 3 per cent in 2002 to 95 per cent in 2010. There are now hundreds of models of gas condensers available and an increasing number of oil-fired ones as well: you can check out models and their efficiency ratings on www.boilers.org.uk.

The key point to grasp about condensers is that they convert more of the gas or oil being burnt by the boiler into hot water to be pumped around the house. The old boilers would convert maybe 75 per cent or perhaps 80 per cent of the fuel into usable heat, the condensers aim to convert more than 90 per cent. The bench efficiencies are recorded on this website.

THE PLUME

One problem that is present with condensing boilers is the plume of water vapour that issues from the waste flue. Its chemical composition is no different to waste gas coming out of conventional boilers but because the gas has been allowed to cool below 54 deg C, the large amount of water vapour present condenses and appears as a white steamy cloud known as a plume. For each kilogram of natural gas burnt, approximately two kilograms of water vapour are produced and a condensing boiler, when working in full condensing mode, can produce about a pint of liquid per hour. Some of this emerges in the plume, some needs to be piped away to the drains. There are certain situations such as flats where the plume has caused problems for neighbours, but in a detached house this should be of minor importance, although it may well be worth locating the flue well away from windows - many condensing boilers allow you to duct the waste gas quite a distance.

GAS SAVER

There is a bit of kit known as The Gas Saver (generically known as Passive Flue Gas Heat Recovery Devices, or PFGHRDS - snappy acronym, if ever) which you can bolt onto the flue of a gas condensing boiler and which extracts heat from the exhaust fumes, and uses this to pre-heat the water coming into the boiler. The company that makes it is called Zenex and it seems it saves something like 30 - 40 per cent of the energy you are pumping out through the flue gases. It costs around £600 and it's compatible with Alpha and Baxi boilers. Google Zenex Energy if you want to know more.

FLUE CHOICES

Where you have a boiler, you must also have some form of exhaust pipe to get rid of the fumes. The flue, as it is known, is actually quite an expensive part of the kit and selecting the right flue is an important step. There are currently three options.

CONVENTIONAL FLUES

This is the old-fashioned, low-tech solution and involves releasing the exhaust fumes into some sort of vertical chimney. However, conventional flues require an intake of air from the outside, which must be built-in somewhere (i.e. you can't just rely on drafts). In a draft-proofed new house it really doesn't make a lot of sense, unless you have a room-sealed boiler or fire — see the section on Wood Stoves and

Chimneys late in this chapter..

BALANCED FLUE

This draws fresh, combustible air in from the same opening through which the exhaust fumes are expelled. Nowadays, this is the preferable option with gas and oil-fired boilers; some balanced flue versions are the same price as conventional flues but most manufacturers add a 15-20 per cent premium. In a new dwelling however, this is almost always going to be much cheaper than building in a conventional flue.

FAN FLUE

Popular in flats where boiler positioning is sometimes difficult. Specifying a fanned flue adds 20-30 per cent to the cost of a conventionally flued boiler, but allows a far greater number of positioning possibilities because the fumes can be expelled a much greater distance.

FLUE POSITIONING

There are masses of regulations about where you can and can't place boiler flue terminals in outside walls: these are in building regs Part J in England. For instance, they shouldn't be less than 300mm below an opening window or under the roof eaves and they shouldn't be less than 600mm from an internal or external corner. Your designer should be aware of these hurdles, but every now and then someone gets caught out and has to reposition the boiler away from its preferred spot. Generally, the regulations are not as stringent for fan flue terminals, and fitting a fanned flue boiler can sometimes be a useful (if expensive) way around an otherwise intractable siting problem.

KITCHEN RANGES

This is an option that appeals to many because of the intrinsic style and feel. The

Aga is the best known, but it is basically just a huge cast iron cooker not a whole house-heating boiler. There are a number of products (e.g. Rayburn, Stanley, Esse, Eastwood) which will fit the bill and provide all three required functions – that is cooking, space heating and domestic hot water (DHW) – from one heat source. The Rayburn Heatranger series is a gas-fired cooker that can provide 23kW of space heating, but is also capable of running on a summer setting that reduces output to around 1kW.

There are limitations in using ranges for all your heating requirements – no mains pressure tanks, relatively unresponsive – but the top models now have electronic time and thermostatic control and Esse even make a condensing model. No way is this a cheap option but if you have your heart set on a cast-iron cooker it is worth considering upgrading to one that does space heating and DHW as well. Having said that, the space/DHW heating capabilities come at a price (£600-£800) for which you could purchase many more efficient gas- or oil-fired boilers as well as more sophisticated controls. It is also little understood that ranges are very expensive to run, whatever the fuel. The gas-fired Rayburn uses around 30,000kWh/annum (cost £1500); this is rather more than the anticipated space heating costs for a large house and nearly twenty times the cost of conventional gas cooking.

OVERHEATING

I have come across one or two examples of people fitting all singing and dancing cast-iron ranges into new houses only to be overwhelmed by the amount of heat they pump out. It's a problem in summer especially when it had been hoped to use the range as a cooker only and yet the cooker won't work without heating up copious amounts of hot water which has nowhere to go except around parts of the radiator system. The better insulated the house, the bigger the problem.

EMITTERS

'Emitters' is a convenient tag to use for the bits of space heating systems that deliver the heat. Go into Plumb Center and ask for an emitter and they'd most likely direct you to the local psychiatrist, but if I just call them radiators (rads in plumber-speak) then I am ignoring all the other weird and wonderful heat emitters that exist. More on those later. Conventional wet central heating systems use rads, so we'll start here.

RADIATORS

These are what go into most central heating systems today and most readers will be all too familiar with them. Functional rather than elegant, there are several well-known makes that tend to compete on price: e.g. Stelrad, Quinn (formerly Barlo), Brugman, Myson, Acova (formerly Worcester), Aeon, Bisque. Plus now there are specialist companies that have sprung up, such as the Radiator Company and Radiating Style. Rather like windows they come in standard shapes and sizes, typically from 300mm to 700mm high and from 500mm to 3000mm long. Most manufacturers produce three or four height options, each available in lengths which increase in 100mm steps. There are also double-panelled and finned versions that give off more heat. Roughly speaking, they produce heat in proportion to their size: the smallest (300H x 400L) will give out 0.25kW, the largest, double-panelled type (700H x 2000L) will give out around 4kW. Having carried out a heat calculation for each room, you will be faced with a choice of shapes and sizes as to how that heat load can be met and here

thought can be given to radiator placing.

PRICING

List prices are, as ever, indicative of where the haggling starts. Discounts off radiators can be huge (60-70 per cent is not uncommon with some manufacturers); look to pay around £50 for each kW of output – discount outlets like Harrison McCarthy can go as low as £40 per kW. Merchants tend to have special offers going and so it pays not to be too fussy as to make. A typical detached four-bedroomed house would use perhaps 15 rads with a total output of 15kW. Piping up the rads with 100m x 15mm copper tube, fittings, valves would cost an additional £300 in materials. Add in thermostatic radiator valves at around £10 each and a bit extra for heated towel rails and the cost sails over £1,000.

ALTERNATIVES

Radiators come in many different shapes and sizes. If you want something different to the bog standard pressed steel, then you can have it. But you will also pay for it. Instead of paying a meagre £50 per kW output, you will be paying out more than £100 and possibly twice as much. Zehnder is a good place to start: this Swiss radiator company doesn't do pressed steel but they do do most other designs: multi-column style (similar to the old cast iron rads), low surface temperature rads (think nursing homes) and sleek die-cast aluminium designer rads in a variety of colours, plus a range of very cute towel rails. All of them well north of £100 per kW output. Another interesting company is Radiating Style who have been shaping and welding all manner of interesting objects into heat emitters for ten years or so, turning radiators into fashion accessories.

Traditional cast-iron radiators are still around and available from an increasing

range of suppliers. In period bathrooms and the like they are just the ticket but they do not come cheap.

SKIRTING RADIATORS

One increasingly popular alternative is to fit skirting radiators. They vary from the functional, rather institutional-looking variety to ones that look every bit as convincing as conventional skirting board. Skirting heating delivers a more even heat than conventional radiators, and yet is just as responsive. However, costs tend to work at over £30 per linear metre and with most detached homes having well in excess of 100 linear metres of skirting, this makes skirting heating an expensive option as a whole house solution. It's probably better suited to renovations. Look out for Discrete Heat.

HEATED TOWEL RAILS

There are hundreds of designs to choose from dozens of manufacturers. Zehnder are still very much a top end option, but even Wickes sells 11 different designs, varying in price from £70 to over £500. And there are several internet outlets which are easily Googled.

In fact, several radiator companies make no distinction between heated towel rails and ordinary radiators. They are, after all, just radiators that happen to be a slightly unusual shape.

UNDERFLOOR HEATING

Available as either water-based (wet) or electric, underfloor heating (or UFH) now widely specified in the UK selfbuild market. The electric systems are most frequently installed as mats in single rooms like bathrooms. Whole houses tend to use warm water piped systems. Overall, its market share in the UK is still small but this is expected to grow dramatically during the next ten years. With an underfloor heating system, the floor itself becomes the emitter and, so as you don't burn your tootsies. The wet systems need to work at lower temperatures than ordinary wall rads and they are very suitable for use with condensing boilers and heat pumps which both work most efficiently at low temperatures. They are mostly laid under a cement screed, which is used as a heat reservoir (like an electric storage heater); this means that the heat is released slowly throughout the day – it is pleasantly draught free and the heat stays close to the floor. Electric underfloor heating is touched on in a following section in this chapter. There are now many businesses offering varying levels of service and most can be found at the selfbuild exhibitions.

Underfloor heating is not a homogeneous product: every system is different and the quotations need to be deconstructed carefully to see whether you are comparing like with like. Watch out to see if significant extras are included – insulation, heating controls, mesh to attach the pipe to. Note that whilst UFH does away with radiators, you still need to find somewhere to fit the manifold - these are large and ugly and are best concealed in a cupboard or a utility area. In cost terms, UFH tends to work out about £1,500-£2,500 more than a standard radiator system in a largish house, pretty similar to using skirting heating or unusual radiators.

UFH UNDER TIMBER FLOORS

Whilst there is some debate about the suitability of UFH under timber floors – wood is regarded as an insulating material – virtually every supplier offers it as an option. There are several methods of installing UFH under timber floors. Some use aluminium plates to spread the heat across the floor: some require a mortar 'pug' to be built as an extra layer in the floor, some use nothing at all, the pipes being clipped to the underside of the floor

after it is laid. Generally the aluminium plate system is rather more expensive than the other systems in terms of materials supplied but the mortar pug system requires a fair amount of extra building work. Some suppliers quote for installation using alternative designs: the mortar pug system usually appears to be significantly cheaper but bear in mind that it will involve other significant construction costs.

PIPE ISSUES

People naturally fear pipe failure with UFH. Suppliers go to great lengths to ensure that the pipe is up to the job, but as it is still a relatively new technique, there is some justification for at least being worried about it. Most warm water UFH is run in PEX pipe, now widely used all over Europe and reckoned to be the safe choice. An alternative is to use one of the polybutylene pipes like Hep2O. It's best to specify one with an oxygen barrier as this reduces the risk of rust getting into the system.

ENERGY SAVING

Many suppliers claim that UFH is inherently energy efficient and will save you money in the long term. I have my doubts. Just because it works at low temperatures, compared to radiator-based systems, doesn't necessarily mean it will cost less to run. You are after all heating up a much larger area, using much more water. When placed in a cement screed, UFH is a very slow response system: it takes a long time to heat up and a long time to cool down. It is therefore best suited to lifestyles where people are around all day; otherwise you end up heating an empty house. Under timber floors the response times are quicker but the efficiency is reduced because of the insulating qualities of timber. Ditto when placed under thick carpets.

One common route taken by

selfbuilders is to run UFH downstairs and radiators upstairs. It makes a lot of sense because a) it's a bit cheaper and b) radiators are not quite such a problem in bedrooms.

DOMESTIC HOT WATER

TRADITIONAL VENTED CYLINDERS

The standard system, used in Britain for most of the 20th century, used a copper cylinder, fed by a tank overhead or in the loft, and heated by copper tubes inside. These tubes transfer heat from the boiler primary circuit to the water in the cylinder: the domestic hot water (DHW) never passes through the boiler at all and thus it is known as an indirect system. All cylinders these days come ready insulated (lagged).

LOFT PLUMBING

In conventional systems, there are two tanks in the loft: one (usually 227lts) feeds the cylinder, the other (usually 18lts) supplies the central heating system. Having to put a tank in the loft – avoiding this is sold as a big plus for other systems – actually costs around £250 for the water storage tank and around £100 for the feed and expansion tank (aka the Jockey Tank). Therefore, any system that does away with all loft plumbing is going to save you around £350.

INSTANTANEOUS HOT WATER

Small instantaneous hot water heaters are still sold but in a new house the normal way of achieving this is by fitting a Combination Boiler (or combi). So many combis are sold in the UK that they are no more expensive than system boilers, despite their capability of heating hot water for the tap as well as space heating. Because of

this, combis have become the cheap and cheerful option for new central heating installations in flats and starter homes.

PLUS: No cylinder; no loft pipework or tanks; hot water on demand, 24 hrs a day; simplified controls; no switching valves needed.

MINUS: Poor flow rate remains the big problem - anything below 15lts per minute is not adequate for a family home and many combis produce as little as 10lts per minute. Also problems with scaling (in hard water areas) in the hot water heat exchanger which reduces flow rates still further.

MAINS PRESSURE HOT WATER

These systems use unvented (i.e. no loft pipework for expansion) hot

There are many methods of fixing underfloor heating pipe. An increasingly popular one on ground floors is to use a plastic backing board into which you press home the pipe, to a designed layout

water cylinders which are strong enough to withstand storing hot water under mains pressure. They answer the problem of low flow rates to showers but a cost of around £500 makes them way more expensive than traditional open vented cylinders and combis. To operate to full effect they need at least 2.5 bar of mains pressure and a mains flow rate of 35lts per minute. Unfortunately, UK water companies are only obliged to provide mains water at 1 bar pressure so many situations will not benefit at all. Phone your water company to determine your local pressure. They come with a whole raft of safety features attached (which is partly responsible for their comparative expense) and a requirement that a qualified person installs them.

PLUS: No loft pipework; mains

pressure hot water delivered to all parts of the house, particularly valued by shower users; a small saving on being able to use smaller bore pipework throughout.

MINUS: Expensive (extra £400 above other options). Don't use with cheap taps: leaks, when they do occur, are much worse when under mains pressure. No back-up storage if supply is cut off. It's worth paying extra for a stainless steel or enamel version if you live in a hard water area.

VARIATIONS

I have outlined three approaches to delivery of DHW. Needless to say there are a number of other options that sort of mix and match these three approaches.

THERMAL STORES

A variation of the unvented hot water cylinder is the thermal store. These systems work by reversing the logic of the standard setup and use a cylinder of hot water to heat cold water channeled through it at mains pressure. Result? Hot water at up to 20lts per minute comes straight out of the hot taps. Thermal stores also usually work without the need for tanks in the loft; instead they come with integral feed and expansion tanks. For a four-bedroom house, expect installation costs midway between using the standard route and using mains pressure unvented systems.

Thermal stores were first developed by British Gas in the early Eighties and are produced by a number of small British manufacturers, notably Gledhill.

Chapter 8

They are particularly good when you want to combine different inputs; e.g. if you have a solar panel or a heat pump supplying hot water as well as a boiler. You can get thermal stores made to order to fit your particular application from a couple of thermal store boutiques, Chelmer Heating and DPS Heatsave. Their downside is that they really need hot water to be stored at 80 deg C in order to get sufficient heat transferred across to the rising main. They also tend to run cold rather more quickly than indirect cylinders and mains pressure cylinders.

SHOWER PUMPS

When all is said and done, the main reason for having mains pressure hot water is to enjoy decent showers - that's the place you really notice the difference. If you want to stick with a gravity system but value a good shower, then you will need to fit a shower pump. There are single impeller pumps that boost the water after the mixing valve, and double impellers that boost both hot and cold before they enter the valve. There is also an increasing number of all-in-one pump and valve shower units. Which you choose is partly dependent on the layout you have. Prices are largely dependent on the power of the pump. They can be purchased for just over £100, but a pump delivering 15lts per minute (equivalent to a reasonable mains pressure system) will cost £180 plus. Most work on a timed switch. Add the costs for extra wiring and fitting and you can see that a shower pump is not a very clever option in a new building, where you would be quids in by starting off with a better DHW system. Leading manufacturers: Mira, Aqualisa.

WHOLE HOUSE PUMPS

A more recent innovation is the whole house shower pump which is a sensible option if you have more than one shower, as the cost is around double that of a single shower pump - look around the £350 mark. The best place to install a whole house shower pump is close by the cylinder which makes the plumbing much simpler.

BACKGROUND

A big bath takes about 70-80lts of hot water and so water storage needs to be above this level (or instantaneous) to be adequate. Hot water cylinders usually hold around twice this amount.

A typical household of four uses between 200 and 250lts of hot water a day, conventionally heated to 60 deg C. Officially. My experience of a household of five, including three teenagers, is that these official estimates are way out of line. The real amounts could easily be double these figures.

It takes 12kWh to heat 200lts of water through 50 deg C (the difference between the temperature of the cold water and the hot water) and the average cost of water heating (by gas or oil-fired boiler) is £250 per annum. Those are the official figures, assuming your notional family uses 5,000kWh per annum on heating DHW. I think, in this age of power showers, a more realistic figure is 2,000kWh per person, which would make it around £100-120 per person in terms of cost.

Just under half of all water consumed in the home is heated.

SHOWERS AND FLOW RATES

A good power shower needs a flow rate of 20lts per minute. This will not be achieved by the conventional gravity-type system. A pump will be required (or else feeble showers endured).

Now our legislators take a very different view. They now regard 20lt per minute showers as an indulgence and have introduced building regs (Part G in England) to restrict shower flow rates. When you build a new house now, you have to account for all the water using appliances and demonstrate that you won't use more than 125lts of water a day for each person in the household. Whereas kitchen sinks, loos and washing machines have a marginal effect on overall volume usage, shower volumes are critical, and so the hunt is now on for low-flow power showers. Which is a contradiction in terms, but there you have it.

The word is that we should be fitting showers of no more than 6lts per minute. Whether this will really satisfy today's teenagers, I have my doubts, but I can give you some pointers.

The Nordic Eco shower is a possibility, and Hansgrohe have a 6lt shower that is said to be OK. Wolseley Sustainable Building Center promotes Mira's Eco handset which, it says, gives a good 6lt shower.

The problem is that unvented hot water systems are set to deliver power showers at 15lts or 20lts per minute. In fact, this is their chief attraction. What is the point of fitting one, if you can't have a high volume shower? You might just as well fit a combi boiler where the flow rate is feeble in comparison. It is unlikely to be much better than 10lts per minute.

Bear in mind that if you are renovating, none of this water calculator malarkey applies. It only applies to new dwellings, so you can fit what you want

RECOVERY RATES

The time taken for cold water from the mains to get to 60 deg C inside the cylinder is referred to as the recovery rate. This rate is dependent on the size of the boiler or the cylinder heat exchanger – whichever is smaller. For instance, a typical cylinder for a four-bedroom house needs 8kWh of energy to heat its 140lts of water from 10 deg C to 60 deg C; an 8kW heater will accomplish this feat in one hour, whereas a 16kW heater will take just half as long. In theory a 32kW heater would achieve the same feat in 15 minutes, but in practice this would not happen unless the boiler was also rated at 32kW, which is unlikely. Here the boiler size becomes the limiting factor in the recovery rate. Unlike boilers, cylinders are not advertised by the size of their heat exchangers; however, some manufacturers sell a 'standard' version which takes about one hour to heat up and a 'quick recovery' version which takes 20 minutes. The latter simply have larger heat exchangers.

EFFICIENCY/HEAT LOSS

All new cylinders are insulated to reduce heat loss to less than 3kWh of heat during a 24-hour period. Effectively, this heat loss can be ignored for six months of the year as it is simply transferring heat from water to space heat; during the summer you might leak something like 500kWh of heat. Many new cylinders (like the Megaflo) are encapsulated by 50mm of polyurethane which reduces heat lost over a 24hr period to under 1kWh – nothing to all intents and purposes.

HOT WATER SOLAR PANELS

A 2-3 sq m roof mounted collector is capable of producing 3,000kWh of hot water for your cylinder during the course of a year, that's maybe equivalent to 500 five minute hot showers for free, albeit between the months of April and October.

The more hot water you use, the better the payback on solar panels. The annual savings are unlikely to be more enormous but subsidies can make solar thermal a very attractive investment. (NB The Renewable Heat Incentive)

Note that to get effective use out of solar hot water panels, you need to have a large cylinder or thermal store, preferably around 50lts per person. The panels tend to produce about 3kW heat at full whack so they require four or five hours to replenish a 200lt cylinder from cold: not quick, but fine if you have adequate capacity. The standard routine is to let the solar panels do their work during daylight hours and then top up the heat in

Chelmer's thermal stores have been at the cutting edge of this technology for many years

the cylinder from your boiler during the night.

You can get more information and possible supplier details from the Solar Trade Association website. Note that if you do want to get any subsidy, you will have to ensure that both the kit and the installers are registered with the Microgeneration Certification scheme.

DEAD LEGS

The hot water piping running between the cylinder and the hot water taps is effectively an extension to the cylinder; water sitting there loses its heat very quickly. An efficiently designed installation would have around 5lts of water sitting in the hot pipes. This may sound insignificant, but bear in mind that every time a hot tap is opened some of this water is replaced and so if every hot tap is turned on just three times a day, then 15lts of extra hot water has to be heated. An inefficient design with much longer dead legs – i.e. bathrooms and kitchen all at opposite ends of the house - might use four or five times the length of hot water pipe. Not only does the cost of supplying hot water to the dead legs then become significant but also you start getting 20-30 second lags between opening the hot tap and getting hot water. Avoid long dead legs if possible.

There is a way around this problem which is to create a pumped hot water loop around the house so that there is always hot water at each hot tap. However you have the added cost of installing and running a circulation pump

Chapter 8

and, to be effective, you have to insulate the hot water pipes to a high standard otherwise you will gain very little.

HEATING CONTROLS

Before the days of central heating (around 1950), heating controls consisted of putting (or not putting) coal on the fire or, at best, an on/off switch on an electric heater. Here is an industry that has grown at a prodigious rate and there is now a bewildering range of options open to the householder. Yet the purpose of controls is quite simple:
- to increase comfort
- to decrease fuel consumption
- safety.

This section concentrates on wet heating systems; other heating systems (warm air, electric, solid fuel) tend to have slightly different control systems, although the logic behind them all remains the same.

PROGRAMMERS

Timers to the layman. These are basically the on/off switch for the whole heating system and, as such, override all the other controls (except safety features like frost thermostats). Digital display has brought big improvements to programmers and now for little more than £30 you can get separate controls for hot water heating and space heating which you can switch on and off 21 times a week. Changing the setting is about as easy as recording a film on the video

– i.e. it helps to be young. Also, plumbers just love being called back to find out why the heating isn't coming on, only to find that you've been messing around with the programmer.

Look for ones with a boost (or 'Extra Hour') facility which allows you to turn the system on at odd times – mostly a standard feature now. A basic electronic programmer is now considered an absolutely essential component of a central heating system. Digital displays are now almost universal, although it hasn't made them easier to use or understand than the older ones with plastic knobs.

THERMOSTATS

Known by plumbers as just stats, these provide a secondary level of on/off switching, controlled by temperature. So if the air or water

Evacuated tubes are a more expensive form of solar hot water panel, contrasting with the flat back panels. The tubes are better at extracting heat on overcast days

temperature is higher than the thermostat setting, these controls will switch the heating system off, even though the programmer says 'run'.

Room stats will cut off hot water to radiators when the set temperature is reached. Placing them requires care. To some extent being replaced by TRVs and programmable thermostats - see below.

Cylinder stats do much the same for the hot water cylinder. Some are integral with the cylinder, some are strapped onto the copper walls.

Boiler stats: Usually integral with the boiler, these set the temperature of water passing through the boiler, which is the hottest part of the system.

Frost stats are a safety device which turns on heating if there is a danger of any components freezing – e.g. boilers in garages or other unheated spaces. It can of course take precedence over a timer which says the system should be off. Malfunctioning frost stats can be expensive to run and difficult to pinpoint.

PROGRAMMABLE THERMOSTATS

These combine the functions of the ordinary programmer (time switching) with that of the room stat (temperature switching). They also allow you to pre-select different temperature maxima for different times of day: very clever but even less user-friendly than the ordinary electronic programmers. A potential energy saver and a potential comfort increaser and no more expensive than a programmer

HEAT PUMPS

Adrian Thurley's Cambridgeshire house, built in 2003, is heated entirely by an Ice Energy heat pump. The heat pump is located in the basement; it's connected to two 200m long pipes that run under the front garden and it is capable of providing 18.5kW of heat, using less then a third of this amount of electricity to do so. It heats the water up to 55degC, to be stored in a large pressurised cylinder. 'It's been fascinating to see it working,' said Adrian. 'I was led to believe that it drew its heat from the ground, which remained at a constant 10degC all year around. But in fact the temperature in the garden loop has changed dramatically through the year, peaking at 21degC in summer and going as low as -1degC in winter. Yet even at -1degC, the heat pump still manages to extract 3deg or 4deg of heat from the pipes. For every one kilowatt of power used in running the system, we get between three and four kilowatts of heat out of it. That's the magic of heat pumps.' It wasn't cheap, costing around £8,000 to install, but part of this cost was offset by a grant of £1,200.

and room stat separately. Whereas ordinary time-only programmers can be placed anywhere that's convenient, once you introduce a thermostat you have to think very carefully about its location and which temperatures it will be measuring.

TWO-ZONE HEATING SYSTEMS
An energy saving idea which splits the space heating into two heating zones – typically upstairs/downstairs – in addition to heating the hot water. It involves using a three-zone programmer such as the Horstmann Channel Plus. Again, the benefits very much depend on lifestyle – i.e. whether you really use your house in a predictable way. If, for instance, you hardly ever went upstairs before 9.00pm then you could have upstairs heating off all day which could conceivably save 10-15 per cent of space heating bills. You could achieve similar results with TRVs but these would need daily manual adjustment. Zoning more complex than upstairs/downstairs is possible, but would probably involve longer and less efficient pipe runs which would tend to cancel out any advantage.

MOTORISED ZONE VALVES

These are what the programmer operates; they are used to switch the flow of hot water around different parts (or zones) of the system. The cheapest systems use a 3-port valve but it is better to use two 2-port valves. The simplest valves switch all water either this way or that and therefore give rise to something called hot water priority, which means that the hot water stops being pumped around the radiators when the domestic hot water is being heated in the cylinder. There are more costly valves that are capable of opening in a middle position which allows a flow of hot water both ways.

A standard set of heating controls (excluding TRVs) for a four-bedroom house would cost around £200. These controls are often sold in packages which usually include a pump, motorised valve, a programmer, a room stat and a cylinder stat. Note that wiring must be provided between all these components.

TRVS

Thermostatic radiator valves (TRVs) are apparently simple little gizmos fitted on to the bottom of radiators that can sense the air temperature and switch off supply to the radiator when satisfied. They are cheap, they increase comfort levels by stopping overheating and they reduce fuel bills. They are now fitted as standard on new radiators.

What's not to like?

Well, there have been problems with the operation of TRVs. Many

people do not understand the principle of thermostatic control and, when feeling cold and seeing a dial, turn the TRVs to 'Max', thinking this will make the radiators hotter. It won't. It simply turns the radiator 'On' at a lower room temperature. Radiators are either 'on' or 'off' — the little TRV dial doesn't make them any hotter, it just changes the temperature they come 'on'. Furthermore, because they require manual operation, there is no way of knowing (other than learning from experience) how high to set them to achieve comfortable space heating in any given room – though note that the latest versions allow you to limit the highest/lowest settings. Mostly people just turn them

Ground source heat pumps are usually laid underneath garden space, at a depth of 1.2 to 1.5m. Conventional wisdom says that the collection area should be around three times the delivery area. Thus a 200m2 heated footprint would require 600m2 of garden

to 'Max' and leave them, which completely negates the point of fitting them in the first place. You might just as well stick with the basic radiator taps which you can turn on and off manually.

Another problem with TRVs is that they are prone to sticking (usually in the off position) and many people have reported radiators not working at all at the beginning of the heating season. I know of someone who took all their TRVs off because they appeared to stop the radiators working at all. Sticking TRVs are often a symptom of having dirty water in the system: if it happens to you, you should get the system flushed and add some corrosion inhibitor.

Fitting TRVs does reduce the

demand on the boiler because, although they won't turn the boiler off, every radiator that turns itself off reduces the demand on the boiler. But a better way of doing this is to have your TRVs working in conjunction with a whole house thermostat (see above) which can override the individual TRVs. This is known as having a boiler interlock. It takes a bit of getting used to, as you don't want the whole heating system to shut down when some rooms are warm and others are cold, but if it's set up right (the positioning of the whole house stat is critical), then it really does save a lot of energy by preventing the boiler from working its socks off when no heating is required.

WEATHER COMPENSATION

Perhaps the most sophisticated of all the domestic heating controls, weather compensation introduces an external thermometer which controls the output temperature of the boiler. If the external temperatures drop, the boiler output increases, and vice versa. The kit is not cheap - costing maybe an extra £150 or £200 - and the claimed for savings are disputed by some, but in theory it should make it cheaper to run boilers, especially condensing boilers which get an efficiency boost if the return temperature falls below 55 deg C and the boiler actually starts condensing.

UNDERFLOOR SYSTEMS

If you want underfloor heating controlled on a room-by-room basis, you have to use wall mounted room stats, which is an expensive option when compared with TRVs.

HEAT PUMPS

Heat pumps are a hybrid heat source. They are run entirely on electricity but they capture additional energy from the external environment, most commonly heat from the garden space around the house (that's ground source) or from the air (air source). They take a few degrees from this low-grade heat and transfer the energy into a smaller volume of water at higher temperatures inside the house. The efficiency of a heat pump system is measured by the coefficient of performance (CoP). This is the ratio of units of heat output for each unit of electricity used to drive the compressor and pump for the ground loop. Typical CoPs range from 2.5 to 4. The critical factors determining the efficiency of the system are the performance of the heat pump itself and the input and output temperatures: the narrower the range of temperature between the source and the house, the more efficiently the system runs. However, heat pumps continue to work effectively even at sub-zero temperatures.

GROUND SOURCE HEAT PUMPS (GSHP)

One of the key advantages of using the ground as a heat collector is that the temperatures stay relatively even over the course of a year. At a one metre depth, the ground temperature in Britain fluctuates between around 5 deg C (in mid-winter) and 12 deg C (in mid-summer); as you go deeper still, the temperature fluctuations disappear altogether. Ground source heat pumps are therefore able to tap into this natural heat store even in the depths of winter and thereby maintain high CoPs throughout the year.

There are three important elements to a GSHP heating system:
1) A ground loop. This is comprised of lengths of pipe buried in the ground, either in a borehole or a horizontal trench. The pipe is filled with a mixture of water and antifreeze, which is pumped round the pipe absorbing heat from the ground. Note that occasionally you are able to extract heat from groundwater directly. Such installations are called water source heat pumps and are usually more efficient than mere ground source ones.

2) A heat pump. This has three main parts:
■ the evaporator – takes the heat from the water in the ground loop;
■ the compressor – moves the refrigerant round the heat pump and compresses the gaseous refrigerant to the temperature needed for the heat distribution circuit;
■ the condenser – gives up heat to a hot water tank that feeds the distribution system.

3) A hot water heat distribution system, no different to a conventional heating system. The house can use radiators but efficiencies are gained by switching to a low temperature underfloor heating system.

HOW MUCH DOES IT COST?

A typical 8kW system costs £6,000-£10,000, plus to the price of the distribution system around the house, maybe another £2,000-£4,000. That's expensive when compared to a gas or oil-fired boiler system, which will set you back maybe £2,500 up to perhaps £4,500 (oil-fired systems are considerably more expensive than gas, partly because of the onsite storage tanks).

PAYBACK TIMES

The issue of payback time is one that is frequently raised by would-be green technology installers. In essence, it's a simple equation, dividing the extra installation costs by the annual running cost savings: if, for instance, a heat pump cost an additional £3,000 to install and it saved £300 a year on fuel bills, there would be a ten-year payback (being £3,000/£300).

Chapter 8

In fact, this example isn't far removed what people who install heat pumps are currently working on: a ten-year payback is reckoned to be pretty good and beats most other renewable technologies.

There are, however, a number of variables that need to be considered, all of which impact on the payback equation.

▓ 1. Fuel costs: essentially you are comparing electricity costs with oil costs and maybe biomass as well. Mains gas is by some way the cheapest option now and you would struggle to justify a heat pump against mains gas on fuel cost savings alone. But with oil at around 50p per litre (translating at perhaps 6p per kWh after boiler inefficiencies are taken into account, then you only need a CoP on your heat pump of 2.0 to make the heat pump win this particular race.

▓ 2. Installation costs: whilst heat pumps are invariably more expensive to install than gas or oil-fired boiler systems, just how much more varies enormously from site to site. It may be £3,000, it could be double or treble. Realistically, all you can do is to obtain quotations for your specific installation and do the calculations after you have some firm prices.

▓ 3. Level of subsidy. At the time of writing, the level of subsidy offered by the Renewable Heat Incentive isn't published, but even if it's small, it's still likely to favour ground source heat pumps over oil or gas.

▓ 4. Demand: The work you require from your heating system is a function of the size of your house, its insulation levels, its airtightness and your lifestyle. By reducing demand, you also reduce the scope for savings in running costs and hence you actually lengthen payback periods for all green technologies.

▓ 5. Actual efficiencies: A good heat pump will easily achieve its stated objective, which is usually to raise water temperatures

in the house by 35 deg C at a CoP of 4. Many systems will do even better than this in CoP terms. But for every 1 deg C extra temperature lift you require, the efficiency of the heat pump drops by around 3 per cent. The temperature lift required is itself dependent on the external ground temperature, which may vary by 10 deg C or more, depending on ground conditions and the depth the ground loop is installed as well as the temperature of the water circulating in the underfloor heating pipes and the storage temperature of your domestic hot water. The effect of increasing the temperature is to reduce the CoP (efficiency) so that the average CoP off a heat pump throughout a year is considerably less than the advertised rate. Obviously, a reduction in the efficiency adds to running costs and hence lengthens the payback time.

Which begs an important additional question. What is the achieved performance of heat pumps? In September 2010, the Energy Savings Trust released the result of a survey of 83 heat pump installations (54 ground source and 29 air source) and found very mixed results. Many were achieving the hoped-for efficiencies (CoP higher than 3.0) but an awful lot weren't and often the CoP went as low as 1.3 – remember an electric fire has a CoP of 1.0! Another data collecting survey I am aware of took place on eight separate installations in Yorkshire and again there was a wide range of outcomes with some ostensibly similar households using twice as much power as others. The best of the Yorkshire sample achieved a CoP of 4, the worst less than 2 – only half as efficient. Two key factors which affect this seem to be the preferred space heating temperature and the demand for hot water: where both these are high, the

CoP is significantly reduced.

USE WITH UNDERFLOOR HEATING
Heat pumps are at their most efficient when delivering relatively low temperatures, typically around 45 deg C. This immediately lends itself to underfloor heating as the preferred delivery method, as this works well at these relatively low temperatures, compared with radiators.

GARDEN SPACE REQUIREMENTS
If you have a large garden, it is cheap to lay pipework in shallow trenches, excavated by digger. But if garden space is tight, there are alternatives available. You can drill a borehole, at an additional cost of around £3,000, which can accommodate all the ground source pipework, in an area as little as 2m x 2m. Ice Energy has also developed a ground radiator collection system that enables large installations to be fed from a single trench. And they have even placed some ground source pipes under the footprint of a new house. Roger Bullivant, the foundation specialists, are developing a borehole system so that you can insert a ground loop at the same time as your foundations are being piled (if of course they are being piled): as the main extra cost of drilling a borehole is getting the equipment on site, this development should reduce the additional cost of a borehole down to near zero.

GROUND CONDITIONS
Trench collectors work best with relatively wet soils, such as clay, where there is a mechanism for the heat taken from the ground to be readily replaced. In dry ground, such as sand or gravel, the ground itself can eventually freeze because the heat being taken out isn't replenished. This, of course, doesn't stop the heat pump working but low ground temperatures do reduce the

efficiency. It can be that the heat transfer from dry ground falls off considerably through the winter, so the best advice is always to get some sort of ground survey undertaken.

COOLING CAPABILITIES

Some systems are capable of being run in reverse so as to provide cooling in summer. Generally this comes at a cost, not only in additional installation fees but in operating efficiency as well. A better option is to pump some of the waste cold air (the fridge in reverse) into cooling units, known as passive cooling. Whilst its not quite as effective as reversing the whole system, it is much less energy hungry.

ADDITIONAL HEAT SOURCES

You may want to harness other power sources to boost your hot water supply. For instance, you may have a stove that can produce hot water, or you may have solar panels fitted. Most heat pumps can accommodate additional heat sources but it is important that the whole hot water supply side is designed correctly at the outset.

SWIMMING POOLS

One of the favorite applications for heat pumps is to provide heating for swimming pools. It's something ideally suited to heat pumps as they work at their best when delivering a constant trickle of heat, rather than a few short sharp bursts which typifies how oil and gas fired boilers work.

DOMESTIC HOT WATER

It's important to assess your domestic

hot water needs carefully because this is an area where heat pumps are arguably not at their best. Most heat pumps are set to deliver around 10kW maximum: this is easily enough to keep even a very large house warm throughout the coldest winter snaps. It is also quite adequate to provide stored hot water for a family. However, the recovery time taken to replace hot water is fairly lengthy in comparison with typical boilers.

The only situation where this is likely to be a problem is if you have heavy use of power showers, which drain the heat out of tanks at between 12 and 20 litres per minute, depending on how hot the water is stored. A heat pump could take an

An air source heat pump at the Milton Keynes benchmark house. This heat pump is being used, primarily, to heat the domestic hot water. Note that the extract from the ventilation system is located right behind the heat pump (it's that square grill in the wall) so that any residual heat being expelled from the house can be recycled through the heat pump

hour or so to replace the hot water, whereas a boiler, rated at 20kWh, would take half the time. If your hot water needs were more modest, then you probably would not even notice any difference.

Again, it is an issue that can be addressed at the design stage. You may be able to install booster heating elements or a secondary hot water storage tank. But the cost, as ever, is a reduced overall CoP.

INSULATION

Standards are becoming progressively tighter but it can't be emphasized enough that the success of heat pump heating systems is very dependent on good insulation levels in the walls, roof, floors and good airtightness levels throughout the house. A really well insulated house requires remarkably little heat to stay warm throughout the winter and by reducing your heat demand, you reduce both the installation costs and the running costs of any heating system you might choose to fit.

NOISE AND SITING ISSUES

Heat pumps behave to all intense and purposes like refrigerators. Although clean – there are no emissions – they are probably best located in a utility room or garage rather than in living space. Most designs work with large water tanks, often around 200 or 300lts, about double the size of a larder fridge. There are very few house designs that couldn't incorporate a heat pump but equally its not something to fit in as an afterthought.

Chapter 8

REQUIREMENT FOR THREE-PHASE ELECTRICITY

Some larger units are best operated off a three-phase supply. The additional cost of three-phase is extremely variable. If it is present nearby, it can often be supplied at no extra cost, and the running costs are identical to normal single-phase supplies. But on some sites the cost of three-phase supply may be many thousands of pounds – effectively prohibitive. In such cases, it is usually possible to work around the supply restrictions.

AIR SOURCE HEAT PUMPS

Seen by some as a poor man's heat pump, the air source heat pump (ASHP) uses the same techniques to pull usable heat from the air, rather than beneath the ground. The immediate disadvantage is that the air temperature is far more variable than the ground temperature and that the ASHP unit is likely to have to do more work, which of course makes it less efficient. However, not having to mess around with pipework under the ground makes ASHP much cheaper to install. Furthermore, advocates of ASHP are moving towards solutions that involve heating tanks of hot water to act as energy batteries for home heating, thus the ASHP doesn't have to work continuously.

There have been many problems associated with ASHP. Not least that in very cold weather, the like of which we have started to get in the UK, air source heat pumps either work so inefficiently that you would do better with an electric immersion heater, or they pack up altogether. However, there are also significant developments in the technology, especially as regards water heating, and products like the Genvex Combi (£6,000 worth of whole house water heater fired by air source heat pump) keep appearing on my radar.

A SWEDISH PERSPECTIVE

Heat pumps are regarded as the standard way of heating homes in Sweden, and have been used widely for 25 years. Partly this is because Sweden has very little fossil fuel and partly also it has good supplies of hydro electricity, which is 100 per cent renewable. The typical Swedish winter throws up temperatures of −25 deg C. Even at this sort of temperature, heat pumps keep Swedish homes comfortably above 20 deg C indoors and also supply all domestic hot water needs. Paul Wurk, a Swedish architect with close connections to the British selfbuild industry via his work with the Swedish House Company, is a keen advocate of heat pumps and finds it hard to understand why we don't use them more often in Britain. 'My 230 $^{sq\,m}$ house is heated entirely by electric heat pump. Although I have a wood-burning stove, I haven't used it for many years. The key to the comfort is the insulation levels we have: my 20 year-old house has 200mm of insulation in the walls and 300mm in the roof and, were I to re-build it today, I would be required to use even more. Even so, my heat pump consumes just 12,000kWh per annum and I reckon my CoP is around 3.'

BIOMASS BOILERS

Modern biomass boilers are not designed to be focal point room fires, but instead aim to replace a domestic gas or oil-fired boiler in a utility space. Many of them are also designed to automate the delivery of fuel, none more so than the wood pellet boilers which can be set up to take fuel from a hopper without human intervention.

Biomass boilers can run on logs, but are more often set up to burn wood chips or wood pellets, which are compressed wood shavings, enabling long distance transportation as a fuel to rival oil. In contrast, log burning only really makes economic sense if the fuel is sourced very locally. Wood pellets are a common form of domestic fuel in some countries (notably Austria and Sweden) and are now becoming widely available across the UK.

Unlike stoves, boilers are designed primarily to heat water, either for space heating or domestic hot water. They are functional rather than elegant, although many models exist which blur these boundaries and would happily sit in a living room.

COSTS

Whereas you can buy wood burning stoves for between £600 and £3,000, biomass boilers tend to be very much more expensive: expect to pay anything between £4,000 and £12,000 for a top of the range, automatic feed boiler.

GRANTS AND INCENTIVES

The Renewable Heat Incentive (RHI) is set to make subsidies available for new biomass boiler installations (as well as heat pumps and solar hot water systems). The original consultation document suggested that biomass heating systems might attract as much as 9p per kWh used for 15 years; this could amount to a subsidy worth £15,000 in total, enough to pay for the installation and the fuel burned. However, the original generosity is constantly being pared down, and in this fast changing field it will do you no favours for me to hazard a guess at what you might actually get. Suffice to say that the Energy Savings Trust website is the place to go if you want current information on the RHI.

SUPPLEMENTARY HEATING

The very essence of central heating is that you don't require anything else to keep you warm. Once your boiler or heat pump has fired up, every room in the house is designed to reach a comfortable temperature within half an hour or so. If you have underfloor heating, the house stays warm throughout the winter whilst you are barely aware you have a heating system at all. And yet self builders still yearn for something more, something a little different, something a little bit less sterile and more social. In short, a fire. The problem is that it's technically challenging to start introducing extra heating into a space that is already adequately heated. What are the options?

OPEN FIRES

Open fires are particularly challenging in modern homes because in recent years there has been much greater emphasis on energy efficiency and airtightness, which makes the installation and operation of a traditional open fire problematic. There are three conflicting requirements at work here:

1 - energy efficiency demands that warm air inside the house isn't allowed to seep out through unwarranted holes in the fabric (like open chimneys!)

2 - ventilation requirements demand that there is a constant supply level of fresh air in a house, enough to keep the air fresh but not enough to supply air to an open fire

3 - an open fire requires a significant supply of air to create a draft in order to keep the fire going and draw the smoke up the chimney. This last point is the killer. An open fire will require a permanently open vent hole of anywhere between

250x250mm up to 500x500mm, depending on the size and design of the fire. That's similar to leaving a window open throughout the winter, not a very appetising prospect when you have just paid a small fortune to insulate and double glaze your new house. This open vent can be sealed up during the airtightness test, so in theory Part L (the energy efficiency regulations) can't stop you having a permanently open vent of this size, but you will be penalised elsewhere by the SAP calculations and have to install expensive additional energy saving features to compensate. It's hard not to conclude that the days of the traditional, Victorian-style open fire are over.

Wood pellets are seen by some as the fuel of the future, but supply is still in its infancy and on site storage also requires some thought

But technology provides a solution — at a cost — by way of the Closed or Room-Sealed Fire. This is a hybrid design, halfway between a traditional open fire and a wood burning stove. It sits within a wall opening and looks like a traditional open fire, but the combustion takes place behind glass in a controlled environment where the air is ducted in and out without ever mixing with the air in the house. The only time the house air mixes with the combustion air is when the glass door is opened for refuelling.

In the past, this wouldn't have been an attractive option because the glass would soon have sooted-up and the pleasure of an open-fire would have been lost behind a wall of blackened glass. But today's clean wood-burners, with their emphasis on energy efficiency, don't release any significant particulate smoke and the glass stays clear, so much so that you are barely aware that the combustion is taking place is a sealed box.

Room sealed fires, such as the M-Design range (costing around £3,300 exc VAT), burn at around 85 per cent efficiency and come with a secondary air ducting system which allows the warm air produced by the fire to be piped around the house.

WOOD STOVES

The wood burning stove is a simpler way of achieving the same thing — having a focal point fire in a centrally heated, near airtight house. Wood burners are available in wide range of styles and a huge price range — anything from around £300 up to nearly £10,000. Whilst the principle remains the same — i.e. to burn wood in a controlled way in a metal container — you do tend to get what you pay for and at the top end of the range, you are buying sleek modern designs with incredible burning efficiencies.

The market has also subtly changed. Stuart Vialls of Anglia Fireplaces commented to me: "Ten years ago, I couldn't sell a dedicated wood burning stove, it had to be a multi-fuel one. Now nobody ever considers burning coal — everyone wants a wood stove." There is a technical advantage here in that a dedicated wood-burning stove tends to burn wood more efficiently and therefore more cleanly. People are also much more interested in the efficiency of the stove which means that products like the German Xeoos stoves, boasting a 95 per cent efficiency level are gaining traction, despite the £3,500 (exc VAT) price tag.

As with the room-sealed fires, there is an issue with air supply to wood stoves. The trend is towards room-sealed supply as well, as no one wants a permanently open vent hole in their living room. The cheaper, traditional wood stoves are designed to work in environments with free air flow and will not suit a new house built to current airtightness standards, so the air supply is a critical factor to assess, if you are considering a wood stove.
But there is a supplementary issue to be resolved here as well, because every time you open the door to reload, the smoke wafts out into the room — the so-called spillage problem. In 2012, I was shown a solution to spillage — a new stove design from Chesney's called the Passiv (retailing at around £1200 plus VAT) which cleverly redirect the airflow when the door is opened to redirect the flue draft. It still

leaves some complex flue arrangements to sort out, but gradually the wood stove seems to be responding to the airtight house.

SOURCING WOOD

Wood burning is the height of self build fashion at the moment, but it's not without its issues. For one thing, wood prices are increasing as rapidly as other fuels, especially now that it's being subsidised for use in power stations. In addition, the current generation of super-efficient fires and stoves depend on burning properly dried timber if they are to achieve their desired effect. Most local timber suppliers are selling green timber which has been felled recently and has a high moisture content. Ideally this needs to be stored for 18 months or two years before it's dry enough to burn. If you haven't got time or the capacity to do this, then you should really be buying kiln-dried wood, but this is much more expensive — often double or three times the cost of a regular load.

Of course, if you have the time and space, the best thing is to create a covered wood store where you can buy two years ahead and dry your own fuel, topped off perhaps with an internal storage feature close to the fire where you can finish off the logs before you put them on the fire. A word of warning: you may be tempted to create a wood store at the front of your house — it can be a very attractive feature — but with rising wood prices this may become a target for organised theft, so it advisable to situate your wood store away from prying eyes.

HANDLING THE OUTPUT

A modern, highly-insulated home requires very little heat to keep warm and you may well find that your "little fire in the corner" ends up overwhelming you and has you

rushing to open all the available windows to cool down. This is especially true if you have installed an underfloor heating system whose output cannot easily be turned down.

One possible solution is to choose a stove with a back boiler, a water-heating element, that can use excess heat to meet some of your domestic hot water demands. As a rule, back boiler stoves use far more fuel (around 75 per cent of the output goes into heating the water) and you may not fancy having to reload so frequently.

Another option is to arrange for the heat output to be ducted around the rest of the house, either in a dedicated system or via a mechanical ventilation system. If it's the latter, make sure that the designers know what your aims are because the register next to the fire needs to be an outlet rather than an inlet.

BUYING TIPS

▓ Don't oversize the stove. Stove outputs are rated in kW and, in an existing older house, 1kW will heat something like 14 cu m of room space. But in a well-insulated new house, a 4kW stove may well be enough to heat the entire house. Several self builders have successfully based their entire home heating strategy on using a mechanical ventilation system with heat recovery to waft around the heat from a 3 or 4kW wood stove. But it doesn't always work: note, ventilation systems are not heating systems and they are usually set up with the living room as an inlet, not an outlet, so the idea that heat from a stove will magically be distributed around the bedrooms is fanciful.
▓ Chimney or flue? In an existing house, you may well be able to use the chimney but ensure that it's swept and free of obstructions. In a new house, you will probably want to fit a stainless steel flue, which is cheaper than a chimney.

▨ Smoke Control Areas: many local authorities now have smoke control areas. Google "Smoke Control Areas" to find out if you are in one. You can still fit a wood stove in a smoke control area but it has to be a clean-burn one if you want to burn logs, or a multifuel stove on which you burn smokeless fuel.

▨ Check out the Log Pile website (www. nef.org.uk/logpile), an online database of stove, boiler and fuel suppliers.

IT DOESN'T HAVE TO BE WOOD!

If all this sounds like too much work and too much expense, you can cheat and install a gas (if you have gas) or electric fire. They remain very popular, though mostly in renovations rather than new builds, and, as with wood stoves, there is a new emphasis on energy efficiency. Gone are the days when people were happy to let three-quarters of the heat escape up the chimney or through the flue, just so they could enjoy the look of a fire. The latest range of Gazco E-box gas fires look and work in similar fashion to the room-sealed wood fires in that the burning takes place behind glass, and they also achieve superb efficiency outputs, similar to a condensing boiler. Another big advantage is that a gas fire doesn't require a chimney — it can work on a balanced flue located directly behind the appliance. With a cost of around £750 (exc VAT) it represents an attractive option if you are on mains gas.

Electric fires are even cheaper and don't even require a flue to operate. However, the flames are never terribly convincing and the cost of operation is always going to be a factor, as electricity costs two to three times as much as gas or wood.

ELECTRIC HEATING

Information about electric heat pumps can be gleaned in the previous section. Here I take a look at the common but non-garden variety of electric heating, the night storage heater, the convector heater, electric boilers and various forms of electric underfloor heating.

Electric heating has one or two things going for it and one very big thing going against it. That big contra-thing is the cost of electricity, by far and away our most expensive fuel source. Not surprising really, as it is still predominately made by burning fossil fuels, mostly coal and gas, and there are large inefficiencies in converting fossil fuels into electricity, not to mention piping it for thousands of miles around the country.

Against this high price, electricity suppliers have held up a trump card, being cheap night-time tariffs. These exist because they can't turn off the nuclear power plants at night and so they have all this power pumping around the system with nowhere to go, so they sell it off cheap as electric heating. Enter the world of off-peak night-storage heating: it is the most uncontrollable, unresponsive heating system ever designed, delivering the bulk of its heat when it's hardly needed. Not to mention the fact that night-storage heaters are usually dog ugly.

To counteract these failings, the supply companies have additional tariffs with off-peak rates for three hours in the afternoon, known as Economy 10 tariffs because they give you a ten-hour split charging period. Also, they now tend to recommend electric underfloor heating topped up with ceiling heaters, which are designed to run on the new Economy 10 tariffs. These developments represent a big improvement in the outlook for electric heating: the pluses that apply to wet underfloor systems apply just as strongly to electric heating. Yet as long as oil and gas remain half the price, straightforward electric heating is unlikely to be many people's first choice.

GREEN ELECTRICITY TARIFFS

Environmentally, electricity is often thought of as a dirty fuel because its production is mostly from fossil fuels burned rather inefficiently and what production doesn't come from fossil fuels comes from nuclear power stations, a few windfarms notwithstanding. But for the past ten years or so, you have been able to buy 'green electricity' from all kinds of sources. Whilst the supply you actually get is identical to normal electricity, the idea is that, for a small premium, you match your usage with renewable supplies. Thus, instead of having to go to the hassle of mounting photovoltaic cells on your roof or putting a wind turbine in the garden, you can get a supply of renewable energy over the grid. On this basis, many people have opted for electric heating systems, feeling that they are not only cheap to install but cause no environmental damage whatsoever. If only. My view is that these green electricity tariffs are an illusion and they actually promote the use of all forms of electricity, whereas a more considered approach would be to reduce electricity demand wherever possible. There is currently a rapidly rising demand for renewable electricity but the cause of this rise is 99 per cent down to government intervention. There is, therefore, a rigged market for renewables and this makes them very expensive, which in turn not only makes buying green electricity a pointless gesture but a very expensive one as well.

WARM AIR

Warm air or forced air heating systems work by blowing heated air around the house in a series of ducts. All you see of it are inlet and outlet grills, usually a pair per room. It's the most common form of heating in American homes but in Britain it's fallen right out of favour after many systems fitted in the Sixties and Seventies proved to be noisy and ineffective.

I don't think any private developers have fitted warm air heating systems into new homes since about 1985. Johnson & Starley are the only firm left producing warm air units in this country, mostly satisfying the retrofit market. They work with a conventional flued, floor-standing gas-fired boiler. The system must be installed by a registered installer and would cost around £4,000 for a four-bedroom house. This would include a gas-fired boiler and all the ducting to push the hot air around the house, but domestic hot water (DHW) would have to be supplied by other means. Perhaps a more serious candidate for selfbuilders is the US firm Unico who are offering a forced air unit which combines with air conditioning. They are usually present at the major selfbuild shows and can be linked up to many different kinds of heat source, including heat pumps.

VENTILATION

Buildings need to be ventilated. Trapped water vapour in particular can be very damaging, causing condensation and encouraging mould growth and wet rot. It's a potential problem in both the external structure of a house - especially under ground floors and in roofs - and the enclosed living space.

The building regulations deal with the need for ventilation in both areas. Underfloor ventilation (only applicable with suspended ground floors) is by way of air bricks; roof ventilation is by eaves or soffit vents and occasionally air bricks too.

The building regs dealing with internal ventilation (Part F in England) specify that habitable rooms must have opening windows fitted with trickle vents (more on these later) and that kitchens, utility rooms and bathrooms must have extractor fans (or 'adequate means of extraction'). A cooker hood ducted to the outside is acceptable in a kitchen or else there must be an extractor fan capable of shifting 60lts/s (litres/second); the utility room requires a fan capable of shifting 30lts/s, the bathroom fan 15lts/s, equivalent to a small bathroom full of air in about ten or fifteen minutes. A separate toilet used to be able to make do with just an opening window but, since 2005, a small fan is also mandatory.

STANDARD SOLUTIONS
Fit trickle vents in the windows. Extractor fans in kitchens and bathrooms.

TRICKLE VENTS
These slimline plastic inserts have now become nearly universal on standard joinery - indeed it is a problem to find windows without them. Trickle vents, which can be open or closed from inside, are slotted into a hole drilled out of the head of the window. Some manufacturers still charge £6 extra for fitting them, some supply windows with just the slots cut out and supply the vents separately at around £6 each.

COOKER HOODS
Normally fitted as standard in kitchens, although they don't have to be ducted outside – they are said to 'recirculate' if they don't. It makes very good sense to make sure your cooker does duct directly outside as it works much better and saves the cost of a second, more powerful extractor fan. Cooker hoods are usually sold as part of a package with hobs and ovens. They start at around £50: automatic versions with humidity controlled switching are available at around £100, but the current

fashion if for rather grand stainless steel ones which typically cost £300 upwards.

BATHROOM FANS
A basic, 15lts/s, fan can be controlled by a pull switch, or linked to a room light switch. Bathrooms without windows have to have models fitted with automatic overrun timers, and where ducting is required a centrifugal fan is recommended. Higher up the range, the fans have humidistats which can automatically switch fans between off, low and high settings dependent on humidity in the bathroom. And at the top

The typical cost of these measures on a four-bedroomed house is around £500, though the trickle vents may not be readily costable, because they are hidden in the charge for windows

WHOLE HOUSE SYSTEMS
MECHANICAL VENTILATION (MVHR)
The building regs allow for radically different approaches to ventilation. One is to do away with trickle vents and to provide both extract and inlet ventilation via a series of ducts controlled by electric fans. A number of manufacturers produce units that will recapture some of the heat being sucked out of the house, mixing it with fresh air being brought in through the loft. A new house has such high insulation levels that the fabric (i.e. walls, roof, floor) lose comparatively little heat. If careful attention isn't paid to airtightness and ventilation, then much of this saved heat will just trickle away. Typically, between a third to a half of the space heating bill goes on replacing unwarranted ventilation.

Enter the mechanical ventilation system with heat recovery (or MVHR). The unit usually sits in the loft and draws fresh air in through a duct and passes it across the outgoing warm air so that the heat is absorbed. It then pipes the warmed air into the 'dry' rooms (living rooms, bedrooms) and the system is balanced by sucking out the warm air from the 'wet' rooms (kitchen, bathrooms). An MVHR system will cost at least £2,500 to install and as much as £50 per annum to run because it is powered by two electric fans on continuously; in addition there will be occasional servicing costs. In terms of power saved v power used (known as the efficiency ratio), heat recovery systems perform reasonably well but, when costed, it turns out that the power saved usually costs about 5p per kWh, whereas the electricity to run the unit is costing around 12p per kWh, so don't expect to save money by installing one. In response to this, manufacturers have been introducing systems powered by low wattage fans (such as VentAxia's HR200V) which improve the overall returns.

When pressed, most manufacturers will admit that the economic return is negligible but will still insist that there are benefits in increased comfort levels. The move towards airtight homes also tends to be accompanied by the use of controlled ventilation systems, and the ultra-low energy Passive Houses all come with mechanical ventilation with heat recovery as standard. In fact, the PassivHaus standard demands mechanical ventilation with heat recovery. When a house starts to get really airtight, you need mechanical ventilation to keep the indoor air quality acceptable. In fact, none of the other ventilation systems cut

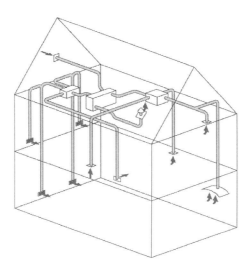

the mustard in this respect.

PASSIVE STACK VENTILATION

This is another option that can be used if you are interested in whole house ventilation. Passive stack ventilation also uses ducts to extract stale air from the house but there the similarity ends. Trickle vents are fitted in all the dry rooms (i.e. living rooms, bedrooms) whilst ducts run from the wet areas (bathrooms, kitchens) up to a vented ridge tile; air pressure does the rest, drawing air in through the house and away through the roof. A whole house system (with four passive stacks) would cost around £1,000. Add a cooker hood (which is recommended) and the overall cost will be around 60 per cent more than the standard route.

There are currently two passive stack suppliers, Passivent and Aereco. Passivent have a couple of variations on the basic module

Installation layout for whole house mechanical ventilation. There are four extracts and five inlets, enough for a small house

including a system that introduces humidistats on both the inlets (trickle vents) and the extract grilles. This effectively cuts down excessive air-changes as the vents close below a certain level of humidity. Strictly speaking, this would seem to be contrary to the building regs standard that half an air-change per hour should take place throughout the house, but humidity levels are a good indicator of the level of use a room is getting (people produce water vapour) and no one seems to be complaining. The 'intelligent system' with humidistats costs around £250 more than the ordinary stack system, by now nearly double the standard route - although still half the price of mechanical heat recovery. For around £400 above the standard solution, you get a system that works without anything mechanical to go wrong and introduces an element of heat saving.

GROUND TO AIR VENTILATION

(aka Earth Pipes) Earth pipes have been used in a number of countries over the years, but only recently introduced to the UK. The system consists of a single length of pipe made of conductive antimicrobial material approximately 200mm diameter laid 1.5 or 2m below ground in a loop around the house or in the garden. One end terminates in a stainless steel tower (about 1m high) where the air is drawn in and the other links up with the supply ducting for the heat recovery unit (or vent supply fan). The costs vary depending on the size of the house: the smaller kits are priced at £2,000 and the largest at £4,000 – this is in addition to costs incurred for installing a mechanical ventilation system.

Why fit earth pipes? They have a marginal positive effect on the efficiency of mechanical ventilation systems when running in heating mode, but they come into their own as a method of passive summer cooling, where the incoming air drawn into the system can be up to 5 deg C cooler than the external air temperature.

COOLING

There are home air conditioning systems available in the UK but whilst new housebuilders show increasing interest in more and more sophisticated ways of staying warm during the 20-odd week annual heating season, there is limited interest in staying cool during the 10-week high summer period.

Why? Well for a starter, it is expensive. An air conditioning system for a detached house would set you back in the region of £5,000. A one-room system would cost around £1,500. The existing models are all electrically powered and a whole house model would consume around 3-5kW of power when going at full blast – typically it would run for only 50 per cent of the time, even on the hottest of days, providing you remember to keep the doors and windows shut. The units also tend to be noisy, though this problem can be reduced if the design of the installation is good. Like boilers, air conditioning needs to have exhaust ducting and this means that the system has to be built-in permanently and is connected to an outdoor unit. To my knowledge, there are no portable air conditioners that you could move around the house with you.

Some of the heat recovery units and some heat pumps offer an air-cooling facility; the Villavent 4 unit provides

something called comfort cooling – it will not turn the house into a fridge like the ones in American homes, but will be able to drop incoming air temperature by several degrees. And some heat pumps can run in cooling mode as well.

Generally, it is felt that cooling isn't really necessary in the UK climate if the design is well-executed. One problem to avoid is solar over-heating in the summer months, the sort of effect that you see in conservatories. Large south-facing glazing may sound like a wonderful idea on paper but it is likely to be quite unpleasant to live with during July and August.

HYBRID HEATING-VENTILATION SYSTEMS

Thus far I have tried to nail everything down into neat boxes. Thus we have heat pumps products, cooling products, ventilation products and water heating products. But you don't have to dig very deep to see that there are degrees of overlap here and that, not surprisingly, there are new products which don't fit into these neat boxes. I've already mentioned heat pumps that can cool as well as heat. There are also ventilation systems that incorporate heat pumps and thus turn them into warm air heating systems.

Take, for instance, the Genvex Combi, an interesting piece of kit that sells for around £6,000. It's a big box which uses an air source heat pump to draw heat from the exhaust air coming from your mechanical ventilation system, and uses this to provide hot water and some warm air heating for your house.

I've seen it installed in a low energy housing development in Somerset and have to say I was quite impressed.

There are others. The PassivHaus standard – which demands whole house ventilation systems – seems to be

encouraging the development of a number of compact air handling units which also provide a small element of heating using heat pump technology to achieve this. If you build a very low energy house, like a Passive House, then you really don't require very much in the way of a conventional heating system, and these ventilation bolt-on heaters seem like a good way forward. The only proviso is that these solutions are certainly not yet mainstream and you may end up being something of a guinea-pig if you fit one.

FIRES & CHIMNEYS

Look around any 21st century housing scheme and you will see lots of clean-cut roofs, with rarely a chimney in sight. That is because chimneys are expensive to build, and stoves or fires are quite unnecessary in a modern, centrally-heated home. Penny pinching developers, quite logically, omit them. If there is a chimney, the chances are it will be a dummy made of GRC (Glassfibe Reinforced Concrete), or some other lightweight material, put there at the insistence of the local planning department.

But self builders sing to a different hymn sheet and most of them long to have a focal point fire. Top of the self build pops is the wood-burning stove, combining as it does elegance and efficiency. Others seeking more convenience will go for a gas fire or, less frequently, an electric fire. Very few people now choose to burn coal in an open grate – it's gone right out of fashion.

Whereas a gas fire can often be fitted with a through-the-wall balanced flue, a wood burning stove or a solid-fuel open fireplace needs a flue and/or a chimney. They are not quite the same thing. A chimney is a masonry structure designed to act as a flue, but you can have a flue without having to build a chimney. What are the choices?

MASONRY CHIMNEYS

Whereas a chimney was once simply constructed in brickwork as an open duct, terminating with a terracotta pot, they are now built around a core of clay or concrete flue liner. For a chimney to work well, it requires a good flow of air and for the flue to maintain as high a temperature as possible, so there are exacting regulations about chimney design. For instance, it's important for chimneys to be insulated as this keeps the smoke warm and lessens the chances of it condensing as tar deposits. This is particularly important with wood burning appliances, as they burn cooler than coal. Material costs for a new chimney start at around £1,000 and can spiral upwards depending on the design. However, there is generally a considerable labour element going into building a masonry chimney, and there is added complexity when wanting to place a masonry chimney within a timber-framed house.

FLUES

■ The budget option with a wood burning stove is to go for a pre-fabricated stainless steel flue. Whereas a gas-burning appliance can use a single-skin flue, with solid fuel you have to use an insulated twin-wall flue section in order to stop the smoke condensing inside the flue. Typical material costs for a 7m twin-wall stainless steel flue are around £1,500. Main manufacturers are Rite-Vent, Poujoulat, SFL and Selkirk.
■ Ceramic twin-wall flues are a more up-market option, and are 30-50 per cent more expensive than stainless steel. Ceramic

flues tend to come with a 30 yr guarantee (rather than 10 yrs for stainless steel flues). Recommended for heavy use, especially with biomass boilers.

Pumice stone prefabricated flues: they provide a very simple way of building a long lasting, insulated masonry chimney system, at a similar cost to a twin-walled stainless steel flue. Instead of having to source components from several different suppliers, these chimney systems are supplied as kits for easy assembly. Names to look out for here are Schiedel and Anki.

In Short
■ Chimneys require foundations. Steel or ceramic flues don't.
■ If you want a traditional pot, then you need a chimney. Flues have terminals instead (ugly?).
■ Chimneys work best with blockwork construction: flues work with any construction type.

RENOVATING EXISTING CHIMNEYS
Many people will want to keep an existing chimney and adapt it for use with a wood burning appliance. You need to check that the chimney is functional and adequate – a good chimney sweep should be able to help here. And it is now commonplace to install flexible flue liners, usually pushing them down the existing chimney from the top. Whilst often not essential, a flexible flue liner will help with the free flow of smoke and make for a more efficient chimney. Expect to pay between £400 and £600 for flexible flue liners plus the labour to fit.

Of course, there may be much more work you need to undertake to bring an existing chimney back into use. The brick or stone work may be weathered and need repair or repointing: the flashings may have to be replaced: the pots may need replacing as well.

GAS FIRES
Most gas fires can be installed using a through-the-wall balanced flue, just like a gas boiler. You can also use powered flues which allow you to duct the exhaust gas over longer routes incorporating bends. This enables you to place a gas fire away from a suitable external wall.

THE REGULATIONS
There are some very precise regulations dealing with chimneys and flues that have grown more complex over the years. Appliances need an adequate air supply, and the flue/chimney must be designed so that it can carry the resulting smoke, and the flue terminal must be placed somewhere where it is not going to inconvenience others. Plus of course there are stringent fire precautions that have to be met.

PLUMBING

Conventionally, plumbers are hired to fit heating and sanitaryware; this includes all above ground waste fittings, but rarely underground drainage or rainwater goods. Traditionally, plumbers also undertook sheet-metal work on roofing, but now this tends to be carried out by roofers. There are a couple of grey areas to be aware of. The first concerns the wiring of heating controls (which is sometimes carried out by the electrician) and the second concerns the installation of kitchen sinks and dishwashers, which is sometimes undertaken by specialist kitchen installers. Be clear, when you are hiring, who is to do what. The situation has been further confused by the move to make electrical work notifiable to building control, which means that many plumbers are no longer qualified to undertake things like the wiring of your central heating controls.

Chapter 8

CHECK THE SPEC

Many contractors have only the vaguest understanding of the ins and outs of heating and plumbing systems and are more than happy to let their plumber design, price and install whatever system they like, and plumbers have become quite used to acting almost autonomously, as long as the kit works and the price is about right. Comparing quotations between plumbers is consequently a very difficult business because the specifications of the competing heating systems are almost bound to be different unless a professional has been employed to design the system beforehand, something which hardly anyone bothers with on smaller residential construction jobs.

Points to watch out for when comparing quotations are:

▥ Are the design considerations identical? What temperature is each room to be heated to? How many air changes an hour have been assumed in the calculations?
▥ What fuel is being specified to run the system? Have the costs of connection and storage been fully taken into account?
▥ What controls are being provided? How efficient will the system be? How easy will it be to service the system? Will pumps and cables be concealed? What insulation is being provided to the hot water pipes?
▥ What sort of emitters are being specified? If standard panel radiators, where will they be sited? Will they have TRVs fitted as standard? If so, will these be in addition to or instead of a whole-house thermostat?
▥ What provision has been made for towel radiators? Heating airing cupboards?
▥ What arrangements will be made for hot water storage? What will hot water flow rates be like?
▥ What sort of pipework will be used? Where will the overflows run to?
▥ What sort of guarantee is offered? Does

the business offer any form of regular servicing contract?

PLASTIC WASTE PIPES

Slowly but steadily, plumbing is going plastic. There are still many plumbers who wouldn't be seen dead using anything other than copper for their water feeds but you will search high and low to find one who uses anything other than plastic for waste fittings.

The whole subject of plumbing in the waste for bathrooms, loos and kitchens is surprisingly complicated and is covered at good length in the building regs (part H, if you must). The problem is that you need to stop smells getting up into the house from the drains: this is (usually) achieved by designing in water traps separating the appliances from the drains below.

There are several different trap designs around, usually named after letters of the alphabet – P and S figure prominently. Were that it was all there was to it and it would be the end of the story but unfortunately these water traps have a habit of failing, often through induced siphonage sucking the water down the pipe. What has evolved is a series of rules dictating how we should lay out our waste runs and where and when the runs should be joined together. The ones which tend to catch people out are the maximum length of basin runs – 1.7m – laid at a fall of between 18 and 22mm per metre run. It seems ridiculously precise; it's borne out of many years analysing just why basins gurgle and loose their water seals.

You can cheat: there are now non-return valves that don't require a water seal — the best known is Hepworth's ingenious HepVO valve.

The main waste runs also cause problems. The general rule is to run the appliances, such as basins, baths and showers, in small pipe sections (typically 32, 40 or 50mm) into a 110mm pipe, called

a stack, which drops vertically down to the underground drain system. Stacks need to be ventilated and at least one stack on every drain run needs to be ventilated to the outside, usually done through the roof.

If you have more than one stack, you can use a short version, known as a stub stack, on the subsequent stacks: these can be topped off with air admittance valves, also known as Durgos. These act in a similar fashion to the smaller HepVO valves used in small bore drain runs – letting air into the system but not letting any out. The HepVO valve actually has a lot going for it and deserves to be better known because it effectively rewrites the way that you are meant to plumb-in bathroom wastes.

At ground floor level, it's usual to run the waste pipes together into an external gulley and thence to the drains. The principle remains the same: to prevent smells from the drains escaping into the house. It's one part of the house fit-out which is routinely tested on completion of the job – the air test usually involves putting a bung into the drains at the highest manhole and another bung somewhere short of the air outlet and then seeing if the system between holds a given air pressure.

Indoor waste pipes have migrated across to plastic almost exclusively now but there is a choice of plastics and a choice of working methods. The DIY route is to use a push-fit system based on either uPVC or polypropylene. Serious plumbers often prefer to use a glued system, known as solvent weld. These are typically made of ABS (acrylonitrile butadiene styrene), a rather more rigid plastic. The average spend in a house on above ground waste fittings is around £200 so it's not a budget buster, whichever system you opt for.

WATER

Indoor plastic plumbing has been kicking

around since the late Seventies and in its time it's come in for a fair amount of stick from the professionals who were content to look at it as just a DIY product. It's also resulted in numerous floodings resulting from duff joints or, more often, lazy installers. However, it's very easy and quick to install; it's mostly push-fit and it comes on a roll so you don't have to bother with soldering joints as you do with copper. So quick and easy that, at long last, it's really taking off in professional plumbing circles as well. Partly it's because it's used exclusively for underfloor heating (where it seems to perform fine) and partly due to new building techniques. The product itself has matured. Hepworth, the originators, have redesigned their joints to make them hopefully idiot proof and there is now competition from other big names in the field like Marley Plumbing, John Guest's Speedfit, and Polyplumb.

It's hard not to come to the conclusion that copper plumbing is on the way out, although it will continue to be used extensively for many years to come. Gas plumbing, for instance, has to be done in copper. One area where plastic plumbing really wins out is when you are specifying I-beam floors: you can't notch I-beam floors (you can actually, but the results are disastrous) so the ability to uncoil the pipe through holes in the webbing is almost indispensable.

9
WIRING

INTRODUCTION

THE HOUSEBUILDING INDUSTRY'S standard for electrical provision has been some way in advance of the minimum requirements for many years. This will surprise many who automatically assume that professional developers always try and get away with the bare minimum, but in fact the building regs don't require any electrics other than smoke detectors and some energy efficient lighting, and the standards set by the NHBC were absolutely basic although, to be fair, they have now uprated them to closer reflect what actually gets installed. If you are building your own house you will probably have views on just exactly what you require and where, but it's worth bearing in mind that even if you choose the NHBC minimum standard for lighting, you will probably spend a lot

more money on lampshades, table lamps and fittings, all of which would attract VAT at 20 per cent, whereas built-in light fittings are zero-rated in a new house.

PART P AND THE BUILDING REGS
The wiring of new and existing homes is now covered by building regs, and is a notifiable event in the life of a house, but the regulations simply insist that the wiring is done either by a competent person or to a standard that is passed as competent by a competent person. If that sounds like gobble-de-gook, welcome to the world of the new building regs. In Scotland, electrics have always been a notifiable event, but England & Wales only fell into line in 2005 when Part P came into effect. Part P is all about notification. The actual requirements are embedded in BS 7671, which itself is pretty much the same as the 17th edition (2008) of the IEE Wiring Regs. But what

has changed is that house wiring now has to be passed by building inspectors OR by qualified electricians so you need to find out if your electrician is 'Part P compliant': if they are, they can issue you with a certificate on completion to say that the work has been carried out to the relevant standard. Very small works are exempt, but anything involving kitchens, bathrooms or externals is notifiable so, for instance, fitting a new kitchen is now likely to come under building regs. If you are undertaking a major project, like a new house, then you will already be involved in a building regs application and you won't be required to do an additional one just because electrics are involved. Here you can simply ask your building inspector to check the wiring, along with everything else.

COSTS
The tables in this chapter show just how

each element of an electrician's quotation would be made up and how this translates into a whole house quotation. Compared to most aspects of construction, electrical fittings vary enormously in quality.
For many years, the market was been dominated by two British businesses, MK and Crabtree: indeed many specifiers indicate that fittings should be by either of these two firms. But there is a huge gulf between MK/Crabtree prices and some very cheap imported gear that you can get hold of. The current TLC catalogue (www. tlc-direct.co.uk) has MK 13amp double sockets at £3.00 each; however, they also have their own brand version (Telco) at £1.50 each. There are lots of options if you want something between these two prices.

HOUSE WIRING
CONNECTION FEES

Electricity connection to new homes is organised by the businesses which used to be the local electricity board but are now known as Regional Electricity Companies (RECs). They are free to set their own connection fees and, being monopoly suppliers of an indispensable power source, they tend to charge a lot. Even a straightforward connection is likely to cost in the region of £300. If you are considering electric heating or an electric heat pump in your house, you may find that the REC offers to halve or even waive the entire connection fee as a sweetener. Long cable runs (say in excess of 50m) can be prohibitively expensive, costing thousands, and should be carefully costed when assessing the plot. Each REC has a New Supplies Department, which is where you should look for quotations; you don't need to own the plot before getting a quotation. Incidentally, it is currently

very confusing for new housebuilders because new mains gas supplies are dealt with through National Grid, who bought Transco, the gas main company, in 2005. Everyone thinks National Grid should supply electricity to homes, but instead it supplies gas!

TEMPORARY SUPPLIES

Some builders manage without temporary electricity supplies, relying on generators and diesel-powered mixers; indeed most of the house superstructure can be easily erected without power tools. However, plumbers, electricians and second-fix carpenters are big users of power tools and you can't have your permanent supply turned on until they're finished so, for most builders, a temporary supply makes good sense.

Current regs insist that the temporary supply board is adequately housed; on most sites this means building a blockwork box with at least a paving slab roof and a lockable door. Budget a day's work and £100 materials to build an adequate shed with consumer unit and sockets on a backing board inside. Care should be given to locating the temporary supply so that long cables are not left trailing over the site where they could be run over by diggers, dumpers or lorries. Discuss your requirements with the REC's new supplies estimator; there will be an extra charge for temporary supply but it's usually not large, provided there are no major cable detours.

METER BOXES

The industry standard is to install white plastic boxes built into the external wall. The RECs like them because they can access the meter without entering the house; builders like them because the RECs supply them free (as they do lengths

of underground ducting) and they can be built into the outer skin brick wall without a lintel. Only problem is that they are ugly, ugly enough to ruin a fancy period facade. If this bothers you then either look to locate the plastic meter box where it won't detract from your kerb appeal or insist that the company supply comes into the house where it can be concealed in a cupboard.

Gas supplies have the same problem but they offer an alternative meter box concealed in the ground; however, this is felt to be unsafe for an electrical supply. Water meters are always concealed in the ground.

CONSUMER UNITS AND RCDS

The consumer unit – what used to be known as the fuse box – is the place where the REC's supply is split into a number of separate circuits for distribution around the house. There are conventions on how these circuits should be arranged, although the exact design will depend on each particular layout. A 10-gang unit will suffice for all but the largest houses and it is recommended not to economise too much on this item. Miniature circuit breakers (MCBs) have now replaced the traditional fuses; instead of fusewire blowing, a little button pops out and reconnection is never more complicated than pressing the button in again.

Another development is the advent of residual circuit-breaking devices (RCDs) – now mandatory – which provide increased protection against electrocution in event of contact with live wires. One drawback of RCDs is that they are very sensitive and can be triggered by thunderstorms or faulty equipment. This in turn may cause problems with things that must not have their power supply

Electrics Costs

ITEM	COST
POWER CIRCUITS/CONSUMER UNIT	
Double Socket	£ 8
Single Socket	£ 7
Fused Spur	£ 8
5-amp Socket	£ 8
Cooker Switch	£ 13
Cooker Outlet	£ 5
Shaver Point	£ 25
Immersion Point	£ 8
External Sockets	£ 15
Consumer Unit	£ 30
Residual Circuit Devices	£ 40
Each Fuse	£ 4
TV/TELECOM WIRING	
Coaxial Point	£ 8
Telephone Point	£ 5
Loft Aerial	£ 20
Door Bell	£ 5
SAFETY	
Smoke Detectors	£ 30
LIGHTING	
1-gang Switch	£ 4
2-gang Switch	£ 6
3-gang Switch	£ 8
Pull switch	£ 6
2-way Switching	£ 2
3-way Switching	£ 4
Central Pendant	£ 4
Fixed Ceiling Light	£ 3
Halogen downlights	£ 15
Wall Light	£ 2
Extra for Light Fittings	£ 25
External Light Points	£ 5
FANS	
Bathroom Fans	£ 50
Kitchen Fan	£ 75

Prices are for reasonably basic kit and the times allowed are for straightforward runs

Electrician

Electrician's charges at £30/hr labour

	Time	COST
Sockets	40mins	£ 20
External Sockets	80mins	£ 40
Door Bells	60mins	£ 30
Light outlet	30mins	£ 15
Each switch	30mins	£ 15
External lights	90mins	£ 45
Extra for light fittings	45mins	£ 25
Fans (inc kitchen extracts)	150mins	£ 75
Smoke detectors	60mins	£ 30
Basic CU	60mins	£ 30
Each circuit	10mins	£ 5
Electric ovens and hobs	180mins	£ 90

cut off – chiefly freezers and smoke detectors. An RCD-inspired power cut-out could have very messy consequences if it occurred during your two weeks in the Algarve, and for this reason it is recommended that freezers are run off separate circuits not protected by an RCD. The net result of all this is that you'll be spending around £100 on your consumer unit whereas in the bad old days it might have cost only £20.

SOCKETS

If you've got deep pockets, fit lots of sockets – but at £20-£25 per outlet this can rapidly become a prohibitively expensive option. If you know how you are going to arrange beds and furniture in each room you can minimise the number of sockets needed; if you want to retain flexibility for each room then you'll probably need a minimum of three sockets per bedroom and four sockets in living rooms. It will cost a lot more to add sockets in the future and not having them where you want them when you've moved in is very frustrating. Also, don't think that you are saving money by fitting single sockets instead of doubles. The work

involved in installing them is identical and the materials price is only pennies different. You can step-up to metallic-finished sockets for an extra £5 or £10 per outlet.

SAFETY ISSUES

Since 2005, electrical work in the home has to be either carried out by a qualified electrician (Part P compliant is the thing to look out for) or passed by your building inspector. It's not made DIY installations illegal, as some claim, but it has brought in a measure of quality control that wasn't there before. There are a number of areas where DIY housewirers – and professional electricians come to that – are prone to make untraceable errors and you would be well advised to steer clear of house wiring unless you have a thorough knowledge of the tasks in hand.

CABLES IN WALLS

Cables buried in walls must be set either vertically or horizontally from the outlets they supply. The idea is that the follow-on trades have some idea where not to drill holes. However, this requirement is frequently ignored in the rush to get jobs done and sometimes even to try and save money by using less cable. Even if you know where the cable is buried and, therefore, think it doesn't matter, don't forget that the cable will still be there long after you've moved on and some poor sucker thirty years hence could be in for a nasty surprise. Technically, you are allowed to run cables within 150mm of internal corners and wall and ceiling junctions, but this habit cannot be recommended.

EARTH BONDING

It is a requirement that exposed metalwork should be earthed to prevent it becoming 'live.' This is normally done with 10mm earthing cable (it's green and yellow). What exactly needs to be bonded?

▓ Water and gas mains as they enter the house
▓ Any exposed structural steel and oil tanks
▓ All services must be bonded together
▓ All metal in bathrooms must be bonded together.

Note that if you are plumbing with plastic pipe (such as Hep2O or Speedfit), the requirement to earth bathroom radiators and steel baths is dropped.

ELECTRIC HEATING
If you are interested in electric heating and heat pumps in particular, have a look at the relevant sections in the Heating chapter. You may have to opt for a three-phase supply.

It's worth making sure that plastic meter boxes are located where they won't be seen every day

FREQUENTLY OVERLOOKED

When designing electricity supplies to a house there are a number of points to watch out for – and easily forgotten at the first-fix, cable-burying stage. Many electricians are used to doing what they are told and no more and will be of little help in designing a better system. Here is a bulletted list of commonly forgotten wiring details:

▓ Loft lights, cupboard lights – do you want them?
▓ Separate freezer circuit – preferably not protected by RCD
▓ Separate garage supply if garage is external
▓ Outside power points, security lights, welcome lights
▓ Kitchen unit lighting – usually fixed below wall units
▓ Check the rating of your electric cooking gear – 30 amps may not be enough
▓ Wiring for electric showers and power shower pumps
▓ Wiring and installation of fans in bathrooms and kitchen

▓ Separate circuit for immersion heater
▓ Outlets left for smoke detectors (now mandatory)
▓ Doorbell wiring
▓ Heating controls wiring: boiler, programmer, thermostats, pump and valves all need to be connected. This work is often undertaken by the plumber but the electrician must leave at least a fused spur to power the controls. If the plumber does this wiring, then a separate test certificate will be needed from him
▓ Fused spurs for waste disposal units and/or water softeners
▓ Wiring to sewage treatment plants or for any external water pumps (water features, swimming pools)
▓ Wiring for electric garage door operators: needs an accurately placed single socket, not really a problem if power is in the garage
▓ Burglar alarm first-fix

Wiring for renewable energy systems, such as photovoltaics or wind turbines, both of which produce power in DC and need inverters to turn this into AC. Also meters have to be adapted if exporting the power you produce.

LIGHTING

The best light is natural sunlight. Lux is a measurement of light density and whereas 500 lux is the generally accepted level of electric light needed for reading, bright sunshine delivers 100,000 lux and even a cloudy overcast day will produce 5,000 lux of light.

The older you get the more light you need. A 60-year-old requires

Model House Wiring

	SOCKETS	LIGHTS	SWITCHES	LIGHT FITTINGS	TV & PHONES	SMOKE DETECTOR	FANS	SHAVER POINTS	TOTALS
Kitchen/Dining Area	8	12	4	12	2	1	1		
Utility	2	1	1	1			1		
WC		1	1	1			1		
Hallway	1	2	2	2		1			
Lounge	8	6	2	6	2				
Bedroom 1	8	4	2	4	2				
Bed 1 En-suite		2	1	2			1	1	
Family Bathroom		2	1	2			1	1	
Home Office/Bed 4	8	2	2	2	2				
Bedroom 2	8	2	1	2					
Bedroom 3	8	2	1	2					
Landing	2	2	1	2		1			
External	1	4	2	4					
TOTALS	54	42	21	42	8	3	5	2	
LABOUR IN HRS	36	21	11	32	5	3	13	1	122HRS
ROUNDED COST OF LABOUR	£ 1,080	£ 630	£ 330	£ 960	£ 150	£ 90	£390	£ 30	£3,700
TYPICAL MATERIAL COSTS	£ 8	£ 15	£ 6	£ 25	£ 8	£ 30	£ 50	£ 25	
ROUNDED COST OF MATERIALS	£ 430	£ 630	£ 130	£ 1,050	£ 60	£ 90	£250	£ 100	£2,700
WIRING TOTAL LABOUR AND MATERIALS									£6,400

ten times more light than a 10-year-old. Apart from brightness, there are two qualities of light that are important.

COLOUR RENDERING
Some light sources show colours close to their natural daylight colours and are said to have good colour render. Other sources – notably orange street lamps – are incapable of showing any colour variations at all. Fluorescent lighting (including low-energy light bulbs) tends to give a washed-out, faded look to colours. This bothers some people more than others, but before you install energy-saving lightbulbs everywhere in your house, make sure you can live with the light quality.

COLOUR APPEARANCE

Or 'How white is your lamp?' The bog standard tungsten lamp which we all know and love – and is seemingly about to be outlawed – is said to be orange white – others say warm; halogen and LEDs are very white – or crisp white; fluorescents give off a milky, cool white, though there are warm-coloured fluorescents available.

This may seem all very technical and uninteresting but the quality of the light source is an important feature of how a room looks. Some lighting designers will actually recommend that a multipurpose room (say an office by day and a living room by night) has two different lighting schemes – fluorescent for business, halogen for pleasure. The feel of the room is then transformed at the flick of a switch.

CENTRAL PENDANT LIGHTING
This is the basic standard lighting scheme much loved by penny-pinching developers. It provides adequate ambient (background) lighting and it will always be the most efficient way of distributing light into a room but it is, generally, a very poor source for reading by or carrying out intricate manual operations because you will tend to be in the shade. It is really only a very good light source when the light is wanted directly beneath it – e.g. dining tables – but most other light sources require multiple outlets in each room to work well and so pendant lighting will remain a cheap and cheerless option.

SPOTLIGHTS
Back in the Sixties the appearance of

spotlights on the scene was a breath of fresh air and they became the first popular form of directional lighting. They are still immensely popular but there are often better ways of achieving the required results. Because the entire fitting is fixed and visible, spotlights have the ability to completely ruin the look of a room, especially when mounted on tracks in the middle of ceilings.

DOWNLIGHTERS

Light sources concealed in the ceiling have the big advantage of being stylistically neutral – i.e. they can blend in with any type of decor. They have the disadvantage of only being able to light a rather limited area and a large room lit entirely with downlighters might need as many as ten – which is expensive. Despite their name, downlighters do not have to point straight down: there are 'eyeball' versions which beam the light off at an angle – in effect sidelighters.

Low-voltage halogen downlighters, which supply a very bright, good quality light, have been fashionable for some time but their use in new homes is becoming problematic due to energy efficiency regs. It looks as though the market will now slowly shift across to LED lighting that achieves much the same thing but with less power – at much greater cost. There are a lot of very cheap downlighters around and it's not a bad idea – if you can afford it – to fit something a little better than the cheapest. For one thing, downlighters make holes in ceilings and these holes do little for your sound-proofing, your fire-ratings, your airtightness or your thermal insulation values. A fire-proofed downlighter comes with a hood over the light and this does afford some measure of protection against all these ills. Check out Snaplite, a small British company that makes really good

downlighters.

UPLIGHTERS

These work by reflecting light off another surface (usually the ceiling) and many people assume that the light quality will therefore be low. However – provided the room has white or near-white ceilings – they are actually a very efficient way of providing ambient light and the light cast down from the ceiling is usually very good for reading under. Uplighters are normally fixed slightly above eye level to conceal the light source and they come in many shapes and forms; one particularly popular one is to fit unglazed ceramic bowls (cost £15-£25) and then to paint them with the same emulsion used on the surrounding walls. This provides stylistically neutral lighting that blends well with natural wood finishes and off-white walls.

SIDELIGHTS AND TABLE LAMPS

People habitually refer to their sidelights as 'reading lights' which suggests that the central light is good for vacuum cleaning and not much else. There is an enormous variety of shapes and styles to suit every taste: table lamps from £5 upwards, floor (or standard) lamps from £30. The one big advantage of independent lights is that you retain the flexibility to arrange your room in any fashion you choose, as long as you've got a socket nearby.

5-AMP PLUGS

A handy idea for living rooms where you want to have a number of sidelights is to fit a series of 5-amp lighting sockets (usually with small round-pin holes to distinguish them from 13-amp mains sockets). These can be linked together and all switched from one point. It's convenient not only because it gives you a master switch to control all the sidelights plugged into the

5-amp sockets, but it also gives you the ability to dim. By arranging the switching next to the door, it gives you the option of doing away with the central pendant lighting altogether.

If you know nothing about the art of good lighting and you are in a hurry and don't want to waste a small fortune, you won't go wrong by specifying a handful of 5-amp sockets. You can create quite sophisticated lighting effects by using side lighting and, without spending a fortune on fittings, you can get pools of light wherever you want them whilst retaining a flexibility to change it all if you get bored and want something different. Downside is, of course, that you have to re-wire all the plugs on your sidelights.

SCENE LIGHTING

This is where lighting meets home automation. Here you programme banks of lights to come on together to create moods or scenes. It's something that is commonly seen in places like conference suites and lecture theatres but is beginning to migrate towards the home (via the USA). Products such as Lutron's Homeworks works with most types of bulbs and allows you to create and recall lighting arrangements, including dimming. Not only can you switch banks of lights on and off with one button but you can also do vacation settings for security. But it comes at a frightful cost, typically around £1,500 per room and as much as £10,000 for a whole house solution. .

DIMMERS

Dimmer switches give you the ability to control the amount of light given off by a bulb and thus set the mood for a room. They are particularly useful in living rooms where you may want to relax in front of the TV, watching the fire. Furthermore, dimmed

Light Bulbs

TUNGSTEN

Ordinary light bulbs (or GLS bulbs): cheap (30p), average life 1,000hrs, power-hungry, good colour rendering, slightly orange light, easily dimmable; available in a huge choice of shapes and sizes (reflectors, tubes, pygmies, candles) which all cost a good deal more than 30p.

MAINS-VOLTAGE HALOGEN

Also known as Halogen A: cost £2.50, average life 2,000hrs, power-hungry, good colour rendering, pure white light, dimmable, fully interchangeable with tungsten bulb fittings.

LOW-VOLTAGE HALOGEN

Come in specialist fittings (spotlights, downlighters) which vary enormously in cost from under £5 to £40 plus. Replacement bulbs cost around £3.50. Average life of bulb, 2,000hrs; consumes around half the power of tungsten bulbs, good colour rendering, pure white light, dimmable with appropriate electronic switch, now widely available. Best LV halogen lights are dichroic with reflectors and they require transformers.

FLUORESCENT

Usually fitted as tubes; miniatures (as used in shaver lights or as kitchen surface lights) cost around £2.50; otherwise tubes up to 2.4m long cost around £7. Average life 8,000hrs; consumes around 25 per cent of power of tungsten, cold flat light with poor colour rendering. Tends to be used in utility, garage spaces.

COMPACT FLUORESCENT

Better known as energy-saving light bulbs: cost £5-£15, performance similar in every way to long fluorescent tubes but compact shape makes them much more versatile when it comes to positioning. Interchangeable with GLS lightbulbs, but do not fit easily inside average light shade and can look cumbersome. Note that they cannot be dimmed by regular methods and so don't try and replace dimmed GLS lights with compact fluorescents. Which? carried out a somewhat damning survey of them in Jan 2004: they all claim to last 6,000 hours but 25 per cent of those tested didn't. They also tend to dim over time and don't work too well when it's cold. However, they do continue to improve as a technology and they do save a lot of electricity. Most reliable makes were Osram and Philips.

LEDS

LED lighting has been around since the Sixties (think of red digital clockfaces) but only in recent years has the technology developed so that green-blue and now, white light can be made from LEDs. They use very low currents and therefore promise very low energy consumption but at the moment LED lighting schemes are still a rarity in the home because the actual lighting units are expensive.

There are a number of other light sources readily available – metal halide, sodium, neon – but their use is rare in the home and is unlikely to be specified by anyone other than a specialist lighting consultant.

---

lights save energy, and if you use dimmers which don't have a push on/off capability, you increase the length of your bulb life by having a 'soft start' – most bulbs blow when you turn them on.

As regular dimmers are only slightly more expensive than regular switches, there is an argument for fitting them just about everywhere. You can dim just about any kind of light but the very basic dimming switches will only work on the standard GLS tungsten lightbulbs.

There are now electronic or intelligent dimmers widely available from around £10 that will handle either mains or low voltage halogen. Other kinds of bulbs require special dimmers which cost upwards of £30 for one-gang switching.

LIGHTING AND THE BUILDING REGS

The building regs now address energy

efficiency and further enhancements are likely in future. They want you to fit some energy efficient lightbulbs. But where? And how many? The requirement for England & Wales is set out in Part L of the building regs:

▓ it asks for 3 in every 4 outlets to be low energy

▓ it relaxes the previous requirement for the fittings to be dedicated, meaning that people will be free to switch over to any old bulb after the building is finalled

▓ the new efficiency threshold is increased to 45 lumens per circuit-watt.

It's not clear (to me at least) where this leaves the various bulbs. Ordinary tungsten bulbs will fall foul of the new regs, as will halogen which is slightly more efficient than tungsten but will never meet the 45 lumens per watt hurdle. Fluorescent and compact fluorescent should be fine but LEDs — the coming light source — have a wide range of efficiencies, ranging anywhere from 20 to 60 lumens per watt. How building inspectors will police these new regs is anybody's guess, especially as you don't have to fit energy efficient lighting everywhere.

ROOM BY ROOM
KITCHENS

Central pendant lighting is particularly inept at providing light for kitchen worksurfaces, and this is one area where task lighting is now considered essential. The conventional place for this is under the wall cupboard units, hidden from view by the decorative downstand known as the pelmet. There is a choice of tungsten or fluorescent fittings; tungsten gives better light rendering but gets hot and tends to 'cook' the contents of the overhead cupboard; fluorescent stays cool and is generally preferable. An alternative is to fit downlighters in the ceiling over the kitchen surfaces, but placement has to be extremely accurate and you risk getting unlit areas under the wall units. If you have an extractor hood, make sure it has a light as well. You can get downlighters that are only 20mm deep and are specifically designed to fit into a cupboard shelf. If your kitchen design doesn't want or need pelmets under your wall cupboards and you don't want exposed lights, then this is the answer for you.

DINING TABLES

A pendant light hanging over a dining table works very well, but make sure that the bulb is well concealed by the shade or fitting. Lighting from the side is much more difficult because of the shadows cast by the diners. As an alternative to a hanging light, go for a cluster of downlighters – the way they do it in fancy restaurants. Avoid fluorescent lighting if you are of the gourmet tendency and like to see what it is you're eating. And if you are the type who goes for candlelit dinner parties, it's very useful to be able to dim the ambient lighting.

LIVING ROOMS

There are no set rules for lighting living areas. Chandeliers, spotlights, uplighters, wall lights, downlighters, table lamps, sidelights – all have a role to play and it's very much a question of taste. Most developers and self builders will be planning fairly conservative interiors, particularly in their living rooms, and an awful lot of the high-tech lighting schemes would be completely inappropriate here. However, the use of concealed fittings, such as downlighters, is compatible with virtually all settings.

Lighting a room with downlighters is generally pleasing to the eye but it is expensive because of the numbers needed. Pendant fittings and wall lights may be preferred but considerable time and expense may go into selecting the right fittings for the room; downlighters actually require less thought. Another option is to go for three or four uplighters or wall lights, which will generally be enough to provide all the lighting needs (including reading) for a largish room; this presents a stylish mid-priced alternative between the expense of downlighters and the poor light quality offered by a central light.

Feature mirrors need to be set where they do not directly reflect lights. A traditional effect like a mirror above an Adam style fireplace will be ruined by a chandelier directly in front of it. Picture lighting is another problem area that you can ruin if you don't get it right.

BEDROOMS

For most people, bedroom lighting will be a mixture of an ambient central pendant and table lamps for reading. Although a central pendant light source will be cheaper to install, when the cost of task lighting is included, the alternative options of uplighters or downlighters look more pocket-friendly, although you must pay attention to switching from the bed as well as by the door.

BATHROOMS

The regulations require that bathroom light fittings should be concealed to prevent direct contact with water. Conventionally, this is done by placing a central light inside some sort of glazed casing. There are some extremely naff bathroom light fittings around and finding a good one can be difficult. An alternative approach is to use sealed downlighters.

Task lighting is also very useful around bathroom mirrors. The standard method is to fit a strip light (combined with electric shaver socket) which is adequate but rarely beautiful. Mirrors with integral lights are a stylish solution but they are very expensive.

HALLWAYS/STAIRWELLS

■ Don't be tempted to hang lights where you can't change the bulb without a ladder.
■ Don't fit uplighters at the foot of stairwells where you can see the bulbs from above.

EXTERNAL LIGHTING

The bane of external lighting is the 500 watt halogen floodlight. In the last few years these have become very cheap (under £20) and very common, yet their effect is blindingly unpleasant, unless well concealed.

Security lighting need not be unattractive. It is worth giving a bit of thought to external lighting – unless you are building next to a well-lit road, you will find that some form of external light is essential just to negotiate the front path. By all means arrange to switch it on a timed Passive Infra Red (PIR) detector, but that doesn't mean you have to blast people in the face with 500W bulbs. PIR switches can be adjusted to trip on at different light levels and for different lengths of time – from a few seconds to several minutes. As alternatives to tungsten halogen floodlights, consider wall-mounted lanterns, outdoor spotlights spiked into the ground, free standing bollards or even brick lights, which replace a standard brick in your external wall.

The energy efficiency regs also address external lighting. They demand that external lights should either be fitted with daylight detectors and timed switches or not use more than a 40W bulb – ideally a compact fluorescent lamp.

BUILT-IN VACUUMS

Why bother to fit a built-in vacuum cleaning system? The big plus with central vacuums is that what gets sucked up stays sucked up. With a portable vacuum, efficiency depends on how well the filter works. Small particles of dust go through the filter and get re-circulated, which is why a house often smells a little bit different after vacuuming. By removing the motor to somewhere like a utility room or, better still, a garage, you are shifting all this dust out there, though it may not do much for the look of your shiny new car. And, by locating the motor out of the way, you also get another plus which is near-silent vacuuming.

The biggest minus seems to be finding somewhere to stash the pipe. The fewer inlets you have the cheaper and easier to install but the longer the pipe needs to be. Many people fit one inlet downstairs and one upstairs which means you need up to 10 m of pipe to be able to get to the far corners of the house. Coiled up this makes a considerable heap – much bigger than a portable vacuum. The solution is to build in a rack, like a hosepipe rack, somewhere handy to get to but easy to conceal. A pipe cupboard no less.

There are a number of small manufacturers moving into this market in the UK, although note that the two most significant players, Beam and Smart, are both owned by Electrolux, the household appliance giant. Most advertise heavily in the selfbuild press and can be regularly found making pitches at the selfbuild exhibitions. If you are interested, most will quote from floor plans you send them. They aim particularly at the new build market because the system is most conveniently fitted at the first-fix stage so that the ducting is easily concealed. Put another way, it's more trouble than it's worth to fit the pipes

into an old house but building into a new home is relatively straightforward. Prices for a built-in vacuum cleaner installed on a four-bedroom detached house are around £500 (excluding labour). Some businesses actually give away the wall ducting with timber frame kit homes, hoping this will create a sale later.

TELECOMS

Of all the sections in 'The Housebuilder's Bible' that have required rewriting over its twenty-year history, this one stands out because it has changed the most. As recently as 1995, this was a fairly short section: you stuck a phone line in, you put a couple of TV points in, an aerial in the loft, maybe a satellite dish and you were away. For many people this will still be a fine solution, but the intervening years have seen the arrival of home office working, the internet, and digital TV, and suddenly the basic house wiring doesn't look quite up to the mark anymore. Now you have to make an educated guess as to what to put in and what to leave out, not only for your own requirements but for any possible future buyers as well. Time to knuckle down and take a hard look at what's in and what's out in home cabling.

WHAT ARE THE KEY CHANGES IN HOME WIRING?

The twentieth century saw the near-universal adoption of three different wiring systems into the home: electricity, telephones and television, with a few homes opting for a fourth system, wiring for burglar alarms. Of these, only the first, electricity, has conventionally been cabled all over the house. Telephones initially came into the house at just one socket, more recently two or three and likewise TV outlets have been restricted to one, two or three outlets.

Whilst the electric cabling routes around the house remain largely unchanged, the demand for more complex phone wiring and TV cabling is causing these other systems to grow and converge. Phone wiring is changing because we want more outlets and because we are using phone lines for more than just conversations. TV wiring is changing because the methods of delivering TV signals are changing. Over and beyond this, the actual cables used for phones and TVs are changing and people are starting to cable for additional reasons: things like security, audio and lighting control.

DIGITAL TV?

TV signals are delivered to the home by three different methods, rooftop aerial, satellite dish and fibre optic cable. If you live in or near to a big city, you will have a choice of all three but fibre-optics are unlikely to be laid out in rural districts, so you need to find out what is available and what works well in your area.

Standard TV signals (the ones we have all grown up with since the Fifties) have conventionally been fed around the house in brown coaxial cable from the rooftop or loft aerial. The standard signal is usually adequate to service three or four TV sets – if you want more you need to add a small amplifier to the system.

Digital TV isn't so different. The signal needs to be decoded in the house, something which used to be achieved in a box of tricks called a digibox, although these days it's

usually done inside a digital TV (that is a TV that has a built-in decoder). You can use just one decoder for all the TVs in the house, but if you want to watch different channels, then each TV will need its own decoder (or be a digital TV).

If you subscribe to Sky or VirginMedia, and you want to watch it on more than one TV, you will need to rent an extra box for each TV, and have a plan to run cable to each one, not to mention a phone line as well.

Designate a place in the house as a central hub (known as the wiring closet) and you can bring all the incoming cables to this point and then distribute them around the house

PHONES AND BROADBAND

Phone cabling around the house has traditionally been a simple affair. Your service provider (traditionally BT) installed a master socket and you could run a small number of extensions out from there. If you started running a business from home, you would install a second line with a fax/phone on it. It rarely got more complicated than that. Surprisingly, the broadband roll-out hasn't changed it that much. If you want to connect three computers, an X-box and a TV to the internet, you can do it all via one phone line. Broadband is now established as a medium for watching TV and video on demand, even though there are distinct signs that the infrastructure is groaning with the demand being placed in it. One of the neatest features of broadband is that you can still make and receive phone calls on the same line whilst uploading and downloading whatever from the internet, something the old dial-up connections couldn't do.

So in many ways, broadband makes life simpler for people working from home who previously would have had to install multiple phone lines.

Cable modems, an alternative way of getting broadband, are available to customers of the cable network which covers 50 per cent of the UK population. The deals are broadly similar to other broadband offerings but link you to the fibre-optic network, run by VirginMedia, which promises much faster speeds.

WIRED OR WIRELESS?

Chapter 9

Self builders have over the past decade or so spent a great deal of money laying data cabling systems around their homes, only to find that the world seems to have migrated to wireless systems, which require nothing more than a single broadband router — usually provided free by the internet service provider – plugged into the phone line. Whereas once, we all used desktop computers (which came with all manner of wires and cables), we now seem to be using laptops, tablets and smart phones where mobility is key. Has the technology moved on to the extent that wired systems are now redundant?

WIRELESS PROS
- It's simple to install
- It's inherently flexible - you don't have to plug into a socket
- It's almost as quick as hard wired connection – strictly speaking not true, as wired connections are capable of much greater data transmission speeds, but the limiting factor is usually the bandwidth coming into the house, not the distribution around the house, so in reality you won't notice any difference
- It's more convenient with mobile devices like iPads and iPhones
- Far fewer cables
- t works up to 100m from the base station
- It's easily and cheaply upgradeable

WIRELESS CONS
- You may get blind spots – it often doesn't work in every corner of the house: aluminium sheeting, in particular (sometimes used with plasterboard or underfloor heating), blocks wireless reception
- Sometimes other devices can cause interference
- This makes it problematic when planning ahead – how do you know whether it will work or not?
- There are many smart home applications which are not wireless – TV and entertainment systems, alarm systems, some home automation.

EXTENDING WIRELESS NETWORKS
There are work-arounds for some of these problems. There are products that enable you to set up booster outlets which take the signal from the main router and relay it to parts of the home (or the garden office) where reception is difficult. Apple's Airport Express is designed to do just this, and it also enables music to be distributed wirelessly as well. The advantage of these products is that they are portable, so that you can move them around until you get the signal strength you require.

Of course, it's not either wired or wireless. There is nothing stopping you playing mix and match, so that some parts of your home network are wired whilst other parts are wireless. It may be that in future self builders will stop flood wiring their homes with data cabling (ie several outlets in each room) and instead run two or three ethernet cables from the hub to strategic points around the house and then rely on wireless connection from booster stations.

POWERLINE NETWORKS
But there is another technology that threatens to make even this amount of data cabling redundant, because now you can transmit data through your home's electrical wiring system. Type 'Powerline' into Amazon and it'll return a dozen or so pairs of plugs at around £40, enabling you to fit these adapters into your electrical sockets and then connect Ethernet cabling. It saves you having to run the cabling all over the house. Again, it's an inherently flexible system because every room

(bathrooms excepted) has electrical sockets and so you can have a cabled internet connection anywhere you want. It's a particularly good solution for outbuildings and garden offices where a wireless connection might struggle.

CAT 5 AND 6 CABLING SYSTEMS
This is the 'conventional' way of doing it, even though just a few years ago it was regarded as cutting edge. It has migrated from offices where it is now as common as electric wiring. Instead of haphazardly running cables from the various input points to the various output points around the house, you designate a place in the house as a central hub (known as the wiring closet or sometimes, annoyingly, as Node Zero) and you bring all the incoming cables to this point and then distribute them around the house to wall mounted data sockets which look very much like electric sockets.

A wiring closet doesn't have to reside in its own purpose built room – unlike the other kind of WC.

The essential element in a wiring closet is a patch panel, a wall hung box the size of a small suitcase. The patch panel plays a similar role to an electrical fusebox in household electrical wiring where the power coming into the house is split up and sorted into different circuits. It is in here that the phone lines and TV cables are all connected. Rather than being connected up in series (or daisy chained) as many TV and phone outlets are in conventional set-ups, each outlet throughout the house is connected directly back to the patch panel. That means a double data socket will have two cables running next to each other back to the patch panel where each will terminate with its own unique number which corresponds to a number etched on the data socket.

CAT 5 COSTS

The Cat 5 cable itself is not expensive, typically no more than electric cable. Similarly the patch panel and the RJ45 outlets are commodity items. The materials to fit out a four-bedroomed house would typically cost around £800-£1,200, depending on the number of outlets that you require. This compares very similarly with the cost of electrical wiring. For many self builders, the cabling is seen as just another DIY task to be completed along with the underfloor heating and the central vacuum system. There are now many companies offering to supply and fit structured cabling systems and prices start from about £2,000 for a basic fit out, though many of the more esoteric uses of structured cabling such as lighting control and multi-room sound systems are expensive extras costing many additional thousands.

The one major weak point with Cat 5 cabling was that it didn't deliver a very compelling TV signal. Because of this it has been conventional to run CT-100 coaxial cable as well as Cat 5 around the house and back to the patch panel.

IN SUMMARY

So the big question remains. If you are about to commission a new home, is it still worthwhile opting for a structured cabling system, based on running Cat 5 Ethernet cables in a star configuration, to every room in the house? The short answer is no. Mobile computing and wireless communication is taking over and few homes will have more than one desktop computer in future. However, it may still be worth running a limited cable network to get reliable access to far-flung corners of the home. And of course, there will still be other features of the smart home (principally entertainment, audio and security systems) which require cabling. But then these never did use the standard data cabling systems in any event.

10
FINISHES

TRADITIONALLY, THE SECOND-FIX stage of house building begins with the internal plastering, even though these days the majority of new houses never get to see any traditional plastering. Up until this time, everything going on inside the superstructure of the house has been first-fixing – constructing walls, roofs and floors, burying pipes and cables. The key difference between the two stages is that the first-fix works will remain hidden in the structure, whilst the second-fix items will be there for all to see when the house is completed. Hence this chapter, entitled 'Finishes,' covers everything from the second-fixing stage onwards.

INTERNAL WALL FINISHES

Plastering is the cheapest way of providing good internal wall and ceiling coverings. There are different systems of 'plastering' but they all come within spitting distance of £12-£15 sq m in price. There are alternatives which can be used when you know exactly what you want – exposed brickwork, timber linings – but they are considerably more expensive than a plastered finish and are normally only built as features.

The big question facing housebuilders is whether to go for a wet or dry system of wall coverings. The wet techniques use wet-mixed cement renders and gypsum plasters: the dry systems use dry-lined plasterboards. The wet techniques are traditional British building – the dry techniques are imported from countries where timber frame is prevalent. Ceilings are almost invariably fixed with plasterboard, but here there remains a choice about whether to cover them with a wet Thistle Finish plaster, to dry-line or

to comb on Artex. Actually, no one combs on Artex anymore, but you could do if you are feeling particularly perverse. Pricewise, there is very little to choose between the systems although I estimate that dry-lining is a little cheaper.

WET PLASTERING

Wet plastering is well understood by builders and favoured by most plasterers; a well-skimmed plaster finish looks fantastic – at least initially. It's problem stems from the fact that it uses a lot of water. Something like one cubic metre of water (equals 12 bathfulls) is being built into the fabric of the house if it is wet-plastered and this must in time dry out, which will take a summer at least. This drying-out results in movement which causes cracking in the top-coat plaster which looks naff and gets builders called back on site to carry out cosmetic repairs. This problem

Plastering: Material Costs

	UNIT	PRICE	DIVIDER	METRE RATE
12.5mm Plasterboard	1200x2400	£ 5.00	2.8	£ 1.80m²
15mm Plasterboard	1200x2400	£ 7.20	2.8	£ 2.60m²
12.5mm Fire Rated Plasterboard	1200x2400	£ 8.25	2.8	£ 3.30m²
12.5mm Fermacell Board	1200x2400	£ 10.60	2.8	£ 3.80m²
12mm Render	Cubic Metre	£ 68.00	80.0	£ 0.85m²
Thistle Skim Finish	25kg bag	£ 4.30	9.0	£ 0.50m²
Monocouche Renders	25kg bag	£9.00	1.0	£9.00m²
65mm Screed mixed on site	Cubic Metre	£ 100.00	15.0	£ 6.60m²
Coving 100mm	3m length	£ 3.60	2.5	£ 1.40m²

Plastering: Square Metre Rates

CHARGED RATE	£ 20 HR	LABOUR	MATERIALS	TOTAL
Render and Skim	30 mins	£ 10	£ 3	£ 13
Render only (scratch coat)	15 mins	£ 5	£ 2	£ 7
Render top coat	20 mins	£ 7	£ 2	£ 9
Tacking (Nailing) Plasterboard	12 mins	£ 4	£ 3	£ 7
Tacking 15mm Plasterboard	15 mins	£ 5	£ 4	£ 9
Dot and Dab (Sticking) Plasterboard	10 mins	£ 4	£ 3	£ 7
Skim Finish on Plasterboard	16 mins	£ 6	£ 1	£ 7
Dry Lined Finish to Plasterboard	12 mins	£ 4	£ 1	£ 5
Fixing External Mesh for Render	12 mins	£ 4	£ 8	£ 12
Two-coat External Render	45 mins	£ 17	£ 3	£ 20
Single-coat monocouche render	30 mins	£ 10	£ 9	£ 19
Floor Screed, 65mm Thick	25 mins	£ 9	£ 8	£ 17
Ready mixed screed	20 mins	£ 7	£ 8	£ 15
Gypsum screeds	Supply and fix only		£ 20	£ 20
Basic Coving (in linear metres)	10 min/m	£ 4	£ 2	£ 6

Model House Costs: Plastering

	AREA	RATE	MATERIALS	LABOUR	TOTAL
Ceilings	140m²	£ 17	£ 800	£ 1,500	£ 2,300
Walls	350m²	£ 17	£ 2,100	£ 3,900	£ 6,000
Floor Screeds	80m²	£ 17	£ 600	£ 700	£ 1,300
TOTAL			£ 3,500	£ 6,100	£ 9,600

is particularly bad when plasterboard ceilings are skimmed with a plaster finish; here the movement in timber behind the boards causes hairline cracks around all the plasterboard joints. None of this cracking is in the least bit dangerous – it doesn't mean subsidence is occurring – and many people live happily with it knowing that these bedding-in problems can be filled in at the first redecoration. However, for many unsuspecting souls it is a source of genuine grievance and complaint.

DRY-LINING?

It's dry – avoiding problems outlined above. It is relatively easy to correct out-of-plumb blockwork – you just adjust the thickness of the adhesive dabs. It also gives a comparatively soft wall with enough give for small children to bounce off unharmed, whereas a hard, plastered wall would bring forth tears.

Dry-lining is not particularly difficult to learn – the plasterboard manufacturers all run cheap two- or three-day training courses – but it can be badly applied, leaving a ridged effect on walls and ceilings. Plasterboard has to be fixed more carefully than is normal trade practice in order to keep the number of cuts to a minimum. The wall finish is similar to what you would get if painting on to lining paper (which is basically what you are doing) and this may not be glossy enough for some tastes. Plasterboard walls are not as damage-resistant as traditional plasters, although repairs can be easily effected.

The other noted problem with dry-lining, and with dot and dab (as used against masonry walls) in particular, is that it is air leaky, which will bother people looking for a low energy home. This air leakiness problem occurs with all forms of construction that use dry-lining, but its significance is greatly reduced when you build in timber-frame, incorporating a vapour barrier in the external walls.

BLOCKWORK V STUDWORK

You can only apply wet render onto a masonry background and it is, therefore, not an option for timber framers. Those using studwork walls will have to fit a wallboard, usually plasterboard – although, as already noted, plasterboard will take a 3mm wet plaster finish. On the other hand, if a dry method is desired in a brick and block house, then the favoured method is to stick plasterboard on to the blockwork using the dot and dab technique which uses specialised gypsum plasters as adhesives. This is the method currently in favour with most professional house builders – just goes to show how much they value not being called back because 'there's cracks in me walls.'

PLASTERBOARD

What is it? Gypsum plaster sandwiched between two layers of paper. It is characterised by being easy to cut, fairly easy to handle and it provides a good backing for paint and plaster. Note that wastage can be high when using plasterboard – up to 30 per cent on small rooms and ceilings, 10-15 per cent on walls. It is available in several different formats: square edged (for wet plaster skimming) or tapered edge (for dry-lining); 12.5mm thick for 600mm spaced studwork and 9.5mm thick for 400mm spacings; foil-backed for providing an integral vapour barrier (it's cheaper to use a separate polythene sheet); small boards measuring 1800x900mm as well as the more normal, room-height, boards which are 1200x2400mm. Since the sound regs were beefed up in 2004, there is a big uptake of heavier boards to get studwork partitions up to the required 40dB sound reduction rating. Sound deadening boards at 12.5mm are what to look out for. None of these formats is expensive: rates vary between £1.50 and £3.50 sq m depending on what you want the board to do.

There are also a number of plasterboards that are laminated for insulation. Make sure you get the right format for the job and make sure that you've used metric spacings on your wall studs and ceiling joists as imperial-sized plasterboard is no longer made.

Plasterboard is a very competitive business with three companies slugging it out for the European market: Knauf, Lafarge and BPB (aka British Gypsum, and now owned by St.Gobain). Consequently, the price hasn't really changed much in 20 years – amazing value if you think about it. There is little to choose between the rivals either on price or quality.

ALTERNATIVES
FERMACELL

Widely used in Germany, Fermacell is, in some ways, very similar to plasterboard and, in others, rather superior. It has a much higher racking strength than plasterboard and is therefore particularly useful when you want to hang radiators and bathroom furniture off timber stud walls and you don't know where the studs are. Fermacell also makes for better soundproofing. However, it is pricey in comparison with plasterboard, two to three times the price. Consequently, it is being used in the UK mostly as a backing board for kitchens and bathrooms. It is usual to glue the boards together and simply paint over them for a finished surface. Another board worth seeking out is Knauf's Aquapanel, a cement particle board which is completely waterproof and can therefore be specified in shower enclosures. Again, it's an expensive beast, costing around £30 a sheet.

EXPOSED BRICKWORK

Exposed brickwork internally isn't widely used these days because it's relatively expensive and it leaves open a problem with exposed elements like door lintels and cabling. These problems mean that feature brickwork is most often seen in small areas such as fireplaces. Also note that a transparent masonry sealer should be applied after drying out – and this is more expensive than emulsion work.

PINE MATCHBOARDING

Pine panelling used to be very popular in the 70s and 80s, but is now rarely seen over whole walls or ceilings, although it's sometimes used as a stained boarding, fixed vertically between skirting and dado rail. It is also an effective way of creating decorative service panels behind which can be run pipework and cabling, although this is a complex matter which ideally needs designing into the building from the beginning. In cost terms, it's intermediate between plaster and exposed brickwork or tiling.

GLASS BLOCKS

One of the most intriguing trends in home interiors has been the re-emergence of glass block walls. They were widely used in the Thirties, mostly on public buildings, but then fell completely out of fashion. You simply didn't see them until about ten years ago when the TV interior shows rediscovered them and suddenly glass blocks are everywhere. You can't get through B&Q without tripping over them. Ballpark materials costs come in at around £60 sq m.

PLASTERED FANCIES

Coving is used to mask the joint between walls and ceilings. It used to be almost ubiquitous in new housing but it's beginning to fall out of fashion. It's not particularly expensive – including adhesive, working out to around £2 per lin m and is fixed for between £3 and £4 per lin m. This may sound like small beer but a four-bedroomed house will tend to have at least 200 lin m of covable joints, so choosing coving could easily add £1,000 to your overall budget. On the other hand, making the joints tight enough so as not to need coving is a little bit more work for plasterers, so they may turn around and demand more money for having a cove-less finish, although it doesn't reflect well on their competency if they do.

NATURAL PLASTERS

There is a small but growing interest in traditional lime and clay plasters which has spread from the conservation market into new build. Clay, in particular, has a reputation for being good in wet rooms because it absorbs moisture when wet and helps control humidity levels. Plus it looks good unpainted.

CERAMIC WALL TILING

Tiling is not strictly speaking an alternative to plastering because it is usually applied on top, so 'addition' might be a better word. Its use is often entirely functional when applied as a splashback behind sinks, basins and baths, but in the Mediterranean you frequently see ceramic tiling in living rooms and bedrooms as well. In the UK wall tiling is seen in more functional terms, partly because wall tiles are so much more expensive here.

Whether you pay under £5 sq m for some unadorned and unnamed white tiles or £80 sq m for some top of the range, hand painted tiles out of the Fired Earth catalogue, the fixing costs remain remarkably similar. The adhesives which you use to stick the tiles down with and the grouts which you spread between the tiles tend to work out together at between £3 and £4 sq m depending on the thickness and specification. The laying costs depend on the intricacies of the task in hand, but on fairly straightforward work, it takes a tiler around one hour to fix a square metre of tiles and about 15 minutes to grout them up later. Big straight runs will be faster than this but most tiling work in kitchens and bathrooms involves a fair amount of cutting.

FLOOR SCREEDS

Traditionally, the floor screeding is undertaken by plasterers. Although it looks simple, it's one of the hardest and most skillful aspects of housebuilding and, as such, is ripe for a little techno-fix. Which is precisely what has been happening in the world of screeding.

Traditional, 20th century-style screeding, involves a two-and-one gang, mixing up a very dry, comparatively strong, 1:3 cement:sand mix and laying it by hand, 65mm or 75mm deep. The screeding gang work on their hands and knees, smoothing out the screed mix, trowelling off the surface, and keeping a very close eye on the levels across the floor. It's very easy to get it horribly wrong and end up with a sloping floor or one with hills and valleys in it, which clients tend not to appreciate very much. In my costing tables, I have 65mm screeding down at being around 25 minsper sq m; at that sort of pace, a two-and-one gang (that's three people!) would take two weeks to complete the downstairs of a detached house. They don't take anything like as long as this (some wouldn't even take two days) but their art/skill is so highly regarded that they can charge two or three times as much as ordinary tradesmen and

Chapter 10

the only way I can make sense of their charging rates is by making it appear to take longer than it actually does.

Anyway, the screed business is slowly changing. Site mixed screeding, as I have just described, is dying out and it now accounts for less than a third of the overall screed market. The bulk of screeds are now delivered readymixed, which is good for quality and does away with a third of the two-and-one gang. But the real growth market is in gypsum-based screeds, which are sprayed out of a nozzle and are self-placing. They have been available in the UK since the 1990s and have captured something like 20 per cent of the market. The cost is about £150 per cu m, as opposed to £100 per cu m for readymixed screed, but these screeds can be laid at half the depth (i.e. 35mm -. except where you have underfloor heating; then its 50mm as opposed to 65mm.) It's particularly suitable for underfloor heating as it doesn't require wheelbarrows with the potential to damage the pipes. Look out for Larfarge Gyvlon, Cemex Supaflo or Tarmac Truflow. Also check out Screedflo, an interesting independent business in this arena that is making a name for itself and has a natty specification called Screedflo dB which is designed to be poured onto intermediate timber floors to aid sound proofing and provide a medium for underfloor heating.

It's still the province of specialist contractors, which makes it rather more expensive than traditional screeds, but not by very much. It also dries a little more quickly. Talking of drying....

DRYING TIMES

Screeds, whether cement or gypsum based, take time to dry and it's important that they are thoroughly dried out, especially if there is a timber floor being laid on top of them. I have seen beautiful oak floor boards buckle and warp because moisture from the screed below was still evaporating. Seventy days is reckoned to be time enough for most screeds: in the summer months it will be a little less. If you have underfloor heating fitted, you can speed the process but only gently: cement screeds must be left for 28 days before any heating is applied at all, and even then it has to be turned on slowly, a few degrees higher each day.

WHY SCREED AT ALL?

You often don't have to. If you are finishing your floor in timber, you may not need to lay an intermediate floor, but if you are laying tiles and/or carpet, you will need a smooth surface to work off and it's hard (though not impossible) to get a concrete slab smooth enough for this. And of course, if you are laying underfloor heating on your ground floor, you need to set it in a screed.

FLOOR FINISHES

Nowhere else in building is there such a great variety of materials at such a huge variation in price. You could carpet a four-bedroom house for less than £2,000 (inc. VAT); equally you could spend over £10,000 and not risk being accused of extravagance. Normally, floor finishes are not included in building budgets unless they are an integral part of the construction; developers rarely fit floor finishes although they occasionally offer to carpet houses as a sweetener to encourage a sale.

CARPET

Even when glued down, carpet is regarded by Customs & Excise as a movable item and therefore subject to VAT as a furnishing – all other types of floor finish are zero-rated in the UK and therefore effectively exempt from VAT when built into a new house. Even so, carpeting still provides potentially the cheapest form of floor covering available – especially the bonded cords which also happen to be reasonably hard wearing. Beware offers of free underlay and free laying; obviously these services are not free and the charge for them is included in the price. Usually priced by the yard, carpet laying can be subject to enormous wastage because of the limited roll sizes. The DIY builder might be happier to lay carpet tiles, but if price is the only consideration, then it will still probably be cheaper to look out for the absolute basic ranges supplied and fitted by one of the carpet warehouses. Some of these carpets sell for a good deal less than a decent underlay (which can cost £3 sq m) so you can imagine what the quality is like.

■ Material. Wool is the traditional and natural material for carpets; it also tends to be the most expensive. Other natural materials you can use include sisal, coir, jute and seagrass, all of which tend to give a faintly bohemian feel to your flooring schemes. Synthetics like nylon and acrylics are now commonplace and much carpet sold these days is a cocktail of wool and synthetics – and people walking on them would not know the difference. The very cheapest material is polypropylene which looks synthetic but may be fine for your needs, especially in bedrooms.

■ Comparing prices over the phone is difficult because a lot of carpet is not branded and as there are so many varieties on the market, very often no two outlets sell the same thing. Sticking to an established name like John Lewis will ensure that you are not ripped-off, but they are unlikely to be selling carpet below £10 sq m, which is higher than many people's budget will allow.

■ Bear in mind this rule of thumb when

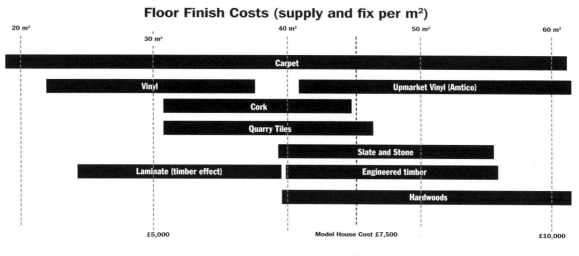

Floor Finish Costs (supply and fix per m²)

20 m²   30 m²   40 m²   50 m²   60 m²

Carpet

Vinyl   Upmarket Vinyl (Amtico)

Cork

Quarry Tiles

Slate and Stone

Laminate (timber effect)   Engineered timber

Hardwoods

£5,000   Model House Cost £7,500   £10,000

Model House Costs: Floor and Wall Finishes

	AREA IN m²	RATE	MATERIALS	LABOUR	TOTALS
Carpet	70	£30	£1,800	£400	£2,200
Oak flooring	60	£60	£2,400	£1,400	£3,800
Floor Tiling	30	£50	£800	£500	£1,300
Wall Tiling	58	£40	£500	£700	£1,200
Combined			£5,500	£3,000	£8,500

estimating cost: you should double the advertised price of a fitted carpet to get an idea of what it will all cost when laid on your floors. This will allow for offcuts, underlay and laying costs.

BATHROOM CARPETING

Avoid woollen carpets in bathrooms as they will tend to go mouldy, especially if they have a hessian backing. Polypropylene carpets with foam backings are cheap and durable and will survive many years of bath time frolicking.

TILES

There are many different materials used to tile or sheet floors and there is not space to cover them all here. In particular,

there are any number of synthetic rubbery plastic type floor coverings which are generally more at home in an industrial or commercial setting than a house. If you want to know more, check out your Yellow Pages under Flooring Services. Here I look at just the three most popular tiled finishes.

VINYL

The very word vinyl sounds cheap but don't be misled, it's not. Either in sheet or tile form, this can vary between the very cheap marble effects (like Polyflor) costing less than £5 sq m – these tiles usually have only a small percentage of vinyl in them – to Amtico floor tiles costing over £80 sq m. The best results are to be had when the immediate sub-floor is covered either with a

5mm latex screed or thin plywood sheeting. Adhesive adds around £1.50 sq m, laying costs between £15 and £20 sq m. There are some pretty convincing wood plank effect vinyls made by Karndean, costing around £20 sq m, which give you the look of a hardwood floor without the grief.

CORK

Back in the Eighties, I laid dozens of cork tile floors in bathrooms and kitchens. Cork was the height of fashion with the so-called Habitat generation. But as Habitat came to be superceded by IKEA, cork tiling slipped off the radar and now it's precious hard to track it down. You don't see it in B&Q, for instance. Which is strange because it's not that expensive,

Chapter 10

it's attractive and it scores highly on environmental grounds. Fashion is a funny thing. Wicanders is the best-known producer: their top of the range Cork Master costs around £25 sq m. Best laid on board; if laid on a cement screed ensure that it's completely dry – this takes around eight summer weeks.

CERAMIC/STONE TILES

Laying costs are higher when specifying ceramic tiles because it is a more involved process, requiring time-consuming cutting and a second pass to grout up the results. Adhesives and grouts can also be very expensive. Whilst you can find plenty of adhesives for under £3 sq m, anything with the word flexible in it causes prices to spiral, up to £10 sq m or more. Grout, of course, is extra. BAL is the big name here. The very cheapest floor tiles are usually imported from Italy or Portugal and are displayed under little known brand names in the DIY sheds and discount tile shops at less than £5 sq m. The cheapest British quarry tiles are available in red at around £10 sq m, whilst Cristal, Pilkington and Wooliscroft produce popular floor tiles from around £9 sq m upwards. At the other end of the scale, Fired Earth and numerous imitators sell a dazzling array of terracotta floor tiles, many of them reclaimed, from around £35 sq m upwards.

Another popular option is to fit a stone floor. I have seen a lot of Indian slate laid recently – it looks good and it's very cheap but it seems to suffer from varying thicknesses which makes a pig of laying. Paving stones or flagstones are conventionally laid outside but they can also make stunning interiors as well; Classical Flagstones produce convincing replica York stone from £25 sq m which is often used indoors.

TIMBER FLOORING

The rise and rise of hardwood flooring is a notable trend in contemporary home design. It was always thought of as an aspirational feature but people used to get put off by the price. It's not got any cheaper but all of a sudden people seem to be quite happily paying £40 - £80 sq m for hardwood floor planking and are being increasingly daring as to the choice of wood – current top of the pops seems to be bamboo which sounds like it might be cheap but ain't. Slightly cheaper options are to use a veneered floor which has a 4-5mm layer of hardwood stuck onto a composite backing. If anything, a veneer floor is going to be more stable because of the backing. However, every time you sand a hardwood floor you strip at least 1mm off the top surface so in the long-term maintenance stakes, a solid floor wins out. But how many times are you actually going to sand a hardwood floor? Cheaper still is to use a vinyl 'wood look-alike' floor cover but this is really cheating now.

There are an awful lot of options and a wide range of prices; oak planks can be anywhere between £17 and £80 sq m, a huge price range for what you might imagine are very similar products. Of course, they're not. One of the key points to watch if you buy a solid hardwood floor is that the moisture content is right down at around 8 per cent when you lay – this is especially important if you want to fit underfloor heating.

Another approach is to use a reclaimed board that has been stored undercover and is, hopefully, dimensionally stable. These vary in price from around £10 sq m up to £30 sq m and will almost certainly involve you in a lot of extra work (de-nailing, sanding, hole filling, more sanding, sealing). The huge variation in prices for reclaimed boards is of course an indication

that there is a huge variation in quality as well. If you go to one of the better salvage yards, such as Machells, near Leeds, you'll find good quality board but prices to match new planks. Another option is to use wood blocks – reclaimed oak can still be picked up from salvage yards for less than £15 sq m – but again be prepared to have to carry out a lot of extra preparation work. However, a wood block floor (sometimes known as parquet) has to be laid on a solid backing, which will generally involve laying some form of extra screed or decking beneath, especially as floor insulation is now mandatory.

MATWELLS

It's always a nice touch to see people thinking ahead and building in a sunken matwell is usually a sign that someone has been. Now that the disabled access regs require level access, usually at the main entrance door, a sunken matwell becomes even more important, as the door now opens just a few millimetres above the floor cover. There is an industry standard matwell (which may surprise some) which is 760 x 460 x 40mm. If you stick to this you can buy galvanised steel surrounds for around £40 and these will take industry standard sized coconut matting. If you are putting down a timber floor, you can of course create your own surrounds.

SECOND FIX CARPENTRY

Second-fix carpentry is a bit of a rag-bag of different activities that covers just about everything that carpenters get up to after the plasterers are finished. It usually includes door hanging and staircase fixing, as well as fixing skirtings and architraves and pipe boxings; often it also includes fitting

Second Fix Carpentry Key Rates

ITEM	UNIT	CHEAP	MID PRICE	FANCY	TIME TAKEN IN MINS	LABOUR @ £18/HR
Window board	m run		£ 5		20	£ 6
Door Linings	5.1m set	£ 11	£ 13	£ 26	45	£ 14
Internal Doors	each	£ 30	£ 140	£ 210	120	£ 36
Double Glazed Doors	per pair		£ 210	£ 450	300	£ 90
Door Furniture	per door		£ 10	£ 30	inc above	
Skirtings	m run	£ 0.75	£ 1.50	£ 3.00	12	£ 4
Architrave	m run	£ 0.55	£ 1.00	£ 1.80	8	£ 3
Cupboard Fit Out	m3		£ 20		180	£ 54
Matchboarding	m2	£ 6	£ 8	£ 15	40	£ 12
Loft Access Covers	each		£ 30		45	£ 20
Loft Ladders	each	£ 30		£ 120	120	£ 40

Model House: 2Nd Fix Carpentry Costs

	RANGE		MATERIALS	LABOUR	COMBINED
Windowboards		20m	£ 100	£ 120	£ 220
Door Linings	Mid	13 sets	£ 170	£ 180	£ 350
Architraves	Mid	130m	£ 70	£ 310	£ 380
Skirtings	Mid	120m	£ 90	£ 430	£ 520
Internal Doors	Cheap	13 No	£ 390	£ 470	£ 860
Door Furniture	Mid	13 sets	£ 130	inc above	£ 130
Loft Access Cover	Mid	1	£ 30	£ 10	£ 40
Loft Ladder	Mid	1	£ 30	£ 40	£ 70
Airing Cupboard			£20	£50	£70
Stairs	Mid	1 set	£ 450	£ 440	£ 890
Balusters	St Steel		£ 750	£ 200	£ 950
Juliet Balcony	St Steel		£ 450	£180	£ 630
Rounded Totals			**£ 2,700**	**£ 2,400**	**£ 5,100**

kitchens, and vanity units in bathrooms, and putting up shelves.

INTERNAL DOORS

The world of the internal door is split between the hollow and the solid. The hollow doors are like sandwiches; the casings are layers of board and the filling consists of a material very similar to egg boxes. Where you would normally place the handle and latch, they put a solid hunk of wood called the lock block and foolish would-be chippies (like me) have been known to hang these doors in a hurry, only to find that the lock block is on the hinge side of the door. If you are observant, you will hang the door on the correct side – there is only ever one lock block in a hollow door and if you look on the bottom edge you will see which side the lock block is located.

This all sounds very cheap and tacky and, generally speaking, eggbox-style doors are, but they can also be purchased with hardwood veneers, usually from some environmentally incorrect species like sapele (pronounced sa-pee-lee), and this pushes the price up to levels at which you can buy solid softwood doors, around the £30 mark. Sapele is in fact by far and away the most popular veneer in this country: the doors have 2.5mm chipboard facing onto which the veneers are ironed or steamed.

The very cheapest doors you can get are eggbox-filled doors which are encased in, wait for it, hardboard. Expect to pay around £15 for one of these but don't ever kick it. A popular variation on this theme is the embossed or moulded door; they are no stronger but they imitate the fielded panels found on timber doors and some of them imitate wood grain texture. The simpler ones cost between £30 and £40 each and they look quite acceptable when painted, which is what they are designed for. Some superior ones use a type of fibreboard for the casing and they are strong enough to take glazing, although doors with glazing panels are much more expensive – around £70. All the major joinery manufacturers have a selection of these doors and, if you want to select a door, get hold of one of their catalogues. Or have a look at the Doors World website — it's an eye-opener.

SOLID WOOD DOORS

For people who like their doors to go clunk rather than thwack when they shut. Not that these doors are that much heavier than their eggbox counterparts; indeed there are a number of incredibly cheap (ie less than £30) imported timber doors available in the DIY sheds which look as though they might actually disintegrate if you shut them too hard. They are usually stored about ten feet above ground level and when you get to see them close up you realise why.

Generally, internal timber doors fall into two categories; stainable and paint-only grade. The paint-only ones are made from inferior timbers that may well have dead knots – which are given to working loose – and are frequently made up of short sections of timber which are finger-jointed together. If you are planning to paint the doors you might just as well settle for a paint-only grade door costing around

£40; the better quality, stainable doors are more than twice as much.

Hardwood is an option as well. Oak and meranti are widely available but expensive at around £150 per door. The hardwood veneered hollow doors are about half this price and are solid enough for most people's demands.

COTTAGE STYLE DOORS

An increasingly popular option is to fit ledged-and-braced doors to all internal openings. This style of door used to be exclusively associated with back doors and outbuildings, but with the fashion for all things cottagey, they are beginning to move indoors. External doors are manufactured with a moisture content of around 18 per cent whereas the ideal moisture content for internal doors is around half this amount. Hanging an external door inside tends to result in them twisting out of shape.

The joinery majors such as JeldWen now carry internal cottage doors (in their case known as an FL&B for Framed Ledged & Braced) but they cost twice as much as the ones designed for exterior use.

MDF DOORS

Another approach, especially as regards fitted cupboard doors, is to make them on site using MDF (medium density fibreboard). MDF is a manufactured timber board which has no grain but can be worked like natural timber; the finish can be sanded to accept paint or even, at a pinch, stain.

Mouldings can be either routed into the board or stuck on to the surface. This is obviously rather labour intensive and the doors tend to be a bit on the heavy side but it is cheap. If you have non-standard sized doorways, which often occurs with alcove cupboards and the like, then MDF is often

a good solution. You need a board that's at least 25mm thick or else you won't be able to hinge it; alternatively, you can stick two thinner boards together and cut bits out of the top one to make decorative panelling effects. A good timber merchant will be able to dimension MDF for you, a facility not to be sniffed at.

DOOR FURNITURE

Door furniture is the phrase used to describe just about everything to do with doors excluding the door itself. That usually means all the bits made of metal, and door ironmongery would be a much easier to understand expression, but the building trade likes the word furniture to be used here. I really don't know why. Perhaps it adds to the mystique of the whole thing or maybe they are just being pig-ignorant. Anyway, I digress.

The point to cotton on to here is that some door furniture is purely functional in that you don't see it or, if you do, you don't notice it; however other bits are very visual and – wait for it – tactile. Yes folks, door handles are sexy. Developers know this and consequently are prepared to spend above the bare minimum to create an impression on the would-be house purchaser. Door handles may indeed be the only part of the house that the viewer actually touches during an inspection and female purchasers are thought to be impressed by something strong and solid which responds readily to their grasp. Or so male housebuilders believe.

STYLE

Most developers fit brass-plated furniture to their doors. There are two basic styles: Victorian (or plain) and Georgian (frilly bits added). Both styles are catered for by builders' merchants and DIY sheds who sell shrink-wrapped pre-packs at fairly

reasonable prices.

These pre-packs have one big advantage going for them in that they've got all the bits you need in the pack; you may be able to buy at keener prices but you risk a) forgetting vital bits, b) having to overbuy on items like screws and c) buying the wrong bits – classic one here is to get the wrong-sized hinges. If your tastes veer away from these mainstream choices you'll have to brave it and go and order your very own door furniture.

DOOR SECURITY

Door security features are dealt with in the Security section in the last chapter of this book. To summarise, current NHBC guidelines recommend fitting 5-lever locks to all external doors but also recommend that the main exit door should be protected by a Yale-type night latch which can be readily opened from inside without a key; this is to make escape easier in case of fire.

5-POINT LOCKING SYSTEMS

These are fancy multi-point locking systems that are fitted, as standard, on uPVC doors, but only because the basic material is so flexible that it would not be secure without bolts top, middle and bottom. The use of 5-point locking systems is creeping into the world of timber joinery and you can fit your own to any timber door simply by routing a slot down the closing edge.

BUYING TIPS

As already mentioned, the door furniture pre-packs are a

Cautionary tale: don't hang external ledged and braced doors internally! When initially hung, these cupboard doors were absolutely plumb with one another. Yet within a few weeks, the twisting was so severe that there is no way of correcting, other than starting again with new doors. This is to do with moisture content: external doors have around 18 per cent moisture content whereas internal conditioned air dries timber to below 12 per cent.

moderately good deal if you are happy to stay within a limited range. If you want more unusual fittings then the DIY sheds have a surprising variety; if you want wood or ceramic knobs this is a good place to look. More specialised still are the Architectural Ironmongers: check the Yellow Pages in your area. A very useful 'Bible' for door furniture is published by Ironmongery Direct (also online).

Another tip well worth pursuing is to order all your external door locks 'to pass.' This means that all your 5-lever locks are adjusted so that they can be opened with the same key. It's not exactly the automated house but it's a big improvement on lugging around identical looking keys, each of which will open only one of your doors. A good merchant will be able to sell you locks to pass at no extra cost although they will take an extra day or two to sort it out.

KNOBS AND LATCHES

Sorry to bring up this sordid subject again but the observant amongst you may have noticed that there are two distinct styles of door opening levers, otherwise known as handles and knobs. Whatever the merits and demerits of the two, there is one painful little trap to watch out for if you go for a knob – you need to fit a longer latch otherwise you will scrape your knuckles every time you open the door. For the technically challenged, the latch, in this instance, is the metal tube that fits inside the door and the hole in the latch determines exactly how far the handle or the knob sits from

Dados And Picture Rails

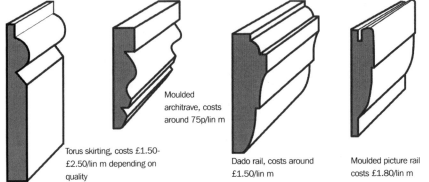

Torus skirting, costs £1.50-
£2.50/lin m depending on
quality

Moulded
architrave, costs
around 75p/lin m

Dado rail, costs around
£1.50/lin m

Moulded picture rail
costs £1.80/lin m

the edge of the door. The standard tubular latch is 63mm long and it's designed for handles; when fitting a knob on an internal door, fit a 75mm latch and an external door knob will require an even longer latch – say 95mm. The pre-packed knobsets normally include 75mm latches, but if you are buying independently then watch out.

SKIRTING AND ARCHITRAVE

The amazing thing about skirtings and architraves is that we don't really need them at all. Indeed, many countries have already done away with them. Yet all the major UK housebuilders and just about every self builder throws good money on fixing largely superfluous bits of timber to the base of all the walls and around all the internal door openings (architraves).

There is (or rather was) a logic behind fitting skirting boards. It used to be standard building practice to leave a 50mm gap between the floor and the bottom of the plaster on the wall so as not to breach the damp-proof course placed in the wall; however, damp-proofing techniques have changed and now floor membranes

are lapped into wall membranes and the rising damp never (in theory) penetrates the room space at all. It still leaves the problem of filling the unsightly crack between wall and floor but the widespread incorporation of fitted floor finishes has made even this problem a thing of the past.

Not that I've anything against skirting boards; I love 'em – the wider the better. They look great and any room without them will look cold and, worse still, European. Both skirtings and architrave are available in a range of styles varying from the very plain to the thick moulded sections beloved by the Victorians. Fixing times don't vary much but as regards material costs, the fancy sections are two to three times more than the utilitarian versions which are around 65p per m.

If you are in a hurry you can use prepainted MDF sections, which are widely available at builder's merchants. These are best nailed into the walls but, alternatively, can be stuck on with an adhesive like Gripfill, a mastic glue which can be used to bond all kinds of materials. Not only could you use it for all your skirtings and

architraves, but it's fantastically useful for sorting out little problems like squeaky stairs. A true friend to the bodge merchant. Not so clever when you want to later remove the skirting without taking half the wall down, but that's another story.

SHADOW GAPS

The fancy modern thing is to go for shadow gaps instead of skirtings and architraves. Rarely can it have been so hard to do so little, because despite the fact that there's nothing there, they are very difficult to pull off well because you can see the gap all the way around.

To get a shadow gap, you start by fixing the door lining and then fix a plaster stop bead into the wall around it, leaving a shadow gap between the door lining and the stop bead of around 10mm. Expamet make shadow gap beads, although you could elect to use a conventional stop bead. You are looking to get the surfaces of the wall and the door lining to be absolutely flush.

However, you might want to use something other than standard door linings, which are supplied with slot joints in the

Door furniture remains firmly rooted in the 20th century. Hi-tech solutions like finger-print recognition keypads are sometimes seen on demonstration projects, but are still a long way from becoming mainstream options

head section, These are designed to be covered over when the architrave is fixed: with no architrave, you will be able to see them. You may also find that the widths of the standard linings don't match your wall and plaster widths. Remember that planed timber is sold in nominal widths (that is before planing takes place) and the actual widths are usually 7 or 8mm less than this. So be prepared to spend a little extra on your door linings: they may have to be made up on site, or purchased as specials.

LOFT HATCH

Every house with an empty loft has one and they are not the most demanding of features. But take a little care in fitting a loft hatch as it is frequently a weak point in your home's battle against draughts. Furthermore, being an outlet for draughts rather than an inlet, you are never likely to be aware of just how much warm air you may lose through the loft hatch. Many an otherwise fastidious greenie (myself included) has insulated the top of the loft trap door – Gripfill is brilliant for this job as well – but neglected to effectively draught proof the strips of wood on which the hatch door sits. In terms of heat loss through loft hatches, effective draught proofing is ten times more important than the insulation. You don't have to do anything dramatic; just make sure it sits tight. Most people now buy proprietary loft hatches made from uPVC which clamp shut: they cost around £50.

LOFT LADDERS

If you've got an open loft and you don't plan a loft conversion, then a loft ladder is not quite essential but nevertheless incredibly useful, even if you only go up there once a year. A decent aluminium sliding loft ladder will cost around £50 and take a competent DIY boffin around two hours to fit. However, if you are interested in making your loft hatch draught-proof, it is really worth carrying out the installation of a loft ladder first because it usually leads to you having to make significant adjustments to the trap door housing.

Whilst we're on the subject, it's worth installing a permanent light in the loft just to make life easy when fixing a loft ladder. You won't regret it.

AIRING CUPBOARD

Airing cupboards are not actually required in houses with central heating but they are still very commonly fitted. There is one major drawback to the contemporary airing cupboard and that is that with the new generation of combi boilers or super-lagged hot-water cylinders, you no longer have a creditable heat source in the airing cupboard; hence, perpetually soggy towels. Well, that's not quite true; any new house will enjoy a much higher ambient temperature than an old wreck and this will tend to dry damp clothes, albeit rather slowly. You can, of course, just put fully dried clothes in the airing cupboard, but this rather defeats the purpose of having an airing cupboard in the first place. Alternatively, you can fit a mini-heater or a 150W light bulb inside. It all seems a bit futile when the cause of your problem is the fact that you've wrapped up the hot water cylinder so well that it no longer gives off any heat.

What's really needed is an effective way of lagging and unlagging your hot water tank, controlled automatically by the relative humidity of air inside the cupboard. But this sounds very expensive and surely the world is full of more pressing problems. Still it's one to ponder on during those long sleepless nights.

BOXING IN

Boxing in the pipes is a new

facet of housebuilding that now forms a significant bit of a second-fixer's work. In the good-bad-indifferent-olde days the pipes were left naked for all to see. The stench pipe in particular was usually run down the outside of the house.

Current fashions are for internal stench pipes – concealed internal stench pipes – and this means boxing is de rigueur. Now, depending on your disposition, this type of job can seem like an incredible almighty drag or a marvelous opportunity to show the world just how creative you can be with a bit of dead space.

Whichever camp you fall into, it helps to plan your pipe runs and attendant boxings well ahead so that the boxing can be incorporated into the overall scheme of things rather than sticking out into rooms like an ugly carbuncle ('monstrous', I hear you saying).

Bathroom boxings are often best tiled over, but you must allow at least some of the paneling to be removable – a trick that's accomplished with mirror screws and flexible mastic joints. If you are painting the finish, then MDF is probably the best material to use, but if you plan to stick ceramic tiles on, then a waterproof 18mm plywood would be a better choice.

Boxing is also widely used in bathrooms to create a fitted vanity unit effect. There are a range of basins (known as semi-countertop) that are designed to sit over a boxed unit, and there are also concealed cisterns which will be proud to flush behind your mini-wall. The usual choice of wall finish will be ceramic tiles but pine matchboarding is becoming fashionable once again, albeit painted not varnished.

SHELVING

The only quotation that The Duchess of Windsor is remembered for is 'you can't be too rich and you can't be too thin'. Had she been a keen builder, she might have added 'you can't have enough shelves' because it is an axiom that, however many shelves you put up, you will still need more. I can discern three approaches to shelving:

n Buy some: go out and buy some ready made up units. DIY sheds have some pretty basic ones; IKEA has some basic ones which are a little better designed. John Lewis have some very nice expensive shelving systems. Free-standing shelving units are not especially cheap but they are removable.

n Bash them up: utility shelving can be extremely cheap to fit. If you use one of the proprietary steel bracket systems like Spur or Element 32 you pay a lot more but you get a system that's very quick to install and easy to alter. It is also readily removable. Materials for a steel bracket shelving system work out at around £30 per lin m which is cheaper than almost any ready made system.

n Labour of love: design your shelving to fit a particular alcove or sit at a certain height. Think a little of the finished look; perhaps add some sort of pelmet and possibly some lighting as well. This sort of detail does not have to be expensive but it does require a certain amount of forethought. If you know what MDF is and know how to wield a router, you should be able to erect bespoke shelving (with no metal brackets showing!) for less than £20 per lin m (materials only).

STAIRS

Designing and installing stairs and landings is one of the less discussed aspects of housebuilding yet a staircase can make or break an interior, and getting it right it can be very challenging and sometimes extremely expensive. So what do you need to know?

There are regulations about how you should set out a staircase so that it works safely. Too few or too many steps and it'll be difficult to climb. Handrail positions, headroom and pitch are also regulated, all with the aim of making staircases user friendly. By and large, it's worth sticking to these guidelines, although they can be relaxed in certain circumstances, such as restricted loft access.

DESIGNING THE STAIRCASE LAYOUT

The first and most critical factor is to work out how the staircase will run. Where will it flow from and to, and whether it will achieve this with a straight flight or with a turn or two. There are practical reasons for choosing a straight flight: it's usually the cheapest option and it usually makes it easier to move furniture up and down stairs. And if at any point in the future, you might want to install a stair lift, a straight flight is much the simplest option.

However, sometimes a turn will fit the available space better. If you want to create a more dramatic entrance with a full height hallway, and space is somewhat lacking, then a staircase with a half landing is a good way to achieve this. And in smaller houses where circulation space is tight, you can reduce the overall space taken up by a staircase and its top and bottom landing areas by engineering a turn or two.

There are often several options on how you can run a staircase and good designer will work through them to see which one flows best. The polite convention is to arrange the stairs so that the base should be somewhere close to the front door of the house and that you shouldn't have to cross a room to get from the front door to the stairs. This is doubly important if there is (or maybe, at some time in the future) a third storey to the house, when the stairs have to

Stairs Key Rates

	SOFTWOOD	HARDWOOD	TIME TAKEN (HRS)	LABOUR @ £18/HR
Straight flight - landing balusters	£ 400	£ 700	16	£ 300
One turn - stair & landing balusters	£ 800	£ 1,300	24	£ 450
Two turns - stairs & landing	£ 1,000	£ 1,500	32	£ 600

act as a fire escape route from the loft.

TECHNICALITIES

Having established the overall staircase design, the next problem is to develop a technical brief for how the stairs are to be constructed.

STEP ONE is to measure the total rise, this is the measurement from finished floor below to finished floor level above.

STEP TWO is to work out the number of steps needed. Staircase builders refer to the horizontal steps as treads, and the vertical connecting parts as risers. It's usually reckoned that the best height for a riser is 200mm, so you want to be as close to this as possible — the building regulations allow you to have risers up to 220mm. Typically you get a 2600mm overall rise and this divides neatly into 13No 200mm individual steps or risers.

STEP THREE is to work out the number of treads and how they will sit. There is always one less tread than the number of risers, as the top of the stairs is designed to be level with the finished floor and you have only a connecting piece, known as a nosing.

STEP FOUR is to work out the tread width, otherwise known as the going. The going is the measurement from the face of one riser to the face of the next riser. The minimum going for a domestic staircase to comply with building regulations is 220mm and the pitch of a domestic staircase must not exceed 42₀.

If you break the stairs with a landing, it's conventional to keep the same rise and going for both halves of the staircase. There

is no restriction with how narrow you can go with a staircase but the width of a standard flight of stairs is 860mm, and this should be regarded as a minimum for a main staircase, though secondary stairs or loft access stairs can still work down to 600mm width.

LANDINGS

The commonest option is to split the staircase into two halves connected by a small landing. A landing that turns a staircase through 180₀ is known as a half landing; unsurprisingly, it's known as a quarter landing when it turns it through 90₀. This arrangement is better when you want a more open stairwell design and often makes it much easier to design the internal layout of the house.

WINDERS AND SPIRALS

Winders (pronounced wine-ders, not win-ders) is the name given to steps that turn corners whilst still climbing; a spiral staircase consists of nothing but winders but a more conventional arrangement uses three winder steps (usually at the top or the bottom of the flight) to navigate a 90₀ turn. They are space efficient: these days they are most commonly used with loft conversions, precisely because of this reason.

HEADROOM

You need a minimum of 2000mm of clear headroom above the pitch line on a domestic staircase to comply with building regulations although this can be relaxed for loft conversions where height is restricted.

Having insufficient headroom can be a problem when the stairwell is located under an area of sloping roof and it's a technical detail that is often overlooked by architects and designers. You may be able to fall back on the reduced height requirements for loft conversions but sometimes it is more effective to redesign the stair layout.

LOFT STAIRS

The regulations recognise that there are certain situations – principally loft conversions – where it just isn't feasible to build a standard staircase. Provided the stairs only lead up to one habitable room (plus an attached bathroom), then you are permitted to use either a loft ladder or an alternate tread staircase. The normal pitch requirements are also relaxed allowing you to fit a staircase into a much tighter space. These stairs are often marketed as space saver stairs.

TRENDS

The role of the staircase is gradually changing. In previous eras, only the grandest houses would have attempted to make a feature out of a staircase. In normal domestic architecture, the stairs fulfilled a purely functional role, and this remains true in the vast majority of developer built homes. Even ten years ago, pretty much the only choice you had to make was whether the timber spindles on your banister were to be plain or carved. But in common with the growing interest in other interior design features, staircases have started to get modern and sexy. Instead of spending

Chapter 10

a few hundred pounds, maximum, on building a staircase, people now seem willing to fork out several thousand pounds for designer staircases, commonly using such materials as glass and steel.

OPEN RISERS

Replacing solid risers (the vertical sections of each step), with open risers is something that features high on many self builders' wish lists. There is a problem here in that the building regulations don't permit any gaps in stairs wider than 100mm, in order to stop small children falling through. This is sometimes referred to as the 100mm sphere rule — the theory being that you shouldn't be able to pass a 100mm diameter sphere through the gap.

The standard solution to this is to have a semi-open riser design, so that each step appears to have a little downstand underneath it, known as a riser downstand. This allows you to see through the stairs as you climb up, whilst satisfying the guarding regulation. An alternative is to have completely open risers, but to fit a horizontal bar at the mid point between the treads.

Nevertheless, you often see photographs of unguarded open riser staircases in magazines. The reason for this may be that the new staircase is a replacement of an older one, and that the work has been carried out outside building control jurisdiction. Alternatively, the guard rails have been removed after the building inspector's final visit.

GLASS

Such is everyone's desire for space

For safety reasons the regulations don't permit any gaps in stairs wider than 100mm

and light that we have witnessed a rise in demand for glass balustrading on staircases and landings. The glass has to be thick and toughed, and consequently the fixings have to be more robust and this adds to costs. If you want the cool, contemporary look of glass around your stairs, it's likely to add between £3,000 and £8,000 to the costs, depending on the scale and complexity of your design.

FUSION

Richard Burbidge introduced the contemporary-looking Fusion stairparts range in 2000 and initially thought that they were launching a niche product, but it's turned into a big hit. The stair parts for a simple staircase with a 2m landing sells for around £550 using Fusion, around £200 more than pine, but it's much quicker to fit, 'requiring an average of just seven saw cuts as opposed to 125 when using conventional stair ballustrading'. Such has been the success of Fusion that other manufacturers have now launched similar products, such as Axxys from Cheshire Mouldings.

MODULAR STAIRS

Generally made in Italy, modular stair kits offer a way of getting a contemporary design on a budget. They tend to specialise in spiral and spacesaver designs and they probably wouldn't suit a main staircase as they generally don't comply with UK building regulations but may be suitable for small loft conversions and mezzanine sleeping platforms.

LIGHTING

It's important to think about how a staircase and landings should be lit, both in terms of daylight and during hours of darkness. In some house designs, the circulation space is in semi-darkness the whole time because all the windows are placed in the living rooms, bedrooms and bathrooms. Good designers will find ways of introducing daylight: traditionally, this was achieved with a glass fanlight placed above an internal doorway which borrows light from the room behind. These days, a more common solution is to set a rooflight above the stairwell. If space is tight, an alternative option is to use a lightpipe.

The stairwell also needs to be lit electrically. The standard arrangement is to have lights both top and bottom, and for these lights to be switched from both top and bottom of the staircase, known as two-way switching. More elaborate lighting is available; typically this will involve low-powered lighting, such as LEDs, used on each individual step, or sometimes set into the wall or handrail.

MATERIALS AND COMPARISON COSTS

There are two essential factors that have a bearing on costs. One is the design of the staircase, the other is the materials used to build it. Generally, the simpler the design, the cheaper the staircase. It also helps to have a standard rise between floors: if the distance between finished floors is the standard 2600mm, then you gain a small advantage in being able to order an off-the-peg staircase.

Straight flights are of course cheaper than staircases that turn, and curved staircases tend to be more expensive still.

As for materials, the cheapest stairs tend to be engineered pine and plywoods. These are best suited for fully carpeted stairs. One step up from this is parana pine, which has been the preferred timber for stair makers for many years. It is a tightly grained softwood with lots of reddy-brown colour variations and it takes a clear coat of varnish. It often gets specified with hemlock stairparts.

Hardwood staircases are more expensive still, although you can get a hardwood look for less money by specifying veneered MDFs. Hardwoods vary in price from two times the price of softwoods, to four or five times the price, depending on the choice of timber. Oak is usually the most expensive.

Other materials used include steel

(popular for spirals), reconstituted stone (also popular for spirals) and glass. Pre-cast concrete is uncommon in individual houses, though it's sometimes used in basements.

Stairplan.co.uk run an amazingly helpful website with lots of guidance on choosing stairs, and they also have an online shop at www.tradestairs.com which allows you to work out prices directly. As a rule, a straightforward flight of stairs with a small, 2m landing, can be supplied for as little as £500 and fitted in a day, but if you want to use cutting edge design and unusual materials, it's not difficult to spend ten or even twenty times as much.

PAINTING AND DECORATING

EXTERIOR WORK

You can avoid exterior decorating altogether by specifying pre-finished materials like uPVC, composites or aluminium coverings. Windows and doors are available with composite finishes: there are masonry alternatives for fascias and soffits and even timber boarding is available in cementitous replica or in species like cedar that doesn't require any paint or stain.

But if regular timber is your thing, then you have to provide some form of protection for it if it's to be used externally. The main choice is now between traditional paint and woodstains. Even though woodstains are more expensive to buy, the cost difference between the two systems is negligible because there is such a high labour content in decorating and, if anything, stains are slightly quicker to apply. What really causes decorating costs to tumble is reducing the number of coats needed to get a decent finish. Many builders do this with stains by dispensing with the third coat, which would be difficult with

conventional paint, but there are now a number of one-coat paints (eg Crown Solo) that enable you to dispense with the undercoat – at a price.

WOOD PAINTS

The traditional way of finishing external timber is with oil-based gloss paint. This is applied in a three-coat system: primer, undercoat, gloss. If you want to use a traditional paint finish you can save money and time by specifying that your joinery arrives on site primed with paint instead of the current industry standard of a basecoat of honey-coloured stain.

Which paint to use? There is a bewildering array of paints available: traditional oil-based gloss, non-drip gloss, one-coat gloss, microporous paints, acrylic paints to name but a few and coupled with the fact that every manufacturer seems to use a different naming system to describe their product it's no wonder the poor consumer gets confused. Which? magazine carries out an annual review of exterior paints (and stains) but it only scratches the surface of the paint market; their survey is just not comprehensive enough to provide a complete picture and, in any event, the canny manufacturers are forever reformulating their products and giving them new brand names so that the chances are, even if you went around B&Q armed with the latest Which? survey in your hand, you'd still not find their recommendations. Or if you did, how would you know it was the same as it was five years ago when Which?'s test started?

WATER-BASED ACRYLICS

Two factors have combined to increase the sales of water-based paints and they are both to do with user friendliness. Firstly, they are very easy to apply – afterwards the brushes can be washed out under a cold

Painting & Decorating Rates

Decorating - Metre Rates (inc Labour and Materials)

	EACH COAT /m²	COST FOR THREE COATS/m²
Emulsion to Internal Plasterwork	£ 1.30	£ 4
Masonary paint to external render	£ 4.00	£ 12
Stain to external cladding	£ 4.50	£ 13
Varnish to hardwood flooring	£ 3.70	£ 11
Paint one face of a window	£ 7.20	£ 22
Stain one face of a window	£ 7.80	£ 24
Paint one face of a door	£ 3.70	£ 11
Stain one face of a door	£ 4.30	£ 13
Paint balusters and stair supports	£ 7.20	£ 22
Stain balusters and stairs	£ 7.80	£ 23
Paint strips	£ 1.00 m run	£ 3 m run
Stain strips	£ 1.20 m run	£ 4 m run
Wallpaper	£ 7.00	

Model House: Decorating Costs

	AREA/LENGTH	RATE	MATERIALS	LABOUR	TOTAL
Internal plasterwork	490m²	£ 3.90	£ 150	£ 1,760	£ 1,910
Timber lengths					
Paint Door Linings	66m	£ 3.60	£ 60	£ 180	£ 240
Paint Architraves	130 m	£ 3.60	£ 110	£ 350	£ 460
Paint Skirtings	120 m	£ 3.60	£ 110	£ 320	£ 430
Paint Window boards	20 m	£ 3.60	£ 20	£ 50	£ 70
Rounded Totals			£ 500	£ 2,700	£ 3,200

tap; secondly, there are increasing concerns over the health risks of using the traditional oil-based gloss paints. The people most likely to benefit from both these factors are the professional painters and decorators yet, paradoxically, they are the ones who are most resistant to using water-based paints, reckoning them to be useless. Expensive more like. Although they are still relatively new (first introduced in the Seventies, but we are talking painting and decorating here), the indications are that water-based paints perform rather better than many oil-based alternatives. What they won't give you is a high-gloss sheen finish, but then most people prefer the matt look these days.

MASONRY PAINTS

As if to emphasise the last point about the durability of water-based paints, standard masonry paints, which are used to cover external render and masonry, are mostly water-based and many will claim to last for 15 years before needing re-coating. They are easy to apply but their application should not be rushed; the underlying cement render must be allowed to dry out thoroughly. This is a drag because many builders are itching to strike the scaffolding by the time the external rendering is done

and waiting for render to dry can take forever. Take the scaffolding down and it'll take you three times as long to paint the house. The moral? Only build houses with external painted panels when the sun shines. Or, better still, opt for a pre-coloured monocouche render.

STAINS

The habit of applying woodstains was a hit with the wood-stripping Habitat generation because the stains enable you to see the natural grain of the timber. Generically, stains are divided into two sub-groups, low-build and medium-build, but you are unlikely to hear these terms bandied about on a building site where they are known by their brand names. The build rating refers to the thickness of the stain and the higher the build the better the protection but the less you see of the underlying wood. The biggest names in this business are Sadolin and Sikkens, now both part of Akzo Nobel, as is Dulux. Sadolin's low-build stain is called Classic and is most widely used on sawn timber which drinks it like a Dublin bar on St. Patrick's night. They do an Advanced One Coat version that halves the application time. Their medium-build stain is called Extra (currently it's called Extra Durable Woodstain) and this is much more oily – treacly almost – and you use this for covering timber joinery. All these stains are available in a range of woody colours - the really jazzy colours are usually restricted to the low-build ranges.

Conventionally, stains have been spirit-based but, as with paints, you can now buy water-based acrylic stains. Sikkens' Cetol BL range is reckoned to be one of the best. The use of woodstains seems to have peeked, as the Habitat generation gives way to the IKEA one. In the mid-Nineties, 60 per cent of timber windows fitted into new homes were getting a stain finish: today, that's fallen back to below 40 per cent.

INTERIOR WORK
WALLS AND CEILINGS
Most interior walls are finished with emulsion paints, which are very cheap and very easy to apply, being water-based. The standard choice you need to make is between a matt finish and a silk finish. Matt finishes are characterised as being thicker (more opaque) and softer; silk finishes produce a harder, glossier look that has the added advantage of being more readily washable. There is no difference in price. Satin finishes are a halfway house between

matt and silk. One tip for new housebuilders is to apply your emulsions immediately after plastering or dry-lining is finished. You can get in and have a relatively free run at bare walls without having to fiddle around with skirtings, architraves, socket boxes, switch plates and radiators.

Another tip, this one for the stylistically challenged housebuilder, is to slap magnolia on everything. White is a bit too clinical for most people's taste; in contrast magnolia has enough cream in it to soften the overall effect without making any loud statements that will clash with furnishing choices made later on. If you are in a hurry and don't want to be bothered planning colour schemes, then magnolia is the answer. It's also a boon in homes shared with small children where walls have an endearing habit of getting drawn on. Instead of trying desperately to clean off the mess, you can just slap some more paint on it and it'll be just like new. Dull but true.

WOODWORK
Interior woodwork gets very similar treatment to exterior woodwork. Traditionally, that meant a three-coat gloss paint system. Increasingly it means that woodstains are used instead.

FLOORS
I'm tempted to say that varnishing is vanishing but I wouldn't be so daft; its use is, however, much more limited than it used to be. Externally – where it is prone to blistering and flaking – it has been replaced by the woodstains. However there is still a place for varnishes indoors on any exposed timbers, most notably hardwood floors. Some you can buy pre-lacquered, which is easy, but most require some form of surface treatment. The quickest route is to apply as hard a sealer as you can find – Dulux's Diamond Glaze is often chosen as

it's as hard as they come. The problem with this approach is that, given time, even the hardest coatings wear through and then you are faced with a re-sand. The other approach is to use an oil and to be prepared to re-apply it regularly. This is fine in rooms like bedrooms but it's an almighty drag in kitchens and hallways. Actually, the truth is that hardwood floors require maintenance if you want them to continue to look fantastic, whichever surface treatment you choose.

SPECIALIST FINISHES
ARTEX TEXTURED CEILINGS
Don't think that Artex is a replacement for painting as well as plastering. It has to be painted to stop the smell, and emulsioning Artex is a good deal more time-consuming than going over a flat surface. Many of the big housebuilders still specify Artex on their ceilings throughout, presumably because of problems they have experienced with cracking in plastered ceilings. Dry-lining, which is now prevalent on internal walls, can of course be applied to ceilings as well but the taping and jointing work needed to finish it is more complicated because there is always a much higher number of cuts and joints on ceilings than on walls.

WALLPAPER
It's not so very expensive but wallpaper is right out of fashion at the moment. You could wallpaper a four-bedroomed house throughout for around £800 over and above the cost of slapping on a basic emulsion.

PAINT EFFECTS
There has been a considerable revival of interest in near-forgotten painting techniques like stippling and rag rolling. If you are at all interested you will probably already have a book by Jocasta Innes and there's really nothing more to add. However, if you want to dip your toes in it but are

afraid that you might get stoned on scumble glazes then you can cheat and use one of the proprietary two-tone paints. However, I don't think Jocasta would approve somehow.

MASTICS

Mastics are something of a new feature in building, or at least the ways we use them today are new. They now tend to get applied to just about every conceivable join between materials; so wherever joinery meets brickwork or a tiled surface meets a worktop or a bathtub, there's a bead of mastic. There are mastics for sealing between plasterboard sheets and decorator's mastics for filling cracks (Painter's Mate); just about the only thing that is common to them is that they are packaged in tubes. Where water penetration is a problem – and that includes most external applications – it is worth paying more for the silicone based ones which, whilst remaining flexible, are less likely to break down.

It is said by some that mastics are the bodger's friend and that if you build to very high standards your joints will all be tight and you shouldn't need mastics at all. While there is some truth that good building standards are usually reflected in tight joints, mastics, particularly the silicone based ones, are now so widely used that it is inconceivable you will not have any need of them at some point. It is, however, very difficult to estimate just how much mastic you will need – that, at least, often depends on how wide your gaps are. And it is also true that mastic is a whole lot easier to apply against tightly

fitting backgrounds. Note that if you are subcontracting decorating, you should make it absolutely clear where you want mastic to be applied and which type of mastic you want to be used.

DRIVEWAYS AND PAVINGS

Driveways are included on the list of external works that are exempt from VAT on new buildings, so there is every reason to finish the drive before occupation. Almost invariably, planning permission for new homes requires provision for off-road car parking (though increasingly for less parking than you would actually like) and this means that some attention has to be paid to both where and how this

The 9th edition benchmark house has a mix of hard paving and decorative aggregate. I kept the same mix for this edition's model house

is to be accommodated. So whilst a garage is arguably a luxury you could dispense with (or postpone), driveways and hardstandings must be accommodated within the initial design.

FOUNDATIONS

Whatever drive finish you decide on, the base you lay should essentially be the same: ideally 100-150mm of hardcore. A 1 cu m void needs 2 tonnes of hardcore to fill it, so:
■ To lay hardcore 100mm thick, 1 tonne will cover 5 sq m
■ To lay hardcore 150mm thick, 1 tonne will cover 3.3 sq m.

A superior method, particularly recommended on clay sites, is to use a Terram or Geotextile sheet underlay beneath the hardcore layer. These allow water to pass through

External Works: Key Rates

	MATERIALS	TIME TAKEN IN MINUTES	LABOUR @ £18/HR	COMBINED
150mm Hardcore base	£ 6 m²	20	£ 6 m²	£ 12 m²
100mm concrete slab	£ 9 m²	25	£ 8 m²	£ 17 m²
Two-coat tarmac	£ 6 m²	30	£ 9 m²	£ 15 m²
75mm Gravel	£ 3 m²	30	£ 9 m²	£ 12 m²
Paving slabs	£ 11 m²	30	£ 10 m²	£ 20 m²
York stone	£ 50 m²	40	£ 12 m²	£ 62 m²
Simple kerbs	£ 3 m	30	£ 9 m	£ 12 m
Plain Block pavings	£ 10 m²	30	£ 10 m²	£ 20 m²
Fancy Block setts	£ 25 m²	30	£ 10 m²	£ 35 m²
Block kerbs	£ 9 m	30	£ 9 m	£ 18 m
Pattern Imprinted Concrete		Supply & Fix only		£ 35 m²
Resin Bonded Driveways		Supply & Fix only		£ 30 m²
Turfing	£ 2 m²	12	£ 4 m²	£ 6 m²
Post and 3-Rail Fencing	£ 5 m	20	£ 7 m	£ 12 m
Palings	£ 4 m	20	£ 7 m	£ 11 m
Picket Fence	£ 8 m	20	£ 7 m	£ 15 m
Close Boarded Fence (1.8h)	£ 20 m	45	£ 15 m	£ 35 m
9in brick wall with piers (1.8h)	£ 120 m run	360	£ 120 m	£ 240 m

Model House Externals

	AREA/LENGTH	RATE	MATERIALS	LABOUR	TOTAL
Base Preparation	160m²	£ 12	£ 960	£ 960	£ 1,920
Decorative Aggregate	140m²	£ 15	£ 840	£ 1,260	£ 2,100
Fancy block paving	20m²	£ 35	£ 500	£ 200	£ 700
Paving Slabs	15m²	£ 20	£ 165	£ 135	£ 300
Post & Rail Fencing	30m	£ 11	£ 150	£ 180	£ 330
Close-boarded Fencing	15m	£ 34	£ 300	£ 210	£ 510
Turfing	140m²	£ 6	£ 280	£ 560	£ 840
Rounded Totals			**£ 3,200**	**£ 3,500**	**£ 6,700**

whilst stopping mud mixing in with the hardcore overlay. Laying hardcore can be done by hand but this is backbreaking and time-consuming. The most efficient method is to use machines to spread and tamp hardcore – digger buckets are particularly effective tampers. It is very useful to have hardcore laid as early as possible on a building job as it aids access and stops the site becoming a quagmire, but drain-laying timetables do not always allow this use of machinery and whether it is worth getting machinery in later just to lay hardcore depends on the size of the driveway.

If you dispense with or skimp on this hardcore sub-base, you will end up with a drive which will initially look good but will rapidly disintegrate. The other problem to be aware of here is rainwater drainage; on flat sites, water will tend to pool if it is not adequately planned for. To this end, it is normal to lay the drive so that rainwater collects in certain points, then drains off to a soakaway. Whilst the falls can usually be constructed when the actual driveway is being laid, the drainage obviously has to be installed before the sub-base. A minor detail? You won't think so if you overlook it.

CONCRETE BLOCK PAVING

Now the most popular way of finishing the front access (and also for doing paths and patios). There are large price breaks available for bulk orders and full loads (144 sq m) should be available at less than £10 sq m in greys or buffs (which makes them as cheap as plain concrete paving slabs and almost as cheap as wet concrete laid 100mm deep). They are laid dry (without any cement) on a 50mm bed of sharp sand, and finished with jointing sand brushed over them and whacked with a compactor plate: dry laying is cheaper than wet and this makes them a cheap and attractive option for patios and paths as well as drives.

Supply and fix prices for plain block pavings tend to come in around £20 sq m (excluding hardcore foundation preparations), but these are at the low end of what you might expect to pay for something fancier. Kerb work obviously has a big impact on the overall costs and the value of this varies from site to site but averages about 20 per cent of the overall costs. Fancy pavers will bump the overall price up by 50-100 per cent. As with bricks and roof tiles, there is a choice between clay and concrete; clay invariably costs more but is said to look better or, more accurately, to wear better.

Builders can usually make significant savings by negotiating paver prices off the back of brick and block orders placed at the beginning of the job and thereby taking advantage of full load deliveries. Money can also be saved by using machines (JCBs etc) to place pallet loads at convenient places; later on this work can often only be done by hand.

PERMEABLE PAVINGS

The last decade or so has seen a growing interest in pavings that are designed to absorb water rather than to direct it elsewhere. Formpave were the first into this market and after a slow start it has taken off with the whole SUDS movement. Now everyone is at it with brand names like Aquapave and Hydropave. It's actually a whole system approach to surface run-off and the pavers form only part of it: you have to use a no fines sub base which will hold water, and there are debates about just where and how many geotextiles should be involved.

On small selfbuild sites, permeable paving systems are unlikely to make a huge difference to the world of storm water management (unlike a Tesco car park, for instance), but you may well be required to build a SUDS-compliant driveway as a planning condition. Usually, it's enough to direct the surface run-off to a soakaway, which can be done with drain gulleys just as easily as fancy permeable paving systems.

GRASS PAVING

On the other hand, you may be attracted to a permeable paving system and there is nothing quite so eco-chiq here as a grass paving. There are several systems available: these vary from block paving with spaces which get planted out, to concrete grids with voids, to plastic cellular systems which contain gravel or grass, and even reinforced turf. It's a specialised area: the acknowledged experts here are Grasscrete.

TARMAC

The preparation is much the same as for pavers; kerbs need to be set in concrete around the perimeter, although these are usually cheaper than the special kerbings used with block paving.

A pukka job should consist of a 80mm base course laid below a 35mm top course, known as the wearing course. A 50 sq m

driveway with 20m kerbings should cost slightly less than a basic block paver.

Some tarmac prices appear to be far lower than this – this is the Wild West of the building trade remember – but the specification is unlikely to be the business and the finished drive may not last very long.

CONCRETE

Base preparations are again similar to pavers and tarmac; kerbs can be ignored in favour of shuttering (or road forms) for which steel formers are available to hire. The designated readymix for driveways is PAV 1 – strong and relatively expensive – and it is normally laid at 100mm depth. Reinforcement should not be necessary. Cheap and cheerless.

PATTERN IMPRINTED CONCRETE (OR PIC)

A number of specialist operators now offer patterned concrete paving where imprints of pavers are set into wet concrete to give a paved effect drive. This technique is widely used elsewhere around the world but is having difficulty catching on in the UK because of the low prices of standard concrete block paving. Having said that, you can't get concrete block paving to look like wood. If you want to see just what you can do with pattern imprinting on concrete, take the family off to Disneyworld – it's full of it.

There are some noted snags with PIC: it can crack (it shouldn't but it does), it can get slimey, it can stain, and you are stuck if you have to take the drive up for drain repairs or something like that. It's also the province of high-pressure sales teams and sometimes the prices quoted can look ridiculous. It shouldn't really cost much more than block paving.

SHINGLE AND GRAVEL

This is the cheapest option and, in many

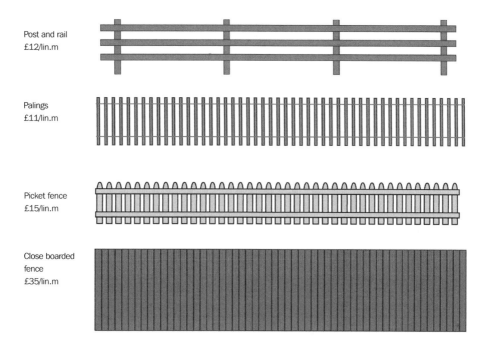

Post and rail
£12/lin.m

Palings
£11/lin.m

Picket fence
£15/lin.m

Close boarded
fence
£35/lin.m

rural situations, the most attractive. However, note that the better gravel driveways are actually labour intensive as they involve laying three or four layers of stones, individually rolled. Edgings need to be placed – treated timber strips are adequate – and the success of the drive overall depends on good hardcore beneath.

Top coat materials shouldn't cost much but laying costs are likely to be high, especially if there's no mechanised plant available.

Quotes to supply and lay a gravel drive often specify a simpler two layer application as this keeps the price down to around the £10 sq m mark (excluding foundation works). There are also a number of much more expensive decorative stone effect gravels you can use — look good, but an easy way to bump up the price.

RESIN-BONDED DRIVEWAYS

Available from specialist firms, these work by sticking small stones into a rigid sheet to give a shingle-look driveway which is as hard and durable as concrete or tarmac. Fantastic product if it's done properly but can be a disaster if not, so check the credentials of the installers. Prices tend to be similar to the Pattern Imprinted Concrete, and minimum charges (often around £2,500) often apply.

FANCY PAVING OPTIONS

There are many other materials available to lay paths and, in particular, patios. Labour costs for laying vary widely (£5-£15 sq m) depending on whether they can be laid wet or dry and whether they need pointing-up afterwards. Wet laying involves using cement (albeit usually a dryish mix)

and tends to be very much more labour intensive. Some hardcore backfill is usually advisable, although when it is designed for foot traffic only it does not need to be laid as deep as it is under driveways. Materials choices include:
▪ Plain paving slabs: £4-£5 sq m
▪ Riven paving slabs (textured surface): £6-£7 sq m
▪ Heritage paving (simulated natural stone): £15 sq m
▪ Natural York stone flags (the real McCoy): £50 sq m
▪ Granite setts: £40 sq m
▪ 75mm Beach Cobbles: £15 sq m
▪ Reconstituted stone: £25 sq m.

Marshalls of Halifax is the largest supplier of manufactured pavings (and garden walling effects). Their brochures, which are widely available at builders' merchants, are a good starting point in assimilating some possibilities. They also have a wide choice of block pavers (both concrete and clay) and paving slabs.

Natural stone slabs, setts and cobbles are widely available although you have to search them out from smaller suppliers and quarries.

SPECIALISTS

Laying a drive should not be beyond the competence of a good builder yet many people prefer to subcontract the whole process to a specialist, typically found in the Yellow Pages under Asphalt and Macadam or Paving Services.

Before you do this, I would like to draw your attention to a 1995 Which? report which revealed a staggering range of prices as well as some uncompromising high pressure selling tactics associated with national companies advertising through magazines and usually (but not always) selling patterned concrete or resin-bonded driveways. In this Which? report, prices for one 60 sq m driveway varied from £329 to £6,210!

Finally a plug for www. pavingexpert.com, a website maintained by paving guru Tony McCormack, where you can find out more than you possibly ever wanted to know about the black art

FENCING AND TURFING

FENCING

If you just want to mark a boundary and are not too bothered about

No ordinary close-boarded fence. The see-through panels at the top are there to offer a little more visibility and hence security

privacy or security, then the cheapest permanent option is the timber post-and-rail fence. This arrangement shouldn't cost more than £12 per lin m; it looks fine and is easily maintained. If you have longish (30m plus) lengths to erect, then the cheapest suppliers are to be found in the pages of Horse & Hound. Alternatively, a chain link fence is cheap, is more secure and should stop dogs and children straying.

Another cheapish option is 1.2m-high chestnut palings which, being vertical, are much harder to get over. They are easily fixed – just whack posts in every 2m or so – but have a temporary air about them which may not appeal to all. The picket fence is similar in design but altogether more permanent in appearance and it costs around £15 per lin m.

If you require privacy and

security then you will have to go for a solid or near solid fence with a height of 1.8m (above head height). The traditional way of doing this is to erect something similar to a post-and-rail fence and then to cover it with vertically fixed, featheredge boarding. This is known as a close-boarded fence. Expect it to cost around £35 per lin m. It is a little cheaper to use ready-made panels of the type you see in garden centres but the result is very flimsy in comparison. There are many variations on the theme of boarded fences; you can set the boards horizontally or diagonally, or alternate the boards between the inside and the outside of the fence posts (called hit and miss fencing). You can achieve quite stunning effects very simply and they don't have to be stained dark afterwards. If you want to investigate further, I recommend you get Jackson's

Good Fencing Guide – it's free from Jacksons, or downloadable as a PDF. They also deal with wire fencing which, I am assuming, is of lesser interest to would-be housebuilders.

BRICK WALLS

Whilst timber fencing is getting expensive at around £30 per lin m, you are not going to get even a whiff of a brick boundary wall under £100 per lin m and, if you use a nice brick and build up to head-height, the cost will be around £200 per lin m. This is a different animal altogether and ideally should be erected along with the main house so as to combine economies of scale – not to mention getting JCBs into the back garden. A 1.8m-high brick wall is actually a rather vulnerable construction, prone to blowing over in howling gales, and best practice advice now recommends that all unsupported walls over a mere 650mm high should be built two brick skins thick (225mm). In exposed locations, a 1.8m-high brick wall should be built 330mm thick. Whether your wall is free-standing or is being built as a retaining wall against some high ground, your building inspector will advise you as to the exact requirements needed. Dry stone walls are, needless to say, even more expensive, costing around £300 per lin m for a waist-high one.

TURFING

A detailed look at landscaping lies beyond the scope of this book, but I feel I must cover turfing at least because most developers consider it part of their remit to make a garden

look acceptable, if not exactly inspired. Indeed, as with fencing, the VAT office allows you to reclaim VAT on purchases of turf when erecting a new house: unfortunately for keen gardeners, the VAT line is drawn at turf.

Of course there's more to it than just laying the turf. After the builders have done their bit, the average plot resembles a World War One battle ground (hopefully without the bodies) and the site has first to be cleaned of debris. Usually, it is then rotavated, leveled and rolled, and normally a selective weed killer is applied to prevent thistles taking over. Turf itself usually costs around £2 sq m to purchase; the preparation work and the laying will cost around £4 sq m, more if the work is particularly arduous or if there are slopes involved. If extra topsoil is needed, this costs around £10-£20per cu m. You can halve the

The builder of this boundary wall, in an exposed position between two properties, chose to add butresses as an extra precaution against collapse

cost of turfing if you seed the area instead but this can be a bit hit and miss: seeding is best carried out in September, though you can often get away with it in springtime as well. You need to be lucky with the rain or else you will have to water for about eight weeks.

11
ROOM BY ROOM

KITCHEN DESIGN

The kitchen is the most expensive part of the house to build. On a unit cost basis, the kitchen is likely to be 5 per cent more expensive to build than a bedroom or a living room, and that's simply because it has so much kit in it.

This is perhaps slightly misleading because only the kitchen and bathrooms are finished at the building stage; everywhere else has to be furnished by the homeowner. But even so, if insurance company figures are anything to go by, the average home has just £20,000 of stealable fittings and, looked at on a pounds per sq m basis, that only adds £250/ sq m to floor area costings. So, whichever way you look at it, kitchens remain the most expensive item in the contemporary house.

What prominence you decide to give to the kitchen is the most difficult internal design decision that you will be faced with. The two extremes to opt for are:
■ the kitchen as utility area (hidden from view and servicing a separate dining room)
■ the kitchen to be the main living area of the home, typically called an open-plan arrangement.

The trend is towards the open-plan kitchen; this suits the kitchen suppliers as it means a) bigger kitchens and b) consumers are more conscious of the way their kitchens are going to look. If you accept the notion that you want your kitchen to be the most important room in the house, then you are probably prepared to spend a much larger sum on making it beautiful. On the other hand, if you want to keep costs down, design your kitchen more as a utility area and have a separate dining room where you eat.

MUD ROOMS AND LARDERS

Many designs relegate the utility area to little more than a laundry room, but for some people, particularly country dwellers, a proper mud room would be far more useful; somewhere warm and light to take off wellies and wet coats, to air clothes, for dogs to sleep in. It's the natural place for a back door, but to do it properly requires a surprising amount of space. They are not called mud rooms for nothing; during the six winter months every year, just going out into the garden is a seriously mucky business and the interface between inside and outside needs thought.

The separate larder is an old idea coming back into fashion. This can be a small room and doesn't need any daylight but to work well it needs to be easily accessed from the kitchen preparation area. In days of yore, the larder enjoyed a completely different microclimate to the kitchen - it was cool,

Kitchen Key Rates

	UNIT	CHEAP	MID	FANCY IN HRS	TIME TAKEN	LABOUR
Kitchen units - flat pack	m³	£ 300	£ 500	£ 700	3.5	£ 70
Kitchen units - rigid	m³	£ 340	£ 700	£ 3,000	2.5	£ 50
Worktops	m run	£ 20	£ 80	£ 250	1.5	£ 30
Kitchen sinks	each	£ 80	£ 200	£ 400	5	£ 150
Hob	each	£ 100	£ 300	£ 800	3	£ 90
Oven	each	£ 200	£ 400	£ 800	3	£ 90
Range Cooker	each	£ 600	£ 1,200	£ 3,000	3	£ 90
Extractor	each	£ 50	£ 150	£ 1,200	2	£ 60
Fridge/Freezer	each	£ 150	£ 300	£ 1,000	1	£ 30
Washing Machine	each	£ 225	£ 350	£ 800	2	£ 60
Dishwasher	each	£ 200	£ 350	£ 700	2	£ 60

The concept of buying kitchen units by the cubic metre may seem alien but it's a great yardstick – pun intended. It includes all the trimmings – pelmets, plinths etc but not worktops nor plumbing and wiring tasks. The labour timings don't change with cost which is a little unrealistic cost-wise. If you are spending £3,000/m³ on your units, you might even get the fitting thrown in 'for free'

dark and even a little damp - but this is hard to achieve in contemporary housing because of the energy efficiency demands. But even a centrally-heated larder is useful if only to store dried food and crockery: it's much cheaper than fitting it all into expensive kitchen units.

GRASPING THE KETTLE

When you've come to some conclusion about how you want your kitchen to work with the rest of the house, you can then get down to the nuts and bolts design-matters of what goes where. It is usual to start with a list of household appliances. If you have opted for a separate utility area, this will be the natural home of washing machines and tumble dryers and, possibly, freezers. The kitchen proper must have a sink, some sort of cooker and a fridge. Dishwashers are now ubiquitous and are conventionally placed close to the sink. The positioning of your appliances around the kitchen becomes the skeleton on which the kitchen furniture is hung. There are some conventional dos and don'ts to consider:
▨ DO locate sinks and plumbed-in appliances where waste pipes can get to the drains. Usually this means placing them against an outside wall.

▨ DO locate cooker hoods against an outside wall where exhaust fumes can be evacuated. You can run ducting to get around this problem but it is a fiddle best avoided.
▨ DO leave worktop space either side of both the sink and the hob (or cooker top).
▨ DO keep the sink, the hob and the fridge reasonably close to each other. Simply for the sake of convenience. Some kitchen planners will go on at length about the importance of the work triangle in the kitchen. Politely ignore them.
▨ DON'T place a hob or a sink in a corner unless you consider an angled corner arrangement (expensive); corners tend to make poor working/storage space.
▨ DON'T place a fridge or freezer next to or under a heat source (hob, cooker, radiator).
▨ DON'T forget to consider the boiler if it needs to be in the kitchen. Not only will it be hot but also there are rules concerning just where you can and can't place boiler flue terminals.
▨ DON'T put wall cupboards over the sink; conventionally, sinks go under windows and for most small- or medium-sized kitchens this will always be the most practical location.

If you're a neat, logical kind of person, having got this far you should be able to draw a layout plan on some graph paper and begin to get an idea of the number of units you will need. Congratulate yourself because you're the kind of client any kitchen supplier would be pleased to have – you actually know what you want!

KITCHEN UNITS

The fitted kitchen is very much a 20th century invention. In the Sixties, a kitchen cabinet was thought of as something to do with Harold Wilson's unique style of government. But shortly thereafter, the fitted kitchen arrived in the home and, bit-by-bit, we have learned to spend more and more money on our kitchens. There are several procurement routes, each with their own pitfalls. Whilst the bulk of the new kitchen market now goes into replacing existing kitchens, a significant chunk gets accounted for by all the new homes built each year. And whilst a penny pinching spec housebuilder may spend as little as £2,000 on fitting a kitchen on a starter home, you only have to open a Sunday newspaper to realise that some people are happy to spend over £100,000 on a fitted (or

Chapter 11

covered with a melamine veneer which serves to make them both stronger and moisture resistant. The cheaper doors, which are hung over these carcasses, are made of similar materials, although here the melamine covering is usually decorated with some trim. Solid timber is a more upmarket door option and there are more adventurous designs using materials such as stainless steel and plastic.

FLAT PACK DIY KITCHENS

There are several ways of getting fixed up with a kitchen. About the cheapest is to go to one of the giant DIY retailers such as B&Q or IKEA and buy yourself a flat-pack. The cheaper kitchens tend to be supplied flat-packed and need assembling on site, a feat which in theory is straightforward but in practice can be damned difficult, especially when it takes you two days to realise you haven't got all the bits.

Another point well worth garnering about flat-pack kitchens is that you are buying the materials, not the fitting out. Consequently, they look much cheaper than all the other options, which come on a supply and fix basis. Now B&Q may well have a few trade cards stuck at the back of the store with names of recommended installers but tread with care here. Installing a kitchen is a complex multi-task of a job involving co-ordinating fitters, plumbers, sparkies, tilers and fitters all over again. It's not just a question of getting hold of some bloke handy with a screwdriver, he must be bloody useful with a mobile phone as well.

perhaps an unfitted) kitchen. Bigger of course, better undoubtedly, but not fifty times bigger or better.

JUST SHELVES WITH FANCY DOORS

When we think of fitted kitchens, we think of how the door fronts look. The kitchen dream sellers are well aware of this and, although the actual units may make up only 25 per cent of the final bill, these are how kitchens are sold to us. New fashions come but don't really go so kitchen design continually expands to incorporate new ideas whilst simultaneously recycling the old ones. The basic manufacturing process is relatively simple and cheap so that no new idea can ever be free from imitators for more than a few months.

The kitchen business is fully metricated and works in modular

units which increase in 100 mm intervals. Thus any given range of floor units or wall cupboards will be available in widths of typically 300 mm, 400 mm, 500 mm and 600 mm; 600 mm is the key one, this is the building block of the fitted kitchen – appliances are conventionally made to fit into 600 mm gaps. The other sizes tend to get used to fill awkward gaps between the 600 mm units. By twiddling the plan about a bit, you can fill any space on any wall to the nearest 100 mm – and they sell blanking-off pieces to cover any little gaps left over. So give a kitchen designer a space that's 3600x2400 mm and they will tend to think of it as six units long and four across.

All but the most expensive kitchen unit carcasses are made from a wood pulp board like chipboard or MDF, usually

Which? magazine surveyed six flat pack kitchens and found that IKEA came out tops. "The best quality units we tested," they wrote, "provided you can follow the instructions."

Model House Kitchen Costs

	UNIT PRICE	MATERIALS	LABOUR	COMBINED
Rigid kitchen units (10m³)	£ 600	£ 6,000	£ 500	£ 6,500
Laminate worktops (10m run)	£ 80	£ 800	£ 300	£ 1,100
Sinks and Taps (2 No)	£250	£500	£ 300	£ 800
Hob/Cooker/Fan		£ 1,300	£ 250	£ 1,540
Fridge/Freezer	£ 500	£ 500	£ 30	£ 530
Washing machine and Dishwasher	£ 350	£ 700	£ 120	£ 820
Total		£ 9,800	£ 1,500	£ 11,300

A 600 x 600 x 700 high base unit measures 0.25m³ so a cubic metre will buy you four base units. A small kitchen (for a flat) probably has around 2m³ of units. The model house has 10m³

THE CONTINENTALS

The more innovative and interesting designs are the preserve of the up-market kitchen. The Germans were the first into this pond in the Seventies when names like Wellman, Allmilmo and, most notably, Poggenpohl came to the UK. Like all things German, they have built up a reputation for superbly crafted kitchens. In terms of style however they've been left in the slow lane. The high-tech, continental look is now led by the French and, especially, the Italians – look out for Boffi's futuristic designs.

SMALLBONE, ETC

Despite exporting barely any kitchens at all (we import about 20 per cent), the British have responded to the threat of mainly up-market invasion by inventing a whole new romantic theme – sometimes known as the English Revival style or, more often, doing a Smallbone. Smallbone – which started as an antiques business in Wiltshire – led the way in creating a new vernacular kitchen, which managed to strike some chord in the English middle-class psyche and led people to pay vast sums to recreate a past that never existed. Using many revived techniques and idioms (rag rolling, marbling, Welsh dressers), they created a magnificent, seductive illusion. To purchase the actual Smallbone marque

is horribly expensive – the average one costs £42,000 – but the style has spawned dozens of imitators. These high prices have proved to be just perhaps a bit too high and Smallbone (and the related Mark Wilkinson Kitchens) went bust in 2009, though they continue to trade under new owners.

This school of kitchen design has grown away from providing modular boxes towards what has become known as the unfitted kitchen – an Aga here, a beech block table there, terra cotta tiles on the floor, wicker baskets hanging on rails, you can almost smell the garlic and olive oil.

Some of these up-market companies must be approached directly, many have just one UK outlet. The nearest thing to a directory exists in the back of 'Kitchens, Bedrooms and Bathrooms' magazine which will give you an overview of the market's top end.

KITCHEN BOUTIQUES

Another approach is to ignore the plethora of manufacturers and concentrate on your local kitchen specialists. Most small towns have at least one, and a regional shopping centre will have several – check Yellow Pages. Most will stock only three or four manufacturers' products but as manufacturers offer sometimes hundreds of options (especially door colours) this

can still be quite bewildering. Typically, they will stock a mass-produced British flat-pack product that they will use to try and compete with B&Q and Co, but the bulk of their showrooms are given over to displaying a more up-market continental range. They make more money on the more expensive kitchens so it is understandable that it is these that they promote.

Many people are rather reluctant to set foot inside a kitchen specialist as they think it would be a) too expensive and b) involve high-pressure selling. By and large, this is not the case; although they probably cannot compete with B&Q on kitchen unit price alone, they are usually owner-managed and tend to give a high level of personal service without resorting to any pressure tactics. Unlike the major retail outlets, prices are usually negotiable and this makes it hard to compare on a like for like basis.

THE BUILDER

If you are fitting a kitchen as part of a much larger project .ie building a house) then it may make sense to keep the work in-house and ask your builder to fit it. That's if you are still on speaking terms by the time you have reached the kitchen fitting. There are several outlets (principally builders' merchants and joinery centres) that aim to sell mainly to builders and they

Chapter 11

have kitchen catalogues available to browse through and sometimes showrooms to visit.

Some of the major joinery firms – Howden, Magnet – produce fitted kitchens although, stylistically, they tend to be the most conservative of all. Their catalogues are easy to get hold of and clearly priced. The builder can buy these units (and the accessories) at discounts of between 20 to 40 per cent off list price and many will be happy to negotiate to share at least some of the discount with you – see section on Contracts in Chapter 5, 'Project Management', in particular find out what a PC Sum is. Even so, the prices from the volume joinery majors, even with full discount, will be slightly more than the cheapest available from the likes of B&Q; but there is one big advantage if your builder fits the units and that is that he will remain responsible for sorting out any snags. If, on the other hand, you supply your own units to your builder and, say, the hinges work loose or there are

unsightly gaps here and there, then you'll have your work cut out trying to convince him it's his fault: indeed you'll have fallen into one of the contractual traps placed along the route.

BESPOKE KITCHENS

Before the advent of Smallbone, getting a joiner to make up a kitchen for you was always thought of as the most expensive option. If you choose to have doors made up out of gale-blown timbers, etc, this can still prove to be expensive enough but, with the advent of MDF, simple handmade and hand-painted kitchens can be surprisingly cheap. Almost all kitchen carcassing (ie the bits you don't see) is made up of chipboard or MDF. You can buy 18 mm thick MDF board in 2.4 m x 1.2 m sheets for as little as £15 per sheet and get it machine cut for under 50p per cut. A sheet will make up an averaged-sized kitchen carcass and door; add a little for ironmongery and knobs, paint or varnish, design a simple trim and

1
If you are looking for kitchen value then ready-built but custom-designed units from www. jamesmayorfurniture.com come already primed and ready to paint. They also do replacement kitchen doors if you're renovating an existing kitchen

2
The kitchen units are Omega's Logica Gloss White. This is a moderately-priced solid kitchen range, complimented by Duropal High Gloss worktops and Bosch appliances. With sinks, taps and an elaborate cooker hood, it came to just over £11,000 inc fitting

plinth detail and – lo and behold – you've got all the materials for our standard kitchen at less than half the price of B&Q's cheapest. Get hold of the Hafele catalogue and you suddenly have access to all the same ironmongery as the kitchen manufacturers do (because they use the same catalogue). Carousels, fancy pedal bins, soft closers, you name it, they are all in there.

Even though a competent joiner would take little longer to assemble this kitchen than he would a flat-pack, there are still remarkably few takers for such a design. This is probably a result of marketing failure as much as anything else. There are many economies in fabricating on site but most people are simply unaware what they might be. There are substantial design limitations – glass doors, friezes, fielded panelling and other complicated motifs are best carried out in factories – but there is, however, undoubtedly a niche for kitchen designers to create simple made-on-site kitchens which will accommodate the limited budget. This would be much closer to the ideal of the Shaker kitchen than those maddeningly expensive ones that carry that currently fashionable title.

COSTS

Strange as it may seem, you can quite easily compare kitchen unit costs by the cubic metre. It's actually quite helpful because it gives you a handle on both basic cost and quantity. You need to carry out a few measurements: basically the length, depth and height of the units. You don't have to measure individually – work in blocks of units.

Floor units are conventionally 700 mm high and 600 mm deep. Over-worktop wall units are also 700 mm high but only 300 mm deep. A small starter kitchen will typically consist of around 2 cu m of units: in contrast, a detached four-bedroomed house is likely to have around 10 cu m.

SINKS
STAINLESS STEEL

Stainless steel sinks now represent the cheap and cheerful option, which is perhaps surprising because in many other contexts stainless steel is regarded as an expensive material. Steel is actually a very good choice of material for a sink; it's strong, lightweight and easily cleaned. However, it is something of a victim of its own success because stainless steel sinks became so ubiquitous in the Sixties and Seventies that people started to

Like all things German, Poggenpohl kitchens have built up a reputation for superb craftmenship

choose other materials just to be different. It also suffered from the fact that it was a one-colour product at a time when kitchens were becoming colour coordinated.

The very cheapest kitchen sinks now tend to be stainless steel; single bowl/single drainers can be picked up for less than £40, a set of taps for less than £20. However, the products from the big names in kitchen sinks (Leisure, Carron, Franke, Blanco) can be every bit as expensive as coloured ones. Expect to pay £120-plus for something as good as a Franke one-and-a-half bowl sink (ed: spotted one on eBay for just £75 inc free shipping!)

SYNTHETICS AND CERAMICS

In the Nineties, a whole bunch of composite materials were used to make sinks but they have pretty much gone out of fashion now. As with bathrooms, where everything is white, kitchen sinks have reverted to either stainless steel or white ceramics. There are still composite products around, and they work just fine, it's just that no one is fitting them anymore.

The old fashioned butler's sink tends to look a wow in the kitchen showroom, particularly when it is inset in a hardwood surround with drainage grooves. It's not changed from the original Victorian design (ie a large white rectangular box) and this adds an air of authenticity to it which nothing else in a modern kitchen can touch, not even an Aga (which hails from the Thirties). Consequently, it's become an item in all Smallbone-inspired kitchens and its very size and weight stand as statements of contempt for the standard mass-produced fitted kitchen. Butler's sinks, such as the Armitage Shanks Belfast, cost between £110 and £150 depending on size. Taps and waste are extra: these sinks are most definitely not sold in packs.

KITCHEN WORKTOPS

The worktop is the name given to the main shelf in a kitchen where all the action happens – the food preparation, the cooking and the cleaning. Everything else is just storage. Getting the worktop right is a crucial part of kitchen design and, although it may not be the first thing you think about when selecting a kitchen, it will be the single most important element in your kitchen. The standard width for worktops is 600 mm, which is sufficient for most kitchen configurations. Peninsulas, islands and breakfast bars may all require wider surfaces; there are a few extra-wide sizes available with two good edges, designed for these types of applications. The cheapest option is 28 mm thick white or near-white laminate that costs around £35 for a 3 m length, available at DIY sheds or trade outlets like Magnet. But nobody fits these anymore. However, if you want irregular shapes or fancy trims then you will need to go via a kitchen specialist and probably have to buy a more expensive laminate.

EXPENSIVE LAMINATES

The patterned varieties are what the kitchen showrooms push. There are a few well-known names like Formica, Polyrey, Resopal, Duropal and Beaumel; the showrooms often try to sell their own versions. They are usually sold in 40 mm thicknesses which gives them a beefy feel – although provided the front is supported every 600 mm the extra thickness is unnecessary. There is a far wider choice of colours and patterns but prices will be around three times the cheapest options – ie they start at around £90 for a 3 m length or, if you prefer, £30 per lin m.

HARDWOOD

These usually appear as thick strips of woods such as beech or oak that are glued and laminated into a solid board, usually available in two thicknesses, either 26 mm or 42 mm. You can either have them shaped up as a series of thin strips all bonded together or as wider planks, maybe 150 mm wide, so that a 600 worktop would consist of four glued planks. Costs start at around

£130 per lin m for beech, the cheapest hardwood, and up to nearly double that for oak. Iroko is a popular mid-priced alternative. Ideally hardwood worktops need a little looking after – occasional oiling – and they also have a nasty little habit of staining if they get persistently wet, such as happens in awkward spots behind sinks.

GRANITE

Granite has come from nowhere to become Britain's favourite worktop surface in the space of a decade. It's bloody expensive, rarely costing under £150 per linear metre run. Normally this supplies a 30 mm thick slab which is sometimes fitted on to a timber sub-base for extra support. Holes can be cut for sinks and hobs (at around £100 per hole) and intricate moulded edges can be applied at £10 per lin m; drainage grooves can be cut at around £20 each.

CORIAN

Corian is a product that is used to make both worktops and sinks. It is best known for making it possible to 'weld' sinks seamlessly into the worktop so they appear to be one and the same item. It remains a bit high-tech for many people's tastes and a bit high priced for many people's pockets. What is it? Well, it's an inert mineral filler fixed in a matrix of methyl methacrylate polymer. Nuff said? It's a synthetic panel product but unlike the regular melamine laminates (which are actually just thin coverings stuck on chipboard) these boys are solid, heavy and smooth. Every kitchen specialist showroom boasts a Corian (or Corian look-alike such as Schock) sink-cum-worktop but they don't actually shift very many. There are an increasing number of alternative makes and some are beginning to get very much cheaper than original Corian. Look out for

Silkstone which looks very similar but costs something akin to a mere £100 per m run, about half the price of Corian.

TRIM OPTIONS

The standard edge detail for laminate worktops is what is called Postform, which gives a curved finish to the front edge. You can get square-edged finishes but they are not recommended unless you are going to add some sort of trim to it. An otherwise cheap and cheerless laminate top can be made to look very much more attractive with the addition of an edge trim. These can be applied by hand but it is difficult to do a professional job on site; if factory applied, it will approximately double the cost of a laminate worktop (budget £50 per lin m). Even more expensive trims are available – like Corian – which would push the price up by over £70 per lin m.

JOINTING OPTIONS

One of the problems in specifying laminate worktops, particularly ones with curved, postformed edges, is how to get around corners. The cheap option is to use metal jointing strips which stand up proud of the worktops and cover the gap where the two worktops meet. They are cheap but seamless they are not. Worktop fabricators offer various options for jointing worktops so that they appear to be one piece; straight runs are butt jointed from about £10; angles get a mason's mitre for around £15.

KITCHEN APPLIANCES

All prices quoted in this section will include VAT. Trade prices invariably exclude it whilst retail outlets invariably include it. Whichever way, new housebuilders in the UK cannot reclaim VAT on kitchen cookers or appliances with the sole exception of cooker hoods, which are regarded as a ventilation item.

COOKING

The standard practice today is to buy a built-in oven with a separate hob and a hood, often sold together as a package. Every supplier offers a choice of gas or electricity for your hob without any effect on price, but a gas oven is more expensive than an electric one. The budget developers' packages are priced at around £300.

Appliances are mostly made to modular sizes so that they slip easily into any kitchen unit assembly so there is no compulsion to source your appliances from the same place as your units. Neither of course is there any compulsion to stick to the same brand of appliances throughout the kitchen, though for convenience many people do.

STAND ALONE/SLOT-IN COOKERS

Go into Currys, and you will still find a range of very Fifties style gas and electric stoves. I don't think very many go into new homes (unless you are specifically going for that Fifties retro-look) but they are very cheap. However, 21st century housebuilders all go for fitted ovens and hobs. The question is which oven, hob and hood? In recent years the choice has multiplied alarmingly making this once simple task extremely taxing.

OVENS

At the basic end you get a single electric oven with a timer clock and two or three functions. That is enough for 90 per cent of us. It'll cook a Christmas dinner, what more can you ask? Well, a lot. What's happened with ovens mimics what's happened with computers. They have grown more functions and controls. Take a top of the range Miele single oven. It comes with ten functions: true fan heat, top heat, conventional heat, bottom heat, intensive bake, fan grill, automatic roast, defrost, full grill, economy grill. It also has ThermoClean plus pyrolytic cleaning with Air Clean catalyser. Don't yer luv this stuff? You need to go on a course just to see how it works and, not surprisingly, Miele, along with a handful of other manufacturers, run cookery demonstration courses.

You can opt for a double oven which gives you a second cooking chamber, useful if you want to cook things at different temperatures but for many people the top oven gets used as an eye-level grill – you don't really need any other functions.

GAS OVENS

Built-in gas ovens are widely available but much less common than electric ones; they tend to be more expensive and don't have many of the features of an electric oven. Their main selling point is low running costs – around 25 per cent of conventional electric cooking. The extra cost of a gas oven will pay for itself within five years if burning mains gas, and ten years if burning LPG.

SPECIALIST OVENS
The relentless rise of the microwave has seen it elevated from being a countertop accessory to being a built-in second oven in its own right. Most people find it far more useful and flexible than having a double oven. Despite being limited in their uses, microwaves are excellent in a number of areas (eg cooking casseroles and fish, boiling vegetables, reheating, defrosting) where conventional cooking is cumbersome. They are quick, clean and energy efficient.

As an alternative to fitting a separate microwave unit, most manufacturers now make multi-function or combi ovens that include a microwave function. You can use these as either conventional only, microwave only or both functions at once which allows you to halve the cooking time for something like a joint or a chicken or roast potatoes but still get an element of crispy browning. However operating them in combined mode is quite complicated – it requires a whole new set of cooking skills.

Steam ovens sell themselves as healthy alternatives to microwaves. They tend to be quite small, not much bigger than a microwave, and they work by boiling water and blasting steam into the cooking chamber (some of them do this under pressure). Like microwaves, they are surprisingly versatile and can do much of the cooking undertaken on a hob as well as useful little jobs like defrosting and sterilising bottles. Again, it's a whole different approach to cooking that has to be learned afresh. Steam ovens are still quite a specialised item and they are not cheap, prices starting from about £600 from de Dietrich or Miele.

HOBS

Where they have a choice, most people go for a gas hob. Gas is fast, responsive and cheap to use: its drawbacks are that they are hard to clean and they have a dislike of pans boiling over. If mains gas is unobtainable, then consider having bottled gas just for the hob. Gas cooking has another big, often unspoken plus going for it in that it continues to work in power cuts, something many rural areas still suffer from frequently.

Whilst electric hobs have been seen as the poor relation, there are a number of developments that make them more interesting. First the ceramic hob came along which was easier to clean, if nothing else, but they perform only slightly better than conventional electric plates. They do, however, make a pleasing orange glow. More recently we have seen induction hobs that work via a magnetic field rather than an element. When magnetic pans are placed on the surface, a field is created which produces heat. The field is only generated where the pan touches so induction cooking is efficient and extremely quick – faster even than gas. Induction hobs are also horribly expensive – expect to pay around £750 for one of these beauties. And buy new cookware – it has to be magnetic.

The more up-market suppliers can also fit you out with specialist hoblets where you can mix and match your cooking surfaces and include griddles and fryers as well as the more usual plates. Most manufacturers also give you the option of having extended hobs if you find the standard 600 mm width a bit limiting.

Be aware that the standard electrical supply for electric cooking in the kitchen is a 30amp cable. This is only capable of supplying 7.5kW of power (you need 4 amps for each kW). Double ovens will use as much as 6kW with everything on and an induction hob or a five or six plate ceramic hob can take as much as 8kW with every ring in action. You can elect to either uprate your supply to 45amp or run separate circuits for the oven and the hob.

COOKER HOODS

In a new, draught-free house,

The Aga has become ubiquitous, but it's high thirst for oil threatens to burst the bubble

condensation and cooking smells will not easily disperse without opening windows, so a cooker hood is nigh-on essential, especially as you have to have some form of extractor fan in a kitchen in order to satisfy building regs. You can have cooker hoods that merely 'recirculate' the air back into the kitchen but these are really nothing more than glorified grease filters. It's accepted as far better practice to enable your cooker hood to extract to the outside which obviously involves knocking a hole in the wall and connecting ducting to it. However, if you have a whole house ventilation system, you may want to hang onto some of the usable heat you are extracting and here a re-circulator may make sense.

Cooker hoods now seem to come in four flavours. The standard version is a rectangular box which sits between 650 and 750 mm above the hob: you get a three speed fan and a light (actually very useful) but they are cheap and usually noisy. There is an 'integrated' variety which gets concealed in an overhead wall cupboard and is activated by pulling the top-hung cupboard door open. Next a slimline or telescopic version which is typically no more than 25 mm deep and these are turned on just by a gentle tug towards you; the fan itself sits in a dummy cupboard above.

The most up-market option is to go for a canopy cooker hood which acts more like a conventional chimney: usually finished in stainless steel, look to pay north of £350 for this type, though much cheaper ones can be found on eBay and the like. If you want to study how basic functional items have morphed into high fashion items, then the cooker hood would be a good subject. You can get one for £30 if you look carefully. You can also pay more than £1,500 if you want, as much as a basic chimney costs.

WHICH MAKE?

There is an awful lot of snobbery about kitchen appliances. Classy kitchens need white goods with German (or at least German sounding) names like AEG, Bosch, Neff or Miele (it's pronounced like Sheila). Very classy kitchens need classy German makes like Gaggenau. British manufacturers like Hotpoint, Tricity Bendix, Creda have reputations based on price rather than quality, as have Philips Whirlpool and most of the Italian manufacturers with the exception of Smeg (yes, they are Italian) who have levered themselves up to Premiership status. The very cheapest appliances often come with little-known brand names and obscure East European origins.

Getting confused? It gets worse. White goods branding is an extremely complicated area. There is much cross-manufacturing of parts and 'country of origin' labeling should more correctly read 'country of final assembly'. As an example, most European cooker hoods are made in Italy and perform to much the same (rather noisy) standard whether they are branded Candy, Neff or Creda. Much of the upmarket German kit is actually assembled in Turkey or Portugal.

No wonder purchasers often subcontract the decision making as well as the installation. Broadly speaking, if you want to create an impression then the brand names have to be German. The very best cookers tend to be German, but don't assume that a German brand name is necessarily a sign of quality. Also, if you want anything unusual like a built-in griddle you will need to seek out the high quality

brand names. However, if low price is your main concern, then you should check out Curry own brands or alternatively specialists selling to developers – Arrow, Allied, or BCG.

AGAS

The Aga remains the item for the complete country kitchen. Despite their exorbitant cost (new price anywhere between £6,500 and £15,000 plus the need for adequate foundations, suitable chimney arrangements and fitting costs) and their exorbitant running costs (around 50 litres of oil or 275kWh of electricity a week – you work it out), otherwise rational people still salivate at the thought of having an Aga in the kitchen. They can't do chips, they can't grill and boiling a kettle takes forever but, to quote the sales blurb: 'An Aga transforms even the most functional kitchen into a warm and welcoming gathering place for all the family. It becomes the heart and hub of your home.' The fact that this description is often spot on usually says more about the state of the rest of the house than any unique attributes of the Aga. Any large radiant heat source will be immensely attractive on a bitingly cold day and it's this aspect of the Aga – over half a tonne of hot cast-iron – which fuels its seemingly unending popularity. A large storage heater would fulfill the same function at a fraction of the cost but, I'm afraid, it would completely lack the necessary style.

If you are contemplating an Aga for your home, you must plan for it from the ground upwards. Though not designed as water boilers, for an extra £300 you can go for an Aga with a boiler capable of heating not less than 400 litres of water a day (ie enough for about eight people) and – provided yours is a new house qualifying for VAT zero-rating – you can reclaim VAT on the purchase which instantly saves around £500. HMRC

are usually happy to accept this distinction and they cannot insist that the boiler is ever connected to your hot water cylinder. Agas come in gas-fired, oil-fired, solid fuel and electric (Economy 7) versions, and it has recently unveiled a biofuel-enabled range. There are a number of cast iron stove makers besides Aga and they are usually quite a bit cheaper. Many of them incorporate boilers so that you can use them as both cookers and house heaters but although this sounds economical, it can be a mixed blessing when it's your only heat source – it's not so much a case of being warm in winter as boiling in the summer.

No way can you reconcile having an Aga with hopes of building an eco house. I am sorry. Much as you might hope to just slip one in as a sop to the wife (that's the usual story), such is the energy consumption of these behemoths that it just can't be done. If you want to see a splendid example of a company trying to defend the indefensible, have a look at Aga's Green Issues web page. 'It's built from recycled materials,' they trill. 'It'll last much longer than an ordinary cooker.' 'It'll store energy from renewable power sources.'' 'Some of our Agas will be biofuel enabled.' Yes, yes. All true and all utterly irrelevant. Denial is a thing of wonder.

RANGES

There are alternatives between the splendour of the Aga and the industry standard 'tin boxes' which are sold as part of a fitted kitchen. When the first edition of this book came out in 1995, hobby cookers were unheard of. Now every kitchen showroom has them on display at prices starting at around £800, even less at Currys. They are now referred to as range cookers and they are about half as wide again as the industry standard 600 mm so you get six rings instead of four. You can get them dual fuel so that you get an electric oven and a gas hob: indeed this is the most popular option.

WHITE GOODS
DISHWASHERS

If you want a dishwasher, the big decision facing you is whether to go free-standing or integrated. If you are buying a fitted kitchen you will come under a little pressure to go for an integrated one which will slip behind a kitchen-unit door so that you wouldn't know there was a dishwasher there at all.

Now, despite the integrated ones having less in the way of metal casing, they invariably cost more although sometimes it can be hard to compare because the models are not directly equivalent. But take a good, solid German make like Miele whose basic 638 model is available as both a free-standing and an integrated unit. Free-standing costs around £350, integrated – you'll do well to get one for less than £450. If you succumb to the allure of an integrated dishwasher, you have a further choice to make. Whether to hide the entire machine behind your chosen kitchen unit door – that's known as fully integrated – or to let the control panel peep out at you in a way referred to as semi-integrated by some and as drawer line by others. Just as girls wearing tight Lycra cycle shorts are prone to exhibit an elastic knicker line, so kitchen units are said to have a drawer line, conventionally located at 200 mm below the worksurface. The semi-integrated or drawer line units have the control panels located above the drawer line (same as the free-standing dishwashers) and leave an infill space below designed to take a matching door panel. In contrast, the fully integrated dishwashers engineer the control panels so that they are actually located on the top edge of the door. You can only get to them by opening the dishwasher.

If you find the distinction between fully and semi-integrated dishwashers all a bit too precious, then save yourself a couple of hundred quid and bung a free-standing one in. And avoid stainless steel and save yourself another couple of hundred quid. Stainless steel looks good, photographs well but as anyone who has lived with one will tell you, they don't half show the fingermarks. If you want the stainless steel look to stay looking clean, then you need aluminium, which is even more expensive.

LAUNDRY

You can get integrated washing machines and tumble dryers but generally these items get placed in a separate utility room and they are therefore normally purchased as free-standing items. Hotpoint remain the biggest name in washing machines, accounting for 50 per cent of the UK market. Their basic stand-alone models start at around £280; their Aquarius range starts at £350 and incorporates a number of green features (less water, less power, less powder). Hoover are one of the very few to offer a machine with a delay timer.

TUMBLE DRYERS

You'd think choosing a tumble dryer would be simple but, of course, it ain't. There are a number of factors to consider, most importantly whether to go for a vented one or a condenser. The difference? The vented ones duct to the outside via a 100 mm flexi-duct, whilst the condensers, as the name suggests, turn all that warm, moist air into water to be either emptied out by you or plumbed into your drains. The condensers have to do more work and therefore use more energy: they also cost between 50 and 80 per cent more than the simpler vented ones. Oh, and they tend to break down more often. So if you are alert and in the planning-ahead mode, a vented

tumble dryer is probably something to go for: there are models that vent sideways but most require at least 100 mm behind them in order to get an adequate duct attachment in. You need to have some extra space behind a vented tumble dryer – many people leave the minimum 600 mm just because that is how kitchens are designed. You also need to think about making a 100 mm round hole through your wall at approximately the right spot. Alternatively, a condenser ideally needs to be plumbed into your waste: not usually difficult if the tumble dryer is located next to (above?) your washing machine.

Which? surveyed tumble dryers in 2005 and found out what everybody would expect: the German brands were a) the best and b) the most expensive. The condensing Miele actually costs a cool £800 but was given five stars. If you are not bothered about such quality, you can pick up a vented tumble dryer for £150. You can still get gas-fired tumble dryers (the brand is White Knight) but, although they promise greatly reduced running costs, they tend to be rather underpowered and, consequently, painfully slow.

WASHER-DRYERS

The trend towards separate utility areas in larger houses has meant that there are few built-in washing machines and no built-in tumble dryers. Instead there are a large number of extremely expensive washer dryers costing from £350 upwards. They do save space but they are not as convenient as you might hope – they are only capable of tumble drying half a wash load at a time so they need unpacking between programs. They are also the most unreliable of all kitchen appliances.

COLD STORAGE

There are numerous options of above- and

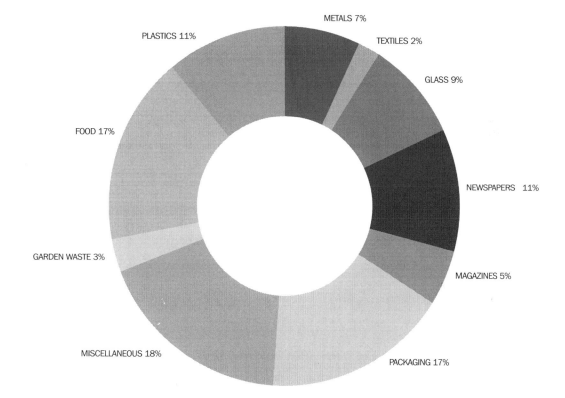

What We Throw Away

- METALS 7%
- TEXTILES 2%
- GLASS 9%
- NEWSPAPERS 11%
- MAGAZINES 5%
- PACKAGING 17%
- MISCELLANEOUS 18%
- GARDEN WASTE 3%
- FOOD 17%
- PLASTICS 11%

below-freezing point storage and there are also numerous arrangements for their housing. You have the same decisions you get with cookers – whether to integrate or go free-standing. Free-standing is invariably cheaper. Or was until the arrival on our shores of the giant American fridges which you haven't a hope of integrating into any MDF kitchen unit. Now a whole raft of new names (to us) like Admiral, Amana and Maytag are selling enormous fridge freezers with ice dispensers and are getting to over £2,000 for some models. Quite a change

from a Whirlpool under-the-counter-job for £125. And Smeg has appeared with some curved edge Fifties style fridges in a range of pastel colours, looking fabulous and definitely not for concealing, especially with an £800 price tag. Ice dispensers: don't forget they need a water supply. All attempts to add value to what are essentially nothing more than cold cupboards. Again, if you are trying to save a little money, consider building an old fashioned larder, located off the kitchen, where you can store even more than you would get in a 26.7 cu

ft Maytag Sovereign. I figure even a small larder will be five times the volume – but where would you put the ice dispenser?

KITCHEN WASTE

The trend towards separating waste has spread right across the country now. Regular bin collections have become more sporadic and we are now expected to sort our waste in-house. This represents a challenge for kitchen designers because it effectively means we have to have two or three different bins in each kitchen. Or at

Chapter 11

Plumbers Rates

LABOUR RATE USED FOR CALCS £30 HOUR

Fix Bathroom Suite (Bath/Basin/WC)	6hr	£ 180
H+C Plumbing to Same	4hr	£ 120
Waste from Suite to Stack	2hr	£ 60
Fit Waste Stack (Ground to Roof)	4hr	£ 120
Shower Fitting (inc H+C, Waste)	8hr	£ 240
Bidet Fitting (inc H+C, Waste)	4hr	£ 120
Fix Cloakroom Suite	4hr	£ 120
H+C Plumbing to Same	2hr	£ 60
Waste from Cloakroom to Stack	2hr	£ 60
Fit Kitchen Sink (inc H+C, Waste)	5hr	£ 150
Fit W/M or D/W (inc H+C, Waste)	2hr	£ 60
Fit Outside Tap	2hr	£ 60

Bathroom Key Rates

BATHROOM FITTINGS - BASIC RATES

Toilet	£ 80
Basin plus taps	£ 60
Bath plus taps	£ 200
Shower Tray	£ 150
Shower Door	£ 100
Shower screen (door and side)	£ 200
Shower	£ 150
15mm Copper pipe (m run inc fittings)	£ 5
Plastic pipe (m run inc fittings)	£ 2
Waste pipe (m run inc fittings)	£ 8
100mm Soil pipe (m run inc fittings)	£ 8

Model House: Bathroom Costs

COST FOR 2 BATHROOMS PLUS DOWNSTAIRS WC

			Materials	Labour hours	Labour cost	cost combined
Family Bathroom						
Toilet/Bath/Basin Set			£ 340	6	£ 200	£ 540
Ensuite Bathroom						
Toilet/Basin			£ 140	4	£ 100	£ 240
Shower (inc Tray and Door)			£ 400	8	£ 240	£ 640
Downstairs WC						
Toilet/Basin			£ 140	4	£ 120	£ 260
Feeds and waste to all the above	m runs	Mat rate				
Pipework	80	£ 2	£ 160	10	£ 300	£ 460
Waste fittings and stack	20	£ 8	£ 160	10	£ 300	£ 460
ROUNDED TOTALS			£ 1,300	42	£ 1,300	£ 2,600

Note that this table only includes the sanitaryware fittings. Much of the bathroom works are included elsewhere: i.e. the tiling, the flooring, the wiring, the fans.

least have a plan for dealing with all the waste.

Much of this isn't terribly difficult to achieve. You just need a few extra bins. If you are really bothered, you can build these into your kitchen cabinets but this is expensive. The cheaper options are to use good looking bins in the kitchen – currently Brabantia are the best established name with their stainless steel offerings – or get a load of plastic boxes and put

them in the utility room or the garage. The trouble with putting bins out of the kitchen is that the act of throwing stuff in bins gets problematic and is therefore prone to high failure levels.

Compost bins are something else. I have lived with compost bins most of my life and, whilst the theory is all fine and dandy, the practice is anything but. Firstly, if they aren't emptied frequently, ideally daily, then they get smelly and fly-blown.

Secondly the compost heap itself needs a lot of attention if it is to work as advertised. Otherwise it too becomes smelly and fly-blown and acts as a magnet to the local rat population. And unless it gets turned over every now and then, it doesn't even make useful compost.

One step is to keep chickens which will dispose of most of your vegetable spoil but then chickens need even more work than a compost heap. Another is to turn

in the opposite direction and get a waste-disposal unit, a gizmo that fits in the bottom of the sink and macerates all animal and vegetable remains and pumps them down the drain. These cost between £100 and £300 depending on power and capabilities.

Whatever route you choose, don't be fobbed off with a kitchen design based around a mini-swing bin of 20lt or less. Even the greenest households need a waste bin that will hold a dustbin liner. If storing great quantities of waste is a problem you can't see an easy way around, consider a rubbish compactor that reduces the volume four or five times. They are an expensive option, costing around £700 and taking up as much space as a large bin! Contact In-Sink-Erator

1
Changes to the building regulations mean that we now have to consider the amount of water that our loos flush. This Eco Toilet To Go was fitted at in the last edition's benchmark house

2
The traditional style takes its design inspiration from the past

3
Bathroom styles have now split into two distinct groups: traditional and contemporary. Contemporary covers everything from the clean lines to really cutting-edge design

BATHROOMS

Big changes are afoot in the sleepy world of bathrooms. In October 2010, a new set of regulations came into effect (in England only) which set out to limit the amount of water we use in our homes. The regs, known as Part G, want us to submit our plans to a Water Efficiency Calculator which will be used to assess whether or not we will be using too much of the stuff. The hurdle rate has been set at a notional 125lts per person per day and the combined effect of our choices should not be greater than this. Now this doesn't actually mean we have to use this much water, but it sort of imagines that if Mr and Mrs Average were to live in the house, this is what they would use. It only applies to new dwellings and, by and large, it's not that difficult to meet the hurdle rate if you pay attention to your bath size and, in particular, your shower flow rate. You'll probably be pleased to know that swimming pools and outdoor jacuzzis are exempt: this does however rather make a mockery of the new regulations.

It might have been easier if they had just said that, in future, baths can only be of a certain size (say max 200lts) or shower should be restricted to 12lts per minute. But they have chosen a more complex route whereby you have to fill in your projected water use into the water calculator (basically a horrible looking spreadsheet) and left it for you to justify your choices of taps, loos and showers.

You can find versions of the Water Calculator online and the one I have been researching on is to be found at www.wrcplc.co.uk/PartGCalculator/Calculator.aspx. And you can find lots of useful advice on how to fill it in at another website called www.water-efficient-buildings.org.uk. here are some tips:

SHOWERS

You need to find showers that have a flow rate below 12lts per minute, preferably even 10lts per minute. This isn't very much flow, in the great scheme of things, as

most power showers like to deliver well over 20lts per minute. More on this in the section on showers.

BATHS

Specify a bath less than 175lts capacity if possible.

TOILETS

All new ones are now dual flush and have a maximum flush of 6lts or less, so these are generally fine.

TAPS

You are looking for taps with a flow rate of 6lts or less; it can be hard to find any information on tap flow rates at all. This may change as Part G begins to bite over the coming years.

APPLIANCES

▓ Washing machines have a default score of 8.17lts per kg dryload. You may find better, but it's not going to make a lot of difference.
▓ Dishwashers have a default score of 1.25lts per place setting. Again, it doesn't make a big difference if you beat this.
▓ Waste disposal units. They don't like these – they all score 3lts per person per day.
▓ Water softeners can be ignored usually – unless they are very inefficient

What we can expect is that over the coming years, suppliers will start labelling things more clearly and even putting together suites of sanitaryware and taps that are designed to meet the Water Calculator requirements. But for the time being, expect confusion to

Contemporary bathrooms are frequently unfitted and often do away with the shower tray, as in this one by Fired Earth. Apart from needing excellent water proofing it is worth considering that other bathroom users may have to walk on a wet floor

rule the day, and for some building inspectors to insist on the letter of the law whilst others completely ignore it.

OVERVIEW

As it stands, the water calculator is going to be little more than a nuisance, as the projected score – 125lts per person per day – isn't that hard to meet, even if it does mean a rather feeble shower. This may lead to the oft seen situation where a feeble shower is installed for the building inspector's final visit, only to be replaced by a water-guzzling monster the next day. But the way the future is projected to go by the powers that be, the water calculator is set to lower the hurdle down to 85lts per person perday, at which point it gets really difficult to find suitable kit. It's still all controversial and may never happen, but you have been warned.

BATHROOM COSTS

The bathroom is a multi-trade zone. Do not be fooled into thinking that bathrooms are all about plumbing-in sanitaryware: that's just the beginning. Ventilation, wall tiling, mirrors, accessories, obscured glazing, enclosed light fittings, pull switches, towel rails (heated or otherwise) and specialised floor coverings all combine to make bathroom fitting a complex and elaborate process – and one that is easy to neglect in the hurry to finish a house. Bathroom planning is even more important in timber frame buildings because timber bearers should be present in the walls to secure all the fittings.

Bathrooms are also expensive. Bear in mind that it's not the size of the bathroom that is expensive but the fittings in it. Big bathrooms are becoming very popular; many people want to fit cupboards and furniture in them and the en-suite bathroom, in particular, seems to be getting bigger and bigger, eating chunks out of its attached bedroom. But there is no need to follow these American-led trends slavishly. Our Continental cousins still prefer family bathrooms and, although the word en-suite would seem to be French, you won't find many en-suites in France.

BATHROOM SUITES

Budget bathrooms are most usually sold as three-piece suites. Normally a bathroom suite includes:
- Bath, bath taps, plug
- Bath panels (to conceal the fact that the

bath is plastic)
- Basin and supporting pedestal
- Basin taps and plug
- WC, cistern, seat, handle.

If you don't buy a suite, you'll have to remember to get all these items separately – items like cistern levers are easily overlooked. If you want to opt for a separate shower instead of a bath you may be able to find a two-piece 'cloakroom suite' (be warned: cloakroom basins are often minute).

A very basic bathroom suite will cost £200-£250. Most bathroom outlets have a range of four or five suites going up in price to around £400; after that, you get into more up-market designs where all items come priced individually.

Prices tend to get softer as they get higher and trade discounts of 'no more than 10 per cent' on budget lines suddenly rise to 30 per cent or more when your spend rises above £1,000.

TAPS

To date, baths and basins have been available with all manner of tap arrangements. The old British standard of hot tap on the left and cold tap on the right has gradually been superceded by various mixer taps which are often extremely unintuitive.

In 2010, the regulations were amended so that, in future, all bath taps will have to be thermostatically controlled. This is to prevent around 20 deaths and 600 serious scaldings that occur every year because of hot water, in bath, in particular. The problem is that hot water is routinely stored at 60 deg C and this is about 18 deg C hotter than you want a bath or a shower. Thermostatic taps premix the hot and cold water and include temperature limiters to stop water going above a preset

temperature.

ACCESSORIES

Most suites offer a wide range of matching accessories (shelves, soap holders, loo roll holders, toothbrush holders, toilet brush holders, towel rails) at prices well over the odds for what you would pay in a DIY shed. Even on a fairly basic suite, you could easily spend over £100 on buying matching fittings, adding another 20 per cent to your suite price. If you want a bidet, expect this to add around 30 per cent to the basic three-piece suite price.

STYLES

You can have any colour you want as long as its white. Just where this craze for white bathrooms arrived from, I am not sure, but it upsets me just a little, because I come from a generation which regarded coloured suites as being mildly sophisticated and now everyone just laughs at us. I can remember in earlier editions of this book giving advice on how to colour co-ordinate your sanitaryware with your tiling scheme. No more. That would look far too dated, far worse than not having the latest regs at my fingertips. But it seems so illogical. How come you can still get coloured wall tiles? Or are they all going to white too soon?

There are still defined groups of bathroom suite styles but whereas it was once a straight toss-up between trad and modern, now it's a little harder to define. Check out bathstore.com, Wolseley's consumer-facing spin out, and see if you can work out which is which. Actually bathstore.com isn't a bad place to start, even though it sometimes gets horrendous reviews from customers: I find its showrooms are well laid out, and its prices are certainly keen.

SHOWERS

Chapter 11

Showers are popular both as attachments to bath taps (known as shower mixers) and in their own right in stand-alone shower cubicles. Apart from style – and there are showers to fit every style – there are two things to look out for: thermostatic control and adequate flow rate.

THERMOSTATIC CONTROL

Thermostatic control automatically adjusts the balance of hot and cold water flowing through the shower head as other taps in the house turn on and off. It is expensive, usually adding around £70 to the cost of a shower. A cheaper alternative is to have a shower with a high-temperature limiter that will avoid scalding but may still leave you drenched in cold water when a hot tap opens somewhere else.

ELECTRONIC SWITCHING

A natty new development is to have a push-button shower. Rather than phaffing about with taps, adjusting flow rates and temperature settings, you can just programme this stuff in and push a button to bring the shower to life. And you can, of course, arrange two-way switching so that you don't even have to be in the shower to turn it on. Aqualisa's Quartz shower (which does all this) has proved to be a big hit, despite it's £400-odd price tag. The switches, which you have to press quite hard, give you visual feedback to tell you when the shower is up to temperature so there is no more dipping in and out of the shower to test whether it's just right. It also works with baths too – you can enjoy a Digital Bath, which tickles me somehow.

SHOWER POWER

There are many routes to getting a good pressure through your shower head. The most effective is to install a mains pressure hot water system or a thermal store (see section on Domestic Hot Water in Chapter 8). The least effective is to install an electric shower or a combination boiler, both of which heat water instantaneously and therefore suffer from low flow rates. In between these extremes come a whole gamut of power showers which aim to add whoosh to feeble pressure from tanks in the loft. There are single impeller pumps, which boost the water after the mixing valve, and double impellers, which boost both hot and cold before they enter the valve. Which you choose is partly dependent on the layout you have and prices are largely dependent on the power of the pump. They can be purchased for just over £100, but a pump delivering 30lts per minute (equivalent to a good mains pressure system) will cost £180plus. Leading manufacturers: Mira, Aqualisa.

If you want a power shower in a new house, you would be well advised to avoid all these products and go for a mains pressure or near mains pressure hot water system. Having taken us decades to accept mains pressure hot water systems in the UK – they weren't admitted until 1987 – they have now pretty much swept the field in new housing: the days of water tanks up in the loft appear to be numbered.

Against this are of course the new regulations which seek to limit the flow of water through showers. They have a point. The average shower uses as much water as the average bath after just ten minutes and many people (OK, teenagers) like to shower for far longer than this. Possible low flow showers which you might want to check out include the Nordic Eco shower and Hansgrohe's 6lt shower. Wolseley Sustainable Building Center promotes Mira's Eco handset which, it says, gives a good 6l shower.

SHOWER TRAYS

Acrylic trays can be had for under £50 but they are not recommended because of problems with leaking caused by the trays flexing. The most popular option is the ceramic stone trays: Matki's are good. For a little more, you can buy them with an under-tile upstand that will minimise any possibility of leakage. The standard size is 760 mm square (which suits the standard pivot doors). There is a significant (100 per cent) cost penalty if you want a larger tray, however note that some people find the standard 760x760 mm size uncomfortably mean.

SHOWER DOORS

You have a choice of building the shower into an alcove (with three side walls tiled), into a corner or free-standing against one wall. Pricewise there is little to choose – the cost of a tiled wall being similar to the cost of a glazed side panel. The alcove option usually looks the most professional; you finish the opening with either a pivot or a bi-fold door Matching side panels tend to be 60-80 per cent of the door price. If your shower is incorporated with your bath, then you have a choice of a simple shower curtain hung from a rail or a glazed shower screen.

OPEN SHOWERS OR WET ROOMS

What price open showers running into a floor drain? It's a detail regularly seen on the Continent and has been widely specified in this country in special needs bathrooms. You dispense with the tray and your enclosure need only be a shower curtain. The key component is the floor drain which has to be able to sit inside a floor void, to be able to cope with the 30 litres per minute which a power shower will throw, to include a trap and yet be readily cleanable which means that the grate and the assembly must be removable. In consequence, shower drains are relatively sophisticated and good ones cost over £100.

Manufactures include Harmer (part of the Alumasc group) and Caroflow and designs allow incorporation with either regular floor tile sizes or sheet materials such as Altro Safety Flooring. Altro's main shower product is Marine 20 which is a 2 mm covering laid over floors and can be continued up walls as well.

The key to getting a floor shower drain to work well is to build in a fall of 1:40 for a metre around the floor drain. In masonry floors, this can be achieved relatively easily with a 25 mm depression in the screed – the Harmer floor drain requires only a 25 mm deep screed. However, you can rarely shave 25 mm off the top of a timber joist without seriously weakening the floor so the usual solution is to build a fall up with firrings laid across the tops of the joists; this leaves you with a 25 mm threshold at the bathroom door which needs to be addressed.

Open showers are not without their problems. Like it or not, you end up with a wet floor after using the shower and subsequent bathroom users don't really appreciate wet floors, especially if they are wearing shoes or socks. There is an increasingly popular halfway house, the doorless shower enclosure, which can sit in the corner of a room and be accessed round a stylish curved glass wall. They are so designed that (almost) all the water is caught by the glass and channelled down into an in-built drain. They are sold as units - tray, enclosure and shower together (though you can opt for different showers if you wish) - and, naturally, they are not a cheap option. Look to pay around £1,000 to £1,200 with the shower attachment, or around £700 to £800 for just the enclosure and tray.

AVOIDING LEAKY SHOWERS

In theory, this is no problem; in practice, tiled shower cubicles often ship water where they shouldn't and tiled floors will tend to fare even worse. It really is worth paying a lot of attention to the construction of shower enclosures generally because their failure is one of the commonest faults in new buildings. Don't skimp on the linings – use a waterproof plywood or a waterproof board like Knauf's Aquapanel rather than regular plasterboard – and use the best adhesive you can afford to fix ceramic tiles with.

The key failure point, however, is the joint between the walls and the floor (or more likely tray) and with most designs you are dependent on a bead of silicone mastic to stop water finding a route through the defence. Your silicone sealant will stand a much better chance of success if the joint is tight and even, something that usually depends on how good your carpentry is. But failures can also occur in the tile grouting and around the shower fitting itself.

One ingenious way around the problem of leaking showers is to install an all-in-one moulded cubicle. Advanced Showers produce a range of elegant, stand-alone enclosures which, whilst not cheap (costing upwards of £600), are very quick and easy to install and will be valued by all those who have experienced the frustrations of shower leaks. Another option is to avoid timber joists in your first floor: it's the shrinkage in these joists (often as much as 8 mm) when the house is drying out that causes most shower leaks. Specify either a beam and block first floor or a timber I-beam floor. (see Chapter 7, section on Floors).

BEDROOMS

For developers, bedroom space is cheap space. All that really has to be provided is enough room to fit a bed and an item of furniture plus enough space to manoeuvre about between them – the technical term for this is swinging a cat.

DESIGN CONSIDERATIONS

You can of course give far more consideration to the whole issue. It's worth visualising the layout of the bedroom furniture so as to work out where to place radiators and power sockets. Also it's a nice touch to arrange light switching so that it can be reached easily from the bed. On the other hand, if you want to maintain maximum flexibility, then fit power sockets on every wall so you can accommodate various layouts. In reality there may only be one sensible place where a bed can go, but there may be other considerations. What is appropriate as a nursery for a toddler is unlikely to suit a teenager and you should consider how the uses a bedroom gets put to will change over the years. Don't always assume that a bedroom will remain a bedroom.

SIZE

It is conventional to rank bedrooms by size. Now, you might think that in a four-bedroom house you would provide a double bedroom for mum and dad (or whoever tickles your fancy) plus three smaller but similar sized rooms for the children. But no; the British way of doing it is to build bedrooms in ever decreasing sizes. It's also the British way of doing things to rank – and price – houses according to the number of bedrooms they have. Almost all developers switch to four bedrooms when the overall floor size creeps over 110 sq m. When you are working with relatively tight floor areas, which goes for 90 per cent of UK housebuilding, squeezing an extra bedroom in is a seen as a vital sales booster, even if the resulting bedrooms are horribly cramped.

Chapter 11

WARDROBES

Not usually included by developers and not usually included in any summary of building costs, the wardrobe is, nevertheless, a near essential item in any bedroom. There are basically three approaches to creating bedroom storage space:

- Use free-standing furniture: it costs but you can take it with you
- Use specialist bedroom fittings
- Make your own.

The last method has one major advantage in that it is regarded as zero-rated for VAT purposes. Typically you would design your bedroom wall partitions with various strategically placed kinks into which you slip a hanging rail and a few open shelves and then hang a door or two in front. It's probably the cheapest option for new housebuilders as the cupboards can be created as you go rather than being added on afterwards.

Budget between £150 and £300 per fitted wardrobe, depending on the size, finish and complexity of the design; this would include shelving, hanging rails and a door or two. Magnet and the DIY sheds sell melamine wardrobe fitting kits, complete with hanging rails, at around £40 each.

THE HOME OFFICE

Pick up any paper or magazine and you're likely to find articles about working from home, as if it had just been discovered as the panacea of all modern ills. This is completely

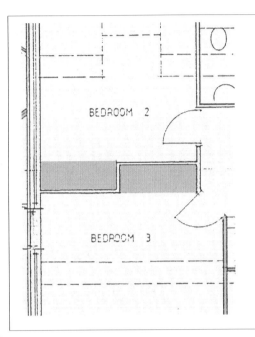

The kinked bedroom wall creates wardrobe space and satisfies the VAT office. It also adds to sound-proofing between bedrooms

daft. Working from home is what most of us always did, long before they invented factories and offices, and there are still loads of trades and businesses which have always worked from home. What is new is that there is a whole host of office workers, who would previously have commuted some distance to work, now padding a few feet down the passageway. Journalists in particular are able to work from home which is, just possibly, why you read so much about it in the newspapers and magazines. But my farming friends just scratch their heads and wonder what everyone is talking about.

What's the upshot of all this? Well, what most people think

when they think of working from home is that they need an office, or at least some office space. The physical requirements for all this are remarkably small, usually satisfied by a few shelves and a working space serviced by a couple of power outlets, a telephone socket and a broadband router. There really isn't much designing to be done, you just take over the box bedroom and have done with it. Even if you are inclined towards the hi-tech office with PCs, faxes, printers, scanners, copiers, routers and the like, you still don't really need anything more in the way of infrastructure – although extra power points and phone sockets would certainly come in handy.

PLANNING ISSUES

However, for many others, working from home will need considerably more thought. You may require meeting space or consultation rooms which are best kept quite separate from the rest of the household in order to maintain a professional atmosphere: sometimes this can be quite neatly achieved with an additional ground floor room which has its own external entrance. On the other hand, you may need workshop space which will create dust or noise or smell and which is ideally situated in a separate building. These are specialised concerns and really no one is going to understand them better than yourself, so it is pointless me wittering on. What I should point out though is that the more specialised and separate your workspace becomes, the more problems you are likely to encounter at the planning stage.

These problems are likely to hinge on whether you can extend the terms of the planning permission to include non-residential uses. Solo home office working is frankly not going to be an issue but anything that a) makes a lot of noise or smell or b) attracts a lot of visitors is not going to be passed through on the nod; in fact, it's probably unlikely to get passed at all if the area is zoned purely residential. However the buzz word of contemporary planning, sustainability, is on your side here. For decades the planning system has worked to separate the residential zones from the industrial zones on the premise that the two don't mix well, but as much of our working activities have become cleaner and quieter, the wisdom of this zoning has been called into question. Now the boot seems to be on the other foot because the car – more particularly the car journey – has become the bête noire of planning departments. Anything that can be done to reduce the number of car journeys is said to be sustainable, which is planning speak for a good thing.

LIVE-WORK UNITS
Most spec housing continues to be built without dedicated office space although this changes as you move up market. In London and some other metro areas, you occasionally come across live/work units that are designed to appeal to mostly to singletons. You might be tempted to use this home working

scenario to gain a little planning leverage – reducing car journeys, etc – but do bear in mind that there are potential tax traps. The house may be deemed to be partially commercial space which will mean that part of it becomes exempt from your principle private residence tax shelter and that you may be assessed for commercial rates.

HOW MUCH CABLE?
Even if you don't want a dedicated home office, future purchasers are likely to have such space high on their wish list, so it is good to plan a little flexibility into the scheme you are designing. Easily written, but what does it actually mean. I think it boils down to whether you

The home office can be fitted into a box bedroom but if you're planning to use it for more than a few hours a day it is worth creating a space that you will be happy working in – and one with plenty of power sockets for computers etc

are going to cable up the house for data. You could just choose to ignore all this if it doesn't bother you. Any future developments in home cabling systems will have to be capable of being retro-fitted into existing houses so you can afford to sit and wait and see what the future may bring. But the growing use of broadband means that it is quite likely that an internet connection in every bedroom becomes the accepted norm within a few years and this is certainly much easier to accommodate whilst undertaking the initial wiring. On the other hand, we now live in a world of ubiquitous wi-fi and most homes can get adequate broadband signal in all rooms from a single wireless

1

2

router, if sensibly placed. See Chapter 9 on Wiring.

GARAGES

Before you commit yourself to spending good money on garage space consider for a moment whether it is really necessary. Although current fashions in house styles tend towards the traditional, there is absolutely nothing traditional about a garage. Its nearest equivalent in pre-20th century housing is the stable or, perhaps, the cowshed; but the housing of cars is an altogether different affair. Furthermore, whilst thirty or forty years ago it was a good idea to keep vehicles undercover to facilitate winter starts and to stop rust, cars these days are made to very much higher standards and it is really not necessary to keep them undercover. Nowadays, security is often cited as a reason for building garages – but

does this really justify spending as much on a garage as it costs to buy a small car? And for many practiced car thieves, a locked garage doesn't really represent much of an obstacle in any event, especially as people tend to be much less security conscious on outbuildings.

Of course, garages have many other uses besides providing undercover car parking, as is shown by the numbers of people who have them but never park their cars inside them. Solid fuel, tools, lawnmowers, gardening equipment, bicycles, golf clubs, baby buggies, deep freezes, paddling pools, paint, you name it, it gets stored out there, and very useful it is too. But if you are designing a house from scratch, you may come to the conclusion that what you need is a larger utility room or a basement, not a garage. Garages are obviously valued by a great number of people otherwise speculative

developments wouldn't include them as a matter of course, but don't just fall into the trap of assuming that a house must have a garage because it's not a proper house without one. Having said all that, you still want a garage. Next question is...

WHEN TO BUILD IT?

You can, of course, decide to leave the construction of a garage until an unspecified later date, provided that it's not integral to the house. If it is included on your planning permission drawings, the right to build it cannot be taken away once you have started the main house. NB This ruling goes for conservatories, swimming pools and any other fancy accoutrements that you aspire to but can't afford. Therefore just drawing the plans might represent a good compromise solution for those who don't really need a garage but worry that the house might be difficult to sell without one. Against this, you should be aware that any building work that takes place after you move into a house will not be exempt from VAT, so it will cost you 20 per cent more to construct. Also, it is worth pointing out that many people find it very useful to build the garage before the rest of the house as it provides a useful and secure store-cum-site hut whilst the main construction forges ahead. Indeed, with a bit of adaptation, you could just about live in a garage for a few months – certainly not much worse than the average caravan.

SITING

By and large, house designers do not like garages. They are difficult. On most sites, access demands that they are located somewhere prominent near the frontage and yet, by their very nature, they are more akin to outbuildings and sheds. Now, polite architectural convention dictates that you don't put a humble shed in the front garden and so you are left with the problem of having to make the garage look good without costing too much.

INTEGRAL

One way around this conundrum is to have an integral garage, that is, one that is built into or at least attached to the main house.

FOR

▓ It makes for a more effective utility room type garage if that's what you have in mind
▓ You can use it to house boilers and freezers
▓ The arrangement fits better on narrow fronted sites (under 15 m wide).

AGAINST

It doesn't usually do much for the look of a house. Most garage doors are better suited to largely unseen parts of your estate – ie they are naff – and placing one

prominently in your front elevation can be very ugly. The problem of the garage door is particularly acute when you are building in a traditional style. One way of alleviating it is to have an 'L' shaped house and to tuck the garage into the bit of the L that projects forward towards the road. This softens the impact of the integral garage on the all important kerb appeal.

DETACHED

Given a site without space constraints, most builders will plump for a detached garage. The main attraction of this arrangement is that it maintains the integrity of the house design but, even so, the siting of the garage can still overwhelm this. Ideally, it will be well away to one side but most plots these days are not large enough to make this a viable option and so very often the house is half-hidden by the detached garage in front of it. Effectively, this means that the garage plays a crucial role in people's initial views of a house, and developers have responded to this by spending more and more money on external appearance, commonly including fancy roofing effects not seen on the main house.

BUILDING COSTS

Many of the costs of building a garage – whether integral or detached – are no different from the costs of building the main house. Garages do not have to meet the standard building regulations as regards insulation and damp penetration and this allows them to be constructed with thinner, single-skin walls. However, groundwork costs and roofing costs are basically identical, and despite the fact that garages are rarely fitted out with all the paraphernalia of a finished house, the construction costs of a garage are still as much as 60 per cent of those of a finished house when compared on a floor area basis.

ALTERNATIVES
CAR PORTS

One alternative approach is just to build a lean-to car port or undercover car parking bay. You need some form of hard standing for the car and then the rest is up to you. The finished result could be anything from a flimsy timber construction which might look better as a garden pergola to a fully-fledged garage without a door.

PREFABRICATED

There are several small manufacturers who produce prefabricated garages at prices way below standard construction costs. But what you are buying is probably little different in quality to a garden shed. That may be exactly what you are looking for of course. They are very utilitarian and would probably be best sited away from the main house.

UNDERGROUND

An underground garage is unlikely to be a cost-effective option unless space is at a premium. Access ramps (budget £8,000) and potential drainage problems make the totally underground garage an expensive luxury. However, the economics look far friendlier when sorting out sloping ground. There are instances where burying car parking below ground can actually free up ground elsewhere for more cost-effective uses (like building extra houses), but this is unlikely to be relevant to many single housebuilders.

GARAGE DOORS

For many designers, the problem with garages begins and ends with the garage door. Until the Seventies garage doors were strictly functional and utilitarian, often made of steel with no attempts at embellishment. Since then, a large number of imitation traditional door styles have sprung up, aping the move back to other traditional forms. The trouble is, that whilst a window or a front door can be made in styles copied from old doors, there are no old garage doors to copy from. Hence a mock Georgian or mock Tudor garage door looks more than faintly ridiculous. Double doors, over 4 m wide, look particularly strange and attempts to mould classical patterns on them merely emphasise how strange and out of place they look.

If there is a traditional British garage door it is the side opening style that you see on houses built in the Twenties and Thirties, made from solid timbers and lit by small square frosted-glass panels, sometimes called a Pattern 301 door.

Garage doors are large and therefore tend to get pricey. It's a specialist business and your best bet is to trawl through Yellow Pages to 'Garage Doors' and seek quotations from there. Steel is much the cheapest material but also the least attractive. Timber and GRP are around twice the price. GRP doors are usually produced to look like timber – in fact they can look incredibly realistic. They can also be stained; their main advantage over timber is that they are (hopefully) maintenance-free, yet many people will prefer to stick with timber.

If you don't like any of the commercially available doors yet still crave the convenience of an up-and-over door, then check out Hormann's sub-frames that you can fill in with your own designs at your leisure. They are called Open-for-Infill doors.

OPENING MECHANISMS

As already stated, most garage doors these days open vertically. But it's not quite that simple. There is vertical and vertical. The simplest type of opening is the canopy or up-and-over door; when open, about a third of the door protrudes outside the frame, forming a canopy. They are usually hand operated and canopy double doors are something you could live without as they can get very heavy and awkward to lift.

As its name suggests, the fully retractable door glides all the way back into the garage on a set of tracks. These are much more suitable for double doors and for remote operators.

The North Americans like to fit sectional garage doors. These split into, typically, four horizontal sections which slide up a set of vertical tracks and then, one section at a time, turn through 90 degrees and end up under the garage roof. The advantage of this is that the door doesn't protrude when opening so that you can park hard up to both the inside and outside face and still open the door.

Finally, there are various makes of Roller Doors around which perform in much the same way as sectional doors. However instead of turning through 90 degrees, these doors roll up like a carpet. They look like steel shutters, which is what they are, and so kerb appeal is limited.

HOW WIDE?

The traditional width for a single garage door in the UK has been 7 ft (2134 mm). It's mean. There are an awful lot of cars around that will struggle to get through such a gap, particularly so if the entry angle isn't dead straight. If you have the room, go for doors that are 7 ft 6 in wide (2286 mm). If space is very tight, you can usually gain a crucial few inches by locating the supporting frame behind the walls rather than between them. Height is also an issue. Some big cars won't fit under a 7 ft doorway.

If you are planning a double garage, you have the choice of a double door or two singles. Two single doors usually work out cheaper; although you have to build a dividing pillar, the cost of this is offset by the extra cost of a 4.5 m lintel to cross the gap above a double door opening. Opening double doors by hand can also be quite a hassle, particularly if the spring mechanism works out of adjustment. On the other hand, if you plan to use an electric door operator you save yourself the cost of installing a second one.

REMOTE CONTROL OPERATORS

An increasingly popular item which allows you to open and close your garage door automatically from both a switch inside the garage and a remote control unit which you can keep inside the car. They are not cheap – coming in at around £400 which includes a remote control device (or two if you are lucky) – but they do make a lot of sense when you consider the hassle involved in opening garage doors manually. All the garage door suppliers sell these and they come in varying levels of sophistication. Hormann and Bosch market multi-function ones that can switch on welcome lights and open entrance gates as well. However, even the most basic ones come with timed welcome lights that come on whenever the door is opened: this is very useful.

Electric operators also come in different flavours. Most work with a geared chain but there are some (Hormann's Supramatic) that work on a Kevlar belt which promise virtually silent opening. They tend not to work on the basic canopy up-and-over doors although Cardale's Autoglide is an exception: in fact it can be retrofitted onto existing doors. If you are going to spend £6,000 plus on a garage, then it's probably worthwhile spending the extra on an operator so that you actually get to use the garage for its intended purpose.

12
ADDING EXTRA SPACE

FOR EVERY NEW house built in Britain, there are something like three or four homes extended and/or improved. The exact figure can only be guessed at but it's a huge industry in the UK, more so than in other countries. Why?

In most other countries, the rate of new housebuilding per head of population is way higher than it is in the UK. And the ones we do build are depressingly small – our average house size is just 75 sq m, the smallest in the EU.

Consequentially, the home improvement market in the UK is enormous, far bigger relative to the overall population than anywhere else in the world. This chapter looks at the options facing you if you are out to extend rather than to build from scratch. Many of the techniques are no different, but the ways of going about things are.

Here, ranked in cost order, with the cheapest first, is a summary of ways you can gain extra living space.

■ 1. Convert existing floor space into habitable space, such as a garage conversion
■ 2. Convert existing loft space
■ 3. Build an outhouse in the garden
■ 4. Extend the existing structure
■ 5. Excavate a basement

Is it possible to put sensible prices onto these? Let's ignore the fitting out costs. Not that these aren't considerable, it's just that they shouldn't vary an awful lot whichever method you use to gain space, ie a kitchen or an office fit-out shouldn't be that different in cost wherever you choose to put it.

I would have said that there is a range of costs between £200 per sq m for upgrading existing space to meet building regs standards for habitable rooms and £1,500 per sq m for creating new cellar space under an existing house. The bulk of this sort of work clusters around the lower end of these two extremes. Anticipate simple loft conversions to cost around £500 per sq m, extensions from between £800 and £1,000 per sq m. And once again, don't forget I am ignoring fit out costs which can sometimes double the basic build cost. What I am trying to say, politely, is that there is a huge range of costs likely to be encountered in this sort of work and it's possibly not that helpful to attempt to boil it all down to "£xx per square metre."

DESIGN

Many of the important things that are to be said about design have already been made in the design chapter. But there are

Typical Extension Costs

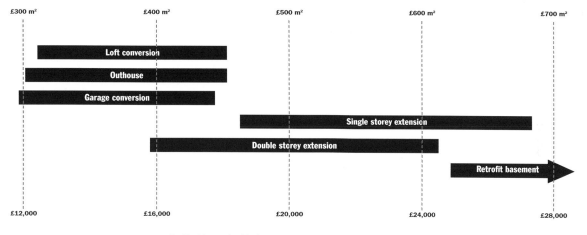

Shell-build costs for 40m². Fit-out can easily double the finished cost

one or two salient points to be boned up on when you are just mapping out small pieces of a house or an outbuilding.

How much individual design, let alone flair, is required to turn an idea and some money into a useable structure is dependent almost wholly on what you are trying to achieve. The projects covered by this chapter include many where the design comes with the product: I am thinking here of garden sheds, stables and sometimes conservatories. At the other end of the scale are projects every bit as complicated as a new house where a good design is required to gain planning permission and to add value to the works. And, in between, will be many projects like simple loft conversions and extensions, where the constraints of the site are such that what design is required is needed simply to facilitate the building

work. In other words, it may not be much more than a glorified shopping list.

Which probably isn't much help to you. You instinctively know this stuff already. What isn't always clear is when to go straight to a builder and when to go to a designer for some interpretation of your requirements and some professional help in turning them into a building contract. Where do you draw the line?

For what it's worth, I reckon that a requirement for planning permission also acts as some sort of litmus test here. By and large, it's the larger jobs that require planning permission. And, by and large, it's the larger jobs that require a little bit more from the design department. For a start, your work is unlikely to gain planning permission without some form of technical drawings and so there is a natural reason to hire a designer. Having done that, it's a much smaller step to

using this same person to put together tender documents for builders to quote from.

The main alternative option is to work with a builder from the off, to create a design and build contract, where the builder also becomes responsible for undertaking the design and maybe sorting out planning permission for you. It can work well even on relatively large and complex jobs: it really does come down a lot to personalities and capabilities.

PLANNING AND RED TAPE

Whereas a new house always requires planning permission, a large amount of remodelling in an existing house doesn't, which is good news for

Chapter 12

remodellers. The bad news is that it's often far from clear just what you can and can't do without going cap in hand to the local planners. First, I'll try and give some guidance on just what you might expect to be able to do without planning permission and then I'll discuss what to do if your proposed work does require permission.

PERMITTED DEVELOPMENT RIGHTS
The basis of our planning regime is the Town & Country Planning Act, which came into effect in 1948, part of the post-war Old Labour 'rebuilding Britain' package that also saw the introduction of the NHS and the nationalisation of much of our industrial backbone. Before that, you didn't have to apply to anyone for permission to build, or so rumour has it.

This 1948 date has become a cut-off point. Whatever had been done to your house before 1948 was said to be 'existing': whatever has been done to it since is said to be 'extending'. It's a long time ago now and the chances are that the house you live in was built long after 1948 but nevertheless it's still a point in time worth being aware of.

The Town & Country Planning Act sought to control what and where we could build. Its intention wasn't to prevent development, merely to enhance it and to ensure it took place in everybody's interest. Ha! So that the local planning department didn't grind to a halt – that took another 50 years – the Act incorporated a provision that allowed you to extend your home up to a certain amount without having to trouble the planners. This provision has come to be known as our Permitted Development Rights, PD Rights for short. It applies to houses at their built-shape in 1948 and it applies to houses constructed since

1948, although there are one or two exceptions. It wouldn't be planning if there weren't one or two exceptions.

To make things even more complicated, the system of PD rights that existed merrily since 1948 was rewritten in 2008, so that several of the old conventions, which everybody in planning was familiar with, were obliterated and replaced with even more complex rules. This is particularly true of extensions and outbuildings where the rules have undergone some subtle changes.

And then the current Chancellor, George Osborne, has sought to relax the rules in 2012 for a period of three years in order to try and stimulate growth. It's out for consultation as I write, but it's pretty much chaos down at the planning department.

And of course, this being the United Kingdom, you can count on the fact that Wales, Scotland and Ireland all have their own versions of permitted development rights. Broadly speaking, they are very similar, but they are different enough to make things very awkward for books trying to explain what is what.

The good news, as far as I am concerned, is that the internet is now a repository of knowledge on these matters and that rather than me trying to point out what you can and can't do, I will simply point you to the relevant web page.

IF IN DOUBT
The advice must always be to run your project past the planners. They should be able to give you a clear indication about whether planning permission is required. In fact, you can apply for a Lawful Development Certificate to make it clear to all and sundry that what you are about

to undertake doesn't require planning permission. The current fees for minor planning applications are £172 , so even if you do have to apply it's not a ruinous amount although it may well take months to sort through.

USEFUL URLS
England: www.planningportal.gov.uk Go to General Public Area, then household planning rules. Visit the interactive houses so you can figure out just what you can and can't do without planning permission. Remember, you may have already used up some of your PD rights if the house has been extended after 1948.

WALES: www.planningaidwales.org. uk Go to General PublicNational Planning PolicyPlanning ApplicationsPermitted Development. There you should find the General Permitted Development Order which you can download. No fancy graphics here, unfortunately. Just pages of rules. Set to be devolved soon and may well have new rules in place.

SCOTLAND: Also under review. You can find the Scottish version of the General Permitted Development Orders at the OPSI website (Office of Public Sector Information) - again no flash graphics, just hard copy. Go to www.opsi. gov.uk and type'"Permitted Development Scotland" into the search field and it will pop into view. This may soon devolve to the Scottish Executive website. Good luck

IRELAND: The Planning Service is what you want. www.planningni.gov.uk. There you will find the local version of the General Development Order in the general advice section.

PD TIPS
If planning permission for what you want to do is at all contentious, you can

occasionally get cute with your PD rights and use them to run rings around the planners.

▓ 1. If you apply for planning permission to extend above and beyond what the PD Rights already give you, you don't get to keep the unused PD Rights. But just suppose you want to extend in two directions, say sideways and backwards. Assume that your PD Rights are still intact but that the additional size of both extensions exceeds the permitted limits. Decide which of the two extensions is the more controversial and apply for planning permission to build the other bit. If this is granted, you can then use your virgin PD Rights to build the controversial bit first without compromising your already granted planning permission.

▓ 2. You can reclaim your PD Rights by demolishing something built after 1948. Say you have a particularly naff attached garage put up in the 1960s without planning permission. If the extension you would like to build takes you over the amended PD Rights limits, because the garage eats up most of the allowed volume, you can reclaim the rights by taking down the garage.

▓ 3. PD Rights are also useful when negotiating a replacement dwelling. Often local councils have guidelines restricting the size of the new dwelling, relating to the size of the existing. Galling when you have a tiny bungalow on an acre plot. If the old bungalow had never used up its PD Rights, be sure to include them in your calculations.

PARTY WALL ACT

More information on the workings of the Party Wall Act is included in the main section on Planning, earlier in the book. It affects all properties in England & Wales but is only likely to have any bearing on your project if you have close neighbours, as you would expect to find if you live in a semi or a terraced house, or an apartment. Do be aware that it comes into effect if you are planning to build off a neighbours wall, as well you might when undertaking a loft conversion, and that it also kicks in if you excavate new foundations, deeper than your neighbour's, within 3m of your neighbour's foundations. This might easily be the case with an extension, especially if the neighbour's property is over 100 years old, before the time that excavations were dug deep.

There is a good explanatory booklet downloadable from the building regs website, which will tell you more than you would ever really want to know. Note that this really should be sorted out two months before the building work starts: otherwise you are courting delay.

BUILDING REGS

In April 2010, I received the following email:

Dear Mr Brinkley,
I have just read your latest book on house building as we are having a kitchen extension done. I am a little disappointed in your lack of information about Building Control. The book makes little mention of Building Control other than the costs. I spoke to East Cambs Building Control yesterday and they told me that there are statutory visits that they must make when a house/extension is being built. I have just printed them off. Should you not at least include a paragraph on these inspections, when they have to start, what they include and the end inspection which, I believe, is a sign off of the building? I can't find mention of these statutory visits, and if

I was doing a DIY job and didn't have all the inspections and the sign off at the end surely the whole job could go seriously awry?

Also, given the proliferation of 'cowboy' builders wouldn't the building control officer pick up that a job wasn't being done properly before too much work had gone ahead?

We managed to build a boarding cattery in Cambridgeshire without consulting Building Control (through ignorance, no one told us we should be using them) and almost didn't get a regularisation certificate as one of the buildings was, in theory, too close to a farmers barn. Hence how I know about building control. So if I were using your book as my 'bible' I am not sure I would know that I had to use Building Control, and at what stages.
Yours
Carole Cooke

I thought the best thing was to include the text in full, as I couldn't make the point any better. In my defence, I touch on building control in much more detail in the chapter on Project Management, forgetting that many people would be dipping into this chapter alone because they are only doing an extension or something similar. So if that means you, then heed this warning now and bear in mind that Chapters 4 and 5 are just as much for you as this one.

But, to re-iterate Carole Cooke's point, if you are carrying out substantial building works, you need to get the building inspectors on board although they no longer have to be local council building inspectors – you can use other approved inspectors, if you can find them.

It's true that there are some minor

works that don't require inspection, but generally, the larger the job, the more chance there is of building regs being required: extensions and loft conversions always require building control approval. On renovation and alteration work, the picture isn't as clear although the tentacles of building control have a habit of spreading wider and wider.

For instance, the introduction of Part P in England & Wales in 2004 brought almost all electrical work within building control for the first time, even when it is carried out in structures like conservatories and outbuildings which are normally building control exempt. And changes to Part L, the energy efficiency regs, have brought replacement windows and replacement boilers within building control.

The trend is clear. The government doesn't want to hire thousands more building inspectors to cover all these extra items: it wants the tradesmen carrying them out to be competent and certified, and for them to sign off their work and for you, the homeowner, to keep the guarantee for when you come to sell the house.

Generally, you are required to apply for building regulations for the following works:

An application needs to be submitted when you intend to:
▨ Erect a building. eg new dwelling
▨ Extend an existing building. eg kitchen extension, attached garage etc.
▨ Make alterations to a building. eg remove a load-bearing wall or a chimney stack, or form an opening in a structural or fire-protecting wall
▨ Underpin all or part of a building
▨ Convert a loft. eg make a new room in the roof space

▨ Install services and fittings.e g installing showers and toilets, or replacement glazing, Central Heating Systems, boilers, flues, laying new drains or altering electrics. (Some of these may be controlled under competent persons schemes)
▨ Change the use of a building. eg convert a house to flats or make more than one dwelling.
▨ Erect a large conservatory. eg floor area greater than 30 sq m (a conservatory less than 30 sq m is exempt provided at least 75 per cent of the roof and 50 per cent of the walls are of translucent material and is thermally separated from the dwelling by walls, windows and doors with U-values and draught stripping provision at least as good as elsewhere in the dwelling.)
▨ Carry out work to thermal elements .eg re-plastering, replacement roof, external rendering/cladding or new ground floor.
▨ Make alterations or extensions to commercial premises, schools, hospitals etc
▨ Carry out work to improve access to and/or provide facilities for disabled people. You can find an up-to-date explanatory booklet from the building regs website. This tends to reside under the planning services part of your local authority website.

EXTENSIONS

Building an extension is like building a mini-house and essentially the very same processes have to be gone through. In some ways, extensions are actually harder than houses to build because there is always the matter of tying onto the existing structure, which frequently creates little teething problems.

BUILDING REGS

The building regs are essentially no different for extensions than for whole houses but in one or two instances they are made a lot simpler because it is inappropriate to use them for only part of the house. In particular:

PART M – THE DISABLED ACCESS REGS

These are designed to be applied to new houses and the essential aspects of Part M, being level thresholds, maximum and minimum socket heights, wider doors and a downstairs WC, don't make any sense when applied to just the extension of an existing house. The one aspect of Part M which may be applied to an extension is if you are somehow contriving to make matters worse for disabled visitors. Thus if your access was level and you were about to make it stepped, or you were to remove a downstairs WC.

If your house was built after 1999, then it should already be Part M compliant – you will be able to tell from the socket heights. If it is, then any additional work on the house will be expected to also be Part M compliant.

PART L – THE ENERGY EFFICIENCY REGS

The regs apply to extensions and to some renovation work but in a much-simplified format. Gone is the requirement for whole house SAP calculations and pressure testing. Instead, you can just design your walls, floors and roofs to meet certain U values, in the traditional method.

Note that boiler replacement and window replacement, two common restoration tasks, are required to meet Part L standards. Your boiler will have to be a condensing one and your replacement windows will have to be FENSA approved to show that they comply with the maximum U values.

ACCESS

Access for building work is likely to be much more restricted than it is for a new build. This is one of the factors that often makes extensions much more expensive to build on a per square metre basis. Specifically, you are often unable to get large plant around the back of an existing house and you therefore find that in consequence foundations may have to be hand dug and materials may well have to be purchased in small loads and barrowed or handballed around the building.

You may also have problems with scaffolding, especially if you are building on the boundary. Your neighbours may or may not take kindly to your building work but even if they do, it can be difficult to even locate scaffolding sometimes.

As a rule of thumb, difficult access may well add up to 20 per cent to building work costs. Extensions can be built from inside if external scaffolding can't be provided, but this is slow and tedious and will add to costs as well. Generally it is worth pointing out to your neighbours, that a brick wall looks far better when it is built from the correct side!

OPENING UP WALLS

The typical extension job requires that you break a hole into the existing structure and use this to form the access to the extension. If it's a two-storey extension, then the hole will open both storeys of the house.

Knocking down walls is an art in itself and most builders are very familiar with such a task. The key points to understand is that the structure which depended on the walls you knock down has to be supported both during the demolition and building work and permanently thereafter. The standard procedure is to support the floor joists, if they run into the soon-to-be-demolished wall, so a beam, usually steel, gets inserted to provide permanent support. If you are just having a door between the extension and the existing, then there is unlikely to be any problem but for any opening over 2m wide, you need to be sure that the loadings are correct. Your building inspector will advise and is likely to require you to hire a structural engineer to prove the beam size.

TYING IN BRICKWORK

The new structure will have to be tied into the existing. If the structure is brick or block, then this can be done carefully by toothing out the existing and building into the gaps, or you can cheat and use stainless steel profiles which you just screw into the existing.

Some people are snobby about profiles and suggest that the traditional and therefore better method is always to tooth into the existing brickwork. But the existing brickwork isn't always as good as you might hope for and sometimes the existing brick courses are unequal, which makes tying in a minor nightmare.

FLASHINGS AND WATERPROOFINGS

Obviously where the roof of the extension abuts the existing, you have to make some provision for rainfall to be collected and channelled away. However, if the wall you are abutting is a cavity wall, you have an additional and extremely fiddly piece of work to undertake, namely the insertion of cavity trays.

FLOORS

The section on floors covers the actual floor construction options. But extensions have one extra problem up their sleeves, which is the matching up of floors between the old and new. Normally, it's just a question of planning ahead carefully and deciding what level the finished floor should be and sort of working backwards from there. Just occasionally you will find that the existing floor is not level and you get left with an awkward decision about how best to get the two floors to match up.

MOVING DRAINS

One frequent problem which arises when working on extensions is drains. Normally drains are routed out of the house as quickly as possible. Typically, they exit out the back of the house or into a side passage and thence to the front. But in many older properties, especially in terraces, the drains are shared with a number of other houses. You can in fact build over domestic drains: the standard routine is to bridge the existing drains when you place the foundations so as to ensure that the drains are not damaged. If there is a manhole or inspection chamber under the floor of your proposed extension, you have a problem but not necessarily insurmountable. You may be able to cover it over and to replace it with a new one outside the extension. You may even be able to keep it there and to have it accessed through the floor, although this is far from ideal. It's a principal of good drain design that you don't want to have to access drains from indoors!

Finally, you may be able to re-route the existing drains around the outside of the extension. There are problems if the drain runs along one of your foundation trenches, but there are often solutions. The one situation that can cause major difficulties is if there is a mains sewer running close to your house: the regs regarding mains sewers are much tighter. Refer to Part H of the England & Wales building regs.

ADDITIONAL HEATING

The extension will require heating in one form or another. Just how this can best be achieved depends largely on what heating you already have in the existing and whether it is man enough to carry the extra load imposed by the additional space. Really only a survey of the existing arrangements will reveal this and it's pretty pointless to speculate about that here. But note that if the boiler is old and requires replacing, the latest regulations require that you use an energy-efficient condensing boiler in its place. Condensing boilers themselves require a drain off point to collect the condensate. This isn't always possible in conventional boiler locations and you may be able to argue for a dispensation to use a non-condensing boiler instead.

However you do it, the chances are that the work will involve some disruption to the existing house.

EXTENDING ELECTRICS

The issues with extending electrics are similar in many ways to extending the heating and maybe plumbing. The newer the house is, the less likely it will be to require a complete rewire, but there is a chance that the installation you already have in place will not be adequate to handle the extra load imposed on it by the new extension, especially if the extension houses power hungry appliances like cookers and hobs.

Again the most useful thing to do here is to get the existing installation surveyed prior to work starting out on the extension.

Note that electrical work is now

covered by the building regulations and has to be certified by an approved installer, although if the electrical work forms part of a much bigger job, like an extension, you don't have to make a separate application. Indeed, you can ask your building inspector to include the inspection of the electrics as part of their service.

ENERGY EFFICIENCY MEASURES

During the last three consultations over energy efficiency regulations, there has been a proposal put forward to insist that anyone doing work on their home which required building regs approval should be required to spend an additional amount, possibly as much as 10 per cent of the overall budget, on improving energy efficiency in the existing structure. Typically, the householder would have been required to:
- undertake cavity wall insulation
- replace the old boiler with something more efficient
- add extra loft insulation
- add draft proofing to windows and doors

There is logic in this proposal. All the energy efficiency regulations that have been introduced since 1976 have been aimed at new build or extensions to existing builds. The situation has now come to pass that new builds are reasonably low in energy demands and it has become increasingly difficult to introduce cost-effective ways of improving matters still further. However, older housing stock remains largely untouched by the energy efficiency drives and it's an anomaly that is beginning to irk our energy saving boffins.

However, to date this proposal had been edited out by various housing ministers, and more recently by the Prime

Minister no less. David Cameron called such a proposal "bonkers," according to the Daily Mail in April 2012.

By and large the building regs have been very careful not to interfere with existing structures and having flirted with this idea they decided that this was not perhaps the best time to start. But the 'consequential improvements' debate hasn't gone away and one or two local authorities have started introducing something similar via their planning departments, so you may yet be faced with demands to undertake works you hadn't originally envisaged.

LOFT CONVERSIONS

The loft conversion is a thoroughly modern phenomenon. A generation ago, nobody thought to extend their living space into the roof. People who wanted more space generally moved house. Their lofts sat gathering dust, holding old photograph albums and abandoned suitcases. But as land values have risen across the country, so the pressure on space has increased. And, as moving on to a larger house has become more and more expensive, people's attention has turned to making the most of what they already have. Increasingly, that has meant utilising the dead space in the roof.

It's little wonder that the past thirty years has witnessed an explosion in the number of loft conversions being carried out in the UK. However, it's important to bear in mind that the loft conversion is not always the best or most appropriate solution. This is especially true with single-storey dwellings that appeal largely to older people who value not having to negotiate stairs. The stairs are a limiting factor, which means that lofts are generally not best suited for dayrooms and kitchens. In contrast, they are excellent for extra bedroom space or quieter hobby rooms or home offices.

INITIAL ASSESSMENT

All loft conversions start with an initial assessment. The easiest way to do this is, of course, to get up there and take a look around. Some people will want a professional to undertake this work for them but much of the initial assessment is common sense and there is no harm in undertaking a preliminary study yourself.

HEAD ROOM

The first thing to look out for is the head room. You need to be able to stand up in the middle and ideally you should be struggling to touch the ridge plate running along the top of the roof. The things which determine the space you have in a loft are the span between the eaves and the pitch or slope of the roof (which in turn determines the height). Most detached and semi-detached homes have a wide enough span and if the slope or pitch is more than 35 deg then you should have enough volume to make a decent sized room. It's something you can tell easily enough just by getting up into the loft space. You need to be looking for a minimum distance of 2.3m between the underside of the ridge and the ceiling below.

If you haven't got this space in your loft, you can't have a useful loft conversion without some alterations to your roof shape

which will obviously be much more costly to undertake. For instance, you may be able to raise the height of the roof and build a box-shaped roof extension.

ROOF SHAPE

The next step is to have a look at the shape of the roof. Generally, the simpler the roof-shape, the better. What loft converters love above all else is a straightforward pitched roof with straight walls or gables at either end. These allow you to easily transfer all the roof loadings onto beams stretching between the gable walls. A hipped roof presents problems but not insurmountable ones. Similarly with roofs which form an L-shape. If the upper floor of your house is built partly into the roof (the so-called one and a half storey house is a case in point) then a loft conversions is likely to be a non-starter as there is rarely enough headroom left above the ceiling to make any usable loft space.

CHIMNEYS

The presence of a chimney may present problems, depending largely where it's located. Anything central is likely to be difficult: it's hardly worth generalising about this because it's likely to be obvious from a cursory inspection whether the chimney is an obstruction or not. If it is, and you no longer use the chimney, it is usually quite acceptable to take it down during the course of the works, although planners and listed building officers might just have a different opinion.

1
Lofts can offer a great way of adding living space – whatever the shape and space available

2
The simplest way to find out whether a loft conversion is feasible is to get up in the loft and see what the headroom is. This is just on the limits of what is sensible

ROOF STRUCTURE

Another important factor to consider is how the roof is built. There are, in generalisation, two main methods of building roofs. The traditional method was prevalent on all roofs until the 1960s and is the easiest to convert. It involves carpenters cutting the roof timbers on site – it is sometimes referred to as a cut roof – and fixing the timbers one-by-one to make up the roof structure. This method was to a large extent replaced by a system of engineered roof trusses, developed in America, which swept through the housebuilding industry in the 1960s because they were quicker and cheaper to erect.

A trussed roof arrives on site on the back of a lorry in large triangular sections. These are hauled up onto the roof and nailed in place side-by-side. It's very much quicker than doing a cut roof and also much less skillful. Because their strength is derived from the fact that the sections are already triangulated, you can use much smaller pieces of timber to make a truss roof. Once you know what you are looking for, it's easy to tell a trussed roof from a traditional one. Look out for thin sections of planed wood, typically no more than 75mm or 3 inches deep. There will be a number of these small timbers running from the top of the truss to the bottom and joined onto the outer timbers by tell-tale rectangular metal plates, easily visible from the side.

In contrast, a traditional or cut roof uses larger sections of sawn (not planed) timber (often 50x150mm) and these are cut on site and usually nailed together. They frequently have supporting beams called purlins located midway under each rafter, running along the length of the roof. Unlike traditional cut roofs where the individual timber rafters are load bearing, the roof truss derives its strength from the combination of all the small pieces of timber working together as one. Altering a truss roof is possible but is a much more involved process than adapting a traditional roof although recently there has been a lot of interest in this field and a number of specialist firms are offering trussed roof conversions at prices not substantially more than traditional cut roof conversions.

ATTIC TRUSSES

In more recent years, truss designs have

grown more complex and you can now have a house built with attic trusses which are designed specifically to leave usable space in the loft but you are very unlikely to have attic trusses in your home without knowing about it – it's a major selling point.

STAIRS

If you have established that your loft can be converted, the major internal design issue is access. One of the largest areas of extra expense when considering loft living is the fitting of a staircase. In three storey designs, because of fire regulations, you ideally want to position the top staircase close to the lower one and this can rather limit your room layouts. When converting loft space in an existing house, the normal staircase regulations are relaxed somewhat to allow for various space saving designs such as the alternate tread staircase which work with a much steeper pitch than regular stairs. However where you have the space available, a traditional staircase is the preferred option – it's both cheaper and far more practical. However it is not always an easy matter to design a traditional staircase under a sloping roof – you may well find that the top of the staircase ends up slap in the centre of your loft living space, which may make the subsequent room division tricky. Each case needs to be examined on its merits but, as with so many other issues with house design, the more space you have at your disposal, the greater are the number of workable solutions.

Occasionally, you will be faced with a situation where the disruption caused by fitting a second staircase is so great that it outweighs the benefit from converting the loft. If you feel this to be a significant stumbling block, you would be well advised to hire a professional designer

to look at the problem because there are often many ways of fitting staircases that are not at all obvious. An experienced professional may be able to see solutions which evade you. It is often surprising just how many variations you can work into a small floor plan.

There are many other issues to be resolved but generally they are of a relatively minor nature. If you have the headroom and you can fit a staircase, then the two biggest obstacles to converting your loft are out of the way.

PLANNING PERMISSION FOR LOFTS

The guidelines about what can and can't be done without planning permission have already been dealt with earlier in the chapter in the section on Design. It's all a question of whether or not you have used your PD Rights. Currently, the planning fee for all domestic alterations, including loft conversions, is £172 in England. Don't press ahead with a loft conversion if you are in any doubt about whether you need planning permission. You will undoubtedly be asked about this if and when you come to sell the house and it may prove very costly to obtain it retrospectively. It costs nothing to check with your local planning department and, if you are in any doubt about whether you need permission or not, it is the obvious first port of call.

BUILDING REGULATIONS

Whilst the planning angle is fairly straightforward, the building regulations covering loft conversions are something of a minefield. Some simpler storage-only loft conversions are undertaken without any reference to building regulations but if you intend to use the new rooms as habitable space you should ensure that the work is carried out in accordance with the regs.

STRUCTURE

If you are altering the timbers in a roof space, you need to be satisfied that the new design will be strong enough to bear the new loads. Usually your existing ceiling joists will not be strong enough to act as floor joists for the loft conversion and there are various ways of beefing them up. The normal method is to leave the existing joists in place – so as to cause minimum disruption to the ceiling below – and place larger joists by their side in order to take the added weight of the new floor. The roof carpentry will also have to be carefully designed to ensure that it stays in place whilst the structural alterations are undertaken and is then adequate for the open roof space you need. This may require the insertion of steel beams to support the new loadings. Alternatively support can sometimes be provided by knee walls, tying the rafters to the new floor joists. The important points to bear in mind are that the new structure must be strong enough to bear the weight of the new loads and also be rigid enough to stop the roof shape deflecting. The building inspector will want to see that some calculations have been carried out to ensure that these aims have been met.

INSULATION

Another area that causes considerable headaches for loft builders is rearranging the insulation so that it follows the roofline, rather than just being laid along the ceiling joists. The required U value (as of 2013) has fallen to 0.15 which translates as a minimum 200mm of foam insulation such as the type made by Celotex and Kingspan. There are more options if you chose to re-roof at the same time as this allows you to use a breathable felt which gives you a little extra room for insulation – you can avoid the requirement

to maintain a 50mm ventilation gap on the immediate underside of the roof. But generally it is felt that whereas once you could get away with just placing insulation between the rafters, now you have to combine this approach with extra layers of insulation on the underside (room side) of the rafters. This has the advantage of providing better insulation – the cold bridge caused by the rafters themselves is eliminated – but there is some resulting height loss in the room; this may be critical in smaller lofts and is something to consider carefully. You also now need to plan for that 50mm ventilation gap to be left to the underside of the rafters in order to get adequate insulation in.

One increasingly popular method of insulation is to use a multifoil type insulation such as Actis Tri-Iso Super 10 combined with a high efficiency foam. The acceptability of these multifoils is still a matter of contention – a few private building inspectors are happy with them, the great majority aren't – but as they are only 25mm thick they do make it very easy in loft conversions. The definitive word on whether multifoils really work is still awaited but the weight of evidence so far makes it look like the more extravagant claims of their manufacturers are just that – i.e. extravagant claims – but there is clearly a place for multifoils when used in conjunction with more conventional insulation. However you design the insulation, in almost every conceivable case, it will now protrude beneath the rafter line and consequently there will some lofts where this loss of height is critical, surely an unintended side effect of the new regulations.

FIRE SAFETY

But perhaps the biggest hurdle faced by loft converters is meeting the onerous

fire safety regulations. When you create habitable space more than 4.5m above ground level, you must allow for the fact that people will not be able to climb out of a window to escape a fire below. You have to provide at least one window that you can escape from via a fireman's ladder – known as an egress window – but in addition to this, you need to provide a fire-proofed route from the loft down to the front door. Half-hour fire-proofing is not particularly difficult to achieve but it will require additional work to be carried out on the doorways leading onto your escape route – typically the bedroom doors opening onto a landing. These doors will have to be treated (either with fire resistant paint or some fireproof board) and they used to have self-closing mechanisms fitted onto them. The best known of these is the Perko door closer, a little sprung chain mechanism that fits snugly into the hinged edge of the door and can be adjusted to ensure that it applies the correct pressure to close the door automatically. The requirement for fitting these was relaxed (in England) in 2007 because so many people disabled them once the building inspector had finalled the loft conversion.

You may face additional problems if your existing stairwell exits into a living room or kitchen, rather than an enclosed hallway. This sort of arrangement is not acceptable and you might have to build an enclosure around the staircase or find another route down to the ground (such as an external fire escape).

SERVICES AND FINISHES

More often than not, there will be water storage tanks in the existing loft that will have to be moved or replaced. Normally these are located in the middle of the loft and sometimes there is enough room to relocate them to the eaves or against

Chapter 12

an end wall. However if you plan to have plumbing in the loft space, either a wet radiator or perhaps a bathroom, you have to raise the tanks above the level of the outlets which may involve putting the tanks on raised platforms. As an alternative, you can switch to a more modern pressurised plumbing system which doesn't require separate tanks: a pressurised cylinder can be located anywhere in the house and can supply central heating as well as hot water. The downside on switching to a pressurised system is the cost: the cylinders alone cost around £600 and the additional plumbing needed to install one can be complex.

HEATING

With such high levels of insulation now required the additional heat required to keep the new loft space warm is minimal and it will almost always be possible to add a small radiator or two without having to upgrade the existing boiler. Alternatively you can fit underfloor heating – either warm water or electric – or small electric storage heaters or convector heaters. Electric heating systems are invariably cheap to install but expensive to run but you are likely to find that the heat loss is so small that they may only ever be needed as a back-up heating system on the coldest nights: most of the loft's heating needs will be met from background sources such as electric lights, sunshine and heat rising up from the house below.

ELECTRICS AND LIGHTING

Electrical alterations can usually be fairly easily accommodated, provided the new loads are generally limited to lights and a few sockets. One feature that may cause problems is the use of recessed downlighters. Whilst this may seem an ideal way to provide light when ceiling height is restricted, the physical breaching of the vapour barrier conventionally placed behind the plasterboard ceiling is likely to cause condensation problems in the roof space behind the fitting. It is generally best to try and separate the internal air from that within the roof construction, wherever possible. Therefore spotlights and wall lights are a better solution for lofts. If you must go for recessed downlighters, make sure they are good ones – look for fireproof ones, or acoustically rated ones.

Wall and floor finishes for lofts are not otherwise affected though because you are working with a timber framed backing it makes good sense to stick with relatively lightweight coverings, such as plasterboard or timber boarding.

SOUNDPROOFING

Soundproofing may be an issue you wish to consider, particularly if there are bedrooms below. There are some very expensive floor/ceiling solutions on the market that may be quite impractical for your loft unless you have a great deal of headroom available. These solutions usually work by adding cushioning layers between the floor joists and the floor covering and, additionally, fixing a false ceiling underneath the existing one. In practice, in domestic situations, you would be far better advised to use a thick carpet as your floor covering in the loft space.

BUILD ROUTE

Few people would feel competent to undertake a complete loft conversion without some professional help. But whether you go with a full-blown architect service or stick with a competent builder is a matter of debate. There are lots of builders specialising in loft conversions — they now have their own section in Yellow Pages, quite distinct from ordinary builders – and for straightforward conversions where there is often not a great deal of intricate design involved a good builder should be fine. The scale of the works may be quite small compared to building a house or even a large extension, but the placing of staircases and the rearranging of the roof structure, especially when dormer windows are involved, is never easy and it's not unknown for a set of expensively drawn plans to have to be reworked by the builders on site. On the other hand, a good designer with a feel for the job can produce an elegant solution in the tiniest of spaces, a skill not to be sniffed at. As ever in these instances, if you have someone recommended to you, whether architect, designer or builder, you would probably do well to seek them out.

Loft conversions are usually tackled from the outside via scaffolding. Not only does this make it easier and cleaner to get materials up into the loft but it means that the messy process of breaking through into the existing living space can be left towards the end of the job when the staircase comes to be fitted. The complexity of the job often depends on whether the windows are roof-lights (which run along the pitch of the roof) or dormers (which stick out from the roof). Dormers are time consuming to construct and expensive to build in comparison but in certain roofs they may add significantly to the overall roof-space. Many lofts are designed with full width dormers on one side and this is a good way to get extra space.

BUDGETING

One way to budget for loft conversions is to take the foot print area of the loft (ie the ceiling area of the storey below) and use this as a multiplier to get a budget figure. Very simple lofts with roof-lights and an easily fitted staircase tend to cost around £300 per sq m (making a minimum cost on a terraced house of £12,000). This figure can double as the shape of the loft becomes more complex: full width dormers, balconies, hipped roofs, plus expensive fittings such as bathrooms will all tend to push the unit area cost up beyond £500 per sq m. So a largish loft conversion in a detached 1930s house could easily cost upwards of £25,000, still cheaper than an extension.

CONSERVATORIES

The conservatory industry exists in its own little bubble. It's obviously related to mainstream building, to home improvements and the world of extensions, but it is the province of specialists who, by and large, don't do much else. There are an enormous number of new conservatories built in the UK each year — at its peak it was well over 200,000 and even today it's still going to be an impressively high number.

The question is why? There are one or two things that conservatories have going for them which can make them a very cheap way of gaining extra space. One is that they very rarely require planning permission. Another is that they very rarely require building regulations. Thus the two big administrative heavyweights, designed to send us bonkers, are, at a stroke, banished from the world

of conservatories. You can just go and order one and you don't have to bother with red tape. Of course, Britain being what it is today, there are numerous exceptions to these rules. 'Very rarely' doesn't mean 'never'. Sir Cliff Richard, no less, was ordered to pull down a conservatory he built in Virginia Water because his Permitted Development Rights had been removed without his knowledge.

In fact the Permitted Development Rights routines used to control regular extensions apply to conservatories in exactly the same way. That is to say that you probably won't need permission unless you have already built a

A conservatory does not need to look like an after-thought, but can be an integral part of the design

substantial extension or maybe a large loft conversion. The situation with building regs is rather more complex. Most conservatories don't need to trouble the building control department but there are some aspects of conservatory building which will come into the building regs ambit, forming a nice grey area (shall I? shan't I?). To avoid having to apply for building regs:

▪ the floor area must be less than 30 sq m (though it's only 8 sq m in Scotland)

▪ the conservatory must not form part of the 'heated envelope' of the house – ie there must be separating doors

▓ the roof is at least 75 per cent glass or polycarb sheeting
▓ the walls are at least 50 per cent glass or polycarb sheeting
▓ the conservatory must all be at least 1m from the garden boundary
▓ it must be at ground level.

Now that does cover the great bulk of bolt-on conservatories, but it might not cover yours. But even if your planned conservatory falls outside building regs, you are still required to comply with the safety glazing directives (in Part N of the building regs) and also if you have any electrics installed, it becomes a notifiable event, if not carried out by a competent electrician who can sign it all off against his insurance. There is also a potentially nasty little problem to do with conservatories being located under means-of-escape or egress windows, which some local authorities seem to be more concerned about than others. This is a complicated area because first-floor windows have only had to be egress since 2002, so it cannot logically be applied to the 95 per cent of the UK housing stock that was never built with egress windows. It is the sort of grey area where you might want to think about installing mains-operated smoke detectors in the house, which is in fact the single most effective fire safety measure you can make to an existing dwelling.

There is no requirement for conservatories to be double-glazed. However, if you want to make the conservatory a 'walk-through feature with no dividing doors, then the price you have to pay is that the conservatory will be assessed as part of the normal living space and it will have to meet exacting energy efficiency standards, which will certainly include double glazing.

WHY BOTHER?

So much for red tape. The bigger question is, why bother to fit a conservatory at all? If you like gardening, why not build a greenhouse? If you like light, why not build an extension with lots of glazing? If you like sunbathing, why not buy a timeshare in Tenerife? Or a sunlamp? Why are there so many conservatories added onto existing homes each year? Could it be that, for most people, it's seen as a cheap way of getting an extension? Yes, I think it just might. For whilst there are the odd aspirational companies around like Amdega who sell a very up-market product at prices way in excess of normal extensions, the great bulk of the conservatory market is made up of the sort of thing you can pick up at Wickes for under £2,500. It'll be built-up off a brick plinth, itself built-up off pretty minimal foundations, and it'll be stuck onto the back of the house with a few screws and the roof will have a stuck-on flashing connecting it to the main house. If it leaks, it's really not a disaster, and if there is a little subsidence, then that won't really matter that much either. In fact, this sort of conservatory is a throw back to how we used to build in days of yore, and how they build shanty towns today in Brazil. Bash it up – it'll do.

Now it's easy to be sniffy about this sort of building, but it does have a place. If you haven't got a lot of dosh and your house is just too cramped, then a bolt-on uPVC conservatory may be just brilliant for you, especially as you don't have to be bothered with the boys from the council crawling all over your house. You know it's never going to feature on Grand Designs, so what?

THE UP-MARKET OPTIONS

There is a yawning gulf between these bolt-on plastic extensions (95 per cent of the market) and the beautiful one-off designs you see in the magazine adverts. There is a surprising correlation with the kitchen market where you can easily put in a fitted kitchen into a modest house for under £3,000, but the top of the range can cost more than ten or twenty times as much. For a start, if the conservatory design tips into the zone where you have to have building control involved – and it will if it is large or there is no thermal break between the house and the conservatory – then the full weight of the energy efficiency regs comes into effect. This loosely means that glazing to have a maximum U value of 1.8, which translates as argon-filled, low-e coatings and large air gaps. The cost of the glazing jumps from around £25 per sq m up to over £80 per sq m, which makes it more expensive than conventional walling or roofing materials. Having spent all this money, you then have to think about having a very cold space in winter (do you provide heating?) and a very hot space in summer (blinds? ventilation?). You can, of course, choose to not use your conservatory when it's either too hot or too cold or too dark, but that's an awful lot of times for a room that's so expensive to build, and it makes little sense when you consider the size of the initial investment.

GARDEN WORKSPACES

The growing trend for home working combined with the relaxed planning rules has led to a mushrooming demand for garden workspaces. Many people will be upgrading existing structures for a few thousand pounds but others will be looking to build new structures. These

Run a cable, insulate, double glaze and your garden shed could be transformed into a home office

can vary from the utilitarian through to individually designed, hand crafted architectural gems. Prefabricated offices are becoming increasingly popular, mirroring the growth in the kit homes market. Most modules use some form of timber framing and this can vary from traditional log cabins through to the hi-tech insulated panel systems. They have the advantage of you having both a design and a price on the table so you can window shop the various systems before committing to spending any money.

If you do decide to build a garden structure, make sure that it is adequate for the job in hand. In particular, if you wish to work in there during winter and you use sensitive equipment like computers, the structure will need to be both secure and warm.

SECURITY

Garden offices are easily and often broken into and if you plan to leave expensive equipment in there think carefully about how it can best be protected. A good 5-lever lock is essential and also think about using laminated glass in the windows as this will deter casual thieves.

Adding an alarm is probably over the top but a passive infra-red switched external light will be a boon both for you on those dark winter evenings and for deterring unwanted visitors. Alternatively, use a passive motion detector set to alert you in the house.

If you plan to use a computer, opt for a laptop which you can take into the house at night. If you go away on holiday, bring the most valuable items from the garden room back into the house and leave the windows uncovered so that ne'r-do wells can see that there is nothing inside worth nicking.

HEATING

You will probably want some form of heating to make the room pleasant to work in. You will also want to keep the night time temperature above 12 deg C inside if you want to prevent condensation and mould growth. Assuming that you aren't able to add onto the hot water system in the main house, your options as regards heating are rather limited

to electricity. You can heat using electricity but it's expensive unless you reduce the demand. And of course the key to doing this is to insulate the office really well: I would take the insulation standards used for new housing and apply them to the office.

Night storage heaters are a good method of supplying heat to garden rooms. They are cheap to run, if you use an Economy 7 tariff, they are good at combating condensation damage and they provide the best of their output during the daytime when the room is probably most likely to be being used. However, they do have their drawbacks, principally that they are very inflexible: you can't turn them up if there is a sudden cold snap and you really need to leave them on all winter whether you are using the room or not.

Other options include electric underfloor mat heating, convector heaters and fan heaters. None of these has the thermal mass advantages of storage heaters (I am assuming here that the structure is likely to be lightweight) and they are likely to leave you with a very cold office overnight, which will be bad news on the condensation front. Either that or you leave background heating on all night during the winter, which I wouldn't recommend.

SERVICES

If you do install electric heating, you will need to lay a on a supply, usually via a buried armoured cable between the house and the garden structure you are building.

Chapter 12

The load will be determined by what you are proposing, and it's likely that the heating load will be the significant feature. Although a structure up to 30 sq m in your garden isn't covered by regular building control, note that laying on an electrical supply is a different matter and this work would have to comply with Part P in England & Wales. This means broadly speaking that the work would have to be undertaken by a suitably qualified electrician.

PLANNING ISSUES

The planning rules are surprisingly relaxed about what they will allow you to put up in your back garden. Well, relaxed for Britain! Provided the structure isn't too high (ie it's single storey), you can cover a large area with buildings. Rules for conservation areas are of course much stricter and Scotland and Ireland have different legislation as well. The best advice is always to check with your local planning department.

BASEMENTS

One of the most significant recent changes in the selfbuild market has been the rise and rise in the popularity of the basement. It's gone from being an expensive problem waiting to trap the unwary, into something approaching a must-have item, an aspirational choice to rank alongside the hardwood floor, the underfloor heating system and the kitchen range. Suddenly the basement is a selfbuild fashion item. What's going on?

A little history is in order. There have been periods in our history when basement building has been common place: you only have to visit many of the 18th and 19th century inner city areas of our major cities to see plenty of examples of homes built with basements or cellars, as they were called in those days. However with the coming of the railways and the opening up of the suburbs and the countryside to housebuilding, building land became cheap and plentiful and the basement fell from fashion.

In other countries the basement has prospered. In the USA and Canada, many new homes are regularly constructed with basements. In some areas, such as the mid-west Tornado alley, they are built as storm shelters as much as anything. But other parts of North America just value the amenity benefits of a basement, a room which is usually used as a utility and storage area. Germany is another country with a strong basement culture: here at least part of the reason is that the planning regime is very strict about house sizes and ridge heights but discounts basement space from the overall living area and so immediately there is a strong incentive for Germany's huge number of selfbuilders to start off by building down. Whilst the number of basements being built in the UK is measured in hundreds per year, in Germany the figure is in tens of thousands. Not surprisingly, the Germans have the developed a number of advanced techniques for building basements some of which are now beginning to appear in the UK.

The renaissance of the British basement seems to be coming about partly through high land prices (which make it worthwhile spending extra money on construction) and partly through the advantages of basements becoming more widely known. Selfbuilders in particular want larger than average homes and planning constraints often prevent them from building out sideways, so the German idea of building down starts making a lot of sense. What every new home in Britain has had for the past 40 years is a garage yet we increasingly use garages for storage and park cars outside. The penny has dropped for many selfbuilders who realise that the typical family home is built with far too little space and adding a basement is an entirely sensible response to this issue.

HOW TO DO IT?

The UK would probably have seen many more new basements during the last century if the knowledge of how to build them hadn't largely died out with the Victorians. Today many architects and builders will try to steer you clear of having anything to do with a basement. There may be lots of head shaking and tut-tutting, accompanied by lurid tales of collapsing trenches and damp walls. The chances are that they will never have built a basement and all these stories are nothing more than this – ie stories. That's not to suggest that there aren't problems in building basements but by and large there is nothing that can't be dealt with if its designed correctly and built according to the specifications. The waterproof element is the key issue in basement design. The structural matters relating to the foundations and the strength of the retaining walls are rarely anything out of the ordinary for experienced engineers and ground-workers. However the requirement to build a waterproof tank – a reverse swimming pool as it's sometimes called – calls for careful design and painstaking installation. In certain conditions, high water tables will exert considerable hydrostatic pressure on the basement walls and any weakness in the tanking details will soon be exposed.

Just how you go about waterproofing the basement depends on a number of factors. These are detailed in a publication called the Approved Document: Basement

for Dwellings that defines four grades of waterproofing. Which grade you go for depends on how you plan to use the space, whether it is acceptable to be musky and occasionally damp or whether it needs to be as dry and airy as above ground living areas. What measures are necessary to achieve your chosen grade depend on a close analysis of the ground conditions you are faced with. However they broadly fall into three categories which Basements for Dwellings defines as Types A, B and C.

Type A waterproofing is often thought of as being the simplest and cheapest to undertake. This involves adding a waterproof membrane around the basement, which is usually applied externally but can also be sandwiched inside the walls. Typically this would involve some form of membrane laid under the floor and sealed to

a tanking layer or sheet running up the basement walls. It is commonplace as well to build in some french drains at the external base of the walls to aid the removal of groundwater. If the basement is on a sloping site, these drains can be directed around the basement and on down the hill but on a flat site the collected water would have to be pumped away at some point.

Whereas a Type A basement walls can be built out of blockwork, a Type B basement has to be built from a water-resistant concrete because the walls themselves become the main barrier to water penetration. Actually many basement builders choose to combine Types A and B so that there are effectively two water barriers, the reinforced concrete walls and the external tanking. Type C basements are most frequently seen in retrofit basements, dug out from under an

1
The foundations for a basement floor use a surprising amount of steel

2
The sump and pump idea design is a feature of retro-fit basements. Rather than attempting to keep all the water out, you let some through and pump it away

existing house. Here, any water penetrating the external walls is channelled away to a sump where it is later pumped off site.

There are several other design considerations to take on board if you are considering a basement. For habitable rooms (usually defined as either bedrooms or living rooms but, interestingly, not kitchens) then you must have more than one fire exit route from the basement. This is easily accommodated on a sloping site but will require an escape window or a door on a fully below ground basement.

Ventilation is another key issue; basements have a reputation for being dank and mouldy; this is due as much to poor ventilation as it is to damp penetration. The solution is to install a background ventilation system which removes the stale air — this is particularly important when building a Type C basement which allows water to penetrate the external walls. Getting light into a basement is also critical: this is relatively easy in a partial basement but may require the construction of light-wells in a fully below ground basement.

ESTIMATING THE COST

One of the major factors holding back the construction of basements is the presumption that they are very expensive to build. Evidence from recent basement studies suggest that, whilst not cheap, basements are little different to above ground building costs although the finished costs are usually very dependent on just what the basement area is used for and how it is finished. Recent British experience suggests that our new build basements are costing between £500 and £800 per sq m, not dissimilar to building on the equivalent extra space as an extension or as a detached garage block.

On the one hand a basement involves specific costs not found in above ground construction such as reinforcement in the walls, floor rafts and waterproofing: on the other hand there are a number of obvious savings such as not having to build an external skin and not having to build a roof.

GETTING PLANNING PERMISSION

Many people wrongly assume that because a basement is barely visible it won't need planning permission. This is not the case. Neither is obtaining planning permission a routine matter. Attitudes to basements appear to vary considerably in different planning authorities. At one extreme, Surrey selfbuilder Richard Evans commented to me: 'I was told any 'underfloor' habitable space would be deducted from my above floor plans and that if I went ahead after planning was

agreed they would slap an enforcement notice on me'. Contrast this with Richard Owen's experiences building a basement in Gwent. 'You could put six cars or a light industrial unit in the basement space we are building. The planners didn't even blink. The only concerns the planners raised were that the patio doors became French Windows and that they reserved the right to approve the colour of the balustrading. I have to say that I was surprised and amazed.'

Several selfbuilders have been stymied in their attempts to add a basement to their house plans. No planning department seems to regard this as a minor amendment – all want an entirely new submission that not only involves much extra cost but also a potential delay of months. The crucial point of dispute seems to be how the local authority regards the extra space added by the basement. Many authorities have guidelines about just what size of house should be permitted on each individual plot and the addition of a basement may be enough to break these space guidelines. It's a strange and, to many, an intrusive aspect of our planning system that gives local authorities such arbitrary powers but it is remains a fact of life that, at the present time, some planning departments are not basement friendly. Indications are however that this attitude is rapidly changing as everybody begins to appreciate the need to use our available building land more effectively.

Another aspect worth bearing in mind is the use to which the basement will be put. Planners are less happy with additional bedrooms or living space, seeing this as unjustifiable overdevelopment. But uses such as utility areas, garages, hobby rooms, gyms and swimming pools are harder to argue against as these could later be placed in independent buildings in the

garden, often without the need for any planning permission.

RETROFIT BASEMENTS

Most basements are constructed under new housing. Yet in London, land prices are so high and loft conversions so widespread, a number of companies have sprung up offering to build a basement under your existing house. They are known as retrofit basements and they are not for the faint-hearted: it's very much an extension of last resort, expensive and difficult to achieve. And whilst £80,000-plus for a basement under a terraced house may sound like an awful lot of money, when the housing is worth well over a million, the stamp duty and estate agent's fees combined mean that it can cost almost as much to move somewhere new.

It's such a specialised area that it would be pointless to go into any the subject here in any depth. The businesses that have got into this market tended to have started life doing underpinning; there is in fact a great deal of similarity between the two techniques. One of the advantages of this is that the bulk of the work can be carried out without breaking through into the existing house: the external walls are underpinned and then the ground is excavated. Most homes with a suspended ground floor are technically able to have retrofit basements, but cost-wise, it really only makes sense in the most expensive areas where land prices are at a premium.

Most local authorities will apply the Permitted Development volume rules on retro-fit basements which means for many that they will require planning permission, as people rarely do a retrofit basement as a first extension.

13
SHOPPING

IF YOU LOVE shopping, it's a given that you'll love housebuilding. One of the secret joys of building homes is that you can indulge yourself on the greatest shopping trip of your life. But successful housebuilders are always canny shoppers, not spendthrifts, and there are a few basic lessons to be learned before you launch into it. Firstly, do not simply get carried away and choose items way beyond your budget. Secondly, know where to look. And thirdly, know how to shop, how to strike a bargain. It's well worth studying the buying process. This is the logic of this chapter. It doesn't cover everything, but it does cover important areas that have been otherwise ignored up to this point.

TAKING OFF QUANTITIES

A bill of quantities is a fancy, construction professional's term for a shopping list. Making a comprehensive one is fundamental to controlling costs and is one of the major benefits to derive from having a properly designed, properly specified job. Many times in the past I have measured off plan to estimate a cost and then gone and measured again on site to order materials. I must also admit to having measured three or even four times when the bit of wood I write the measurements on gets nailed into some studwork or gets painted over. If I had taken the advice that I'm offering now I'd be a little bit richer and a little bit fatter. It may just be that you have built so inaccurately that your house does not resemble the plans that were drawn up, but if this is the case then you're playing in a different orchestra to me and there's no help to be proffered; go ahead and skip the rest of this section.

Now, serious construction professionals will engage the services of a quantity surveyor (known on site as 'the QS') to work out what is needed. However, QSs don't come cheap and many small builders work on their own rules of thumb for estimating the right quantities. These are not usually as accurate as a QS would get them but they are much better than nothing.

FREE TAKE-OFFS
If you've no experience of this sort of quantification work, then I would tend to steer well clear unless you have loads of time and patience, particularly as many builder's merchants now offer a free or at least cheap take-off service, ideally suited to the needs of rookie builders. Or check out one of the very cheap internet estimating services, like Estimators Limited – £150 for a house, £90 for an extension.

Much of the repetitious grind of

measuring and recording is carried out by computer and, provided the job is relatively straightforward, they are pretty accurate. The closer you stick to industry standard solutions, the better the outcome and they are quite capable of generating accurate results from a basic set of plans and elevations.

TRADITIONAL ROUTE

Let's compare it with the traditional way of doing a take-off. Traditional here means that your source document is a written schedule of works (often known as the spec), not the plans. You use the plans to calculate the areas and volumes but you work methodically down the written list so as not to miss anything out. To give you a flavour of what I'm on about, here is a clause taken from a house built in 2005.
▓ External (house) walls of 25- 28 0 mm 3.5N clinker blockwork cavity work incorporating 10 0 mm Rockwool or similar full fill cavity insulation and 20 0 mm s/s butterfly brick ties at max 90 0 mm horizontal and 45 0 mm vertically and at every block course adjacent to openings. Additional 10 5 mm skin of face brickwork (bricks to client's choice) forming plinth wall and tied to blockwork with s/s butterfly ties as described above. Plinth wall extends 10 courses above DPC.

Hardly a riveting read, but it's clear enough. The job of the QS is, if you like, to rewrite this specification with the quantities added in so that it might read:
▓ 158 sq m double skin external (house) walls of 275-28 0 mm 3.5N clinker blockwork cavity work incorporating 145 sq m x 10 0 mm Rockwool or similar full fill cavity insulation and 580No. 20 0 mm s/s butterfly brick ties at max 90 0 mm horizontally and 45 0 mm vertically and at every block course adjacent to openings. Additional 55 sq m x 10 5 mm skin of

face brickwork (bricks to client's choice) forming plinth wall and tied to blockwork with 130No. s/s butterfly ties as described above. Plinth wall extends 10 courses above DPC.

You don't need any specialised equipment. All you need are your finished plans, a decent ruler, a calculator and a pen and pencil (rubber would be handy). And bags of common sense. If you've got a computer and you know your way around a spreadsheet you'll save yourself a bit of work, but not that much.

MEASUREMENTS TO TAKE

Take your measurements from your detailed plans (which are now conventionally drawn in metric scale which makes scaling up a damn sight easier). If the distance you want is referred to on the drawings then use it, otherwise you must measure off plan in millimetres and scale up to get actual sizes; thus, if drawings are 1:50, then you multiply your measurement by 50 to get the actual measurement.

Many of the dimensions you need will be written in on the plan so you won't need to measure. Where an area is needed you multiply the two sides together, but when this area is not a simple rectangle you must split the overall area into a number of smaller rectangular boxes and add these together. Remember that the area of a triangle equals half base x height.

For all but the very largest houses all this measuring should take about four to six hours. Complicated building details like split levels, curved work, dormer windows or raked ceilings make the measuring much more complex too and it is well worth double-checking as a mistake here will have costly ramifications on down the line. Oh, and don't forget to write the answers down where you won't lose them.

I also find it incredibly handy to make little notes next to the calculations, which remind me what assumptions I have made when doing the calculations. Typically these read as 'have assumed no skirtings in conservatory' or 'have allowed for three courses of face brickwork below DPC.' It's a good idea to decide whether your derived quantities are 'as measured' or whether you have added an allowance for waste. It really doesn't matter which method you employ but you must be consistent otherwise you will end up adding 15 per cent to the quantities several times over and you will over-order by miles.

The further your house gets away from the good old box shape, the more complicated it gets to measure out and, if a feature like a bay window or a fancy chimney is difficult to quantify, then you can bet that it will also be difficult to build.

WORKING THROUGH THE SPEC

You work methodically through the spec quantifying everything that is quantifiable. You then have to sweep through the whole thing a second time to generate a shopping list; some of the things you have quantified will have to be amalgamated with other sections, others will have to be broken down still further.

Blockwork is a good example. It usually appears in several different places, such as external walls, garage walls, some internal walls, around chimneys and sometimes in the floor (as in beam and block flooring). Presuming that they are all the same species of block (unlikely), add them all together to get an overall total for blockwork. And then consider that blockwork includes not just the blocks themselves, but the sand and cement making up the mortar, not to mention the labour to lay them with. These totals

Chapter 13

have to be extracted from the blockwork total and added to the brickwork total which, to add to the confusion, will have different square metre labour rates and uses different volumes of mortar.

WRITTEN SPECIFICATIONS

Well, that's the traditional route. It's time consuming but it works. If you plan to do your own project management it may even be worth going through this exercise to familiarise yourself with the job in hand. However, many housebuilders never bother with anything so elaborate as a written specification of works but just make do with plans on a couple of A1 sheets. This is fine if you know what you are doing, but using a set of plans without a written spec can be a bit like trying to cook a new dish for which you have a list of the ingredients but no instructions on how they go together. Arguably it doesn't matter which order you measure quantities in but the danger is that if you don't work methodically through a list, you will miss whole chunks out. If you have skimped on this stage of the design process, then this is where your chickens come home to roost.

APPLYING MEASUREMENTS

From all these measurements plus various details drawn in on the plans you should be able to construct a reasonably accurate bill of quantities. You may not actually want to make up a shopping list for paint at the planning stage, but the point is that by having taken all these measurements you shouldn't have to keep taking them throughout the job. You have the figures. From these figures plus a little close scrutiny of your house plans you can work out quantities for:

- Excavation
- Concrete (approximate)
- Flooring materials
- Walling materials
- Roofing materials
- Insulation
- Plasterboarding and plastering
- Decorating materials
- Skirting and architrave
- Covings
- Scaffolding
- Guttering and downpipes
- Whole house heat-loss calculations.

Joinery is treated rather differently. If you've got a pukka written spec, there will be a joinery schedule attached that will list all the opening sizes and the window and door styles which will fit in the openings. I find it helpful to start with the joinery: I work out the overall areas and use this sum to subtract from wall areas. The joinery schedule can also be used to calculate approximate quantities for glazing, lengths for lintels and cavity breaks and a subsidiary schedule for door furniture.

AVERAGE PRICES

The rates I quote throughout the book are all rates current for building work in southern England in 2013, especially around my home town of Cambridge. The key rate is £18 per hour, equivalent to just under £150 per day, £700 a week, or just over £30,000 per annum, typical wage for good tradesmen. Your area may (almost certainly will) have different prices in operation by the time you start building, but bear in mind that Cambridgeshire is close to the national average on building costs.

Early editions of this book (it first appeared in 1994) were able to neatly summarise both material and labour costs right across mainland Britain – only Ireland diverged significantly. But since then, labour rates in boom areas seem to be up by 50 to 100 per cent whilst slack areas are little changed from the Nineties. London in particular is very expensive but there are other parts of the country where labour can be just as difficult to get hold of, let alone wring sensible prices out of. It's certainly not exclusively a South East of England problem – Edinburgh appears to be almost as expensive as London – but the result is that many of the labour rates will have to be adjusted up or down by 30 per cent or more – I have tried to pitch them somewhere in the middle. In any event, my prices are intended only as a guideline by which you can compare your own quotations.

WASTAGE

If you manage to work out the theoretical quantities of just about everything you need, you are still faced with the problem of knowing how much extra to order to cover wastage. Wastage is a wonderfully vague term that covers just about any and every mishap that can occur on a building site from defective materials being delivered to perfectly adequate materials apparently walking off site. There's really no way of knowing in advance what your wastage rate will be, but experience suggests that you'd be wise to over-order by between eight and ten per cent on heavyside materials like bricks, blocks, sand and cement and also plastering materials. You should be able to work out timber quantities exactly, but here you will probably be blighted by timber quality not being what you require and again you would do well to add extra lengths to your totals. Buying more than you actually need is, of course, expensive but so are the frequent shopping trips that happen when you buy too little.

ENTERING THE BAZAAR

The British consumer is used to being able to see what something costs. Visit any high street or supermarket and the price you pay will be clearly labelled on the goods or, at least, on the shelf underneath. Haggling over the price is something that you might do on holiday in Morocco or Turkey but it's thought not to be part of the British way of life.

This is far from the truth. Step off the high street and into the world of commerce (or house buying or even car purchase) and we Brits are out there haggling with the best of them. Generally speaking, when there are three or more zeros on the end of the price tag, the gloves come off and any pretence at civilised shopping goes out of the window. Anyone responsible for purchasing building materials would do well to bear this in mind because a well-organised buyer can achieve savings of 20 per cent or more over the unprepared novice.

It helps to be an established builder. To have a proven trading record stretching back over some years and, better still, to have had a record as a prompt payer will stand anyone in good stead with their suppliers. But, these days, merchants are keen to attract any custom (except the doubtful payers) and if you can establish your credit worthiness and the fact that you might be a substantial customer, if only temporarily, then you will have a strong bargaining chip.

INSIDE A BUILDER'S MERCHANT

Like any business, builder's merchants and all the related building trade suppliers are buying in goods and selling them on at a mark-up. The services that a merchant

provides for this mark-up are:
- accessibility
- delivery (usually free)
- advice.

After a round of take-overs and mergers, there are only three national chains left. Jewson is the largest: it took over Harcros in 1997 and Grahams in 1999, and was itself taken over by the French conglomerate St .Gobain in 2000. Travis Perkins (which swallowed Keyline in 1999 and Wickes in 2005) is No 2 and Builder Center (part of the giant Wolseley group) comes in a distant third. In addition there are around thirty regional operations (typically with five to ten outlets) and still a fair number of small independents, one- or two-branch outfits which may well turn over less than £1million per annum. There are also many specialist trade outlets dealing with plumbing, electrics, roofing, joinery, ironmongery and glass. Whether they are any good or not depends an awful lot on the quality of the staff working in any particular branch and, especially, the branch manager. Needless to say, the smaller operations tend to give a more personalised service but can't always match the prices offered by the large chains.

A general merchant will hope – indeed need – to make an average mark-up in excess of 50 per centto stay in business. Thus, if they purchase some paint for, say, £100 then they will need to sell it for £150. An awful lot of their business is conducted with preferred clients at mark-ups much lower than this 50 per cent and so to balance this out they must sell a great deal at mark-ups of 70, 80 or even 100 per cent. So, one of the keys to getting good prices from a builder's merchant is to become known as a preferred client. Step one is to open an account.

TRADING ACCOUNTS

To set up an account with a builder's merchant, you would normally be asked for a bank reference and two trade references. The bank reference shouldn't be a problem (depending on your relationship with your bank, of course) but trade references could prove difficult if you've never had a trading account. Instead, write a letter of introduction saying who you are and what your project is. This will carry far more clout if you include a copy of the plans, which they may well offer to quote on.

If you've never had a trading account (and if you are not in business on your own account there is no particular reason to have had one), they operate under a very simple code. When you pick goods up or have them delivered you get a dispatch or delivery note. The tax invoice arrives a few days later by post (this is the one you must keep for VAT records) and every month you are sent a statement of account which summarises all the invoices you have run up on your account in the previous calendar month. Normal terms are that you must pay off the outstanding balance on your account at the end of each subsequent month, so if you spent £500 on account with Jewsons during April, you would be required to give them a cheque for £500 at the end of May. In effect you get between 30 and 60 days' credit depending on whether your purchase happened at the beginning of the month or the end of the month. Sometimes postponing a purchase by a day or two – so as to avoid the month end – can get you an extra 30 days' credit. Builders merchants know all about these tricks and they consistently get more sales in the first week of a month than they do in the last week.

Don't just open an account and start

Chapter 13

purchasing materials as and when you need them – you'll pay top whack this way. If you've got the whole job priced up you know that you will have some serious prices back because they suspect you will have got prices from the competition. You may well be able to improve on these quoted prices. A question you occasionally get asked over the phone by a builder's merchant is 'Is this a job you are actually doing?' Probably sounds rather silly but they are sounding you out: if you're just estimating you get one price, if you are buying you get a better price. They quite expect you to go the rounds of local suppliers and they want to have a bit of fat they can lose on the next call.

This practice of haggling over prices is common to almost all areas of building supplies except the DIY sheds (Homebase, B&Q, etc.). It's partly volume driven (that is, if you buy 150 sheets of plasterboard you'll get a better rate than if you buy just one), but it also has much to do with the cosy understanding that exists between builders and their suppliers, which goes to make builders' rates look cheaper than they actually are – or to put it another way, to discourage the DIY enthusiast from getting out of bed. The levels of discount vary from product to product and just to make it complicated some merchants operate two, three or even four levels of discount off the retail price. Some products are sold with a list price from which you have to negotiate the biggest discount you can get; other products have no list prices and the prices paid for them just come down to negotiation. Purchasing well is an art. Get too pushy and the merchants will get annoyed and shut up shop. Too relaxed and they'll squeeze whatever extra they can get out of you.

Now, once upon a time, what I have just written would have practically barred me from ever setting foot in a builder's merchant again. But slowly the worm is turning and the trade merchants are far more aware of a) the competition from the DIY sheds and b) the growth of the selfbuild market. Most merchants I talk to are only too willing to supply one-off builders at somewhere near their best prices. They have had too many cosy relationships with 'trusted trade customers' turn horribly sour and now the order of the day is to do any business which pays. So even if you are a coven of Bangladeshi single-parent lesbians, don't feel you'd not be welcome – although you'll probably still get funny looks in the cement shed.

If this is all too much for you, then maybe a Buildstore Trade Card is the answer. It promises access to the Wolseley group businesses (that's anything ending in Center), Magnet, PTS, Sheffield Insulation and one or two others at trade prices. One further point. Don't assume that your work is done after you have agreed some good prices. You have to check that you are invoiced correctly: builder's merchants, large and small, have an annoying little habit of ignoring agreed prices and invoicing you at top whack. Keep your quotes somewhere handy and cross check against them when the invoices arrive. To hazard a guess, I would reckon that ten per cent of invoices from builder's merchants come with prices higher than agreed – never lower!

BUYING DIRECT

This whole question of who supplies whom is still a pretty murky area. Most manufacturers take the view that they should support the established distribution channels (ie the general merchants) and consequently you will have to shop there for the product. For instance, you can't buy plastic drain ware direct even if you are Barratt Homes. On the other hand, there are manufacturers like Rytons (who produce roof ventilation) who readily sell via mail order to all comers but who, consequently, tend to get blackballed by builder's merchants so that their product is little known.

As a general rule, manufacturers do not deal direct with end users except where they set up their own distribution channels, such as Magnet. To make the whole picture thoroughly confusing, you will find that some distributors (notably Jewsons) will have own brand items on sale, which suggests that they are manufacturers. Just like Sainsburys are farmers. But this doesn't mean you are buying direct. What really matters is not which brand or where you bought it from but was it cheap and was it any good?

B&Q AND HOMEBASE

One of the reasons for the success of the edge of town DIY sheds is the perceived unfriendliness of the builder's merchant to non-trade customers. The Saturday afternoon patio-building brigade have long felt that they have been treated as second-class customers at trade outlets and, what is worse, have been forced to pay over the odds for this dubious privilege. How much more convivial to shop at a place where the prices are actually displayed, even if they aren't particularly cheap, and where the staff probably know even less than you do.

As a rule the DIY sheds are not very competitive on heavyside, bulky materials but tend to be pretty good on the finishes, provided you are not looking for anything fancy.

One exception I've found is Wickes, whose prices are keen right across the board. Wickes is a hybrid between a

builder's merchant and a DIY shed; the prices are close to (and sometimes better than) a regular builder's merchant's trade prices but they are also on full display – a big advantage to rookie builders. Wickes have been taken over by Travis Perkins but they continue to run quite separately to the main chain. Don't pull up to a Wickes branch and expect to put things on your TP account. Wickes is a cash business, just like B&Q.

Screwfix is another outlet to be aware of. It started life as a mail order ironmongery specialist but, since being taken over by Kingfisher, owners of B&Q, it has expanded both its remit and its way of selling, so that they now have a lot of trade counters dotted around the country. I'm not sure it would be the ideal place to score

B&Q has started it's own trade business – Tradepoint – which runs alongside it's exiting consumer business. Larger stores carry the full range of building materials in stock. Trade prices are only available to Tradepoint card holders

heavyside, but they do operate trade accounts, which must gain some traction on Wickes.

SPECIALISTS

The general builder's merchant is to the building trade what a convenience store is to the high street shopper. You can get just about anything you want there and the prices are reasonable. However, for the serious shopper, intent on sniffing out bargains, there are any number of specialist suppliers who can usually undercut the general merchants in their own areas. The trouble is they take some hunting out, and often they don't want to be bothered by small fry, one-off housebuilders, let alone amateurs. You could spend an awful lot of time tracking down specialist suppliers and not save

more than a few hundred quid overall, and it may well be that you decide the convenience (and often helpfulness) of a local builder's merchant is worth hanging on to.

However, I would not be doing my duty if I weren't to make you aware of how the professionals do it. Where do they go shopping? Anyone with a broadband connection (does anyone not have one now?) will probably head straight for Google and start their enquiries there. In the old days, you would have started by opening the Yellow Pages and, in truth, this still isn't a bad way of approaching things as this is where you will find many of the best local contacts, and subcontractors too for that matter. They are online too, of course, at yell.com. The general builder's merchants do still get a look in. They are particularly strong when it comes to supplying cement, drains, timber, plastering materials and joinery, but they tend to be out-priced by specialists in most other areas. However, do bear in mind that whilst the general merchants are to some extent geared to Wallies asking stupid questions, the specialists usually expect you to know what you are talking about. Ask a steel stockholder what you should use to reinforce your garage floor and you'll probably get told some crap mother-in-law joke.

SAND AND AGGREGATES

Straight from quarries or via specialist hauliers. Check Yellow Pages under Quarries.

Chapter 13

Scaffolding Key Rates

▨ Scaffolding is conventionally hired out for eight weeks at a time on a supply and fix basis.

▨ To estimate a price, first work out the length of the scaffold run (usually the perimeter of the building)

▨ Then work out the number of visits required to fit and to re-arrange the scaffolding

▨ Roughly speaking, this equates to the number of storeys you are building

THE METRE RUN RATE IS FOR THE STANDARD EIGHT WEEK HIRE

Single storey	£ 30 per metre run
Two storey	£ 45 per metre run
Three storey	£ 60 per metre run

Subsequent weeks are normally charged at eight per cent of the first eight weeks' rate over eight weeks, so add eight per cent per each extra week

Model House Prelim Costs

Perimeter of House and Garage	40m
Two storey scaffolding rate	£ 45 per metre run
House rate x perimeter	£ 1,800
Overrun cost	£ 145 (8% of total)
Extra weeks taken	10
Overrun cost	£ 1,450
Rounded Scaffolding Total	**£ 3,300**

OTHER PRELIMS	COST PER WEEK	NO. OF WEEKS	TOTAL
Site Security Fencing	£ 15	24	£ 360
Storage Container	£ 15	24	£ 360
On Site Mixer	£ 10	10	£ 100
Portaloo	£ 20	25	£ 500
Skips	£ 170 ea	8 No	£ 1,400
Total			**£ 2,700**

CEMENT, LIME

General merchants are usually the best place to buy unless you want one of the speciality limes in which case you want either a local producer or an eco-merchant.

BRICKS, BLOCKS, PAVINGS

Besides the general merchants there are a number of specialist brick wholesalers (or factors) who specialise in supplying full loads direct to site. Look out for Brickability, particularly good for sourcing block paving. Also check Yellow Pages under Brick Merchants.

BUILDING STONE

Either direct from quarries or via brick or stone merchants. Check Yellow Pages under Stone Merchants.

READYMIX CONCRETE

Direct from Readymix outfits. Check Yellow Pages under Concrete – Ready Mixed.

DRAINAGE

General merchants do well, although there are some specialists who are worth checking out. John Davidson Pipes (now JDP) are good for Osma and Burdens are good all round groundworks suppliers.

JOINERY

Mass-produced joinery is usually best sought out via the general merchants. Magnet Joinery, which is characterised by being 'good value', is alone amongst the major producers in being only available from its own depots, which run a sketchy delivery service. For workshop joinery, look in the Yellow Pages under Joinery Manufacturers

TIMBER AND TIMBER BOARDS

General merchants tend to do well here although some are conspicuously better than others. There are some specialist timber merchants and these are the places to look for unusual species. We like Vincent Timber, based in Birmingham. Check Yellow Pages under Timber Merchants.

ROOF TRUSSES

Many timber merchants run up roof trusses as a sideline and this is a good line of approach. There are specialists although they are few and far between. One with a good reputation and near nationwide coverage is Scotts of Thrapston.

INSULATION

There are many specialist suppliers in this field and they usually undercut the general merchants. Check Yellow Pages under Insulation materials. Don't overlook the Insulation Installers section; many of these offer very good value either for supply only or supply and fix.

ROOFING

Another area where specialists reign supreme as both suppliers and subcontractors. Most Yellow Pages have several pages of both Roofing Materials and Roofing Services.

GUTTERING

Buy from general merchants unless you want something better than the industry standard uPVC fittings.

LINTELS

Again buy from general merchants.

STEEL BEAMS, REINFORCING

Usually the steel stockholders offer the best value. They have their own Yellow Pages section.

GLASS

Again the specialists usually offer the best value, certainly cheaper than buying your glass with your joinery. Check Yellow Pages under Glass Merchants and Glaziers. Norman & Underwood have a good reputation for sealed units and supply to most of southern England.

PLUMBING

Plumbers buy from specialist plumber's merchants who get their own Yellow Pages section.

Scaffolding arranged in three lifts. The lower two for the brickies, the top one for the roofers

ELECTRICS

Look in Yellow Pages under Electrical Supplies Wholesalers or Retailers.

KITCHENS

As the section on kitchens, hopefully, makes clear, your kitchen could come from any one of a huge number of sources: joinery shops, general merchants, kitchen specialists, you name it. There are also worktop specialists, appliance wholesalers and more than 1,000 kitchen unit manufacturers, many supplying direct to the public. Details of some of these suppliers are in the section Kitchens in Chapter II.

PLASTERING

General merchants pick up the great bulk of sales to plasterers. However the Yellow Pages, Plastering & Screeding, is a good source of contacts for hiring plasterers and dry-liners.

PAINTS, STAINS

Decorators' Merchants get a listing in Yellow Pages but for many people a general merchant or even a DIY shed will be just as cheap and more convenient.

IRONMONGERY

There are specialist stockists offering wholesale prices but a one-off housebuilder is still going to do better by buying the right amounts rather than chasing extra keen prices. General merchants discount heavily on bulk orders and do well here. Also check local Bolt and Nut stockists in Yellow Pages. The mail order specialists tend to do quite well. Screwfix, owned by B&Q, is the big name here. Prices are keen but prompt delivery seems to be a problem and orders often seem to be incorrectly processed. Ironmongery Direct have a smaller range (door furniture is their speciality) but are better at it.

CERAMIC TILES
Check under Tile Manufacturers & Suppliers.

GARAGE DOORS
Check under Garage Doors.

This list is by no means exhaustive but I hope you have gleaned that in many cases the Yellow Pages, or its internet equivalent Yell.com, is an essential reference tool both for digging out materials and for finding subcontractors. For items like central vacuum cleaners, underfloor heating and heat recovery units, where there may well be no local agents, the obvious place to look is in the selfbuild magazines, where the nationwide businesses actively seeking work are likely to be advertising. Also the selfbuild exhibitions are a great place to make contact with new and unusual suppliers.

eBAY
It's there and you already know about it. It's an incredible source of materials and a great place for smaller suppliers to access the national market, rather than staying local. You'd struggle to build a whole house from eBay, but when it comes to finishing materials, it's often hard to beat. Bear in mind that the big downside of

buying off the internet is that damaged items, wrong items and returns are much harder to deal with.

SALVAGE
One other important area I've not touched on is the salvage yard. Time was when salvage yards were a source of cheap building materials, but there has been a flight to quality in this market and these days you are much more likely to be sniffing around expensive architectural gems which you probably won't be able to afford. If you are seriously into using salvaged building materials, you would do well to identify as early as possible what exactly it is you are going to get because incorporating changes to materials specification during construction can be very costly. There are hundreds of reclaimed building materials yards all over the country, varying in size from a couple of sheds in a back garden to multi-acre sites better equipped than the average builder's merchant. If you want to look further afield than your local Yellow Pages area, contact Salvo who keep a good database of material recyclers all over the UK.

HIRING IN PLANT

Tool and equipment hire is a rather specialised area that deserves a section to itself. As with most things in the field of project management, a little planning beforehand will reap dividends along the way. What equipment you need to hire (or buy) depends very much on how you plan to manage your build. For instance, if you are entrusting the whole shooting match to a main contractor, then you really shouldn't need anything at all. But if you are acting as the main contractor and hiring subcontractors to complete

the various trades, you will need to discuss each subcontractor's requirements beforehand.

It can be a confusing area. For instance, some subcontractors – notably plumbers, electricians and most carpenters – tend to come fully fitted out with toolkits and access equipment; others, typically bricklayers, expect you to provide everything other than their trowels and their levels. With groundworks, you tend to hire the kit and the labour together as a single unit – thus when a JCB is quoted at £200 a day you are getting both a JCB and a driver for that price.

SCAFFOLDING
A specialised area of plant hire that is normally undertaken by either dedicated scaffolders or sometimes roofing gangs. A standard scaffolding contract would specify an agreed price for a hire period of eight or, perhaps, ten weeks; if the hire continues beyond the agreed period, a surcharge is levied – typically eight per cent of the original price per week. The original price would include for three or sometimes four visits from the scaffolders to erect the different levels (known as lifts) needed for the other trades to put up the house.

Single-storey houses (and detached garages) will typically need only one lift but its level will have to be adjusted between brickwork and roofing; a two-storey house needs two lifts, each being adjusted in level at some point. Guide prices for scaffolding are £30 per m run per storey and to calculate the relevant metre runs add 15 per cent to the perimeter measurements of the buildings you wish to scaffold to get the scaffolder's lengths. The guide price for a small four-bedroomed house with detached garage would be around £2400 for ten weeks' hire, followed by a £100 a week surcharge for longer hire periods. If you want to take control of the scaffolding process itself, there is a system called Kwikstage by Kwikform UK which just slots together, rather similar to erecting an aluminium tower scaffold, making it particularly suitable for those who are taking a more hands-on approach and want to have scaffolding erected for much longer than the normal time span. Kwikform provide some training for people who have never used scaffolding before or, alternatively, can provide an erection service. Rental prices for a four-bedroom house sized project work out at around £50 a week.

SKIPS

Part of your build plan should involve a close look at how you plan to dispose of waste; for many small builders a skip is a practical and economical solution. The basic cost of a builder's standard sized skip has more than doubled since the introduction of Landfill tax in 1996. By 2012, this tax had risen to £64 per tonne, and as most skips hold a tonne or three, it has had a significant impact on prices. It's not all bad news: skip companies are able to recycle some of the typical skip waste, such as timber and metal, and this reduces the effects of the Landfill Tax.

SKIPS COME IN THREE SIZES:

▨ LARGE hold 6.2 cu m (8 yards), which is a maximum 7-8 tons and will cost £150-£200 for one week

and £10 extra for each subsequent week

▨ MEDIUM hold 3 cu m (4 yards), equals around 5 tons and will cost £100-£120 for one week

▨ MINI-SKIPS hold 1.5 cu m3 (2 yards), equals up to 2.5 tons and are usually only hired for two or three days max, at a cost of around £80-£100.

If you want a skip on the road, there is red tape and a permit involved, often around £25 for a fortnight. You can save a little money if you can guarantee that you will be filling a skip with inert waste, and even more money if you can fill it with usable hardcore. And you can also use skips to get sand and aggregates delivered to site, which saves on added transportation costs.

The rental element is usually

Even though they are undoubtedly expensive, most professional builders still use skips to organise their waste

surprisingly small (typically £10 per week) and so you don't save money by delaying the arrival of a skip – you simply end up having to handle your rubbish twice over. Given that all building sites produce copious quantities of rubbish, I think that having a skip on site (certainly during the latter stages of the build) is essential: if you disagree, then at least have some coherent alternative strategy worked out for waste disposal.

SITE FENCING

There are an increasing number of sites where some sort of perimeter fencing is advisable, if only to stop unwanted visitors clambering all over your building site and walking off with your tools. The CDM health and safety regulations have also meant that professional builders are being forced to examine their policies in these areas because of accidents occurring with children playing on sites. Although a selfbuilder will be largely exempt from these regulations, that is no reason for ignoring their importance and if you are unable to provide round the clock supervision to a site, you should consider some form of fencing if your site is vulnerable.

You can hire steel fencing for about 50p per metre per week (less for long periods) but it is the province of the specialist. Check out Heras Readifence, which is about six-foot high and is very easy to assemble yet surprisingly secure. If you need security fencing for more than five months, it will probably pay you to buy it and resell when you have finished.

TOOL HIRE SHOPS

If you want to stay ahead of the game, then make sure you have opened trading accounts with a couple of tool hire shops because you will save yourself an awful lot of faffing about. For many novice project managers, tool and plant hire is one of those things that you just stumble into once the project is up and running. But after you've been and hired three things and left £50 deposits which did or didn't get credited to your final bill and anyway you've gone and lost the paperwork which was in the front of the car but now you can't find it...you'll wish you had opened a trading account at the hire shop too. If you do, you will be able to take tools for as long as you want without having to pay any deposit. Deliveries and collections are also much easier to organise – most hire shops will deliver and pick-up for a small charge (around £5-£10).

Generally, the hire charges are structured so that you pay the highest rate over the first 24 hours, then the daily rate falls significantly if you hire for longer periods. After about ten weeks you will have paid as much in hire charges as it would cost you to buy, so hiring really only makes sense over shorter periods. The number of things you can hire never ceases to amaze me and rather than bore you with a long list, if you are interested get hold of a catalogue yourself – Hewdens is particularly good.

HIRING V BUYING

Which begs the questions: what should you hire and what should you buy? There are a few basic bits of kit that it would seem near essential to have with you permanently and therefore you should buy if you haven't already got them. I would include in this basic hand tools like a 5m tape measure, hammer, saw, screwdriver, 1.2m spirit level, the sort of thing you need to put up shelves or assemble flat-pack kitchen units. I would also place a good, beefy (£70+) power drill, a good extension lead (£10) and a 6m ladder (£120) on my list of essentials; this equipment will be useful for ongoing maintenance, not just for housebuilding.

How much else it is worth buying is really only a question you can answer. It depends on how quickly you plan to build, how much direct involvement you will have in the building process and whether or not your selected subbies will have their own equipment. A brickie gang will, for instance, very often expect you not only to supply tea but also a cement mixer, and it may well make good sense to buy one that you can sell on at the job's end (though don't expect very much for a used mixer). If you work in the trade or have serious DIY pretensions, then you will probably have all of the above plus a lot more and you may view your project as a wonderful opportunity to expand your range of tools. But if you don't intend to carry on building after you've finished your house, then it is pointless to lay out thousands to buy tools which will only ever fill up your precious storage space and provide rich pickings for would-be thieves.

Whether you hire or buy, the proportion of your total bill going on either hiring or buying equipment is large (often around two per cent of total build costs) and can be one major hidden cost to creep up on the unwary. Also note that selfbuilders are not able to reclaim VAT on tool purchases or tool and plant hire, including such items as scaffolding and fencing.

TRUCKING

Moving materials around the country is expensive. A lorry with an off-loading crane (usually a HIAB, pronounced high-ab) and driver will cost around £250-£400 to make a trip of more than half a day – although this will be less with an ordinary flat-back truck without a crane. This sum will be the same whatever the load and so from the buyer's point of view it makes good sense to get as near to a full load as possible. The best economies come when ordering 20 tonnes, which is usually a full payload.

WHAT'S IN A FULL LOAD?

A 20-tonne lorry can shift:
- about 8,000 standard bricks
- or 7,200 block pavers (144 sq m)
- or 1,440 dense blocks (144 sq m)
- or 2,400 clinker blocks (240 sq m).

Aerated blocks (like Thermalite or Celcon) are so light that the capacity constraint on haulage tends to be volume rather than weight. 20 tonnes of super-lightweight blocks would be about 6,000 blocks, which would be 36 double packs.

There are no industry standards as to how masonry materials should be packed, although there is a tendency to use shrink-wrapped plastic (which keeps watertight) and to pack in weights and quantities that fit on to a pallet. A forklift can handle more than two tonnes and a common pack size is around one tonne (which allows two packs to be lifted at once). When ordering direct loads, you'll have to accept the nearest pack size quantity so if, for instance, you wanted 8,000 bricks and your selected brick is packed in 410s (as many are), you would have to settle for either 19 packs (19 x 410 = 7,790) or 20 packs (20 x 410 = 8,200).

Packs will either come palletted or with fork holes for forklift off-loading. The chances are a fully laden 20-tonner will not be able to get off the road, so hire of a rough-terrain forklift may be the best solution for unloading. A rough-terrain forklift and driver should be available at around £150 for a half day and is usually money well spent if the site is big enough to warrant one. Bricks and blocks can (sometimes) be set around site, making labouring much quicker and easier. A JCB with forks can be used as an alternative to a rough-terrain forklift.

PLASTERBOARD

The plasterboard manufacturers all pack in the same sizes. Better prices are usually negotiable on full packs. A 22-tonne direct load would be enough for three or four large timber frame houses – probably a bit too much for your average individual builder – however, by buying in full pack sizes you should be able to make savings.
▓ 1200 x 2400 x 9. 5 mm plasterboard comes in packs of 80 (1.76 tonnes)
▓ 1200 x 2400 x 12. 5 mm plasterboard comes in packs of 60 (1.66 tonnes).

TIMBER

Timber has to be purchased in 20 cu m lots to take advantage of bulk discounts. 20 cu m is an awful lot of timber. Furthermore, CLS studwork, which is perhaps the commonest size of timber used in timber frame buildings, has to be ordered in 40 cu m lots. The average timber frame house uses around 1,00 0 m of CLS – a paltry 5 cu m! Full loads of timber can undercut merchants' best prices by as much as 30 per cent, but you have to have some site going to justify such orders. By and large, you'd do better to try and concentrate on buying good rather than cheap timber.

PALLETS

Many builder's merchants now charge a £15 deposit on pallets supplied to site with tonne loads of cement or whatever. This can soon mount up to a substantial sum. Reclaiming the deposit is straightforward if your paperwork is in order – ie you can't just take the pallets back, you need to prove that you actually paid a deposit before they will refund.

The practice of charging a deposit on pallets does not yet appear to have extended to supplies which arrive direct from the manufacturers so you may well end up with some pallets which have a deposit on their heads whilst others are free spirits.

CONCRETE
SITE MIX V READYMIX

One person working with an electric or diesel mixer will mix 1 cu m of concrete in about an hour. That's fine for odd bits and pieces but hopeless for major projects like foundations. As a rule, readymix will be cheaper when more than 2.5 cu m is needed. Readymix loads are always going to be preferable where consistent concrete

strength is important. Really, for anything other than laying the odd patio, it has to be site-delivered readymix concrete every time.

STRENGTHS

Traditionally the design strengths of concrete have been expressed in ratios of volumes cement:sand:gravel (as in 1:3:6). However, things are stirring in the sleepy world of concrete and there are now at least three other labelling systems in operation. If you are mixing concrete on site, the old ratio system, as described, is fine and is actually very useful as you can use it to gauge how many shovels need to go into the mixer, although note that it is usually most convenient to have a sand and gravel mixture delivered to site – ask for 'all-in ballast'. If, however, you phone up for a readymix delivery you may do well just to explain what it is you want the concrete for and let them work out which mix it is you need:

Foundation mixes: 1:3:6 is traditional for on-site batched concrete. In readymix terms, this is now known as a GEN 1 mix.

Floor slab mix: 1:2:4 is the traditional volume way of looking at it – it's a bit stronger than the foundation mix. The readymix equivalent is usually referred to as a GEN 3. If you are screeding over your slab, you may be able to use a GEN 1 instead of a GEN 3. Basically, the lower the GEN number, the cheaper the mix. GEN 3 and GEN 4 are about five to ten per cent more expensive than GEN 1. There are lots of other more specialised mixes around. Reinforced work requires reinforced mixes, designated RC. Driveways and paths have their own mix known as PAV 1. If in doubt, ask the readymix rep.

When you add water to readymix, you weaken it. It often leaves the readymix yard in a perfect condition and is watered on site, making a joke of its original spec. Watered concrete is the biggest single cause of concrete failure.

If you take any of this on board you will already be ahead of the game. My friendly local readymix supplier, Allen Newport, told me: "99 people out of a 100 who phone up here haven't got a clue what type of concrete they want. Even with the professionals, it's only about 50 per cent who know what they need."

CHARGING FOR AIR

Readymix lorries mostly carry 6 cu m, though some are 5 cu m. Much of the cost involved with readymixed concrete is transport so the amount you pay depends very much on how far the truck has to travel so it pays to buy local. But be aware that on your first two truckloads you will be charged something for the empty carrying space on each lorry. So if you were to order 8 cu m of GEN 1, for instance, you'd pay for 8 cu m of concrete and 4 cu m of unused capacity, often at around a third the price of the concrete itself. If you order over 12 cu m (more than two loads) this charge is usually waived but be sure to find out beforehand how it is to be applied.

CONCRETE PUMPS

To hire a concrete pump, allow around £200-£250 per session. They pump a full load (6 cu m) in 20 minutes, about three times quicker than three men barrowing might do. Concrete pumps make financial sense on jobs with more than 30 cu m of concrete to be poured but there are other reasons

for using them, notably when speed is important or access is difficult. If using a pump be sure to let the readymix supplier know, because the mix design is wetter and the through-put of lorries is much faster than on a normal job. It's also a little more expensive.

SELF-PLACING CONCRETE

This attempts to do what concrete pumps do straight out of the tin. It saves on having to barrow, dump or pump concrete around your foundation trenches. It sells for ten per cent premium but they reckon you can claw back the costs through labour and/or plant savings. Look for Lafarge's Agilia mix.

STEEL

Steel can be used in a wide variety of applications in new housebuilding and there are moves

Concrete pumps reduce the amount of labour required to pour readymix

afoot to introduce steel framing as an alternative to timber framing. However, most housebuilders use it sparingly, preferring to use the traditional materials brick, concrete and timber wherever possible. Steel is the No 1 choice for standard fixings like nails and screws but elsewhere its use is restricted to a few specialised areas.

REINFORCING

The commonest form of steel reinforcing used in housebuilding is A142 anti-crack mesh, which is often set in concrete floor slabs to add strength. Note that you'll need bolt croppers on site in order to cut it. It is usual (though by no means universal) to lay this in garage floor slabs. It needs to be located towards the bottom of the concrete layer in order to do its work properly. There are many other forms of steel reinforcing used in concrete but you are unlikely to come across them in housebuilding unless you have to lay specialised foundations.

LINTELS

Even though reinforced concrete is much cheaper, for many years now steel has been the preferred material for bridging the openings in outer walls made by doorways and windows. The problem with concrete is that, in insulated new houses, it remains a large cold bridge through the wall, which is bad news thermally and attracts condensation. Also, when viewed from outside, concrete lintels look crude and cheap. In contrast, steel can be insulated and the outer leaf support is hidden seamlessly over the top of the window or door. The market was dominated by two Welsh steel businesses, Catnic and IG, and designers still routinely specify their products. But Catnic is now part of Tata Steel and IG was taken over by Irish competitor Keystone, so the way is open for alternative suppliers. The most commonly used IG lintel is the L1/S, very suitable for bridging openings in cavity work with cavities up to 10 0 mm. There is a heavy duty version, known as the L1/HD. They are made in lengths from 60 0 mm to 480 0 mm and they increase in 15 0 mm increments. The minimum end bearings must be 15 0 mm so that an opening of 900 would need to be bridged by a lintel of 900 + 150 + 150 = 120 0 mm.

In contrast, concrete lintels still tend to be the preferred choice to bridge internal doorways in masonry work only. Here the lintel is completely covered and the heat loss/condensation issue is irrelevant. The steel lintel manufacturers do produce an internal door lintel but it is not widely used. Timber framers tend to use timber lintels, but note that where a brick skin is specified for the external wall, there are special steel lintels designed to do the job of just supporting the outer skin.

CAVITY WALL TIES

Where the facing material is brick, block or stone you need approx 3.5 wall ties per sq m. If the inner skin of the cavity is timber frame rather than blockwork, the wall ties are a different shape and you need slightly more (about 4 per sq m). Since 2004, you have had to use stainless steel wall ties rather than the cheaper galvanised. Go for stainless steel rather than cheaper galvanised. Wall ties are seen as a significant cold bridge and moves are now afoot to use steel as the preferred material. The PassivHaus builders seem to be using the Teplo Wall Tie from Magmatech, made of basalt fibre and therefore not a cold bridge.

MORTARS

The standard building cement, packed in 25kg bags, is known as OPC, which stands for Ordinary Portland Cement, and sometimes this is referred to as Portland Cement. The cement (and concrete) market is dominated by a small number of firms, once all British, now all foreign owned. RMC is now Cemex (from Mexico), Blue Circle is now Lafarge (France), both ARC and Castle Cement are now Heidelberg (Germany). It being a mature industry, you'll find that there is remarkably little variation in cement prices – although cynics may have an alternative explanation for this. By all means shop around – current prices are hovering around £150 per tonne (£3.60 per 25kg bag) – but note that it is worth sticking with the same manufacturer once you've made your decision; cement colours vary and you can ruin face brickwork with a nasty change in mortar colours. A detached four-bedroomed house, built of brick and block, will require something like 6 tonnes of cement (excluding concrete) so, with a total value of under £1,000, cement purchase is never going to be a bank-breaker.

MIX DESIGNS

How strong do you want it? Strong mixes (one part cement to three parts sand, henceforth 1:3) are used where the mortar must stand on its own (a floor screed) or is likely to get very wet (underground work); for brick and blockwork and for wall renders, it is important not to get an over-strong mix and also to get some plasticity into the mix. This is usually accomplished by using additives (such as FebMix or Cementone) or by substituting lime for some cement. Given the choice, many bricklayers like to work with hydrated lime in the mortar but it's not universally admired; it's bulky and easily wasted and transporting split bags is a pain. Also mixing has to be carried out more accurately as the addition of a third ingredient adds to the likelihood of changes in mortar colour.

MASONRY CEMENTS

There are several other options available, all designed to make on-site gauging a little easier and a little more accurate. Masonry cements can be used in all the major cement applications (concrete, brick mortars, renders and screeds) and will go fatty enough in a mixer to be used without any additional additives. One brickie I know is very uncomplimentary about them, to the extent that if I were to print his comments, all you would see would be a whole bunch of asterisks. Look for names like Mastercrete and Multi-cem.

A better alternative is a product from Buxton Lime Industries called Limebond

Chapter 13

Mortar Tables: Key Costs

Cement (OPC)	£ 3.60 25kg bag	£ 0.14 kg
White Cement (OPC)	£ 8.40 25kg bag	£ 0.34 kg
Hydrated Lime	£ 9.00 25kg bag	£ 0.36 kg
Hydraulic Lime	£ 8.00 25kg bag	£ 0.32 kg
Lime Putty	£ 10.00 per 20 lts	£ 0.50 lt
Sand	£ 20.00 per tonne	£ 0.02 kg
Plasticiser	£ 1.00 per lt	£ 1.00 lt

What's in a Cubic Metre of Mortar

COST PER M³		SAND LTS	TONNES	COST	CEMENT LTS	KG	COST	LIME LTS	KG	COST	PLASTICISER LTS	COST
Screed Mix (1:3)	£ 99	1000	1.6	£ 32	330	462	£ 57					
Masonry cement mix (1:5)	£ 72	1000	1.6	£ 32	200	280	£ 40					
Plasticiser mix (1:6)	£ 68	1000	1.6	£ 32	175	245	£ 35				1.2	£ 1
Snowcrete mix (1:6)	£ 116	1000	1.6	£ 32	175	245	£ 82				1.2	£ 1
OPC/Lime mix (1:1:6)	£ 105	1000	1.6	£ 32	175	245	£ 35	175	105	£ 38		
Hydrated Lime Mix (1:3)	£ 103	1000	1.6	£ 32				330	198	£ 71		
Hydraulic Lime Mix (1:3)	£ 100	1000	1.6	£ 32				330	198	£ 63		
Lime Putty mix (1:3)	£ 200	1000	1.6	£ 32				330		£ 165		

How far does a Cubic Metre of Mortar get you?

	m³ OF MORTAR LAYS		m³ MORTAR/ m²	LTS MORTAR/ m²	TYPICAL COST/m²
Bricks, single skin work, with frogs up, 10mm bed	1800 No	or 30 m²	0.033	33	£ 2.40
Bricks, single skin, frogs down or no frogs, 10mm bed	2800 No	or 47 m²	0.021	21	£ 1.55
100mm Blockwork, single skin, 10mm beds	800 No	or 80 m²	0.013	13	£ 0.90
12mm Render		80 m²	0.013	13	£ 0.90
50mm Screed		20 m²	0.050	50	£ 4.90
65mm Screed		15 m²	0.067	67	£ 6.60

Model House: Mortar Costs

		AREA IN m²	m³ NEEDED	COST PER m³	TOTAL
Brickwork	Masonry Mix	200	6.7	£ 72	£480
Blockwork	Masonry Mix	255	3.2	£ 72	£ 230
65mm Screed	Screed Mix	80	5.3	£ 99	£ 530
ROUNDED TOTAL FOR ALL MORTAR					£1,240

Mortar Mix Chart

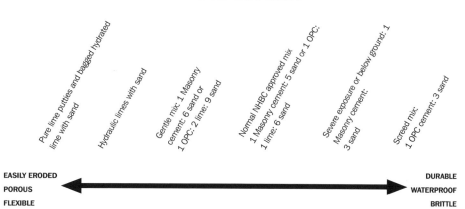

Pure lime putties and bagged hydrated lime with sand	Hydraulic limes with sand	Gentle mix: 1 Masonry cement: 6 sand or 1 OPC: 2 lime: 9 sand	Normal NHBC approved mix 1 Masonry cement: 5 sand or 1 OPC: 1 lime: 6 sand	Severe exposure or below ground: 1 Masonry cement: 3 sand · Screed mix: 1 OPC cement: 3 sand

EASILY ERODED — **DURABLE**
POROUS — **WATERPROOF**
FLEXIBLE — **BRITTLE**

which, as its name suggests, uses lime and not fillers and is in effect a pre-gauged package to which you just add sand. Note that Limebond is just a little specialised and many merchants have never even heard of it. Yet another option is to use a pre-mixed mortar .ie even the sand is mixed in for you) – RMC (OK, Cemex) can supply these at either in skips or tipped off lorries or in small bags.

LIME

There is no compulsion to use cement for the construction of new buildings and there are many restoration projects where it would be advisable to avoid it altogether. The use of cement in housebuilding did not become widespread until the 1920s. Before that, people used lime-only mortars which never set as hard as cement, and one of the big advantages of lime mortars is that the mortar can be cleaned from the brick, making it possible for some bricks to be reused in other buildings. In contrast, most cement mortars cannot be removed from bricks and cement-bedded bricks

are good for nothing more than hardcore. Another advantage is that lime mortars remain slightly plastic and this provides a certain amount of flexibility to walls, which helps to withstand subsidence and cracking.

However, it's not that simple just to switch to lime as a replacement for cement. The really traditional limes, sold in liquid 'putty' format in tubs, are around six times as expensive as OPC cement and cannot readily be used below temperatures of 10,C: use that on your external brickwork and you'll be hanging around forever waiting for the stuff to set. There are different types of bagged lime available which you can use instead: hydrated lime is relatively cheap and readily available from builder's merchants but lacks strength without a little cement to bind it, whilst hydraulic limes can be used instead of cement but usually have to be imported from France.

If you want the lime look without the lime hassle, then you can cheat big time and use white cement, sold as Snowcrete.

It's twice the price of OPC but still much cheaper than using lime.

TIMBER

You rarely see the price of timber advertised and you rarely see it on display in timber yards. This is because there is a wide range of prices charged for timber. The regular trade prices are usually around 33 per cent less than those charged to casual in-off-the-street customers and large orders will get another five to ten per cent off the regular trade prices. The way to get good prices is invariably to send your (hopefully) large order in for quotation at least two weeks before you require it. By all means include second-fix items like skirting boards which you may not need for several months; it makes you look more like a serious customer.

CARCASSING

Most construction grade carcassing timber is spruce, usually referred to as carcassing, whitewood or deal presumably because it's a good deal. It is relatively cheap and easy to work but it suffers from being one of the least durable timbers available. Of more interest to the builder is the strength of any particular piece of timber and there are several grading systems run by the timber trade for assessing this. The commonest form of grading at present is to see timber labelled as SC3 or SC4. SC4 timber is the stronger and the advantage of paying the five per cent more for SC4 timber is that you are allowed to use them over longer spans. For instance the longest distance you can bridge with a 50x17 5 mm section of timber is 317 0 mm in SC3, but this length rises to 338 0 mm in SC4. SC3 and SC4 are British Standards and moves are afoot to replace them with Euro gradings, Cl6 and C24 respectively.

KILN-DRIED TIMBER

In 1995, it became compulsory to use low moisture timber in all internal structural applications – which means joists, studwork walls and roofs. Low moisture is defined as having a moisture content below 20 per cent and in effect this means using kiln-dried timber. The advantage of kiln dried timber is that it is dimensionally stable – it will not twist or warp as cheaper timber will, especially if it's been treated – and that it is regularised, which means that it has all been milled to an accuracy of 1 mm. It is thus very much quicker and easier to put up accurate studwork and to fix flooring joists; non-regularised timber can sometimes vary in depth by 5 mm or more and this is very noticeable when flooring is being laid over it. Having said that, there is a lot of supposedly regularised timber around which varies by plus or minus 5 mm, sometimes even more, so the term is regularly abused. And in truth, 20 per cent moisture content is still much higher than the final settlement level reached in a centrally heated house (about eight per cent), so shrinkage still takes place. But kiln-dried timber is still a step in the right direction.

TIMBER TREATMENT

Spruce is not classified as a durable timber and this means that it is liable to rot if exposed to continuous damp. This has led to the increasingly widespread use of timber preservatives to add durability. These preservatives can be applied by brush on site but more normally the timbers are immersed in a vacuum-pressure tank, which leads to them being referred to as having been 'vacuum treated'. There are two rival systems in regular use in the UK, Tanalising and Protimising. There is little to choose between them in price – they add around 10 per cent to the cost of the raw timber – but they do perform rather differently.

Tanalising is a water-based treatment which tends to dye the wood a light green colour although there is now a brown-dye version as well (useful if you plan to use brown or black stains); Protimising is spirit-based and usually leaves the wood uncoloured, although sometimes a red dye is added. You can usually tell if timber has been Protimised from the pungent, petrol-like smell. Generally tanalising is preferred in applications where there is contact with the ground, like fencing, and protimising is preferred for structural timber (and joinery) because it is less likely to cause the timber to twist. Tanalising used to use arsenic as one of its ingredients; it has been reformulated to avoid this particular gremlin and is sometimes referred to by a different name, such as AC500. However, it will take a good few years before British builders get around to calling it anything other than tanalising

JOINERY GRADE REDWOOD

The other commonly used wood in UK housebuilding is pine, or redwood as it is known. This is a denser and slightly more durable timber than spruce, and it is commonly used to manufacture windows and internal applications like skirting boards, floorboards and matchboard walling. It is more easily worked than spruce and it is most frequently seen in timber yards with a planed finish, usually referred to as Planed All Round (PAR) or Planed Square Edge (PSE). Scandinavia is the major supplier of redwoods.

You can use cheaper whitewoods for internal applications but they suffer from having what are called dead knots, which tend to work loose and fall out with time. Your mice may appreciate the odd dead knot in your skirting board but you will probably prefer to have timber with live knots that move with the timber as it expands and contracts.

SPECIALIST SOFTWOODS

There are a number of more specialised softwoods:

■ Douglas Fir is particularly resinous and durable and it performs as well as many hardwoods. It is a favourite in high specification windows although one problem is that it doesn't hold paint well: wood stains are the solution.

■ Hemlock is another North American speciality softwood that is mostly used in door construction.

■ Cedar is particularly durable and really doesn't require any sort of on site treatment at all. However, its use is very limited, tending to be restricted to external claddings such as garage doors, and roofing, and increasingly, weatherboarded exteriors.

■ Parana Pine. This is a lovely looking South American timber, popular in several internal applications such as window boards and staircases. It is anything but durable and is very prone to buckling.

HARDWOODS

Generally, hardwoods are not an alternative to softwoods. Rather, they tend to get used in particular applications like flooring and kitchen worksurfaces where softwoods are not commonly used. Joinery is the obvious exception to this rule: see the section 'Windows' in Chapter 7, Superstructure, where the pros and cons are examined. Also check Chapter 13, 'Green Issues', for the low down on tropical hardwoods.

14
GREEN ISSUES

MOST OF THE interest in this field – and indeed, most of this chapter – is to do with saving energy. Our fascination with this topic really began during the 1974 oil crisis when people assumed – incorrectly – that we were facing a permanent fuel shortage and consequentially rocketing fuel prices. However, in more recent times, concern has grown that the ambient temperature of the entire planet Earth is gradually increasing, a phenomenon known to us all now as global warming. Despite many people claiming that this could be a natural phenomenon, a very large finger of suspicion is pointing at us and, in particular, our dirty habit of burning masses and masses of fossil fuels and thereby releasing carbon dioxide (CO_2) into the atmosphere.

Reckoning that it is probably better to be safe than sorry, governments the

world over have been signing accords to reduce levels of carbon emissions although, as environmentalists point out, not by very much and sometimes by nothing at all. As private households contribute about a third of our national CO_2 emissions, the effect of these undertakings is trickling down to the Building Regulations in the hope that stricter codes for new building will bring about some reduction in our energy consumption. Hence many of the recent changes to the building regs are to do directly with reducing carbon dioxide emissions.

Energy saving is, however, not the be-all and end-all of environmental concerns and I'll start the chapter by taking a look at some of the other issues, including an assessment of how much energy is used in actually constructing a new house.

CONSTRUCTION AUDIT

This book may be green-tinged but it is not what anyone would call an eco-handbook. If you want to know more about green options then there are dozens of other titles available and I can especially recommend 'The Whole House Book' by Pat Borer and Cindy Harris, which gives a good overview of the many different ways there are to build and Tim Pullen's 'Sustainable Building Bible' which covers the materials and technology in greater depth than I have here.

Whatever your personal views on green issues, what can't be denied is that the green perspective has caused mainstream housebuilding to examine just what it does, and to look at ways it could be improved. For most of the twentieth century, housebuilding in Britain was driven by the

Model House Construction Audit

Material Quantities and Energy Used to Construct House

Materials	Energy used in manufacturing (in kWhs/tonnes)	Material quantity	Multiplier	Weight (in tonnes)	Energy used (in kWhs)	CO$_2$ RELEASED (in tonnes)
Concrete	300	25 m³	2.3	60	18,000	3.6
Bricks	2,000	12000 No	0.003	36	72,000	14.4
Aerated Blocks	1,000	255 m²	0.1	25	25,000	5.1
Concrete Floor Beams	500	95 m²	0.15	10	5,000	1.0
Sand	30	25 t		25	800	0.2
Cement	1,200	5 t		2	6,000	1.2
Natural Slates	80	122 m²	0.05	6	500	0.1
Concrete Paving	500	35 m²	0.15	5	2,500	0.5
Hardcore and Gravel	80	50 m³	1.6	80	6,400	1.3
Timber	2,000	12 m³	0.5	6	12,000	2.4
Chipboard/Plywood	2,750	5 m³	0.5	2.5	6,900	1.4
Plasterboard	800	490 m²	0.01	5	4,000	0.8
Steel	7,000	1 t		1	7,000	1.4
Double-Glazing	5,000	35 m²	0.02	0.7	3,500	0.7
Plastic/uPVC	20,000	0.25 t		0.25	5,000	1.0
Sanitaryware	8,000	0.4 t		0.4	3,200	0.6
Others Materials	5,000	1 t		0.2	1,000	0.2
TOTAL				**270 T**	**180,000**	**36 T**

COMPARISONS

Energy used/annum	kWh/annum	Tonnes CO$_2$
Annual energy use in Model House Built to 2010 standards	20,000	3.9
Model House Built to Passivhaus standards	6,000	1.2
Benchmark House Built to 1975 standards	80,000	15.0
Family Car Doing 20,000km/annum	20,000	4.0
Family of 4 flying to Spain and back	20,000	2.4

desire to make houses cheaper and easier to construct. Now the agenda is subtly shifting so that at last we are beginning to worry about what it is that we are building. Is it any good? How much damage does it cause in order to get built? How long will it last? Can it be safely disposed of when we've finished with it? In a word, sustainability. How does a typical new house stack up?

TRADE BALANCE

Materials going into a masonry-built detached house, such as our benchmark Chapter 2 example, would weigh around 200 tonnes, the vast majority of which will have been produced within 200 miles of the house. Timber (15 tonnes) is the only significant import by weight, although copper (used extensively in plumbing and wiring) and kitchen appliances are also imported. Traditional housebuilding remains an overwhelmingly British business. It is low-tech and uses a lot of very bulky materials that are costly to transport. Even where foreign companies achieve market penetration in Britain, production is usually UK based.

As a rule, Britain runs a trade deficit in building materials. We are net exporters of steel, wallpapers, paints, sanitaryware and even a few bricks (mostly to Japan), whilst timber accounts for around 90 per cent of our net imports, with heating and plumbing gear being the only other significant contributor on this side of the account. Take out timber from the equation and everything else pretty much balances out.

EMBODIED ENERGY

Energy use involved in building any house can be divided into three areas: material production, transport and construction. Broadly speaking, the less a material is processed, the less energy it takes to produce, and the less distance a material travels the less energy is used in getting it there. On-site construction energy use is remarkably low, unless heating and lighting are employed, and even this is unlikely to make a huge difference. The Construction Audit table su mmarises the energy used in constructing the benchmark house and it is based on the following figures, taken from Bath University's ICE (Inventory or Carbon & Energy) project.

Natural materials take the least energy to produce. Sand, stone, and gravel come into this group: energy used in production is typically under 100kWh per tonne.

Cement is a relatively high energy consumer but it is never used on its own. Cement-based products like concrete and render are surprisingly low on energy use because they have a high proportion of natural sand or stone mixed in with the cement. Concrete products consume around 300 – 500 kWh per tonne.

In contrast, clay-baked products like bricks and clay roof tiles use around three to five times as much energy in production, 1500 – 2000kWh per tonne. They have to be fired at very high temperatures and this is the main reasons they are more expensive than concrete imitations.

Aerated concrete blocks (i.e. Celcon, Thermalite) use much more energy to produce than standard concrete products, between two and three times as much. But because they are pumped full of air, they are much lighter and so a tonne of these blocks goes a lot further – two to three times further, neatly canceling out the difference in energy consumed in manufacture.

Timber is an interesting case. The Bath project reckons on a figure of around 2000kWh per tonne. Part of this is explained by the energy costs in transportation and in kiln-drying, but it's also partly explained by the carbon present in the timber itself. Many sources regard this as sequestered or captured carbon and go as far as claiming that timber as a product is therefore carbon positive. Bath take a different view and suggest that it ignores the fact that eventually this carbon will be released into the atmosphere (possibly as methane which is even worse for global warming than carbon dioxide). Furthermore, they take a view that on a global scale timber is still being used faster than its being replaced, so that it's just plain wrong to count it as a renewable material. You can see that this embodied energy stuff is not straightforward. Not straightforward at all.

Timber products like chipboard, OSB and plywood score even worse than sawn timber. However, bear in mind that timber is relatively lightweight so a tonne

goes a long way.

Other typical scores include:
■ Plasterboard, around 800kWh per tonne
■ Glass: uses 5,000 kWh per tonne
■ Steel: uses around 7,500 kWh per tonne
■ Copper, brass, zinc: use between 10,000 and 15,000kWh per tonne
■ Aluminium: uses 40,000 kWh per tonne
■ Plastic (including uPVC): uses 20,000 kWh per tonne – but a tonne goes a long way.

A word about these figures. I have used the kWh per tonne figures unchanged since the first edition of the book back in 1995. In this edition, I have, in addition, converted the kWhs to tonnes carbon dioxide released, which is arguably the whole point of this embodied energy exercise. However, the conversion rate is also a matter of guesswork as we really have little idea just how the goods were actually made. I have assumed that all the fired products .i.e. cement, bricks, glass, steel) will have been cooked with gas. It's probably safe to assume they didn't use a microwave. My big point is, however, all these figures should be treated with caution. Although this is 'The Housebuilder's Bible', they are not gospel!

COMPARISONS
The table breaks down the embodied energy that went into the benchmark house, which I calculate at around 100,000 kWh, equivalent to 20 tonnes of carbon dioxide. This sounds like a lot but let's put the figure in context. 20 tonnes of carbon dioxide equates to around six years motoring in a family car, or flying the family to Australia and back twice. More pertinently, the UK releases around 10 tonnes of carbon dioxide per head per annum, and the very energy efficient

benchmark house, with three residents, will be expected to release about two tonnes. In it's older, pre-insulated state, this two tonnes would be as much as 10 tonnes so a new house is saving a lot of carbon dioxide compared to the older housing stock. Were it to be a replacement dwelling, it would claw back the 20 tonnes of carbon dioxide released by building it within three years. But of course, it's not a replacement dwelling so even though it is relatively energy efficient, its very existence is still adding to the overall national carbon emissions.

Bear in mind, finally, that when we hear talk about our housing stock producing 30 per cent of our national carbon dioxide emissions, it's not actually our housing stock but the people who live in our housing stock. Left to its own devices – i.e. empty – our housing stock doesn't produce anything.

ENVIRONMENTAL AUDIT
EXTRACTION OF AGGREGATES
Around 80 per cent by weight of the benchmark house is composed of sands and gravels and clays, much of it bound together with cement. With 100,000 new houses being built in the UK each year, something like two cubic miles of materials are being extracted annually to meet this demand. That's an awful lot of holes in the ground and it's one area where new house building is particularly greedy. Quarries pose no long-term health risks and, arguably, the scars of quarrying are actually healed remarkably quickly. However, that doesn't make quarries attractive to nearby residents and new quarrying proposals are always hotly disputed.

TIMBER
The weight of timber used to construct houses is minute in comparison with

masonry/concrete products. The benchmark house uses about 15 cu m (8 tonnes) of wood and wood-based products. Were it a timber-frame build, this figure would probably double. On the face of it, building with timber would seem to be very desirable but there are a few snags:

■ Logging often has more in co mmon with mineral extraction than agriculture; even so-called sustainable sources are often permanently damaged after the virgin crop is removed to be replaced by monotonous, species-thin plantations.

■ Almost all structural timber has to be imported into Britain, making it the one major building component not to be sourced in the UK.

TROPICAL HARDWOODS

The problem with using tropical hardwoods is to do with the way in which they are harvested (or plundered) with acres of virgin rainforest being destroyed often to fell just one particularly nice mahogany tree. By and large this land is then cleared and used for rather poor cattle grazing. This sort of wanton destruction is going on all over the tropics and, in truth, is as much to do with burgeoning population growth as it is with extracting hardwoods, but there is no doubt that the hardwood trade plays a significant part.

However, the environmental problems resulting from using these hardwoods in new housebuilding should not be exaggerated: their use is rare precisely because of their expense. Brazilian mahogany is specified as standard as a cill detail on timber door frames but otherwise you have to go looking for materials – chiefly joinery – made out of tropical hardwoods. Another area where you may stumble across them is

as constituents of better-grade plywoods (Far Eastern) and blockboards, but these are more co mmonly used for shelving than construction; MDF can be used as a cheaper substitute.

HEALTH RISKS
FORMALDEHYDE

This glue is used to bind timber panel products, chiefly chipboards, MDF and plywoods. Some people are known to react badly to the fumes that are released very slowly over a period of months after manufacture, a process known as off-gassing. However, adverse reactions are rare and exact causes are difficult to pinpoint. Almost all volatile organic compounds (VOCs) have come under suspicion – including carpets and clothes – and it remains a complex and poorly understood area. You can, of course, build and furnish a house from entirely natural materials but it is an expensive option.

SOLVENTS

Solvents are used in oil-based paints, stains and varnishes, as well as adhesives and mastics. Many people actually like the smell of solvents but long-term exposure to them has been linked with brain damage. Occasional users probably need not be alarmed, but be aware that solvents are likely to be far more damaging to young children than to adults; if youngsters (and pregnant women) are present then you would do well to consider using water-based paints and stains indoors.

WOOD PRESERVATIVES

One normally associates timber treatment with remedial work carried out on old houses, but a great deal of new timber gets pre-treated with either water-based tanalith or solvent-based protim. The tanalising treatments used to be based on

the copper-chrome-arsenic compounds (CCAs) whilst the spirit-based systems use a cocktail of chemical nasties such as lindane, pentachlorophenol (PCPs) and tri-butyl-tin-oxide (TBTOs). Neither is particularly pleasant and the tanaliths have been reformulated as AC500 (minus the arsenic). They serve a dual purpose: one is to reduce risk of fungal infestations such as dry rot, the other is to reduce risk of insect attack such as woodworm and death watch beetle. The idea is that treated timber will taste so foul that insects and fungus will steer well clear: the danger is that these chemicals won't do us much good either.

External joinery is pre-treated as a matter of course and NHBC regulations require that timber in exposed walls is treated. There is a potential long term hazard, although this is rather along the lines of the formaldehyde and VOC threat – i.e. no one can say what it is – but there is also a more i mmediate danger to site carpenters who inevitably come into physical contact with treated timbers. Wearing gloves is not really an option for a chippie: the best precaution is to ensure that the timber is dried properly before it is worked; sometimes it arrives on site still dripping with the chemical preservatives, having just come out of the vacuum tank. Some co mmentators maintain that if the design detailing is good then the timber does not need preserving, but preservation is now an industry standard. Note that timber frame kit houses tend to come with pre-treated timber specified everywhere, whether it's actually needed or not.

ASBESTOS

Asbestos was widely used in the UK building industry through most of the last century. It was only during the Eighties that it started to become blacklisted and it was still being used, mixed with cement,

Chapter 14

through till 1999. It was used in all kinds of places: Artex (which was 2 per cent asbestos until 1984), asbestos-cement roofing sheets, inside airing cupboards and around stoves and boilers, pipe lagging, ironing boards, night storage radiators, fire doors, artificial slates, wall boards. One of the most dangerous formats was a board made by Cape called Astbestolux, later replaced by an asbestos-free version called Supalux. There is a lot of asbestos about and if you get involved with demolition or renovation of an old building, you need to know how to handle the risk.

There are some fairly exacting requirements in place for co mmercial enterprises, including builders and demolition contractors. Every co mmercial building is now meant to have an Asbestos Register detailing if and where asbestos is located. But the situation with private householders is still largely unregulated, which means that if you have asbestos in your house you can more or less dispose of it as you wish. Except you can't just take it to any old tip, but to one designated to take hazardous waste.

My local council, South Cambs, offers sealable sacks to householders in which to place their own asbestos remains and there is one tip in the county you can take it all to, for which there is no additional charge. I guess they have to consider the alternative: fly tipping.

MDF

The problems related to formaldehyde have already been touched on and are not unique to MDF. However MDF is the board that gets worked most and it tends to produce the finest dust which sails through the average dust mask as if it's not there. This combination is reckoned (by some) to

make MDF a hazard on a par with asbestos and moves are afoot to produce a similar board made with safer resins. Passive consumers of MDF products are unlikely to be at risk but you should look out if you work with a lot of MDF dust.

CEMENT

Human skin does not react well with wet cement and concrete mixes; there is no instant sign that burning is taking place and many people assume that it is therefore harmless. It's not; prolonged exposure will cause very nasty burns. Bear in mind, that much the same thing happens with lime as well.

GLASS FIBRE

Glass fibre insulation, together with the closely related mineral wool, are unpleasantly itchy on skin, and eyes like it even less. Thought by some to be similar to asbestos in effect, others claim that the fibres are generally too large to cause lethal irritation. Whoever proves to be correct, it makes sense not to be macho about it. Wear gloves and a mask when insulating. Or use sheep's wool, if you can afford it.

uPVC

The use of uPVC has been growing steadily in housebuilding. You will find it in plastic guttering and drainage pipes, in electric cable and, of course, uPVC windows and doors. However there is a vociferous campaign (led in this country by Greenpeace) against the use of uPVC, principally on the grounds that its production is a dirty, polluting business leading to the release of dioxins and the dumping of chlorine. What is not clear is whether uPVC manufacture is any worse than the rest of the chemicals/plastics industry.

THE ENERGY EFFICIENCY REGS

The building regulations regarding energy efficiency in the home have grown progressively more complex over the years. In England & Wales (but shortly Wales is going to cut free), the building regs are broken up into Parts that are lettered from A through to P (with the odd confusing letter like I and O missed out). Part L is the one that deals with energy efficiency and Part L is now a complex beast which hardly anyone understands. Let's look at Part L.

It used to have a table in it that told you what U values you needed to meet, and it was a fairly simple calculation to get from that to a particular depth of insulation. No more. In it's sixth iteration, the 2006 version, it moved everything across to a whole house heat calculation approach and asked for the sum of the heat loss for the whole house to be no more than a certain figure, known as the Dwelling Emission Rate. Technically, this is a superior method of going about things because it allows you to trade off one poorly performing element against a better one somewhere else in the design. But from the point of view of simple comprehension, it is a disaster because no one really knows how to meet the regs anymore, and they have to hire expensive consultants to work it out.

In 2010, Part L changed to yet another version and the complexities grew a little bit more. I'll outline what I can in a minute, but first realise there is an end point that Part L is now aiming for and that is the so-called zero-carbon house which will become the building regs standard in 2016. There is now a roadmap which suggests that there will be one more intermediate step (planned for 2013) before Part L arrives in its final iteration. After all, you can't get more energy efficient than a zero-carbon house, can you?

Well actually, yes you can, because it turns out that ever since the zero-carbon house was first mentioned by government (back in 2006), the exact definition of what this means has been subject to hot debate. The Labour government flunked it and left office in May 2010 without ever having resolved this issue. Would the Coalition drop the idea altogether? Apparently not. Instead, they have watered it down some way from what was anticipated back in 2006. At time of writing (Jan 2013) the final definition is still not clear, but it looks as though it's going to settle for something that's only just slightly better than what we have now. The real deal, in terms of energy efficiency, is being left to a German performance standard known as PassivHaus. More on this later.

So what's in the new Part L, the 2010 version? It's split into four sub-parts, known as L1A, L1B, L2A and L2B. The L1s deal with housing, the L2s with everything else. The 1s deal with new builds and the 2s deal with renovations and conversions. You can download them for free at the Planning Portal website (Celtic territories have their own websites too).

So L1A (new homes) basically requires that any new house you build is 25 per cent more energy efficient than the version you would have built before 2010. It leaves it up to you how to do that, but your design has to be measured against a document known as SAP 2009 which indicated the likely energy loss from all manner of details.

Once upon a time, you could go through this exercise with a pencil, filling in values into boxes, but now it's all done by spreadsheet. Every aspect of the build, from the shape and dimensions, through the orientation and the shading, to the way its actually built and heated, gets fed into the spreadsheet, and the answer has to be below 'x' to get a pass. If your answer doesn't meet the target, then you have to go back and redesign the house until it does. You get penalised if you plan to burn anything other than mains gas or biomass, and therefore have to make the structure even more energy efficient. And there is still a table with limits on your design standards:

■ The roof must have a U value of 0.2 or less
■ The walls must have a U value of 0.3 or less
■ The floor must have a U value of 0.25 or less
■ Any party wall must have a U value of 0.2 or less
■ Windows, roof lights and doors must have a U value of 2.0 or less
■ Air permeability must be 10 air changes an hour under pressure or better

Now these are not the standards. If you were to build to these levels, you wouldn't meet Part L 2010. You'd have to be better, but exactly how much better is difficult to tell. Gone are the days when we could safely say 'stuff 80 mm on mineral wool in the wall cavity and you'll be fine'. But when all is said and done, there will end up being standard solutions – probably about 150 mm of mineral wool insulation in the walls.

L1B is a bit different. As it deals with how you insulate an existing structure, you can't really go around doing whole house heat loss calcs. So it's rather more like the older versions of Part L in this respect. In fact, lurking inside Part L1B is the table that tells you what U values you should be using, the one that is so annoyingly hidden from view in Part L1A. It goes like this:
■ Walls – U value 0.28
■ Pitched roof (insulation at ceiling level) – 0.16
■ Pitched roof (insulation at rafter level) – 0.18
■ Flat roof – 0.18
■ Floor – 0.22

There has been a move to introduce consequential improvements for home extenders, so that you would be forced to spend additional money on upgrading the energy performance of the rest of the house, but this has never been implemented, due to fear of negative 'Daily Mail' type publicity. In fact a recent attempt to introduce consequential improvements into the 2013 Part L resulted in a successful front page campaign by the Daily Mail to have it withdrawn.

PERFORMANCE METRICS

A word about how these energy efficiency standards are measured. Back in the old days (before 2006), we had gotten used to talking about walls with such and such a U value. Generally, the lower the U value, the more energy efficient the house was likely to be, as the way to lower the U value is to stuff insulation everywhere. But whereas U values can be good indicator of how individual elements, like walls, behave, they don't tell you an awful

R Values of Building Materials

Section Through a Brick and Block Cavity Wall, showing the R value of each element

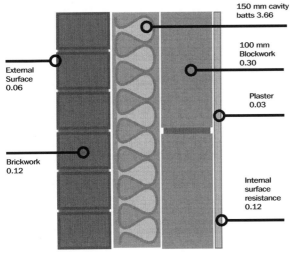

150 mm cavity
batts 3.66

100 mm
Blockwork
0.30

External
Surface
0.06

Brickwork
0.12

Plaster
0.03

Internal
surface
resistance
0.12

R VALUE TOTALS	
External Surface	0.06
Brickwork	0.12
150mm Cavity Batts	3.66
100mm Blockwork	0.30
Plaster	0.03
Internal Surface Resistance	0.12
Total of all R Values	4.29
U Value of Wall	0.23

To calculate the U value,
you first total all the R
values of your wall/roof/
floor

Step two is to divide the
number 1 by the total of
all the R values

lot about whether the whole house is energy efficient or not. So the move is now underway to describe the energy efficiency levels in terms of how many kilowatt hours a year (expressed as kWh per sq m/annum) it takes to keep a house warm and comfortable. At the moment, it is reckoned that the 2010 building regs will come out at around 70kWh per sq m/a: the PassivHaus standard looks to score no more than 15kWh/ sq m/a. The level suggested for our zero carbon homes in 2016 is 39kWh per sq m/a for flats and mid-terraced houses, and 46kWh per sq m/a for detached houses, end terraces and semis.

At the moment, this is for the future. Part L 2010 version doesn't mention any of these metrics.

UNDERSTANDING U VALUES

You can't really get to grips with the concepts behind energy efficiency in buildings without having an understanding of what a U value is. So now is a good place to digress into the world of building science and to try and establish just what a U value might be.

Like most of the other values in our society, U values are declining; however, in this case, declining values are broadly welcomed. You see, a U value is a measure of heat loss and a material with a low U value loses less heat than one with a high U value. In many ways, that's all you need to know. However, a U value is not like a moral value which you either have or

haven't got; it's actually a scientifically derived measurement and knowing your U values will help you make a whole lot more sense of your decisions about how to build and heat your house.

A U value is a measurement of the heat flow (measured in watts) through a square metre (sq m) of a building element for every 1 deg C temperature difference between the inside and the outside. That reads like the horrible sort of definition you had to learn for Science A-levels, which is why you never did one. It's actually got three different bits to it and in an algebra lesson they'd call them a, b, and c and make it even more unintelligible. However the point that it's trying to make is dead simple: some things are better at retaining heat than others. It's something you know instinctively without ever having to ascribe a value to it – after all you know just how many clothes you need to wear to feel comfortable. The U value is just some poor sod's attempt at quantifying this fact.

In fact the U value of just about everything you could ever think of using to construct a house has been worked out under laboratory conditions. What they do is establish how quickly heat leaks out of any given material – the boffins call this thermal conductivity. The answer is expressed as a value, known as the lambda value, which is in fact the same as the U value for a one metre thick slab of this material. The better the insulator, the lower the leakage rate.

Our best insulators, things like polyurethane foams, have a lambda value of 0.025watts whilst a poor insulator like granite has a value of 2.9watts. From which you can deduce that polyurethane is around 100 times better than granite as an insulator or, put another way, a 1 mm strip of polyurethane would keep you as warm as a 100 mm wide granite brick.

The final U value of a material is found by dividing the lambda value of the material by its actual width in metres. Thus 50 mm (or 0.05m) of polyurethane foam (lambda value 0.025 remember) has a U value of 0.025 0.05 = 0.5.

Now that's all fine and dandy but there is a mathematical problem to be faced here. A wall is conventionally made up of maybe

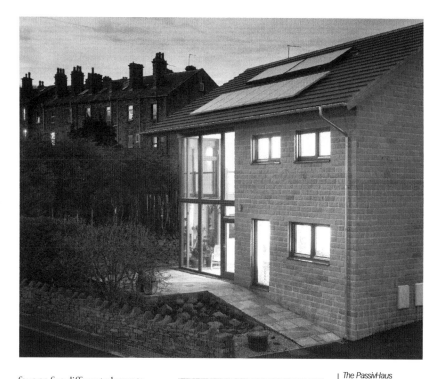

four or five different elements. Each one has its own U value and each contributes in some way to the insulating capabilities of that wall. In order to work out the cumulative U value of the wall you need some method of combining these values. You can't just add the U values together or subtract them from one another; you get a nonsensical answer. The trick is done by switching U values into R values, resistance values. R values are a mirror image of U values – the higher they go, the more they resist the passage of heat.

To switch between U values and R values you always divide the number you are working with into

1. So a U value of 0.5 is an R value of 2.0 (i.e. 1 0.5 = 2). And an R value of 4 is the same as a U value of 0.25 (i.e. 1 4 = 0.25). Unlike U values, you can add R values together and get a coherent answer. When you've added all the R values

The PassivHaus movement took flight in Germany and is rapidly spreading around the world. The one pictured above in Denby Dale featured as a case study in the Ninth Edition of The Housebuilder's Bible. Right: The PassivHaus (Passive House) certificate. Note the English spelling. We can't quite make up our minds and it seems neither can the powers that be...

together to give you a cumulative R value figure, you can then convert this total back to U values. It's not that difficult.

Interestingly, the Americans prefer to work everything in R values and you rarely see them refer to U values. Note, however, that if you get hold of some US building literature and you think their R values look amazingly high, it's not because they only build eco-cabins but because they use imperial measurements. A metric R value is worth 5.68 imperial ones. R values are arguably a simpler concept than U values – the higher the better – but U values are more useful because you can use them for whole house heat calculations.

COMMENTARY

The R value table covers most of the regular building elements that you might meet in constructing a new house. You can use it to roughly work out your own construction's U values by adding all the R values together and dividing 1 by the result. I have used the most regular thicknesses, but if you are not using one of these, remember that R values can be scaled up or down directly in proportion to the thickness of the material so that you can readily calculate your own. And also bear in mind that in more complex layers, such as a timber stud wall where the voids are filled with insulation, you have to work out the average R value based on the proportions of the area that are timber and insulation – typically 20 per cent is timber and 80 per cent is insulation.

Eagle-eyed readers will be asking 'Where's the glass?' Glass is a special case; when it's sunny, it gains heat - indeed it's specified as a heat source in passive solar designs. Windows tend to get attributed U values depending on the performance of the overall glass and frame combo; they also get marked up or down depending on

the orientation.

GROUND FLOORS

U values for ground floors are also a special case and the process for calculating them is quite different, largely because heat has difficulty traveling in a downwards direction. However the cold bridging effect around the edges of the floors is pronounced and so the key calculation is concerned not with the R values of all the bits of the floor but in establishing a ratio of the edge or perimeter of the floor with the area of the floor. You measure the length of the perimeter walls (heated area only) in metres and divide the result by the area of the floor (heated area only) in square metres. It makes no difference if your ground floor is suspended or ground bearing, timber or concrete. On the typical house the calculation looks like this:

Perimeter walls of house (excluding garage) are 43m long; ground floor (heated area only, again excluding garage) is 90 sq m. Calculation is 43 90 = 0.48.

This ratio has to be looked up on a table from which the R value and the U value can be read off - remember the U value = 1 R value. Deconstruct the table and you can see that the bigger and squarer the building, the less heat it loses through the ground floor.

HEAT CALCS AND ENERGY RATINGS

So if we are required to undertake a heat loss calculation by the building regs, let's look at what this involves. I have run some simplified heat calculations through the spreadsheet showing how it's all done. The measurements are taken for one of my

old benchmark houses but the U values and the ventilation rates are adjusted with some license. I then compare the building standards.

The 1975 house reflects how we built homes then, with little or no insulation. As you might suspect, it leaks heat.

The 2010 house is built to the standards in place in England and Wales at the time of going to press (2013).

The Eco House or Passive House standard is an example of an ultra-low energy dwelling which requires very little heating. The principles are always the same. Increase the insulation levels to such a degree that lightbulbs, appliances and body heat (the so-called incidentals) cover the vast bulk of the heat loss for the house, right down to your designed-for minimum external temperature.

THE CALCULATIONS WORK AS FOLLOWS:

▦ 1. You start with measuring the areas of the different parts of the house fabric - i.e. walls, roof, floors, joinery. NB The walls and roof figure should exclude the area taken up by the joinery.

▦ 2. You then attribute a U value to each of these areas.

▦ 3. You multiply each area by its U value. The result is the specific heat loss (SHL) for each area.

▦ 4. You add a bit on to account for thermal bridging – that is unanticipated losses through bits of the structure which are not quite so well insulated as you might hope: for instance, through wall ties, lintels, junctions, meter boxes.

▦ 5. You then work out the specific heat loss for the ventilation. To do this you need to know the volume of the heated air space in the house in cubic metres. And you need to factor in the number of air changes per hour. This used to be very hit and miss

R Values Of Building Materials

Material	Thermal Conductivity	Thickness in Mm VVv	R Value
Insulation			
Fibreglass/Mineral Wool			
Loose Quilt	0.04	100	2.50
	0.04	150	3.75
	0.04	200	5.00
Cavity Batts	0.038	50	1.32
	0.038	65	1.71
Timber Frame Batts	0.038	90	2.37
	0.038	140	3.68
Expanded Polystyrene	0.04	25	0.63
	0.04	50	1.25
	0.03	25	0.83
	0.03	50	1.67
Polyurethane	0.025	25	1.00
	0.025	38	1.52
	0.025	50	2.00
Vermiculite	0.075	100	1.33
Other Materials			
Softwood	0.13	25	0.19
	0.13	50	0.38
Hardwood	0.18	25	0.14
	0.18	50	0.28
Plywood/Chipboard	0.13	9	0.07
	0.13	18	0.14
	0.13	22	0.17
Plasterboard	0.25	9.5	0.04
	0.25	12.5	0.05
add for Foil Backing			0.20
uPVC	0.4	2	0.01
Clay Brick	0.77	102	0.13
Blocks			
Clinker Blocks	0.57	100	0.18
Aerated (Celcon)	0.18	100	0.56

Material	Thermal Conductivity	Thickness in mm	R Value
Concrete Blocks	1.9	100	0.05
Granite	2.9	100	0.03
Limestone	1.7	100	0.06
Sandstone	2.3	100	0.04
Clay Tile	1.0	10	0.01
Concrete Tile	1.5	12	0.01
Roofing Felt	0.2	2	0.01
50mm Screed	0.4	50	0.13
65mm Screed	0.4	65	0.16
100mm Concrete Slab	1.3	100	0.08
150mm Concrete Slab	1.3	150	0.12
Render	0.57	12	0.02
Finish Plasters	0.57	3	0.01
AIR GAPS			
Cavity 25mm plus			0.20
10mm or less			0.10
Ventilated Loft Space			0.20
SURFACE RESISTANCE			
External			0.05
Internal			0.10

R values for Ground Floors

Ground floor heat-loss calculations are a special case (see previous page). Edge:Area ratio is calculated by dividing the GF perimter length in metres by the GF area in m²

EDGE: AREA RATIO	R VALUE	U VALUE
0.2	2.8	0.4
0.3	2.0	0.5
0.4	1.6	0.6
0.5	1.4	0.7
0.6	1.2	0.8
0.7	1.1	0.9
0.8	1.0	1.0

If you want to improve on these 'as built' U values, you need to add insulation. To recalculate the new U value, add the edge:area R value to the R value of your chosen insulation, then calculate the U value

Chapter 14

affair but the latest changes to the building regs bring air tightness to the fore and require you to undertake an airtightness test, even though the standard required is not very exacting. If you are building a new home you could probably hazard a guess that you would get to around the half air change per hour mark. Multiply the air changes per hour by the volume and you get the volume of new air passing through the house every hour. Multiply this figure by 0.33 Watts, the specific heat of air (or the heat required to lift 1 cu m of air through 1 deg C) and you have a specific heat figure for your ventilation requirements.

■ 6. You then add all these figures together to give you a specific heat loss for the whole house. This is the amount of heat, in watts, that it takes to lift the entire house through 1 deg C. This is the critical figure in the calculations, known as the specific heat loss. It's sort of a sum of all the U values. The lower the SHL, the better insulated the structure is. As it's a measurement in watts, you can easily apply a multiplier to it to find out how much heat you need to keep the house warm on the coldest day. Normally we work to a design temperature of -1 deg C in England and Wales and -4 deg C in Scotland. Although you are under no obligation to stick to them, the industry standards for desired temperature in each room are as follows:

■ Living rooms/kitchen

21 deg C

■ Bedrooms

18 deg C

■ Hall/stairs

16 deg C

■ Bathrooms

22 deg C

To make the calculations a bit simpler, you can even all these temperatures to get an average temperature of around 18

deg C, maybe 19 deg C if you're a bit of a wuss. In order to keep our homes say 18 deg C warmer than the minimum design temperatures you would multiply the SHL by 19 deg C in England & Wales and 22 deg C in Scotland. The results are always surprisingly small. Try and persuade your plumber that you only need a 5kW boiler in your five bedroom house!

ENERGY RATINGS

Energy ratings take the heat loss calcs one stage further and attempt to speculate about how much energy you will actually burn in your home each year. A full-blown energy rating on a house is a complex beast involving many different interlinked calculations. The standard one used by the powers that be is the SAP Rating. Its full title is the Government's Standard Assessment Procedure for Energy Rating Dwellings, and it's forever being tweaked here and there as new products come on to the market. The building regs are supported by an upgraded SAP procedure, known as SAP 2009. From these figures it's possible to make a stab at your probable energy usage per annum expressed in units of energy, financial cost and carbon dioxide emissions.

It's very easy to pull holes in energy ratings, if you want to. Much of it is incredibly detailed to an altogether anal degree. Yet other bits use broad-brush assumptions that can only ever approximate real energy use. For instance, hot water use is estimated to rise in proportion to the house floor area. Anyone can see that it's actually more likely to be affected by the number of people living in the house but a dumb spreadsheet can't speculate about that, can it? So in order to be able to compare one house with another, floor area is used a lot. Yet energy ratings are a useful exercise if only to help

us understand just how houses work and how they do and do not burn energy.

Rather than go through the SAP calculations step-by-step, I have built a very dumbed down version in the table 'Benchmark House: Energy Ratings' which shows the basics. The big variables are the Specific Heat Loss (already worked out for three different standards in the table), the fuel used and the boiler efficiencies. Common sense really.

Here are a few notes on the table to help make sense of it.

■ A: Specific Heat Loss (SHL). This is calculated in the table 'Benchmark House: Calculating Specific Heat Loss.' It is the basis of the energy rating. Normally it's expressed in watts but here I've divided the watts by 1,000 to express it kilowatts because it makes better sense later on in the table.

■ B: Incidentals. This is the heat that you pump inadvertently into the house by way of lights, appliances, solar gains from sunshine, all those standby lights on computers and TVs and, of course, body heat. A person at rest gives off just over 100 Watts, whilst moderate physical exercise gives off around 400 Watts. In all incidentals probably contribute between 2,000W (2kW) and 3,000W (3kW) to a typical household. Like much in the world of energy rating, incidentals are very variable and so a vague approximate figure is used. Gains from the residents themselves are ignored.

■ C: Incidentals divided by the Specific Heat Loss. Why? The SHL represents the rate of heat loss from the house for every 1 deg C temperature difference between inside and outside. If you wish to keep the inside of the house 20 deg C warmer than the outside, then you will require twenty times more heat than the SHL to achieve this. But if your incidentals

Model House: Heat Loss Calculations

Calculating Specific Heat Loss

ELEMENTS	AREA	U VALUE	1975	2010	PASSIV HAUS
A: UPSTAIRS FLAT CEILING	80m²				
1975 - little or no insulation	x	0.8	64w		
2010 standards 180mm Pu	x	0.18		14w	
Passiv Haus standard	x	0.12			10w
B: EXTERNAL WALLS	200m²				
1975 - no insulation	x	1.5	300w		
2010 standards	x	0.22		44w	
Passiv Haus standard	x	0.12			24w
C: WINDOWS & DOORS	35m²				
Single Glazing	x	5.0	175w		
Double Glazing to 2010 standards	x	1.4		49w	
Triple Glazing	x	0.8			28w
D: FLOOR	80m²				
No Insulation	x	0.7	58w		
2010 standards	x	0.18		14w	
Passiv Haus standard	x	0.15			12w
E:Add allowance for THERMAL BRIDGING		100w	100w	50w	
F: VENTILATION	430m³				
Specific Heat of Air		0.33w/m³			
Heat required for 1 air change/hr		142w			
1 air change/hr(c 1975)		1.0	142w		
2010 standard (0.6 air changes/hr)		0.6		85w	
Passiv Haus standard (with MVHR)	0.2				21w

WHOLE HOUSE HEAT LOSS

		1975	2010	PASSIV HAUS
Specific Heat Loss	A+B+C+D+E+F	840w	310w	140w
Heat load required for 20°C uplift	SHL x 20 ÷1000	17kW	6kW	3kW
20° uplift/m³	Heat load ÷ volume	34w	13w	7w

are already providing some of this heat, then you need to subtract this amount from your overall heating requirement. So this figure tells you how much of your heating load will be accounted for by your incidentals. And the answer can be expressed in degrees Celsius because each SHL unit is 1 deg C. Neat, isn't it?

■ D: Degree days, which are an indicator of how much heat we need to get us through a winter heating season. Every day it goes below an agreed temperature (15 deg C) counts towards the annual total, and the lower it gets, the more it counts. For instance, If it gets down to zero, then that day would clock up a degree day score of

15, because it was 15 deg C below the trigger. Total it up for the whole year and you get an annual degree days total. In Britain it varies from 1,800 DD at Land's End to 3,000 at John O'Groats. The figure of 2,500 DD is taken here, just above average. It's the figure embedded within the SAP calculations – a sort of national average.

Chapter 14

MODEL HOUSE ENERGY RATINGS

			1975 HOUSE	2010 HOUSE	PASSIV HAUS
A	Specific Heat Loss (1°C temp diff)	kw	0.84kW	0.31kW	0.14kW
B	Incidentals Heat Gains(body heat, electrics)	kW	1 kW	1kW	1kW
C	Incidentals ÷ SHL	B÷A	1.2°C	3.2°C	7.1°C
D	Base Temperature for heating		19.0°C	19.0°C	19.0°C
E	Required uplift after Incidentals	D-C	17.8°C	15.8°C	11.9°C
D	Degree days of heating (look-up in tables)	look up	2,500dd	1,560dd	600dd
G	Annual space heating demand	F x 24 x A	50,000kWh	12,000kWh	2,000kWh
ADD FOR DOMESTIC HOT WATER					
Ha	say 4 people at 1500kWh ea/annum		6,000kWh	6,000kWh	3,000kWh
Hb	Passiv Haus uses solar panels (50% off)				3,000kWh
H	Net use for DHW	Ha-Hb	6,000kWh	6,000kWh	3,000kWh
I	Combined total for space heating and DHW	G+H	61,000kWh	19,000kWh	5,300kWh
GAS					
J	Allowance for boiler efficiency		68 per cent	90 per cent	90 per cent
K	kWh actually consumed	I ÷ J	82,000kWh	20,000kWh	5,600kWh
L	Unit cost of gas/kWh (in pence)	4.5 p			
M	Annual cost (exc standing orders)		£ 3,700	£ 900	£ 250
N	Carbon emissions for gas	0.18kg/kWh			
P	Carbon emissions in tonne/annum		15 t	4 t	1 t
Q	Carbon emissions (kg per sq m)	160 m²	95	23	6
OIL					
J	Allowance for boiler efficiency		70 per cent	90 per cent	90 per cent
K	kWh actually consumed	I ÷ J	80,000kWh	20,000kWh	6,000kWh
L	Unit cost of oil/kWh (in pence)	6.2 p			
M	Annual cost (exc standing orders)		£ 4,900	£ 1,200	£ 370
N	Carbon emissions for oil	0.27 kg/kWh			
P	Carbon emissions in tonne/annum		21 t	5 t	1.6 t
Q	Carbon emissions (kg per sq m)	160 m²	130	33	10
DIRTY ELECTRICITY					
J	Allowance for efficiency		100 per cent	100 per cent	100 per cent
K	kWh actually consumed	I ÷ J	56,000kWh	18,000kWh	5,00kWh
L	Unit cost of electricity/kWh (in pence)	14.5 p			
M	Annual cost (exc standing orders)		£ 8,000	£ 2,500	£ 700
N	Carbon emissions for elelctricity	0.54 kg/kWh			
P	Carbon emissions in kg/annum		30 t	10 t	2.7 t
Q	Carbon emissions per square metre	160 m²	190	60	17
ELECTRIC GROUND SOURCE HEAT PUMP					
J	Efficiency (assumes CoP of 3.0)		300 per cent	300 per cent	300 per cent
K	kWh actually consumed	I ÷ J	18.500kWh	6,000kWh	1,600kWh
L	Unit cost of electricity/kWh (in pence)	14.5 p			
M	Annual cost (exc standing orders)		£ 2,700	£ 850	£ 240
N	Carbon emissions for electricity	0.54 kg/kWh			
P	Carbon emissions in kg/annum		10 t	3.3 t	1 t
Q	Carbon emissions per square metre	160 m²	60	20	6

Degree Days

Degree Days taken from SAP 2005

Base Temp in °C	Degree days	
1	0	
2	60	
3	120	
4	185	
5	265	
6	360	
7	480	
8	620	
9	775	Eco House (Norfolk)
10	950	
11	1140	2010 house (Cornwall)
12	1345	2010 house (Norfolk)
13	1560	
14	1780	2010 house (Caithness)
15	2015	
16	2250	1975 house (Norfolk)
17	2490	
18	2730	
19	2970	
20	3210	

Your degree day score varies with your location (it's colder up north) and how well insulated your house is. Your insulation levels determine how much of your heat load is met by incidental heating, which reduces demand for space heating.

house whereas in the 1975 house the same amount of incidental heat is (I can't resist it) virtually incidental.

Back to the task in hand.

■ H: Domestic Hot Water (DHW) requirements. As already discussed, this part of the calculation is largely guesswork. But 4,000 kWh is enough for 180l of hot water every day of the year, about 2.5 bath fulls. That's probably what four people would use. I have given the Eco House some credit (2,000 kWh) for having half their hot water being supplied by solar panels – it's the sort of thing Passive House people would do.

■ I: Combine space heating and DHW and you have an estimate of annual energy demand (in kWh).

■ J and K: Boiler efficiency. Now boilers are not a 100 per centefficient. They have been getting more efficient and the latest, state of the art, condensing boilers have broken through the 90 per cent efficiency barrier, but you still need to factor the boiler efficiency into the calculations. I have included a separate calculation for electric heat pumps which I have assumed work at 300 per cent efficiency, which is what a CoP of 3.0 look like when expressed as an efficiency ratio.

■ L and M: Fuel costs. Now we have a figure for consumption, we can calculate a fuel cost.

■ N to Q: Carbon emissions. Each fuel has a carbon emission factor. From this you can readily work out the total carbon dioxide release for each house type, by fuel type. And divide by the floor area to get a kg of carbon dioxide per sq m, which is how the Dwelling Emission Rate (DER) is worked out. The SAP worksheets have used several targets over the years. Originally, the final sum was known as a SAP rating and this was based on likely fuel costs. Then came the Carbon Index in 2002, which has now

■ E: Reduction due to incidentals. Now here's a tweak and a half. Read this one carefully. If your incidentals can be expressed in degrees of heating (see above), then it follows that they can be subtracted from the number of degree days you need to cover. In effect, they lower your 15 deg C base temperature. Each degree less heat required because of your incidentals amounts to roughly 200 degree days less over a year - in fact the relationship isn't directly proportional but this is a dumbed-down table – what did you expect?

■ G: Having done this calculation, you can then have a healthy stab at how much heat you will actually need in your home to keep it warm throughout the heating season. You take the adjusted degree days,

you multiply by 24 because there are 24 hours in every day and then you multiply this by your SHL figure. Voila. You have an answer in kilowatt hours (kWh) used per annum.

What is fascinating here is to momentarily reflect on the role of incidental heating in all this. Although the actual amount of incidental heat doesn't alter a great deal between the three different houses I have examined, the reduction in degree days rises dramatically as you increase the insulation levels, thereby reducing the SHL. In the extremely well insulated Eco House, you need just over 1kW of incidental heat to cover the anticipated heating requirements for the whole

Chapter 14

Passivhaus Standard

Maximum annual space heating requirement	15 kWh/m² /annum
Max annual energy budget	120 kWh/m²/annum
Max heating load	10 watts/m²
Max U value for roof and walls	0.15
Max U value for windows and doors	0.8
Minimum efficiency on heat recovery systems	80%
Max air changes per hour (tested by blower door)	0.6 @ 50 Pascals

The Passivhaus standard is the gold standard of low energy housing. Developed in Germany in the 1990s, it has become internationally recognised not only for its exacting performance standards but also because it insists on a level of quality control unknown in the vast bulk of the UK building trade.

been abandoned: just as well because no one understood it. Now it's down to carbon dioxide emissions per sq m of internal floor area, similar to the Passive House standard although the current regs are of course nothing like so exacting.

LIGHTWEIGHT V HEAVYWEIGHT CONSTRUCTION

Is timber frame more energy efficient than masonry build? It's a selfbuild perennial, this one, and there really isn't a simple answer to it.

The one big plus that timber frame has going for it is that it is largely hollow and this provides lots of space in which to stuff insulation. In contrast, masonry is invariably solid, which means that the insulation has to be placed either inside, outside or, more co mmonly, within the cavity between the two skins. Whilst this isn't necessarily a problem, it means that masonry walls tend to be a little thicker overall, and this is generally regarded as a bad thing because thick walls eat floorspace.

However, even this point is contentious because it is possible, by judicious substitution of one insulating material for another, to build brick and block walls no thicker than 350 mm that are well able to satisfy the insulation standards of

2010. With the timber frame industry now switching over from 90 mm to 140 mm wall studs, this is only about 25 mm more than a timber frame wall with a brick facing skin. Timber frame can get external wall thicknesses down below 250 mm overall but only by switching to a lightweight cladding such as weatherboarding or render.

But this is an argument about wall thicknesses, not energy efficiency. Insulation levels are critically important when it comes to determining energy efficiency but they are not the be all and end all. As our insulation standards have risen over the years, it has become apparent that other factors play a crucial role as well. And because insulation thickness is subject to the laws of diminishing returns, these other factors have become more significant as we have now moved to a world where the building regulations demand that all new buildings are well insulated, at least by historical standards.

AIR TIGHTNESS

One factor that has leapt to the forefront is air tightness. The British have never been overly concerned about air tightness. In Canada and Sweden this issue is taken very seriously but then they regularly get winter temperatures of minus 25 deg C and consequently unwanted drafts are a matter of life and death. In contrast,

we have grown up in a culture where it remains co mmonplace to sleep with the windows open, throughout the depths of winter. Trying to impose Scandinavian levels of air tightness on us is seen as somehow alien and just possibly unhealthy. But from an energy saving point of view, airtightness is critical because an extra 50 mm of insulation in the walls and the roof is utterly pointless if the occupants subsequently leave the windows open. There is little the legislators can do about this but they can insist that buildings are constructed in such a way that they don't inadvertently leak. To this end, in 2006 the energy efficiency regs introduced an airtightness test for new houses. The required standard is not very onerous: in fact, it would have to be a very poorly built house to fail the test, but it is a marker for the future, and it is sure to be made more stringent as time moves on.

So how do the two building systems compare on air tightness? Generally speaking, it's not the walling systems that are the issue with air tightness. Rather, it's the insertions that puncture them and the junctions that enclose them. We are talking about ill-fitting windows, doors, meter boxes and loft hatches and poorly detailed eaves. Paradoxically, one of the most significant causes of air leakage is the connection between timber and masonry elements. Not only do they have differing rates of thermal expansion but timber tends to shrink significantly as it dries out to the background moisture levels in the building as a whole. This means that gaps can appear around joists built into masonry walls and at wallplate level under roofs. A house built entirely of timber or entirely of masonry wouldn't suffer air leakage in this way but such houses are extremely rare: in reality our timber frame homes tend to use a lot of masonry and our masonry homes use a lot of timber.

THERMAL MASS

The other energy saving issue bubbling away in the background surrounds the concept of thermal mass. Put quite simply, thermal mass is the capacity of a material to store heat. Heavy materials, like concrete, brick and cement screeds, will store a lot of heat – typically around 60kWh/ cu m – whilst lightweight materials, like timber frame walls covered in plasterboard, store as little as 2kWh/ cu m. Masonry homes have high thermal mass and because of this they take much more energy to warm up from cold. But having warmed up, they have become like giant night storage heaters and will keep warm much longer than a lightweight house because of all this extra heat stored within the walls and floors.

Now if a house is kept at a constant background temperature throughout the winter, it shouldn't really make any difference to energy consumption whether it is a high or low thermal mass. Once the heavy masonry house has achieved equilibrium, which may involve storing as much as 500kWh of heart within the structure, it motors along all winter, evening out the warm and cold periods. But high thermal mass houses have a trick up their sleeve here in that, if the interrelationship of the glazing and the high thermal mass elements is correct, they can

absorb significant amounts of free radiant heat from the sun during the daytime. This is the effect known as passive solar heating.

How much heat can be absorbed this way? In some climates where there is an abundance of clear sunny days in winter, passive solar design can provide the bulk of a house's heating load. Unfortunately, the British Isles rarely enjoy such weather and so passive solar heating is realistically only ever going to contribute a small proportion of what is required to keep warm.

But it's a plus for the masonry house builders. And in the see-saw arguments that rage over which system is better, the masonry boys are quick to crow about this benefit. But there is a downside to high thermal mass homes as well, which they are much less likely to acknowledge. This concerns the lifestyles of the occupants or, to put it another way, how a house is driven. High thermal mass homes work best when the building is constantly occupied, as there is always someone there to enjoy the heat radiating from the walls and floors. But a typical DINKY (Double Income No Kids) household may spend less than a third of their waking hours in their home and for them all this thermal mass is largely wasted, keeping an empty house warm. For them, the extra heat required to get the house warm in the evenings will more than cancel out any free heat gained from passive solar. And if you go away for a week's winter break and turn the heating off, the stored heat in the walls and floors will leak away and you will have to replace all 500kWh on your return. The heavier the house, the longer it takes to return to a comfortable temperature.

You can build a low energy structure using either masonry or framed building methods. And I don't think one system is inherently more energy efficient than the other. If anything, heavy structures have

an edge when the buildings are occupied during the daytime only. Lightweight structures will do slightly better when occupation is intermittent. And the average house? Probably somewhere between the two!

RENEWABLE TECHNOLOGIES

I can't have a chapter on green issues without mentioning renewable energy. But renewable energy isn't central to the issue of green building, despite what you might think, so I am not going to labour the topic too much. Besides, it's a topic which has become as much about harvesting subsidies as it has about the technologies themselves, and the decision about what if anything to specify on your build is now largely down to how much money is on offer. Which I don't like. For one thing, I end up having to write about the subsidies in more detail that the technology, and the capricious government has, in any event, a nasty habit of changing the subsidies at a whim, so that anything I write is almost bound to be out of date before this edition hits the shelves.

The Seventh edition had the Clear Skies grants. This was replaced in the Eighth edition by the Low Carbon Buildings Progra mme grants (with different versions for Scotland and N Ireland). That went as well. The Ninth edition had to take on board the Feed-In Tariff and the Renewable Heat Incentive. These are still going ahead during the Tenth Edition but they are seemingly constantly in flux, so much so that I'm not even going to bother to quote the level of subsidy. The up to date figures can be easily enough gleaned off the web — OFGEM and the Energy Savings Trust are the sites to go to.

Chapter 14

THE SUBSIDIES
FEED-IN TARIFFS

Introduced in the UK in April 2010, the feed-in tariff rewards people who install small-scale renewable energy plant. There are four different technologies covered by the scheme, being Solar PV, Wind, Hydroelectric and Micro CHP. For most people in most properties, hydro and wind are not going to be options; micro CHP might be, but probably won't. Which leaves roof mounted solar PV, or photovoltaics.

▨ You have to bear all the installation costs yourself. Both the kit and the installer must be MCS certified

▨ The output is metered and you are paid for every kilowatt hour of electricity you produce.

▨ Further to this you are paid an additional amount for electricity that you export, rather than consume at home.

▨ These payments are inflation-indexed, tax-free and will last for 20 years

▨ In addition, you will be spared paying for the electricity that you would have purchased from the Grid had you not been using your home-made electricity

SO IS IT WORTH IT?

You have to estimate how much it will cost you, how much electricity your plant will generate, and what income/savings you will receive.

As a rule of thumb, it seems that most people are opting for a 1.5kW system, and it's costing around £3,500 to install, down from around £10,000 before FITs were introduced. It's a good benchmark to start from. A 1.5kW system is quite large – it will probably involve 10 or 12 sq m of PV on the roof.

Let's assume it's around 1,250kWh/annum. Maybe that's a little generous – it rather depends on where you live - but we'll leave it here. It means that the PV arrays operate

at an average of around 20 per cent of peak power in daylight hours.

Generally, FITS are a moderately attractive investment. The installation costs have more than halved in two years, but so has the value of the tariff. And as there may well be further price reductions in the coming years, it's pointless to undertake an actuarial calculation here, except to say that the Government has designed these tariffs to make a modest return on investment over the lifetime of the panels, which may be 20 years or longer.

What you do get, which people like, is a way of generating electricity which protects you against the ravages of higher fuel prices.

RENEWABLE HEAT INCENTIVE

The Renewable Heat Incentive (the RHI) sets out to do something similar to the Feed-In Tariff but for different technologies – namely biomass heating, heat pumps and solar hot water. Arguably, it's of more interest to self builders because it concerns heating systems, which aren't optional. Without subsidy, these heating methods are at best marginal choices; none of them have a sensible payback against mains gas condensing boilers, but they all start to look more interesting when compared to the more expensive oil-boiler systems that you would have to chose if you live off the mains gas grid.

The technologies covered by the RHI are all dealt with in Chapter 8, Plumbing & Heating, and so I won't touch on them here.

PHOTOVOLTAICS OR PV

PV arrays convert sunlight into electricity. They normally sit on the roof, although they can be mounted in arrays on the ground or built into wall claddings. A PV cell consists of two layers of a semi-

conductor, invariably silicon, and when exposed to sunlight, electrons start flowing between the layers creating a small electrical current. The current is direct and has to be converted to AC for normal domestic use, or exported back to the grid. This is done with a bit of kit called an inverter.

The reliability of PV cells is good as there are no moving parts. However it is reckoned that the potential to produce electricity will decline over time and cautious observers reckon that they may need replacing after just 20 years if they are to continue to perform adequately.

The PV market is expanding quite rapidly and we are beginning to see it arrive it different formats. One that is attracting attention is PVT which combines the two kinds of solar panel (photovoltaics and hot water) into one unit. This carries an efficiency advantage because the heat gets drawn away into the hot water system which makes the PV operate more efficiently. However, it carries a disadvantage too in that you end up with far more hot water than you can sensibly use in su mmer. One for those with a heated swi mming pool, methinks. Look out for Newform Energy: they are nothing if not innovative.

WIND TURBINES

We are all familiar with the huge windfarms, which cause so much controversy around the countryside. The domestic wind turbine is the junior relation, which sits in your garden or, just possibly, on your roof. It is connected to a generator which produces direct electricity – same problem as PV cells here — but the cost per peak kW is somewhat less than PV cells, estimated to be around £2,000. Like PV cells, domestic wind turbines have an anticipated lifespan of around 20 years. The main and obvious drawback of wind turbines is that they only produce power when the wind blows and so the output is unpredictable, which hardly makes them ideal for creating a cohesive energy strategy. They are also far more visible and intrusive than roof mounted PV cells and there are consequently planning issues with wind turbines: as a rule, neighbours do not like them.

Unfortunately, it seems to be that the smaller the wind turbine, the less effective it is. Most of the roof mounted ones struggle to produce any meaningful amount of power: the pole mounted ones, designed for paddocks and the like, perform much more reliably.

Both PV cells and wind turbines would benefit greatly if there was a readily available domestic battery that could store the electricity. However, this is a case of watch this space. At the present moment, no such option exists.

COMBINED HEAT & POWER (OR MICRO CHP)

CHP isn't a renewable technology as such in that the kit being developed burns mains gas or sometimes oil. The trick it does, as its name suggests, is to produce electricity as well as hot water and so offers some savings over grid-delivered electricity. Like many of these technologies, there is nothing very new about CHP: something like it was introduced by the Victorians who used the heat generated by power stations to supply piped hot water in parts of London. In Denmark, spiritual home of CHP, around 50 per cent of all homes have a piped hot water supply form a district grid, and small grid systems are now being built into innovative estates in the UK.

What is new on the CHP scene is the development of kit for single homes, known as micro CHP. We've seen kit come and go over the years (where are you, Whisphergen?) but currently what waves are being made are being made by the Baxi EcoGen, the first widely available wall-hung domestic micro-CHP boiler in the UK. It costs around £5,000. The boiler produces up to 1 kWe of electricity per hour and what doesn't get used in the home can then be sold back to the local network. Micro-CHP units are also included within the Feed-in Tariff scheme.

HYDROGEN FUEL CELLS

Fuel cells are an interesting and evolving technology that produce both electricity and heat, similar in that respect to CHP. Potentially, it's much greener because the fuel used is hydrogen. Just how renewable this is depends on how the hydrogen is produced and unfortunately most hydrogen manufacturing is very energy intensive. Research and development into fuel cells is a huge international business – take a look at www.fuelcelltoday.com for a flavour of what is going on – but as yet there is nothing available co mmercially aimed at the domestic market, although British Gas are currently working with Ceres Power on developing a CHP unit to be run on hydrogen fuel cells. If it gets going soon, it will be the world's first mass market application for fuel cells, but to date this is still in the 'Watch This Space' category.

HYDROELECTRICITY

Water mills, by any other name. This is of course another very well established technology – hydroelectric damns and electricity generation have been around since Victorian times. It's also very green in that it's all powered by falling water – gravity in other words. However its use in the domestic sphere is limited by the requirements for falling water on site, not something widely seen in many new estates although it may well suit some remote off-grid sites. If you have a site that's suitable for hydropower, there are a number of co mmercial businesses which can build and install plant for you and the costs per peak kW are reckoned to be as little as £500.

Check out www.british-hydro.org.

MECHANICAL VENTILATION WITH HEAT RECOVERY (MVHR)

This is a technology that is not encouraged by government grant, even though it is based around using heat pumps. MVHR is felt to be essential in many low energy house designs: the Passive House standard insists on it. There are other green technologies, like Dwell-Vent triple-glazed windows and certain tubular light tower designs which could arguably be added to the list of grant-boosted devices, but I suppose they have to draw the line somewhere...

LOW ENERGY LIGHTING

Lighting is a significant part of the energy load of a new house so it's not surprising that it falls under the remit of Part L, the energy efficiency regs. It first appeared as a controlled item in 2002 and the requirements have changed quite a bit over the intervening years. In the 2006 version of Part L, you were required to have one in every four lights as a low-energy fitting, and for the fittings to be dedicated ones so you couldn't simply take out the bulbs and put ordinary ones in. But in the 2010 version of Part L, this has changed to three out of every four fittings but, at the same time, the requirement for the fittings to be dedicated has been removed.

Chapter 14

WHY?

Well it seems that it's something of an unworkable requirement. One of a number of building regulations where people will happily comply until the building inspector has been and gone for the last time, and then revert to what they wanted to do all along. If people want to fit low energy fittings, they will: if they don't, then building regs won't make them. Even dedicated low energy fittings weren't sufficient deterrent: they can easily be replaced.

There's more. The regs extend to external lighting. You are no longer allowed to rig up permanent lighting without it being energy efficient. You can fulfill this requirement either by using CF bulbs or by installing it with daylight and movement sensors – i.e. so it's only on occasionally.

Lighting is energy intensive and relatively expensive because a) it is inefficient (95 per cent of the energy coming out of a standard GLS light bulb is heat) and b) it is using peak-rate electricity. In terms of kWhs burned, lights rarely lift above 15 per cent of the overall usage, but this can be a much higher percentage when expressed in carbon emissions because electricity is of course a carbon-rich power source. So it does appear quite logical for the building regs to concern themselves with lighting efficiency. But there is a considerable hurdle to jump which is that compact fluorescent bulbs are not interchangeable with tungsten or halogen lamps. They can't be di mmed (though ones are now coming to market which can be, after a fashion – look out for Varilight). And the light quality is quite different. Downlighters and spotlights are designed to be directional: fluorescents, by their very nature, can't be. So whilst there are fluorescent downlighters available, they don't really do the same job as a halogen downlighter. Bear in mind also that whilst you get something like four times the light output from a CF pendant light for the same power level, the light output is subtly reduced with downlighters so that you would probably require an 18w CF bulb to replicate a 50w halogen one.

Substituting fluorescent light for tungsten light also makes for subtle changes in atmosphere, and ill-planned installation can end up putting people off energy-saving lamps for good. Energy-efficient lighting doesn't have to be bad lighting but for too many people this is exactly what it becomes when they swap over to a compact fluorescent bulb. However technology has moved on since the early days of CF bulbs and the current crop are smaller, more efficient and give better light quality.

The fact is that many office buildings and hotels are now lit almost exclusively by CF lights and no one bats an eyelid, so perhaps the question is will they, in time, become compulsory in new homes? According to the government, they wish to phase out tungsten bulbs in about three or four years, which will be interesting.

INTELLIGENT SWITCHES

Don't overlook the fact that one of the best ways to save lighting bills is to turn lights off when they are not being used. However, if you've got a house full of stroppy teenagers this may not be quite as easy as it sounds. You can, of course, fit time switches in hallways and stairwells but they tend to be a bit institutional. We are now quite used to seeing PIR switching used for external security but its use indoors to control lighting is still rare, but no more expensive than external PIRs (prices from around £25).

ARE LEDS THE ANSWER?

Very likely. LED lighting has come on leaps and bounds in the past few years and is now achieving lighting efficiencies way better than fluorescents. Indeed, the use of LEDs in spotlights and downlighters is rapidly becoming the fashionable thing as people are much happier with the light quality. The main barrier to uptake is still the cost. An LED downlighter retails at around £25, compared to £8 for a CF energy saver and £2 for halogen. That's still a big gulf.

KITCHEN & LAUNDRY

Together with lighting, household appliances are the great unseen energy consumers. An examination of the fuel costs for a new home reveal that, even without specifying super-insulation levels, fuel bills are actually higher for kitchen appliances, cooking and lighting than they are for space and hot water heating. And even when looked at in carbon emission terms, they still rank almost equal to space heating and hot water. Yet with a little application it should be possible to reduce running costs by nearly half.

COOKING

Gas cooking is way cheaper than using electricity. Many people prefer cooking on a gas hob (and most developers' packages offer them as an alternative at no extra cost) but gas ovens have an undeservedly poor reputation and they are now few and far between, particularly in the built-in market. Electric controls and electronic ignition have greatly improved the traditional gas oven and if you use a main oven or grill more than one hour a week, it will be worth paying the extra £150 to install a gas oven. Stoves, Canon, Parkinson Cowan, New World still produce them; British Gas

Household Appliances Energy Use

				Mains gas	LPG	Electricity
Fuel costs in pence per kWh				4.5p	6.6p	14.5p

APPLIANCE	RATING IN WATTS	HOURS USED/ ANNUM	KWH USED PER ANNUM	ANNUAL RUNNING COSTS		
Hobs	2000	200	400	£ 18	£ 25	£ 60
Oven	2000	300	600	£ 25	£ 40	£ 85
Microwave	2000	100	200			£ 30
Dishwasher	1200	400	480			£ 70
Washing Machine	1200	350	420			£ 60
Tumble Dryer	1000	300	300	£ 15	£ 20	£ 45
Small fridge (120lt)	25	8760	220			£ 30
Fridge/freezer	50	8760	440			£ 65
Kettle	3000	100	300			£ 45
Iron	2000	50	100			£ 15
TV	100	1500	150			£ 25
Computers	150	1500	230			£ 35
Stand-by equipment/chargers	10	8760	90			£ 12
Heavy use GLS lightbulb	60	1500	90			£ 12
Heavy use energy efficient light	18	1500	30			£ 4
Medium use lighting	60	500	30			£ 4

showrooms (now called Energy Centres) display them although they are not cheap places to shop. If mains gas is not available, then LPG models will still produce a significant saving on electric cooking.

If electric cooking is the only sensible option, there is currently very little one can do to reduce costs. Energy efficiency has yet to make any significant impact on this area, but note that microwaves are very efficient at cooking small quantities. Microwaves are quick and work at much lower power than conventional electric cookers: on the other hand, food bought ready for microwaving is expensive. It all depends on how you use them. The induction hob, described in Chapter 11 'Kitchen appliances', would also seem to offer efficiencies over an ordinary ceramic hob.

Note that cast-iron stoves – and Agas in particular – are very heavy users of fuel. A gas or oil-fired Aga kept on all year will cost over £400 per annum to run.

HOT AND COLD FILL

Look for dishwashers and washing machines which can be filled from your hot water pipes rather than heating their own water. This is now standard on new washing machines but is still rare on dishwashers. If using machines on delayed night-time switching, then separate H&C fill is of little benefit as the disparity between the costs of off-peak electrically heated water and boiler heated water is reduced.

ENERGY EFFICIENT?

Many manufacturers are jumping on the bandwagon in claiming to produce machines that save on electricity, water and detergents. This is a complicated area and many of the claims are at best marginal and depend on the user understanding just what is expected of them. To help spread a little light into this murky area, fridges, freezers and washing machines are now routinely energy labelled to help the customer make an informed decision about how much power they use. A visit to my local Curry's revealed a wide range of scores: a Bosch Economic fridge freezer scored A and reckoned to use just 120kWh per annum (cost £20) whilst a giant Hotpoint power guzzler scored G, estimated to use 540kWh per annum (cost £85). Whilst the accuracy of energy labelling (which is carried out by the manufacturers) has been called into question, the fact that there is now a comparative yardstick available on a range of white goods is a big boon.

Although these savings may not look individually very large, careful purchasing should be able to save £100 or more per annum of peak rate power and metered water. Water saving washing machines actually save remarkably little in cash terms and yet it is this feature which tends to be the strongest selling point on 'Green' appliances.

For most buyers, there will be a number of other factors which will determine which machines they purchase – notably servicing costs and standards, reliability record, easy-to-use controls or perhaps it just all came with the kitchen – and you may well be right to base your decision on these criteria, but don't be afraid to ask about water and electricity use.

USE OF APPLIANCES

Considerable savings can be achieved by using your appliances efficiently. Really these are no more than co mmon sense measures such as drying clothes on washing lines whenever possible, setting washing machine temperatures as low as possible and turning off lights when rooms are empty. If you've a genuine interest in energy conservation – or just don't like paying bills – then at least part of the solution is in your hands.

SUMMARY

Energy-efficient appliances – or more particularly energy-efficient use of appliances – can be planned into a new house. The presence of gas on site makes for large cost savings but, even on remoter sites where gas is not available, there are numerous actions you can take to increase fuel efficiency. There is a cost penalty (though it is hard to quantify because there are so many variables) but there are also appreciable savings to be made. However, unlike installing insulation or

efficient heating systems, saving energy in the kitchen requires you to interact intelligently with your machines and for many people this is just too much hassle.

SAVING WATER

Although 75 per cent of UK property is still charged for water and sewage by a rating system, newly constructed housing in England & Wales is invariably metered (not so in Scotland and N. Ireland). Living with a metered water supply is a novel experience for many of us and it takes some getting used to. If you are connecting your drains into the main drains as well as tapping into the local water supplies, your bills will be broken down into four sections:
■ Standing charge for water supply
■ Volume charge for water supply
■ Standing charge for sewage disposal
■ Volume charge for sewage disposal.

Properties that dispose of waste by other means (usually septic tanks) will have other costs to pay instead of sewage charges – see section on Drains, Chapter 6, 'Groundworks'.

METERING: HOW IT WORKS

Only the water supply is metered. The volume of discharge you pour back down the drains is worked out from the amounts of water you consume: some companies reckon it to be 100 per cent, some 95 per cent and some 90 per cent. If yours works on a 95 per cent figure then, if you were to consume 100 cu m of water, you would be charged for 95 cu m of sewage.

A four-person household will typically use and discharge 185 cu m of water/annum (equivalent to 2300 baths, that's just over six baths a day). This 185 cu m figure is very much an average and a new house with lots of thirsty appliances like dishwashers and

power showers, not to mention children, could easily use 50 per cent more. When I was living in a house with three teenage sons present, we used as much as 365 cu m per annum, the main culprit, I believe, being the teenagers love of power showers lasting ten minutes at a time, consuming around 20l per minute, maybe 400l per day or 150 cu m per annum. I don't think our family was that unusual and I suspect that the quoted average figures probably underestimate a typical user. Heavy users with swi mming pools, water features and garden sprinklers and the like would propel your annual usage way over even these suspect usage figures.

COMPARISONS

The charges for average water usage are larger than the anticipated heating bills for a new home. Assuming an average of 250 cu m per annum is consumed by our notional four-person household, the average bill, including standing charges, will be over £650 per annum. The pie chart illustrates how we consume our water.

What i mmediately stands out about these figures is how little water actually passes into our bodies (three per cent) compared to how much is consumed largely to keep us and our homes clean and hygienic. Part of the justification for higher water prices is the cost of maintaining drinking water standards but, on reflection, it seems extraordinary that we should go to such trouble to purify our water supplies in order to pour 97 per cent back down the drains. In theory, at least, there is ample scope to use non-potable water (ie non-drinking), and ample savings to be made by avoiding relatively expensive metered supplies.

USE LESS

Before delving into esoteric water-saving schemes, there are a number of co mmon sense ways that water consumption can be reduced without making you smell:

▨ Don't stand under the shower for ten minutes every day

▨ Check out lo-flow shower heads. More and more suppliers are offering them. Indeed, if you are building a new home, you will be required to fit them in order to meet the building regulations. More on this in Chapter 8, Plumbing & Heating.

▨ Fit the smallest WC cisterns possible – the industry standard is now down to six litres per flush, thanks to a recent change in the water bylaws, but you may be able to source even smaller cisterns. Dual flush at 4l/6l are widely available

▨ Buy A+ rated appliances. A water-efficient washing machine will use around half as much as an older model. Same goes for dishwashers

▨ Don't run washing machines and dishwashers unless they are full

▨ Look to fit water efficient taps to basins and kitchen sinks

▨ Don't water lawns; water plants in the evening to avoid evaporation

▨ Use water butts (although attractive ones are hard to find)

▨ Don't build a swi mming pool.

PART G

The building regulations now make water efficiency mandatory – in England the relevant section is Part G. This requires us to undertake a water calculation when designing the house to show that our overall consumption shouldn't average more than 125lts/day, a feat achieved largely through specifying small baths and/or low flow showers. There is more on Part G and the water calculator in the Bathrooms section in Chapter 11.

WATER SAVING

Water-saving schemes are so mmat else.

They can be divided into two areas: rainwater collection which replaces water you'd normally buy through your water meter, and grey water collection which recycles some of the water you have already used.

RAINWATER HARVESTING

Even in dry lowland England (average rainfall equals 750 mm per annum) a four-bedroom house plus detached garage will get around 60-75 cu m of rain falling on to it during the course of a year. That sounds like a lot but it's probably only around what one person consumes in a year, or enough for a household of four or five to flush the loos. The calculation is as follows: take your average annual rainfall in metres and multiply it by your catchment area in square metres. So if you have a 100 sq m roof and 0.75m of rainfall per annum (that's 30 inches) then you might hope to collect 75 cu m of water. Actually, rather less, because inevitably a significant amount gets spilled or lost via evaporation. In wetter areas to the north and west this figure could easily double as rainfall levels are so much higher. The potential is there; the problem is that rainfall is not only unpredictable but sporadic whereas household usage is basically quite constant. You need to build a reservoir capable of holding enough rainwater to supply basic household needs, which is exactly what your own water company does on a much larger scale. Starting your very own water supply business may be an appealing prospect for some but it is likely to prove expensive to build and time-consuming to run. The bigger your reservoir, the more effective your own supplies will be in replacing your metered supply, but the more problems you are likely to have with construction and maintenance.

Rainwater harvesting has become quite

trendy in no time at all and a surprising number of self built homes are fitting tanks, filters and pumps so that they can reuse at least some of their free rainfall in a similar fashion. The Germans have been doing it on a domestic scale for twenty years and three of their systems – IRM, Wisy and KSB – are now available in the UK. Prices quoted are between £2,000 and £4,000: for this you get underground storage tanks (either plastic or concrete), filters to take out most of the leaves and twigs and a pump to lift the water back up to the house. Most people use it just for flushing loos, installing a second plumbing system supplying the cisterns from the storage tanks, but there is no reason you can't supply the bulk of your taps with rainwater. You can rig it up so that the storage tanks never empty – the mains water cuts in when the level falls too low. More sophisticated arrangements with some onsite treatment allows rainwater to be used as drinking water but this requires on site treatment which is a more complex affair.

Whether it is really worth doing from an economic perspective is debatable. It only makes sense if you have a water meter, for a start. Even then, a 1,000l of water, which is by definition a cubic metre, is currently charged at anywhere between 80p and £1.20, depending on your water company, so your maximum saving is unlikely to be more than about £80 a year.

GREY WATER

Grey water is the term given to waste which is reusable, notably the waste from baths, showers and wash basins. There is potential to recycle this water in the garden and especially for flushing loos. Because the waste from baths and washing is much more regular than rainfall, the storage facilities do not have to be nearly

as large to be effective. A large bath-sized tank will be enough to flush ten loos and should get refilled most days.

As with rainwater harvesting, there has been a small explosion of interest in grey water recycling and there are now proprietary systems available using pumps and a small holding tank that can be placed in the loft. The grey water is treated with cleaning agents and passed through a carbon filter. Grey water requires much less storage than rainwater harvesting to be effective but there are potential problems with contamination that need to be addressed.

BOREHOLES
There is another way of avoiding

water company charges – and infrastructure charges – and that is to sink your own borehole and draw your own water supply up from under the ground. It's where most of the water comes from in SE England and in many other areas besides and, whereas your local water company has a monopoly on piped supplies, there is nothing to stop you tapping into the enormous natural groundwater reservoir directly. That's an oversimplification; there is the small matter of installation costs that can vary from £2,000 to £20,000, depending on such matters as the depth of the borehole and the water pressure. For most people, that makes it an extremely expensive way of going

Jeff Tanner (L) inspects the two linked loft tanks which carry rainwater and greywater. The rainwater is drawn from an underground storage tank into the upper tank here (behind Jeff's left hand) and this is used to fill the lower greywater tank if there is a shortage of grey water. A mains supply into the rainwater header tank ensures that both tanks remain full in the event of rainwater and or greywater running low

about getting water and sends them straight back into the arms of their local water company.

If you are one of the small number who plan to draw their own water supply from under the ground, then you will be responsible for your own water quality. That's not to say that you won't have to submit your water for analysis to the local Environmental Health Inspector: indeed most councils will be around testing you every couple of years or so. Simple bacteria tests tend to be done in local hospitals and cost around £30; however tests for pollution are more expensive – I was quoted £100 for a nitrate test. The Environmental Health Inspector has the power to condemn your supply but this rarely happens because almost everything can be filtered out – at a cost. My local inspector reckoned that ground water pollution was something of an overstated problem and that when he did come across it, it was very often the house itself that was the cause of the pollution; he advised not to use ground water supplies in conjunction with a septic tank. Obvious really.

PAYING FOR LEAKS
Whilst the problem of a dripping tap is well known (and costly for metered households), it palls into insignificance compared to the potential nightmare of an underground leak. You, the householder, are responsible for all water consumption downstream from the water

How We Use Water In The Home

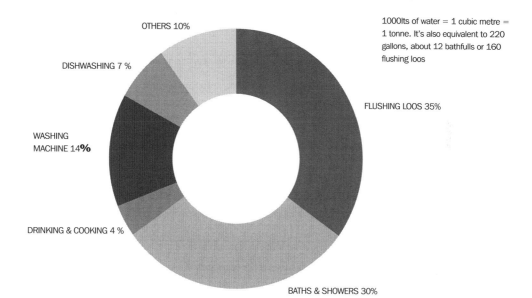

OTHERS 10%

DISHWASHING 7 %

WASHING MACHINE 14**%**

DRINKING & COOKING 4 %

1000lts of water = 1 cubic metre = 1 tonne. It's also equivalent to 220 gallons, about 12 bathfulls or 160 flushing loos

FLUSHING LOOS 35%

BATHS & SHOWERS 30%

meter – which is conventionally located outside, close to the plot boundary. Spring a leak underground between the meter and your internal stop tap and you may know nothing about it until a massive water bill arrives on your doormat (as much as six months later); if you are lucky, the water company will let you off paying the sewage charge, but even so a bad leak might lose as much as 20 cu m of water a day which would cost £1,500 by the time you get your water bill. Be warned that sloppy installation (and loose connections) of metered mains supplies can be very expensive.

WATER TREATMENT

There are two very distinct processes here. You soften (or condition) water

in an attempt to prolong the life of your domestic appliances, whereas you filter water in an attempt to prolong your own life. Both techniques are surrounded by a veil of mystery and intrigue which is hard to penetrate, and the whole subject is so rife with claim and counterclaim that it makes the job of the humble co mmentator akin to negotiating a minefield. Wish me luck as I go in.

SOFTENING AND CONDITIONING

If you live in a soft water area (which includes most of Britain above a line drawn between the Humber and the Severn) then this section is one to miss. If in doubt, phone your water company to get figures on local conditions. Even if you live in a hard water area there is

no need to panic. Households have been known to function quite adequately for years without so much as a hint of any water softeners about. However, many sane people swear by water softeners and insist that they produce tangible benefits – even if it's only to reduce the amount of soap powder they use in their washing machines

TRADITIONAL SOFTENERS

For between £600 and £1,000 you get a big box into which you add salt – you need around three 25kg bags of salt per person per annum, so this alone will cost you £15 each every year. Softeners work by separating out the hard bits in the water, exchanging them for softer sodium bits. The box needs an electrical supply and a drain-off point. It also needs, ideally, to

Water Bills in England & Wales

ANNUAL CHARGES/M³			WATER	SEWAGE	COMBINED
Average Standing Charges			£35	£45	£80
Average Volume Charges			£1.50	£1.80	£3.30

WATER USED BY 4-PERSON HOUSEHOLD			ANNUAL VOLUME CHARGES		
ACTIVITY	Litres/day		WATER	SEWAGE	COMBINED
Drinking/Cooking	20	3%	£11	£13	£24
Baths/Showers	300	44%	£164	£197	£361
Flushing Loos	150	22%	£82	£99	£181
Washing Machine	70	10%	£38	£46	£84
Dishwasher	35	5%	£19	£23	£42
Others	100	15%	£55	£66	£121
TOTAL	675	100%	£370	£443	£813
STANDING CHARGES + VOLUME CHARGES			£405	£490	£895

VARIATIONS					
4-person household, Highest charging area (South West)				£1,000	
4 -person household, Lowest charging area (Northumbria)					£600
Average for 3-person household					£690
Average for 2-person household					£490
Average for 1-person household					£280

be located somewhere close to the rising main so that it's relatively easy to plumb in. 'Under the utility sink' is an obvious place but, be warned, most water softeners require a fair bit of space around and above them in order to be got at for maintenance and weekly salt refills. You may have to adjust your utility worktop to suit. The long-term benefits include reduced water heating bills and savings on soap powders (combined unlikely to be worth more than about £25 per annum). Evidence that water softeners increase the lifespan of hot water appliances is – careful now – inconclusive but almost everyone who has one reckons they do make the water feel softer and the laundry appears cleaner. In 2005, I installed a water softener, never having had one before: I actually don't like the 'feel' of the water as much as genuine soft water, but one place where the chemically softened water is really appreciated is in the bathrooms where limescale is a thing of the past, making cleaning a doddle. If you plan to install glazed shower screens in a hard water area, then you will really appreciate a water softener.

As these boxes actually chemically change the water supply, their output should not be drunk or cooked with. Design your plumbing so that the kitchen tap, at least, comes direct from the mains.

PHOSPHATE CONDITIONERS

These are a sort of junior version of the big water softeners. They are designed to stop hot water appliances from scaling up and they are usually sold in conjunction with combination boilers and/or mains pressure hot water cylinders. You will see them in plumber's merchants – look for names like Combimate and Combicare.

They work by adding phosphate solution to the incoming water, which inhibits scale formation – they don't 'soften' the water as such but they are reckoned to prolong the life of water-heating equipment in hard water areas.

They cost around £80 and they don't need power or drainage facilities but the phosphate cartridges need replacing every year (cost £15 a time). Again the treated water is not ideal for drinking but these conditioners are normally only fitted to water heating devices.

INHIBITORS

Unlike the two preceding methods – which are chemical treatments – inhibitors act by passing a magnetic or an electrical charge through the water which – it is claimed – prevents the hard bits in the water from sticking to the pipes. They are relatively cheap (£30-£60), easy to install and need no maintenance. Also they do not affect drinking water qualities. Some need electrical power, most operate without. But do they work?

You may figure they are so cheap that there is nothing to lose in trying and you may well be right. But how will you know that your investment does the biz? Another thing to ponder on during those long dark nights.

FILTERING

In the last few years, there has been an enormous growth of interest in the subject of tap water quality. Whereas the Victorians basked in the glory of the technical achievement of providing clean drinking water to all homes, we have now become blasé about this and tend to worry that much of this water runs through lead pipes and, in any event, doesn't taste very good. Added to which there are fears (in lowland England at least) that we are now getting nitrate and pesticide residues in our tap water.

There is a huge choice of water filters available, ranging from the free standing plastic jug affairs which can be picked up in Boots for a few quid to expensive, in-line purifiers. There are no British Standards for water purifiers ('tap water's just fine, old boy') and there is little concrete evidence on the effectiveness of the various methods. There is also concern that many filters may themselves be health hazards, providing spawning grounds for micro-bacteria.

Nevertheless, interest in water filters continues to grow and one of the more innovative companies working in this field is Culligans who supply the whole range of water treatment gizmos from softeners and scale reducers to filters and ultra-violet disinfection units. If you remain unconvinced but would still like a source of filtered water, you could do worse than snap up a Brita Filter kettle for about £40.

Rainwater collection tanks are routinely buried underground, but there is no reason why they can't be incorporated in above ground, as in this set up

CODE FOR SUSTAINABLE HOMES

In December 2006, the Labour government published the Code for Sustainable Homes. Over the intervening six years I have grown to be a harsh critic of this document but one thing I must admit right at the outset is that it's been hugely influential and widely reported. Anybody with even a passing interest in housebuilding has heard about it and most have a pretty good idea that a Code Level 6 house is the tops. By 2016, the government wants (or at least once wanted) every new house in England to meet Level 6. Wales has opted for an even tighter timetable. Scotland has been a little wiser, and isn't setting quite such ambitious targets.

And as if to confirm the fact that the Code has arrived, it's now been made mandatory for all new homes to have a rating against the Code, although initially you can simply opt for an 'Unrated' option. Methinks not for long. Eventually, the Code will either be absorbed into the building regulations or it will become a mandatory accessory. It's the future of housebuilding, as far as we can tell.

The Code didn't arrive out of the blue. It built on something similar called Eco Homes which, like the Code, came out of the resources of the Building Research Establishment in Watford. These are essentially checklists with which to measure just how eco your eco house actually is. Points are awarded for all kinds of green features, and although energy saving grabs the headlines, there is also water saving to be done, recycling and various other good design features.

The way the Code has been set up, it's divided into six levels. Level 1 is already history as far as energy saving is concerned: in 2010 the

Chapter 14

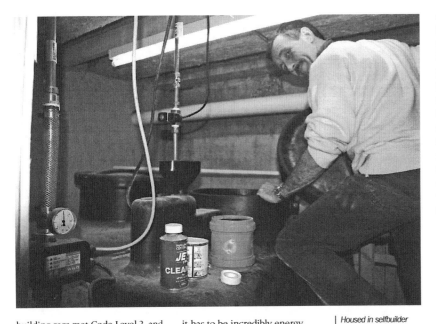

building regs met Code Level 3, and they are due to reach Code Level 4 in 2013 (though this may not happen quite as planned!).

There are other features of the Code that aren't touched by the building regulations. In fact energy efficiency only accounts for around a third of the available credits. There's an additional 10 per cent for saving water, and the rest of the points are divided up across seven categories. Code Level 6, the top level, requires a score of 90 per cent. You can read all about it at your leisure by downloading the Code Technical guidance from the Planning Portal website.

So how would you go about garnering enough percentage points required to lever your house up from Code Level 0 to Level 6? The basic thing is that

it has to be incredibly energy efficient. The insulation and airtightness levels have to get close to Passive House standards and then you have to fix the house up with some renewable energy devices, like solar panels or wind turbines, and possibly something like a ground source heat pump. I won't dwell on these features here because they have been written about at length elsewhere in the book. What's perhaps more interesting about the Code is all the other things you have to do. You have to garner loads more points for being generally eco and good. Some are relatively easy:
▥ Provision for cycle storage – score 2.5 per cent
▥ Provision of a home office – score 1.25 per cent
▥ Provision of recycling bins and a

Housed in selfbuilder Adrian Thurley's basement are three rainwater harvesting tanks, supplied by Freewater UK. The cost for the whole system was around £2,500; it takes rainwater from the guttering and reuses it to flush the loos and to fill the washing machine. Adrian commented: 'When it's working, it supplies about 60 per cent of our household water. I calculate it's saving us about £7 a week which I am delighted with. The two tanks together hold 7500 litres and it takes just an inch of rain to fill them up.'

compost bin – 4.75 per cent
▥ Use EU approved insulation – 0.6 per cent
Others are more taxing and potentially a lot more costly
▥ Build to Lifetime Homes standards – 4.75 per cent
▥ Build to Secured by Design standards – 2.25 per cent
▥ Improve on Part E sound regulations – 4.75 per cent
▥ Use A+ rated materials from the Green Guide for Specification – 4.5 per cent
▥ Build into the basement or the loft space – 2.65 per cent

You can only afford to lose 10 per cent of the credits available if you want to qualify for Code Level 6. As there are likely to be some areas where your site cannot score at all, the likelihood is that designers will be forced to incorporate practically every feature mentioned in the Code. The elbow room for trade-off is remarkably limited.

This is where the Code gets into sticky ground. A lot of these features – there are 34 tests applied in all – are concerned with good design and best practice, but not necessarily to do with sustainability. For instance, having your builder signed up for the Considerate Contractors Scheme (worth 2.25 per cent) is all very well but doesn't really make much difference to climate change. So why is it being included in the Code?

And the requirement for A or A+ rated materials is effectively going to blacklist an awful lot of

C rated materials. I am not sure the PVCu manufacturers have yet twigged this, but the Code has it in for them.

THE FUTURE

Just where we are headed with both the general building regulations and the Code for Sustainable Homes has become a matter of political debate. Ever since I've been involved in construction (30 odd years), the regulations have been getting tighter and more green. The 2016 Code Level 6 target was seen as the ultimate destination on the road map to green building. But Code Level 6 was conceived in different times and five years of recession has changed the agenda somewhat so that many (on the right) now want to see a watering down of these standards because they are seen as a barrier to growth. Whatever the rights and wrongs of this debate, there is every chance that what we get in 2016 will end up being a pale imitation of what we were supposed to be getting when the Code was first formulated. On the ground, endless behind-the-scenes Westminster lobbying translates as deadlines for the introduction of new regulations being delayed or postponed. It's not clear whether the 2013 changes to the energy efficiency regs will be happening in 2013, and the 2016 goal is looking even shakier. Amazing as it may seem, but the definition of what a zero-carbon house actually consists of has never been agreed.

In the meantime, many forward thinking builders are starting to concentrate on the Passivhaus standard as a viable alternative to this Code for Sustainable Homes malarky. Passivhaus is an internationally (alright, German) agreed technical standard which more or less guarantees not only very low energy consumption but very high building standards. It just concentrates on energy use: if people want to add water efficiency measures or renewable energy devices, that is up to them. And it's not subject to the vagaries of politics.

APOCRYPHA

GROUNDWORKS IS THE term used to The original Aprocrypha was written at the same time as the Holy Bible but was felt by the editors of that work not to be quite up to the mark, so they published it separately. This Bible's Apocrypha consists of a few odds and ends that simply don't fit into the rest of the book. Analysing housebuilding as an activity is a bit like trying to figure out where every strand of spaghetti begins and ends. Some are easy to spot, some take some figuring out and some you just can't do, no matter what. So these are the bits to go into the Aprocrypha. All essential stuff of course, but it just doesn't fit neatly into the jigsaw.

BEWARE BUILDING COSTS

You may have a very good idea of what you can afford but, unless you are an experienced developer, you are unlikely to have much idea of how much and what sort of house that money will build. The going rate for new homebuilding varies as you travel around the land – the magazine 'Homebuilding & Renovating' publishes a useful table showing average build costs across the country – search for their Build Cost Calculator – which vary from over £1,830 per sq m for a top notch job in the London area down to under £620 per sq m for a basic job with lots of DIY input somewhere cheap.

Novice builders often make the mistake of clutching at building costs like these and assume that they should divide their budget by the going rate and the answer is the size of house they should build. For instance, if your building budget is £160,000, then – by dividing £160,000 by say £1,000/sq m – you could build a 160 sq m house. You may be very happy with this outcome, but it is also just possible that a 120 sq m house built to a much higher specification would have suited you better. You don't just judge cars by their size and you shouldn't judge houses that way either.

Trouble is that all of the figures that are casually bandied about – none more so than unit area build costs expressed either as £ per sq m or £ per sq ft – are themselves very casually defined. There is no British Standard number to define what a building cost actually is and there isn't really such a thing as an industry standard either. Neither is there complete agreement on just how floor areas of houses should be measured. Different businesses use different methods and this makes a minefield out of the task of comparing costs and setting budgets.

Which Method of Measuring?

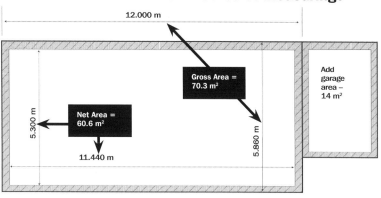

One bungalow, three different methods of measuring it. The net area – I think this is the correct one – shows a floor area of 60.6 sq m. The gross area adds the external walls and comes out at 70.3 sq m. Whilst the third way adds the attached garage, making the floor area total nearly 40 per cent more than the net area.

External walls are 280mm thick, usually 12-15% of the gross floor area

MEASURING FLOOR AREAS

You might at first think that how you go about measuring a floor area is a little bit academic. It is, if you aren't basing your budget and/or designs on some cost per unit area, but the evidence is that a huge number of builders do just that. And for those contemplating buying a timber frame kit, the floor area measurements are habitually used to compare one supplier's product with another, despite the fact that there is every chance you will not be comparing like with like.

The most widely used floor area measurement in Britain is the one which refers to the internal floor area of the house. It expressly excludes the area of the external walls, although (largely for convenience when carrying out the measurements) the area taken up by the internal partition walls is included. This measurement is also known as the net floor area.

GROSS V NET

There is another floor area measurement commonly in use, the gross floor area, which includes the area of the external walls. The effect of including the external wall areas in the calculation is to increase the apparent size of the building by up to 15 per cent as external walls are, these days, usually constructed at thicknesses of 300 mm – more on heavily insulated houses. On the Continent, it's the gross floor area that people usually refer to and many of the kit home suppliers use gross floor areas in their sales literature without being explicit about the fact and there is often no way of telling which area they are talking about other than by measuring it up yourself with a ruler. Using a gross floor area will appear to reduce unit area costs by 15 per cent.

GARAGES

Garages should not be regarded as living space, even when they are integral to the rest of the house. Again, there is no check other than you and your ruler and you need to be very careful when evaluating sales literature of kit home suppliers to see that any integral garage is not included in the overall floor area. In contrast, detached garages are unlikely to be included as part of the floor area of a house in such literature, but here the trick is to exclude their building costs from any overall budget calculations. As a garage will typically cost anything upwards of £6,000 to build, either its inclusion in floor areas or its exclusion from building costs will have a dramatic (and wholly misleading) effect on apparent unit area cost.

Added to possible confusion over net and gross floor areas, the lack of a consistent benchmark for measuring floor areas means that a four-bedroom house with an integral garage could be given as 150 sq m by one method and as much as 200 sq m by another.

GREY AREAS

There are a number of other features worth examining. When you get into the swing of measuring house sizes off plan, you will undoubtedly come across features which are not clear cut. Again there are no hard and fast rules but I would suggest the following assumptions are fair.

■ Cupboard space: storage space such as

under-eaves cupboards which are common when your upper storey is built into the roofspace, should be excluded from internal floor area. However, built-in full height wardrobes should be included as normal living space.

▓ Utility Areas: normally these would be included as part of the living space. Sometimes it is hard to judge where a utility/storage area ends and a garage begins; if you're in this position don't worry too much because at least you understand what the issues are.

▓ Internal Walls: conventionally, these are measured straight through and they are included as part of the internal area.

▓ Stairwells: normally measured straight through on both floors and therefore included as internal floor area as if it was regular circulation space. The exception comes when you have a large open plan arrangement, not often seen in new houses but common in barn conversions where large openings have to be preserved. How do you decide when your ordinary stairwell becomes extraordinary? The rule is that if the upper floor opening is restricted to just the functioning stairwell, then measure straight through on both floors; if the open area extends beyond the immediate staircase, then you must exclude the entire stairwell area from the upper floor area.

BUILDING COSTS

So much for defining the internal floor area. The 'building costs' are even harder to define. There is no official standard but there is a sort of British way of defining building costs. Making long lists and producing definitions is all very well, but what I am trying to get at is that building costs are really just a subgroup of development costs and that to concentrate on building costs to the exclusion of

other costs is potentially disastrous. Like building costs, development costs can vary enormously and in this respect there is no greater variant than the price paid for your building plot. Some building plots are far more expensive to develop than others; problems can arise with bad ground, slopes, difficult service connections, difficult access, trees, legal covenants, intransigent planners – you name it! Now, the art of property developing is to be able to predict these problems and to negotiate a price on the land that reflects the cost of getting around them.

All housebuilders must pay close attention to these extra costs. One advantage a selfbuilder has over a professional is that they have more potential to control the project cashflow. For instance, you may not need to build a garage at all, which could bring substantial savings. You can defer certain non-essential works such as landscaping for many years if cash is tight. You can substantially reduce your financial commitments by roughing it a little bit whilst the house is being built. And, of course, you can reduce costs by undertaking some of the work yourself. But all of this will pale into insignificance if you fail to budget the project correctly in the first place; to achieve significant savings, you need to buy and develop your plot appropriately, be very organised and able to stick tightly to a budget.

ACCESSIBILITY

Provision for disabled access in housing became part of the building regulations in 1999 – in England it's all in Part M. Part M was greeted with enthusiasm by disability campaigners but has had a lukewarm reaction from both the housebuilders and

the general public who feel that this is political correctness run riot. Personally, I'm torn between the extremes.

The little Tory in me reacts negatively to having meddlesome legislation shoved across my soon-to-be-levelled doorstep; then a few days later I find myself talking with a builder whose wife is confined to a wheelchair and, as he describes the struggles they both have in coping with her disability, I suddenly chide myself for being so mean-spirited and wish that the regulations went much further than they do.

Although Part M has been phrased in such a way as to make you think they are designed solely for wheelchair users, the groups who benefit from the changes are far reaching, including the blind and partially sighted and families with pre-school children.

Part of the problem is that there are actually very few severely long-term disabled people around, so making every new house conform to a rigid set of standards in order to meet their requirements seems both expensive and illogical. Perhaps. Perhaps not. It actually costs very little extra to build a Part M compliant house – in contrast it's always frighteningly expensive to retrofit such measures into an existing house. We are building homes that may well have a life expectancy stretching well into the 22nd century and during this lifespan there is every chance that several occupants will come to appreciate some aspect of Part M.

WHAT'S IN PART M?

To comply with Part M every house has to have one level threshold – ideally, but not necessarily, the front door. This doorway should have a minimum clearance of 775 mm between frame and opened door, which translates as having to use an 838

mm door (the old imperial 2 ft 9 in size). A level threshold is defined as one which has a bump of no more than 15 mm under the door.

This entrance should be easily approachable from the outside. In practise this means there should be no steps and no incline of more than 1:20.

Every home must have a downstairs toilet. This room doesn't have to be big enough to accommodate a wheelchair. It's just the door has to be wide enough to get a wheelchair through (2 ft 9 in or 838 mm again).

Ground floor corridors and doorways must be wide enough to allow wheelchair users easy access. There is a trade-off here; wider corridors can have narrower doors but the rule of thumb that seems

Level threshold at under construction. The matwell behind the door is recessed in order to get the levels right and allow the door to open

to have developed is to have all ground floor doors 838 mm wide and to have corridors at least 1050 mm wide.

Power sockets and switches must be placed no lower than 450 mm and no higher than 1200 mm above finished floor level throughout the house.

LEVEL THRESHOLDS

The standard (pre-1999) British front door involved stepping up from the ground into the house – indeed the internal floor level is typically 150 mm – that's two brick courses – higher than the external ground level. Like many standards, this front step had never been a regulation but was simply a detail that had evolved, primarily as a way of keeping water from flowing in under the door. The level threshold changes all. It requires the doorstep to be re-engineered. Many builders will chose to provide a ramped access up to the level threshold but in situations where this is not possible, it will be necessary to sink the entire house by two brick courses. Don't shout it out too loudly but there is actually a small potential cost saving here.

Detailing a level threshold so that it is watertight is in itself a challenge. One of the authors of Part M, Andrew Burke, admitted in a seminar I attended that there were no designs that were totally foolproof: I find that worrying. You need to pay attention to rainwater ingress and to rising damp – the damp proof course around the door needs careful attention, as does thermal cold bridging and,

in some cases, radon and methane penetration into the surrounding cavity. It's easy to install waterproof barriers underneath the front door only for the carpet fitters to come and rip them off later when they find that they can't actually open the door once the carpet has been fitted. This is another problem to be faced. If you pay close attention to your front door detailing, you will probably be fine but, traditionally, it's been a part of housebuilding design that has usually been sorted out on site. Traditionally front doors open inwards and traditionally floor covers have not been an issue because of the step. But level thresholds force you to consider carefully how you will finish the floor internally. Consider it carefully. A sunken mat well seems to be a good solution for many. This covers the area where the door opens.

In fact, we have accumulated a wealth of experience in building level thresholds, mostly in the social housing sector. Habinteg is a housing association which has been specialising in special needs designs since 1970. They have fitted level thresholds to thousands of properties and have not experienced any notable problems. Occasionally, they have to fit a gully across the threshold to collect rainwater but this can normally be avoided by creating a small (one in 40) slope away from the door.

Habinteg's standard detail satisfies the requirements for waterproofing, draught proofing and thermal bridging as well as level access. Instead of a timber

Chapter 15

cill, they use a precast concrete threshold, chamfered on the leading edge so that water runs off. Unlike a conventional timber cill, this concrete threshold sits below the damp proof course – the damp proof membrane is lapped up the inside face of the threshold. The cold bridge is stopped by a 20 mm strip of insulation placed against the inside face of this threshold: this in turn is bridged by quarry tiles.

The joinery manufacturers all produce Part M compliant entrance frames which take most of the sweat out of how to specify them. However, it still leaves the problem of providing a level access up to the door. The way that most builders are 'doing level thresholds' is by

Another way of getting a level threshold is to build a ramp up to the front door.

putting in a ramp outside the front door. This can look completely ridiculous and can also be something of a hazard itself.

The regulations about ramp gradients and corridor widths are spelled out in the approved document and house designers are now up to speed on how these measures should or should not be incorporated into the home.

What is less clear is just how and where exceptions are to be made. Officially, Part M excludes only extensions and alterations to existing dwellings. All new dwellings in England and Wales are meant to comply with Part M access whether they be new builds or conversions. However, there are a number of cases where there

may be an opportunity to waive at least some of the obligations. Most prominent amongst these is the issue of people building flats: there is no requirement to provide lift access to the upper stories, so effectively the disabled will be no better off. There is also expected to be some provision for steeply sloping sites which otherwise might not be developable, without recourse to using stepped access.

LIFETIME HOMES

From the point of view of the disabled, Part M is very tame. It concentrates on making new homes 'visitable' but it does little to make them more 'usable.' The future would seem to lie with a more advanced version of what is already in Part M, known as the Lifetime Homes standard, developed by the Joseph Rowntree Foundation in 1991. There has been a lot of debate about whether this standard should become incorporated into the building regs, but at time of writing this remains unresolved.

What would turn a Part M compliant home into a Lifetime Home?

It's a set of 16 features intended to make homes readily adaptable for disabled users.

■ 1 Car parking space should be easily capable of enlargement to attain a width of 3300 mm
■ 2 The distance from the car parking space to the home should be kept to a minimum and should be level or gently sloping
■ 3 The approach to all entrances

should be level or gently sloping

▥ 4 All entrances should be illuminated and the main entrance should be level and covered

▥ 5 Communal stairs should provide easy access and where levels are reached by lift, the lift should be fully wheelchair accessible

▥ 6 Doorways and hallways have to be at least 750 mm wide, or at least 900 mm wide when the approach is head-on

▥ 7 Dining and living areas should have space for turning a wheelchair and there should be adequate circulation space for wheelchair users

▥ 8 The living space should be at the level of the entrance

▥ 9 If homes have two or more storeys, there should be space at entrance level which could be used as a convenient bed space

▥ 10 There should be a WC at the entrance level of the property and, in larger properties, there should be drainage provision enabling a shower to be fitted in the future

▥ 11 The design of the property should provide for a reasonable route for a potential hoist from a main bedroom to the bathroom

▥ 12 The design of the property should incorporate a provision for a future stair lift and a suitably identified space for a through-the-floor lift from the ground to the first floor

▥ 13 Walls in the bathrooms and toilets should be capable of taking adaptations such as handrails

▥ 14 The bathroom should be designed to incorporate ease of access to essential amenities such as the bath, basin and WC

▥ 15 Living room windows should begin 800 mm from the floor or lower and be easy to open

▥ 16 Switches, sockets, ventilation and service controls should be situated between 450 mm and 1200 mm from the floor

Whilst many people bridle at the thought of being told how their house should be designed, most of these steps are easily incorporated into a new house and cost either very little or nothing at all. They really only become difficult to incorporate in smaller homes where some of the space requirements become hard to meet, in particular the requirement for a downstairs bathroom to be capable of adaptation for wheelchair users, plus the requirement for a shower drain in the downstairs bathroom.

SECURITY & SAFETY

The average private dwelling currently suffers an attempted break-in every 12 years and over half of these attempts are successful. Of course, it all depends on where you live. Some quiet locations still exist where no one locks their front doors, whilst there are some inner city areas which seem to get burgled regularly.

Wherever you live and whatever the future holds, burglary is not a problem that is likely to go away and anyone considering building a new house would be foolish not to consider the matter very carefully.

THE BURGLAR

As you might suspect, the typical burglar is a young male but you might be surprised to learn that he is not part of a well-organised gang but usually a lone wolf whose break-in is often done on the spur-of-the-moment, when he sees the opportunity arise. There is really no reason to adopt a fatalistic attitude because,

although it's entirely true that if someone really wants to get into a house they can, 90 per cent of the time they won't bother if you go to the trouble of making life difficult for them.

Our young burglar's main concern is not to get caught in the act and to this end he values being able to get in, and out, quickly and preferably unseen. Another surprising statistic thrown up is that as many as 40 per cent of burglaries take place while the home is occupied. You'd think this would be amazingly risky for our burglar but it only takes a few seconds to come in through an open door and walk out again with something like a radio or a smart phone and you may not even realise that you've been burgled. If you are worried about this sort of thing happening, get a dog.

With regard to new housebuilding, current thinking focuses on the following areas:

▥ Site layout
▥ Preventing access to the rear of the house
▥ Decent locks fitted to ground floor windows and doors
▥ Burglar alarms where risk is high
▥ Security lighting.

SITE LAYOUT

Although this area has more relevance to estates than to single dwellings, it's worth mentioning what they are on about. Dark corners and unlit alleyways should be avoided and houses should be sited where their neighbours can see who is coming and going. There is often little the individual housebuilder can do about this, though it is possible that consideration can be given to the issue when there are two or more houses to be sited near each other.

One obvious point that the

Chapter 15

professionals have tended to overlook is to locate the most widely used room in the house – usually the kitchen – at the front, so that the occupants can see who is coming and going out on the street. However, this arrangement remains an extremely unpopular layout in this country; we still prefer our kitchens to be by the back door.

RESTRICTING ACCESS

The rear of the house is the preferred area of entry for burglars. This is largely because the back of the house is almost always more private and is often screened from neighbours. A burglary often starts with a casual casing of the front of the house; if it looks as though there is no one at home, the second stage will be to go round the back and take a closer look. Only when they're convinced the coast is clear will the break-in proceed. If access to the back of the house is impeded, then the would-be burglar may abort the job at this early stage in the hope of there being easier pickings further up the road.

A 2 m fence and a stout gate – even without a bolt – will provide a considerable measure of defence against unwanted prowling. A tip from my 2010 Milton Keynes benchmark house is to use a 2 m fence but to have the top 300 mm made up of a see-through trellis which is just as difficult to get over but allows you to see who is walking along behind it. Back gardens can be protected, to a lesser extent, by walling or hedging them in. Plan in any obstructions that will at least slow down the progress of a potential burglar. However, bear in mind that a fully enclosed garden, once breached, makes an ideal spot for our burglar to force an unseen rear entry so if your garden is going to be enclosed for security reasons, you need to do it well.

ROBUST LOCKS

It is an NHBC standard to have five-lever locks on all external doors and to have window locks as well. The relevant standard here for door locks is BS 3621: you may even get a small discount from your insurers if your locks meet this standard. At least one exit – usually the front door – must be protected by a night latch (Yale-type locks), which can be opened from the inside without a key; this is to aid escape in case of fire. The idea is to lock the door on the night latch when the house is occupied and to use the five-lever mortise lock when the house is empty. Window locks used to be fitted as standard on volume joinery, but a change to the fire regs in 2002, calling for all first floor windows to be openable internally, has thrown this all into a state of confusion. Ideally, you want downstairs windows to be key-lockable and upstairs windows to be openable easily without having to find a key, but the chances of your joinery supplier getting all right are not high!

FRENCH AND PATIO DOORS

It is marginally easier to force a door inwards than to prise it out but it is likely to be rather noisy. Most front doors open inwards. However, note that double-doors (French doors) are particularly easy to force in or prise outwards; most French doors open outwards and if you fit them be sure to fit decent sliding bolts to the top and bottom of both doors. For extra security, make these lockable bolts. Sliding patio doors are generally a much more secure (and draughtproof) alternative (though not half as elegant); however, many break-ins have occurred where the patio door frame has been levered out of its seating, having only ever been held in by six short screws or, sometimes, nothing more than mastic sealant.

GLASS

The current building regulations will ensure that you have to fit double-glazed sealed units, and the safety standards on glazing insist that safety glass is fitted to all doors, windows next to doors and all glazing less than 800 mm above the internal floor level. Safety glass is expensive, costing nearly twice as much as ordinary float glass. It comes in two varieties, toughened or laminated, and they perform slightly differently.

Toughened is harder to break but when it breaks it collapses into small nodules, whereas laminated glass has a sheet of plastic sandwiched between two layers of ordinary glass; this makes it harder to break through (from the burglar's point of view) and is therefore slightly more secure. The police are big fans of laminated glass, and suggest that it should be fitted wherever there is glass next to an accessible lock, but as this includes virtually every ground floor opening window it would be an expensive option.

NEW SECURITY STANDARDS

Factory-glazed windows are available which meet a new British security standard, BS 7950, also known as Secured by Design. Rather than just testing the individual locks or the glass, BS 7950 tests the whole window assembly in situ. Typically such a window will have laminated glass on the external face and shootbolt espagnolette locking mechanisms. To get windows to this standard, they really need to have been factory glazed but this doesn't mean they have to be plastic – most of the big timber joinery manufacturers now produce BS 7950 windows.

BURGLAR ALARMS

There is a huge variety of different alarm

systems out there and it's not easy deciding what to fit. It is usually cheaper to install a wired system, which is particularly well suited to new housing as the wiring can be concealed during first-fix stage. Installation quotes for a four-bedroom house are likely to vary from £500 for a basic system based on a mixture of internal infrared detectors and contact points to over £1,000 for external vibration detectors which are triggered by interference with doors and windows. Should you not want to go to the expense of installing an alarm, as an alternative, the wiring can be first-fixed in a day for between £100 and £200, so that the intruder detectors can be fitted at a later date without disruption to the decorations. Burglar alarms are eligible for zero-rating of VAT when building a new home.

Fixing a burglar alarm should not be beyond the capabilities of a competent DIYer and there are a number of systems designed for just this. DIY alarms usually consist of a control panel, the detectors and an external siren. The wired systems are the most reliable and are probably best suited to new builds. However, wireless alarms have their advocates and are easily fitted as an afterthought. The standard wireless systems still need mains connections for both the control panel and the siren but the latest generation work entirely on radio signalling: the siren and the control panels are solar powered and you activate the alarm by using a remote control.

More features tend to add to the cost but it is still possible to get a well-featured wireless system for under £200, such as Yale's High Security Alarm System which can handle up to 24 zones. Zones are the areas covered by individual detectors and most burglar alarms allow you to arm or disarm any of your zones individually. This is useful if you have pets or if you want only the downstairs armed when you are upstairs at night. Better systems have a capability of checking that all component parts are working – a feature sometimes referred to as a 24 hour zone.

DETECTORS

The detectors on which burglar alarms are based come in a number of guises. The two commonest are the passive infrared (PIR) detector, which is triggered by movement across its path, and the door or window-opening detector that is set off when a magnetic contact is broken. You can also get detectors based on pressure pads – typically these would be under a doormat and would be triggered when someone unexpected treads on it. You can give great thought to just which detector to put where and still get it all wrong.

Many a break-in now occurs via an upstairs window: the thieves never go downstairs because they reckon it will be alarmed, so they just ransack the bedrooms before leaving the same way they came in. So maybe it pays to have lots of detection zones but possibly only if you are very confident in your ability to operate the system.

If you've never lived with a burglar alarm, you might be forgiven for thinking that they are the last word in home security. However, the consequences of fitting an alarm can be fairly tortuous for the householder and their neighbours. All systems are set to make a loud noise for a few minutes; false alarms will make you very unpopular and false alarms do happen, so a burglar alarm is not without its problems. A recent police estimate reckoned that no less than nine out of ten ringing alarms are actually false alarms and the police now have a policy, in effect in most areas from 2006, of withdrawing their response after more than three false alarms.

MONITORED ALARMS

If you have a very remote site or are not entirely happy about a 105-decibel alarm ringing when a mouse crosses the floor, the next step up the security ladder is to get a monitored alarm. These link your house via the phone lines either to the local police or to a security firm. If you want the police to monitor your alarm, then the system must be installed by a company approved by one of two bodies; NACOSS (National Approval Council of Security Systems) or SSAIB (Security Systems and Alarm Inspection Board). Needless to say NACOSS or SSAIB approved systems cost rather more than unapproved ones. Or as one wag put it to me, it's daylight robbery what these guys get away with. Monitored systems also carry an annual charge which is likely to be in excess of £150; they are only available if two key holders besides the occupants live close by and are prepared to be called out in the middle of the night.

MOVEMENT SENSORS

Alarm systems don't have to just concern themselves with making loud noises or sending messages off to police stations. You can also rig up detector beams running across the front and the back of your house which set off a buzzer inside when they are crossed. They vary in sophistication from simple passive infrared beams like the ones used to trip lights, to multi-height beams running between two concealed posts which aim to be cat and fox proof. The well designed systems will give you fairly reliable intruder alerts: a poor system, tripping out every time a bird flies by, will just make you paranoid.

Why bother with a movement sensor? Well, I would have tended to ask the same

Chapter 15

question until my mum had one installed a few years back. She loves it; she has one out the front and one out the back and she can tell the difference between the postman and the paperboy by the time they take to cross the beam. At night, the system is switched from buzzer to warning light in the bedroom and once it picked up a prowler round the back of the property and enabled her to alert a neighbour before any damage was done.

CAR PARKING

Both integral and detached garages can be included in whole house intruder alarm systems, but this tends to be very inconvenient; the car has to be left outside whilst the alarm is deactivated (usually inside the house). It rather defeats the purpose of these remote control devices for garage doors.

OTHER MEASURES

Door chains (from £3) and viewers (from £4) are becoming more common, and are recommended by the police. Surely the most cheeky is the fake 'Protected by Burglar Alarm' bell casing which you screw on to your outside wall. Available at around £8 from DIY sheds.

SECURITY LIGHTING

Passive Infrared (PIR) detectors, similar to the ones used on internal movement sensors in burglar alarms, are also used on external lighting. These can be very useful around dark entrances although the halogen bulbs (sometimes 500W) can be so bright that you dazzle passers-by and tend to make them think you live in a high-security prison. There are some very cheap versions on the market (at around £10-£15) which are best avoided; at around £30 you start to get ones where it is possible to change the bulb. Better

forms of external lighting exist that can be wired to PIR switches, as well as manual override switches, which give pleasant external illumination as well as some form of security .

There are also a number of products that can be used to give the effect of occupation when the house is empty. For around £20, you can buy a gizmo which fits in between a lightbulb and its lamp holder that acts as a light-sensitive switch, useful for simulating occupation when you are away.

SHUTTER PROTECTION

To fit security roll-down shutters to every opening on a detached house would cost over £6,000 so no way is this a cheap and cheerful option. Indeed it looks pretty severe as well, but if you are away a lot and have particular reason to fear intruders, then shutters are very secure. They don't work well with outward opening windows (think about it) and are best designed around either sliding sash style or tilt and turn windows. On the Continent, shutter protection is often taken as a given, but then on the Continent windows only ever seem to open inwards. Strange to reflect how different something as basic as a window can be.

SAFES

Home safes are available from £150 for a wall fitting one and from £200 for one bolted to the floor. Placing a safe in an existing house can be awkward but in a new house it's a doddle – if you've planned ahead for it.

FIRE SAFETY

The fire brigades get called out to around 60,000 house fires every year and around 500 people die each year in house fires in this country. And many of these deaths

could be easily prevented with a few basic precautions. Fortunately, most of these have been encoded in our building regs so if you are undertaking a newbuild or a major renovation, you will have to build them in.

The purpose of the fire safety regulations is not to stop buildings burning down but rather to allow the occupants time enough to escape from them when they do start burning down. One of the long held prejudices against timber-frame building is that people think it will be more likely to catch on fire but this really is not so as the timber elements are almost always enclosed in a layer of inert plasterboard which is enough to delay the onset of fire by around half an hour.

The real danger in house fires is caused when soft furnishings catch fire, and the smoke quickly engulfs the occupants. Whilst there has been a steady introduction of non-flammable materials into the home furnishing market, the biggest step forward in the world of housebuilding came in 1992 when smoke detectors became mandatory. Since then, all new homes have been required to have smoke detectors not just fitted but mains-operated with a battery backup as a fail safe.

Smoke detectors cost around £20 and can be wired into the house lighting circuit. Electricians are by now au fait with what's required. The regs are that there should be smoke alarms on each storey and that they shouldn't be further than 3 m from any bedroom door, so that some larger designs will require two or more on the upstairs landing.

What the regs don't go into is the different types of smoke detector you can choose. The cheapest and commonest are the ionisation detectors which are very sensitive to small particles of smoke produced by flaming fires, such as chip pans, and will detect this type of fire before the smoke gets too thick. But you can also specify optical ones which are more effective at detecting larger particles of smoke produced by slow-burning fires, such as smouldering foam-filled upholstery and overheated PVC wiring. Optical detectors are more prone to going off in error; either the mirror gets dirty or thunderflies get in.

A third and possibly more useful type is the heat sensor which gets triggered when temps reach around 55 deg C – fit it in the kitchen but not too near the cooker. Whatever you choose, they have to be interconnected so that when one is triggered, they all go into action. Some smoke alarms have additional capabilities, such as emergency lights and silence buttons to override false alarms.

Other safety features you might choose to look at are the provision of fire blankets in the kitchen and extinguishers in garages and near open fires. Your best bet is to stick with local firms which offer maintenance: look in Yellow Pages under Fire Extinguishing Equipment.

THREE-STOREY HOUSES
Provided every room opens onto a hallway or corridor, a two storey house is not going to have any problems meeting fire safety regulations. But there is a critical safety level, defined as having a floor 4.5 m above ground level, when it becomes necessary to beef up your escape procedures. One of the principal requirements relates to how your main staircase runs through the house. Ideally, the staircase should lead directly to the front entrance door within an enclosed hallway: what is frowned upon are open-plan arrangements, particularly when the staircase exits via the kitchen (reckoned to

be the highest risk area).

You also need to consider how to protect the stairwell from encroaching fire. You have to make the entire stairwell what is called a fully protected enclosure; this means that the walls around the landing and stairwell must be rated at 30 minutes fire resistance and the doors opening onto the landing must be rated at 20 minutes. You also need to consider the floor construction which also needs to meet the 30 minute fire rating.

If you are undertaking a new build or a major renovation, it's not difficult to meet these standards; in fact in terms of walls and floors it's quite difficult not to meet them. The only place where you are likely to come unstuck is on the doors that need to be uprated to fire door standard, although this is achievable with a suitably-rated paint or varnish. The requirement to fit door closers was dropped in the last iteration of the fire regs, partly because no one ever kept the damn things on once the job had been finalled, and partly because of the success of smoke detectors.

SPRINKLERS
In 2010, Wales passed legislation requiring all new properties to be protected by sprinklers. The new requirement is due to come into force in late 2013. And there is every likelihood that other parts of the UK will follow suit, although nothing is currently going through the legislative process.

WHY BOTHER WITH SPRINKLERS?
The short answer is that they save lives. Sprinklers also reduce the number of serious burns and injury cases, and the amount of damage caused by house fires. The latest research from the American National Fire Protection Association shows that the death-per-fire rate is dramatically

reduced when sprinklers are present, and that property damage is reduced from an average of $17,000 per fire down to $4,000. Furthermore, when sprinklers are installed, subsequent fires are almost always contained in one room, whereas in homes without sprinklers, fire spreads to other rooms in 75 per cent of cases. Fire fighters take time to arrive after a fire has started, and end up using far more water to put out the fire, which itself causes damage, so sprinklers actually work to reduce the risk to lives and property.

HOW DO THEY WORK?
Fire sprinklers are only activated when the temperature in the room in which a fire is burning exceeds the preset temperature of the sprinkler head - nominally 68 deg C. Sprinklers operate as individual heat sensors, meaning that water is only released in the area where there is a fire. They are not activated by smoke. Often, in a room with two sprinkler heads, only one actually operates. Sprinklers typically deliver 60l/minute (compared to 1000l/min from a fire hose): systems are usually plumbed with copper pipe or rigid cPCV pipe, teed off the rising main. Ideally they require a 32 mm cold feed into house as the systems need a good flow.

All that you see in the house is a series of 100 mm white discs, protruding down just below the ceiling. The typical area covered by each sprinkler head is 15 sq m, so only the largest rooms would require more than one outlet.

COSTS
In a new dwelling, the cost works out at around £15 to £20 per sq m, or around £200 per outlet. That's equivalent to approximately £3,000 to cover every room in a four-bedroomed house. In addition to this, there are also the costs of an annual

Chapter 15

maintenance contract. However, advocates point out that the use of sprinklers can sometimes reduce costs elsewhere, especially where there are expensive fire doors to be installed instead.

THE DOWNSIDE

There are numerous objections to enforcing the uptake of sprinkler systems. Unsurprisingly, the main ones are connected with the costs involved. New housebuilding is already incredibly expensive and it's constantly being loaded down with additional costs being imposed by government regulations — insulation, acoustical works, safety glass, thermostatic taps, disabled access requirements, etc. And the existing building regulations already call for the use of smoke detectors and various passive fire protection measures which have been extremely effective in reducing the number of fatalities and injuries.

Whilst no one would argue that sprinklers can't be a good solution for certain designs (such as open plan areas and loft platforms), there is a widespread feeling that the wholesale adoption of sprinklers is akin to using a very expensive sledgehammer to crack a small nut. Newly-built homes are inherently much less at risk from fire damage than most of the existing housing stock, and there is a feeling that adding two to three per cent to their build cost in order to make them safer still is focusing resources in the wrong area.

There are also worries about sprinkler systems malfunctioning. Industry literature suggests this is unlikely: 'Data collected over 30 years suggest that the chances of a sprinkler head malfunctioning are estimated to be extremely remote, perhaps no more than 1 in 16 million'. Whilst this may appear to be a reassuringly unlikely

possibility, it doubtless doesn't account for cases where systems are triggered by malicious tampering or by accidental damage.

There are also construction-related issues to consider. A sprinkler system requires a 125 mm depth ceiling cavity, which is easier to incorporate into some designs than others. Solid floor and ceiling systems (pre-cast concrete, SIPs) already work with added service voids, but these are typically less than 50 mm deep. Having to widen these voids to 125 mm would make their use unviable in many cases. To be fair, there are often ways around these issues: sprinklers can be ducted through walls and set to release sideways if ceiling location is difficult. One solution may be to install a partial system, although the cost saving may not be pro rata.

If you decide to install a sprinkler system at home, do ensure that the company you choose is working to the industry standard (BS9251) and is preferably FIRAS accredited. A useful starting point of contact is the Fire Sprinkler Association 0118 971 2322 or www. firesprinklers.info.

SOUND ADVICE

Our appreciation of sound is very personal and therefore highly subjective. What annoys some people gives pleasure to others. There are sounds which most people wouldn't even notice that can drive others completely nutty. How do you legislate for such a state of affairs? With a great deal of difficulty, of course. It falls on Part E of the Englishbuilding regs to provide guidance and it is a very complicated part indeed.

This section of the Housebuilder's Bible looks at the background behind sound reduction measures for builders. Guidance on how to achieve better soundproofing is

to be found lodged in two earlier sections on internal walls and internal floors, both back in Chapter 7. But do try to wade through this section before you decide what to do about your walls and floors; I think it will be worth it, if only to learn what the hell a decibel is. Or dB.

Do you know why the "B" in dB is capitalised? It's because the unit is named after Alexander Graham Bell, who invented the telephone and then founded Bell Laboratories where it was launched, if you can do such a thing as launch a measurement unit. Now go figure why a kiloWatt also has an intercap.

ACOUSTICS FOR BEGINNERS

Sound is a form of energy. It moves in waves through the air and it can be absorbed and transmitted through solids as well. The human ear is adept at picking up sound in a range of frequencies and at different volumes. There are more qualities to sound than just frequency and volume but we'll concern ourselves with just these two, as it's their interplay that makes much of the debate about soundproofing so intriguing.

Frequencies are measured in hertz (Hz) and kilohertz (kHz): these correspond to the wavelengths that various sounds travel at. Low frequency sound has a very long wavelength; high frequency sound consists, conversely, of energy moving at very short wavelengths. Humans tend to hear sounds between 50 Hz and 15,000 Hz (15 kHz); this upper limit reduces with age.

Sound energy is measured in decibels, routinely written down as dB. The decibel scale is non-linear: it doubles every 3dB . However, what we perceive as sound is a little different: humans perceive a doubling or halving of volume roughly every 10dB. Thus a 60dB noise would sound, subjectively, twice as loud as a 50dB one, which, in turn, sounds roughly twice as loud as a 40dB one.

Whilst the ability to hear sounds is regarded as one of life's more pleasurable experiences, we also worry inordinately about hearing noises we don't want to hear. Noise is defined as unwanted sound. As regards building design, our concerns are usually to minimise sound transfer through walls and floors.

Sound energy is said to transfer through buildings in three different ways. The easiest to understand is airborne sound. This is how sound gets to us when we speak to one another. If there is a wall between us when we speak, then some of the airborne sound gets absorbed by the wall and the amount of sound absorbed by the wall is said to be so many decibels of sound reduction. Thus, if a wall is said to have an airborne sound reduction level of 40dB, it means that, should a 60dB conversation be taking place on the other side of it, you would only hear about 20dBs on your side.

But sound is capable of travelling through solids as well. In certain instances, walls and, in particular, floors have a nasty habit of not absorbing sound at all but instead acting as a conduit for sounds. Impact sounds, as we call them, are usually mechanical in origin: tapping, hammering, drumming or just walking across floors with hard heels. The actual volume of the sound may not be that high but a floor without adequate impact sound insulation might as well not be there.

Paul Goring, head of NHBC's acoustic department, seen here with an impact sound testing device

The third method of noise transfer is called flanking sound. It occurs when airborne or impact sounds get to you via an indirect route. Consider for a moment a wall between two adjacent rooms. Now suppose that you soundproofed this wall so well that no noise was capable of travelling through it. You would still be able to hear noise in the other room because sounds can travel via other routes. Maybe via the corridor shared by the doorways of these two rooms, or via their windows, or transmitted through the ceiling overhead. These are flanking sounds.

Another way of looking at flanking sound is that is represents the difference between the sound reduction performance of an element (i.e. a wall or a floor) tested in a laboratory and the as-built situation. There is a close parallel here with what happens with thermal insulation when the designed-for U value of an element is compromised by cold bridging.

It wasn't until I spent an afternoon witnessing an acoustic test that I really began to understand the difference between the different sorts of sound transfer. Paul Goring, currently NHBC's head of acoustics, was testing a floor between two flats in a newly built nurses' hostel and it took him a good couple of hours to do it. On floors, it is routine to test for both airborne sound and impact sound and the procedure for testing them is a little different and worth describing.

To measure airborne sound transmission through a floor, he placed a multidirectional loudspeaker in the upper room and set it to pump out 100db of noise: 'pink noise' it is referred to as, a horrible cocktail of every audible frequency you can think of. At 100db you really don't want to be in that room for a moment longer than you have to be: even with ear defenders on, it's physically unpleasant.

The measuring equipment was in the room below. Airborne sound insulation is measured by taking the difference between the output from the pink noise and the sound in the receiving room. Your decibel rating for the floor in

Chapter 15

Wall and Floor Sound Reduction

Engineered 'i' joist minimum depth 240 mm supported by timber framed walls

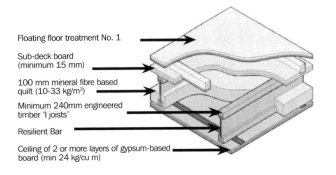

Floating floor treatment No. 1

Sub-deck board
(minimum 15 mm)

100 mm mineral fibre based
quilt (10-33 kg/m³)

Minimum 240mm engineered
timber 'I joists'

Resilient Bar

Ceiling of 2 or more layers of gypsum-based
board (min 24 kg/cu m)

The Robust Standard Details show methods of building in 50dB sound reduction into walls and floors. Here's the RSD for timber I joist floors, showing that it can be done, even if it is multi-layered and therefore rather expensive

question is the difference between the two measurements. Straightforward enough. The airborne tests consist of five different samples from around the receiving room, each taken from two different locations for the pink noise box in the room above.

Impact noise is measured in a different way. The noise is made by a series of hammers inside a wooden box, resembling a mechanical drum machine, which you sit on the floor and then let rip. Impact noise is conventionally measured directly: you don't subtract the noise made in one room from the noise received in another: you just make a British Standard sort of impacty-noise from the drum machine and measure how much gets through the floor. Impact noise is only ever considered on floors.

So there is an important distinction here. When you see decibel-rating tables, the airborne decibel ratings are for sound reduction capabilities. Therefore the higher the decibel rating on airborne sound reduction, the better: a 50dB-rated floor is much better than a 45dB-rated one. But for impact sound ratings, the reverse is true.

The rating just tells you how much sound got through the floor: the lower the figure here, the better.

Flanking sound isn't measured directly, but it contributes to the overall scores and makes significant differences to the scores between lab tests and field tests. You don't experience flanking sound as something different to airborne sound or impact sound but when there is a lot of noise being made, you can sometimes be aware of it. In my case, I was able to actually feel the walls vibrating when the pink noise machine was on. This was flanking sound in action.

MEASURING UP

The equipment that measures sound – or noise, as it would be referred to in this instance – is expensive and sophisticated. Paul Goring uses a Danish system costing around £15,000. It measures sound at 16 different frequencies and gives 16 different readings that have to be interpreted and analysed. This is where things start to get very complicated. Legislators want a yes or no answer to the question, 'Does this floor

or wall meet a defined sound reduction standard?' The regs invariably hone in on a pass rate expressed in decibels but the data comes in measured over 16 different frequencies, some of which may look OK and others not.

What has evolved over the years is a number of calculations that offer a 'best fit' answer to the riddle of how much noise is being made at any one time. None of them are perfect and there are big debates about which measuring systems should be used. Normally, this really wouldn't be of concern to anyone outside the cosy world of acoustics but during 2003 this debate took centre stage in the formulation of the latest set of building regulations, because the different ways of sampling decibels give some widely different results.

There are four main methods of measuring sound reduction used in Britain. If proof were needed that acousticians do not come from this planet, these different methods are referred to by a complex sequence of letters and punctuation marks, some italicised, some suffixed. When they speak English, these labels roll off their tongues in capitals and don't sound so weird, so I will be anglicising them, if only to help my typesetter.

The simplest rating, written as Rw and referred to by all as 'RW', is derived from laboratory measurements of airborne noise. It's a useful tool for considering the best performance you can get out of a particular construction detail but it doesn't look at the likely performance of a wall or floor in a building: flanking noises are ignored. By way of example, the simplest (and cheapest) timber joist floor with 18 mm chipboard over it and 12.5 mm of plasterboard nailed under it, will have an RW sound reduction rating of around 35-38dB.

The next sound reduction rating, written as DnT,w (known as 'DNTW') is worked out from the measured airborne sound reduction through a wall or floor element on site, rather than in a lab. Not surprisingly, the DNTW ratings tend to be lower than the Rw ratings, usually by around 5dB. That's the flanking sound effect. DNTW ruled the roost as far as the building regs went until the 2003 changes. But because of various bits of research undertaken in recent years, it was felt simple DNTW didn't adequately reflect the types of noise that are currently being made through our party walls and floors so a variation, giving far more emphasis to low frequency sounds, has been unveiled, known as the Ctr or CTR bias.

Ctr is additional to, not a replacement for, DNTW so that the new regs require you to provide 45d of airborne sound reduction (DnT,w + Ctr). It's complicated, but not that complicated, and if you look at it long enough you can begin to see the funny side. The point about DNTW plus Ctr measurements is that it creates a higher standard to meet because low frequencies are harder to block. However,

the Ctr effect is not uniform: on some structures, it may make the figure just 2 or 3dB lower; on others it may be as much as 10 or 15dB lower. Our basic timber floor is particularly badly affected by Ctr bias: its sound reduction rating, depending on the low frequency performance, can fall to around 20dB.

There is a fourth measuring scale used solely for impact sound. It's written L'nT,w: gets called LNTW. Impact sound is only measured on floors and, as already discussed, is measured directly rather than being subtracted from a source sound, so the lower the dB rating, the less noise gets through the floor.

In summary, let's take our very basic floor and see how it stacks up on the different scales. It's a timber-joisted floor with just a chipboard cover and plasterboard nailed to it underneath. It scores:

▓ 38db on the RW airborne scale
▓ 33db on the DNTW airborne scale, (roughly −5dB difference between lab and field)
▓ 20dB on the DTNW plus CTR airborne scale (Ctr of, say, -13dB)
▓ 70dB on the LNTW impact scale

None of these are any good at all! To find out how to improve them, check the section called Sound advice back in Chapter 7.

MINISTRY OF SOUND

You can, hopefully, see that sound reduction levels expressed in simple decibels don't actually mean very much unless you know which scale they are referring to. The latest switch to the added Ctr measurements has divided the acoustics community; although everybody agrees that bass sounds are more prevalent, not everyone agrees that this new

measurement system is the best way of approaching it.

When the building regs were revamped in 2003, the actual sound reduction levels demanded by the regulations appeared to get less but this was because of the new method of measuring them. However, the changes are not uniform and there are some constructions that would have failed the old regs that now pass the new ones, so the improvement in standards is neither consistent nor universal.

However, it was another aspect of the changes in regulations which took centre stage in 2003. That was the insistence that not only should party walls and floors be built to the new standards but that they should be tested on site to show that they had in fact achieved these standards.

But when the powers-that-be first ran their suggestions past the housebuilders, pandemonium broke out. Not only was acoustic testing reckoned to cost around £600 per test, but also rectifying failures in already completed schemes would be a nightmare. Years of acoustic testing had shown that there is often a large gap between the designed-for sound reduction and that actually achieved. The acousticians felt strongly that it wasn't enough simply to tighten the old standards: to improve matters significantly, you had to test, which, coincidentally, was jolly good news for acousticians.

Well a fudge was worked out. After much badgering and a very rushed research programme during 2003, the government accepted a Super Level sound proofing standard, to be known henceforth as the Robust Standard Details or RSDs. This sets an airborne soundproofing target a full 5dB better than that required just to meet the regs for new party walls and floors but − crucially − doesn't call for any testing.

So what emerged when the regs were

Chapter 15

set in stone were four different levels of soundproofing:

▦ Level 1: 40dB (Rw scale) airborne sound reduction. Applies to internal walls and floors within individual homes. No testing required.

▦ Level 2: 43dB (DNTw + Ctr scale) airborne sound reduction plus (floors only) 64dB (LNTw scale) maximum impact noise. Applies to party walls and floors between flats and attached houses when they have undergone renovation. Requires testing.

▦ Level 3: 45dB (DNTw + CTR scale) airborne sound reduction plus (floors only) 62dB (LNTw scale) maximum impact noise. Applies to party walls and floors between flats and attached houses if they are newbuild. Requires testing.

▦ Level 4: 50dB (DNTw + CTR scale) airborne sound reduction plus (floors only) 57dB (LNTw scale) maximum impact noise. A series of approved robust standard details (known as RSDs) that can be used by new builders (only) who wish to avoid the expense of testing.

How you go about meeting these new standards really lies beyond the scope of this book. If you want to use the RSD route to compliance, you have to buy a copy of their handbook (currently £65) and you also have to register each plot for £30 as a way of showing compliance. The business running it is called Robust Details. The RSD documents have details for walls and floors made out of timber and steel as well as the more obvious masonry materials. What is worth pointing out is that there is a big jump between Level 1 and Level 2. It may look like a mere 5dB difference but notice that the scales are different and 40dB on the Rw scale is probably only about 30dB on the more exacting DNTw + CTR scale. So there is lots of room to improve the very basic

standard found in Part E2 of the regs, which applies to individual homes.

BARN CONVERSIONS

Many people reading this book start out with a dream of living in the countryside in a house built to their own designs. It's a widely shared aspiration but, for the majority, it will never become more than that. Britain has some of the tightest rural planning rules in the world and it's simply not possible to pitch up in Chipping Butty and build a house in Farmer Giles's meadow. What building plots do come up are more likely to be the back garden of an existing house which may not be quite what you had in mind.

But there is a chink in the planning armor. Whilst the planners won't countenance building from scratch, they are keen to see existing rural buildings get a new lease of life. There are several hundred thousand farms dotted around the British countryside. Virtually every one has outbuildings used to store cattle or grain or for various farmy-type things and a huge number of these are now lying empty and unused. Now conservation bodies love these old barns and want to see them survive in some form but there is simply no call for them with modern farming. Such is the demand for rural building plots that people are willing to pay enormous sums to convert these barns into homes. In doing so, they have created an entirely new form of housing that seems to be unique to Britain. It is both ancient and modern. Ancient in that it involves restoring centuries old structures often using traditional techniques. Modern in that the space being created is often far more like an urban loft apartment than a

traditional home as served up to us by the mass market developers.

The world of converting redundant buildings is very different to new housebuilding. You have to be prepared to have things imposed on you which you might think are unreasonable and unfair. The very fact that we are allowed to convert redundant buildings rather than just pulling them down demonstrates that we are engaging with the British obsession with preserving the past, and the planners have a number of ways of making sure that certain rules are adhered to in exchange for the right to create a home in a place you otherwise would not be able to. Chief amongst these is the idea that what you build should continue to look like what was there before. And not in any way look like a conventional house. This goes for conversions of nearly all redundant buildings with some degree of historic interest; chapels, schools and pubs to name but three. But the bulk of single home conversions are going on in rural barns as these are by far the commonest rural structure up for conversion.

THE RULES

▦ reuse existing doorways, even if they were designed for carts

▦ don't block up existing openings

▦ no masonry chimneys – stainless steel flues acceptable only if kept away from the ridge

▦ as few new windows as possible – and any new windows should be as plain as possible

▦ no changes to the roof. Certainly no dormers and preferably no rooflights. If rooflights, preferably on the side no one sees

▦ repair the original material wherever possible.

▦ If replaced, use something similar. If

it's timber, it must be timber that matches the old style.

What a lot of barn designers end up doing is building in a large glazed screen area where once stood the main barn door. This is often inset into the structure – this borrows a little extra light for the rooms opening off the hallway behind the glazed screen. No matter that what you end up with doesn't look a bit like a farm building, but it does make a very attractive structure. In fact the barn conversion, particularly the timber barn conversion, has rapidly attained iconic status as a fashion item in its own right. Whilst the history of the original barns has been documented by the likes of RW Brunskill, the history of barn conversions has yet to be written.

Barns tend to come in two distinct flavours, timber and stone. Timber predominates in the south and east where they tended to be built for threshing and storing corn.

Before and during. The above shot, taken in Feb 2000, shows a timber barn on its last legs. By June that year, the whole structure had been transformed. You could easily be mistaken for thinking this was a new house taking shape: basically, it is. Only the original posts and beams remain from the original structure

Stone barns are more common in the north and the west – the Scots refer to them as steadings – where they were most often used as cattle sheds. As cattle don't like going up stairs, the stone barns tend to be single storey, the timber ones are routinely two storey or, more accurately, high enough to accommodate a second storey. There are of course masses of exceptions to this rule of thumb and there are also masses of sheds and barns built of other interesting materials like cob and clay lump.

After a penal brick tax was removed in 1857, a lot of brick barns were built which are also now ripe for conversion. I have even seen steel framed agricultural buildings (you can hardly call them barns) dating from the Fifties getting the modern barn conversion treatment, complete with stained weatherboard exterior. Another example of planning gone mad, perhaps. But why not?

If you see a barn on the market with planning permission for conversion, the chances are that it has already been subject to a thorough examination in order to have that permission obtained.

Unlike virgin building plots, you can't get Outline permission on a barn conversion – it has to be Detailed which means that the design is closely scrutinised by the planners before any approval is granted. The planners would ideally like to see redundant farm buildings given over to some commercial use with the hope of creating some rural employment. In fact there are grants available for conversion if you can find a viable business use for the building – this can include farm shops, workshops or even holiday lets. Diversification, that's the name of the game. Trouble is that for a huge number of barns there simply isn't any viable option other than residential conversion for resale.

Chapter 15

However, in order to prove this, you have to carry out a business viability survey, assessing likely income from the converted building.

Brian Belton, a surveyor with Durrant & Sons, based in Diss in Norfolk, handles a large number of these applications every year and he says: 'I've yet to find a barn in my patch, the Waveney valley, where the economics of a commercial conversion stack up. You need to show a return of 14 or 15 per cent before banks will be willing to finance and you only ever seem to get around 7 or 8 per cent returns showing through on the surveys, even with grant money thrown in'.

Only by showing a commercial conversion is unviable do you open the door to a residential conversion. But before such permission is forthcoming, a detailed structural survey also needs to be undertaken to see whether the barn is 'permanent and substantial'. In Durrant's practice, this involves measuring every timber and inspecting all the joints. Most timber barns are in need of a large amount of restoration but very few are unsalvageable. The rule seems to be if it's standing, it's salvageable. Typically the timber along the bottom edge – the sole plate – has rotted and sometimes twisted, causing the base of the barn to move outwards, but the sole plate can be replaced and the plinth can be reset. The very fact that a barn has stood for so long is usually a testament to how well it was built in the first place but sometimes decay can be rapid, especially if the roof cover has been removed or has blown off. On occasion, conversion has to be carried out in double quick time in order to save the building. If it collapses beyond repair, there will be no hope of obtaining permission to rebuild.

This raises another intriguing problem: insurance. Redundant buildings are intrinsically liabilities, not assets. What's of value here is the development potential, not the structure itself. But the development potential hangs on the structure continuing to at least exist. There's a danger of buying a barn for conversion and losing everything when it burns down or gets blown over before you've started work. Currently, there appears to be no one covering this as an insurance risk, so you'd better not hang around too long before starting work.

Sometimes the damage to the structure is self-inflicted. I am indebted to a reader in Buckinghamshire who told me the following horror story. He bought a dilapidated barn with permission to convert. He hired a builder to undertake the work and he specifically instructed the builder not to dismantle more than was strictly necessary to effect repairs. The builder assured him he knew what he was doing, having already done several barn conversions. Nevertheless, he went too far and, within a week of starting, a planning officer called by the site, at the behest of a disgruntled neighbour, and instantly withdrew the planning consent on the grounds that the barn had ceased to exist in any meaningful way. £250k in debt, asset stripped away, our reader was in a desperate state. Getting angry with the builder did no good. As far as the planners were concerned, it was an ex-barn and that was his problem. It took three years to obtain a renewed planning permission and, even then, he only won it due to the councillors taking pity at his plight. The moral is...be very careful, especially with timber barns.

TIMBER BARNS

With a little luck, your barn survives long enough for you to make a start on the conversion. What needs to be done? Start with the foundations. Rarely will any of these buildings have what we now call foundations in any shape or form. Stone or brick plinth walls just tended to spread a little below ground; there were never any attempts to dig down a metre or so on to hard bearing ground. However the barns have stood the test of time so the principle to be observed is that, if you don't change any of the loadings, there really shouldn't be any need to alter what exists. Given that the alternative is underpinning and that underpinning tends to cost a minimum of £500 per linear metre (likely to work out at over £20,000 for a barn), then it's well worth avoiding new foundations if possible. So if you wish to build in an upper storey, you have to find a way of keeping the added load of this new floor off the existing walls. The solution lies in building a platform inside the barn; this can be achieved with stud walls underneath or, more commonly, using a series of beefy posts which themselves get bedded on concrete pads.

Then consider the ground floor. The condition of these varies from compacted earth through to level concrete in good condition. Concrete sounds like an advantage but bear in mind that in order to meet the latest U value requirement for floors you will almost certainly have to put insulation on top of it and consequently you may be losing significant height; sometimes it is better to dig out an existing floor and put in a new one.

There are two additional points to consider here. You don't want to go down so deep that you expose the base of the walls otherwise you will suddenly find yourself in an underpinning situation – a couple of exploratory test digs should reveal how far down your walls go under the ground.

On the other hand, if you are planning on building an upper deck, you may find that you have to negotiate a tie beam, tying the roof trusses together. Ideally you want your finished ground floor level to be at least 4.5m below any tie beams otherwise you will have to go on hands and knees to get under the tie beams when you want to go to the bathroom.

Incidentally, there is no minimum height for rooms or doorways encoded in our building regs, but realistically you need 1.8 m clearance on doors to make them comfortable to pass through. If you haven't got a reasonable clearance there may be ways around the problem by gaining access to the different bays from half landings or maybe installing a second staircase. Physically, you may be able to lower the floor a little or you may even be able to jack the entire building up a little – although for God's sake keep quiet about this, the planners would have a fit!

Actually, it is perfectly acceptable to jack a timber structure up when carrying out restoration work. Expected even. The procedure is to strip away everything that you don't intend to keep. Often this means reducing the barn to nothing more than a timber skeleton. You then build an internal scaffold cage and then place pins under the header plates at the top of the walls which take the weight of the roof. The whole structure then gets lifted gently off the supporting walls at the bottom and this then allows you to get to work restoring these walls and go about replacing the sole plates.

If all the bottom joints between the sole plate and the wall studs have rotted, it is standard practice to cut the wall studs shorter and fix a new sole plate

(usually green oak) in a slightly higher position than the old one.

If other pieces of the original frame are missing or damaged, now is the time that the replacements are made. You will then have to add a couple of courses of brick or stone onto the plinth wall underneath to make up the difference. At this point you would be expected to let the structure down again to sit on the repaired plinth.

From here on in, the timber barn conversion becomes a new build. The walls will normally get covered in plywood or something similar and you need to add insulation to the structure – in this respect a converted barn must perform to the same standards as a new house. In timber barns, most people want to see as much as possible of the original timbers and therefore the tendency is to find insulation systems that wrap around the exterior. Normally a timber barn will get a new weatherboarded exterior.

STONE BARNS

Stone barns pose rather different problems. There will certainly be no jacking up of the structure, rather there may have to be a painstaking repair of what is there. And the requirement for good insulation levels means that one face, usually the inside, will have to be covered over. You may need to underpin, especially where new openings are formed and the wall loadings are altered – it very much depends on the ground conditions beneath.

An additional problem is to make the structure watertight, something which it was doubtless never designed to be in the first place. A typical stone barn consists of two skins of sorted stone separated by a rubble filled cavity. The existing walls will often be as much as 450 mm thick so, on most barns, it's quite impractical to build

another skin on the inside. So you have to work with what is there. It's difficult to install an effective damp proof course and it can be difficult to stop rain penetration through the walls as well.

The planners are unlikely to accept a waterproof render being applied to the outside face, the best you can realistically hope to do is to point up the gaps between the stones. And accept, perhaps, that you are not living in a new build and that you may have to put up with the odd damp patch from time to time.

COST

Barn conversions cost rather more than new housing on a square metre basis. On a like-for-like basis, the unit area rate works out at between 30 per cent and 50 per cent more than new builds. An upper deck will be slightly cheaper to construct on a square metre basis making two floor barns cheaper than single storey ones. But the saving is not that great.

Stone barns will tend to be a little more expensive because stone is always time consuming and therefore expensive to work with. Modern (brick) barns will be cheaper because the structure is usually in better condition. The more exceptional the barn, the more it is likely to cost to convert.

Most barns are not listed unless they happen to be in the grounds (or the curtilage, in planning speak) of a listed farm in which case there may well be extra features to consider (such as thatch). Generally speaking, most barn conversions are undertaken by selfbuilders. Spec builders tend to shy away from them because they don't like the unpredictability – although one or two plucky ones will go as far as importing barns from France in order to get the right feel in a property.

BRINKLEY'S SNAGGING LIST

One of the many things that bedevils building work is quality. If you buy a new car or a computer, you can usually sort out any quality issues at time of purchase or shortly afterwards, under guarantee. But with building work, it's not quite so easy because for starters it's often quite hard to tell when a building job has finished and even then there are often tell-tale snags which crop up at any point. Doors which fitted fine start binding, stairs develop a squeak, gaps open up, and things that looked fine at first turn out to be not so fine when you live with them for a while.

With the best will in the world, a good builder is still going to leave behind them a long list of items to be rectified, which is why the building contracts have developed over the years to include a retention clause withholding some money, usually 2.5 per cent of the contract fee, for six months after completion. This work is all part and parcel of building work and is sometimes referred to as third fixing.

It's a particular problem for new homebuilders because they are in the business of selling 'the perfect home' and common sense tells us that they are not really in the position to deliver snag-free houses. The best builders manage the buyer's expectations and ensure that any follow-on snags are dealt with promptly but nevertheless the whole subject causes loads of grief for both new home buyers and their builders. A lot of this flack gets directed at the warranty providers, such as the NHBC and Zurich, and even though their warranties specifically exclude minor snagging, it still takes a lot of their time and also causes a lot of bad publicity.

In an attempt to manage this process more systematically, in 1999 the NHBC produced a document called a Consistent Approach to Finishes which set about trying to define acceptable standards for new housebuilding. In 2006, it was further refined and placed within the main NHBC Standards book, getting a chapter all to itself, No 1.2 right up the front end, so they must be quite pleased with it and I think they have every right to be because this potentially has the capability of both raising finish standards for builders and reducing needless disputes with disgruntled homeowners. This document is available for free download from the NHBC website on their publications page. It's only five pages long, so it's worth getting hold of.

I make no bones about drawing heavily from this document with the blessing of one of its authors, Neil Smith, because it also has the potential to appeal to a much wider audience than new homebuyers. Because here is a template for assessing the quality of all domestic building work, and that is something the building industry has been lacking. I have also combined it with a snagging guide which you can use to make your own judgements about whether the building work you have had done for you is of an acceptable standard.

If you are project managing, you can also use this guide to look at the work of your subcontractors. But use it with care. As the NHBC's guide states: 'This guide is not intended to deal with every situation that may arise and discretion should be exercised in its application in specific circumstances'.

EXTERIOR WALLS, GENERAL

▇ Check to see if the damp-proof course (DPC) has been correctly installed (150 mm above Ground Level)
Ideally needs to be checked as it's built. After completion, DPCs can be difficult to detect. The DPC is usually a plastic or felt-based layer that is embedded in the mortar on face brickwork or blockwork. It can alternatively be done with two courses of engineering bricks (shiny surface, either dark blue or blood red). Sometimes you can see evidence of a roll-type DPC sticking through one course of the mortar but it's not always visible. If you can't see anything, it doesn't spell disaster. But if you can see it, make sure that it's all above ground level at the base of the wall, otherwise it won't work as a DPC.
▇ Airbricks (if any) should not be blocked
Airbricks will only be installed with a suspended ground floor, so an absence of airbricks doesn't spell disaster (though it might, if you have a suspended ground floor. Do you? Often the presence of airbricks is the easiest way to tell.) Airbricks are usually arranged so that the outside airbrick in a cavity wall is set above the internal floor and is joined to a lower, inner airbrick by some plastic ducting placed in the cavity, a feature called telescopic venting. How do you tell if the airbricks are blocked? With difficulty. But at least check that, like the DPC, the external airbricks are not buried below ground.
▇ Cavity trays installed correctly
Cavity trays exist to deflect water from the inside face of a cavity to the outside. They are required where you have junctions and abutments, such as a single storey roof being built off a two storey cavity wall. Missing them out or installing them incorrectly, so that they don't actually drain water across to the outside face of the outer skin, is a very frequent error on building sites, but there is no way of checking this after the wall is enclosed, so it has to be checked on site as the walls or roofs are being built.
▇ *Again this is something you can only*

realistically check as the walls go up.

▨ Expansion gaps (if any) should have been neatly filled

What is, and where would you find, an expansion gap? Most houses won't have an expansion joint, aka a movement joint. It's a feature of masonry walls, usually external ones, and they are put there to prevent movement and cracking. However, you need a big wall before you need get too concerned about movement joints. In clay brickwork, the wall needs to be more than 15 m long – if it turns a corner, it's not regarded as one wall anymore, so it has to be a 15 m long straight run, which is going it some.

When the external wall is blockwork, typically rendered over, you should have a vertical expansion gap every 6 m, which is quite likely on many medium to large houses or extensions. Expansion gaps should be vertical, run the full height of the wall and should be filled with some material which will have a bit of give in it like fibreboard or foam rubber. In external work, these can be filled with mortar for appearance sake, but they should be visible. Often hidden behind downpipes.

▨ Look for gaps around pipes coming through walls

There shouldn't be any! If there are it may provide unwanted air leakage points or, even worse, access for rodents.

n Are there gaps between walls and roof? Gaps between soffit board (if any) and walls should be tight and/or sealed with insect mesh

Air leakage issues plus access for winged creatures you may or may not want.

▨ Check that nothing is attached to the walls that shouldn't be there (nails, screws)

▨ Check that the wall is plumb, straight and true

The NHBC provides some detailed guidance on this.

a) An external wall should be horizontally straight 10 mm over 5 m. Use a string line on blocks to establish this.

b) An external wall should be plumb 10 mm each storey, 20 mm on overall height. Use plumb bob on spacer to assess.

▨ Check for blemishes

The NHBC provides guidance on this issue. They suggest that you should view walls in daylight (ie not shining a torch) from a distance of 10 m. If you can't see it from that distance, it's not an issue worth mentioning.

BRICK AND STONE WALLS

▨ Look for mortar snots (piling) on walls

The NHBC guidance is clear. You should be able to notice it from 10 m in daylight.

n Mortar overall should be a consistent colour

Ideally, yes. In practice, it's unlikely to be perfect throughout because mixing mortar is often done by hand (at least it is on small sites) and sometimes the mortar and the sand change during the build, causing subtle and not-so-subtle variations in mortar colour. It's also an extremely difficult snag to rectify – if you repoint, you risk damaging the brickwork. This is a problem best picked up during the build process where it's easy to fix, not at handover stage. You may have to be prepared to accept a little variation in colour.

▨ Look for efflorescence

It looks awful but it's harmless and should be ignored. It will work itself out over three to five years.

▨ Look for chipped or damaged brickwork or stonework

NHBC: 15 mm is the 'action size'. Below this, ignore

▨ Look for gaps in the pointing

These should be filled. Sometimes a sign that the brickwork hasn't been done as

carefully as it might have been, sometimes it's just holes left for scaffold poles that simply haven't been filled.

▨ Brick courses should be level, and perps should be reasonably aligned

NHBC: bed joints should be level: 10 mm for walls up to 5 m long, 15 mm for walls longer than 5 m. Bed joints should be even: max variation 5 mm over eight successive joints. The perps (the perpendicular joints in the brickwork) should align all the way up a wall; in practice it often gets knocked out by window openings - this doesn't signify anything amiss.

RENDERED WALLS

n Rendered finishes should be a consistent colour and texture and have no cracking

NHBC: minor cracking and crazing is acceptable and that visible patches and daywork joints are acceptable as long as they don't affect performance and are not unduly obtrusive. This is a difficult area because render will often crack a little as the background moves, especially with new structures. It doesn't signify major damage. Normally, cracks need to be wider than 3 mm before you need to get worried about subsidence.

OTHER CLADDINGS

▨ Other claddings (boards, tiles etc.) should be suitably finished (colour, levels, cracking)

NHBC: accept that external finishes will change colour over time.

GARAGES

▨ Check garage doors - do they work? – are they blemish free? – is the lock working?

▨ Check other garage joinery – does it work? do the locks work?

Chapter 15

NHBC: blockwork in garages: cracks up to 3 mm are acceptable in unplastered work

RAINWATER GOODS

▨ Check guttering all around the house – look for open joints or misaligned sections, or missing clips

▨ Check that downpipes are attached to the wall regularly

▨ f possible, check how guttering works in a rainstorm – look for leaks and spills and misaligned downpipe connectors

▨ If you can view guttering from above, check to see that the gutters are not blocked and that the roof underlay overhangs the guttering

Checking on rainwater gear is far easier to do when the scaffolding is still in place. Generally, it's a good idea to use a hosepipe to simulate rainfall.

ROOF

▨ Check roof edge details wherever possible – neatly finished?

▨ Check roof cover visually for obvious defects. *If your ridge tiles are mortared, the mortar shouldn't have stained the tiles below but, with the best will in the world, this sometimes happens if it rains soon after the flaunching is carried out. Should the roofer be responsible for replacing sections of the roof because it's rained and the mortar hadn't set? It's a difficult one to call – the NHBC offer no guidance on this. Generally, I think that if the staining isn't too bad, it will weather in over time and you can probably afford to ignore it.*

GARDEN AND EXTERNALS

▨ Check that garden gates are working and in order (locks and bolts)

▨ Check for defects in walls and fences and posts

▨ Paving slabs should be stable underfoot

NHBC: variations up to 10 mm on a 2 m straight edge are OK: subsequent settlement is the responsibility of the owner.

▨ Pavings shouldn't be chipped, cracked or discoloured (cement stains) and shouldn't present a tripping hazard

▨ Manhole covers should be undamaged and flat

NHBC: 10 mm settlement in hard paved areas around manhole covers is acceptable.

▨ Paving should drain away from property

▨ No standing water in driveways - it should drain away

NHBC: one hour after rain has stopped, a puddle up to 1 sq m and 7 mm deep is acceptable, anything bigger is not

▨ Check to see that garden is free from builders' rubble. If turfed, check condition of turf

This really depends on the nature of the contract you have signed up to. If you are buying a spec-built house, then these are standard snagging checks you need to make but if it's already your property, the builder may well be expecting you to dispose of waste and to repair the garden.

▨ Check boundaries are correct

Again, this is something that would normally fall under the pre-contract work, but it's relevant if you are buying a spec-built house.

DOORS

▨ Check that doors are hung correctly: they shouldn't open or close on their own accord, unless sprung or hung on rising butts as you would expect of a fire door, used in bedrooms with houses with third storeys or loft conversions

▨ Check that doors don't bind on hinge side or rub on closing edges.

NHBC suggests a gap of up to 5 mm around the doors is acceptable, although

they state nothing about evenness of this gap. They also suggest that for double doors the max gap should be 5 mm between doors. NHBC suggests that gap under doors is 5 mm min and 22 mm max (on unfinished floors)

▨ Check that hinges don't squeak, and that every hinge has all its screws in place.

▨ Check that keys, locks and catches all perform smoothly

▨ Check that doors are flat and plumb

Just how flat and how plumb? With many materials, such as moulded MDF, GRP, plastic and steel, there is no real reason for doors to be misshapen at all. But timber doors are a different kettle of fish and they will all be subject to a certain amount of movement and distortion both before and after being hung. So there has to be a 'degree of flexibility' here. The NHBC suggest that doors should not be more than 10 mm out of plumb and also suggest that the max distortion for doors is 5 mm across width and 9 mm over height. These measurements would be taken in relation to the frames in which the doors sit.

▨ Check that the door styles and door furniture are consistent throughout the house (if applicable – obviously not if some parts are new and others old)

▨ Check that the door linings, door stops and the architraves are properly fixed and that the styles are consistent

▨ Check the stain or paint finish on doors. Look for 'tears' and knotting stains. Check that the edges haven't been planed to fit after the decorators have left, leaving you with exposed timber.

NHBC guidance states that resin spots from timber knots are acceptable. Maybe.

▨ Check that glazing is sound and isn't scratched or marked – see section on glazing for greater detail

▨ On external doors, check to see that

the draft proofing has been fitted and the frames have been adequately installed and sealed

▨ Check that external door frames do not distort when opening and closing

If there is a level threshold, required by building regs on new homes since 1999, then check to see if it's been adequately installed and that water won't come in under the door.

GLAZING

▨ Look for scratches

How fussy can you get? It's a frequent complaint of new homeowners and extenders that the expensive new glazing has been scratched by the builders. It's easy to do and it happens all too often. And it's very expensive and time-consuming to fix. The NHBC has come up with some guidance about how big a scratch should be before it becomes 'actionable'. They say that you should view the glass in daylight, from inside the room, at right angles to the glass from a distance of 2 m for ordinary glass and 3 m for toughened or laminated glass. Why the distinction? I have no idea. Having done this, you have filtered out most of the really small blemishes. Now if you can see stuff from this distance, you may have cause to complain. BUT, they urge you to accept manufacturing bubbles, blisters and particles trapped within the glass, plus fine scratches less than 25 mm long. And all marks within 6 mm of the edge. Only then do you have legitimate grounds for concern.

So effectively what they are saying is that you must be able to show a scratch longer than 25 mm that is visible from at least 2 m, if not 3 m. That's quite a long scratch, and many customers won't be happy with scratches slightly smaller than this.

WINDOWS

▨ Are the window reveals, both external

and internal, sealed, and true?

▨ Check that the cills are true and that drainage details are correct

NHBC suggest that the cill should be no more than 3 mm out of level over both internally and externally.

NHBC guidance also suggests that you should also be looking at 'squareness' of the openings. The window reveals should not deviate more than 6mm in the vertical over a 1 m span and that the reveals and frames are not out of plumb by more than 6 mm over 1.5 m, or 10 mm if over 1.5 m. The openings should not be more than 8 mm out of square.

▨ Check that mastic or glazing tape is in position and is not damaged

▨ Check that the draught strip is in place

▨ Check that the glass labelling is removed

▨ Ensure windows all open as planned, don't bind and that locks work

▨ Check that trickle vents, if present, are not blocked and that they open and close

▨ If the windows are timber, check that the frames are painted or stained well and that they are not blemished

ELECTRICS

▨ Check that the work has been passed by building control or been carried out by a competent electrician

This is now a building regs requirement. You may need to show that the electrical work was 'compliant' when you come to sell the house, so getting the paper trail sorted is important. It should also provide some measure of quality control to ensure that the installation is safe.

▨ Check that any built-in fittings are connected and work: look at ovens, immersion heaters, alarm systems, smoke detectors and anything else

▨ Check that fans work and that they vent to outside (look for flaps opening)

▨ Check light fittings all work and that

switching is correct. Also that sockets work

▨ Check that faceplates are not damaged and are screwed home securely

HEATING & PLUMBING

Heating systems are growing increasingly complex and it's really a good idea if you get some instruction on how to operate them effectively. In particular, programmers can flummox ordinary mortals and you should make yourself familiar with just how they work before you settle down to live with them. It's also grown more complex in a regulatory sense because the electrical control systems frequently have to be installed or at least checked over by qualified electricians, where once they were done by plumbers.

It can be difficult to know sometimes whether a heating system is working as designed. Signs to watch out for that all may not be as intended include:

▨ Larger than expected fuel bills – may indicate a boiler malfunction

▨ Cold spots – emitters not working correctly

▨ Noises – often air trapped in the system

▨ No hot water – pumps or valves malfunctioning

▨ Check to see that the pipes running from the boiler are insulated

On the plumbing side:

▨ Check that fittings and pipework have been securely fixed and are level and unmarked

▨ There shouldn't be excessive gurgling noises from the waste pipes – check this by running water through the appliances. This is also a useful check for any leaks which might have been overlooked

▨ Check that grouts and seals are in place

▨ Check that appliances – loos, showers, baths – work as designed and that features like shower doors work properly

Chapter 15

WALLS & CEILINGS

▨ If boarded out, ideally you shouldn't be able to see the joints between the boards and nail fixings should not be visible

NHBC guidance suggests that nail holes should not be visible and no cracking acceptable on handover. After this, hairline cracking is an acceptable blemish as the house dries out. Any subsequent cracking up to 2 mm in width is acceptable.

▨ Surfaces should be smooth with no scoring or indentations. Paint should be consistent colour, without brushmarks or roller lines

NHBC guidelines on this: view surfaces in daylight, with electric lights off, from 2 m; should be no brush marks or runs; but tool marks in plasterwork are acceptable; the surfaces should be 'reasonably uniform' with 'minor textural differences around lights and other fittings'

▨ Surfaces should be flat: 5 mm over a 2 m straight edge

▨ Walls should be plumb: 10 mm deviation allowable over 2.5m drop

▨ Check for squareness on internal and external corners using 500x500 square, max deviation should be no more than 15 mm

▨ Ceilings should be flat: 6 mm over a 2 m straight edge

▨ Skirting, dado, coving – ideally, you shouldn't be able to tell where the joins are; they should be free from blemishes and properly decorated; the styles should be consistent

▨ Skirting gaps: *a 5 mm gap between floor and skirting is perfectly normal. A gap up to 15 mm is acceptable when drying out has occurred. Shrinkage gaps are part of 'normal household maintenance'. Many people would baulk at these standards*

and say they are not remotely acceptable. But often gaps will appear at the midway point of a wall as the floor deflects when furniture is loaded onto it.

EMPTY LOFT SPACE

▨ Check insulation is in place throughout – look for gaps

▨ Check that loft hatch is insulated and sealed – no draughts

▨ Check that you can't see daylight from inside

▨ Check that pipework and extracts in loftspace connect at both ends

STAIRS

▨ Check that the staircase doesn't squeak

NHBC guidance suggests that squeaking on timber staircases is inevitable because of shrinkage. It suggests that 'squeaking should not be excessive'.

▨ Check banisters and handrails are secure, and well decorated

▨ Check headroom is adequate

It should be, of course, but what the hell do you do if it isn't? Short of rebuilding the stair enclosure, often there isn't much you can do. It's a check that the building inspector should be making in any event as stair height is something governed by the building regs. As are banisters, handrails, stair angle and widths. But not, unfortunately, squeaking.

KITCHEN

▨ Check that appliances work and that they are not damaged.

▨ Check that all the fittings are present.

▨ Check that integrated appliances are secured to the kitchen units.

▨ Check that drawers open and close smoothly and have stops fitted.

▨ Check that doors open and close correctly and are aligned.

NHBC guidance suggests that the doors and shelves should align vertically, horizontally and in plan and that gaps should be uniform, but doesn't go as far as suggesting any dimensional tolerances. They do suggest that you view matters from 2 m.

▨ Look for signs of leaks from sinks and appliances.

▨ Check the kickboards are secure and aligned and have no gaps.

▨ Check that worktops are properly fixed and that, where joined, they are level

FLOORS

▨ All floors should be flat and free from blemishes.

But how flat? And what constitutes a blemish? The NHBC guidance suggests that floors up to 6 m wide can be out of level by up to 4 mm and that floors over 6 m wide can be out of level up to 25 mm overall.

Also consider the overall flatness of a floor. The NHBC guidance suggest that you use a 2 m straight edge to establish that no floor should be more than 5 mm out on finished floors, or 8 mm on unfinished screed/concrete

▨ Timber or boarded floors, check for squeaks and blemishes, and gaps

Ah! The dreaded squeaky floors! How squeaky is squeaky? It's perhaps impossible to permanently stop squeaking from timber floors but the squeaking shouldn't be so bad that it drives the inhabitants bonkers. All the NHBC can come up with here is that 'the squeaking should not be excessive' because 'squeaking is inevitable because of shrinkage'.

▨ Check that any floor ducting is properly installed. Above all, it should be level and should not protrude above the finished floor level.

CRUCIAL MEASUREMENTS

WHAT'S IN A TON?

Conventionally when the word is written Ton it refers to an imperial ton. When it's written Tonne, it's a metric ton(ne). The old imperial ton was 20 cwt (hundredweight): the metric tonne is 1,000 kilogrammes. The imperial ton is just 1.6 per cent heavier than the metric tonne and therefore, to all intents and purposes you can ignore the difference.

Not so the differences between cubic metres and tonnes. Now quarries or merchants can sell by using either method. In fact many suppliers use both – volume up to 10 cu m and tonnes above that level.

The conversion on sand is 1cu m equals 1.6 tonnes but be warned that sand is much heavier when wet and so you'll be getting up to 20 per cent less if you are buying by weight in wet weather. However, at £6-£10 per tonne for 10 tonne loads, it's cheap enough to not worry unduly over. Other importaant volume to weight conversions are noted in the Material Densities section of the adjacent table.

Note the critical one is water, which is used to define the relationships between metres, litres and tonnes. Materials with a density greater than 1 are heavier than water and will sink, whilst materials with a density less than 1 will float. Try dropping a Celcon areated block in a bath full of water: it will amaze the kids, if nothing else.

Getting It Square

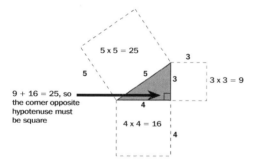

Only in a right-angled triangle is the square of the hypotenuse (the long side) equal to the square of the two shorter sides. This basic rule of geometry (Pythagoras' Theorem) allows us to get our corners dead square using nothing more than a tape measure. Most carpenters are taught this bit of geometry via the 3-4-5 rule which they use for squaring up frames but it is just as useful when setting out foundations. The classic 3-4-5 triangle calculation is demonstrated in the diagram but, of course, the calculation will work with any lengths, just as long as you can work out the squares. Tip: get a calculator with a square root function.

Measurements

Weight	
1lb =	0.454kg
1kg =	2.2lbs
1 imperial ton =	1016kg = 1.016 tonnes

Length	
1 millimetre (mm) =	0.039 inches
1 metre (m) =	39.4 inches = 1.094 yards
1 inch =	25.5mm
1 foot =	305mm
1 yard =	914mm = 0.914m

Area	
1 sq. metre (m^2) =	10.76 sq.ft
1 ft2 =	0.93m^2
1 hectare =	10,000m^2 = 2.47 acres
1 acre =	4047m^2 = 0.4 hectare
Area of triangle =	half base x height

Volume	
1 UK gallon =	4.5 litres
1 cubic metre (m^3) =	1000 litres = 220 gallons
1 m^3 of water =	1 tonne

Heat	
1 kiloWatt (kW) =	3410 British Thermal Units
1 kilowatt hour (kWh) =	1 kW burned for one hour
1 joule =	1 watt burned for a second
1 gigajoule (GJ) =	278kWh
Specific Heat of Air =	0.33watts/m^3/1°C

Material Densities	
1m^3 water @ 4°C =	1 tonne (by definition!)
1m^3 of dry sand =	1.6 tonnes (+20% wet)
1m^3 of aggregate =	1.8 tonnes
1m^3 of cement =	1.4 tonnes
1m^3 hydrated lime =	0.6 tonnes
1m^3 concrete =	2 tonnes
1m^3 clinker blocks =	1.6 tonnes
1m^3 bricks =	1.2 to 1.6 tonnes
1m^3 aerated blocks =	0.6 tonnes
1m^3 softwood =	0.45 tonnes
1m^3 hardwood =	0.65 tonnes

For more conversions, check out www.simetric.co.uk

THE STORY OF THE BIBLE

Mark Brinkley

THE HOUSEBUILDER'S BIBLE first saw the light of day in 1994. It has always been my brainchild and, over the past fifteen or so years, its success has transformed my life from being that of a working builder into becoming a full-time writer. How did it come about?

From 1980 to 1994, I worked as a carpenter, small builder and developer in and around my home town of Cambridge, fifty miles north of London. That is what I would probably still be doing had it not been for the economic downturn in the early Nineties. This book is very much a by-product of that recession.

In 1986, I went into partnership with Robin Gomm, a designer-builder, and together we began buying up plots and development opportunities, borrowing money to finance the bulk of the deals. In common with tens of thousands of small builders and developers (and millions of homeowners), we were caught out when the property market turned sour

at the end of 1988. During that fateful year,

we were building a four-bedroomed house a few miles outside Cambridge and we had lots of interest. I remember turning down a cash offer of £180,000 on the house in the summer, deciding to hold off till we were completely finished in the hope of netting £200,000. But by the time we had finished, the market sentiment had turned and all deals were off. We ended up selling it for £154,000, virtually cost price, eight months later. At least we sold. Many developers refused to sell at these apparently knockdown prices and hung on far too long. They mostly went under.

Among the other bits of land we had accumulated was a building plot in Weston Colville, a small village east of Cambridge. We'd picked it up for £45,000 in 1986, seen its value double and then halve again. We decided that rather than try and build a house there for resale, we would just sell the plot. But in 1989 there were no takers, not even at £40,000. After a year on the market without

an offer, it became obvious that it was time for a rethink. For during this period I had also got married and together was in the process of fathering three children in four years. A family house in the country suddenly seemed quite an appealing prospect. And whilst there was no market for rural building plots, even in 1990 it wouldn't take too long to sell a terraced house in central Cambridge. Thus we decided to go and build a house for ourselves on this unsaleable plot.

My business partner was meanwhile winning quite a bit of work from some farming contacts we had. A large new house, a series of barn conversions, some renovation work. It wasn't developing, it was design and build, but it kept us busy and paid the bills. My project took a back seat for a couple of years whilst we cracked on with the jobs in hand. It enabled us to spend a little time thinking about what we would build, how we would build it and how much we would hope to build it for. It was also during this time that the genesis of the Housebuilder's Bible occurred:

initially just a little furtive note taking.

Work started on the house in Weston Colville in 1992, after the planners had had their say and re-worked many of our original thoughts. It was a sloping site, unusual for Cambridgeshire, and I was unprepared for just how much spoil we had to shift off site to get a level footprint. More note taking, plus a few calculations — the origins of Brinkley's Slope Law that features in Chapter 6. I took an active part in the groundworks and drainage, I serviced the brickies for a month and then worked as part of the carpentry team erecting the timber frame upper storey. After fourteen weeks we had the superstructure built and covered in. I then had to stop work whilst we negotiated a sale on the terraced house, whilst simultaneously helping my wife with the arrival of our third child. Finally we threw a whole mass of people at the house for eight weeks to enable us to move in before Christmas 1992.

Despite being the sixth house I had been directly involved in commissioning and building, I had found the process of housebuilding for myself and my family an amazingly rushed and frustrating experience. There simply wasn't anywhere to go to get a handle on the choices to be made, their costs and their pros and cons. There was at the time just one major book on selfbuild, Murray Armor's 'Building Your Own Home', which had sold in vast quantities since it first came out in the 1970s. It was, and indeed remains, an excellent book but it doesn't really deal with the technicalities of building. My idea was to put together a book that more or less started where Murray Armor's book left off — actually analysing the process of housebuilding from a builder's point of view.

The analogy of travel guides kept coming to mind. Imagine being dumped in a foreign city where you don't speak the language. You want to see the sights but you have no idea where they are or how to get to them. You have three days. You rush around like a whirling dervish, checking out likely looking buildings, catching buses all over the place and generally being pretty frantic. When the time comes to leave, you know you've 'done' Rome or Barcelona or wherever it was you went, but you really don't have a clue whether you've seen the best bits or not. That was what it was like building a house in 1992. And so I figured there must be a market for a guide book which would list the attractions, the admission prices, and the directions. That is more or less what the Housebuilder's Bible sets out to do.

I started the book-writing project by approaching a couple of publishers to see if there was any interest in such an idea. 'Absolutely no way,' said the first, 'it's far too specialised'. 'Absolutely no way,' said the second, 'anything with prices in will date far too quickly'. If anything, these responses just strengthened my resolve. I react well to being told I am crazy. I decided I would self-publish and concentrate on selling the book directly by mail order and at selfbuild exhibitions. First I had to write it.

All I had in 1993 was a series of notes on an Amstrad PCW, the machine that made Sir Alan Sugar's fortune, plus masses and masses of price data in the office. It seemed a mammoth task to turn it into a readable book, especially with a young family to look after, a new house to finish off and an existing business to keep going. Looking back on it, I am not too sure how I got it all from an idea to a physical book in just 18 months with all that going on in the background. As I said, this book is a by-product of recession and recessions make you work that much harder. A key figure in all this was undoubtedly my mother who believed me when I said I was going to write a book and who kept us afloat during 1994 when I was taking three days a week off from the building business to get the first draft completed. I couldn't really work at home because of the distractions of three pre-school boys padding about the house. So I took a leaf out of the notebook of one of my heroes, singer songwriter Randy Newman, who, whenever he had to produce a new album, went and hired an office, put a piano in it and shut himself away for eight hours a day until the work was complete. Like Randy, I found a room in a village office complex and shut myself away. It worked. That is where I cracked it. Thank God the world wide web didn't exist back then: there were no such distractions.

Come November 1994, I had something worth putting down on paper. I had bought an Apple Mac and taught myself how to use PageMaker and Photoshop, the tools of the desktop publisher. I had the costs all worked into one unwieldy Excel spreadsheet. It wasn't going to be glossy but I was sure it would be useful. My first print-run was tentative, a few hundred run out on a DocuTech machine, a sort of up-market photocopier. Had they sat around for ages, I would have written off the whole project to experience and gone back to join Robin in the building business. But the first edition sold. They sold off the page in the selfbuild mags and they sold by the hundred at a selfbuild exhibition at the NEC. Within a couple of months I had to do a reprint and the Housebuilder's Bible was on its way.

For the first couple of years I tried to get a presence in the major bookshops, making several appeals to WHSmith and Waterstones to stock my baby. But they were not in the least interested in such an amateurish product without a major publisher or a TV series behind it. Despite this, the sales kept climbing and the book sold very well through the selfbuild magazines and also through some professional titles as well. It surprises many who think of it primarily as a selfbuild

Chapter 15

title that nearly half the sales are made to 'professionals' - small builders and tradesmen, architects, surveyors, even estate agents. The fourth edition, the Millennium one, finally broke through into the retail market albeit via amazon. co.uk, the internet bookseller, whose sales depend to a large part on customer reviews. The Bible had some good ones – and no, I didn't write them myself!

During this period, I have also turned my hand to a little journalism. Michael Holmes, the long time editor of the leading selfbuild magazine Homebuilding & Renovating, was an early fan. He asked me to write for his magazine in 1996 and I have been contributing pieces to it ever since. And David Birkbeck and Jo Smit, editors of Building Homes, were also very supportive. Thanks to them I have published over 400 articles, many of them deepening and expanding areas I had covered in the Bible.

In 2003, the book had become just a little bit too much for me to continue with on my own and I joined forces with a new business partner, Mark Neeter, to start a publishing venture called Ovolo, which has taken on the publishing of this book in addition to commissioning new work in this field.

In order to cover these aspects more thoroughly, I have taken to blogging, which is an ideal medium for a sporadic newsletter. My blog can be found at both my own website, www.markbrinkley. net and you can search it for

updates and new developments, information that is supplementary to what is in this book.

Housebuilding is a vast topic and no one can hope to know everything there is to know about it. I am no exception and I am aware that in some areas I am barely doing more than skating over the surface, handing out a few pointers. The value of a book like this derives in great part from pooling other people's expertise into one accessible source. Every edition of this book improves on the one before and many of these improvements are as a direct result of readers contacting me about little things which are unclear, misleading or just plain wrong. So I will finish with an offer of thanks to the many hundreds of people who have helped me with this project over the years and a plea to keep the feedback rolling in.

Dedication to:

David Thomas, my best friend from school days and university who met an untimely end, aged just 36, in a fateful accident in Kuwait in 1991, where he was reporting on the aftermath of the Gulf War for the Financial Times. He was an inspiration to me; it was partly his death which persuaded me to drop the hammer and learn to play the keyboard and start writing.

Mark Brinkley
March 2013

Index